GREENLAND
CANADA IN
D1132126
1920
EEWATIN
HUDSON BAY
ATLANTIC OCEAN
LABRADOR 1949 (NEWFOUNDLAND)
St. John's
NEWFOUNDLAND
QUEBEC 1912
P.E.I. 1769
Charlottetown
1784
ONTARIO 1912
Port Arthur
Fort William
LAKE SUPERIOR
Quebec
St. John
NOVA SCOTIA 1784
Halifax
NEW BRUNSWICK
Montreal
Sudbury
L. HURON
Ottawa
ATLANTIC OCEAN
L. ONTARIO
Toronto
UNITED STATES
LAKE MICHIGAN
L. ERIE
Scale of Miles
0 100 200 300 400

FROM SEA UNTO SEA

"A MARI USQUE AD MARE"

Books by W. G. Hardy

THE CITY OF LIBERTINES

THE UNFULFILLED

ALL THE TRUMPETS SOUNDED

TURN BACK THE RIVER

FATHER ABRAHAM

(ABRAHAM, PRINCE OF UR *in the U.S. edition*)

FROM SEA UNTO SEA

CANADA—1850 to 1910
The Road to Nationhood

W. G. HARDY

1960
DOUBLEDAY & COMPANY, INC.
GARDEN CITY, NEW YORK

Library of Congress Catalog Card Number 60–13528

Printed in the United States of America
First Edition

TO THE MEMORY
OF MY WIFE

ACKNOWLEDGMENTS

IN this attempt to present the vivid personalities and stirring events of the Canada of 1850 to 1910, there is a heavy dependence on the works of those scholars who have written with authority and competence about the period. Books which I found helpful are listed in the Selected Bibliography. I should like, however, to make particular reference to Donald Creighton's excellent biography of John A. Macdonald; to Douglas Mackay's *The Honourable Company;* to G. F. G. Stanley's *The Birth of Western Canada;* to J. A. Roy's study of Joseph Howe and to J. B. Brebner's article about Howe's Crimean War venture in Volume XI of the *Canadian Historical Review;* to M. S. Wade's dramatic story of "The Overlanders of '62"; and to J. F. C. Wright's careful and interesting picture of the Dukhobors in *Slava Bohu.*

There was assistance elsewhere. Miss Irene McAfee, Head of History and General Information Division of the Vancouver Public Library, and her capable staff were most kind in clearing certain points with reference to British Columbia. From Calgary, Hugh Dempsey, Archivist of the Glenbow Foundation, provided information about the Indians of the Canadian plains. When it came to the story of the building of the Canadian Pacific Railway, D. B. Wallace and H. T. Coleman of the Public Relations Department of the C.P.R. were most courteous in answering questions. I should like to acknowledge, too, the kindness and help of Thomas B. Costain, the editor in chief of this whole series, of George Shively, editor of Doubleday & Company, and of Professor Lewis Thomas, Head of the Department of History, University of Alberta.

I am particularly indebted, however, to Professor Morden Long, formerly Head of the Department of History of the University of Alberta, and to Associate Professor T. S. Webster of the Department of History of the University of Manitoba. Both of these scholars were kind enough to read the book while it was still in manuscript form and both made valuable suggestions and corrections.

W. G. Hardy

CONTENTS

FROM SEA UNTO SEA

"A MARI USQUE AD MARE"

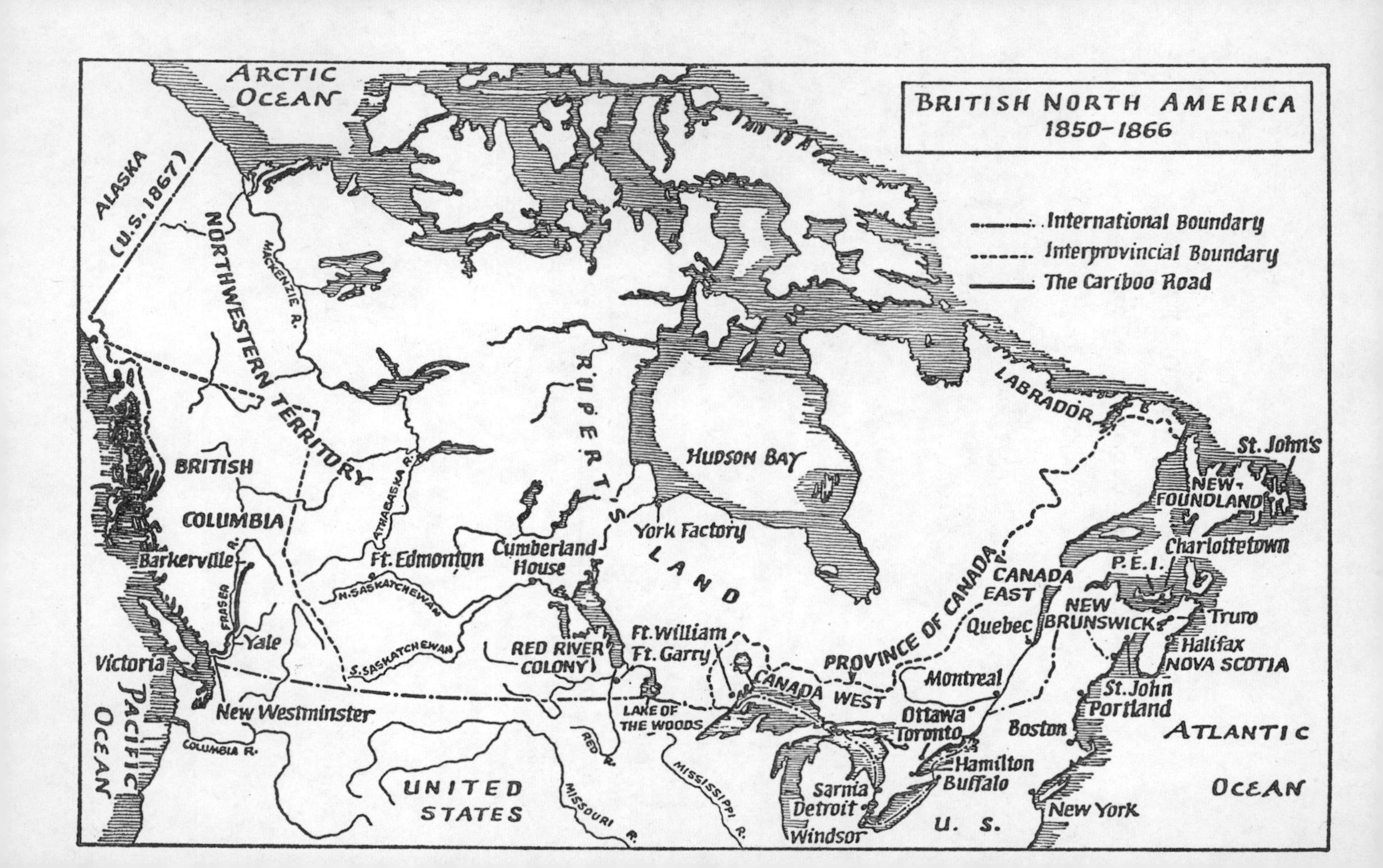

BRITISH NORTH AMERICA
1850-1866
International Boundary
Interprovincial Boundary
The Cariboo Road
ARCTIC OCEAN
ALASKA
(U.S. 1867)
NORTHWESTERN TERRITORY
MACKENZIE R.
BRITISH
COLUMBIA
ATHABASKA R.
RUPERT'S LAND
HUDSON BAY
York Factory
LABRADOR
St. John's
NEW-FOUNDLAND
Charlottetown
P.E.I.
Truro
Halifax
NOVA SCOTIA
NEW BRUNSWICK
St. John
Portland
CANADA EAST
Quebec
PROVINCE OF CANADA
Montreal
Ottawa
Toronto
CANADA WEST
Hamilton
Buffalo
Boston
New York
Sarnia
Detroit
Windsor
U. S.
ATLANTIC OCEAN
Cumberland House
Ft. Edmonton
N. SASKATCHEWAN
S. SASKATCHEWAN
Ft. William
Ft. Garry
RED RIVER COLONY
LAKE OF THE WOODS
RED R.
MISSOURI R.
MISSISSIPPI R.
UNITED STATES
Barkerville
FRASER R.
Yale
Victoria
New Westminster
COLUMBIA R.
PACIFIC OCEAN

CHAPTER I

1850

British North America at Mid-Century—Ceremony at Fort Victoria

1

IN mid-nineteenth century the future of British North America still teetered in the balance scales. To the south the United States was a waiting leviathan, glutted for the instant by the huge mouthfuls she had gouged from her sister republic in the Mexican War of 1846–48 (practically all the vast expanse which is now Arizona, New Mexico, Utah, Nevada, along with parts of Colorado and Wyoming and the major share of California) but with her "awful swaller for territory" not yet fully sated. For the moment the watchful jealousy between slave and anti-slave states prevented her from doing more than roll covetous eyes northward at the eastern British colonies. But most of her citizens remained complacently confident that, when the time was ripe, those colonies and the rest of British North America would slip into the maw of the United States. The doctrine that it was the "manifest destiny" of the Republic to occupy the whole continent "for the free development of our yearly multiplying millions" was by no means dead. It was merely taking a breathing spell.

Meanwhile, in Europe, the revolutionary hopes of 1848 had been nipped by the chill frost of reaction. Italy, once more enslaved, was to wait until 1861 for liberation and unification. In central Europe, as in northern Italy, the Austrian Empire was again paramount, though its future challenger, Prussia, was sharpening a saber to the north. In France another Napoleon was about to vault into the saddle. (On December 2, 1851, Napoleon

III seized power by a *coup d'état* and a year later was crowned Emperor of the French.) Across the Channel the crackpot 1848 Young Irelanders' rebellion had been crushed. In England, in the same year, the agitation of the Chartists for, among other demands, manhood suffrage and the abolition of all property qualifications for members of Parliament had petered out.

The backwash of the 1848 revolutionary year was to have its effect on British North American thinking. But in Britain, tight-laced in Victorian respectability, and with its Industrial Revolution already an article for export, mercantilism and empire were both out of fashion. The Little Englanders in power at Westminster were fascinated by their new panacea, Free Trade. Under its spell and sunk in that welter of vague internationalism and universal good will which, periodically, appears to overwhelm the Anglo-Saxon, they were quite content to envisage the eastern colonies, and ultimately all their possessions in North America, gliding down the expectant gullet of the United States. "These wretched colonies," the future archimperialist Disraeli snapped petulantly in 1853, "are millstones around our necks."

Those "wretched colonies" had by 1850 achieved, or were close to achieving, self-government, even though it was a self-government still tied to Britain's apron. But they remained separate entities. At the mouth of the St. Lawrence, Britain's oldest colony, Newfoundland, was a sulky cat, its back turned to the mainland and its wistful gaze so firmly fixed on England that it was to play only a minor role in the development of British North America. Meantime, southward, the three Maritime Provinces were intent on their farms, their fisheries, their forests, and on the splash of newly built wooden ships in every cove and harbor.

Those ships were already carrying spars, square timber, and deals (three-inch planks) to the Mersey and to London Pool and Southampton Water. They were freighting flour, potatoes, salt fish, lumber, and cordwood to the New England ports and to the West Indies, there to trade their cargoes for rum and molasses. They were even sailed by adventurers to the gold fields of Australia and California and out over the Seven Seas.

Climate, geography, and similarities of occupations and of ethnic groups (chiefly Britishers commingled with United Empire Loyalists) along with an intense devotion to the Crown gave Nova Scotia, New Brunswick, and Prince Edward Island a basic unity. The hard facts of economics and geography made them adjuncts of New England. Apart from the "tribune" of Nova Scotia, the stocky, blunt-faced Joseph Howe, most Maritimers were too busy with their own concerns to look northwestward. There, chopped off from them by the Appalachian highlands, the New Brunswick forests, and the 1842 Webster-Ashburton Treaty, in which a British negotiator had presented Maine with a blunt fist thrusting up almost to the St. Lawrence, the two Canadas were a snarling dog and a prickly porcupine, locked into the same cage by the 1840 Act of Union.

Wheat—thirteen million bushels of it in 1850 in Canada West—and the red and white pine were the chief exports. Up the mighty St. Lawrence to Quebec City each May sailed the green- or red-hulled timber ships from Europe and Britain, as many as seventy on one tide and a thousand in a season. Down the river floated the winter-cut logs (the upper Ottawa region was the chief source) in huge rafts, sixty feet in width and two hundred to three hundred feet in length, and ridden by red-shirted, singing French-Canadian lumberjacks. Around Quebec and up the St. Charles River the sawmills screeched. In every cove and inlet near by the Irish timber stowers cursed and sweated as with cant hook and pike pole they manhandled the square timber and the deals into the cavernous holds of the great droghers. Under the clear outline of Cape Diamond, in the crowded groggeries of the Lower Town, seamen, timber stowers, and lumberjacks drank and wenched and fought. Meantime, during the fifties as in the forties, the boats dumped British immigrants on the quays.

Through the timber trade and the immigrant ships, Quebec retained something of its old-time cosmopolitanism. So did the upriver port of Montreal. Here, a group of bankers and merchants, the successors to the wide-ranging Nor'wester fur barons, strove valiantly against New York for the trade of Canada West and of the newly opened lands west of Lake Michigan. By mid-century, though, the canal, lake, and river route they had just completed as far as Sault Ste. Marie had already been bypassed by the railroads south of the border.

In spite of a few pathetic attempts, Montreal had not yet succeeded in meeting that challenge. Throughout the two Canadas transportation was still by water or else by coaches rolling along the turnpikes of the "Front," that thin streak of settlement on the north shore of Lake Ontario, or struggling over the dirt trails and corduroy roads of the back country. Further west, in sleepy elm-shaded Toronto and in Hamilton, crouching under its "mountain," were energetic groups of businessmen. But most of Canada West was either only a generation past the pioneer stage or still in it; while across the Ottawa River the habitants clung like limpets to race, religion, and their ancient way of life. In each of the two Canadas few lifted their heads from the scythe or the plow except when Canada West Protestant yelped at Roman Catholic and French Canada spat back. There was, however, one bond of unity. Both Canadas cherished a suspicious hostility toward the United States.

The depth of that hostility and suspicion may seem incomprehensible, especially to Americans, in these days of friendship on both sides of the border. In the nineteenth century, however, in French Canada there was a fear (which continues to the present) that absorption by the United States would mean the disintegration of their race, religion, and language. In Canada West, that conglomerate of United Empire Loyalists, settlers from the United States, and Irish-tinged British immigrants, the Americans themselves had fostered a nascent Canadianism by their invasions during the War of 1812 and by the 1838 raids of the Hunters' Lodges into Canadian territory from bases on American soil. In spite of the abortive Montreal Annexationist Manifesto of October 1849, the Republic, without realizing it, had made Canadians decide that they had no wish to be Americans. It had also instilled in them an intense suspicion of American greed and an extravagant loyalty to the British connection, two impulses which were finally to be decisive in bringing about the union of British North America.

In any future junction between the East and the British Northwest, Canada West would be, by its very location, the key area. At mid-century, though, there seemed to be little hope for a federation of even the eastern colonies. Newfoundland was out of the picture. The Maritimes and Canada West were divided by geography and by a touchy French-Canadian enclave. The whole region was thinly populated (less than two and a half million people straggling from the Atlantic to the Great Lakes), and each province was too intent on its own affairs for suggestions of union to be more than pious New Year's resolutions.

If, at mid-century, to think of a federation of even the Maritimes and Canada was to walk with dreams, to hint at a Dominion stretching from ocean to ocean was to stamp oneself as a fevered visionary or a madman. Canada and the Maritimes were inhabited and adjacent to each other. Between the last chimney of Canada West and the curling smoke of the tiny Red River settlement around Upper Fort Garry (some five thousand whites and half-breeds in 1850) was wedged, as if by malignant fate, a thousand miles of lake, forest, muskeg, and barren rock. In the days of the tough Nor'westers there had been a toilsome canoe and portage route from Montreal across that wilderness to Fort William at the head of Lake Superior and thence to Red River and the West. When, in 1821, the Nor'westers and the Hudson's Bay Company merged, the route lapsed, because the Company brought its goods out from London and took its peltries back by sea from Hudson Bay. As a result the only ingress and egress to and from Red River Settlement was via St. Paul and the cart trails leading north to Fort Garry. By 1850, even to Canada West, the British Northwest and Pacific West might almost have been on another continent.

And here was the heart land of the Hudson's Bay Company, an empire stretching from Labrador to the Pacific and, except for a paw of the Russian bear planted negligently on Alaska, from the two Canadas and the 49th parallel to the Arctic. From Red River to the Pacific no settler's cabin crouched. Over the leagues of grass the buffalo thundered. Northward, amid the park land and the dark forests and over the barren tundra, the Indians trapped and hunted; while the igloos of the Eskimos were scarcely within man's ken. Still further west, in range after range of snow-tipped peaks, the mountains threw up a corrugated barrier between the prairies and the lush, deeply indented Pacific coast.

It was by no means an unfruitful realm. Fish swarmed in its multitudinous lakes and flowing streams and in the mighty rivers, with their trumpet names—the two Saskatchewans, the Mackenzie, the Peace, the Columbia, the Thompson, the foam-spattered Fraser. Elk, moose, deer, bear, and beaver were a few of the game animals to supplement the shaggy masses of the buffalo on the prairie and the rippling carpet of the caribou over the Barren Lands. Swans, geese, ducks, and turkeys were clouds in the air or unnumbered dwellers on the sloughs and lakes, while everywhere was the darting flight of the prairie chicken. Though few suspected it, it was also rich for settlement, much of it fertile to the plow, and concealing beneath its surface mineral treasures of which the extent, even today, has scarcely been appreciated.

Yet in mid-century it was almost uninhabited. In 1857 the H.B.C.'s estimate was of an Indian population of 139,000, of which it placed 85,000 west of the Rockies. Furs and settlers are, moreover, mutually incompatible. The company of "Adventurers of England," its trading posts dotted like pin points on the skin of this almost prehistoric subcontinent, preferred it to remain little known and empty of settlement. But what was to happen when the Americans digested the new empire they had won from Mexico? In 1818, with the aid of complacently ignorant British negotiators, they had grabbed the major portion of the rich Red River Valley. Their 1846 Oregon seizure had been another huge bite. Only the Mexican War had made them content with that much of a meal, since, originally, they had claimed the whole Pacific coast as far as Russia's Alaska.

To any logical person, the ultimate future of the whole British West was evident. The Americans were already casting sheep's eyes at Red River Settlement and at the valley of the Saskatchewan, as well as at the British Pacific coast. Union with the eastern colonies was manifestly impossible. When the right moment came the Americans would roll northward as easily and, from the Canadian point of view, with as little regard for legalities as they had flooded into Oregon.

History sometimes fails to hew to logic. In this same 1850, on March 11, at faraway Fort Victoria, on the southern tip of beautiful Vancouver's Island, as it was then called, a formal ceremony was to prove itself the first tiny and fumbling step toward thwarting the American dream.

2

The skies were gray over Fort Victoria that March 11. A foot of wet snow blanketed the shores of the harbor and mixed with the mud in the rectangle of ground inside the wooden palisades and bastions of the fort. There in the "big room" of the principal building were gathered the servants and officials of the H.B.C. along with a handful of British residents and the officers, decked out in full uniform, of two British men-of-war, H.M.S. *Driver* and H.M.S. *Cormorant,* which were riding at anchor in James Bay. In front of that group a lean and comparatively young man with a high brow, an aquiline nose, and a heavy military mustache was reading from a parchment. On that parchment was the seal of Queen Victoria.

The lean young man, with, as Dr. Tolmie of the H.B.C. at Fort Nisqually on Puget Sound later recorded it, "a pale, intellectual countenance," was Richard Blanshard, well-to-do London merchant and a man who, in his own words, "had been in one or two of the West Indies Islands" and "in British Honduras" and "in India," though there is no proof that he had ever been an administrator. The parchment from which he read was his commission as the first governor of the colony of Vancouver's Island, a colony which had been established in London in January of the previous year. Towering amid the group facing him was the giant-statured, mask-faced, swarthy-skinned James Douglas, chief factor of the H.B.C. and the real power along the British Pacific coast.

Blanshard, who had arrived the day before on H.M.S. *Driver*, was to be only a bit player. He was soon to discover, if he had not already realized it, that this colony was a colony with practically no settlers and little prospect of them. There was no salary for his office. In London there had been talk of a thousand-acre estate. To Blanshard, this may have suggested a mansion with broad, sweeping lawns and strutting peacocks. What he found was a thousand acres still in primeval bush and rock which he was to clear at his own expense. Furthermore, he was to have only the use and not the ownership of what had seemed a princely estate. At the moment there was no lodging for him on shore. When, on March 11, he finished reading his proclamation, there were, according to a spectator, "three hearty British cheers." Then Blanshard went back on board H.M.S. *Driver*, cursing the snow and mud and, it is almost certain, already repenting his blithe acceptance, in London, of this governorship.

The man who was to be his bête noire must have watched Blanshard leave with sardonic eyes. James Douglas had been the first suggestion for governor. At forty-seven he had already been groomed by events for a rendezvous with Destiny. Said to be a descendant of the famous Black Douglas, he had come out at an early age, like so many of his compatriots, to British North America in search of fortune. The Nor'westers took him on. At Fort William, Destiny gave its first shove. Douglas won the favor of the burly, violent-tempered Dr. John McLoughlin. When the H.B.C. swallowed the Nor'westers, McLoughlin, as part of the deal, went as chief to the Columbia Department of the Company's fur empire. There, for over two decades, he ruled a kingdom stretching from Spanish California to Russia's Alaska.

McLoughlin, the "white-headed Eagle of the Oregon," did not forget his protégé. Young Douglas was given seasoning in the Athabaska District and later, from 1824 to 1828, in New Caledonia in what is now the northern part of British Columbia. He learned to handle furs and Indians and to conceal his emotions and his deep religious feelings under a mask of imperturbability. He married, *en façon du Nord,* the pretty half-breed daughter of Chief Factor Connolly. He won a reputation for integrity, for absolute loyalty to the Company, and for nerves of steel. On one occasion, it was said, instead of escaping—as was possible—he turned and faced down singlehandedly a hundred and twenty Indians who were yelping for his scalp.

In 1828 McLoughlin brought him to his capital, Fort Vancouver, on the Columbia River, ninety miles from its mouth. Within five years Douglas, at the age of thirty, was a chief factor and McLoughlin's second self. He checked the trading posts. He established new ones. It was he who in 1840 set up at Yerba Buena the H.B.C. post which stood where San Francisco's busy Montgomery Street runs today. It was he who in 1842, when both Simpson and McLoughlin became suspicious that Britain might yield the Oregon territory to the United States, picked the site of Fort Victoria on beautiful Camosun Harbor as a spot to which the covered wagons could not roll.

Those years with McLoughlin put a stamp on Douglas. Fort Vancouver is still on the map today, a few miles to the north of the busy city of Portland. Not many who pass through it realize that it was once the center of a kingdom. Here in the eighteen thirties and early forties, McLoughlin sat in a banquet hall which no woman was allowed to profane. Douglas was at his right hand. Behind them kilted pipers stood. To it came visitors—from the United States, from Canada, from England, from Alaska, even from the Sandwich Islands. From that fort McLoughlin reigned from the Rockies to the Pacific and from Mexican California to Alaska. The Company had its own three vessels to run to London. It had others—notably the schooner *Cadboro* and the steamer *Beaver,* both armed with cannon—to maintain order on the Pacific coast and to carry on the trade with Alaska. For, by an 1839 convention, the H.B.C. had rented the Alaskan Panhandle from the Russian-American Fur Company for 2000 otter skins a year. In return the Russians in Alaska had agreed to purchase only those goods and supplies brought in Company bottoms. It was again James Douglas who was sent in 1840 to establish posts on Russian territory.

The Company's bargain was a shrewd one. At one stroke it wiped out American competition along the Pacific coast and provided a market for itself. To meet that market and to supply its own posts, its farms and ranches in the Oregon territory were expanded. When Governor Simpson, the "Little Emperor" of the fur trade, visited the Columbia posts in 1841 during his celebrated journey around the world, he found, according to his account, 120 farms along the Willamette River, which flows into the Columbia below Fort Vancouver. In that year those farms provided 35,000 bushels of wheat as well as corresponding amounts of oats, peas, barley, and potatoes. The count also showed 3000 cattle, 2500 horses, and a multitude of hogs.

These farms were run by retired servants of the Company along with, in 1841, sixty-five new settlers from the United States. Their only market was the H.B.C. The Company had, as well, 1200 acres under cultivation at Fort Vancouver (4000 bushels of wheat in 1841, weighing, according to Simpson, "65 to 68½ lbs. per bushel") and other farms and ranches on the Cowlitz River and at Fort Nisqually on Puget Sound at the mouth of the Nisqually River. These last it turned over to a subsidiary, the Puget Sound Agricultural Company.

Farms, ranches, ships, far-scattered fur posts, Indians—this was the kingdom McLoughlin ruled and in which James Douglas was crown prince. Their one superior was Governor Simpson. The "Little Emperor," the illegitimate Scots lad who had won the North American governorship of the H.B.C. and a knighthood from Queen Victoria, was a ruthless, efficient, and touchy administrator. Small and neat-limbed with finely cut features until age made them florid, an amorist who was popularly said to have peopled the fur empire, he and the burly, independent McLoughlin were bound to clash. The open break came when McLoughlin's son was killed in a drunken brawl in 1842 at Fort Stikine in Alaska and Simpson, who arrived from Honolulu soon afterward, let the murderer go. From this time forward the two men quarreled, chiefly about McLoughlin's charitable treatment of the American invaders in Oregon.

The advance guard of the newcomers were missionaries.

Throughout the thirties they converted Indians, took up farms, and on visits back East preached the necessity of the United States' laying hold of the Oregon territory. To them the American eagle was God's chosen bird of prey. Soon the immigrant wagons were rolling West along the Oregon Trail, the confessed purpose, as Peter Burnett, later to be the first American governor of California, expressed it in 1843, that "with our trusty rifles we should drive out the British usurpers"—and this, although British fur-trading posts had control of the country and, since 1818, the United States and Britain had agreed upon joint occupancy.

John McLoughlin was not ruthless enough to hold the line. Later, he was accused of betrayal of their interests by both the Company and Great Britain. Though Simpson in 1841 sent in 116 settlers overland all the way from Red River, the Americans kept coming—in 1843 more than 1000 of them, 1400 the next year, and 3000 in 1845. On May 2, 1843, they formed a provisional government. The next year James K. Polk was elected President of the United States by the slogan of "Fifty-four forty or fight."

This meant that the United States was claiming the whole country west of the Rockies as far north as the Russians in Alaska. The British negotiators, though their legal and moral position was strong, were, as usual, quite content to sacrifice what they regarded as faraway and useless country for a nonexistent American good will. Fortunately for the Company, in 1846 the Mexican War was brewing. With a richer prey in view the United States settled for a boundary at the 49th parallel and even agreed to Vancouver's Island remaining British.

These events had made a deep impression on the James Douglas who watched Blanshard read his proclamation of office. Douglas had had a firsthand experience of nineteenth-century American continental imperialism and of its disregard for any rights except its own desires. He realized that any boundary line was of no importance if immigrants could flood over it and then demand annexation or raise a cry about the violated rights of American citizens. He had watched McLoughlin lose his kingdom, resign from the company, and retire to Oregon City. There he begged for American citizenship and lingered on for eleven years, a forgotten man. To Douglas, the fault lay in McLoughlin's failure to serve the Company with single-minded loyalty.

Douglas was from a different mold. After 1848, standing, in effect, in McLouglin's vacated boots, and with what is now Washington, Oregon, Idaho, and part of Montana lost to the Company, he made Fort Victoria the new center and began to withdraw from the territory south of the boundary. By the time Blanshard arrived to take over the colony, the H.B.C. and the Puget Sound Agricultural Company already had seven farms, totaling 3048 acres, in operation on the island. A seam of coal had been worked at Fort Rupert at the northern tip. In October 1849 the first cargo of lumber for export, 42,270 feet, cut by a Company sawmill, had been shipped to San Francisco.

The H.B.C. was digging in its heels. Douglas knew well, for that matter, on that March 11 of 1850, that the proclamation of the colony was the Company's and Britain's feeble gesture to hold the Pacific coast against the Americans. As such, the colony was a hybrid creation. The island had been granted to the Company in perpetuity subject to a repossession by the Crown at the end of five years or when the H.B.C.'s exclusive license to trade in the Indian territories lapsed in 1859. The Crown was to be represented by a governor and an appointed council, and, later, there was to be an elected assembly. But it was the H.B.C. which was to own and develop the resources of the island and to use the returns, after a deduction of 10 per cent for the Company, to bring out settlers and establish roads, schools, churches, and the like. The fur-trading Company, naturally, was none too eager for settlers. It had set the price of land at a pound—or five dollars —an acre, though the going rate in Oregon was a dollar an acre. It had put aside large reserves for itself. It had ordained that for each twenty acres of land one laborer must be brought by the settler.

Under these circumstances, as Blanshard soon discovered, he was the governor of a colony without colonists. In dispatches to London he complained of the H.B.C. monopoly of land and prices and stated that there were only three bona fide settlers on the island. Of these three, the most picturesque was Captain W. Colquhon Grant. He had descended on Fort Victoria in June of 1849 with eight laborers, coaches and carriages for nonexistent roads, sets of cricket equipment for nonexistent playing fields, and, fortunately for the island, with the seed of the golden gorse and broom.

Grant settled at Sooke. After a short trial, he sold his property to the Muirs, who were coal miners brought out by the Company, and returned to England. Blanshard, frustrated at every turn, also gave up. On November 18, 1850, he sent in his resignation. When, nine months later, he got word of its acceptance, he sailed back to London's fogs, there to vociferate against the H.B.C. and James Douglas. It must have been salt in the wound when Douglas was appointed as governor in his stead at an annual salary of £800. Meantime, Douglas was still chief factor of the H.B.C. and agent for its Puget Sound Agricultural Company. Under him the embryonic colony of Vancouver's Island was not even a crack in the power of the H.B.C.

The inauguration of the colony on March 11, 1850, must have seemed an almost useless move. Yet, though neither Blanshard nor Douglas could know it, it was the moment of the conception of the future British Columbia. The existence of that province instead of an American territory reaching to Alaska was ultimately to make possible a British Dominion of Canada from ocean to ocean. Though it is very much of an oversimplification, it could almost be said that in 1846 the United States won Oregon and lost the northern half of the westland.

CHAPTER II

1850–52

Politics and Railroads in Canada—George Brown, John A. Macdonald, and A. T. Galt—Howe and the Seven Million Pounds

1

THE final decision as to whether one or two flags should wave over the subcontinent west of the Great Lakes and of Hudson Bay was still in the future. In the early fifties of the nineteenth century not even Canada West had more than a casual glance for the unknown Northwest or a thought to spare for the tiny settlement on the southern tip of Vancouver's Island. In Canada, in the fifties, the trumpet call was railroads.

Yet, though the genial leader of Canada's High Tories, the portly, red-faced Sir Allan MacNab, once said: "Railways are my politics," not all Canadian politics were railroads. The 1840 Act of Union had made the French- and English-speaking Canadas into recalcitrant bedfellows. Each successive government of the two-bodied province had to have two heads, one French and one English. Furthermore, ever since the burning of the Montreal Parliament Buildings in the 1849 riots, which, thanks to the square-faced, intelligent Lord Elgin, had ushered in Responsible Government, the Canadian House perambulated in alternating three-year terms between Quebec and Toronto.

In 1850 the administration of Baldwin-Lafontaine was in its last year of office. That government was an uneasy mixture of Canada West Reformers with Canada East *Rouges*, the political descendants of the 1837 rebel leader Papineau. The Opposition, led by the portly MacNab, was a combination of High Tories, who were the unreconciled remnant of the old family Compact, and the *Bleus* of Canada East. The *Bleus,* in turn, were an alliance of Montreal merchants with the powerful Roman Catholic hierarchy.

Each party had its thorn in the flesh. For Sir Allan MacNab it was a group of moderate Canada West Conservatives whose chief leader was John A. Macdonald. The Reformers had a sharper embarrassment. In 1850 at a vociferous convention at Markham, near Toronto, with a rising young newspaperman, William McDougall, as one of its principal spokesmen, the Clear Grit faction had been formed—"all sand and no dirt, clear grit all the way through," as they described themselves. Their program came in part from the 1837 Rebellion, but it also borrowed from the 1848 Chartist agitation in England. Some of the planks in their platform were abolition of property qualifications for M.P.s, vote by secret ballot, secularization of the Clergy Reserves, and a demand—about which, sloganized to "Rep. by Pop.," a great deal was to be heard later—of representation according to population.

The Clear Grits, further, were characterized by a militant anti-Catholicism. Both the Baldwin-Lafontaine government and the Reform Hincks-Morin administration, which replaced it in the fall of 1851, leaned heavily on Roman Catholic support. Yet here among its own followers was an anti-Papist splinter group.

It can be seen at once that any Canadian First Minister in the fifties and sixties had to be a circus acrobat. Within each party were Catholics and Protestants in days when neither had even tasted the cup of tolerance. In addition, each strong man in the House, such as John Sandfield Macdonald, the Glengarry Catholic, or A. T. Galt, the *Rouge* Montreal promoter, had his own "tail" of followers; and each strong man had a disconcerting habit of jumping suddenly from one political bed to another.

The age of the party whip and of conformity was as yet only a dim flush on the horizon. In the early fifties, though, the most chilling threat to the Reform government was its own supporter, the terrible-tempered George Brown.

This Scot from near Edinburgh had emigrated with his father to the United States in 1838, there to found two newspapers in the days when an editor was anybody with two hundred dollars and ambition. In 1843, however, when on a business visit to Canada West, Brown was converted by the country and the Baldwin Reformers. The next year his father and he established the

Toronto *Globe,* still one of the most influential papers in the Dominion. Its first issue appeared on March 5, 1844.

In George Brown's hands the *Globe* rapidly became a political force. So did its editor. Red-headed, dynamic, six feet four inches in height, straight as a ramrod and just as stiff in his convictions, an ardent Free Kirk Presbyterian and an intolerant anti-Papist, Brown had nothing but contempt for compromise. In the fight for Responsible Government he had flung his paper behind Baldwin, Lafontaine, and Lord Elgin. But when, on October 7, 1850, Cardinal Wiseman published in England a pronouncement of the papacy, "From Out the Flaminian Gate of Rome," dividing English counties into Roman Catholic dioceses, Brown's stout Free Kirk soul blazed with indignation. On November 4 of that year, Britain's Prime Minister, Lord John Russell, stigmatized the papal brief as "insolent and insidious." In December, Brown followed suit. All winter long, careless of the difficulty he was creating for his friends Baldwin and Lafontaine among their Roman Catholic supporters, he continued an intemperate onslaught on the papacy. Then, in April 1851, he lost a by-election in Haldimand. Brown distributed the blame for his defeat among the Clear Grits (he called them "Calebites," from Caleb Hopkins, one of their leaders, but was himself shortly to become their shepherd), the Papists, and the failure of the Baldwin Reformers to give him the proper support. It is interesting to note that Brown's successful rival in the by-election was William Lyon Mackenzie, the gnomelike leader of Upper Canada's 1837 Rebellion and now a Clear Grit, who had by this time returned from exile.

The dour George Brown, as much of a terror to his friends as to his enemies, was to be one of the giants of Confederation. His great antagonist, the man who more than any single person framed the Dominion of Canada, was also on stage. John A. Macdonald had been brought to Kingston from Glasgow by his Highland Scottish parents in 1820 at the age of five. At mid-century he was a tall, lanky, loose-jointed lawyer-politician with a mop of dark curly hair, somewhat inscrutable, heavy-lidded eyes, and a nose of almost Cyrano-like proportions.

Both Brown and he were Scots in a day when the Scots had established a near monopoly in the business and political life of Montreal and Canada West. Both had been fortunate in a classical education, inclusive of Latin and Greek. There the similarity ended. Adaptable where Brown was rigid, too innately cosmopolitan to be taken in by the shibboleths of either religion or politics, though subject to sudden fits of Celtic rage, Macdonald seems to have learned early that to manage men one must guide them by indirection. In 1850, at the age of thirty-five (Brown was three years younger), John A. had been the Conservative member for Kingston for six years. He had also served briefly in the Cabinet of that Draper-Viger Tory government which had been overthrown by Baldwin and Lafontaine. Later, though a violent opponent of the Rebellion Losses Bill, he had been too wise and too British to sign, as both MacNab and Galt had done, the 1849 Annexationist Manifesto.

In Brown, the dour Lowlander, and Macdonald, the Celtic Highlander, were the newcomers who were to thrust their predecessors off the political stage. The two were bound to clash. Curiously enough—or, possibly, not so curiously in those days of strong friendships and touchy dignities—it was no matter of high principle but personal and party manipulations which began the feud. In 1848 the Reform administration had appointed its strong supporter, Brown, secretary of a Prison Commission. In the fall of that year the Commission suspended Henry Smith, the warden of Kingston Penitentiary, and proceeded to prepare an indictment of 300 folio pages of manuscript against him.

The Smiths were Kingstonians and Henry Smith, Jr., was the Tory member for Frontenac. In the sessions of 1849 and 1850 John A. Macdonald sprang to the defense of Henry Smith, Sr. (he had by this time been dismissed from office), demanding a special committee of inquiry and accusing George Brown, as secretary of the Prison Commission, of juggling the evidence against the erstwhile warden. Brown began to snort and fume. On June 24, 1851, with remarkable pertinacity, Macdonald again moved for a special committee, asserting that Smith had been dismissed by the Ministers of the Crown "from their cowardly fear of George Brown, who had so completely bullied them." Baldwin and Lafontaine, in justifying the Prison Commission, made no specific defense of their appointee. Brown, already smarting over his defeat in the by-election in April, wrote a seething editorial attacking both the government and John A. Macdonald.

The two antagonists had flung their first darts at each other. Brown, at first, forged ahead faster than Macdonald. That same year, 1851, the Hincks-Morin Reform administration had replaced the tired Baldwin and Lafontaine. It had won a decisive victory at the polls. The Tory party seemed in eclipse and the Reformers in for a long term of power. But George Brown, when, finally, he appeared in the Canadian House as member for Kent in the session of 1852–53, was a wolf baring his fangs at anybody, and supported by a tail of Brownites. In 1853, a bill giving more privileges to Roman Catholics, the Ecclesiastical Corporations Bill, drew his fire. It was opposed by some of the anticlerical *Rouges* of Canada East, though normally they were government supporters. The government, lately so secure, barely squeaked through with a vote of 39 to 33–and this only because the Clear Grits betrayed their anti-Papist principles for the sake of office.

The fatal rift between Catholic and Protestant was once more in the open. That same year came the Gavazzi incident to widen it.

Gavazzi's Canadian career began in an atmosphere of pleasurable excitement. The Toronto of 1853 was a respectable-sized community of about 40,000 souls, with sleepy houses along elm-shaded streets straggling northward from the harbor and the three red-brick buildings on Wellington Street which, in alternating three-year periods, housed Canada's peripatetic Parliament. Life was geared at a leisurely tempo. Lectures were an event. On May 31 and June 1, Torontonians crowded together to listen with hypnotized attention to a tall stout man, costumed in a long black robe with one purple cross on the breast and another on the shoulder. This spellbinder was Father Gavazzi, an Italian ex-friar and a veteran of those Italian 1848 revolutionary uprisings which had shocked the formerly liberal Pius IX into the arms of the reactionaries. His theme was the overthrow of the Pope and popery.

To the Torontonians, this was a much to be desired objective. Gavazzi's error was to carry his mission to Catholic Canada East. In Montreal, on the evening of June 8, he tried to address a gathering at Zion Church in Maymarket Square. A hostile mob ran together. The military were called out. In the dimly lighted square someone gave the order to fire. By a coincidence which was, at least, remarkable, the bullets cut down, in the main, Gavazzi's anti-Catholic supporters.

The shots set off a turbulence which proved conclusively, if it needed to be proved, that freedom in the expression of religious views was not desired in French Canada. The windows of Protestant chapels were smashed. Protestant clergymen were assaulted. The municipal and provincial authorities did nothing. Immediately, in Canada West, George Brown's *Globe* and the Orange Lodges began to fulminate against the Catholics. George Brown had by now come close to taking over the Clear Grit wing of the Reform party. An alliance between them and the Orangemen, who were, normally, Tory supporters, suddenly appeared possible. Within two years of its victory in the elections, the Hincks-Morin administration was in serious trouble. The final blow to it, however, came, not from the religio-racial split in the Canadas, but from railroads.

2

The Canadian railroad boom of the fifties was an exercise in unthinking enthusiasm. It was patent that railroads were essential. By mid-century the United States had already opened 9022 miles of track. In the whole of British North America, in spite of a number of abortive attempts, there were only some 66 miles of short roads in operation. If Montreal was not to become a mere suburb of New York, something had to be done.

Out of this feeling had come the project of the St. Lawrence and Atlantic Railway, which was Montreal's desperate search for an ice-free port. Portland, Maine, and Boston competed for the honor. Thanks to a Portland promoter with the quite misleading name of John A. Poor, who organized a midwinter sleigh race from the two ports to Montreal and saw to it that his home city won, Portland got the nod. The company to build this, the first international railroad in history (in the United States it was called the Atlantic and St. Lawrence–Punch and Judy changed to Judy and Punch), was organized in 1845. By 1849 only 40 miles of road had been completed.

It was at this point that A. T. Galt, later to be the "John the Baptist" of Confederation, moved into politics. Personable, agile-minded, accountant-brained, Galt was the son of that Scottish novelist and land agent who had much to do with the almost million-acre settlement of the "Huron Tract," inclusive of Guelph, in Canada West.

The son was even more capable than the father. From 1844 onward, he had already made an enviable record as commissioner of the British American Land Company. Its holdings, for which it courted settlers, were centered below Montreal around Sherbrooke in the Eastern Townships of Canada East, and through this district the new railroad was to run. It was to speed the development of the area that Galt put one foot and then two into the St. Lawrence and Atlantic Railway. His election to the Canadian House as member for Sherbrooke in 1849 was not unconnected with the fact that the railroad had bogged down, financially.

In that same year another projected road, the Great Western —planned to run from the Niagara River via Hamilton to Windsor and Sarnia as a profitable link between the New York Central at Buffalo and the Michigan Central, which was pushing west to Chicago—had also fallen on evil financial days. Its president, by happy chance, was the leader of the Canadian Opposition, the genial but somewhat greedy Sir Allan MacNab. In 1848, as chairman of Canada's Railway Commission, Sir Allan MacNab had listened most sympathetically to a plea for government help from Sir Allan MacNab, president of the Great Western. To preserve impartiality he had hearkened with equal concern to Galt's cry for aid for the St. Lawrence and Atlantic. The next year, he and Galt found an ally in Francis Hincks, at that time Inspector General in the Baldwin-Lafontaine ministry. Another willing coadjutor was George Etienne Cartier, also destined to be a pillar of Confederation. It was Cartier who in February of 1849 presented to the government a petition for help from the St. Lawrence and Atlantic. It was Hincks, seconded by MacNab, who in April put through a bill that the government of Canada would guarantee the interest at not over 6 per cent on an issue of bonds, for not over half the cost of the road, of any railway over 75 miles in length as soon as one half of it was completed.

With this guarantee Canadian politics leaped into railroads and the two railways were in business. Late in the same year Galt took over the presidency of the St. Lawrence and Atlantic. Teamed up with him were three other Montreal promoter-politicians, Luther Holton, John Young, and David Macpherson. Fifth in the new quintet of energy was Casimir Gzowski.

Gzowski, of noble birth and a man who had had a hairbreadth escape from his native land after the 1830 Polish insurrection, was by this time chief engineer of the St. Lawrence and Atlantic. Within a couple of years, he, Galt, Holton, and Macpherson were united in the Gzowski and Company firm of railway contractors. They all made fortunes, and the exiled Pole was knighted by Queen Victoria. In Canada wealth can play stately organ music.

Meanwhile, by 1852 the St. Lawrence and Atlantic was almost completed. In the previous year, with help from the capitalists behind the New York Central, not to mention the assistance of the American railway promoter and political boss Zimmerman, a Pennsylvanian turned Canadian, the Great Western got under way. Hincks' bill to guarantee bonds had likewise given a blood transfusion to the Toronto, Simcoe and Huron (later to be called the Northern) from Toronto to Georgian Bay. In 1851, too, charters were granted for roads from Toronto to Hamilton and from Quebec to Richmond, which was on the St. Lawrence and Atlantic route. The first Canadian railroad boom was in full swing.

The sweet smell of money had led to the sudden burgeoning. Railroads were the oil and gas pipelines of the day and promoters and politicians were convinced that fantastic profits were in the offing. And then in June of 1851 up to Canada came Joseph Howe, the stocky tribune of Nova Scotia, with seven million pounds sterling in his pocket. Hincks' keen nose twitched. So did the predatory instincts of the greatest railway contractors of the day, the English firm of Jackson, Peto, Betts and Brassey.

3

The fantastic story of the seven million is almost a novelette. It begins with that incurable optimist John A. Poor, the Portland promoter. In July of 1850, now that Hincks' guarantee had assured the completion of the St. Lawrence and Atlantic from Montreal to Portland, Maine, he got together a railway conference in his home city. There were delegates from Nova Scotia, New Brunswick, and several New England states. Bands played and sweated in the hot summer streets. The flags of both countries were intertwined. Liquor flowed and so did floods of Websterian oratory. Stripped of verbiage, the hard kernel of Poor's proposal was a North American and European Railway from Portland to St. John, New Brunswick, and thence to Halifax, a total distance of 550 miles. Thus, if one looks at the map, by the long way around —Montreal to Portland, Maine, and Portland to St. John and Halifax—Montreal would cast its outlet to the ice-free ports of St. John and Halifax. Halifax and St. John would in turn share not only in that trade but in the profits to be made along the New England coast; while Portland would outstrip both Boston and New York.

It was an attractive scheme. It was true that an Intercolonial

Railway to join Halifax, the "Warden of the North," with Quebec, the citadel of the St. Lawrence, had been mooted. This had stalled when the British-surveyed "Robinson line" for it, shrinking as far as possible from the American frontier, had left the New Brunswick ports out of the picture. Poor's scheme brought St. John, New Brunswick, in. Drunk with oratory and New England spirits, the Maritimers voted "yes." When they got home, the morning-after question of finance chilled them. Poor's scheme would have died except for Joseph Howe, at this moment Provincial Secretary of Nova Scotia.

The seemingly impossible was always a challenge to Howe. At the time, with the Maritimers sailing the Seven Seas in their wooden ships, there was only one six-mile railway in the Maritimes, serving a coal mine at Albion, Nova Scotia, though in 1847 turf for a road from St. Andrews on the New Brunswick side of the Bay of Fundy to Quebec had been hopefully turned. Howe's agile mind saw the possibility of uniting Poor's scheme with the all but defunct Intercolonial Railway project. In this way, Britain, concerned about a road to unite the Maritimes with Canada for purposes of defense, might be interested; while Halifax with two roads running into it would become the great port of British North America.

All that was needed was money. On November 1, 1850, as official representative of Nova Scotia, Howe embarked for London on the Royal Mail steamship *America,* his objective to persuade Downing Street to finance both roads.

It was tabbed as a hopeless enterprise. The Tribune didn't know the meaning of the adjective. At the same time—for Howe was a very human as well as a very great man—he was prepared to enjoy the trip. In his diary is a list of people he felt he "simply had to meet," one which included the names of Thackeray, Carlyle, and Dickens. He set down notes of presents—"Box and Cuffs to Ellen," for "grandma" a black satin dress—for himself "12 shirts, 6 pair socks, 6 lawn handkerchiefs, 2 silk do., 1 white vest, 1 holland do., Surtout—dress coat—2 pair pants—and a velvet vest." He also catalogued in five pages the titles of stories to tell, such as "Tailor in the Well," "Borrowing a Congregation," "Shooting an Orangeman"—and Howe's taste in anecdotes was earthy.

The passengers on board were at first "grim and distant," but later a parson from Bermuda turned out to be "a capital fellow full of anecdote," and the captain, "a fine Scotch sailor, with good stories." Three widows attracted Howe's attention. One, from Barcelona, is noted as "not being very interesting" and "too old for flirtation," but the others appear to have been more to his liking.

That was Howe at forty-six years of age, full of sanguine energy, a man for a glass and a good story and a pretty face yet, withal, the statesman of the greatest force and vision in the Maritimes. He was in England from the eleventh of December until the fifth of the next May. In the intervals between his dealings with the Imperial Government he drank in a hodgepodge of experiences. He went to Brighton and to Ryde. He saw Macready as Brutus in the Haymarket Theatre. He spent an evening at the Argyle rooms, where there were "whores and rogues galore," attended a soiree at Lady Grey's (Earl Grey was Colonial Secretary), gave a great and important speech at Southampton, which forced the British Government to give heed to his mission, met, among others, Cobden, Thackeray, and Hackett, dined with Dickens, Landseer, Macready, and others and "had gin punch and lark pudding," saw the Pantomime at the Olympic, visited Carlyle, attended a levee at St. James's, and was presented to Queen Victoria.

To read Howe's diary of his trip is to turn the pages of an album in which all the faces are dead—and so is the way of life which those faces thought so unshakable and permanent. Yet, contrary to all expectations, Howe was successful. By mid-May of 1851 he was back in Nova Scotia with an Imperial Government guarantee for a loan of seven million pounds to build the road from Halifax to Portland and the Intercolonial from Halifax to Quebec, provided that Nova Scotia, New Brunswick, and Canada would all participate in the Intercolonial. It was, moreover, stated in Earl Grey's letter that the roundabout Robinson line for the Intercolonial need not be followed, though any changes would have to be approved by the British Government.

The guarantee in Howe's pocket soon assured the participation of Nova Scotia and New Brunswick. Then he and Chandler, the Premier of New Brunswick, set off for Canada. It was a triumphant visit. In Toronto on June 15 the urbane Lord Elgin assured Howe that Canada would assume its share of the Intercolonial project.

The Tribune's progress thenceforth was that of a conquering hero—speeches in Toronto and Quebec, fireworks and a public banquet in his honor in Montreal, and still more speeches. Howe touched on Confederation of the Maritimes and Canada, with the Intercolonial as an essential preliminary. He dwelt on the necessity of French and English living in amity. He said all the inevitable things to cheering crowds amid immense applause.

Behind the applause the promoters and politicians of Montreal and Toronto were sniffing around the British guarantee for a loan of seven million pounds. Of that sum it was estimated that Canada's share would be four million. True, the loan would have to be paid back sometime, but this, it was expected, could easily be achieved out of profits. A little work with pencil and paper suggested to Hincks, the Inspector General of Canada, that this four million would build both Canada's share of the Intercolonial to Quebec and a trunk line from Quebec or Montreal to Hamilton. At Hamilton, the line could latch on to Sir Allan MacNab's Great Western from Niagara through Hamilton to Windsor.

The Grand Trunk Railway had been conceived. Obviously there would be pickings. Hincks, a man who believed that a piper should be paid for piping, licked his lips. The mouths of Galt's group watered, and they applied for a charter to build from Montreal to Kingston with the intention of going on to Toronto. The cagey Hincks, who became Premier in the fall of 1851, had a bill passed in which he gave himself room to maneuver. His first alternative was for the government to build the trunk line from Montreal or Quebec to Hamilton out of the four million pounds, with the proviso that, if the Imperial guarantee didn't materialize, the money could be put up by the province and by the municipalities along the route. This was really giving himself two strings to his bow. His third was construction by private companies with a provincial guarantee for one half the cost, covering both principal and interest. Charters in the meantime were granted for the Montreal-to-Kingston and the Kingston-to-Toronto projects, it being provided, however, that neither charter could go into effect without a provincial proclamation.

Meanwhile, Howe, apparently quite unconscious that his guarantee of seven million pounds had set the fingers of greed twitching—there was never any suggestion that Howe ever feathered his own nest out of public funds, even indirectly—had returned to Nova Scotia, his grand project, apparently, assured. It did not disturb him particularly when an emissary from Jackson, Peto, Betts and Brassey came to call.

The villain of the piece had now made his first overt move.

Jackson *et al.* was a company of contractors which had built one third of Britain's railways as well as roads in France, Spain, Italy, Prussia, and India. Behind them stood those two famous London banking firms which kept pulling the strings behind the scenes throughout the nineteenth-century history of British North America. (They appear, too, in Hervey Allen's gargantuan novel of the Napoleonic period, *Anthony Adverse.*) These were Baring Brothers and Glyn, Mills and Company. To all three firms the seven million pounds was like a nice plump bird sitting on the lawn to a cat behind the shrubbery—and Jackson was M.P. for Newcastle-on-Tyne in the British House of Commons.

His emissary proposed to Howe that Jackson *et al.* should build and finance the Intercolonial. Howe, a determined proponent of government ownership, refused and, apparently, thought no more of it than if he had brushed off a fly. His completed arrangements meant two routes from Halifax to Canada and thence a trunk line from Montreal to Windsor. Federation, he believed, would soon follow. It seemed of no moment that Jackson's emissary went on to Toronto. A man as honest and as single-minded as Howe had little conception of the depths to which the greed of businessmen will take them. Suddenly, on December 29, 1851, he was informed by Lord Grey, the Colonial Secretary, that the Imperial Government had never intended its guarantee to be used to subsidize any part of the railway from Portland to St. John and Halifax. Yet in his crucial letter to Howe of March 10, in that same year, Lord Grey had written:

"The British government would by no means object to its forming part of the plan that it should include provision for establishing a communication between the proposed railway [the Intercolonial] and the railways of the United States."

So Howe was not to blame. It is difficult to resist Howe's own suspicion that Jackson, M.P. for Newcastle and member of the railway construction firm, had used his connections to bring pressure on the British Government. And what pressure! Baring Brothers and Glyn, Mills and Company had before this time determined the course of empire. Lord Ashburton, of the Webster-Ashburton Treaty, had been one of them. Later in this same century other members, such as Lord Revelstoke and Lord Cromer, were, to quote Lower in his *Colony to Nation,* to become "custodians of Imperial policy and the disposers of Imperial Domain." Earl Grey had had to back down.

Howe was the sufferer. His dream had been shattered, since, once the Portland-to-St. John-to-Halifax scheme was killed, New Brunswick, left out in the cold, withdrew.

There was an attempt to salvage the plan. Early in 1852, Hincks, as First Minister of Canada, whose three alternatives in 1851 for his trunk line suggest that he had had some inkling of what might happen, came to Halifax. To keep New Brunswick in, it was arranged that the Intercolonial, instead of following the Robinson line via Chaleur Bay, should run from Halifax to St. John and thence to Quebec. To get the Imperial Government's consent to this change of route, Hincks and Chandler of New Brunswick sailed for England. The British refused. Jackson, "shrewd, fluent, daring, unscrupulous," to quote Howe's estimate of him, set to work. Before Hincks and Chandler left for home, Jackson had the assurance for his firm on its own terms of the contracts for building the railways in Canada and New Brunswick. The *quid pro quo* in Hincks' case was reported to have been £50,000—and Jackson returned with him to make sure the deal went through.

Howe held out a while longer. In the next year he, too, had to concede. Jackson got the contracts for Nova Scotia as well. It is justice of a sort that in 1854 a panic on the London stock market forced Jackson *et al.* to abandon at a loss its projects in Nova Scotia and New Brunswick. But the machinations of that firm had wrecked the Intercolonial for the time being and, probably, had delayed Confederation for a decade. To complete the story in the Maritimes, Howe, as commissioner in chief of the Railway Board of Nova Scotia, now took up the task. By 1858 he had finished the Halifax-Truro-Windsor Railway, a total of 93 miles. When its first section was opened on February 8, 1855, a contemporary wrote exuberantly:

> Flags were flying everywhere. A salute of 18 guns was fired . . . by the Halifax artillery. . . . Thousands of Haligonians lined the track on which the "Mayflower" engine moved like a thing of life . . . there were merry feastings and junkettings and towards evening an interesting event occurred. The western coach arrived with half a dozen passengers from St. John, New Brunswick. The visitors were promptly invited by Mr. Howe to take part in the festivities. They did so . . . and finished the journey to Halifax by rail—in good time to connect with the Cunard steamer.

Nine years later an extension from Truro to Pictou was built, so that Halifax was linked with both the Bay of Fundy and the Gulf of St. Lawrence. At Confederation these, plus the six-mile Albion line, were all the railroads Nova Scotia had.

CHAPTER III

1852–54

Canada's Railway Boom—The Reciprocity Treaty —The Liberal-Conservatives in Power

1

IN 1852 Jackson and Hincks had returned to Canada in high fettle. Jackson was to finance and build the Grand Trunk from Montreal to Toronto; Hincks was to put through the necessary legislation.

They reckoned without Galt's group. Colonials though they might be, they had no intention of being pushed away from the loaded table without a portion, at least, of the roast turkey. When, on August 7, the charters of the Montreal–Kingston and Kingston–Toronto roads were declared in force, and stock books opened for the Montreal–Kingston section, not Jackson, as the plan had been, but Galt's group subscribed every farthing of the £600,000 capital authorized and so got control of the projected Montreal–Kingston line.

Hincks was embarrassed. Jackson was an apoplectic purple. Canada's ambulatory government was meeting that same August in Quebec. As a countermeasure to Galt's move, Hincks brought in a bill to charter a new company, The Grand Trunk Railway Company of Canada, to build a road from Montreal to Toronto. Meanwhile, MacNab, as his portion of the pie, had been presented with the charter from Toronto to Hamilton so as to tie in with his Great Western.

The weather in Quebec was torrid. So were the scenes in the corridors and in the hotel rooms. Jackson blustered of millions to members of Parliament. Zimmerman, the Pennsylvanian, Canada's behind-the-scenes political "boss," lent his influence to the Britisher for a share in the contract, which he prudently sold for £12,000. The Galt group protested at being asked to withdraw in favor of "strangers and foreigners" and John A. Macdonald supported them.

In all the lobbying no one considered the taxpayer. And Hincks had the votes. Jackson got his contracts for the road from Montreal to Toronto, for part of the Intercolonial from Quebec to Trois Pistoles, and for the line from Quebec to Richmond on the St. Lawrence and Atlantic, the whole at a guarantee of £3000 a mile. He sailed for home on October 28. On the same boat was Howe on his way to London to investigate tenders made for the Nova Scotian railroads. He tells us that Jackson insulted Nova Scotians and "talked at" him, trying to pick a quarrel.

In Canada, Galt was not yet beaten. He now prepared to amalgamate his St. Lawrence and Atlantic with his projected Montreal-to-Kingston line, of which he held the charter, and to build a bridge at Montreal to connect the two. Thus, Hincks and Jackson were to be faced with a road competing with their yet-to-be-built Grand Trunk. They rapidly decided that Galt's group ought, after all, to have a slice of the melon.

The final fusion was a masterpiece of railway artifice. The terms were arranged in London in 1853 among, as chief negotiators, George Carr Glyn and Thomas Baring for the bankers (these firms were Canada's financial agents in London as well as being Jackson *et al.*'s backers and so could carry a hopeful pail on each shoulder), Peto of Jackson's company, Galt, and the Honorable John Ross, Solicitor General of Canada and president of the Grand Trunk.

The "robber barons" had foregathered, each intent on his own interest. The first step was to amalgamate both sections of Galt's St. Lawrence and Atlantic Railway by leasing the Maine section to the new Grand Trunk Company for 999 years at an annual rental of 6 per cent of its cost. Meanwhile, the shares of the Canadian section, which were considerably below par, were exchanged for an equal number of Grand Trunk shares at par, while the bridge at Montreal was to be built by the Grand Trunk. The Quebec and Richmond Railway got the same terms as the Canadian section of the St. Lawrence and Atlantic, except that Galt took advantage of this part of the deal to squeeze out an extra £75,000 for his own shareholders. It was also agreed that the Grand Trunk of Canada East should build not merely from Lévis opposite

Quebec to Trois Pistoles, but right to the New Brunswick border. For this extension it was to receive a subsidy of a million acres of land. Meanwhile, the contract prices for Jackson *et al.* for building were set at £6500 a mile for the Trois Pistoles section and at £9000 a mile for the road from Montreal to Toronto. For the Victoria Bridge at Montreal, the English firm was to receive £1,400,000. Everyone was happy, but later, at an awkward moment, Francis Hincks, First Minister of Canada, was to be asked who had paid for the 1008 shares of Grand Trunk stock he owned, and whether he had known when he bought shares of the St. Lawrence and Atlantic that it was certain to be incorporated on profitable terms in the Grand Trunk, and on what information he had purchased a piece of government property which was very close to the future junction of the railway at Lévis opposite Quebec.

These questions seem as modern as this year's and last year's newspapers. However, by the amalgamation, the Grand Trunk had become a going concern except for the section from Toronto westward. The intention had been to absorb Sir Allan MacNab's Great Western from Toronto to Windsor. The Great Western asked too much. Galt, always a man with a quick eye for either a dollar or a pound, knew the answer. Another company had recently received a charter to build a road from Toronto through Guelph to Sarnia. By a happy coincidence Gzowski and Company (the "Company" it must be remembered, was Holton, Macpherson, and Galt) had the contract to construct this road. So, at Galt's suggestion the Grand Trunk took over the charter of this Toronto–Sarnia road, and the contract, too—but the contract price was raised to £8000 a mile.

Thus, the Grand Trunk was born, with Hincks, First Minister of Canada, as one of the directors. According to its prospectus, it was to stretch from Portland, Maine—and eventually from Halifax by both the southern and the northern route—to Sarnia, a distance of 1112 miles. An annual profit of 11½ per cent was envisaged. To add to the mood of happy expectancy, the Imperial Government, so stern with Howe, had proved receptive to a suggestion that it guarantee the cost of the sections of the line from Trois Pistoles to Halifax, that is, the rest of the Intercolonial. The fact that six sevenths of all the construction contracts were in the hands of Jackson, Peto, Betts and Brassey may have had something to do with the British Government's sudden amiability.

The bonds for the Grand Trunk were floated with a total capitalization of £9,500,000, though the bankers, the Glyns and the Barings, insisted that only half the stock be issued at first. It is a proof of the mad railway fever which had by this time seized Canada and Britain that the bonds, with money at 3 per cent, were oversubscribed twenty times. Construction began, with rails and equipment brought from England and with navvies pouring in. At one time, in these boisterous days, there were 14,000 men employed in Canada West alone. By July 1853 the last gaps in the St. Lawrence and Atlantic were filled in. In the next year the Quebec–Richmond line was opened. On October 27, 1856, the first train steamed from Montreal into Toronto, with groups gathered all along the way to cheer. By 1860 the Victoria Bridge at Montreal was completed and the Grand Trunk was in operation from Sarnia in the west to Rivière du Loup, 120 miles downstream from Quebec. There, because of the failure of Jackson *et al.*'s operations in the Maritimes, it stalled.

The financial picture was not as rosy as the construction achievements. For one thing, the Crimean War of 1854–56 had intervened. In the boom created by it (wheat at from two to two and a half dollars a bushel) money had risen from 3 to 7 and 8 per cent, and land, materials, and labor went up in proportion. For another, English methods of construction failed to suit Canada, while the estimate of returns from the road's traffic proved to have been highly optimistic. It is again a chuckling justice that the English contractors, who took their pay in stocks and bonds which depreciated in value, claimed to have lost a million pounds on the jobs they had intrigued to get, while Galt, Holton, Macpherson, and Gzowski, who insisted on cash, all made fortunes. More serious was the fact that the Grand Trunk had to keep appealing to the Canadian Government for aid, beginning in 1854. By Confederation, in principal and interest over £26,000,000, a huge sum for the time, had been donated to it. When one looks at the history of its inception and construction one does not know whether to be disgusted at the greed of promoter and politician or to compliment them for a venture beyond the Canadian resources of the day.

The story of the Grand Trunk is an illustration of Canada's railroad boom of the fifties. Speculation fever seized the country. Some of the roads were economically sound. The Great Western, for instance, completed in 1854 from the suspension bridge at Niagara (which was opened in 1855) to Windsor, and from Hamilton to Toronto in 1856, almost repaid the government loan made to it. The Northern, finished from Toronto to Collingwood in 1855 and with a fleet of steamers running into Lake Michigan, seemed a logical money-maker. By 1859 it was bankrupt and had to receive further government aid before it achieved stability.

These railroads, and the Grand Trunk itself, were gilt-edged bonanzas compared with the rash of ventures which dotted the face of Canada after Hincks passed his Municipal Loan Fund Act in 1854. By this act, in essence, municipalities could share in the credit of the province. The Ontarian of today is regarded as stodgily conservative. In the fifties he went hog-wild, quite convinced that the way to get rich was to build a railroad. The town of Port Hope borrowed $740,000 for railway investments, and Cobourg and Brantford dipped into Hincks' pool for $500,000 each. Brockville took out $400,000. Yet at the time none of the towns had five thousand people in them. Counties followed the example of the towns. Railroads, going nowhere in particular, crisscrossed Canada like a crazy grid.

Most of them failed, and the province had to pick up the tab. Railroads in the fifties cost the enormous, for that time, sum of $150,000,000; and the contractors and promoters made the profits. Those who accuse John A. Macdonald of introducing corruption into Canadian politics should take a second look at the railway boom of the eighteen fifties. It was then that the principle became blatant that the politician was entitled to what he could make out of government-sponsored enterprises, provided he was not found out too publicly.

Meantime, Galt, Holton, Young, MacNab, the Hamilton promoter Buchanan, and others had learned the lesson, never forgotten since by Canadian promoters, of how to make a fortune from government-backed enterprises—and even private ones—without risking a cent, or at least more than a few cents, of one's own capital. In the fifties, the system was to form a company, keep the controlling interest, sell the rest to the public, and award fat contracts to the "insiders." At times, one feels of Canada that *plus ça change, plus c'est la même chose.*

Yet the achievement was tremendous. In the decade of 1850–60 railway trackage in the Maritimes and Canada mushroomed from 66 to 2065 miles. Most of this was in Canada West. Wind and water and the graveled or dirt road gave way to iron tracks and the puffing engine. The back country was opened up for settlement. Villages and towns and industries sprang up along the rails. The immediately pre-modern age began. Prosperity, until 1857, accompanied the boom—though to this the Crimean War and the 1854 Reciprocity Treaty contributed. In the political field, railroads brought the downfall of the Hincks-Morin ministry and the formation of the Liberal-Conservative party. Most important of all, when Confederation came, the East had been made ready for the concept of an all-Canadian transcontinental road. In the fifties the Grand Trunk turned its back on the natural north-south economic geography of North America and decided on an east-west all-British line. The whistle of the first train pulling into Sarnia was to re-echo, decades later, in Vancouver.

2

While Canada was nearing the peak of its railway frenzy and the Hincks-Morin ministry was staggering about the political ring like a punch-drunk boxer, in Washington, "during the last five minutes of the 5th of June and the first five minutes of the 6th" of 1854, four men sat in a "spacious chamber lighted by six wax candles and an Argand lamp," their faces "expressive of deep and earnest thought, not unmixed [with] suspicion."

This eyewitness description is from the memoirs of Laurence Oliphant, secretary to Lord Elgin. The midnight meeting concerned the proposed Reciprocity Treaty between the United States and the five eastern British provinces. The other two participants were Mr. Marcy, Secretary of State of the United States Government, and his secretary. As Lord Elgin read the treaty "the aged" Marcy was "observed to wink from consciousness [*sic*] cuteness or unconscious drowsiness." Then, Lord Elgin signed. Next "the venerable Statesman," Marcy, took the pen.

"His hand does not shake," wrote Oliphant, "though he is very old, and knows the abuse that is in store for him from members of Congress and an enlightened press. . . ."

The American press was to charge that Reciprocity had been "floated through on champagne." There was some truth in the statement. But not, by any means, more than a portion of the truth. Behind that dramatic midnight meeting, which was to aid in bringing prosperity to Canada and the Maritimes and to endure until the United States denounced it in 1866 at a proper moment to give a boost to Confederation, lay years of negotiation, a close approach to armed conflict, and the activity of a remarkable presidential aide, Israel De Wolfe Andrews.

It was the 1846 repeal of the British preferences for Canadian wheat, flour, and timber which put fire under the Reciprocity pot. The first effect of this Free Trade move was a sharp depression in Canada. In an 1849 dispatch, Lord Elgin wrote: "Property in most of the Canadian towns . . . has fallen fifty per cent . . . three fourths of the commercial men are bankrupt . . . a large proportion of the exportable produce of Canada is obliged to seek a market in the United States."

It was this slap in the face which was a compelling cause of the Montreal Annexationist Manifesto. Yet, since by 1849 the eastern forests of the Republic had been decimated, there was a market for Canada's timber south of the border. By that year one third of her exports in this field were going to the States. The Republic wanted sawed lumber, so sawmills began to screech on Canada's waterways. To a lesser extent the Americans were also absorbing Canada's wheat and the fish, timber, and agricultural produce of the Maritimes.

But there was a 20 per cent U.S. duty as a barrier. Hence Canadians (and prominent among them was William Merritt, of St. Catharines, the man who had promoted the Welland Canal) agitated for a free exchange of goods between the two countries. Lord Elgin himself was convinced that Reciprocity was Canada's salvation.

Promising beginnings came to nothing. It was the United States which held back. Its southern states were convinced that Reciprocity would be the prelude to annexation and, whatever the North might feel, the South would have no part of anti-slavery British provinces.

Another stumbling block was the vexed and tangled question of the offshore fisheries of British North America. The War of 1812 had ended American privileges in the area. By an 1818 convention American fishermen were permitted to engage in deep-sea fishing on the Banks off Newfoundland, in the Gulf of St. Lawrence, and along the coasts of the Maritimes but could dry and cure only in certain specified locations; while they could not, in general, fish, dry, or cure within the three-mile limit. The Americans, however, claimed that the three-mile limit followed the windings of the coast, so that they could fish inside the wider bays, while

Nova Scotia insisted that the base for the three miles ran from headland to headland.

This dispute did not matter too much, since the Americans both fished inside the three-mile limit whenever the chances looked good and ran into the bays and inlets of the Maritimes after herring and mackerel. But their vessels were liable to seizure if they were caught. In 1851 when a sudden storm blew up, an American fishing fleet, instead of running into harbor on Prince Edward Island and admitting their infraction of the law, stood out to sea. Over 100 boats were lost and some 300 fishermen were drowned.

The United States, therefore, demanded that a fisheries agreement be flung into the Reciprocity pot. Meanwhile, Nova Scotia and Canada agreed in 1851 to co-operate in enforcing the three-mile-limit law. The next year the British, perhaps to put more punch into the stalled Reciprocity negotiations, sent over armed vessels to assist.

The American reaction was belligerent. President Fillmore, a Republican, valiant in the protection of the illegal actions of American fishermen, ordered Commodore Perry, the man who in the next year forced open Japanese markets to the blessings of American trade, to take a naval force to the fishing grounds. The Secretary of State, Daniel Webster of oratorical fame, on July 25 of 1852 told an audience at Marshfield, Massachusetts, that:

> The fishermen shall be protected in all their rights of property. To use a Marblehead phrase they shall be protected hook, line, bob, and sinker. . . . It is not to be expected that the United States will submit their rights to be adjudicated upon in the petty tribunals of the provinces. – No, No, No!

Webster must have known that the American fisherman had infringed the law. But the American eagle was screaming and no politician could afford not to squawk.

The British had by this time a naval force of thirteen ships in the fishing waters, one of them a 74-gun frigate. Except for the forbearance of the British admiral, war might easily have flared. The mere show of force, however, had a salutary effect on the American Congress. In order to solve the fisheries imbroglio it began to cast thoughtful glances at the Reciprocity it had scorned. In March of 1853 the Democrat Franklin Pierce replaced the Republican Fillmore as President of the United States, with Marcy as his Secretary of State. That same year, in July, the British minister at Washington, John Crampton, was called in to discuss a combined Reciprocity-Fisheries agreement.

Crampton, to quote a contemporary account, was "constitutionally indolent." Besides, though Canada wanted this treaty, the other four provinces were either unenthusiastic or opposed. Nova Scotia and New Brunswick, in particular, were afraid that their fishing preserves would be put on the sacrificial altar to win Reciprocity for Canada. Under these circumstances, Mr. Pierce, in the traditional pattern of American Presidents, appointed his own special agent, Israel De Wolfe Andrews, to grease the way to the treaty he and Marcy now desired.

Andrews was a whole public relations staff wrapped up in one dynamic package. He had been American consul at St. John, New Brunswick. In December 1850 he had completed a report for the U. S. Treasury on the trade, commerce, and resources of the eastern British provinces. Since, for years, he himself had advocated Reciprocity, he knew the prominent men and the strings to pull on both sides of the border. To him, as a realistic idealist, money would make the mare go. He managed to get it both from Marcy and from Lord Elgin. How masterfully and cleverly he operated to reduce Maritime, Newfoundland, and Canada East objections to the treaty can be seen by extracts from his accounting to Washington for the funds advanced to him. In his statement for April 1854 (by which time he had spent $3483 of $5000 placed to his credit on April 15) occur these items, as quoted in Tansill's *The Canadian Reciprocity Treaty of 1854:*

Paid to confidential agents for special purposes . . .	$825.00
For four agents whose services were necessary to accomplish special objects of an important and delicate character . . .	730.00
Dinner parties, coach hire, and other extraordinary expenses of a like character which I was called upon as a matter of course to defray . . .	575.00
Confidential agents in the country districts . . .	300.00
Paid for procuring valuable and necessary information from Public departments . . .	300.00

This is all somewhat mysterious in the best cloak-and-dagger tradition. His next expense account, however, is more explicit and is supported by vouchers. A few excerpts read:

No. 1. *W. H. Needham*, Fredericton, 1st May 1854. For £210 paid to him for certain purposes of a government and legislative character . . . $840.00

No. 3. *E. G. Fuller*, Halifax, April 22nd, 1854 . . .

To the *Sun* and other papers for publishing editorial articles.

To contributors for preparing articles.

To secret agents for special services.

To active persons in Country Districts.

To influential persons in Fishing Districts.

Contributions to Election Expenses for Gov't candidate etc. . . . $3,900.00

Other items include $313.20 to J. P. Keefee of Montreal for a journey to Quebec to see the Honorable Ross, Attorney General of Canada East, and Mr. Taché, the Commissioner of Public Works, and of $1115 to P. L. Little, "Member of the Provincial Assembly of Newfoundland, since appointed a delegate from that Colony to the British Government" and also "a delegate to meet Lord Elgin in Quebec." About Little, Andrews comments: "He has done this government [the United States] and the Treaty good service." Further items, unspecified, refer to a sum of $2683.00 which he was to pay when he returned to the three Maritime Provinces, and in "the lower part of Canada," and to a sum of $3000 expended in Washington. Less mysterious is an amount of $4218.00: "Paid privately and by myself to officials, leading persons and the press and to others from whom it was not proper to ask for, or to expect, vouchers," in Quebec, Montreal, Halifax, and elsewhere in the Maritimes.

The sum total of this second account was $18,720.15. The sort of effects Andrews was after is shown by his explanation of Voucher No. 1:

"Mr. Needham presented resolutions in the New Brunswick Assembly adverse to the surrender of the fisheries."

It is interesting to note that after his meeting with Andrews, Needham became an eager supporter of Reciprocity. Those who believe that international or national issues are determined entirely on their merits or by idealistic arguments should ponder the story told by Andrews' accounts.

In British North America, Andrews' job was to persuade those who opposed Reciprocity to a better point of view. In Washington, at Lord Elgin's behest, he lobbied and spent money with a generous hand. It was he who "sold" the southern Democrats on the argument that, far from Reciprocity being a prelude to annexation, the only way to prevent Canada from being compelled by economic conditions to sue for admission to the Republic was by granting Reciprocity, while northern Democrats and Republicans, who wanted annexation, were told that, in spite of what the South might think, Reciprocity would mean annexation. When these arguments were backed up by the $118,000 paid out by Andrews to some 90 persons in Washington, they became alluring.

Lord Elgin had, in the meantime, been on a visit to an England which was all agog with the initial stages of the Crimean War. While there he was appointed British Commissioner to settle both the Reciprocity and the Fisheries questions—and Andrews took credit for his appointment. Unlike most British negotiators, Lord Elgin had a thorough knowledge of Canada and a deep interest in the welfare of all the colonies. His opinion of the Americans was typical of the Anglo-Canadian of the day. He writes of their "capacity for turning rank greed into something savoring of righteousness" and adds in another letter:

"It is one of the admirable contrivances of the singularly complex system of the United States that it secures to the citizens the privilege of molesting unoffending neighbours with absolute impunity, except when the said neighbours are sharp enough to catch them in the act."

When Lord Elgin, accompanied by representatives of all the five eastern provinces except Nova Scotia and by his secretary, Oliphant, reached Washington in May of 1854, he was too urbane to let these opinions show. With Andrews busy behind the scenes, Elgin plunged into a round of festivities, his objective the winning over of senatorial opponents to the treaty.

"Got away from the French Minister just in time to dress for dinner at the President's," writes Oliphant. "More senators and politics and Hard Shells and Soft Shells [divisions of the rural New York Hunkers' faction of the Democrats, the Soft Shells being willing to take back into the Democratic fold the radical "Barnburners," the Hard Shells refusing]. I much prefer the marine soft shell crab . . . to the political ones. Then with a select party of senators, all of whom were opposed in principle to the treaty, to Governor A's, where we imbibed more champagne, carefully avoided the burning question, and listened to stories, good, bad and indifferent, until 2 a.m. . . ."

Lord Elgin was a master of racy anecdote and brilliant repartee. After ten days of this sort of thing he was able to tell Mr. Marcy that he could assure President Pierce of a majority in the Senate in favor of Reciprocity, inclusive of several prominent southern Democrats. Andrews had carried the ball downfield. Lord Elgin took it over the goal line.

The treaty which Marcy and Elgin signed at that midnight hour of June 5–6, 1854, and which came into effect on May 16 of the next year, was triple-barreled. Americans were allowed to fish within the three-mile limit in the fishing grounds of the eastern British possessions of North America and to land anywhere "for the purpose of drying their nets and curing their fish." Similar rights of no practical value to them were granted British North Americans on the eastern shore of the United States as far as the 36th parallel of latitude.

The fears of the fishermen of the Maritimes, Newfoundland, and Canada East had proved prescient. Their rights had been bartered for Reciprocity. Another term of the treaty was free navigation of the St. Lawrence River and of Canada's canals by Americans in return for free Canadian ingress into Lake Michigan.

From Lord Elgin's and Canada's point of view both these concessions were far outweighed by the reciprocity clause, admitting free of duty across the border in either direction a wide variety of raw products, such as grain, flour, livestock, fish, poultry, fruits, vegetables, horns, manure, timber, lumber, pelts, wool, fish oil, and, to suit the southern states, pitch, tar, and turpentine. It was an advantageous deal for the Maritimes. In Canada, it provided the long needed second market. For a few years, until nationalism and the greed of manufacturers intervened, economic geography functioned freely in primary materials and the mass of the people benefited. When this coup was added to the railway boom and the rise in prices created by the demands of the 1854–56 Crimean War, the total sum was a skyrocketing prosperity for the three years from 1854 to 1857. "Look through Ontario with eyes to see," writes Stephan Leacock in his *Canada: The Foundations of Its Future,* "and you will mark in many old brick houses set behind straggled lilacs and broken hedges, the memory of the Elgin-Marcy Treaty and the Crimean War."

3

In the summer of 1854, in spite of the signing of the Reciprocity Treaty, the Hincks-Morin administration was on its last legs. It may seem unjust that, of all the promoter-politicians who had made money from railroads, the man who had done the most, governmentally, to make the boom possible was the only principal character to flounder into hot water because of it. But Irish-born Francis Hincks, a neat, sharp-eyed, quick-witted man, was not called "Emperor Francis I" for nothing. Openly contemptuous of Parliament, he was equally barefaced in peculation. In the summer of 1853 the Opposition press had been commenting slyly on the First Minister's sudden prosperity. Hincks paid no attention. Then, in September, a suit by the city of Toronto against its mayor, John Bowes, uncovered the "ten-thousand-pound job."

The suit revolved around a grant in municipal debentures of £50,000 to the Toronto, Simcoe and Huron Railway (Northern Railway). The debentures, because issued on defective authority, had depreciated in value. To rectify the situation, the mayor had moved a refunding operation to redeem all the city's former and defective debentures at par. To enable this to be done, Hincks had sponsored a Consolidation Act in the Canadian House.

This all seemed quite ordinary until it leaked out that Hincks and Bowes had bought up the depreciated and defective debentures for £40,000 and then, by their own legislation, exchanged them for new bonds worth £50,000.

The sin was not in making the £10,000 but in having been found out. In February of the next year the Montreal *Gazette* pounced with the delayed questions about the 1008 Grand Trunk shares Hincks owned, about his speculations in depreciated St. Lawrence and Atlantic shares, when he knew that by his own arrangements that road was to be amalgamated with the Grand Trunk, share for share, and about former government land close to the junction of the Grand Trunk at Lévis conveniently acquired by him.

There were other questions, notably about the 50,000 pounds alleged to have been presented to him by Jackson, Peto, Betts and Brassey in return for Hincks' pledge of the contracts for the Grand Trunk. In those days Canada still had a certain amount of public conscience. When Parliament met in Quebec for the 1854 session, the government was defeated. In the ensuing election neither Reformers nor Tories had a clear majority. On September 8 the Hincks-Morin administration resigned.

It was a crucial moment. The Gavazzi incident of the previous year had sharpened the clash between Protestant and Catholic and had made an alliance between the Brownites and Canada West's normally Conservative Orangemen possible. The Montreal *Gazette* and the Toronto *Globe* and Brown himself, now the acknowledged leader of the Clear Grits, hoped for a coalition of Brownites, the *Rouges* of Canada East, and what were coyly termed John A. Macdonald's "advanced Conservatives." The forceful Brown seemed about to don the purple mantle Hincks had dropped.

There was still John A. At thirty-nine, while not disapproving of the railroad boom, he had, at least, kept his boots out of the financial mire which had soiled Hincks. Meanwhile his talent for manipulating men and motives had sharpened. What suddenly emerged was one of the unlikeliest coalitions of all—Hincksite Reformers linked with the High Tories and the moderate Conservatives.

To this—in George Brown's eyes, conscienceless—combination was blandly given—and we can scarcely doubt that the oxymoron was John A.'s invention—the title of "Liberal-Conservatives."

It was a coalition which, with Macdonald as the pilot, was, through many shifts and phases, to rule Canada, except for a few intervals, until John A.'s death in 1891. By its formation the man who came to be called "Old Tomorrow" made Canada's tomorrow his own.

For the moment the titular heads of the new government were MacNab, the High Tory who had helped suppress the 1837 Rebellion, and Morin, a *Rouge* who had followed Papineau, a leader of that rebellion. George Brown, now the herd bull of the Clear Grits, was left penned in his western Canadian pasture. That John A. Macdonald, now Attorney General of Canada West, was the power behind the throne made the grass taste still more bitter.

The era of Macdonald had begun. Hincks, the aroma of public scandal rich around him, was a liability. Yet he was, actually, a very capable man, whose energy and foresight had done much for Canada. Through Lord Elgin's help, in true British fashion, he was kicked upstairs into the governorship of Barbados and the Windward Islands. Thence, he went on to administer British

Guiana and to return, knighted, as Macdonald's Minister of Finance for the years 1869–73. In Anglo-Saxondom, wealth, however acquired, always purifies.

This and the Reciprocity Treaty were Lord Elgin's last services to the Canada in which his stubborn signature on the Rebellion Losses Bill had affirmed Responsible Government, once and for all. On December 19, 1854, he vacated the governorship to go on to further successes as a negotiator and administrator in China and India. In his stead came the former lieutenant governor of New Brunswick, Sir Edmund Walker Head. In him the precise, thoughtful scholar replaced the forceful statesman.

Elgin had been somewhat too intimate with the Reformers, Baldwin and Hincks, for John A. Macdonald and his Liberal-Conservatives to sit cozily by the fire with him. Head, colorless but efficient, suited the new era. John A. could have his head.

CHAPTER IV

1854–56

Clergy Reserves and the Seigneurial System—
Howe as Secret Agent in the United States—
Macdonald versus Brown

1

WHAT sort of man was John A. when, nearing forty, his era began? Still tall and loose-jointed, his generous nose reddened by his fondness for the bottle, his wallet full of bawdy stories and "soft sawder," his active, cynical mind always a jump ahead of his associates, he was a multiplumaged bird among sober crows. French Canada will permit her leaders to be *bons vivants*. Anglo-Canadian politicians must, in public at least, take their pleasures sadly. John A. broke that rule. A man who could stagger out in front of an audience and announce that he knew they would sooner have John A. drunk than George Brown sober had none of the mandatory hypocrisy in him. That same man could leap up in the Canadian Parliament, rush across to his onetime pupil, the priggish, capable Oliver Mowat, and roar in white-faced Celtic rage, "You damned pup, I'll slap your chops."

Macdonald made a lifelong enemy of Mowat. But those he set out to charm rarely failed to fall under his spell. He seemed, as George Brown felt indignantly, to have no principles at all other than the attainment of immediate objectives. Yet no hint of politics for personal wealth ever tainted him. He did not, like Hincks or MacNab or Galt or even Cartier, make money out of the government preoccupation with railways.

Behind his gaiety and flippancy were constant financial difficulties, the death of his first son from a fall when he was two, a dearly beloved but invalid wife who was never well enough to be his chatelaine, and the care of an infant boy. More than once, in fits of discouragement, he wanted to be rid of politics. The whip of a brilliant mind which saw more quickly than anyone else what could be done and how to do it, pulled him back; that and the desire of any capable man to excel and to dominate and to score off his rivals. No one but John A. in the political welter of 1854 could have ruined every calculation of George Brown and come up with the Liberal-Conservative coalition.

Like most great men, he was at times an exercise in contradictions. Unrivaled as a rule in finding solutions for crises, there were still occasions when, under pressure, he simply went to bed with a bottle and stayed there. In spite of his later vision of a wide Dominion, he had to be pushed into Confederation. And in 1854 he still lacked something of the smoothness of manipulation he showed in later years.

The wind blew fair for the new Liberal-Conservative administration in its first session at Quebec. The triple boom raised by railroads, the Crimean War, and Reciprocity was surging forward. Meantime, two problems which had vexed the two Canadas for decades, the Clergy Reserves and Seigneurial Tenure, were solved.

These problems seem dull to us today. In 1854 each of them was a clamorous shout. The 1791 Canada Act had set aside lands equal in value to one seventh of the grants to private individuals (which were enormous) "for the support of a Protestant Clergy."

But what was "Protestant"? The pugnacious and diminutive John Strachan, a Presbyterian turned Anglican, the first bishop of Toronto, and a central figure in the ill-famed Family Compact, demanded all the huge pumpkin (there were millions of acres involved) for his adopted church as the only "Established Church." The Presbyterians promptly put in for a slice. So did the Methodists through the young and fiery Egerton Ryerson, later, in 1844, to become the capable Superintendent of Education in Canada West. In 1836 Strachan persuaded the governor of the day, Sir John Colborne, to endow 57 Anglican rectories from the Clergy Reserves. Of these, 44 were established before indignant yells from the other denominations halted the rape.

Meanwhile the Reserves remained, year after year, as blocks of untouched bush in the townships, impeding the development of roads and schools. In their 1850 Markham convention the Clear

Grits had demanded their secularization, the resulting funds to be used for education. George Brown took up this cry. The Conservatives, among them John A., opposed.

Part of the price of the Hincksite-Tory marriage was the withdrawal of the Conservative opposition to secularization. So John A. Macdonald brought in a bill to secularize the Clergy Reserves, though the existing rectories were to be provided for, and the funds were to go not for education but to the municipalities according to population.

To George Brown, whose thunder was now stolen, this action of John A.'s was another proof of his lack of principle. The bill passed on November 23, 1854. On the same day, as another part of the bargain with the Hincksites, the Conservatives joined in abolishing Seigneurial Tenure in Canada East.

This system was a holdover from the French regime. The French Crown had granted "Seigneuries," large or small tracts of land, to favored individuals or to religious corporations, such as the Jesuits, "*en fief*." In return the Seigneurs were to clear the forests, establish a tenantry as "vassals," and pay dues to the Crown.

At a cost, finally, of $3,500,000 to the province to buy out the rights of the Seigneurs, the habitants were permitted to purchase farms or to rent them for a fixed sum. It might be noted, however, that Roman Catholic Church lands, about one quarter of the whole, were exempted from the act.

2

When, on May 1, 1851, in the Crystal Palace in Hyde Park, Britain's Great Exhibition was opened by Queen Victoria, it seemed that everything was for the best in the best of all British worlds. But three years later Russia and Turkey were at war. To prevent the Russian bear from planting a paw on Constantinople had long been a cornerstone of Britain's foreign policy. In France the new emperor, Napoleon III, felt impelled to offer his subjects a simulacrum at least of his great forebear's victories. Quite suddenly the Crimean War was blazing, with France, Britain, and Sardinia moving against Russia.

As a result of that war, on the night of March 9–10, 1855, while the Liberal-Conservative coalition was still tooling along a level road in Canada, the unpredictable Joseph Howe sat in Georgetown, Delaware, in the home of the indolent Mr. Crampton, the British minister to Washington. It was a somnolent turtle closeted with an active and inquisitive raccoon. For Howe, untaught by the puncturing of his gaily colored railroad balloon by Britain, was here, quite determined, singlehanded, to win the Crimean War.

That war, after the victories of Alma and Inkerman, had bogged down before Sebastopol. The Russian winter had stripped naked for all to see the deplorable inefficiency of the British supply and hospital services (an exposé which was to lead to Florence Nightingale's mission). There was also a shortage of reinforcements. To meet the latter, on December 24 of 1854 the Imperial Parliament passed an ill-considered "Act to Permit Foreign Enlistments," its principal objective to secure recruits in the United States, even though the Republic, at the outbreak of the war, had declared its neutrality.

The act became current knowledge in the United States around the New Year. There was unemployment aggravated by a depression. Applications to enlist poured in to Mr. Crampton and to the British consuls in Boston, New York, Philadelphia, and elsewhere. Some were from ex-Britishers. Many were from revolutionary *émigrés*. Crampton, with no instructions from London, refused all offers of service.

London, however, was informed of the applications. In the last week of February the Colonial Secretary sent a copy of the act to Sir Gaspard Le Marchant, lieutenant governor of Nova Scotia, and also inquired about the possibility of a depot at Halifax for recruits from the States. At the same time the British Government's Foreign Secretary forwarded a copy of the dispatch sent to Le Marchant to Crampton, asking the latter to get in touch with Le Marchant but warning him that the "laws of the United States should be scrupulously respected." Meantime, Le Marchant had consulted with Howe.

Howe's loyalty promptly reached the boiling point. By March 3 he was on board ship for Boston, with careful instructions from Le Marchant to do nothing more than investigate the recruiting situation in the States and to report on it unless Crampton had further instructions. Howe, in fact, was ostensibly traveling as commissioner in chief of the Railway Board of Nova Scotia to look into the U.S. labor market.

Crampton had no further instructions. But to investigate was, to the sanguine Howe, permission to act. On that night of March 9–10 (the conference lasted from 8 P.M. to 2 A.M.), instead of Crampton giving Howe orders, Howe told Crampton what to do. Before he left, the irrepressible Nova Scotian had developed a full-fledged plan to enlist men in the States and send them to Halifax, where all advertising for enlistments and the payment, maintenance, and training of the recruits was to be carried out. In this way, Howe told Crampton, the U. S. Neutrality Law would not be breached.

The indolent Crampton blinked and left the whole thing to Howe's discretion. On the next day, indeed, he consulted his American legal adviser, J. M. Carlisle, to learn that by an 1818 act of Congress any form of recruiting by any foreign agent was scarcely possible in the United States. Crampton then warned Howe that he would have to move "within very narrow limits" and advised him to wait for a further conference before "any decisive measures."

Howe received this warning in New York on March 16. The sanguine Tribune brushed off the advice as if it were a bothersome mosquito. Rushing in bull-like where even bulls might fear to tread, he had already set up a recruiting machinery in New York. Then, by March 10, he was in Philadelphia at the Mount Vernon Hotel, looking for agents. Three days later, all agog over his cloak-and-dagger role, as he conceived of it, he was at the Jones Hotel, but not before he had made contact with a certain Hertz, who had already visited Crampton with offers to help, at a price, though claiming to be a Dane who hated the Russians.

"One of the greatest rascals that I have ever met," Howe wrote in his journal. ". . . May be useful and must be tried, but I think . . . for thirty pieces of gold this rascal would sell the whole British Army. His wife, a Hamburgh [*sic*] Jewess, with great lustrous eyes [a typical touch from Howe] and rather pretty, a fair accomplice."

In these same few days in Philadelphia he saw the Bavarian consul and a baron, "a tall, soldier-like fellow . . . said to be a coward and a thief."

These were the sort of men Howe picked for recruiting agents. By March 14 he was back in New York, still sizzling with energy, with headquarters at Delmonico's, the famous restaurant. He interviewed a miscellaneous riffraff, chiefly Germans, Poles, and Hungarians. A proclamation announcing Halifax as the "Foreign

Legion's" depot was printed. Recruiting pamphlets were circulated. Cards with "N.S.R." were put out. "N.S.R.," by a schoolboy's attempt at deception, was to stand for either "Nova Scotia Regiment" or "Nova Scotian Railroad." Thus, boasted Howe, who, it should be remembered, was Nova Scotia's railway commissioner, he got around the U.S. law which forbade anyone to "hire or retain" recruits for service abroad. The cards were to be given to the recruits. The recruits were, in turn, to present them to shipping agents in Philadelphia, New York, and Boston for free transportation to Halifax. Then the agents were to use the cards to get their money in Halifax.

It was a wildly impossible melodrama, with Howe dashing around in cabs with the curtains drawn, changing from hotel to hotel, and using assumed names. He was also short of funds until Le Marchant sent him $1200. When Le Marchant and Crampton inquired anxiously what he was doing, Howe fobbed them off. He informed Palmerston and Crampton that there ought to be 3000 recruits in Halifax by April 1. He went up to Sharp's rifle factory at Hartford and promptly wrote to Palmerston, the British Prime Minister, advising him to scrap the antiquated arms of the British Army and buy the whole stock from Hartford—sound advice but one can imagine Palmerston's face when he read it.

By this time the American authorities were alerted to what was going on. Howe sank himself still further in his self-imposed role. "Heather on fire," he wrote on March 24. "Newspapers blazing away and everybody frightened. . . . Must start for Washington at 6. Crampton evidently frightened."

In his visit to Crampton, Howe still dominated. Shortly afterward he was in Philadelphia dealing with Hertz, who wanted "all expenses and $8 per man. . . . Back he comes and will take $1 per head." That same evening the excited and indefatigable Howe went to the circus and then, having met two newly found friends, records: "Ten hours sit at the club. Drank them all drunk. . . . Off to New York at one. What a man suffers in the cause of his country. . . ."

From New York, on March 27, certain that U.S. secret service men were after him, Howe moved to the Hotel Napoleon in Hoboken, under the alias of "Mr. Earle of Newhaven." Next day he learned that Hertz had been arrested, along with an Englishman, Perkins. On the thirty-first, his most trusted man, Bucknall, was pulled in, and Howe heard on the thirtieth that a bill of indictment against himself had been prepared. Howe had already moved to Jersey City. Other arrests followed. Howe's whole recruiting machinery was destroyed. Still full of patriotism and excitement, Howe rushed about like a bee in a bottle, entranced by a new scheme to send foreign officers to Halifax to be trained and returned to the States to recruit. In this plan a polished Hungarian nobleman, Count de Kopornay, whom Howe had met in Hoboken, was prominent. Kopornay became his chief of staff, and a hatter's establishment in New York (the hatter was a friend of Kopornay's), the Chapelline Parisienne, Howe's headquarters.

In the meantime there had been attempts to enlist the interest of Sir Edmund Head, governor general of Canada, in the recruiting scheme. Head had refused to bite. But now the British consul at Cincinnati thought that a thousand men could be raised on the western frontier of the States. So, on the eighteenth of April, Howe was off to Buffalo. Thence he crossed to Niagara Falls and telegraphed to Head to see if he could send recruits into Canada. Head turned down the proposal. Howe re-entered the States as "Mr. Vail," returned to New York, and, completely on his own authority, commissioned Kopornay to raise and command a regiment of 600 Kentucky riflemen. Two other counts (Smolenski and Lanckorowski) received a similar commission for Boston. Then, quite abruptly, by the fourth of May, Howe was back in Nova Scotia to defend his seat in the provincial elections, against Dr. Tupper. When Howe left the States, Crampton himself took over the recruiting and on June 22 the British Cabinet decided to wash out the whole experiment.

The actual production from Howe's whirlwind nightmare was meager. His biggest group of recruits, some 120 Irish-Americans who were sent to Windsor, Nova Scotia, to enlist in the "Foreign Legion," were persuaded by the president of the Nova Scotian Irish Charitable Society not "to fight for England" and had to be hired for railroad work. Other recruits were taken off ships in New York and Boston.

The whole venture was a ghastly mistake, though Howe seems to have been too insensitive to realize it. On the ground of his "services" he importuned the British Government for either an undersecretaryship in the London Colonial Office or for a governorship such as Francis Hincks had received. Howe, unlike Hincks, had no private fortune and, besides, London had little use for the bumptious colonial who, in season and out, presumed to give Englishmen advice. What Howe got in 1862, after years of begging which lessened his stature, was a mean appointment as Commissioner of Fisheries. Yet as late as May 22, 1867, in a speech attacking Dr. Tupper, he accused his rival of electioneering while he, Howe, was risking his life.

". . . This," he added, "I did for England in the hour of her extremity and never received a pound for my services, or asked one."

One immediate result of Howe's American melodrama was his defeat in the 1855 Novia Scotia elections by the young and forceful Dr. Tupper. Years later this upset was to lead to Howe's opposition to the Confederation which he had been one of the first to prevision. Another effect, delayed until 1856, was to stir up American hostility to Britain and British North America.

3

It was late evening of February 26, 1856. Canada's ambulatory government was meeting in Toronto. Outside it was a bitter winter's night. Inside the red-brick building on Wellington Street, the gaslights flared down on crimson carpets and hangings and on yawning, bored members. It was a routine debate on the Speech from the Throne, but George Brown was going on interminably, his right arm sawing stiffly up and down as he expatiated on the shortcomings and lack of principle of the MacNab-Morin administration. No one noticed Macdonald leaning forward, white-faced, his wide mouth set in unfamiliar grimness. Scarcely had Brown finished, shortly before midnight, when John A. was on his feet. Suddenly, to the shocked amazement of everyone, Macdonald, in an almost hysterical flood of words, was away from the subject and pouring out his old accusations of 1850 and 1851 that, as secretary of the long forgotten Prison Commission, Brown had browbeaten old Henry Smith, had used the testimony of convicted criminals, and had, in short, falsified the evidence.

It was an almost unforgivable exhibition. Brown got up. In a few dignified words he announced that he would ask for a committee of inquiry, a committee which, incidentally, exonerated the Freekirker.

The feud between the two Scots now seemed too bitter to heal. But what had led to Macdonald's explosion? For one thing, he had discovered that the road of any coalition is beset with pitch-holes. Within a year of the formation of the Liberal-Conservative combination, the Hincksites were chafing at lying down any longer in the same stall with the High Tories. For another, with the first fine frenzy of the railroad boom over, within the Conservative party itself, a group of malcontents, headed by an old rival of John A.'s, John Hillyard Cameron, was intriguing against him. To give the situation poignancy, Macdonald's wife, who had joined him in Toronto late in the preceding year, in the hope that, at last, she could make a home for him, had been struck down by her recurrent illness.

John A. had enough worries on his mind. Meantime, always, ever, there was George Brown hammering away. In February 1855 his *Globe* had swallowed William McDougall's *North American* and McDougall had joined the *Globe*'s staff. In the following September, Brown had gulped down the Hincks-founded *Examiner*. The rigid Freekirker, leader of the Clear Grits and the most potent newspaper voice in the two Canadas, never ceased to attack the alleged iniquitous alliance of railways, Liberal-Conservative politicians, and Montreal financiers (a theme dear to farmers at any time and in any place). He assaulted popery. He preached Rep. by Pop.

The 1851 census had shown that Canada West's population was 952,000 to Canada East's 890,000. So to Canada West representation in Parliament according to population seemed eminently reasonable. Canada East howled dissent, also with good reason. For in 1841, when the Act of Union had come into force, though Canada West had 170,000 fewer people than Canada East, Canada West had been granted an equal number of members (42, later increased to 65 for each section) in the new House. George Brown and his followers, moreover, openly proclaimed that Rep. by Pop., by giving Canada West more members in the House than Canada East, would end the domination of government by French Canada. No longer, they cried, would Roman Catholicism be able to rivet Catholic Separate Schools on Canada West or to obstruct the Clear Grit planks of universal suffrage, the secret ballot, abolition of property qualifications for M.P.s, and the like or to make selfish inroads on revenues provided by Canada West.

The Separate School Bill of 1855, which, by votes from Canada East had further extended the privileges of Roman Catholic schools in Protestant Canada West, was a prickly case in point. Western Canadian members, whether Clear Grit, High Tory, or moderate Conservative, were under pressure from their constituents and, in general, from their own emotions, to approve of Rep. by Pop. French Canada, for the same religious and racial reasons in reverse, could never agree, since the Clear Grits were refurbishing Lord Durham's 1840 solution, the absorption of French Canada by Anglo-Canada. Not even the *Rouges,* Brown's natural allies, dared support him on Rep. by Pop.

In season and out Brown kept up his assaults. To Macdonald, striving desperately to prevent the four horses of the moderate Conservatives, Canada East *Bleus,* High Tories, and Hincksite Canada West Reformers from bolting off in four separate directions, and sick with worry about his wife, the rasping, self-righteous voice of his enemy was abruptly too much. On that February 26 his control broke.

Yet something had to be done if the coalition was not to dissolve. That same winter of 1856 the fatal rift between the two Canadas was made evident once more. An Irish Protestant, Edward Corrigan, was murdered in Canada East. In the trial of several Roman Catholics for the killing, before a Roman Catholic jury, after a charge by a Roman Catholic judge which, in effect, told the jury to disregard the evidence, the accused were acquitted. In the Canadian House it was not the Clear Grits but the Conservative John Hillyard Cameron who moved for a copy of the judge's charge to the jury.

This mutiny in the ranks was quashed. Then, in a debate on a permanent capital for Canada, Quebec was chosen. Toronto, Kingston, and Montreal government supporters were alienated. A blood transfusion for the government was necessary. The portly MacNab, leader of the High Tories, was selected as the sacrificial goat. By May 24 he and Morin were out and the Taché-Macdonald administration was in. Macdonald, Attorney General of Canada West, was the government leader in the House.

The inner significance was that John A. had maintained his position, in spite of the intrigues within his own ranks. John Hillyard Cameron and the High Tories were pushed into oblivion. George Brown gnashed his teeth. He had to attack a new façade in place of the one which had been crumbling.

In the midst of these somewhat tedious intrigues, in the spring of 1856, almost exactly a year after Reciprocity had come into effect, a sudden threat of war with the States blew up.

It had taken the Americans this whole year to realize that they were outraged—and quite justifiably—by the 1855 recruiting activities of Howe and Crampton. They demanded and got Crampton's recall—and Howe pointed out bitterly that Crampton's reward was knighthood while he, Howe, was left holding a bag of empty promises. The attack on Crampton, however, was only a symptom of a quite extraordinary anti-British sentiment which flamed in the United States like a forest fire driven by a high wind. As usual, there was a sudden annexationist fever. The talk was of sending armies into Canada, where, according to the usual American belief of that day, they would be welcomed as liberators.

The danger seemed real. The Canadian militia was called out. Since the Crimean War was over, Britain hurried out five regiments along with military stores.

The war fever sank as quickly as it had arisen. To the extraordinary Americans, it was an unimportant incident, an exercise in their favorite sport of twisting the British lion's tail in the comfortable assurance that the beast would never do more than snarl. To Canadians, it refreshed the memory of 1812. The problem of the defense of the Maritimes and Canada and, indeed, of the whole of British North America was brought to the fore once again. The United States, without realizing it, had given a small assist to lead Canadians toward thoughts of union in the East and to raise their eyes beyond the mists of Lake Superior to a vaguely-guessed-at Westland.

CHAPTER V

1856

Western Canadian and British Interest in the Northwest—Vancouver's Island from 1851 to 1856

1

THE vital area for any westward expansion of British North America was Canada West. The 1846 Oregon seizure had awakened a few to the American threat to Rupert's Land. In the next year George Brown's *Globe* had published in full a lecture by Robert Baldwin Sullivan, pointing out how by a sudden rush of American migrants Canada could be hemmed in by the United States to the northwest as well as to the west and south. In 1848 there had appeared the first of a series of articles and pamphlets advocating an Atlantic-to-Pacific railway to make possible the defense of the whole of British North America against American aggression, a solution first put forward in 1844 by Sheriff Treadwell of L'Orignal in the Ottawa Valley. From this time forward, for those who thought about it, fear of an American rape of the Northwest was tied in with the notion of Canadian expansion westward and of some sort of communications route to the Pacific Ocean. In a very real sense, as has been noted, fear of the Republic to the south initiated the Dominion of the North.

The early suggestions on these points were academic only. But by 1856 free land was reaching its end in Canada West. Besides, an odor of profits began to drift to the noses of Toronto merchants. To St. Paul, it was said, the cart trains from Red River were bringing a million dollars' worth of profits a year, and in those days a million dollars was not a sum to be dismissed with "What's a million?" For the first time Anglo-Canadians began to listen to the retired fur traders among them who had for years been harping on the potential wealth of the Northwest. Now these men began to find an audience, particularly in William McDougall and George Brown. These two started to campaign for expansion to the Northwest, partly from true vision and partly in the hope that by adding it to Canada West the Roman Catholics of French Canada could be snowed under. So great was the sudden surge of interest that Head wrote to the Colonial Office in 1856:

> All sorts of dreams and speculations are floating in the public mind here [about the Northwest] even among sober and good men. We do not, as I have told them, now govern properly the territory belonging to Canada, but it seems to be assumed in some of the papers that there is an inherent right on the part of Canada to some of the spoils of the Hudson's Bay Company.

The assumption was that of George Brown and his Clear Grits. The "spoils" were in the picture because by the summer of 1856 it was known through a visit of Robert Lowe, vice-president of the Board of Trade in Palmerston's Cabinet, that the British Government intended to set up a Select Committee to review the whole question of the H.B.C.'s control of Rupert's Land and the Indian territories; this because in 1859 the Company's exclusive license to trade in those territories would be up for renewal.

Head's own contrary view reflected John A. Macdonald's opinion. John A. knew that French Canada was unalterably opposed to an acquisition of a Northwest which would weaken their position, and he had enough difficulties without adding to them.

In December, however, there came from London the official announcement of the British Select Committee, which was to meet in February of 1857, and a formal invitation to Canada to send witnesses and to make representations. John A. had to act. As Canadian representative he nominated Chief Justice Draper, First Minister of Canada from 1844 to 1846, under whom John A. had had his first cabinet post.

Even before this invitation arrived, a group of Toronto merchants had arranged to send William Kennedy to Red River to investigate trade possibilities and to stir up a demand for union with Canada. Kennedy, the half-breed son of the H.B.C. factor at Fort Cumberland and, later, himself a clerk in the Company's employ at Fort Chimo in Ungava, had since 1854 been lecturing in Canada West on his Arctic experiences and, in an unexpected change of pace, on Temperance. He spent the winter of 1857 in Red River Settlement. When he returned in June of that year, he brought with him protests from Red River against Simpson's evidence before the British Select Committee and a petition for incorporation into Canada signed by 575 Red River settlers. But a North-west Transportation and Navigation and Railway Company, which was formed in 1858 in Canada West to try to tap the trade of Red River, with Kennedy as one of the directors, came to nothing.

The eyes of both London and Toronto, then, had suddenly been focused on the forgotten empire. But what had led the British Government, which in 1838 had granted a renewal of the H.B.C.'s license to exclusive trade with a casual wave of the hand, to take a hard look at the Northwest and the Pacific West?

2

A humble pig or two scamper from time to time through the early history of Vancouver's Island. Over that colony, since Blanshard's disgusted departure in 1851, the statuesque James Douglas had sat supreme in his dual capacity as governor and H.B.C. chief factor. The Indians were handled with a firm but objective hand. Douglas bought the land from Gordon Head to Point Albert west of Esquimalt from the Songhees for £103 14 *s.*, or roughly $515, and the territory of the Clallum tribe from Point Albert to Sooke Inlet for $150 (£30 8*d.*). The Sooke Indians were content with £16 8*s.* 8*d.*, about $80.

It is quite true that the Indians had no concept of what they were surrendering. Still, there was no irresponsible seizure of their land and they were left to themselves as long as they kept the peace. When, however, on November 5, 1852, Peter Brown, a shepherd on the H.B.C. station at Christmas Hill in Saanich, was murdered by two Indians and the surrender of the killers was refused, Douglas took a party of 130 marines and sailors from H.M.S. *Thetis* (Douglas had the right to utilize such forces) and a group of Voltigeurs on board the Company steamer, the *Beaver*.

The Voltigeurs were a local militia organized by Douglas from retired Company servants. Uniformed in boots or moccasions, long worsted stockings, buckskin trousers, blue capotes and caps, and broad red belts, these colorful scouts drew down a dollar a day—

high wages for the period—and rations which, for the officers, included sugar, tea, cakes, salt beef, potatoes, home-cured hams, and live sheep.

Failing to find the murderers at the Saanich Indian village, Douglas transported his forces to Cowichan Bay, arranged a parley, and landed his forces. He had a tent pitched on a little knoll, seated himself on a campstool in front of his troops, and lighted his pipe. This was in January of 1853. Suddenly, to the thump of drums, a flotilla of canoes, filled with Indians in war paint, appeared from the river and moved along the shore past the troops, the Indians "whooping like demons" and beating with their paddles against the sides of the canoes. Douglas kept on smoking. The Indians landed below his post. Then, the whole mob, yelling and brandishing spears and guns, rushed up the incline. Except for a sharp order to his men not to fire, the Governor sat there stolidly. The warriors, outfaced, stopped. After a two-hour parley one of the murderers was surrendered. The other had fled to Nanaimo. Douglas followed him there and secured him, after another parley. The two natives were taken to Fort Victoria, tried, and hanged, to quote Douglas' words, "in the presence of the whole Nanaimo tribe, the same appearing to make a deep impression on their minds."

In the same style, when a settler, Thomas William, was severely wounded by a Cowichan chief, Douglas again landed 18 of his Voltigeurs and 400 men loaned from two British warships on the shore of Cowichan Bay. An equal number of painted warriors faced him. Douglas walked straight toward the man he wanted. The chief lifted his musket to fire. According to one account, his weapon misfired. According to another, the Indians next to him knocked the tribesman's barrel upward. In either case it was the act of a man of iron will and supreme self-confidence. Once again the Indian was tried and hanged in the presence of his tribe, but this time to the nearest suitable tree.

It was rough justice. But by measures such as these the steel-nerved Douglas kept the peace and avoided indiscriminate massacres of the natives; while to the south, in Oregon Territory, the soil was soaked by a succession of disgraceful Indian wars. Except for the treatment of the Beothuk Indians in Newfoundland and except for the Cypress Hills slaughter of Assiniboins by Americans in 1873, there is nothing in the annals of British North America to compare with the resolution in Idaho Territory, as quoted in Begg's *History of British Columbia,* appointing three men "to select twenty-five men to go Indian hunting," and setting "for every buck scout . . . $100, and for every squaw $50, and $25 for everything in the shape of an Indian under ten years of age."

In other respects Douglas served the H.B.C. and Britain well. In 1852, for instance, he wrote jubilantly to the Colonial Office that three beds of coal had been found at Nanaimo, of which the third measured "fifty-seven and a quarter inches in depth of clean coal. . . ."

These beds, still worked at Nanaimo, were discovered because an Indian, known afterward as the Coal Tyee, saw the blacksmith at Fort Victoria tossing coal on his forge fire and observed that he knew where there was plenty of that "black stone." In the year of its discovery the first export shipment of 1840 barrels went to San Francisco. The lumber business was also developed, the Company farms and ranches extended, and a vein of gold in the Queen Charlotte Islands worked until the fierce Haida Indians, the "Vikings" of the Pacific, put an end to it.

Douglas' handling of the settlers was not as happy. Settlement had, in any case, proceeded at a turtle's pace. In 1853, according to a petition sent to London, there were only 56 landed proprietors on the island. The next year the whole white population was only 450 and most of these were either servants, active or retired, of the Company or miners, laborers, and the like brought out by it. Douglas had a council of three to help him. But he made his appointments and laid down the law with a high hand.

In this small community centered around Fort Victoria, the business of any one person was the business of all. Inevitably Douglas was called "tyrannical." It was claimed that the Company's interests were always paramount. Finally, the appointment of his brother-in-law, David Cameron, as chief justice, while Douglas in his role of governor in council was the Supreme Court of Appeal, brought the gathering storm of criticism to a head.

It is here that the pigs scamper in. The leaders of the opposition to Douglas were James Cooper, a member of the governor's council, and the Reverend Mr. Staines.

Staines had come out in 1849 along with his wife to be the Company's chaplain and to start a school. The Reverend, a man of choleric temper, had apparently, like Captain Grant, been under a complete misapprehension about conditions on Vancouver's

Island. When he and his wife landed neither of them could restrain their disappointment at the crudeness of the pioneer life. Planks had to be put in the mud to get them to the fort, the accommodations were not what Staines had been led to expect, and Company prices, he felt, were too high. Later he and Douglas disputed fiercely when Staines put up the banns for a woman who, Douglas claimed, was married to another man.

But Staines had a hobby—pigs. He raised them on a farm near Mount Tolmie. In 1853 came the day when he suspected a French Canadian, Emanuel Douliet, also a swine fancier, of stealing a couple of his pets. There were at the time four justices of the peace, all appointed by Douglas. To one of them Staines made a complaint and got a court order authorizing him to investigate Douliet's farm. In wild excitement Douliet rushed to Douglas, alleging that the preacher had stolen his, Douliet's, pigs and demanding justice, but claiming that no J.P. would act against the Reverend Mr. Staines. Douglas sent him to his brother-in-law, Cameron, appointed a J.P. by suspicious coincidence on that very day. Cameron arrested the Reverend Staines. Then Douglas named Cameron as chief justice. The case of pig stealing against the Reverend Staines was thrown out but the outrage of arrest remained.

The whole affair amounted to the escape of two pigs from a pigpen. Yet the incident drove the opposition to Douglas into clamorous and official protest, with the appointment of his brother-in-law as a main point in the indictment. The Reverend Mr. Staines was selected to carry the anti-Douglas petition in person to London. The pigs intervened again. Staines was on his way to take ship at Sooke Harbour when news came that his pets had got out. Staines turned back and missed his boat. The vessel on which he finally embarked had scarcely started when it was struck by a squall off Cape Flattery. Everyone on board was lost except for one survivor, and the survivor, unfortunately, was not Mr. Staines.

In his dispatches to London, Douglas smoothed over the charges against him. Yet the loud and incessant complaints made the Colonial Office prick up its ears. In 1856 Douglas was ordered to hold the elections for the legislative assembly which had been provided for in the original grant.

It was, in a way, an absurd order. At the time there were about 300 male whites on the island and only some 40 of these owned the twenty acres of land laid down by Douglas as a property prerequisite for the franchise. However, he divided the settlement into four electoral districts, to elect seven members. This first parliament to meet in British North America west of Toronto was called together on August 1, 1856. Before its seven members, Douglas, a self-made man, spoke as if in front of a thousand, congratulating the colony on its "slow but hardy growth" and warning the members to "live strictly within our means." "Within our means" meant within an annual income from liquor licenses of from three to four hundred pounds.

Vancouver's Island was still a colony in miniature with a few hundreds of white population, a toy assembly, a couple of schools, as many churches, and a few short roads leading out into the untouched and glorious wilderness of huge trees and romantic, flower-gay glens, while to the south, across the blue island-studded sea gleamed the white peaks of the majestic Olympic range. Life in this seeming Eden had a charm which the next few years were to destroy. Here even school examinations were a public occasion. On July 30, 1855, in a letter to Dr. Tolmie, John Work, a retired H.B.C. clerk, describes the ceremonies at the school on the Company's Craigflower farm:

". . . Mr. Douglas was there with Mr. and Mrs. Cameron and some of the officers and many others. Craigflower had triumphal arches erected at both ends of the bridge leading to the School [over Victoria Arm] and an elegant device put up with VR in the middle of it, and to finish, at the hour of meeting, a Salute of twenty-one guns fired. . . . [It was] finished off with a repast to the company of wine, cakes and other dainties. The examination is said to have gone off well. . . ."

Such was life for Governor Douglas, a round of petty though often pleasant official duties mingled with the more serious business of developing the resources of the island and making certain that the H.B.C. retained all its powers and privileges. He was a monarch in these years. Only lip service was due to either the British Colonial Office or even to that emperor of the fur trade, Governor Simpson. Quite obviously, when emergencies poked up their sudden heads, Douglas had to act first and report afterward. This type of procedure was actually the rock on which the Company's control of its huge empire rested. Their chief factors, lacking both the long-distance telephone and the telegraph, had to follow their own best judgment.

The system bred despots who were men of action. Thus, when

in 1852 rumors of gold on the Queen Charlotte Islands had brought a rush of American miners, Douglas, though he had no authority, promptly issued a proclamation that all metals there belonged to the Crown and demanded that the miners buy licenses. His actions were recognized by the Imperial Government's appointing him lieutenant governor of the islands.

The gold petered out, but a principle and method of procedure had been established which was to serve Douglas and Britain well when, in 1858, the Fraser gold stampede threatened to swamp the British title to the Pacific coast.

By 1856, however, the complaints against Douglas and the H.B.C. monopoly on Vancouver's Island and the strictures about the slow growth of the colony, along with rumors of gold, were among the reasons which led the Imperial Parliament to set up its Select Committee of 1857. The same type of protest from Red River Settlement and a newly born distrust of any monopolistic control had also made the government decide to take a long, hard look at the H.B.C.'s rule of the Northwest and the Indian territories. That control rested on the twin pillars of the 1670 charter to the "Company of Adventurers of England trading into Hudson's Bay" and the exclusive license to trade in the rest of the area. Was it time to cancel both? There was one man to say an emphatic "no," Sir George Simpson, governor of the North American holdings of the Hudson Bay Company.

CHAPTER VI

1850–57

Sir George Simpson and the Fur Empire—Buffalo-Hunt and Cart-Train Years—Simpson before the British Select Committee—The Palliser and Dawson-Hind Expeditions

1

FOR decades the word of George Simpson had been the ukase from Labrador to the Pacific and from the 49th parallel to the Arctic. This illegitimate Scots lad from Ross-shire got off to a dull start as a clerk in the London firm of an uncle whose daughter, in the style of Horatio Alger's heroes, he was later to marry; although there were items in Simpson's career of which Alger would have disapproved severely. But in 1820, at, according to what appears to be the best account, the age of thirty-three, through the interest of an H.B.C. official, Andrew Colville, Simpson left London for Norway House on Lake Winnipeg. He took to the fur trade like a cage-cooped panther to the wilderness. Once the Nor'westers and the H.B.C. had amalgamated, he shot to the front with greyhound speed. By 1826 he was acting governor for the Company in North America. It was only putting the seal on an accomplished fact when the position was made permanent in 1839.

Energetic, tireless, ruthless, a man who swept from post to post in his state canoe, wearing a top hat and a cloak and accompanied by his kilted piper, the "Little Emperor" made the fur trade pay as it had never paid before. He kept a "character book," in which he put down uninhibited judgments of the men under him, referred to by code numbers to preserve anonymity. He promoted and demoted with but one concern, what was best for the Company. He struck down possible rivals, such as Dr. McLoughlin, described by Simpson after their first meeting as "such a figure as I should not like to meet in a dark night in one of the bye lanes in the neighborhood of London." He raised up loyal souls such as James Douglas, who was set down as "a stout powerful man of good constitution and respectable abilities." He noted how the production of each post could be bettered and saw to it that it was done. During his earlier years no one knew when he might descend, and woe to that chief factor or trader whose handling of affairs did not suit his quick, decisive eyes. To give an illustration, during his 1824–25 trip from York Factory to the Columbia and back to Fort Garry (Simpson always traveled at what was, for the Northwest, Napoleonic speed) he noted with reference to Chief Factor John McLeod at Kamloops that:

"It is a lamentable fact that two Chief Traders out of three now in Columbia say that Mrs. [Misters] D— and M— are so much under the influence of their women and so watchful of their chastity that what they say is Law, and they cannot muster sufficient confidence in their Ladies to be 5 minutes in and out of their presence and even for that short time they keep them under Lock and Key, although they have more than once discovered that 'Love laughs at Locksmiths.'"

The "Ladies" referred to were Indian women married "according to the custom of the country." Soon afterward John McLeod was relieved of his post by being given permission to go "east of the mountains."

It was, however, not a question of morals. The Little Emperor himself, quite unconcernedly, recognized at least seven of his own children born out of wedlock. What he demanded was to put the Company first. For almost forty years he was the terror of the fur empire and the delight of the stay-at-home governors of the Company, sitting in their smoke-blackened board room in London.

With age, however, respectability began to beckon. In 1830, on one of his visits to London, he married the daughter of the uncle who had been his benefactor, though she was twenty-six years his junior. For the winter of 1831–32 he brought his young bride to Upper Fort Garry, where, it was related, with an eye to her husband's former amours, she was afraid to look about her too closely for fear of "seeing something disagreeable." His intention was to settle there. For that purpose, he refurbished Lower Fort Garry.

But the death of their first-born son on Easter Sunday 1832 saddened his wife and himself. He removed to Lachine, just above Montreal. Here, in a great stone house, sixty feet by sixty, he kept in touch with affairs in London and Canada. In January of 1841 he was knighted by Queen Victoria in Buckingham Palace and from thence embarked for his journey around the world.

Though he now sat in Lachine, Simpson did not loosen the reins in the Northwest. Almost every spring until his death in 1860, he set out for Fort Garry in his great canoe along the old water-and-portage route of the Nor'westers. In 1854, when he was sixty-seven, George Simpson, as Moberly, who accompanied him that year, tells us in his *When Fur Was King*, was still rousing at 1 A.M. to travel onward, first taking a preprandial dip in the freezing water of the lake or river by which his camp had been pitched.

This was the man who tried to hold back the waters of change in the Northwest. Each spring he met his councils in Fort William and at Fort Garry or Norway House or York Factory. Each spring and summer he traveled the waterways or the cart trails to his far-flung posts.

While Canada was preoccupied with railways and the Maritimes with their ships, the Northwest was still a fur-trading and a frontier land. The posts were flung like a coarse-meshed net from Fort Garry at Red River and Norway House on Lake Winnipeg and York Factory on Hudson Bay up the valley of the North Saskatchewan to Fort Edmonton. Thence another net was tossed up to the Peace River country and still another across the mountains into New Caledonia. From this last net, loops cast down the valleys of the Fraser and Thompson and the Columbia reached to the posts in Oregon Territory and to Fort Victoria. In all, in 1856, when the Select Committee was decided upon, the Company had 152 establishments, 16 chief factors, 29 chief traders, 5 surgeons, 87 clerks, 67 postmasters, 500 voyageurs, and 1200 permanent servants, besides the personnel on their ships.

The posts in Oregon and in the southern part of present-day British Columbia were supplied—and the peltries taken back—by boat from England and by horse brigades along the river trails. For those in the northern area of the mountains and in Rupert's Land, the goods and furs traveled to and from England via Hudson Bay. From York Factory or Norway House or Fort Garry, the traffic to and from the interior was by York Boat or, later, by cart and horse brigade. It was a tough and a rough life "tracking" the boats upstream or guiding the screeching Red River carts over the rutted trails and bridgeless streams. But there was a frontier freedom which appealed; and to the Company's fur trade, it must be remembered, were added its farms and ranches, its trade with the Russians and Honolulu, and its ventures on Vancouver's Island, which, with Douglas in charge, was still in its domain.

Fort Victoria was the capital of Douglas' kingdom. At Fort Edmonton, the most important post between Fort Victoria and Fort Garry, the burly Irish-Catholic John Rowand ruled until his death in a fit of temper at Fort Pitt in 1854. Of him, Simpson wrote in his character book:

"Warm-hearted and Friendly to an extraordinary degree where he takes a liking, but on the contrary his prejudices are exceedingly strong. Of fiery disposition and as bold as a Lion. An excellent Trader who has the peculiar talent of attracting the fiercest Indians . . . while he rules them with a rod of Iron. . . . Will not tell a lie publick is very uncommon in this country but has sufficient address to evade the truth when it suits his purpose. . . ."

Through Rowand and through Fort Edmonton we can glimpse how the H.B.C. at its height, scarcely more than a century ago, managed its vast and thinly populated empire. The fort itself, after several shifts and changes, had finally been planted on a two-hundred-foot-high natural bastion on the north bank of the swift-flowing North Saskatchewan, just below the Provincial Legislative Building in the modern city of Edmonton. Hexagonal, with a twenty-foot palisade, it commanded a magnificent view over the winding, wooded banks of the almost mile-wide and empty valley below it. Where now a city stands it had farms for raising barley and potatoes (in 1855 the potato crop was 1600 bushels) and two horse guards (in all some four hundred horses) two miles north of the fort and a racecourse near by, added by John Rowand for excitement. At water's edge was a saw pit and boat yard for the building of York Boats, either twenty-eight or forty feet in length, and made of hand-picked spruce, which had to be felled, floated to the yard, and whipsawed by hand into planks. Sternposts and bowposts of these river freight cars were cut at an angle of 45 degrees so that they could be pushed easily off snags or mud bars.

These occupations were only part of the normal round. As in every other post of the Company, there were blacksmiths with horses to shoe, stoves to make, and even their own rectangular hand-cut iron nails and spikes to fashion. Hundreds of pounds of whitefish had to be caught at Lac Ste. Anne, some fifty miles away, as food for the officers, the servants, and the dogs. Hunters went out for moose, deer, and, in particular, for the buffalo, from which the women made pemmican, the fur trader's staff of life. In 1847, when Paul Kane, the earliest painter of the northwestern scene, visited Fort Edmonton, one hundred and fifty people swarmed to the Christmas Day festivities in Rowand's great banqueting hall, and we may take this to be close to the normal staff of the fort.

But when the Indians moved in to trade (because of the constant warfare between them, the Blackfeet came north in the summer and the Crees and Stoneys during the autumn and winter) or when in the fall the brigades pulled in from the East with the trade goods or when the peltries arrived from the Peace, and from Rocky Mountain House and New Caledonia in the spring—then the fort and its environs seethed with dogs, tribesmen, voyageurs, and bright-eyed Indian or half-breed belles. Inside the fort's palisades Rowand had built a three-storied house, sixty by seventy feet. Called "Rowand's Folly," its most striking feature, apart from windows of real glass, was the decoration of its great hall. Of it, Paul Kane wrote:

"The walls and ceiling are boarded . . . but these boards are painted in a most startling, barbaric gaudiness, and the ceiling filled with centre pieces of fantastic gilt scrolls. . . ."

It was here that Rowand overawed the Indian chiefs. Here, too, great balls were given, especially when the fall brigades arrived. There was no lack of fiddlers. The great hall, now vanished, rang with their lilting as the voyageurs and servants of the Company swung the starry-eyed belles to the reels and jigs. Often in the morning, we are told, after such a night of festivity, shyly smiling brides, taken to wife *en façon du Nord,* would appear with their grooms before the factor for ratification of the unions. Otherwise the bride, and, later, the family, would not receive rations from the Company.

All this was a part, though only a fraction, of the way of life which Simpson strove to retain. There was also the open trail and the sudden storms of summer and the winter's deep snow and savage cold—twenty to thirty below zero a commonplace—and the violent blizzards in which dog team and man found it difficult to survive. It required a tough breed of man. Possibly that is why the fur trade was almost a preserve for the Scots. They took to the freedom of this adventurous wide-ranging life and they were stout and stubborn enough to endure. A chance at fortune was an added flick to their strong pioneering instinct. Where else but in the fur trade, for that matter, could a George Simpson have risen to a fortune, a knighthood, and an empire?

The Scots got along with the Indians and intermarried with them as freely as the French fur traders had intermingled. (The Cree women were regarded as the best-looking, most moral, and docile.) For it was still an Indian land. In the Northwest the Indians fought their tribal wars unmolested, even under the very palisades of Fort Edmonton. They still fed off the buffalo, the moose, the elk, the caribou, the beaver, the geese, ducks, and swans of the plains and park land and caught the fish in the lakes and rivers. True, they had come to depend on the white man for knives, guns, and rum. The white man's diseases, and in particular, the dread smallpox, had decimated them time after time. But they remained, in essence, free and proud. The early missionaries, on the whole, agree in describing the prairie and park-land red man as splendid in physique and as practicing a code of conduct which, in some respects, could have given lessons to the whites.

Among the mountains and, in particular, on the Pacific coast, the Indians, thanks to the salmon, were better organized and more "advanced" in culture. Even in the interior, though with notable exceptions, they tended to have more permanent settlements than their brothers on the prairies or in the northern forest. On the coast they lived in huge communal halls, like those of the Samoans, and were divided into nobles, commoners, and slaves. The totem pole was the pride of family and religion, and the potlatch, in which he who gave away most won, the touchstone of wealth and power. They were likewise more jealous of property rights and more ill-disposed to the whites.

The Company's policy of firmness and a justice which was stern but objective, as exemplified by Douglas, prevented any serious or wide-ranging clashes. On the prairie, even the fierce Blackfeet, in whose country no permanent post had ever been established, kept the unspoken truce between the white man and red. Lack of settlers was, in part, the reason why no wholesale massacres such as those south of the border disgraced the history of the Company. But credit, too, must be given to its wise policy of noninterference and, if the unspoken laws were broken, of a stern but just punishment.

To these good relations the missionaries contributed. It was in 1818 that Father—later Bishop—Provencher established the first Roman Catholic mission at Red River. Two years later, the Company brought out the Anglican Reverend John West, also to Red River. In 1840, the Methodist Reverend James Evans, who invented the Cree alphabet and printed the Bible on birch bark, with type made of lead secured from the Company, set up a mission at Norway House, while eleven years afterward the first Presbyterian divine, the Reverend John Black, arrived. From Red River, the missionaries, both Protestant and Catholic, fanned out over the Northwest, notable among them the frail Methodist Robert Terrill Rundle, posted at Fort Edmonton in 1840. Father Thibault set up a mission at Lac Ste. Anne in 1843. Father Lacombe, the "Black-Robe Voyageur," arrived in September 1852, became Rowand's close friend, and began a long life of service in what is now Alberta. Then, in 1862, came the dean of Methodist missionaries, the Reverend George McDougall. He and his two sons, John and David, were to stride large in the early Northwest.

With all these ardent apostles to the pagans the Company worked in harmony, often utilizing them to keep the Indians quiet. From the objective point of view, they planted the conflicting creeds of Christianity among the natives and contributed to the breakdown of a way of life which had been sufficient for them. They, along with the H.B.C. posts, prepared the way for the inevitable destruction of Indian freedom by what is called civilization. But in that era of unquestioning faith the missionaries, whatever their denomination, were selfless and devoted men, enduring the dangers and discomforts of the open trail and the Indian camps in their thirst for souls.

Such, in brief outline, was Simpson's empire, one in which he was the autocrat, a dangerous man to cross but of stanch loyalty to his friends. When Rowand died in 1854, Simpson had his body dug up and boiled and the bones taken to Red River to be put in a keg of alcohol. He shipped that keg via England to Canada East for burial. It was of this event that W. S. Gladstone, who at the time was a carpenter at Fort Edmonton, wrote to Miss Hughes, author of *Father Lacombe,* in September 1910:

"Well, the next spring," Gladstone related, "they were tolded to dig up the body and send the bones to St. Boniface so they got an indian to dig it up and boil the flesh of it was sayed that wimmen of the fort made soap with the fat of the pot . . . there was not a man at boath forts [Fort Edmonton and Fort Pitt] that done any crying for him everybody was glad. . . ."

In that extract from Gladstone's letter is the toughness of the days of Simpson's rule. His empire, however, had its Achilles' heel, the Red River Settlement.

Since 1836, as the District of Assiniboia, defined as a circle with a radius of fifty miles around Fort Garry, Selkirk's old settlement had been administered by a governor and council appointed by the Company. By mid-century it was a Quebec in miniature. Its farms straggled in long narrow strips back from the Red River, as if it were another St. Lawrence, for about thirty miles. Other settlements ran west along the Assiniboine River as far as Portage la Prairie, sixty miles away. The center of the settlement was, naturally, the Company's Upper Fort Garry, on the western bank of the Red River at its junction with the Assiniboine. Most of the 5000 settlers were half-breeds. The Scots and English were Protestants; the French, Catholics.

Difference in blood carried with it a difference in temperament. The English-speaking breeds tended to be sober, serious farmers. The French *métis*, the *Bois-Brulés*, as they often called themselves, were, in general, lighthearted, indolent, and improvident. For them the excitement of the hunt was infinitely preferable to the dullness of the plow. It was these *métis* who believed themselves the "New Nation," the owners of the soil by natural right. And it was they who, by the annual buffalo hunts—a spring and a fall one—were the chief providers of the Company's pemmican.

In the buffalo hunt the spirit of the "New Nation," which was later to challenge Confederation, found full expression. It is, likewise, a reminder of how near its romantic but almost forgotten past is to the Canadian prairie of today. The hunt was practically the whole *métis* community on the march, accompanied by its priests. There were the hunters, each riding an ordinary pony but leading two or three blooded and highly trained buffalo runners, their saddles of elaborately beaded cloth in scarlet or blue. For the women and children there were the Red River carts, built entirely of wood, with high, dished wheels. Around and everywhere were the barking, yelping dogs. In the 1840 hunt 1210 carts, more than 4000 men, women, and children, and some 500 dogs participated.

The wheels screeched on the wooden axles. The convoy wound over the wide prairie. At the first night's encampment the president of the hunt and the "soldiers" were appointed. The laws of the hunt were proclaimed, including observance of the Sabbath and prohibition of theft. For the first violation, the sinner had his saddle cut to pieces. For the second, his coat was torn from his back. For the third, he was flogged.

Here was the quasi-military organization which Louis Riel was later to find ready to his hand. It was all preliminary to the day when the buffalo were sighted. Then the hunters rode slowly forward over the crocus-studded plain in a great semicircle. When the president dropped his upraised arms, the run was on. Ahead thundered the shaggy mass of buffalo, the cows, the preferred meat in the van, the bulls a compact phalanx at the rear. Into that mass charged the hunters, firing from the saddle and reloading at the gallop, their only safety from badger or gopher holes or from the press and horns of the maddened herd, their own alertness and the skill of their ponies. Two or three runs by each hunter was the rule. By that time hundreds of the huge brown bodies were humps on the prairie grass.

After the thrill came the labor under the hot prairie sun. There was the stripping off of the robes, the cutting out of the tongues, and the hacking off of the choice meat. The Red River carts shrieked between the hunt and the camp. There the women slashed the meat into long strips, pressed it by hand into quarter-inch thickness, and hung it on wooden frames to dry. The flesh of the tenderloins, humps, and undershoulders were made into sixty-pound bundles for winter use; the rest was flayed into pemmican—a mass of meat and tallowy fat which could be cut with an ax and which only a fur trader or a *métis* or an Indian could stomach. Bones were split and boiled for their marrow. The tongues were usually sold on the spot to traders, who salted them and then painted them with molasses for sale in St. Paul to the luxury tables of the East. From the 1840 hunt 1,089,000 pounds of meat was brought back, and nearly as much wasted; but in those days the buffalo seemed inexhaustible.

Though the hunt was tied in with the Company's needs, Red River Settlement was still, in Simpson's view, a nest of wasps in an otherwise orderly household. He tried to keep it within bounds by enforcing the Company monopoly—all goods to be purchased from the H.B.C. and no furs to be sold to any market other than the Company. Until the American advance down the Red River Valley, the Company was able to enforce its rule. But in 1844, Norman Kittson, a Canadian born at Chambly in Canada East, but now in the service of John Jacob Astor's American Fur Company, set himself down at Pembina, just across the frontier. The next spring, according to what seems to be the most logical account, he led a six-cart train, loaded with "free trade" peltries, to St. Paul, which, originally called "Pig's Eye," had become a thriving frontier town.

The serpent of Free Trade had wriggled into the Company's Eden. Soon there were other American posts along the frontier to which the *métis* could smuggle their furs for higher prices than the Company would offer. The buffalo hunters had never recognized the 49th parallel, imaginary line as it was, any more than the buffalo did. American Pembina became one of the *métis* centers. But in August of 1845 a body of U.S. cavalry turned back the annual hunt at the border, suggesting that the *métis* had better come across to freedom. There was a corollary. In October of that same year Simpson wrote to Pelly, the London governor of the H.B.C., that "a petition . . . was being sent around among the Settlers for signature, praying Congress to assist and protect them in a settlement at Pembina."

The instigator was a John McLaughlin, who had resided in St. Louis. Simpson believed him to be a U.S. agent. In June of the next year a petition against the Company, signed by 977 settlers, was sent to Queen Victoria. Never a man to sit down when his authority was challenged, on the pretext of danger from the Oregon dispute of 1846, Simpson got some 500 officers and men of the 6th Royal Regiment of Foot sent in. He used them to enforce the Company monopoly. As Alexander Ross, present at the time, comments, "All those disaffected with the existing order of things sneaked across the boundary line to the land of freedom."

When the troops left after two years, the dam Simpson had built against trade with the Americans burst. The crisis came on May 17, 1849, when Pierre Guillaume Sayer and three others were on trial for selling furs elsewhere than to the Company. On that spring day a mob of British and French half-breeds, brandishing their rifles, milled in and around the courthouse which stood just outside the walls of Upper Fort Garry. Prominent among them was the elder Louis Riel, the "Miller of the Seine." That Seine had little similarity to its famous counterpart in Paris. This Seine was a small and muddy stream flowing into the Red River near St. Boniface.

But the temper of the mob outside that courthouse partook of Bastille Day. Sayer was found guilty. The chief factor of the Company did not dare ask for punishment. Instead, he said he would be content with no penalty at all and would drop the charges against the other three. As the crowd inside the courthouse gasped, someone—later it was said to be Louis Riel the Elder—rushed to the door of the courthouse.

"*Le commerce est libre!*" he bawled to the waiting throng. "*Le commerce est libre. Vive la liberté.*"

2

The Hudson's Bay Company monopoly was broken. And meantime, the tide of American expansion was flowing north. In 1848 Wisconsin had become a state, and in the next year, cheers and the firing of guns in St. Paul signalized that Minnesota had been made a territory. It stretched up to the 49th parallel. By 1854 some 30,000 settlers had poured into it, while American traders and gold seekers pushing up the "Big Muddy" had established posts as far as Montana. Soon the cart trains were screeching south from Red River in a crescendo—1500 of them a year to St. Paul by 1854 and in 1858, 6000.

The Red River cart, which could be floated across streams and repaired anywhere en route, was the schooner of the prairies. It had been invented for the buffalo hunt. It was equally well adapted to the trade with St. Paul. Each cart could carry 800 pounds of freight and in those vanished days, cart, ox, and harness cost only $80. Three of them were driven by one carter—practically always a *métis*—his wage a mere $20 a month—while the fortunate owner could charge up to $105 a trip for freighting each 800-pound-load to St. Paul. A new type of merchant, the cart-train potentate, came into being. When one of them traveled with a cart train he rode the finest of buffalo hunters and took his luxuries with him. We read of one merchant's huge padlocked chest, divided into compartments, which were stuffed full with tea, sugar, spices, cheeses, jams, brandies, and fine wines.

To the Easterner, the cart train was a colorful frontier community on the move. As in the buffalo hunt, men, women, children, and dogs all went along. The priests accompanied their flock, and the carts were divided into parishes. A governor was in charge of the whole train, and once assembled (the usual forgathering was at Pembina on the American side), the train set out each morning at first light. It halted in midafternoon, this for fear of attacks from the prairie Sioux. The carts were lined up in a rough circle. Inside the corral tepees were flung up. The oxen and horses grazed until dark. Then they were herded into the enclosure and guards stood to arms all night. As the darkness fell, the cooking fires were lighted. After the meal the fiddlers scraped and dancing feet thudded on the prairie.

It was a six- to eight-week picnic journey to St. Paul. When the cart trains came shrieking down the bluffs of the Mississippi every merchant in that frontier town threw open his store to reap his profit from the Red River peltries and from the goods—clothing, implements, women's finery—he sold the *métis* in exchange. For a week or more the moccasins of the *métis*—handsome and dashing in their wool capotes of bright blue, bound round with sashes of red and crimson, and in their beaded caps—padded the streets of St. Paul before they turned to the journey back. Tourists came up in droves on the paddle steamers of the Mississippi to gape at the *métis* and the trade they brought. The more than $250,000 worth of raw furs was only one item. There was also pemmican, buffalo tongues, and buffalo robes. In one single year in the fifties more than 184,000 robes sailed down the Mississippi to St. Louis while buffalo tongues and steaks became an accustomed delicacy on eastern tables.

It was the reports of the profits from this trade which had inspired Toronto merchants to send William Kennedy in January of 1857 to Red River to see if Canada could get in on the bonanza. The inner significance of the cart trains escaped them. Geographically, Fort Garry and St. Paul were the northern and southern poles of a single and natural economic unit, the valley of the Red River. With American settlement reaching toward the 49th parallel, that imaginary line which meant nothing to either the buffalo or the *métis*, the tiny colony around Fort Garry had already a closer connection with the Minnesotans than with any British province. The only bar to American occupation was the H.B.C., but the Company could not hold the vacancies of Rupert's Land against settlers forever. By 1856 it was clear that unless something were done, Red River Settlement would inevitably become American. When that happened the whole Northwest would be lost to Britain and to Canada.

Among Canadian leaders, George Brown and William McDougall had the clearest comprehension of this danger. Their solution was for Canada to take over Red River and for Canada West to pour in settlers. The H.B.C., as usual, dragged its heels. What led to the British Select Committee was, however, the already mentioned dislike in Britain of any monopolistic institution such as the Company was and the complaints from both Red River and from Vancouver's Island. The 1846 petition of 977 Red Riverites demanding free trade and protesting against the H.B.C. monopoly and government had reached the Colonial Secretary, Earl Grey, through a London lawyer, Mr. Isbister, son of a former officer of the Company. In 1849, when the colonization of Vancouver's Island was being entrusted to the H.B.C., there was violent opposition and a good deal of criticism of the Company. In 1850 the American ambassador in London brought in a hypocritical complaint from the whisky-selling American fur traders that the H.B.C. was trading spirits to the Indians. Meanwhile an element in Red River kept, through Mr. Isbister, protesting against the Company.

The evidence seems clear that the Imperial Government did not set up its Select Committee because of fear of American expansion. Little Englanders still ruled their policy and, if the Northwest were lost to the American republic, it would, in their opinion, be far from a disaster. But the constant complaints against the Company made it necessary to do something, especially since William Ewart Gladstone was spokesman for the group which was bitterly opposed to the Company's monopoly. Once that committee was established, an irrevocable step had been taken. It was a notice to all that the days of the fur empire were numbered.

3

On February 26, 1857, Sir George Simpson took the witness stand before the Select Committee in London. He was seventy, but, except for poor eyesight, vigorous and unrepentant. On the Committee he faced in that dingy, fog-filled room were some of the most important men in the British politics of the day—Labouchère, Colonial Secretary, as chairman; Lord John Russell, Prime

Minister from 1846 to 1852; Lord Stanley; and William Ewart Gladstone, at this time forty-seven years of age and himself a former Colonial Secretary. The Committee's questions ranged widely over the administration of the Company, the possibility of large-scale settlement in Rupert's Land, and the future of Vancouver's Island. The members were courteous, but it was clear that on the whole they were the prosecution and Sir George the defense.

For two days the old lion met the challenge. The Committee seemed shocked to discover that, except where its own interests were concerned, the H.B.C., which governed an empire, did not pretend to govern. They were politely skeptical of Simpson's contention that no part of the Company's territory was really favorable for settlement. Mr. Gordon of the Committee read Simpson extracts from his own *Journey round the World* about the beauties of Rainy River and the extraordinary returns from the "black mould" of Red River of forty bushels to the acre of wheat. Simpson slid around the difficulties with tales of grasshopper plagues, droughts, and early frosts. By the time he was through he had made the last stout defense of the Company's monopoly.

Simpson was only one of twenty-five witnesses, pro and con, inclusive of Blanshard, the frustrated first governor of Vancouver's Island, examined by the Committee during eighteen meetings from February to July of 1857. In all, its verbatim report ran to 550 pages. When Chief Justice Draper appeared before it for Canada, he was tied by his instructions from John A.'s Cabinet. Though in January the Canadian Executive Council had passed a minute that "the general feeling here is that the western Boundary of Canada extends to the Pacific Ocean," Draper's instructions were to protest against the renewal of the Company's license and above all to impress on the Committee "the importance of securing the North-West Territory against the sudden and unauthorized influx of immigration from the United States' side."

In this clause resided the constant fear of American aggression felt by Canada and John A. Macdonald. Apart from these two representations, Draper was apparently left to his own initiative. He requested the right for Canada to explore and settle freely west of Lake Superior and asked for a determination of the boundary line between the H.B.C. and Canada—this without taking up the Clear Grit contention that the H.B.C. charter was invalid. Of a transcontinental railway, he said, in words which seem to have been borrowed from Joseph Howe:

"I hope you will not laugh at me as very visionary, but I hope to live to see the time . . . when there is a railway going all across that country and ending on the Pacific."

The Committee labored and, apparently, brought forth a mouse. It granted Canada the right to settle and even to take over the Red River district. Canada, thanks to the stubborn refusal of French Canada, which foresaw itself overwhelmed by any westward expansion, did not look with kindly eyes at the offer. The Committee suggested that, in lieu of incorporation with Canada, Red River might be made into a Crown colony. Again, nothing was done. Though, in 1859, acting on the Committee's report, the Imperial Government offered the H.B.C. a renewal of its license to trade—first for only one year and then for two—when the Company refused, again nobody did anything. The Company's monopoly remained as before. Only in the change of the status of Vancouver's Island and the Mainland in 1858 did any direct result emerge from the Committee's report.

Appearances, however, were deceiving. When that Select Committee sat down in its comfortable chairs for its first meeting, that very fact determined that the fur trader's control of the Northwest was to disappear. The only question was whether Canada or the United States was to inherit the empire.

4

In Alberta's Calgary today, the Palliser Hotel welcomes oil millionaires, ranchers, pipeline magnates, American tourists, farmers, and royalty itself in a courtly yet, withal, free and easy manner. Further west the traveler by train or automobile through Kicking Horse Pass stares downward into the tumbling waters of the river which gives the pass its name or gazes upward with a momentary touch of reverence at the castellated peaks. Both names are mementos of one of the by-products of the Select Committee. For, even while the Select Committee was meeting, the Imperial Government, on March 31, 1857, ordered Captain John Palliser to survey the settlement and railroad possibilities of the British Northwest. A handsome and, except for sideburns, a clean-shaven sportsman, Palliser's chief qualification for the job was a season's hunting, ten years before this, on the American prairie.

However, he had efficient colleagues, the most effective being the Edinburgh geologist Dr. James Hector. It was Hector who was kicked by his horse in the pass which took its name from the incident and, as he tells us, left "senseless for some time." His Indian guide, Peter, adds that his fellow natives, fearing attacks from hostiles, hastily dug a shallow grave, put Hector in it, and were about to shovel in the dirt when his eyelids flickered.

For two years Palliser and his colleagues roved the prairies, in danger every now and then from the Blackfeet, and explored the Rockies. Palliser reported against a railroad from Canada to Red River but thought a wagon road through the Rockies possible. Four passes, among them the present Kicking Horse and Yellowhead, were investigated. Not too many years later this notion of a wagon road was to capture the interest of the English promoter and imperialist Edward Watkin.

As for settlement, Palliser's chief findings were the classic division of the prairie country into three levels, the announcement of a "Fertile Belt," and his "Palliser's Triangle" of semi-arid land, unfit for settlers, in much of the southern part of modern Alberta and Saskatchewan.

Meanwhile, Canada, which in the spring of 1857 had received a spate of petitions to annex Rupert's Land, had sent out that same year a surveyor, S. J. Dawson, and a chemist and geologist, Dr. A. Y. Hind, of the University of Toronto. They, too, stayed for two years. Dawson picked out the canoe-and-portage route between Lake Superior and Red River which was to be known later to Wolseley's 1870 expedition to Fort Garry as the "Dawson Road." Hind, working further west, accepted the "Palliser Triangle" but found 11,100,000 acres of first-class arable land.

From this time forward there was no longer any real doubt about the suitability of the Northwest for agricultural settlement, even though the fear of its climate persisted. At the same time the Red River settlers were made conscious of faraway Canada. To add to the tenuous link, on June 22 of 1857 at Quebec, 120 officers and men of the Canadian Rifles embarked for the long journey down the St. Lawrence and around Labrador and Ungava and into Hudson Bay to York Factory and Red River. The troops were in high spirits. They were being sent at the request of the Imperial Government, because on August of the previous year another force of American cavalry had again turned back the annual Red River buffalo hunt at the border.

The Rifles reached Red River in October. They stayed until 1861. During those four years these Canadians and the Red Riverites got to know each other. Letters about the new land went back to Canada. Canadian parents became conscious of their sons in a distant country of which they had seldom thought. Other Canadians, and among them the redoubtable Dr. John Christian Schultz from Kingston, were led to migrate to Red River. A "Canadian" party was formed. Whether John A. liked it or not, a bond between Canada and Red River had been forged. That bond did not break when the Rifles returned home. The Northwest was at last within the ken of Canadians. It took a dramatic turn of local politics to make its acquisition, along with Confederation, an official part of Canadian Government policy.

CHAPTER VII

1857–60

Brown Attacks the Grand Trunk—Double Shuffle —Galt and Confederation—The Bluenoses Roam the Seas—The Prince of Wales' Visit

1

IN the spring of 1857 George Brown leaped into a new crusade. He had been thundering for Rep. by Pop. As chairman of a committee to examine petitions from Canada West towns and municipalities for acquisition of the Northwest, he was propagandizing for the taking over of Red River so as to smash Roman Catholic control over Canada. Now he had a new incitement to indignation: the iniquitous conspiracy of John A.'s government, Montreal finance, and the Grand Trunk Railway to fatten themselves off the farmers of Canada West by high freight rates and by provincial subsidies to the railroad.

"The G.T.R. governs Canada at this present moment," his *Globe* blustered on April 22, ". . . the Ministry are mere puppets in its hands."

There was enough truth in the accusation to bite. Since 1854, year after year, the Grand Trunk had been getting handout after handout from Canada's Parliament and in 1857, like Oliver Twist, it was back again. Cartier, the principal leader of the Liberal-Conservatives in French Canada, was its chief solicitor, Taché, the titular head of the ministry, was financially interested in it, and others of the government were on its board of directors. The G.T.R. seemed to have Canada's Parliament in its pocket.

George Brown, when on a crusade, hewed at the log and let the chips fly. He got himself appointed chairman of a committee to investigate the Grand Trunk. The personable Galt was still in the House along with his financial comrade, Luther Holton. Both had made fortunes through the amalgamation of the St. Lawrence and Atlantic with the G.T.R. and also from Gzowski and Company's contract for that portion of the line which ran from Toronto to Sarnia. Both, too, were technically *Rouges*, chiefly because of opposition to Roman Catholicism, and were therefore political allies to George Brown.

That last fact made no difference to the enraged Clear Grit. In the committee meetings and in the House he unleashed violent onslaughts on both for alleged bribery and sharp dealings.

"There was once a time," he thundered on May 12, pointing an accusing finger at Luther Holton, "when the honorable gentleman opposed the Grand Trunk as strongly as I did, but that opposition ceased when he got a Grand Trunk directorship and a Grand Trunk contract."

To new-made millionaires, the truth is a bitter herb. By September 2, Holton was suggesting to Galt in a letter: ". . . Have you and I any particular inducement to play the Opposition's game after the treatment we received? . . ." Meanwhile John A. Macdonald, whose sleepy-lidded eyes had marked Brown's political error and who had estimated Galt as the most influential in his group, was writing under the date of November 2:

> My dear Galt:
>
> . . . You call yourself a Rouge. There may have been at one time a reddish tinge about you but I could observe it becoming by degrees fainter. In fact you are like Byron's Dying Dolphin, exhibiting a series of colours—"the last still loveliest"—and that last is "true blue," being the colour I affect. Seriously you would make a decent Conservative . . . so pray do become true blue at once: it is a good standing colour and bears washing.
>
> Yours always,
>
> John A. Macdonald

In 1857 John A. was still the dominant figure and master manipulator. By November he had to face another change. Etienne Taché, the kindly and gentlemanly First Minister, resigned. In place of the Taché-Macdonald administration was put the well-nigh irresistible combination of Macdonald and Cartier.

In Cartier, Macdonald had at last discovered his ideal complement. Stocky, impetuous, and almost terrifying in his blunt energy,

Cartier, a collateral descendant of Jacques Cartier, was the embodiment of French Canada. In his youth he had written for the revolutionary *Fils de la Liberté* a marching song, "*Avant tout je suis Canadien.*"

That song was the text of his life. He joined the Papineau-inspired Lower Canadian Rebellion of 1837. He went into exile. On his return he attached himself to Lafontaine. Entering Parliament in 1849 as member for Verchères, he became Provincial Secretary in the 1854 MacNab-Morin ministry. Soon he stood out as the leader of all French Canada, except for the extremists of the Left. The Catholic hierarchy accepted him because he was loyal to race and religion. His compatriots felt instinctively that he was one of them and admired him because he was clever enough, as exemplified by his solicitorship for the Grand Trunk, to force "*les sacrés Anglais*" to make a place for him. As long as Cartier stood at his side, John A. did not need to fret about votes from French Canada.

That fact was soon put to the test. December elections followed the establishing of the Macdonald-Cartier ministry. George Brown, with his cry of Rep. by Pop. to end French-Catholic domination, swept the western part of Canada West. John A., almost crippled by another and, this time, hopeless recurrence of his wife's illness, held Kingston and a few other seats. But in the upper Ottawa Valley his almost namesake, John Sanfield Macdonald, the Glengarry Catholic whose recipe for Canada was the "Double Majority," that is, to pass each proposal by a majority from each of the two divisions of the province, was elected along with a tail of followers. The government's fate depended on Cartier.

Cartier did not fail. Holding firm to the principle of equal representation from each section, Canada East gave Cartier enough members to counterbalance George Brown's gains. The Macdonald-Cartier ministry was back in power. But it owed its somewhat precarious majority to French-Canadian votes. As if to underscore for John A. the vanity of triumph, on December 28 his wife died. In spite of this deep personal tragedy, Macdonald had to take up again his attempt to keep some sort of government going; and this with George Brown at his most vigorous and self-righteous self. There was one straw of comfort. The *Rouges* of Canada East, and notably Galt, who had been elected as an Independent, were cautious about following Brown.

John A. managed until July of 1858. His downfall came over the question of a permanent capital for Canada. Back in 1856 Quebec had been chosen. But the Legislative Council had thrown out the appropriation for parliament buildings. In March of 1857, John A., already becoming "Old Tomorrow," had had the problem referred to the Queen for decision. In January of 1858 her choice of Ottawa was a New Year's gift which pleased few and offended the *amour-propre* of the Canadian members. George Brown saw the chance of detaching a bloc of French Canadians from the government. He attacked the Queen's choice. On July 28, on a motion that "the City of Ottawa ought not to be the permanent seat of government of this Province," enough of Cartier's French Canadians deserted to defeat the administration by 64 to 50. Brown leaped up, exultant, to move adjournment. The French Canadians switched back again. His motion was, in its turn, voted down.

It was all petty politics. John A. could have taken the second vote as authorization to stay in power. He chose instead to interpret the defeat of the government on a matter of government policy as a necessity to resign. Brown was called upon by Sir Edmund Head to form a ministry.

A more cautious man would have hesitated. As the second vote had shown, Brown did not have a majority in the House. Moreover, by Canadian procedure, as soon as he and his Cabinet were installed they had to resign their seats to seek re-election, thus reducing their strength in Parliament still further. Brown's obvious course was to form a ministry and then seize the first chance to ask for dissolution in the hope that a new general election would give him a mandate, a course followed with great success a century later by Mr. Diefenbaker and his minority government in the winter of 1958.

The catch lay in the fact that it was the prerogative of the governor to grant or refuse dissolution, and Head warned Brown verbally and in writing that there was no assurance of his granting it.

Such a warning would have given John A. pause. Brown was too eager for the purple. He formed a ministry. At last he sat on the throne which John A. had, in his opinion, usurped.

He was not to sit there long. At noon of August 2 the Brown-Dorion administration (Dorion was the leading *Rouge*) was sworn in. That same afternoon, in stifling heat in the red-brick building on Wellington Street in Toronto, it was defeated by a majority of 40. The next day Brown asked for dissolution. Head refused. On August 4, what John A. was to call "His Excellency's most ephemeral administration" resigned.

It is difficult not to suspect some sort of unspoken complicity between John A. and Head. The Brownites charged open collusion. It seems more likely that John A., knowing both men, gambled on how each of them would react, and won. In this gamble he set a trap for Brown and Brown fell into it. In any case, the John A.-arranged comedy played two further scenes. Galt was asked to form a government. When he failed, Cartier was called in. On August 6 the Macdonald-Cartier administration was back in power as the Cartier-Macdonald ministry. For John A. had once more reached into his bag of tricks. He had remembered that in the previous year a law had been passed that if a cabinet member resigned his post and within a month took a new one, it was not necessary to resign his seat and seek re-election. It was only eight days since the Liberal-Conservative Cabinet had resigned. Now the same men were sworn in again, but holding *new* posts. They held these new offices one day only, then reverted to their former posts. Thus John A. was for one day Postmaster General. Next day he was back in his old position as Attorney General of Canada West. The dance step of "Double Shuffle" had been pulled off. It did George Brown no good to cry "trickery" and "collusion." He was out.

There were only two real changes in the new Cabinet. One was that Cartier was now First Minister. The other was the inclusion of Galt, the former *Rouge,* as Inspector General. Galt made it a condition of his entrance that Confederation of the five eastern provinces and the acquisition of the Northwest become official planks of the Liberal-Conservative platform. For Galt, a man of independent mind, anti- rather than pro-British, had become a convert to both these ideas. What was even more important, he had converted Cartier—and with him French Canada. On August 7, in announcing the program of his ministry, Cartier stated that:

"The expediency of a federal union of the British North American provinces will be anxiously considered and communications with the Home Government and the Lower Provinces entered into forthwith on this subject."

Head, another convert, picked up the same theme when he prorogued the House on August 16. On September 9, he wrote to the new Colonial Secretary, the novelist Bulwer-Lytton, best remembered for his *The Last Days of Pompeii,* and to the lieutenant governors of the other four eastern provinces to open up the subject. In October, Cartier, Ross, and Galt sailed to England to take up with the Imperial Government the allied questions of Confederation, the Intercolonial Railway, and the acquisition of the Northwest. Out of the dull vagaries of Canadian politics Confederation had at last become official policy. But John A. as yet regarded it with the cynical eye of a schoolmaster who was willing to let the boys have their fun.

2

In 1858 Confederation did not even get as far as a blueprint. Britain had little interest. Neither had the Maritimes. Why should they? Canada might have political and economic difficulties to which Confederation and a western empire might seem a solution, but by this time the Seven Seas were the hunting grounds for the "iron men and the wooden ships" of Nova Scotia, New Brunswick, and Prince Edward Island. Their forests, harbors, and geographical situation had always invited the Maritimers to lumbering, fishing, and shipbuilding. In the fifties the 1851 discovery of gold in Australia and the Crimean War had led in Britain to a cry for ships and yet more ships. In their extremity British shipping lines turned to the shipyards of Quebec and the Maritimes. Great timber droghers, built originally for the trade in square timber and deals from St. John and Quebec to Britain, were now bought by British owners for transports and passenger liners. Soon the Quebec and St. John yards were building for the British market. To give one example only, the *Marco Polo,* of 1625 tons, said to be the "fastest ship afloat," was launched at Marsh Creek in Courtenay Bay near St. John in 1850. A three-decker of 185 feet in length, it first carried a load of timber to Liverpool, then went for cotton to Mobile, and on its return was bought by the British-owned Black Ball Line for the Australia trade. The timber drogher, which had had the figurehead of Marco Polo as its sole decoration, was converted into a luxury liner with ornate staterooms and public rooms. Of its dining room, the *Illustrated London News* of that day wrote enthusiastically:

"It is ceiled with maple and the pilasters are panelled with richly ornamented and silver glass, coins of various countries being a feature of the decoration."

The *Marco Polo* was only one of scores of such ships put together for the British. In 1852 alone, Quebec launched twenty-one vessels and New Brunswick yards twenty. All of them were built of pine, tamarack, black birch, maple, and North American oak. But they were soundly built.

The great majority of Maritime ships, though, were framed, especially in Nova Scotia, to be owned and run by Maritimers. They were of all sizes. The Bluenose farmer (Nova Scotians reserved the term for themselves, but outsiders were inclined to apply the name to all Maritimers) had long been famed as a man who could cut timber from the bush, build his own schooner, load her with home-grown potatoes and cordwood, and then sail her down to Boston. Now, in the fifties and sixties, the coves and creeks on either side of the Bay of Fundy and along the southern coast of Nova Scotia echoed to the thud of mallets and the ring of axes and the screech of saws. Throughout the fifties, sixties, and seventies, until the iron freighter cut in on them, the wooden sailing ships of the Bluenoses foraged the Seven Seas, their clippers vying with those of New England in speed and beauty, and their skippers famed for enforcing a tough discipline with fist, marlinespike, and belaying pin. In 1864–65 the *Speculator*, a Yarmouth ship of 747 tons, ranged from home to Montevideo in Uruguay, to Ceylon, to Calcutta, to Rangoon, and to Mauritius, surviving a full-fledged hurricane en route. Hong Kong, Sydney, San Francisco, all the ports of the seas, saw the Bluenose canvas whitening their harbors. As early as 1852 the tonnage of Nova Scotian vessels alone was nearly one third of that of France. Later, Maritime tonnage was to put the new Dominion in fourth place among the shipping nations of the world. In 1867 Joseph Howe tells of seeing the photographs of seven sons in a Yarmouth home, all of whom, the mother told him in quiet pride, "command fine ships and have all been around Cape Horn."

Those romantic decades are, today, part of the Bluenose past. In 1858 the Maritime Provinces, with Reciprocity in force and with prosperity from fisheries and shipping perched on their shores, had no need of union with Canada. In New Brunswick the roistering lumberjack had long taken precedence over the dull farmer; and no one worried about what would happen when the pine stands were all cut down. Prince Edward Island, her forests depleted, had turned to a farming that was cursed with absentee-landlordism. For both of them, fishing and shipbuilding were luxuries in the larder. Meanwhile in Nova Scotia an almost perfect trinity of fishing, farming, and shipbuilding had been achieved. What, then, had Canada's problems to do with the Maritimes? In 1858 even Joseph Howe failed to raise a potent voice for Confederation. In Canada itself, once Cartier, Ross, and Galt had returned, crestfallen, from England, Confederation was tucked away in a closet. Canada turned to the problems at hand.

These were sufficiently severe. A bad harvest in 1857 had coincided with the collapse of the Crimean War boom. The next year the harvest was an almost complete failure and at the same time the soaring railway balloon was pricked. Prices of wheat, cheese, timber, and the like dropped. More and more municipalities defaulted on the money they had borrowed to build railways running nowhere. Thanks to Hincks' 1854 Municipal Loan Fund Act, the province had to assume the debts. By the end of 1859 Canada's indebtedness totaled $58,292,469.81, a mere breakfast egg for Canada's government today, but a century ago, for a population of some two and a half million brought up in a tradition of "pay as you go," a staggering amount.

Out of this debt and the current deficits was born the excuse for Canada's first protective tariff, under the plea of "tariff for revenue." Behind that excuse lurked smugly the manufacturers of the province. At the time of the Reciprocity Treaty the tariff against foreign goods had been 12½ per cent, which in 1856 was raised to 15 per cent. But the boom years from 1854 to 1857 had produced a small but thriving Canadian industrialism. In April of 1858, with Isaac Buchanan of Hamilton, the promoter of railways, paper money, and high tariffs, as the energetic spirit, an "Association for the Promotion of Canadian Industry," the precursor of the present-day Canadian Manufacturers' Association, was formed in Toronto. It squalled for the protection of Canada's "infant industries."

To a layman, a 15 per cent duty might seem a sufficient protection for all but the greediest of hogs. To Canadian manufacturers, no duty is ever quite high enough. Their ideal is a captive Canadian buying public, compelled by tariffs to purchase only Canadian-produced goods at prices set by Canadian manufacturers rather than by competition in a free market. In first Cayley, and then Galt, Canadian industrialists found men with sympathetic ears. In 1858 the Cayley tariff levied 20 per cent on many manufactured imports and 15 per cent on all goods not specified. The Galt 1859 schedule raised the duty on certain imports to 25 per cent and on practically all the rest to 20 per cent. All duties, too, were ad valorem, that is, levied on the value of the article where it was last bought before coming to Canada. By a curious fact not unconnected with Galt's residence in Montreal, this ad valorem specification was, to quote an article in the *Canadian Merchant's Magazine* of March 1859, "to the Montreal merchant . . . a veritable balm of Gilead; to the merchant of Toronto, Wormwood." Toronto merchants, it appeared, bought their tea, coffee, sugar, and molasses in New York and so paid duty on a higher price than Montreal importers, who purchased the same articles at their point of origin, where their price was cheaper; for instance, molasses in the West Indies. Galt had not forgotten his Montreal friends. Beyond that he aimed at compelling imports to come in via Montreal instead of New York.

This first protective tariff was not yet perfect from the industrialists' point of view. Since Reciprocity was still in force, it could not be applied to the raw materials, such as grain, timber, and the like, which still flowed freely each way across the border. The tariff, however, did violate the spirit, though not the letter, of the Reciprocity Treaty. In 1854 no one had dreamed of a group of Canadian manufacturers powerful enough to influence government policy, and on June 24, 1851, in discussing Reciprocity, the British minister in Washington had assured the U. S. Government that Canada would always hold to a "most liberal commercial policy." So American manufacturers, quite justly, protested.

The Cayley-Galt tariff was the first step to the abrogation of Elgin-Marcy Reciprocity Treaty. It was also a declaration of fiscal independence. When Britain's Free Traders objected, Galt declared that:

"It is . . . the duty of the present government distinctly to affirm the right of the Canadian legislature to adjust the taxation of the people in any way they deem best."

In a similar move of independence, in 1858 Canada formally adopted a decimal currency based on the American dollar. Until this time there had been the sterling pound, roughly equal to five dollars, the Halifax pound of four dollars, and the York shilling, as well as other currencies. It took a while for the dollar to win out but the decisive step had been taken. One other small item was cleared. In 1859 the capital was finally set at Ottawa, though it was agreed that Quebec was to have Parliament for a final session. Even so, Sicotte, the most important French Canadian next to Cartier, resigned from the Cabinet in protest.

And so the fifties came to 1860. In the Maritimes a prosperity based on Reciprocity and shipbuilding continued. In the political life of the day, Joseph Howe, since his troop-recruiting venture and his defeat by Tupper in the 1855 election, had been in temporary eclipse. He was also involved in a bitter dispute with the Irish Roman Catholics of his province, whom he accused of attacking the public-school system and everything British. In spite of this quarrel he was soon back in the legislature. On August 3, 1860, he crowned his political career by the premiership of Nova Scotia. In that same year Yarmouth held a centenary celebration.

"Off at daybreak," Howe writes. "Road lined with people going to the festival. Black horse passed them all. . . . Bowing and shaking hands all day. Parades of volunteers and Firemen. . . . Arrangements for speaking frightful. . . .

"General congratulations [for his speech]. . . . Fireworks poor.

"Street full of feathers. A fellow from Shelburne tarred and feathered the night before, for being too free with some Captain's wife. Served him right. He had carried the woman off and when she was recovered by her father he followed her from Shelburne to Yarmouth. . . . He caught a tar-tar instead. . . ."

At fifty-six Howe was still Howe and Nova Scotia was still Bluenose, with no interest in federation with Canada. In Canada the decade had seen great changes. When it opened, except for Quebec, Montreal, and Toronto, Canada was still not far from the pioneer way of life. Along the "Front," it is true, from Montreal to Toronto, and the Niagara and southwest peninsulas, there had been cities and towns and graveled or plank highways. Frame or brick or stone dwellings had replaced the log cabins of the early settlers. Canals, eight feet of water on the sills, on the upper St. Lawrence and through the Niagara Peninsula had made it possible for schooners and barges to come from Sault Ste. Marie all the way to Montreal. Steamers had curled up their bluish smoke on the Ottawa River and between Montreal and Quebec, while luxury vessels had handled the passenger and freighting trade on Lake Ontario.

But in Canada West, in the fingers of settlement reaching north from the Front and the southwest peninsula, it had still been the clearing and the log cabin and fields among the stumps and seeding by hand and the scythe and the cradle and the flail. There had still been Indians roaming and cedar swamps and wolves and bears and wildcats mingled with the porcupines and the cottontail rabbits and the muskrats and the foxes. The saddlebag circuit riders still rode and social life was the barn-raising or the quilting bee. In the more settled districts, the tavern competed for souls with the churches. Common-school education, however, under Egerton Ryerson had got a good footing. Canada East remained settled in its habitant way of life. But in Canada West there had been a ferment, with immigrants, predominantly Irish Protestants, still pushing in.

That influx continued during the fifties. Between 1850 and 1867 upward of 450,000 immigrants entered by way of Quebec. Close to half of these found their way to the States. Those who stayed opened up the back country of Canada West. It was in 1857 that the new counties of Waterloo, Wellington, and Grey were carved out of the Queen's wilderness. The same development took place in the county of Victoria and in the Bruce Peninsula and elsewhere.

To this opening up of the fringes of Anglo-Canada the railroad contributed. It also began to change the whole way of life. By 1860 Canada West was crisscrossed by tracks. Along these, villages grew up. Wind and water and the turnpike highway or rutted dirt trail and corduroy road began to be replaced by rail and steam. There was more communication and with it a spread of knowledge and an increase in education. In Canada West the primitive way of life was still close. But it had been pushed back to the outskirts.

These years—the years of the railroad frenzy and the Reciprocity Treaty and the Crimean War and the Indian Mutiny and of "Double Shuffle"—had seen Canada consider Confederation and look northwestward for the first time. Imperial and Maritime apathy and the perennial religio-racial conflict in the two Canadas had, apparently, killed both projects. When in 1860, Edward, Prince of Wales, later to be Edward VII, visited the eastern colonies, Confederation and westward expansion seemed a brace of dead ducks.

3

It was on July 9 of 1860 that the Prince of Wales, accompanied by the new Colonial Secretary, the Duke of Newcastle, and the usual coterie of anxious minor officials, boarded the *Hero* at Southampton. An invitation for the Queen herself to visit Canada had been presented in person the preceding year by Henry Smith, Jr., Speaker of the Canadian House and son of that Henry Smith whose dismissal as warden of Kingston Penitentiary had initiated the Brown-Macdonald feud. The Queen was sending the Prince in her stead.

To the Prince, at that time nineteen, the tour was a welcome escape from the tedious restrictions of his mother's court and the strict supervision of Albert, the Prince Consort, who, to his dismay, had discovered that his son thought that life ought to have more in it than the cold porridge of duty and the yawning boredom of study. To British North Americans, it was an excitement which would have been sneered at by them as "American" if shown south of the border. At St. John's, Newfoundland, and at Halifax, at St. John, New Brunswick, and at Charlottetown, there were almost hysterical demonstrations. In Canada, the principal objective of the tour, the preparations exhibited the same neurotic lack of restraint.

As the *Hero* left Halifax the Canadian Government steamer, appropriately named the *Queen Victoria*, awaited her at Gaspé Harbor. On board and all of a dither lest the *Hero* slip by, were Governor Head, Cartier, Macdonald, and members of the Cabinet. The conclusion was happy. At the apogee of a glorious Canadian sunset on Sunday, August 12, the *Hero* and her escort of ships swam smoothly into Gaspé Harbor. Soon the whole cortege was gliding up the broad St. Lawrence, the fields and towns and steeples on the banks shimmering in the sun. On August 18 the Prince reached Quebec. The mayor and his council were waiting. The Canadian cabinet ministers sweated in the summer heat, looking, as the *Globe* sneered, "as uncomfortable as so many pigs in armour."

The uniforms laid down for the colonial ministers were of dark blue cloth, decked with gold braid and complete with sword and a cocked hat.

"A great deal of time," said the *Globe* with a healthy colonial scorn—or does one detect a note of spite in a George Brown who, except for "Double Shuffle," might have stood in John A.'s shoes? —"has been wasted by John A. in learning to walk, for the sword suspended to his waist has an awkward knack of getting between his legs, especially after dinner."

To those who knew John A.'s skill with the bottle, the reference in that last phrase was obvious.

The regal tour began auspiciously at Quebec. There was a triumphal procession through the Lower Town, its narrow streets decked out with bunting and evergreen arches, to the Parliament Buildings. These had been remodeled into a sort of palace to furnish apartments for the Prince and his suite. There was also a dining room and a reception room, covered, we are told, with a yellow-and-purple velvet carpet. The boring procedure of speeches and presentations followed, with ecclesiastical dignitaries and members of Parliament crowded in sweating proximity.

Quebec was jammed for the occasion. Hotel rooms had been raised to the unheard-of, for 1860, price of four dollars a day. Tickets to the formal ball on the twenty-first of August were squabbled over. The ladies swarmed about in the bustles and crinolines under which, in Queen Victoria's day, the female figure had concealed itself. With other royal visits of our own time in mind, we scarcely need to smile at the bowing, scraping, and ill-concealed nervousness.

"King worship" was in full spate. From Quebec the royal flotilla moved toward Montreal. Church bells rang in the villages along the banks. Small boats, decked with evergreens and signs of welcome, dashed out to greet the flotilla. Montreal strove to outdo Quebec. There were "allegorical and emblemical transparencies" illuminated by gas jets. (Gaslighting had been introduced into Montreal in 1836.) There were mechanical designs and locomotive wheels ornamenting Victoria Bridge, which the Prince formally declared open. In the evening the Prince and his suite joined incognito in the street dancing and watched the fireworks.

It might have been 1959 instead of 1860. At the inevitable ball the Prince, who was, after all, only nineteen and having his first taste of freedom, danced until 4 A.M., reminding us of another Prince of Wales who visited this country and was just as popular.

One event in the Prince's stay in Montreal, however, ties in with an older day. On the twenty-ninth of August the Prince and his suite drove to Dorval, where today the great planes take off for overseas. In 1860, when the airplane was not even a dream on a drafting board, Dorval was a sleepy village set amid elm-shaded farm fields. On the banks of the river, one hundred Iroquois, painted and feathered, the elite of the H.B.C.'s boatmen, were drawn up in canoes. They escorted the Prince to a parklike island. On the landing Sir George Simpson, the "Little Emperor" of the fur trade, was waiting. There was a luncheon in Sir George's country home on the island. Afterward, the whole party in canoes, with the royal standard flying, drove "at a rapid pace" to Lachine, where Sir George had his official residence.

This event was a fitting close to the life of the illegitimate Scots lad who had become an emperor. Three days later Simpson was struck down by apoplexy. After seven mornings he died, fortunate in that he did not live to see the dissolution of the fur empire he had striven to hold.

Meanwhile the pattern of the royal tour had been established. The universal program, as one reporter expressed it—since, as in today's tours, the press accompanied the royal progress and found itself hard put to find enough trivia about which to write—was "spruce arches, cannon, processions, levée, lunch, ball, departure; cheers, crowds, men and women, enthusiasm, militia, Sunday school children, illuminations, fireworks, etcetera, *ad infinitum.*"

Except that the men were in Prince Alberts and bowler hats, their faces usually concealed behind a shrubbery of mustaches and beards, and the women as distorted by bustles and crinolines as by the trapeze line or the "sack," and except that horses and buggies and steamers took the place of automobiles and airplanes, the Canadian welcome did not differ too much from celebrations of today. Railways were, however, still a prideful novelty. As was done in 1939 for the trans-Canada tour of King George VI and Queen Elizabeth, a special train was prepared for the future Edward VII. The salon coach was done in white walls with gilded moldings and cornices. Its sofas and armchairs were of heavy curled maple, decorated with carved maple leaves and beavers. Upholstery and curtains were in blue. The ironwork was bronzed and the handrails plated in silver. The royal armchair had the Prince's crest carved in it.

There were the items the press, even as now, served up to its readers. It also described the escort which came from Ottawa to meet the Prince's steamer—150 canoes paddled by 1200 painted Indians and blue- and scarlet-shirted lumberjacks. In a huge inverted V these escorted the steamer. At Ottawa, under an evening sky that threatened rain, a huge crowd was waiting. When the Prince arrived, the artillery fired, massed school children piped up in the national anthem, and the rain poured down.

In Ottawa the Prince laid the cornerstone of the new Parliament Buildings, admired a lumberman's arch of 200,000 feet of planking without a single nail (reminding one of Johnson's statement about a woman preaching being like a dog standing on its hind legs, not done well, but you wonder that it is done at all), and shot down the Chaudière timber slide. All was sweetness and light in Canada East. In Canada West there was the Orange Order and a slap in the face for John A. Macdonald.

English diplomats have often been extraordinarily stupid in dealing with Canadians. The Duke of Newcastle was no exception. In Canada West the paraphernalia of the Orange Order was part of the ordinary scene—its banners, its uniforms, its parades, its Orange Master on a white horse, and the bands piping up "Protestant Boys." Its members were fiercely loyal to the Crown; and Orangemen had become the backbone of the Canada West Conservative party.

In England such parades were not the fashion. Nudged on, undoubtedly by Roman Catholic ecclesiastics, to whom, naturally, the Battle of the Boyne and Irish Protestantism were equally repugnant, the Duke of Newcastle, who had shown special favoritism to Roman Catholic dignitaries and processions in Canada East, decided that the Orange Order was illegal. Before he reached Canada West he wrote Head that there must be no Orange demonstrations of any sort anywhere.

Head sent the warning on to the mayors of Kingston and Toronto, and the Orange fat sizzled in the fire of Orange excitement. John A. did his best to make the Duke see reason. When the royal party got on board the steamer *Kingston* at Brockville on the night of September 3, after their carriages from the train to the boat had been "accompanied by firemen who carried lighted torches" with a "throng of people following, cheering and hallooing" and all the houses of Brockville illuminated, Macdonald at 11 P.M. led a delegation from Kingston, headed by the mayor, to interview the Duke. Far into the night the argument continued. The Duke set a stubborn British chin. Orangemen could not parade.

The Orangemen were just as stubborn. When, on the next afternoon, the steamer neared Kingston Harbor, John A.'s own constituency, Orange banners, an Orange arch, and a mass of Orangemen in full regalia waited on shore. The Duke's face swelled, turkey red. The steamer pulled up. The mayor was summoned. The Orangemen were given until morning to bow their heads to the Duke's ukase. In the morning the Orangemen were reassembled in even larger concourse.

There they stood and there they stayed, as sturdy in colonial independence as the Duke was adamant in British formalism. The Prince never did land. After twenty-two hours in the harbor, the *Kingston* steamed away.

John A. Macdonald, though in charge of the Anglo-Canadian part of the tour, was no longer with it. To some, he stayed behind to protect his political stake in the Orange Order. It is just as probable that he felt as stubborn and as annoyed at British stupidity as his constituents. While the Prince's party was in Toronto, he remained in Kingston, leaving the tour to shift for itself.

The tasteless comedy continued. In Toronto the Orangemen tried to work into the reception route a few references to King William and the Battle of the Boyne. The Duke previewed the route and had the offending decorations torn down. We can imagine the "tut-tuts" and the scurrying aides with solemn faces. That night the Duke of Newcastle and the governor general, Head, were burned in effigy. Later, the Grand Master of the Orange Order, John Hillyard Cameron, who at one time had intrigued to get the leadership of the Conservative party away from Macdonald, traveled to England to present a petition against the Duke signed, it was said, by 100,000 Orangemen.

In retrospect it seems a tempest over a teacup—but by such tempests are politics often determined. Macdonald joined the tour again at Hamilton. The Prince, innocent bystander in the disturbance, went on through the western part of the province, laying cornerstones, opening that typical Anglo-Canadian institution, the fall fair, holding receptions, and dancing at balls. Finally, after a day at Niagara Falls, he and his party passed over to the United States, there to receive the wildly adulatory reception which republican Americans always seem to accord visiting royalty.

The tour had two repercussions. The Duke of Newcastle, though one would scarcely have expected it after his obtuseness over the pestilential Orangemen, was acute enough to observe, or to have pointed out to him, the inherent anti-British feeling in the United States, even as its citizens bowed and cheered. The result was to make him a strong proponent of a transcontinental British route to defend British North America and of the transfer of the H.B.C.'s territory to Canada.

This was another unseen step toward Confederation. The more immediate effect was to weaken Macdonald's political strength in Canada West—and this with an election in the offing. John A. dipped again into his bag of tricks. He introduced into Canadian politics the formalized speaking tour.

It began at Brantford on November 9, a few days after the election of Abraham Lincoln as President of the United States. It was a day of strong winds and heavy rains, yet almost 300 sat down in Brantford's Kirby House to trencherman their way through half a dozen courses, drink a half score of high-sounding toasts, and listen to almost as many political orations before Macdonald came on with the speech of the evening, one that began with the British Empire and the glorious Conservative party before it descended to the iniquities of the Grits. On the next day he met a number of the "intelligent gentry" of the district to charm them with the Macdonald brand of "soft sawder" and with stories, nicely fitted to each of his victims.

So successful was the experiment that it grew until in twelve meetings, ending at Millbrook on December 7, 1860, John A. had covered most of western and central Anglo-Canada. There were banners and streamers. There were bands and songs. The ladies either watched the festivities from a gallery or added themselves to the company after the first toast was drunk. To a country which had no movies, no radio, and no TV, a Macdonald meeting, dinner speeches and all, was as good as a show, if there had been a show to see. At the levees the real work was done. By the time the tour was over, John A. could hope that he had repaired the damage done by the Duke of Newcastle's spurning of the Orangemen. Brown, ill and dogged by financial reverses, was absent when the 1861 session opened. But the cry for Rep. by Pop. was none the less clamorous. For in the meantime the new decennial census had proved that Canada West now outnumbered Canada East by some 285,000 people. This revelation shook the Conservatives of Canada West. They began to come out for Rep. by Pop. But this was a proposal which Cartier and his associates could never permit. They dug in to defend the principle of equal representation, no matter what the population figures were.

Out of this conflict came deadlock, and political deadlock was the final key to Confederation's door. But Confederation, when it came, was almost too late to save the Northwest and Pacific West from the Americans. For, in the meantime, time, to use the cliché, had been marching on.

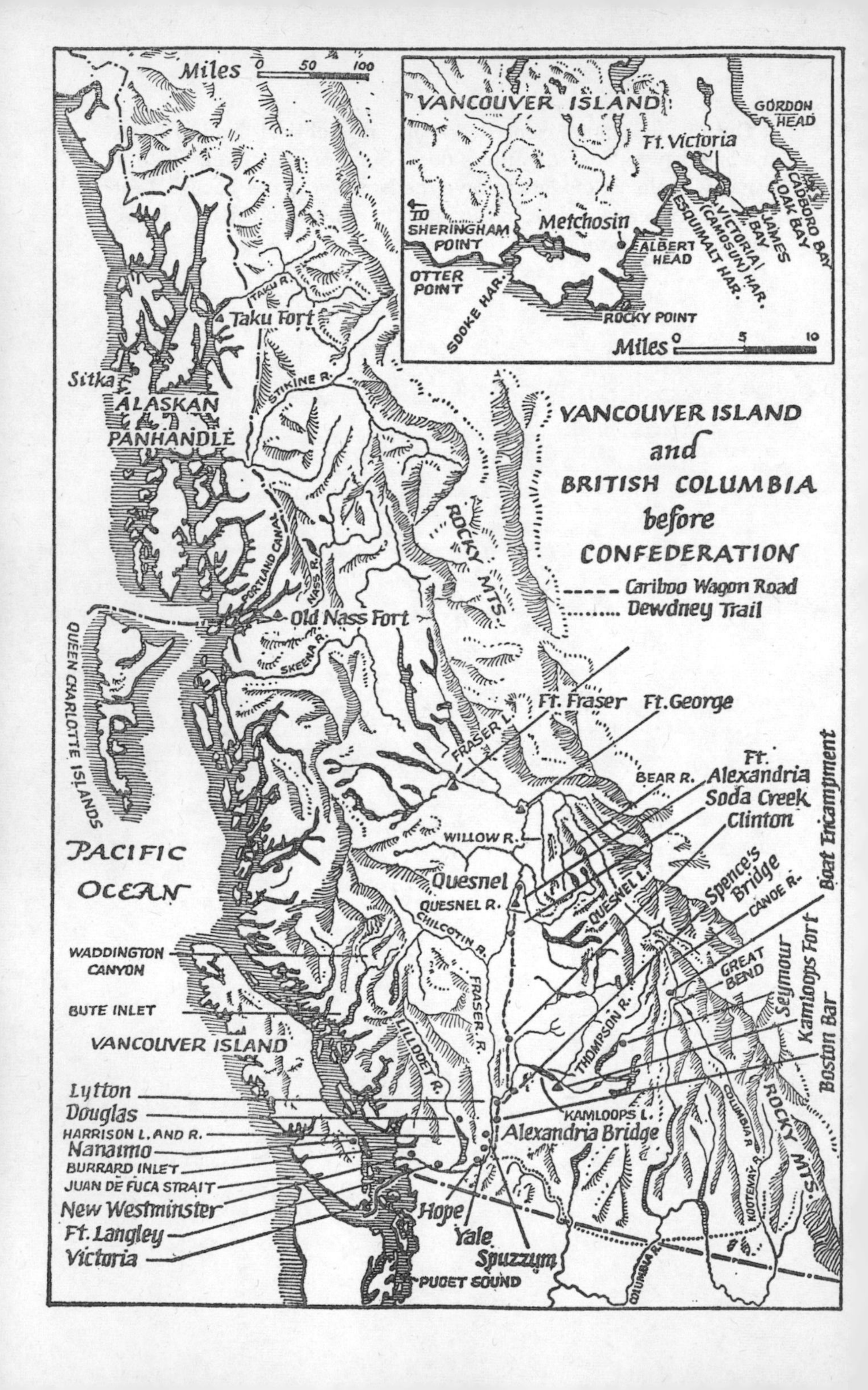

VANCOUVER ISLAND
and
BRITISH COLUMBIA
before
CONFEDERATION
----- Cariboo Wagon Road
.... Dewdney Trail
Miles 0 50 100
VANCOUVER ISLAND
Ft. Victoria
GORDON HEAD
CADBORO BAY
OAK BAY
JAMES BAY
VICTORIA (CAMOSUN) HAR.
ESQUIMALT HAR.
ALBERT HEAD
Metchosin
TO SHERINGHAM POINT
OTTER POINT
SOOKE HAR.
ROCKY POINT
Miles 0 5 10
Taku Fort
TAKU R.
Sitka
ALASKAN PANHANDLE
STIKINE R.
PORTLAND CANAL
NASS R.
Old Nass Fort
SKEENA R.
QUEEN CHARLOTTE ISLANDS
ROCKY MTS.
FRASER L.
Ft. Fraser
Ft. George
Ft. Alexandria
BEAR R.
Soda Creek
Clinton
WILLOW R.
Quesnel
QUESNEL R.
QUESNEL L.
CHILCOTIN R.
Spence's Bridge
CANOE R.
Boat Encampment
PACIFIC OCEAN
WADDINGTON CANYON
BUTE INLET
VANCOUVER ISLAND
LILLOOET R.
FRASER R.
THOMPSON R.
GREAT BEND
Seymour
Kamloops Fort
Boston Bar
KAMLOOPS L.
COLUMBIA R.
ROCKY MTS.
KOOTENAY R.
Lytton
Douglas
HARRISON L. AND R.
Nanaimo
BURRARD INLET
JUAN DE FUCA STRAIT
New Westminster
Ft. Langley
Victoria
Alexandria Bridge
Hope
Yale
Spuzzum
PUGET SOUND
COLUMBIA R.

CHAPTER VIII

1856–60

Gold on the Pacific Coast—The Founding of British Columbia—"Tale of a Pig" on San Juan Island—Steamers on the Red River and American Expansion Northward

1

GOLD! That was the magic word which put an end to the isolation of the British Pacific coast. There had been the elusive discovery of the precious metal on the Queen Charlotte Islands in 1851.

That discovery had been a flash in the pan. But in 1855, according to Angus McDonald, in charge of the H.B.C.'s Fort Colville, "at the mouth of the Pend d'Oreille [River] where it leaps with a bound of about ten feet into the Columbia," just north of the international boundary, and not too far from the modern center of Trail, gold was found. In the next year American miners from the Columbia followed the old fur-trade route northward. At Tranquille Creek, near old Fort Kamloops, at the junction of the Thompson and the Fraser rivers, a prospector, James Huston, found his pan full of nuggets. Before the next year was out gold had been discovered all along the Fraser as far as the Pacific. The Fraser River was about to fulfill its destiny.

In the East the St. Lawrence had been the highway to lead the first explorers to the Great Lakes and beyond. It had then become, with the Great Lakes, the dividing line between the United States and eastern British North America. The Fraser, in the meantime, had been a well-nigh unregarded river, though the H.B.C. had planted posts along its length and in the early forties Simpson had visualized its lower stretch as the line to be held when and if the Columbia territory was lost to the Americans.

Even Simpson had not visualized the part the Fraser was to play. Eight hundred and fifty miles in length and shaped like a child-drawn, elongated S, its sources are three hundred miles north of the 49th parallel and close to the Yellowhead Pass and the boundary between the present provinces of Alberta and British Columbia. At first it runs northwestward. Then it turns to flow due south for league on league between the mountain ranges. At last, swollen by its tributaries, and particularly by the Thompson, at Hope it bursts through its narrow canyons—the water from 85 feet deep at its lowest to 175 feet in the summer freshet, and the current on occasion at the speed of 24 feet to the second—to pour, fast-flowing, westward through its lush, almost hundred-mile-long delta to the ocean. Ten to twenty miles south of that delta is the international boundary.

This was the river of which the gold was to lure men north and east deep into the unexplored interior of the western mountains. By 1857 Company employees were already joined with Indians and with Americans from Oregon to hunt its yellow treasure from Fort Kamloops to the Pacific.

In 1857 Victoria, though incorporated in that year, was still a sleepy trading post. But Douglas could now foresee his rendezvous with Fate. On December 29 he reported to the Colonial Office that he expected a rush of gold miners in the spring. Since he himself had already sent 800 ounces of fine gold to the San Francisco Mint, he could be quite sure of it. For in California the gold fields which had brought in the forty-niners were either worked out or occupied. San Francisco was jammed with disappointed and bankrupt miners asking what next. To them the news of the strike in the Fraser Valley was manna from the god of luck.

In the spring of 1858 the torrent poured in. One stream came overland from the interior of California to join the river flowing in from the Columbia District via Okanagan to Kamloops. A train of ox-drawn wagons, for instance, from Portland overcame the Okanagan River by swimming the oxen across and freighting over the wagons and their contents on canoes lashed together. A company of some 159 men from California and Oregon moved in with pack horses. The Oregon Indians were by this time, with good reason, hostile. This party was attacked. Three Californians were killed and seven wounded.

The overland migration was a trickle compared to the multitude which flooded up by sea. In Oregon farmers left their farms, sailors their ships, and soldiers their regiments to join the throng pouring up by boat from Puget Sound.

These Oregonians were the advance guard for the wave from San Francisco. The *Commodore* with 450 adventurers aboard was the first ship to leave the Golden Gate. Soon every vessel that could swim—many of them worm-eaten hulks which had brought out the forty-niners—was off to the Golconda of the North. In steamers the first-class fare was $65. For steerage it was $35. Sailing craft charged from $25 to $60. The official figures record that 14,689 miners left from San Francisco alone in the months of May, June, and July for the gold bars of the Fraser. Add to these the contingents from Puget Sound and, to say nothing of the hordes traveling in by the overland route, Douglas found his tiny settlement submerged by a seeking, insatiate torrent of some 20,000 red-shirted, bearded adventurers, the bulk of them an experience-hardened lot who had known no law except the survival of the toughest. Most were miners, eager to get on to the gold fields and wanting only supplies and transportation. Sprinkled among them were merchants, traders, gamblers, saloonkeepers, and adventurers of more dubious purposes.

They all landed at either Victoria or Esquimalt, which housed between them some 200 startled people. A town of tents sprang up along the shore. Land values skyrocketed. On June 19 the journal of Commander R. C. Mayne of H.M.S. *Plumper*, who was on the scene, recorded the sale of 16 acres at Esquimalt. Lots which had been bought for £16 ($90) went for $2000. On the twelfth of July in an auction at the same place 25 lots were sold, the highest going to Ah Gim, a Chinese merchant from San Francisco, for $1450, the lowest fetching $375. Lumber leaped from $15 to $150 for a thousand feet. Muddy trails became muddy streets. Wooden, false-fronted stores, shacks, hotels, and saloons were flung together. The Victoria *Gazette* and, later in the year, the *British Colonist* were started. Douglas upped the fees for liquor licenses. The *Gazette* tells us that a retail license for selling liquor was £120 (or $600) per annum, a wholesale license £100, and a beer license £50.

And still the torrent kept tumbling in. On June 27 the *Republic* arrived with 800 passengers, on July 1 the *Sierra Nevada* with 1900, and, shortly thereafter, the *Orizaba* and *Cortez* brought in

2800. Overnight sleepy Victoria and Esquimalt had become roaring, brawling, bustling frontier towns. The stage was set for another San Francisco Barbary Coast. But Victoria was not in American California. Somehow Douglas kept order. Fortunately, there were two British men-of-war at Esquimalt, H.M.S. *Satellite* and Mayne's H.M.S. *Plumper*, both engaged in surveys. Later, Admiral Baynes arrived in H.M.S. *Ganges*, and H.M.S. *Tribune* was with him. Under A. F. Pemberton a police force was formed. When necessary, the Navy was asked for help. The whole situation, in fact, was an illustration of how, time after time, British sea power contributed vitally to the survival of British North America as a separate entity. Even with the Navy's aid, however, it was difficult to keep the peace, with hawk-eyed, greedy traders and riotous, surging miners erupting in brawls from the hotels and the stores and the saloons into the mud or dust of the unpaved streets. Somehow, it was done.

Douglas was aided by the fact that most of that red-shirted, tousled throng wanted to get to the Fraser gold bars. Their only interest in Victoria was supplies, boats, and licenses. The steel-nerved Governor met the situation with the iron imperturbability learned over the years. It was by a rush such as this that in the forties he had watched the Americans wrest the Oregon territory from Britain and the H.B.C. He was resolved not to permit this to happen in the domain he controlled. As early as December 28, 1857, although he had no legal jurisdiction over the mainland other than his headship of the Western Department of the H.B.C., he had taken a precedent from his action during the small gold rush to the Queen Charlotte Islands by issuing a proclamation that no one could disturb the soil in search for gold "without having been duly authorized in that behalf by Her Majesty's Colonial Government"—and this though no such government over the mainland existed. This meant that every miner had to have a license from Douglas, priced at first at ten and later at twenty-one shillings a month.

It was all quite illegal. But it worked. From the start the Americans were made aware that the mainland was British and subject to British law. On May 8 of 1858 Douglas went further. On the ground that the H.B.C. had the exclusive license to trade on the mainland, he issued a decree that all ships which entered the Fraser without a license from the Company and clearance from the Victoria customs would be liable to seizure.

Since the Company had at the moment only the *Otter* and the *Beaver* for transportation and to clear American ships through Victoria took time, he had to compromise. His compromise was that licenses would be issued to vessels to go up the Fraser directly but no passenger could be taken unless he had a mining license and had paid a two-dollar head tax to the Company. The fee for a decked ship was $12, for a canoe or rowboat $6. To enforce the regulations he placed H.M.S. *Satellite* at the mouth of the Fraser River.

Douglas' actions shocked the conventional souls at the Colonial Office. Even so, it was admitted that it was well done. The head tax and the ukase that no passenger who lacked a mining license could visit the mainland were disallowed. His other actions were approved and Douglas was given carte blanche to keep order on the mainland. By the time these instructions arrived from London, his regulations had already maintained control.

Meanwhile, the miners had been pouring from Victoria to the Fraser Valley. Rowboats, canoes, and even rafts were pressed into service. Hundreds, it is said, were drowned in tide rips or swamped by sudden squalls.

Those who passed the barrier at the Fraser's mouth found themselves in a broad, powerful stream bordered in those days by a junglelike density of huge trees. Working the sand bars as they poured along, they paused for supplies at the H.B.C.'s Fort Langley, twenty-seven miles from the river's mouth (Fort Langley on the south bank of the Fraser had first been founded some two miles further downstream in 1827 and then moved to where fragments of it, partially reconstructed, still stand). At Fort Victoria the Company's Roderick Finlayson took in $2,000,000 from the miners. In Fort Langley they spent up to $1500 a day. It is interesting to note that at Fort Langley the Company organized nightly dances for them, conducted "with decorum." In those two words is the difference between Douglas' regime and the Barbary Coast.

The hundred-mile length of the Fraser delta could not hold the miners. As in the blind rush of the spawning salmon, the red-shirted, rough-bearded adventurers surged on to the rugged canyons which at Fort Hope begin to pin in the defiant Fraser. Ten miles above Fort Hope and almost opposite Fort Yale at Hill's Bar, on March 23, the first big strike was made. In all the bars the gold was coarse and in pockets, easy to extract through surface mining by home-built sluice boxes or with the cradlelike rocker or even with a pan. The miners streamed on up the canyons. As early as May 1 the tumultuous throng was spread along the river as far as Lytton, where the clear blue-green of the Thompson drives into the dirty brown of the Fraser. Thirteen bars in all were alive with picks, shovels, and rockers.

The exact number who rushed into the country in 1858 can scarcely be determined, especially since when the summer freshet hit the Fraser in late May, covering the bars and making mining impossible, the majority "pulled foot" in disgust back to Victoria or to the States. By mid-August Douglas reckoned that there were 10,000 in the Fraser Valley, of whom 3000 were "engaged in profitable mining." In October, however, there was another rush. All in all, a fair estimate is that in four months some 20,000 adventurers landed at Victoria and Esquimalt, while another 13,000 poured into the mainland by other routes.

Most of them were Americans. The omnipresent danger was that, as in Oregon, they would form a provisional government and appeal to Washington. To make the menace more threatening, a personal representative of President Buchanan, John Nugent, reached Victoria, his nose sniffing around for a chance at annexation. He incited riots. He demanded ambassadorial privileges. Douglas refused. Then Nugent issued a proclamation to American citizens, promising them the Republic's protection against Douglas' "injustice."

The eagle was screeching provocatively. But Douglas was not the softhearted and somewhat befuddled McLoughlin of the Oregon territory. By his regulations he had already clamped down on the miners. In the spring, though he still had no official standing, he went up the Fraser. At Fort Langley he confiscated sixteen canoes which had no licenses and held them until $5 apiece was paid. At Hill's Bar he appointed George Perrier as justice of the peace. Foreseeing trouble with the Indians, whose cousins were at the moment fighting the Americans in Oregon and who also, quite naturally, believed this land and gold to be theirs and were afraid, besides, that mining would interfere with the salmon run, he called the chiefs to a council.

To Douglas, handling Indians was routine. He gave the chiefs power to bring any Indian offender before Justice Perrier and promised that if any white injured an Indian the white magistrate would give the Indian redress. Then, to the startled and incredulous Americans, the giant-statured Chief Factor announced that they were in the country on sufferance, that no abuses would be permitted, that no liquor was to be sold or given to an Indian, and that the "laws would protect the rights of the Indian no less than the white man." Douglas also appointed Richard Hicks, an Englishman, as revenue officer and Assistant Commissioner of Crown Lands. Both Hicks and Perrier were later, when they failed in their jobs, set aside by the iron-willed Governor.

All this was still a quite illegal use of authority. For the moment it worked. But the miners kept pouring in. A visitor to the upper Fraser found on July 28 "probably 2000 men . . . on Gassy Bar, Emory's Bar, Hill's Bar, Texas Bar and other places." At Hill's Bar he "counted forty log houses already built." It took him "a little less than nine hours" to cover the ten miles upstream against the millrace current from Fort Hope to Fort Yale by canoe, the Indians charging $6.50 for the trip. Fort Yale, situated "on the west side of the river, on a bend, a mile and a half below the lower big canyon," impressed him. On the flat below the bluff on which the fort was placed, with "high mountains" on every side shutting it in, there were "700 or 800 people . . . living in canvas tents and waiting for the river to fall." But there was "no drunkenness or lawlessness of any kind," a tribute to what Douglas had accomplished. There was one public eating house, its diet, invariably "bacon, salmon, bread, tea and coffee and the charge $1 a meal," a high price for those days. "The eating-house," we are told, "is kept in a log house partly covered with bark, and with a dirty floor," there being but one room and it being "not more than 12 × 14 [feet]."

This traveler went up to the "lower big canyon," wore out the seat of his trousers "slipping over rocks," tore off his fingernails, and wrecked a pair of boots. Just a little below the canyon and about two miles above Fort Yale was New York Bar, "settled mostly by a party of New York and San Francisco boatmen—chief among whom is the notorious Martin Gallagher . . . being one of the men expatriated [by the Vigilance Committee] . . . from San Francisco."

These were the sort of men whom Douglas had to keep in order and yet not give the waiting United States an excuse to pounce. While the writer of the account quoted above was at Fort Yale, the *Umatilla,* the pioneer steamboat on the Fraser above Fort Hope, made the first trip. "On her upward passage," he records, "she was welcomed by the miners on the banks of the river with shouts of joy and the firing of guns and pistols all along the route."

It was while the high water interrupted operations on the bars that Douglas somehow persuaded the miners to build a rough freighting road to supply the camps along the canyons. The miners worked without pay. What is even more incredible is that each of them put up $25 as a certificate of good conduct. Their one reward was that, when the road was done, they got back their $25 in goods at Victoria prices instead of at the exaggerated rates of the camps.

In the meantime the $25 apiece provided the capital for building the pack trail. Since boats could at high water go up the Fraser and thence by the Harrison River reach the head of Harrison Lake, the trail was driven from present-day Douglas at the head of the lake to Lillooet above Lytton. From July to November, 108 miles with more than a hundred bridges and culverts were built by hand and with free labor. Douglas put a toll on the freight carried over it. By the next spring the trail was paid for.

The mask-faced Douglas was more than meeting the crisis. While road building, keeping law and order on the mainland, and enforcing his system of licenses, he also had to keep a firm hand on the brawling newcomers in Victoria and Esquimalt. The Assembly of Vancouver's Island met to consider such matters as streets, water supply, and gas as well as the spiraling prices. Mr. Finlayson, treasurer of the H.B.C., was authorized to receive gold from the miners for safekeeping. The flow of traffic to and from the mainland was carefully regulated. Craigflower School held its annual examinations; though a brief but significant note tells us that "the Governor, who had always been present on former occasions, was hindered from coming by business."

It was an *annus mirabilis* for the taciturn, strong-minded Governor. But in August the anticipated trouble flared on the mainland. When the high midsummer water on the Fraser receded, the miners surged up the canyons beyond Fort Yale. Here the Indians were definitely hostile to the "Boston Men," a term which went back to the stupid cruelties of the first New England traders on the Pacific coast. They attacked. Swollen bodies came tumbling down the river. A force of about two hundred miners from Boston Bar, above Fort Yale, then tried to force a passage through to the Forks of the Thompson and the Fraser. On the fourteenth of August near the head of Big Canyon a skirmish was fought over the slippery rocks and among the big trees above the foaming rapids far below. Seven Indians were killed but the miners retreated. Soon they were out of the canyons. Then an expedition was formed at Fort Yale under H. M. Snyder. There was a brief and savage Indian war. Some thirty Indians were killed. Snyder, fortunately, was eager for a peaceful settlement. By the twenty-fifth of the month he was back at Yale with treaties of peace as far as the Forks.

Douglas, who had hurried across from Victoria with thirty-five sappers and miners and twenty marines from H.M.S. *Satellite,* for once was not needed. But he met the Indian chiefs and assured the peace. By the time winter set in, the peak of the crisis had been met and mastered. Douglas had saved the British Pacific coast from the Americans.

2

Today the automobiles pouring toward New Westminster, some sixteen miles away, pass through the two partially reconstructed segments of Fort Langley. The ferry from Albion brings other carloads to visit the one original building which is left. On November 19, 1858, the pristine palisade and bastions stared down through the mist and rain toward the landing place below it on the south arm of the Fraser River where it encircles a wooden island. Out of the mist swam the *Beaver,* the H.B.C. boat which had been the first steamer in the Pacific. From it stepped James Douglas, governor of Vancouver's Island, Rear Admiral Baynes, Chief Justice Cameron, Douglas' brother-in-law, and the towering, black-bearded Matthew Baillie Begbie. At the landing place a guard of honor of Royal Engineers commanded by Captain Grant snapped to stiff attention. The party plodded up the steep and muddy slope to the gate of the fort. As they reached the top of the bank, a salute of eighteen guns from the *Beaver* boomed dully over the sodden trees and the river. On the flagpole of the fort the H.B.C. Red Ensign came down and the British flag went up. This November 19 was the day of the formal inauguration of the new Crown colony of British Columbia.

It was on August 2 of this same year that the colony had been set up in London. New Caledonia could not be its name because the French had a colony so titled. British Columbia had been chosen by the Queen herself. At the same time, the connection of the H.B.C. with Vancouver's Island, which in November 1861 began to be called Vancouver Island in Douglas' documents, was terminated and so was its exclusive license to trade both on the mainland and on the island. The governorship of both colonies had been given to Douglas on condition that he sever all connection with the H.B.C. In response to Douglas' request in the spring for a "naval or military" force, a company of Royal Engineers was sent out. The advance guards of this force—20 and 12, respectively—had arrived on October 29 and November 8. The main body was not to come until the next spring. It should be noted that 160 marines were also brought from Hong Kong. These, however, did not land at Esquimalt until February 13 of 1859.

The greatest gift—and that an accidental one—was the tall, black-bearded Begbie, who on this November 19 followed Douglas through the gate into the rain-sodden compound of the fort, stepping carefully to avoid the puddles in this, the lower, part of the enclosure. At the far end, up the knoll, were the officers' quarters, the biggest building of those which lined the inner sides of the eighteen-foot wooden palisade. The party made for it.

Begbie had arrived at Victoria from London only four days previously. He must have looked about him with curious eyes. At thirty-nine he was regarded in London as a failure. He had lost his sweetheart to his brother. His own success at the law was such that he made his living by reporting the courts for the *Law Times*. So when he was offered £800 a year to become chief justice in the new colony of British Columbia, he jumped at the chance. Now, he was probably wondering, like Blanshard in 1850, just what he had let himself in for.

Blanshard had succumbed to Douglas. Begbie, a Scot like Douglas, had his own share of iron. As big a man as the Governor, full-bearded where Douglas was clean-shaven, wearing his clothes with a deceptively casual air while Douglas always moved ponderously as if on self-conscious parade, the first glance at Begbie might have suggested a reflective dreamer—and indeed he was given over to music, art, and literature. That air of amiable kindliness was misleading. As a judge, he was to be as autocratic and as disdainful of precedents as the governor of the two colonies. Begbie's view of the law could be boiled down to one simple belief—if a man committed a murder, he must hang for it. Neither he nor Douglas knew it yet, but they were to complement each other as neatly as if Providence had designed them for that purpose.

On this November 19, 1858, all this was in the future. The ceremonies had been planned for the fort's enclosure. The dripping rain from the gray low-hanging clouds made this project impossible. As many as could (about a hundred in all) crowded into the big room of the officers' quarters. James Douglas administered the oath of office to Begbie and installed him as chief justice of British Columbia. Begbie, as his first official act, all solemnity, administered the oath of office to Douglas and announced him as governor. One or two other minor officials were installed. Next Douglas read proclamations declaring the new colony, terminating the H.B.C.'s exclusive license to trade, indemnifying himself and all the officers for any irregularities committed up to this point, and declaring British law to be in force.

Thus British Columbia was established. One wonders if, during this ceremony, Douglas spared a thought for that hour of March 11, 1850, only eight and three-quarter years before this, when at Fort Victoria the colony of Vancouver's Island had been born and this new colony of British Columbia conceived. In any case, the British Pacific coast had, for the moment at least, been saved from the hungry republic to the south. To that extent "Black Douglas" had fulfilled his rendezvous with Destiny.

3

Gold had been the midwife for British Columbia's birth. Gold continued to nourish the infant. In 1858, in four months, seven hundred and fifty thousand dollars' worth of it had been shipped out of the Fraser Valley, to say nothing of the huge amounts never declared. There was hope of more to come.

Gold, though, brings in more than miners. Of all the strange characters the yellow lure attracted, none was more striking than the tall-browed, big-nosed, luxuriantly-bearded editor who on December 11, 1858, brought out, in Victoria, the first issue of the *British Colonist*. Born plain William Alexander Smith in Nova Scotia, he had in California—which then as now sometimes put strange ideas into otherwise unremarkable heads—officially changed his name to Amor de Cosmos—"Lover of the World." Now he undertook to attack Douglas for failing to establish towns, farms, mills, and roads in the six months from June to December.

From this time forward Cosmos was a gadfly buzzing around the Governor's ears.

Douglas, who in the meantime had laid out townsites at Forts Yale, Hope, and Langley, let the gadfly buzz. He himself had picked the site of the first Fort Langley, under the name of Derby, as the capital of the new colony. At a sale of lots in Victoria, $70,000 was realized from those eager to get in on the ground floor. When the commander of the Royal Engineers, Colonel Moody, arrived on December 25, he objected to the site. Derby was on the south side of the river and, therefore, in his opinion, too liable to capture by the United States. Douglas found that Moody, a quiet-mannered man with a big mustache and Dundreary whiskers, would not yield—and to Moody had been given by London the duty of selecting the capital. In January he picked what was at first called Queensborough, and a year later, renamed New Westminster. The site on the north bank of the Fraser made it defensible and it was closer than Derby to the mouth of the river. Those who had bought at Derby were allowed to exchange for lots at the new site. On July 16, 1860, New Westminster was incorporated as a city. Douglas, as usual, had the last word. As governor of both colonies he proclaimed Victoria as the port of entry for both—so that customs and other officials made their homes there and New Westminster was relegated to second place.

These were minor details. Gold was still king. By May of 1859 the search had moved 400 miles northward up the Fraser to the Quesnel River. By fall, miners had found pay dirt deep in the Cariboo Mountains and at Cariboo Lake. In the same autumn, a party which was surveying the 49th parallel for the international boundary discovered gold on the Similkameen River—six dollars' worth from six pans. In the next year, 1860, Americans rushing in overland made a rich strike at Rock Creek, south and a little east of the bottom tip of Okanagan Lake. Here, too, men were said to have taken out $1300 in nuggets in six weeks.

The indefatigable Douglas traveled in, called the almost five hundred miners together, explained the law to them, and appointed an Irishman, Captain William Cox, Assistant Gold Commissioner and Stipendiary Magistrate. Then, following the pattern already established, he persuaded the miners to help build a road of sorts from Hope into the area—the "Dewdney Trail"—and put a toll on travel over it.

In spite of the strikes at Rock Creek and in 1859 at Horse Fly Creek flowing into Lake Quesnel, the first fine fervor of the gold rush was over. The bars along the Fraser had been worked out. So were the creeks in the Quesnel area. No new outstanding find had been made. The tide of invasion began to flow back to California and Oregon, the river towns fell on evil days, and in Victoria the newly established merchants, their stocks gathering rust and moths on the shelves, stood at their doors, looking for trade.

There was a renascence of interest when, in 1860, far in the interior, "Doc" Keithley found rich pay dirt on Keithley Creek in the Cariboo area. That fall, close to winter, four men, of whom "Doc" Keithley was one, were still searching. They were on the point of turning back, exhausted, when one morning they tried one last stream, a stream only twenty-five miles distant from Keithley Creek. It was with little hope that they dug and washed the first pan of gravel. To their unbelieving eyes, the residue was gold, twenty-five dollars' worth. Four wildly excited men washed gravel all that day—and one pan is said to have gone as high as seventy-five dollars.

Antler Creek, the first of the spectacular creeks of the Cariboo, had been found. There was a foot of snow on the ground by the next morning. In spite of the snow, the news flashed across the ridges of that rugged terrain. Men rushed in on snowshoes through four feet of snow to stake claims. The Cariboo gold rush, which was to draw adventurers from all over the world, including the '62 Overlanders from Canada, had begun. Before it ebbed almost the whole length and breadth of British Columbia was covered by the prospectors. In the wake of the prospectors marched the settlers.

4

The two western colonies were not to reach 1860 without another "Tale of a Pig." The pig in question was the victim of an ambiguity in the 1846 Oregon Treaty. By its terms, once the coast was reached, the boundary was to be "to the middle of the channel which separates the continent from Vancouver's Island and thence southerly through the middle of the said channel and of Fuca's Straits to the Pacific Ocean."

But which channel? Apart from a middle and little-used channel, there were two recognized passages through the Archipelago de Haro Islands, south of Victoria. Both connected the Gulf of Georgia with Fuca's Straits. The southern one, Rosario Strait, was the one in use in 1846. If this was the passage meant, San Juan Island, the most westerly of the Archipelago de Haro group, belonged to the British. The H.B.C., therefore, which had occupied the island in 1843, continued to keep cattle, pigs, and sheep—5000 of these last—on it. In 1851 the Company, using Indians, established a salmon fishery there.

Unfortunately, there was the other channel, the Canal de Haro, through the islands, closer to Vancouver Island; and San Juan was south of this passage. In 1852 Oregon Territory claimed the island. Various attempts were made to collect customs dues from the Company. In 1854, a collector of customs, I. N. Ebey, landed. Douglas promptly came down from Victoria in the *Otter*. No solution was reached. The next year, Elias Barnes, sheriff of Whatcom County, seized and sold at auction thirty-four Company sheep for alleged back taxes. The Company promptly presented a bill for a compensation of, according to Begg in his *History of British Columbia*, "about $15,000." This led the U. S. Secretary of State to tell Governor Stevens to "pipe down."

By 1859, there were twenty-nine American settlers, chiefly disappointed miners from the Fraser diggings, squatted on San Juan. The Company's staff, meanwhile, consisted of a clerk, Mr. Griffin, and eighteen servants. In June, according to what seems to be the most reliable account, a Company pig got into the potato patch of one of the squatters, a man called Cutler. Cutler took one look at what the pig had done to his potatoes, got his rifle, and shot it. The Company assessed him $100 for the pig. Cutler refused to pay.

Into this stalemate walked a fire-eater, General Harney of the U. S. Army. Harney had been "suppressing Indians" by destroying bands, peaceful or otherwise, whenever he came upon them. On receipt of a petition signed by twenty-two Americans, including Cutler, on July 19, Harney sent over Captain Pickett—the man who later, in 1863, led Pickett's charge against the Union lines at Gettysburg—with sixty soldiers to occupy San Juan. The news reached Victoria. There was intense excitement. Three British warships appeared off the island. With superiority of forces, the British could easily have blown Captain Pickett and his sixty men off the island. But Rear Admiral Baynes "refused to go to war for the shooting of a pig." Harney, however, tried to stir up a conflict. He reinforced the troops on the island, asked for a naval force, and sent false reports to Washington.

Washington, with events moving inevitably toward the giant struggle between the North and South, took a second look. General Scott was sent out to replace Harney. In 1860 it was agreed that there should be joint occupancy until the ownership of the island was decided by arbitration. To complete the story, in 1872 the German Kaiser, in spite of the previous occupancy of the island by the H.B.C., awarded San Juan to the United States.

5

On November 19, 1858, at Fort Langley, the H.B.C. had lost its exclusive sway over its kingdom west of the Rockies. Earlier in the same year Minnesota became a state in the Union. It already had a population of 172,000; while Red River Settlement, though it was forty years since Lord Selkirk had planted it, numbered only about 10,000. Hungry eyes began to look across the border. In a surprise move of this same year, Sir George Simpson, abandoning the old supply route from Hudson Bay to England, arranged for Company goods to be transported in bond across the United States via St. Paul to Fort Garry. On the principle that if "you can't lick 'em, incorporate 'em," he picked the Canadian-born Norman Kittson, the man who over a dozen years before this had led the first cart train south to St. Paul, as his agent. Kittson, later to be one of the founders of the C.P.R., soon established a near monopoly over the St. Paul–Fort Garry route. It ought to be noted that, two years before this, another future C.P.R. founder, J. J. Hill, had reached St. Paul from Rockwood, Canada West. He was only eighteen in 1856. But he was to go far.

In those days the very winds at Fort Garry seemed to breathe of change. In 1857–58 the Palliser and Dawson-Hind expeditions were ranging the country from Lake Superior to the Rockies. The 120 officers and men of the Royal Canadian Rifles were still in the settlement. By this time, too, a few shacks, the nascent Winnipeg, had been flung up to the west of Fort Garry in the forks between the Red and Assiniboine rivers, while across the Red, the stone towers of St. Boniface Cathedral thrust themselves into the sky in rivalry to the Anglican cathedral at Kildonan.

There was talk of annexation by the United States among the

small group of Americans who had pushed into the country. In 1859, too, that enthusiast for Minnesota extension, James Wickes Taylor, had been commissioned by the U. S. Treasury to report on the route via Red River and the valley of the Saskatchewan to the British Columbia gold fields. Then, in 1860, George Emmerling, a German-American peddler, set up a hotel in Winnipeg. His bar became the rallying point for the "American" party.

There was also, as has been noted, a "Canadian" party, which was helped by the presence of the Royal Canadian Rifles. In 1859 Henry McKenney from Canada West called a log shack the "Royal Hotel." Shortly afterward there arrived that violent titan of a man, McKenney's half brother, John Christian Schultz, the physician from Kingston. Wherever Schultz strode either the grass withered or the snow melted. He was soon the herd bull of a group denouncing the validity of the H.B.C. charter over Rupert's Land. At first, since Canada seemed to have little interest in acquiring the Northwest, he bellowed for a Crown colony. Later, it was for annexation to Canada.

And he had a press. In 1859 two young English immigrants, Buckingham and Coldwell (they were twenty-seven and twenty-five years of age and had worked on the Toronto *Globe* and Toronto *Leader*, respectively) full of faith and ambition, started out with type and a press from Toronto. They reached St. Paul, completed their equipment, and bought a stock of paper. From St. Paul, their wives sitting atop the bales, they drove an oxcart all the way to Fort Garry. The first issue of their *Nor'Wester* came out on December 28, 1859.

The winds of change were blowing. And what of the native-born settlers, most of them of mixed blood? The English and Scotch half-breeds stuck doggedly to their plows and let the winds blow. All they wanted was assurance of the titles to their farms.

The French *métis*, the "New Nation," had no relish for what was in the wind. The Earl of Southesk, when he visited Red River in 1859, spoke of them as "tall, straight and well-proportioned," and they were the true riders of the horizonless prairies. They could run after their sleigh dogs in winter "fifty or sixty miles a day for a week together." To them the buffalo hunt and the cart trains screeching to St. Paul were sufficient. Lighthearted and hospitable, though often improvident and reckless, given to wild bouts of dancing and drinking, they were the true descendants of the old *coureurs de bois*. They wanted their world to stay as it was.

The Roman Catholic Church reinforced their attitude. To its hierarchy, there was the chance of another and even purer French-speaking Canada East on the banks of the Red River. But in May of 1859 the mournful blare of a steamboat's whistle put an end to the partial isolation of Red River Settlement.

Behind the whistle which stampeded the cows along the Red and brought men, women, and children to the banks to gape, lay a small epic. The cart trains were still screeching into St. Paul. But with Kittson and the H.B.C. entering into the picture and Toronto showing an interest, the merchants of St. Paul decided on a bold move to cement to themselves the trade of Red River. Steamboats had long threshed the Mississippi. In 1858 the St. Paul Chamber of Commerce accepted the offer of Captain Anson Northrup to transfer his ship, the *North Star*, from the Crow Wing River to the Red. The price was two thousand dollars.

By late February of 1859 Northrup had dismantled his boat. It was 150 miles cross-country, through a wilderness deep with snow, to the Red River. Northrup lashed the segments of his ship to horse- and ox-drawn sleighs. In spite of temperatures at times well below zero, through drifts and blizzards, and later through rain and mud, he got engines, boilers, framework, stern-wheel paddles, and all to Georgetown by the first of April. Seven weeks later, the antiquated hulk, renamed the *Anson Northrup*, floundered in the muddy waters. In early June its threshing paddles startled the settlers of Fort Garry.

"Its arrival," writes Bishop Taché, "was treated as quite an event, and, to the surprise of the public, cannon thundered and bells pealed forth chimes. . . ."

The blare of the *Anson Northrup*'s whistle signaled the approaching end of the cart trains. To the thoughtful observer, it also served warning that the Americans would soon spill across the border. And why not? Red River Valley was a natural unit and the imaginary boundary line no barrier. The interest of Canada West was checked by the thousand miles of barren wilderness and by French-Canadian hostility to western expansion. When that steamboat arrived in early June of 1859, it seemed to make it inevitable that St. Paul would swallow Fort Garry, and the United States the whole of the empty Northwest and, ultimately, the Pacific West as well.

But on the night of October 16 of that same year, far to the south, the fanatic abolitionist John Brown, with twenty-one followers, white and colored, seized the arsenal at Harpers Ferry up the Potomac from Washington. His plan was to set up a stronghold in western Virginia from which he could foray into the low country to release slaves.

His plan collapsed under the bullets of a party commanded by Colonel Robert E. Lee, a name soon to be blazoned abroad as the great general of the Confederacy. Brown and six of his followers paid for their failure on the scaffold. Less than two years later the Confederate guns firing on Fort Sumter were the inevitable consequence.

The dull thudding of those guns on April 12, 1861, and not any action by Canada or Britain, saved for the moment Red River Settlement and the Northwest from the American dream. Those guns did more. They helped turn Canada's reluctant face toward Confederation.

CHAPTER IX

1861–63

The Drift toward Confederation in the East—
The American Civil War and the Trent *Affair—*
Watkin and the Purchase of the Hudson's Bay
Company

1

IN 1861 the Macdonald-Cartier team still dominated Canada. Yet, even though George Brown was missing from the House, Rep. by Pop. was a rock on which the Liberal-Conservative coalition seemed in danger of foundering. In October of this year, too, John A.'s faithful coadjutor, Sir Edmund Head, was replaced by a new governor general, the portly, heavily bearded Lord Monck.

Monck, as yet, understood little of the eternal split between French and English Canada. But, meanwhile, the thunder of the guns to the south was beginning to make the dullest of Canadian politicians realize that Canada's future might be determined by the vicious struggle between Confederates and Unionists.

Across the Atlantic, though the British masses were sympathetic to the North, the ruling classes in both England and France tended to favor the Confederacy. On the thirteenth of May 1861, Britain's declaration of neutrality, which recognized the South as a *de facto* government, had already roused the hostility of the North. As usual, that hostility was directed against British North America.

In the Maritimes and Canada opinion was, as in England, divided. The military and naval groups in Halifax, Montreal, and Toronto, along with many of the High Tories, were, in general, sympathetic to the South. The French-Canadian habitants had, as usual, no interest in anything so remote from their parishes. But, as in Britain, the ordinary English-speaking public was for the North. Both Lincoln and Davis might be reluctant to state that slavery was the principal issue in their civil war. The average men and women simplified the struggle into slavery versus anti-slavery. When Lincoln finally issued his Emancipation Proclamation on September 23, 1862, they were justified. It is ironical but natural that the boom in Canadian wheat and timber, brought on by the war, strengthened the ties with the North.

Union sympathy was strongest in the Maritimes, so closely tied to the New England states by trade bonds, and in the south-western peninsula of Canada West, where so many Americans from the northern states had settled and where, too, had been the exit for the Underground Railroad to freedom for fugitive Negroes. Here, as early as 1848, under Lord Elgin's sponsorship, a tract of 18,000 acres near Lake Erie had been set aside as a refugee settlement for escaped slaves. All in all, it is estimated that 40,000 British North Americans—among them a son of Joseph Howe—enlisted in the armies of the North.

One would have thought that the North would have recognized this help and been grateful for it. Instead, as soon as the *Trent* Affair flamed, Canada became its whipping boy.

It was on November 8, 1861, that the U.S.S. *San Jacinto* under the command of Charles Wilkes, took James Mason and John Slidell, two Southerners on their way to represent the Confederacy at the courts of St. James's and Napoleon III, respectively, from the deck of the *Trent,* a British mail packet.

The North, forgetful that the War of 1812 had, ostensibly, been fought because of the British search of American vessels during its blockade of Napoleon, hailed the capture with shouts of joy. Wilkes was the hero of the day. On the other side of the ocean, the British Prime Minister, Palmerston, exploded into belligerent rage. His original note to Washington might easily have brought war, with the Maritimes and Canada as the battleground. It was modified by Albert, the Prince Consort, as one of his last acts before his death.

Even so, the note demanded an apology and the return of the envoys. The States received it with incredulous howls. The New York *Herald,* in the usual ignorant American assumption that all that was needed to acquire British North America was to free its people from the "tyranny" imposed by a small British garrison, revived the old cry that it was "Manifest Destiny" that all North America should belong to the United States—and meantime the North was forging a powerful military machine.

There was a real danger of war in that November of 1861. Throughout the month both Canada and Britain worked feverishly. Transports carrying nearly 14,000 troops rushed from England for the St. Lawrence. The ice turned them back. With no railway available, the troops were landed at Maritime ports. Through the winter's cold sleighs carried the soldiers over the snow-deep Témiscouata route from New Brunswick to Canada East.

Meanwhile, in Canada 40,000 of the Sedentary Militia were called up. All over Canada West the farmers turned out with shotguns, old muskets, and even pitchforks, brimful of the chauvinistic notion that one Canadian could lick seven Yankees. A new portfolio of Militia Affairs was created with the indispensable John A. as minister.

Fortunately for Canada's patriots, Lincoln knew that the North already had all it could chew in the gray-uniformed armies of Lee and Stonewall Jackson. The captured diplomats were returned, though without an apology. But Canadians still kept casting uneasy glances over the border. Fear of the United States was a nudge toward Confederation. An immediate and unexpected result was the defeat in May of 1862 of the Cartier-Macdonald government.

The instrument of their fall was a militia bill, inspired by the *Trent* Affair, which provided for a fivefold increase in defense expenditures and compulsory as well as volunteer military service. Up until this time the militia had been summoned for a ridiculous one-day jamboree each year. The new bill included a provision to call out in its first year of operation 30,000 men for two weeks' training. Anglo-Canada was in favor. French Canada grumbled. The crisis was over. So why bother? Besides, French Canadians had an almost pathological objection to compulsory military service, for fear of becoming involved in Britain's wars. As the opposition mounted, John A. locked himself in his room with a bottle. "He has one of his old attacks," the *Globe* reported blithely.

John A.'s bouts of compulsive drinking seem to have been his way, when he sensed defeat, of evading reality and responsibility. When, on May 20, pale and jittery, he returned to the House, a bloc of French-Canadian members changed sides. The militia bill was defeated by seventeen votes. The government was out. But George Brown was not the new First Minister. Brown was still not a member of the House. Instead, John Sandfield Macdonald, the Glengarry Catholic, with Sicotte, the French Canadian who had deserted the Liberal-Conservatives over the choice of Ottawa as the capital, came into power.

It was only a stopgap government. By 1863 it, in turn, was defeated and Macdonald and Cartier were back. Political deadlock was becoming another nudge toward Confederation.

2

The next shove came from Edward Watkin. This genial British railway promoter had come to Canada to find out for the British investors why the Grand Trunk Railway failed to pay dividends. His immediate solution was to resurrect the old Intercolonial Railway project. A conference between Maritime and Canadian delegates was held at Quebec in the fall of 1860, "the forests," according to Howe, "everywhere weaving varied tints of autumn." In Quebec when Howe arrived he found everyone, except Tilley of New Brunswick, who was a teetotaler, and Watkin, "half-seas over." After the conference was completed the delegates were carried on visits "everywhere in special trains in the Prince's car." (The visit of the Prince of Wales was just over.)

Nothing came of this attempt or of another conference held in London in 1862. In the meantime, Watkin had succeeded Thomas Baring of Baring Brothers as president of the Grand Trunk Railway, and a new and energetic Britisher, John Charles Brydges, was general manager. Watkin's visits to British North America had also convinced him, as he wrote to a friend, that the G.T.R. could be made to pay only "through the extension of railway communications to the Pacific." In this way, he thought, China and Japan would be opened to British commerce and the gold fields of British Columbia and California brought within reach—and he envisaged the prairies as a wheat-growing country.

Watkin's views were symptomatic of a new British imperialism, which was being slowly forged by events. The Indian Mutiny of 1857 had brought India directly under the Crown. By the sixties China and Japan had been opened to foreign trade. In Europe, Italy had been unified and Prussia was ready to weld Germany into a single state. Moreover, industrialism, imported from Britain, was raising up competitors to her. Mercantilism, the theory that colonies existed only for the benefit of the mother country, had begun to go down the drain at the time of the American Revolution. But while possessions in Africa and elsewhere supplied Britain with raw materials and provided markets, could not colonies such as those in British North America and Australia serve in a system of defense and also help expand British commerce?

This new concept of imperialism was still not quite ready to seize the reins. But Watkin had the right friends. Thomas Baring and George Carr Glyn, the heads of those two banking firms that keep popping up in Canadian history, along with the Colonial Secretary, the Duke of Newcastle, whose 1860 chaperonage of the Prince of Wales in Canada had so infuriated the Orangemen, backed him in forming the Atlantic and Pacific Transit and Telegraph Company. The project of this company was nothing less than a telegraph line across British North America and a wagon road from Red River to the Pacific Ocean.

This project came smack up against the H.B.C. monopoly. Newcastle approached Berens, the twentieth governor of the Company, for land for the route. On the fifth of September 1862 Berens agreed to concede. In a later interview, however, he is said by Watkin to have exclaimed: "What! Sequester our very taproots! Take away the fertile land where our buffalos feed! Let in all kinds of people to squat and settle! . . . If these gentlemen are so patriotic, why don't they buy us out?"

Watkin took him at his word. The International Finance Company was formed with Thomas Baring and George Carr Glyn as the principal figures. By the end of June 1863, to everyone's shocked surprise, the old H.B.C. had been bought out for £1,500,000—that is, at £300 a share for shares which were worth around £200 each. Along with the shares went the 1670 charter and the title to Rupert's Land. The new governor was Sir Edmund Head, ex-governor of Canada. The capitalization of the Company was immediately raised from £500,000 to £2,000,000 and its shares put on the market. In effect, the "Gentlemen Adventurers of England trading into Hudson's Bay" had ceased to exist.

The news of the sale hit the Northwest like a thunderbolt. No provision had been made for those who had always been given a part of the profits of the Company—the chief factors and the chief traders. Upset and uncertain about their status, they tended to relax their control. The *métis* of Red River were unhappy. There had been no recognition of them, either. They began to look more definitely to Minnesota.

In the final issue, Watkin's telegraph and wagon road never got off the planning board. But his purchase of the H.B.C. paved the way for acquisition of the Northwest by the new Dominion, when it was formed. Rupert's Land had been bought once. It could be bought again.

CHAPTER X

1861–64

The Cariboo Gold Rush–Overlanders of '62–The Cariboo Road–The "Hanging Judge"–Separation of the Colonies of Vancouver Island and British Columbia and the End of Douglas' Regime

1

IN the early sixties the gold which had made British Columbia into a province had also spread its fame abroad. The first rush to the Fraser had faded. In the spring of 1861 the strike in the previous fall at Antler Creek brought the stampede back again. Once again Victoria was overrun. Soon Douglas' Harrison–Lillooet Trail was jammed as the tide of miners poured toward the isolated and rugged terrain of the Cariboo. From Antler Creek the torrent surged to the other creeks running north into the big bend of the Fraser. Up until this year it had been surface mining. Now on Williams Creek, flowing into the Willow River, "Dutch Bill" Steitz and his partners burrowed like ground hogs through the gravel into the clay. They came up with a thousand dollars' worth of gold from their first washing. The secret of the creeks was out. Not surface scratching but deep diggings meant fortune. Soon four thousand hysterical, sweating miners were driving holes into the clay along Williams Creek. The daily yield on one claim, according to Judge Begbie, gave its owners thirty to forty pounds of gold each twenty-four hours. Miners had to tote their sacks of gold to their claims each day and stand guard over them each night. Billy Barker, a Cornishman who had jumped ship at Victoria, sank a shaft which tapped Eldorado.

Around his claim sprang up the legendary Barkerville, now a

ghost town, but in the early sixties a mile of false-fronted cabins, stores, saloons, and dance halls on a single street squeezed between the creek and the hillside. On other creeks near by, such as Lightning and Lowhee, rich strikes were made. On Lowhee, so Douglas records, from one claim, $46,800 was taken out. The official statistics for the gold mined in 1861 showed a total of $2,666,118, but to this must be added the immense amounts never reported. By the spring of the next year there were some 6000 miners in and about Barkerville, that fantastic center which it took 600 plodding miles from the coast to reach and where flour cost $300 a barrel.

The Cariboo gold rush was on. It brought men of all types and conditions—actual and would-be miners, packers, storekeepers, gamblers, saloonkeepers. It brought camels on the trail and German "hurdy-gurdy" girls for the dance halls. It lured adventurers from the United States and from Britain and Europe. It brought the Overlanders from Canada.

2

The Cariboo fever was in the air that spring of 1862, as catching as measles. All over Canada West groups were formed, their fantastic project to march overland to the British Columbia gold fields. They had no thought of themselves as the modern Argonauts, but that is what they were. Husbands left their wives. Farmers abandoned their farms, storekeepers their stores, policemen their jobs. There was even, finally, a pregnant woman with three children marching with the Overlanders. For all of them the Cariboo was the Golden Fleece.

All the groups, as pointed out in M. S. Wade's excellent *The Overlanders of '62*, furnished their own equipment. The best-known of them is the McMicking party of twenty-four, organized at Queenston. In it, each man had to pay a five-dollar fee and to agree to a code of rules and regulations.

This party boarded the train at St. Catharines on April 17, 1862. Another group was the Redgrave expedition of forty-five, got together in Toronto. Its leader, Stephen Redgrave, was an Englishman who had been educated at Rugby, had mined in the gold fields of Australia, and served on its Colonial Mounted Police force. Later, in 1859, he had taken his family to South Africa and thence to England. His restless foot then brought him to Toronto to become a sergeant of police.

At thirty-one, Redgrave's thirst for adventure was not yet quenched. Before his party left Toronto on April 23, it was joined by the Huntingdon group of twenty-five from Canada East; but all the names were Anglo-Saxon. John M. Sellar, the diarist of this company (there were those in each party who set down day-by-day accounts of the odyssey), gives us a hint of the feelings of the Overlanders as they set out, their misgivings mixed with the thrill of the unknown adventure.

". . . we finaly . . . assembled at Mr. Millen's Inn at four O'Clock," he writes on April 22, "where they were met by upwards of some two hundred of their City friends. . . . 5 A.M. we performed the last becoming duties to our fair City and Citizens, by taking an affectionate farewell of Home & all that was dear. . . . this was rather a trying task for many of us, especially those who had Wives and families to leave behind. At 5:30/60 got all on board of some veicals [Sellar's spelling is "progressive"] . . . & started for the Rail Road at Chateaguay, the road being almost impassible on account of mud & water. . . ."

After describing the junction with the Redgrave party, Sellar mentions a stop at Port Sarnia: "Where we arrived at 7 P.M. When all those who partake of the Eliments of Padies eye water, joined in a rabbelling Toast to Brittan and British subjects. And then all joined in singing God Save the Queen & three Brave & hearty cheers for our homes & for Canada's Son's, and then embarked on the Steamer for to cross the St. Clair River to Port Huron & from whence we took cars for detroit. . . ."

This was the way of the departure of the Overlanders in quest of their Golden Fleece. Besides the parties from Toronto, Huntingdon, and Queenston, there were also groups from London, Acton, Whitby, Waterloo, Ottawa, Montreal, Goderich, and other points, including seven from Ogdensburg in New York State. Later a group was sent out from England by the "British Columbia Transit Company," which promised that the total cost from Glasgow to the British Columbia gold fields would be £42. Needless to say, the assurances of this company were never fulfilled.

For the Overlanders their route to Fort Garry was of necessity through the United States. Down to the south, the armies of the Union and the Confederacy were locked in combat like two stags meeting. There is not a hint of this in the diaries of the Overlanders. Some went from Detroit to Grand Haven and thence by steamer to Milwaukee. The Redgrave expedition passed through Chicago, where, according to Sellar, "we had dinner & a general spree." All of the companies finally found themselves on the paddle steamers threshing up the Mississippi to St. Paul. That town of some 10,000 people was "some 6 or 8 feet deep with water" because of spring floods and Sellar notes disapprovingly in true Canadian fashion that "there is but little respect shown for the Sabath on the Mississippi for all kinds of business is attended too . . . while the few who do abstain . . . only do so in order to get a days recreation and sport at Billiards amongst the Saloons, or loafing amongst the grogries."

At St. Paul the Canadians divided themselves into squads of ten. They traveled to Georgetown on the Red River in small groups by stagecoach, admiring the farmhouses which were soon to be burned in the August 1862 uprising of the Sioux. The journey took about twelve days. Alexander, of the Redgrave party, writes:

"Pitched our tent and got a lot of Prairie Hay, then lit our fire and I kneaded the flour, made some bread, boiled our tea and then had supper. Prairie Fowl formed a part of it and it is not at all bad to eat. Had prayers and then turned in."

Sellar comments about one night at Baillie's stage station that "we aranged for to pass the night as best we could on the soft side of a plank." Of a dinner at a place called St. Joe, he remarks that "the people of the Village are all French and Jermans, so that dinner was no grate shakes." Sauk Centre at the time, says Alexander, was "one house and is situated on a prairie which seems to have no end." About Georgetown, at this time an H.B.C. post and the embarkation point for Fort Garry, Sellar notes: "Georgetown . . . is composed of one Store at which you can buy nothing, one Hotel at which we could neither buy grog nor victuals, one Barricks & some three or four Indian wigwams & one dwelling House."

At Georgetown the Overlanders had to wait while the Burbank Company of St. Paul finished the steamship *International.* The *Anson Northrup,* after its initial trip to Fort Garry, had been taken over by the Burbanks but in 1860 had been rebuilt and renamed the *Pioneer.* By the end of that year it was useless. So the Burbanks bought the wreck of the *Freighter,* which had run aground in an attempt to get it to Red River, took the boiler and engine to Georgetown, set up a sawmill, and began to build the *International.* While the Overlanders were waiting, Dallas, James Douglas' son-in-law and the new H.B.C. governor, arrived with his family and his servants. The Overlanders, armed with rifles, marched to his lodging, lined up, and fired a salute. Dallas had his valet, who was also his piper, play for them. It is quite evident that, by this time, Canadians were almost pugnaciously conscious that they were Canadians.

Finally, on May 20 at 2:15 P.M., the *International* set out. But the Red River bores through the land like a giant corkscrew. At the very first turn the current swept the 150-foot length of the steamer against the trees on the point. Shortly afterward, and only two miles from Georgetown, she again crashed into the trees and had two of her funnels smashed down and her pilothouse damaged. It took until 2 P.M. the following day to make repairs. An hour later the engines broke down and the boat was hung up until 6 P.M.

Such was travel by stern-wheeler on the Red River in 1862. The passenger list, by the way, included Bishop Taché, Judge Black, later to be a delegate to Ottawa to initiate the province of Manitoba, and Dallas and his party. On the twenty-sixth of May the Overlanders reached Fort Garry. In the diary of Archibald Thompson of the McMicking company, we learn that "it cost us fifteen dollars and sixty-five cents from Suspension Bridge [at Niagara] to St. Paul and twenty-five dollars from St. Paul to Fort Garry."

In those days a cent was a cent and five dollars a week's work. The real odyssey of the Overlanders was now to commence. At Fort Garry they bought horses for $40 a head and oxen at from $25 to $30 each, Red River carts for $8 apiece, harness of raw buffalo hide at $4 a set, as well as supplies of flour and pemmican.

The way in which pemmican, the staple food of the plains, was made fascinated the Canadians. The lean meat of the buffalo—or, further west, of the moose—was cut into thin strips, partially roasted, sun-dried until brittle, and then beaten with sticks into powder. Meanwhile, the green hides were shaped into bags and the fat of the animals rendered. The last stage was to mix the powdered lean meat with the hot fat and pour the result into the bag. This produced 100 pounds of highly concentrated food which would keep for years, but as in the case of Greek *retsina,* a taste for it had to be developed.

On the third of June the McMicking party began to straggle out of Winnipeg to a rendezvous at White Horse Plains, twenty-five miles to the west. Ahead of them was the trek to Fort Edmonton, covered each year, of course, by the H.B.C. brigades but new to the Canadians. Sellar tells us of the first day: "We had many a strange scean . . . such as Oxen running off with their drivers & never failing to rid themselves of their entire tackling. . . . I have seen as many as 6 or 8 all in one of those rearing, tearing fitts att once. . . ."

From White Horse Plains, the groups moved on to Long Lake. There were 138 people in all in this company. Seven from Red River had joined them. Among these was the Schubert family—the husband, the pregnant wife, and their children: August, six years old; James, three; and Mary Jane in between. There were also seven of the Redgrave party and all of the Huntingdon group, to which Sellar belonged. New accessions before Edmonton was reached raised the party to 150.

Here at Long Lake a meeting was held on the open prairie with Thomas McMicking of the Queenston party in charge. His chair was a water cask. Wallace from Toronto was secretary and "sat on the ground and wrote on his knee." The rest stood or sat around.

It was democracy in its simplest form, reminiscent in a less tense way of the meetings of Xenophon's ten thousand Greeks on their epic march back to the sea from the heart of the Persian Empire. Thomas McMicking, a schoolteacher from Queenston, a clean-shaven man with a direct gaze and an open, intelligent face, was elected captain with a committee of thirteen, one from each of the various groups, to help him. Fourteen resolutions in all were passed. Among them was one that there should be no liquor used among the Indians and another that if any person offended "an Indian or Indians," in case the Indians asked for him, "he shall be handed over to their discretion," a reminder that in this country there were no troops or police but only the H.B.C. reputation for fair dealing to protect the Overlanders from the natives.

This meeting was at 10 A.M. of Thursday, June 5. At 2 P.M. the trek began. The cavalcade was made up of 97 Red River carts, wooden wheels shrieking to heaven on wooden axles, and 110 horses and oxen. In close order it stretched for half a mile. By noon of Friday, the sixth, the expedition was at Portage la Prairie.

By the evening of Saturday, the seventh, after the first experience of crossing streams and pushing through the mire of sloughs, it encamped on the banks of the Soft River, described as a clear, rapid little stream, its banks shaded with poplars. On Sunday, the Overlanders stayed in camp and held a religious service—prayers, hymns, reading of the Scriptures, and a sermon on a text from the Bible. The pipeline workers of today, if they could be taken back through time, would marvel at this Sunday scene, so alien from the modern way of life.

The Overlanders were aiming for Fort Ellice, near the boundary between present-day Manitoba and Saskatchewan. By Saturday morning, June 14, after crossing the Little Saskatchewan by a ford and after shooting ducks and taking fish in the river (the Little Saskatchewan is a beautiful stream about forty feet in width and with banks two hundred feet high), they came in sight of Fort Ellice.

By this time the Overlanders were becoming toughened to the new experiences of the march over the untamed land. Through their eyes we glimpse the Northwest before the white man marred it with civilization. The Overlanders were almost awed by the beauty and the expanse of it. Here in front of them, as they record it, was a lush valley in which the Assiniboine met the Qu'Appelle River and Beaver Creek, while topping the hill across the river was the only sign of habitation, Fort Ellice. Through their accounts runs the fresh wonder of explorers.

From Fort Ellice the caravan moved north to Fort Carlton through park land swarming with ducks and thickly dotted with sloughs. The mosquitoes of the West impressed the Easterners. On June 26 Sellar comments with heavy humor, "Before bed time it was found necessary to tie our Mosquitoes nets fast around our necks so as to keep the mosquitoes from flying away with them as they were about the size of humming-birds in Canada." At 11 A.M. on July 1, after crossing the South Saskatchewan—here only a few miles from the northern branch, though the two do not join until further on as if flirting coyly before their wedding—they reached Fort Carlton.

Fort Carlton was the post near which the two Englishmen Milton and Cheadle, in their search for a "North-West Passage by Land," spent the winter of 1862 before moving on to the Pacific the next year. By this time the Overlanders were some five hundred miles out from Fort Garry. Though they had no suspicion of it, their journey so far had been a city street as compared with the troubles ahead. By 10:20 P.M. of the day of their arrival, in spite of a thunderstorm, they had crossed the North Saskatchewan on an H.B.C. scow at a cost of 12½ cents per cart, en route to Fort Pitt, between Forts Carlton and Edmonton. At first all went fair. On July 4 at the "Lumpy Hills" they found carpets of ripe strawberries. The wolves prowled around them, "forming the rear-guard . . . during the day, and entertaining us at night with repeated concerts."

At Fort Pitt the party again crossed the North Saskatchewan to follow the trail along its south bank. On the next day, July 11, it began to rain and it kept up for eleven days more. For three days the Overlanders camped, soaked to the skin, with wood too wet for a fire and, as McMicking notes, the "Dirt of the cattle" making the camp unpleasant. On July 12 a party of Blackfeet was thought to be near. On the fourteenth the Overlanders went on through the rain, passing over on the next day, as Sellar tells us, "the Battle ground of a Battle which had only been fought 3 days prior to our arrival between the Blackfeet and the Cress [Crees]." On the sixteenth a meeting was held for the unexpected purpose of getting up a "musical Association."

Troubles multiplied. Between the eighteenth and twenty-first of July the Overlanders had to build eight bridges because the streams had been swollen by the rains. There were many others which had to be forded. Under the nineteenth of July, Sellar observes: "The traveling was desperate both for Cattle & men we pushed on Knee deep in water till 7:20 when all of a suden we droped into a creek up to the armpits & as there was no timber about, we had to raise our loads on top of our cart boxes. . . . the rain fell in torrents. . . . Every person was wet to the skin."

That night, as the "water had raised some 4 inches in our Tents," Sellar and the six others with him "cut small brush & built a pile 2 feet high" and put their tent over this. At last, about 8 P.M. on July 21, the travelers unexpectedly "popped out of the bush on the river bank opposite Edmonton." Because the river was in flood, so that the boats had been carried downstream, it was not until the twenty-fourth that they got across to the fort.

"It is a nice place," Archibald Thompson of the Queenston party wrote of Fort Edmonton to his brother. "I think I could live here quite contented if I could get provision but they do not raise enough for themselves. They live most of the time on pemmican and potatoes . . . there are some pretty girls here."

But Hunniford of St. Catharines thought it "a very dirty establishment." *Tot homines, quot opiniones.*

What of the rest of the Overlanders? Rumors of gold to be got in the Saskatchewan River split the Redgrave party. But it and the Symington group finally reached Edmonton only to discover that the McMicking expedition, except for twenty-five who stayed behind to wash for gold in the North Saskatchewan, had left Edmonton for the Yellowhead Pass on July 28. Most of the McMicking party had sold their carts and oxen and bought saddle and pack horses. Toughened though they were by this time, they found the mountain trails difficult. Some of their animals slipped from the paths. Their provisions ran short. Thomas McMicking, on August 27, dined on roast skunk. Finally, on August 27, the party reached Tête Jaune Cache on the Fraser River, weak and almost starving. Fortunately they came on a camp of Shuswap Indians, who traded to them huckleberries, battered salmon weighing twenty-five to thirty-pounds each, dried mountain sheep meat, and dried skunk meat.

Meanwhile, some thirty-five of the Redgrave party also decided to join the gold seekers along the North Saskatchewan. On August 12 the remaining twenty-five followed Redgrave to the Yellowhead. Their trek was even more difficult. Young Alexander, a Scots lad from Toronto who at eighteen had joined the Overlanders, records on September 9 that ". . . all we have had since Sunday [September 7] is about a pint of soup made of Pemmican per day for a man, and a Carrion Crow which Jones shot today that divided among four of us. I thought it tasted remarkably good eating."

It was a stiff experience for a lad who had been educated at Edinburgh Academy and Upper Canada College. He and the rest of the group reached Tête Jaune Cache by September 16, while some of the Symington party had arrived ten days before.

In this fashion the three main parties had reached the Fraser River. But how to get to the Cariboo? From Tête Jaune Cache the Fraser throws a 200-mile loop northward before it flows south for about another hundred miles to Quesnel, the jumping-off town for the Cariboo; and yet Quesnel is almost due west from Tête Jaune Cache. The Overlanders had no real concept of the dangers before them. The McMicking party determined to split. Thirty-six of them, including the pregnant Mrs. Schubert, were to herd

130 horses and cattle over toward the North Thompson and thence either to the Cariboo or to Kamloops. The rest, with a few cattle, knowing nothing of the canyons of the river, decided to build rafts or dugouts from cottonwood to float down the Fraser to Quesnel.

The rafts were about forty by twenty feet. They had fireplaces of stone and clay and were named from the passengers' home towns. On these the remaining oxen and horses were put, and on September 1 this group of the Overlanders set out. At first all went well. Then, they reached the Grand Rapids. Four dugouts were lost and one man, Robertson, from Goderich, a young engineer of high promise, drowned. The rafts, by some miracle, got through. The Overlanders faced another stretch of rapids. After that it was clear sailing until they reached the huddle of cabins which was Quesnel.

Meanwhile, the land group, driving its herd before it, toiled across the divide to the headwaters of the North Thompson. It attempted to hack its way down the west bank. The huge cedars and firs defeated them. In all, in seventeen days the party had made 60 miles and Kamloops was 200 miles to the south. *Faute de mieux* they decided to entrust themselves to the river. They killed most of their oxen at "Slaughter Camp." They built rafts and canoes from the huge cedars. They loosed most of their horses. One group of seven, though, built two rafts. On one they put seven horses, an ox, and four men. On the other traveled the remaining three men with their equipment. "On the second day," as Archibald Thompson tells us, "the raft with the animals struck a snag." The animals were put off. The men got through but were "two days and one night without anything to eat." They got the horses back on, but at the Murchison Rapids were overset and Strachan, of London, Canada West, was drowned. They had to portage their goods to the end of the canyon and build a new raft.

Such were the experiences of this party. Potatoes from an Indian encampment, which had been deserted because of smallpox, kept them alive. Some of them had to walk the last 120 miles to Fort Kamloops. The rest floated in by raft. Mrs. Schubert was one of those who came in by raft on the thirteenth. She had her baby, a girl, the next day.

The Redgrave and Symington parties both tried the Fraser River route to Quesnel in canoes. The young Scots lad, Alexander, was in a canoe which was swamped in the Grand Canyon. One of his four companions, Carpenter, was drowned. Alexander himself barely escaped.

"At last," he tells us, "after swimming a distance of about three-quarters of a mile I touched the shore but was so benumbed with the cold I could not hold on to it but drifted off again. Soon, however, I made the shore again and dug my hands among the pebbles and pulled myself out of the water and lay there."

After that one hairbreadth escape from death, he had to swim back across the canyon to rejoin his surviving comrades. Even then the four of them were "200 miles from Fort George, with . . . only eight ground-hog between us. . . . We went at once upon rations, the allowance being one ground-hog a day, each man getting a piece about the size of your hand."

Alexander's account is, perhaps, a fitting glimpse of the last lap of the 3000-mile five-month journey of the Overlanders, though there were still others on the trail when he reached Quesnel. How many lost their lives en route is not known for certain. But it took tough adventurous men, and one pregnant woman, to make the trip.

And what of the gold at the end of the rainbow? By the time the Overlanders reached Quesnel a line of bearded and disappointed men was coming in on their way to the coast. They all told the same story. There was gold in the Cariboo creeks but too many hunting for it. Every claim or possible claim was staked and prices were out of sight. Those Overlanders who had reached Kamloops heard the same tale.

A few of the hardiest of the new Argonauts made the trip in to the diggings. R. B. McMicking, the brother of Thomas McMicking, the schoolteacher from Queenston, was one of three who walked in as far as Cottonwood on Lightning Creek. There on September 14 they found "3 or 4 houses and some tent stands." They saw "lots of persons . . . making their way as fast as possible down to the Ocean, most of them about strapped. . . ."

The three returned to Quesnel and started down the Fraser. By the twenty-sixth of September, R. B. McMicking was working for a road-building company as cook at $50 per month. John Hunniford of St. Catharines set out with sixteen other Overlanders and seven Californians to raft down the Fraser. After four hours his raft stuck on a snag and he "had to give an Indian most my clothes to take me off." He camped in the bush with no "dinner nor supper" until the Ottawa raft picked him and the others up and carried them to Alexandria. Thence they traveled "16 miles to Mud Lake" and Hunniford "slept on the Bar room floor all night in company with Packers and Miners." Next day, the fifteenth of September, they plodded twenty miles to Williams Lake, to see the mining. That was enough. Hunniford started work on the road being built from Clinton to Soda Creek. Sellar, the diarist from Huntingdon, after reporting the depressing news from the miners, records:

"As most of us were pretty well played out of money we concluded to sell our animals, Picks & shovells & what clothing we did not wish to pack on our backs & rase enough to take us to some other country where we could afford to live as no person at Carriboo could pretend to live, they mearly stayed and starved."

He and his comrades took a contract to cut forty cords of firewood at Lillooet for $400. "Such," concludes Sellar, "was our first job & commencement in the far famed Colloney of British Columbia." On the eighteenth of the November this group left for San Francisco.

Such was the end of the quest for the Golden Fleece. Some, like John Hunniford, who returned to St. Catharines to become one of its leading merchants, went back home. Many settled in British Columbia. Thomas McMicking, for instance, made his home in New Westminster. In 1866 the Fraser, whose boiling canyons he had survived, drowned him while he was trying to save his little son, Frank. Stephen Redgrave, the restless-footed Englishman, lived on to become sheriff of Kootenay and Stipendiary Magistrate at Golden. None of them mined. It was as if the quest in itself had satisfied them.

3

The roads on which many of them found temporary employment were part of Douglas' master plan. In 1858 the miners had built for him the Harrison–Lillooet Trail and in 1860 the Dewdney Trail. The miners, too, had improved the old H.B.C. track through the canyons of the lower Fraser from Yale to Spuzzum and had continued it to Boston Bar. From that point Douglas had had the path bettered as far as Lytton. But the Cariboo strike of 1861 meant that these attempts to supply the mining camps were all outdated, though by 1863 Gustavus Blin

Wright had extended the Harrison–Lillooet route by way of Clinton as far as Soda Creek. Thence, by steamer up the Fraser, there was a connection with Quesnel, from which a track of sorts plodded in to Barkerville.

The route was at best a *pis aller*. It involved constant changes from coach or shanks' mare to boats. The canyon trail from the head of navigation at Yale was more popular for all transportation except for the heavy freight. Along it, pack-horse and mule trains served the Cariboo. A mule train varied in number from sixteen to forty-eight mules, handled by a boss, a cook, and one man for each of the sure-footed carriers of the canyon trail. Each mule carried 250 pounds of freight and made $250 for each round trip. One freighter, Frank Laumeister, in the spring of 1862, brought in twenty-one camels, each of which could carry 1000 pounds. They were not a success. Their stench set mules and horses bucking and the pads of their feet wore out on the canyon rock. Some of them were sold and the rest turned out to grass on the Thompson Flats, east of Cache Creek.

The makeshift routes, the massive Douglas decided, would not do. If the miners of the Cariboo were to be supplied, if settlement was to be encouraged and taxes collected, government enforced, and, above all, trade encouraged to flow from the merchants of Victoria and New Westminster into the interior instead of coming up from the States by way of the Okanagan, a Cariboo road must be built.

It seemed an impossible task. Where was the money? And how could a road be built along the canyons of the lower Fraser, where even today the traveler shrinks within himself as he stares from the railway coaches to the depths of the gorges below him? Fortunately, Douglas was too far from London for the Colonial Office to stop him. He traveled over his proposed route. Then, on October 24, 1861, he wrote to the Duke of Newcastle that he had decided to build the road, "thereby securing the whole trade of the colony for Fraser's river and defeating all attempts at competition from Oregon." To finance this plan he proposed to raise "a loan of fifteen or twenty thousand pounds" in the colony itself.

Before the Duke of Newcastle could interfere Douglas had set Colonel Moody's Royal Engineers to work blasting an eighteen-foot-wide roadway through solid rock from Yale up the west bank of the Fraser. For the rest of the job he let out contracts, notably to Thomas Spence and Joseph W. Trutch. From Yale the

Royal Engineers hewed the six miles upstream to Pike's Riffle out of the canyon wall. From that point Spence continued the road to Spuzzum. There Joseph Trutch threw across a suspension bridge with a span of 300 feet made out of bales of wire carried to the spot. This bridge carried the road over to the east bank and was used for half a century. Thence the road ran along first the Fraser to Lytton and then to Spence's Bridge along the North Thompson. There were two more bridges until, north of Clinton and the junction with the Harrison–Lillooet Trail, the road swung through the jack pine to reach the Fraser again at Soda Creek. It took until 1863 to get to Clinton. By 1864–65 it had reached Barkerville.

The fantastic project had been completed. It was a 385-mile wagon road, eighteen feet wide, sometimes at giddy heights above the gorges and supported by pilings or dry rockfalls or gigantic wooden cribbing; at others at water level, now crossing gossamer-like bridges, now skirting the mountains or threading the passes or running on the flat. Along it, in those vanished days of Cariboo gold (within seven years twenty-five million dollars were officially shipped out) rolled a ceaseless traffic—long lines of mules, heavy freight wagons, six-horse passenger coaches, clumps of plodding miners, "rich man, beggarman, Indian, thief."

Its cost, according to Joseph Trutch, was only $1,250,000. Before it was done most of it was already paid for, thanks to Douglas' method of allowing the builders of the two main bridges to levy tolls (from which both Spence and Trutch made fortunes) and of collecting government tolls. The tolls from New Westminster to Barkerville totaled $53 a ton, or over 2½ cents a pound. Yet the Cariboo Road brought the cost of transport to the gold fields down from $1.25 a pound to 15 and 18 cents a pound.

Along it, at every stopping place, the mile houses of the road mushroomed, numbered like the mile posts of the Roman Empire, not from Rome, but from Yale. The expressmen, such as F. G. Barnard, became the new heroes. Barnard covered the road with his freight wagons and devoured it with his stagecoaches, on which the horses were changed every thirteen miles so as to complete the route from Yale to Soda Creek in forty-eight hours. Indians, miners, Chinamen, hurdy-gurdy girls for the dance halls, ministers, judges, gamblers, packed those coaches cheek by jowl. Then, when the gold rush was over and Barkerville a street of ghosts, the Cariboo Road carried in and supplied the new settlers, the farmers and ranchers and businessmen who were to make British Columbia permanent. By the Cariboo Road alone, James Douglas justifies his title as "Founder of British Columbia."

If Douglas was the new colony's Romulus, Begbie was its Numa Pompilius. In the California gold diggings, banditry, murder, vigilance committees, and the outrageous Barbary Coast had made a mockery of all law and order. Begbie saw to it that there was little of this brand of "liberty" in British Columbia. He was a peripatetic judge, the law on horseback. During his first years, traveling with a string of twelve horses, he slept where night overtook him and held court wherever there was trouble. Legalities rarely troubled him. He himself on occasion would act as prosecutor, defense counsel, and judge, all in one. On occasion, he refused to accept the verdict of a jury. There is a story, oft told, of a case in which a jury, in spite of Begbie, brought in a verdict of manslaughter instead of murder.

"Prisoner," Begbie fluted in his high, shrill voice, "it is not a pleasant duty for me to sentence you only to prison for life. . . . You deserve to be hanged. Had the jury performed their duty, I might now have the painful satisfaction of condemning you to death. You, gentlemen of the jury, you are a pack of Dallas horse thieves, and permit me to say it would give me great pleasure to sentence you to be hanged, each and every one of you, for bringing in a murderer guilty of manslaughter."

On another occasion, when a man had been sandbagged in a Victoria saloon but the jury acquitted the man guilty of the crime, Begbie turned and said:

"Prisoner at the bar, the jury have said you are not guilty. You can go, and I devoutly hope that the next man you sandbag will be one of the jury."

Such was the man who boasted that he hanged Americans by the verdicts of American juries. Actually, there were few hangings, simply because the terror of Begbie's name made the Americans toe the line. Behind him stood a mere fifteen police constables, chiefly Englishmen, poorly paid but incorruptible. Their caliber is illustrated by an incident in a rough American camp at Wild Horse Creek in the Kootenay area in 1864. In a Fourth-of-July spree a man was shot dead. A party was formed to avenge him by lynching two characters with the improbable names of "Yeast Powder Bill" and "Overland Bob." Another group, claiming to be the party of law and order, assembled with the avowed intention of trying the two men before a judge of their own selection, and hanging them "legally." By the time Gold Commissioner and Magistrate Haynes and his constable, Young, rode in, there was a shouting, excited, and armed mob of some hundreds.

"But," D. M. Drumheller, who was present, tells us in his memoirs, "one little English constable with knee breeches, red cap, cane in hand, riding a jockey saddle and mounted on a bobtailed horse, quelled that mob in fifteen minutes."

The two accused men were tried, acquitted, and advised quietly to leave Wild Horse Creek, which they did.

With the help of these constables but chiefly by the force of his own Cromwellian personality, Begbie maintained the law throughout the wide-flung mining camps. Yet this same many-faceted man built himself in Victoria a rambling house with wide gardens, in which he had his Chinese servant tie cherries to the trees for his guests to pick. It was he who on Saturday nights first held a soiree for the clergymen of the town but at nine o'clock replaced them with a group of cronies who played cards all night. When he died in 1894, knighted and full of honors, it was discovered that for years he had been supporting a group of poor people. By his own instructions his grave was marked by a wooden cross on which was this inscription only: "Lord, be merciful to me, a sinner."

Begbie left a deep stamp on British Columbia. Only Douglas, the benevolent but determined dictator, surpassed him; and Douglas had his roads and his treasury and his new towns and all the minutiae of administration to occupy him. Opposition was to him simply a wave to override. In 1859, in spite of protests, he put up the first government buildings of brick and wood in front of the site on which the Parliament Buildings now stand. Amor de Cosmos called them "goosepens." In 1862, in that high summer of the Cariboo gold rush, he welcomed the "Bride Ship," with some sixty marriageable girls on board and a matron in charge.

The "Bride Ship," a steamer called the *Tynemouth*, was the work of Miss Burdett-Coutts, whom Joseph Howe had met while in England during that same summer of 1862. On his return to Nova Scotia he was appalled to discover that she had sent him 120 emigrants to look after because, in his exuberance, he had described his province as "a Paradise." With the same spinsterish enthusiasm, hearing that there was a shortage of respectable women in the gold fields of British Columbia, she got together a church committee to send out "desirable females as domestics." Romance soon bloomed. As the women were paraded off the ship, one ardent bachelor stepped up, took one of them by the arm, and asked her to marry him. In a few days most of the "domestics" were brides. Another ship, the *Robert Lowe,* followed. In all, nearly a hundred women reached Victoria on the "Bride Ships."

Meanwhile the gold output continued, but with a difference. Williams Creek had replaced the easy surface mining with deep diggings. These required equipment. The surface miners had to turn laborers or else hunt for new areas. They drifted off to the north to the creeks of the Peace and Stikine rivers or else into the Kootenay and Big Bend country. As early as 1863 the total number of Cariboo miners had dropped to 1393.

And meantime opposition to Douglas was swelling to a volume which the Colonial Office could not disregard. Vancouver Island had an assembly and legislative council and the buzzing gadfly Amor de Cosmos. In British Columbia, Douglas was, by the initial order in council, the sole authority. There were shouts of "dictatorship." There were complaints because the governor and his officials, including Begbie, lived in Victoria. There were cries about a top-heavy civil service, residing "in a foreign land." Merchants and real estate speculators saw all the plums going to Victoria as the "port of entry" for both colonies. There were demands that the government of the two colonies be separated.

In 1863, therefore, the Colonial Secretary, the Duke of Newcastle, informed Douglas that British Columbia would be enlarged to include part of the Stikine territory to the north, that the two colonies would be divided, and that a partially representative legislative council of fifteen would be set up on the mainland to consist of one third government officials, one third magistrates, and one third elected representatives of the residents.

It was a mere spoonful of representative government. Douglas divided the mainland into five electoral districts—the sole qualification for the franchise being British citizenship—held the elections, and met the new Council for the first time on January 21, 1864. His term as governor of Vancouver Island had run out in September of the previous year but he stayed in power until the new governor, Arthur E. Kennedy, arrived from London. On March 14, 1864, twenty-one years to the day from the moment he had landed to begin Fort Victoria, Douglas, who had now been knighted, laid down his power. The colony underwent a change of heart. There were public addresses and dinners and crowds accompanying Douglas to his ship and cheers and bands playing.

Douglas probably took these demonstrations at their worth. A month later, at New Westminster on April 20, he turned his authority in British Columbia over to Frederick Seymour. Then he returned to a banquet for him in Victoria before he left with his family for a visit to his Scottish homeland. At sixty-one the "grand old governor," as he was now called, could feel that he had builded well. He had saved the British Pacific coast from the Americans. Over and above that, on the mainland he had laid the foundation for a new kingdom, not of furs, but of farms and merchandise and lumber and coal, as well as of gold. The gold would, ultimately, be worked out. But agriculture and the infant industries would endure until at last Canada would be ready to reach a steel finger across the wilderness and across the prairies to the mountains and the Pacific. Nor was it surely mere coincidence that in the same year that Douglas finished his work the Charlottetown and Quebec conferences were ringing up the curtain on Confederation.

CHAPTER XI

1864

Stalemate and George Brown—The Charlottetown and Quebec Conferences—Confederate Raid on St. Albans

1

ON Tuesday, June 14, 1864, the Taché-Macdonald government, which on March 21 of that same year had ousted the John Sandfield Macdonald–Sicotte administration, was defeated in the House by two votes. Canada's caravan Parliament was meeting in this year at Quebec. An almost exasperated sigh went up from the members. Since 1862, within the space of two years there had been two general elections and three administrations. This last government, in spite of John A.'s skill, had lasted less than three months. What the members faced was dissolution and still another election. That election would simply return the warring factions in approximately the same strength to form another ephemeral administration.

It was to this impasse that the conflict between Lord Durham's "two nations warring in the bosom of a single state" had finally brought Canada. On the next day John A. Macdonald rose in the House to announce that the Cabinet had decided to communicate with the governor, Lord Monck. Everyone knew that this meant dissolution and a general election. Suddenly George Brown was on his feet.

The rigid Freekirker, having recovered from his illness and his financial reverses, was more potent than ever. In the spring of 1863 his towering rage over the passage by Canada East votes of the Scott Bill to extend still further the privileges of Roman

Catholic Separate Schools in Canada West had compelled the then First Minister, John Sandfield Macdonald, to take three Brownites—Oliver Mowat, John A.'s old pupil, Luther Holton, the Montreal railway promoter, and Antoine Dorion, leader of Canada East's anticlerical *Rouges*—into his Cabinet. Among the three members dropped by Sandfield Macdonald to make room for the Brownites was a five-foot-three Irishman with a fringe of beard framing a flat, undistinguished face.

That Irishman was D'Arcy McGee. Newspaperman, rebel (he had escaped to the United States after the 1848 Young Irelanders' revolt, disguised as a priest), McGee, in the spring of 1857, at the age of thirty-two, had moved his family and himself to Montreal. That same fall the Irish vote had elected him to Canada's legislature. As a dutiful son of Mother Church, he had opposed the Orange Order, supported Separate Schools, and fought against Rep. by Pop. Somewhere along the line he had fallen in love with his adopted country and had become converted to Confederation. Whatever McGee clasped he embraced with a consuming affection, and he was a flamboyant, silver-tongued orator. John A. had had his eye on him. So in 1863, when Sandfield Macdonald kicked him out of his Cabinet without troubling to pad the boot, there was John A. full of Celtic charm and soft sawder. By December of that same year the two were stumping together in a by-election which the Conservatives won.

McGee was the most eloquent of those in whom events had compelled realization that the only solution to Canadian political deadlock was some sort of Confederation. His antithesis, George Brown, Presbyterian and huge-statured, who had come back into the House in 1863 to tell Parliament: "I have killed more than one Ministry in my day," had finally perceived that Rep. by Pop. would never find acceptance in an isolated Canada. In the spring of 1864 he had chaired a select committee of nineteen, which included Cartier, Galt, John A. Macdonald, and D'Arcy McGee, to discuss Canada's constitutional problems. That committee on June 14, the very day of the defeat of the Taché-Macdonald administration, had reported in favor of "a federative system applied either to Canada alone or to the British North American Provinces." It is significant that John A. was one of the four committee members who voted against that resolution. The other fifteen were for some sort of federation. The Northwest, and even the Pacific West, was no longer beyond the ken of Canada, and

Confederation in the East had become in men's minds more than an orator's trick of speech. For south of the border a storm cloud lowered. By June of 1864 it was clear that the North would win the Civil War. What, then, would she do with her battle-hardened armies, the greatest military force of the day? Turn them against Canada?

It seemed quite possible that she might. The 1861 *Trent* Affair had lighted a fire of resentment against Britain. That flame had been fed by Britain's intention to propose mediation in 1862 and, still more, by the launching of Confederate commerce raiders, such as the *Alabama*, from British shipyards. A picture of the *Alabama*, was given wide circulation in the North, and underneath was the inscription: "Built of English oak, in an English yard, armed with English guns, manned by an English crew and sunk in the English channel." In a mood of bitter resentment and upswelling confidence, the Union press was already talking of seizing and annexing Canada, once southern resistance had been obliterated, as a sort of picnic excursion for the Grand Army of the Republic. And what was there to stop that army if it marched?

There was the specter which brooded in the House on the afternoon of Wednesday, June 15, as Macdonald made his announcement and his rival, George Brown, got to his feet. Nearly everyone expected an exhortation to the defeated government to pack up its papers and be gone. In private, however, Brown had already let it be known through Conservative intermediaries to John A. and Galt that he would be willing to co-operate with any government to try to cure Canada's constitutional ills. Now, in the House he suggested that his enemies "should be allowed every opportunity to consider what course they should pursue." Brown's allies, John Sandfield Macdonald and Dorion, were furious. John A., who only the day before had been against Confederation, saw a chance to save the Conservative government. He lunged at the olive branch. On Thursday he asked Brown for a conference. On Friday, at one o'clock in the afternoon, he and Galt walked into Brown's hotel. There were only two hours to go before the House met. When the House did meet, John A. announced that the ministry was reserving the permission for dissolution which had already been granted by Lord Monck in order to carry on discussions with the member for South Oxford—that is, Brown—and proposed adjournment.

Dorion and John Sandfield Macdonald opposed it. Then Brown

rose to his finest hour. Had it been John A. the members might have suspected a political trick. But when George Brown assured them that only extreme necessity would make him negotiate with his political enemies and that there would be no secrecy, the House believed him. Adjournment was granted. Nothing shows more clearly the feeling in Parliament that this was a "last chance" moment than Sir Richard Cartwright's recollection of how he saw "an excitable elderly little French member rush across the floor, climb up on Mr. Brown, . . . fling his arms about his neck and hang several seconds there suspended to the visible consternation of Mr. Brown. . . ."

The "excitable elderly little French member" was Mr. Dufresne of Montreal. In such an atmosphere there was no possibility of failure. It was decided to attempt a federation of all the B.N.A. eastern colonies. A coalition government was formed in which George Brown and John A. sat cheek by jowl but with Sir Etienne Taché as the visible head. Included in the Cabinet were two other Clear Grits, William McDougall and Oliver Mowat. The Confederation train had at last got to the blueprint stage.

This was on June 30. On the same day Governor Monck wrote to the lieutenant governors of Nova Scotia, New Brunswick, and Prince Edward Island to ask if Canada could send a delegation to attend a proposed Maritime Conference on Maritime Union. The answer was in the affirmative. The date was set at September 1 and the place as Charlottetown, Prince Edward Island.

September 1 was too long for the ebullient McGee to wait. He had been in the habit of spending his summers in the Maritimes. So he arranged an August excursion of some hundred Canadian M.P.s, railway men, merchants, and journalists. This ill-assorted group traveled through sultry summer heat in suffocating coaches—air conditioning was still far in the future—from Montreal to Portland. The sweating, shirt-sleeved excursionists drank, smoked, told jokes, and jumped off at every stop. At Portland, where there was a heavy rain, the boat was delayed. Some of the D'Arcy McGee ambassadors of good will turned back. Enough waited so that a sizable group was received by the St. John Board of Trade and welcomed again on August 13 at Halifax. Joseph Howe, who had resigned his premiership for an Imperial post as fisheries commissioner, was there on the government vessel *Lily*. Though his party had been defeated in the Nova Scotian elections of May 1863 by his nemesis, Dr. Charles Tupper, the old Tribune could not resist getting in on the act. He arranged a sail for the McGee party on the *Lily* and addressed them at a banquet at the Prince's Lodge. In that speech he used words he was later to rue.

"In conclusion," he said, "I am pleased to think that the day is rapidly approaching when the Provinces will be united. . . ."

Maritime hospitality, chiefly liquid, created a fine glow of friendship in everyone. There were, however, little or no practical consequences to the McGee expedition. When, on the morning of September 1, the *Queen Victoria*, the same vessel which had met the Prince of Wales in 1860, steamed up the channel to sleepy Charlottetown with eight members of the Canadian Cabinet on board (John A., George Brown, Cartier, Galt, McDougall, McGee, Campbell, and Langevin), there was no one on the dock to greet it. W. H. Pope, a Prince Edward Island M.P. happened to be about. He hurriedly commandeered a rowboat and went out to welcome the Canadians.

It was an *opéra bouffe* start. When the Canadians came ashore, there was still no official welcome. There were no lodgings either.

This was partly because the *Heather Belle* had brought in the Nova Scotians on the afternoon of the previous day, while the *Prince of Wales* had landed the New Brunswickers a little before midnight. One may suspect that on the morning of September 1 most of the Maritimers were recovering from a typical Bluenose celebration.

The other reason was that the first circus to visit Charlottetown in twenty-one years had arrived. So, from far and wide, the islanders had driven their wagons and buggies over the rutted red-earthed roads between the heavy-foliaged trees into Charlottetown to crowd every hotel and boardinghouse. Most of the Canadians had to stay on board the *Queen Victoria*. The Maritimers, however, once they realized the presence of the Canadians, were prepared to listen. On Friday and Saturday, September 2 and 3, the formal case for Confederation was presented by Cartier and Macdonald until, at 3 P.M. of the Saturday, the Conference adjourned to the *Queen Victoria* for luncheon. It was in that luncheon, which with toasts and talk went on and on, and in informal conversations later with, naturally, a bottle within easy reach, that agreement began to appear. Brown and Galt spoke on the Monday. On Tuesday it was decided to meet again at Halifax.

With the larger issue before them the Maritimers ran into

trouble over Maritime Union, especially since Prince Edward Island demanded Charlottetown for the capital. On Thursday, the eighth, the Charlottetown Conference ended with sherry, claret, and champagne flowing in an assembly hall decorated for dancing with flags, flowers, mirrors, evergreens, and gas jets. The Confederation train was beginning to be assembled. When in Halifax a last attempt at Maritime Union stalled, it was agreed to hold an official Confederation Conference at Quebec on October 10. George Brown's action of June 15 had snowballed so rapidly that he himself must have been surprised.

2

Day after day thirty-two delegates from the five eastern colonies sat at Quebec in a building which had once been a general post office but, fortunately, was perched in the Upper Town. Day after day rain blurred Cape Diamond and the St. Lawrence and the trees along its banks.

The rain suited the mood. At Charlottetown and Halifax there had been a gay enthusiasm and a sense of high design. At Quebec the task was to give form and substance to the generalities of wine-flushed vision; and John A. Macdonald was the chief architect. He had been dragooned by political deadlock into accepting Confederation. Once he embraced it, he never faltered. Behind him stood two stalwarts: Tupper, the black-headed, black-bearded, square-faced Nova Scotian, and Lemuel Leonard Tilley, Premier of New Brunswick, a short, neat man with the alert features of an inquisitive fox.

It was quickly decided that the provinces should retain their own provincial assemblies and also elect members for a central legislature, from which in turn the Cabinet, or Executive, would be chosen. In this way the Chief Executive, the Prime Minister, along with his Cabinet, would, as in Britain, be directly responsible to the electorate. Thus, the elaborate procedure for electing a Chief Executive in the United States, as ritualistic as that of a barbarian tribe, was avoided. The name "Senate" was chosen for the upper house. But Canadian Senators were to be appointed for life and not elected. The United States was, in fact, to John A. the horrible example as to what to avoid in effecting a federal union.

The Canadian federal setup, then, was to be stark in its simplicity as compared with the continual round of elections across the border. In Canada, as soon as a Prime Minister fails to command a majority vote in Parliament, he is out of office, but general elections are, as a rule, infrequent.

The question of Senate representation was prickly. It was solved by giving Canada East, Canada West, and the Maritimes equal representation, with four additional Senators for Newfoundland. For the federal Parliament, Brown's principle of Rep. by Pop. was adopted. Canada East, now Quebec, was assigned a permanent representation of sixty-five members. This number, divided from time to time into the population of Quebec, was to provide a unit number of electors by which, in turn, the number of members from the other provinces would be decided. This much had been settled by October 20. Tempers were wearing thin and the thorny problem of provincial versus federal powers had not been decided. At this moment, however, the Confederacy and Governor Smith of Vermont combined to give Canadian Confederation an assist. On October 19 some twenty-five Confederate soldiers, out of uniform, crossed the Canadian border south of Montreal and raided the little village of St. Albans in Vermont.

It was a small and ill-managed incursion. The raiders robbed the bank, looted a few buildings, set fires, wounded two people, one of them fatally, and fled back across the border.

When in 1838 the Hunters' Lodges, operating from American bases, with the help and connivance of American citizens and officials, had launched a full-scale invasion of Canada, the Republic had shrugged off the occurrence as a boyish prank. Now that the shoe pinched its own toe the United States yelped as if a whole foot had been smashed to pulp. On the twentieth of October, Governor Smith wired Governor Monck as if an army of outlaws, fostered and equipped by Canada, had wiped out St. Albans. General Dix, the American commander of the area, ordered his troops to pursue the raiders, if necessary across the border. Seward, the U. S. Secretary of State, instructed the American ambassador at St. James's to give notice of the abrogation of the Rush-Bagot Agreement, which in 1817 had limited naval forces on the Great Lakes.

The furor died down when, a few days later, Canadian police captured the Confederate raiders. But the Quebec delegates had heard the American threat. It was Confederation or else. Though there was a bitter debate about provincial rights, John A.'s point of view won. The federal government, taking a warning from the American Civil War, was made strong and all powers not expressly assigned to the provinces were reserved for it. To the provinces went only control of minor and local affairs and, even so, the federal authority had the right to disallow provincial legislation. To Galt was given the job of making the loss of revenue to the provinces, particularly from tariffs, palatable. It was agreed finally that the national government should pay a grant to each province equivalent to eighty cents per person of population. Other resolutions provided for the appointment of judges for life, the guarantee of an Intercolonial railway to the Maritimes, and an arrangement that British Columbia, Vancouver Island, and the Northwest could be admitted to the new union on terms satisfactory to all parties. By October 27 all except three of the seventy-two Quebec Resolutions had been passed. The Confederation train was built and a fire had been lighted under its boiler. But Confederation still had to be approved by each of the five provinces and then submitted to the Imperial Parliament for an enabling act. The train had some distance to go before it reached the station.

After the work, the feasting. Rain still dulled the scarlet and gold of beech, maple, and elm as a special train carried the delegates and their wives to Montreal (where the final three resolutions were passed), Ottawa, Toronto, Hamilton, and then on to St. Catharines. The tour was typically Anglo-Saxon–sight-seeing, speechmaking, eating, and drinking. The menus were as lusty as an old-time Methodist fowl supper, only refreshments were alcoholic as well as gustatory. Soup, fish, entree, followed by roasts and game dishes and topped off by pastries and a continental selection of wines and liqueurs, put the men (the ladies, in Victorian style, were not expected to do more than sit in the gallery and watch) in the proper state to endure the speeches. By November 8, the triumphal tour, which had incidentally served to publicize what the Quebec Conference had done, was over and the last of the Maritime delegates were on their way home.

3

The high moment was over. The Confederation train was started on its way toward its goal. Now it began to meet obstructions on the track. Its greatest immediate assistance came from the United States over the St. Albans affair. The first protests by the States had been calmed by the arrest of the raiders and besides, in November, the North had been caught up in the excitement of a presidential election. Lincoln was returned. Then, on December 15, the raiders came before a Montreal court, which was to decide whether, in accordance with the demand of Secretary Seward of the United States, they should be extradited. The presiding magistrate never got to that question. Instead, he claimed that because of defects in the Webster-Ashburton Treaty he had no jurisdiction. The raiders walked out, free men.

If the North had howled before, it now shrieked. The press again advocated the annexation of Canada as a pleasant jaunt for the Union armies as soon as the tag ends of the Confederacy were wiped off the map. Congress and the Executive were just as belligerent. On December 17 for the first time passports for persons entering the U.S.A. from British North America were required. Both the Senate and Congress took up the question of abrogating the 1854 Reciprocity Treaty.

Canada went in for hurried appeasement. It pursued and recaptured the raiders. It stationed volunteers along the border to prevent a repetition of the raid, and John A. organized a preventive police force to patrol the frontier from Toronto to Sarnia. This force, under the leadership of Gilbert McMicken, was later retained as a counterespionage body.

By March of the next year, 1865, the immediate agitation had died down. On the eighth of that month, having had second thoughts, Seward notified his ambassador in London that the United States would allow the Rush-Bagot Agreement to remain in force. Two days later the requirement of passports at the border was canceled. But the Reciprocity Treaty was doomed, particularly since the Cayley-Galt tariff had already impaired its popularity in the United States. On March 31 of 1866 it lapsed. Still, the brief flurry over the St. Albans affair had confirmed the Colonial Secretary in London, Cardwell, in his conviction that a confederation of British North America was essential if it was to be saved from the maw of the United States. For opinion in Great Britain had now definitely begun to change. In the fifties the mother country would have been quite pleased to abandon British North America to the Republic. Now, in the early sixties—partly because of the American Civil War and partly because of the beginnings of the new imperialism, in which the colonies might come to be profitable for British industrial capitalism, as seen in the notions of Edward Watkin—some Britishers began to think of holding on to them. Cardwell was one. From the start he was strongly in favor of confederation. His help was a rock to which the Canadians clung.

CHAPTER XII

1865

Opposition to Confederation—Its Passage in Canada—The Canadians in London

WHEN the delegates to the Quebec Conference left for their various homes, it was with a sense of high achievement and in the full expectation that banners and plaudits would greet them. Instead, they met the chill east winds of criticism. In Newfoundland, the first reactions were favorable. When the Assembly met early in January 1865, the two delegates, F. B. T. Carter, Speaker of the House, and Ambrose Shea, leader of the Opposition, painted a glowing report of the advantages of Confederation. The Assembly appeared to concur, and Governor Musgrave, formerly lieutenant governor of Nova Scotia and later to be sent to British Columbia, was in favor. But a petition from a public meeting of the citizens of St. John's urging a general election first, made the Assembly pause. On the seventh of April it was decided to submit the question to a general election to be held in November of 1865.

In Newfoundland the Confederation train was slowed down. Meanwhile, in Prince Edward Island, where the initial conference had been held, early in February the islanders turned against Confederation. Suddenly, of the seven delegates to Quebec, two, Coles and Palmer, began to speak against the Quebec Resolutions. Into the fray leaped David Laird, founder and editor of the *Patriot*. Six feet four inches in height (they seem to have bred them tall in those days) with a voice like a bull of Bashan, he was opposed to Confederation both because the absentee-landlordism which plagued the island had not been settled and because he thought the financial arrangements meant loss. His claim, to be specific, was that Prince Edward Island would be $93,780 worse off each year.

The debate went on for weeks. Finally, shortly before the end of March 1865, by a vote of 23 to 5 the Assembly rejected Confederation. In P.E.I. the train had been pushed off the rails. Tilley, in the sister province of New Brunswick, also ran into difficulties. Though it had been agreed that Confederation should be slipped through the provincial legislatures without any appeal to the electorate, Tilley allowed himself to be maneuvered into a general election.

The pressure for this had come partly from his own colleagues as well as from the Opposition and partly from the lieutenant governor, Arthur Hamilton Gordon, son of that Earl of Aberdeen who had been Prime Minister of Great Britain from 1852 to 1855. Gordon himself had been secretary to Gladstone. This was his first colonial appointment. In his middle thirties, with a long, Tudor face and heavy-lidded Tudor eyes, he disliked colonial life and colonials; particularly since the latter did not always accord him the submissive deference one ought to accord one's superiors. As a believer in Maritime Union, he was opposed to Confederation until a dispatch from Cardwell made him see the light, or pretend to. It was he who pressed on Tilley an immediate dissolution. On January 19, 1865, the same day as the Canadian Parliament opened in Quebec, the decision was taken.

This was disturbing news for the Canadian leaders. Even more frustrating was the opposition in Nova Scotia. Here the great road block was the erstwhile missionary of a Federation from the Atlantic to the Pacific, Joseph Howe.

If Howe had been at the Charlottetown and Quebec conferences, he would, almost certainly, have been one of Confederation's strongest boosters. He had been asked to be a delegate to the Charlottetown meeting. His duties as fisheries commissioner had interfered, though he had hinted that, if the conference were postponed, he could attend it.

Apparently, he was miffed when the meeting was not put back to suit his convenience. At sixty-three the old Tribune was a disappointed and frustrated man. While politicians such as Hincks had received governorships, he had been fobbed off with an unimportant fisheries-commissionership. Still worse, he, who had always been foremost in the Nova Scotia scene, was a back number. Not he, but the whippersnapper Dr. Tupper, the man who had seized the opportunity, while Howe was raising recruits in the States for the Crimean War, to alienate the electorate and give Howe his first election defeat, had in the matter of Confederation spoken for Nova Scotia. That, the Tribune felt deeply, ought to have been his right, he who had been one of the first to conceive of a Dominion from sea unto sea.

"If you had a circus," he is reported to have said to a friend, "and had got together a good show . . . how would you like it if that fellow, Tupper, came and stood by the door and collected the shillings?"

These were the thoughts on which he brooded, shut up on H.M.S. *Lily* with a gentlemanly Captain Heneage and a squabbling George Perley, a man who never breathed a sober breath except by accident or compulsion. To be out of the limelight was not to be endured. There was one remedy, to go into opposition, along with the Halifax merchants, who foresaw their profitable trade cut down by Confederation. From January 11 to March 2, 1865, Howe ran a series of public letters in the Halifax *Morning Chronicle* attacking the "Botheration Scheme." Since his fisheries-commissionership ended in the spring of 1866 and he received no further appointment, he was soon touring the country denouncing Tupper and Confederation before enthusiastic audiences and demanding the submission of the Quebec Resolutions to the electorate. Once again Howe was in the limelight and he loved it.

What Howe did was to give expression to a very real feeling that Confederation was a Canadian scheme that was good for Canada but bad for the Maritimes, and for Nova Scotia in particular. In the sixties the Maritimes were almost at the peak of their sea-borne commerce. So why should not the taxation of their own resources bring them more revenue than Confederation's eighty cents a head? The Northwest was of no interest to them except that the Maritimers would be milked for expenditures on railways and defense works of benefit only to Canada. The loss of Reciprocity was scarcely feared, since they had convinced themselves that licenses on their recovered fisheries' rights would make up the difference; and they had lived so long in amity with New England that the Yankee bugbear seemed a mere Halloween pumpkin. So, why, economically, should they throw away sure prosperity for the mirage of Confederation?

Nor did they want to be absorbed in a larger community. The

Maritimers had an intense local patriotism. A Nova Scotian was a Nova Scotian first, last, and always, and his only respectable cousins—and they to be patronized a little—were New Brunswickers and Prince Edward Islanders.

Joseph Howe might be, in theory, an internationalist. His core was still Nova Scotian. To his delight, he had discovered that his name was still magic among his own people. Teamed up with Annand, editor of the *Morning Chronicle,* he was no cobweb menace. Before long Tupper was afraid either to submit Confederation to the Nova Scotia legislature or to appeal to the people. He ducked into hiding and pulled the cover over him.

In Nova Scotia, then, the Confederation train was stalled. It was only in Canada that under the triumvirate of Macdonald, Cartier, and Brown, with yeoman help from Galt and D'Arcy McGee, Confederation went according to plan. The debate, beginning at Quebec, February 6, 1865, ran for nearly five weeks. In that time almost every member put himself on record. The opposition of French Canada was led by Antoine Dorion of the *Rouges,* who expressed the fear of many of his confreres that Confederation would mean their diminishing importance and that the Intercolonial part of the scheme was simply a handout to the Grand Trunk interests. Had it not been for Cartier, the French-Canadian members might have bolted. John Sandfield Macdonald and his tail from the Ottawa Valley took the same attitude about the Intercolonial. A hairsplitter from Montreal, Christopher Dunkin, was opposed because he feared the fate of the Protestant minority of Canada East if that section got its own local parliament. Undersized and, like Tilley, an early advocate of Temperance, he took an immoderate length of time—all the evening of February 27 and the whole afternoon and evening of the next day until close to midnight—to analyze the weaknesses of the Quebec Resolutions point by point.

The bored triumvirate of Macdonald, Cartier, and Brown scarcely troubled to answer. Cartier's favorite reply to objections had always been: "Call in de members," and he felt quite sure of the majority. But on Saturday, March 4, the results of the New Brunswick elections began to come in over the wires.

It was a complete and shattering defeat for Confederation. Every cabinet minister, including Tilley, had been defeated. Of 41 seats, his party had won only 6. The charge that New Brunswickers were being sold down the St. Lawrence to Canada for eighty cents a head had carried the day. Behind the scenes, as Macdonald and his cohorts knew, the American railway capitalists of the northeastern United States, combining with those St. John merchants whose interests lay in the New England market, had put money into the election to defeat the Intercolonial, that is, to defeat Watkin and his Grand Trunk.

It was a staggering blow. Canadian Confederationists went ahead. By March 11 the Quebec Resolutions to provide for Confederation had been passed in the Assembly by 91 votes to 33, with a majority from both sections of Canada, and in the Legislative Council by 45–15. It was the last meeting of Canada's Parliament in Quebec. Next fall the government removed to the new capital at Ottawa.

Whether it would ever be the capital of a federated British North America was still in doubt. When, late in April 1865, Galt, Cartier, Brown, and Macdonald sailed for England to discuss Confederation with the Imperial Government, Canada stood alone. Prince Edward Island and New Brunswick had defeated Confederation. In Newfoundland the question would not be decided until November. In Nova Scotia, though he had avoided an election, the cautious Tupper had had to trim his sails before the gale raised by Howe. On April 10 he had moved in the provincial House: "Whereas under existing circumstances an immediate Union of the British North American colonies has become impracticable," there should be another attempt to negotiate a Maritime Union.

The Confederation train was more than blocked. It was practically derailed. That it ever got on the tracks again was in part because of the pertinacity of the British Government. When the members of the Canadian delegation arrived, they were entertained and feted. On May 16 they were presented to Queen Victoria. There was a spate of dinner parties and receptions. On the last day of May they went to the Derby, along with D'Arcy McGee, who had now arrived. In a letter of Galt to his wife we learn that there was a party of eleven, inclusive of Russell of the London *Times* and Brydges, general manager of the Grand Trunk.

"We had," writes Galt, "a basket of lunch and wines from Fortnam and Mason and two carriages with postillions." Lunch was in the Shed and Stand of "Mr. Todd Hentley, the wine merchant. . . . He opens it on the Derby Day to his friends, who are all the nobility. He provided a magnificent lunch, turtle soup and champagne cup. You would have been horrified to see the champagne go, it was emptied into large barrels, holding seventy dozen each!! and by a little arrangement of pipes there was a champagne fountain flowing in the middle of the shed. Besides the turtle, there were all the delicacies and substantials of the season."

They did themselves well in those days, when in England it was still the best of all possible worlds—for Englishmen. The French horse (it was Gladiateur, and John A. had a bet on it) won. After the race the Canadians "went to see the sights of the course, gypsies, music, mountebanks, games of all kinds, menageries of savage animals, and shows of Irishmen disguised as savage Indians," until it was time to start on the "Road" back to London.

"Picture us, then," Galt tells his wife, "first providing ourselves with tin tubes and sundry bags of peas, little wooden dolls, pincushions filled with bran, then . . . cigars lighted . . . prepared to enjoy the fun of the Road."

We can picture John A., McGee, and Cartier, who had sung French-Canadian songs, unabashed, to the Prince of Wales in 1860 on the boat up from Quebec to Montreal. It is a little difficult to visualize the stiff and serious Brown shooting peas through tin tubes at the crowd. Yet John A. bought a bag of peas for him and "the convenanting old chap," as John A. sometimes called his dour colleague, for a few hours showed himself a good shot with a peashooter. It took five hours to cover the sixteen miles back to London.

In between was hard work. For, on the ninth of April 1865, Lee had surrendered to Grant at Appomattox, and it was clear that except for bits and pieces (Johnston surrendered to Sherman on the twenty-sixth of the same month and by the twenty-sixth of May it was all over) the Civil War was finished. Where would the Americans turn their Grand Army of the Republic? Against British North America?

This was the urgency which made the British Government quickly come to terms with the Canadians about defense questions—though that agreement was one of delay and postponement—and covenant to do all that was in their power to forward Confederation.

Yet when the delegates did return Confederation still seemed stuck in a morass. In the field of minor catastrophes, the gentlemanly Sir Etienne Taché died on July 30. Since Brown refused to serve under John A., a figurehead for Premier had to be found.

Sir Narcisse Belleau was chosen. Meanwhile there were disturbing rumors from the Northwest. To the south, in St. Paul, after the interlude of the Civil War, Manifest Destiny was beginning to get up off the ground. Though Canada had no time to realize it, the future of half a continent was again trembling in the balance scales. The ownership of the Northwest was soon to become a race between Confederation and the clutching fingers of the United States.

CHAPTER XIII

1866–67

Brown Resigns—The Fenians Invade the Niagara Peninsula—New Brunswick Reverses Itself—The Westminster Conference and the British North America Act.

1

IN the summer and fall of 1865, Confederation, in spite of Britain's support, seemed doomed. A by-election in New Brunswick on November 6 brought a gleam of hope. With the help of $5000 from Canada, asked for and received by Tilley, Fisher, a Confederationist, was elected.

It was a ripple to suggest a possible change in the current. In November, too, the Newfoundland election was in favor of Confederation. These slight gains, however, seemed to be canceled out by the loss of George Brown.

Brown had never felt happy in the coalition Cabinet. John A. ran it and Brown was never meant to be a follow-my-leader man, especially when that leader was John A. He himself had sacrificed his political identity for Confederation. When he looked about him, it seemed that the only person who had benefited was John A. Macdonald. So Brown was happy to seize upon a dispute with Galt over the form an attempt to renew Reciprocity should take, as an excuse to resign from the Cabinet. It is a curious commentary on the essential and deep-seated antipathy between him and John A. that although, as John A. commented, during their brief association, "we acted together, dined at public places together, played euchre together in crossing the Atlantic, and went into Society in England together," from the moment Brown resigned, John A. and he "went back to their old relationship and did not speak."

Brown re-established his Clear Grit party. He did not abandon Confederation. Against his own principles he even offered $500 toward the New Brunswick election fund. Meanwhile the gleam of hope in New Brunswick brightened. Of the two anti-Confederation leaders, the one, Wilmot, resigned because he had been converted to the idea of union. In the same month, January of 1866, delegates from Canada, Nova Scotia, and New Brunswick—the New Brunswick delegate was Smith, the anti-Confederation premier—received in Washington a final and somewhat insulting refusal to any attempt to continue Reciprocity.

This refusal meant difficulty for Smith's program of an extension of trade with the United States in lieu of Confederation. On his return, on February 15, he declared that he was not opposed in principle to union. Gordon, the lieutenant governor, promptly put a noncommittal reference to Confederation in the Speech from the Throne. This was passed in the Legislative Council of New Brunswick by 13 to 5. The governor, breaking precedent—since the Speech from the Throne ought now to have gone without comment before the Legislative Assembly—read a prepared answer to the Legislative Council, expressing his satisfaction at their action. The Smith government resigned in protest.

This was in April of 1866, about a year and a month since union had been beaten decisively at the polls in New Brunswick. The chance for Confederation, which had seemed dead, suddenly revived. In Nova Scotia, too, on April 17 of this same year Tupper had succeeded in getting passed an innocuous resolution to authorize the Nova Scotia government to continue negotiations for a federal union. The New Brunswick elections were the crucial thing. Into them Canada poured a campaign fund of between $40,000 and $50,000; while the American capitalists countered with similar ammunition.

At this moment Confederation, though revivified, was still a tossup. It was the United States which once again unthinkingly provided the decisive push. Its Grand Army had been demobilized. But, as early as the fall of 1865, reports through McMicken's counterespionage organization had come in of a projected invasion by the Fenians.

2

Among all the crackpot organizations, past and present, which the North American continent spawns or nourishes, the Fenians hold high rank. The brotherhood had been begun in Ireland after the abortive 1848 revolt, its objective to liberate the Irish. When it reached North America in 1858 the change of climate turned it to fantasy. Its chief American head was John O'Mahoney, a well-educated man but so mentally unstable that he had twice sojourned in insane asylums. His particular dementia was a belief that he was in touch with Irish giants of the past, who told him what to do. The first attempt of the American Fenians put a shipload of invaders aiming at Ireland in jail in England.

With this sort of leader the light of unreality flickered around the Fenian movement. It was composed of cells, or circles, each of them under an organizer who took orders from the head center in New York. What, abruptly, made it dangerous was not its Irish romanticism but the Irish veterans of the Civil War who flocked into the brotherhood and the apathy or sympathy of American officials. The United States, which had squawked like a setting hen robbed of its eggs over the St. Albans raid, seemed to see nothing wrong in the Fenians' making open preparations on its soil for an invasion of Canada. It had not as yet occurred to anyone on either side of the border that a peaceful conquest through industry was as effective as force of arms or that an allied country could be more useful than actual incorporation of Canadian territory into the United States.

The original aim of the O'Mahoney Fenians had been revolt in Ireland. But a faction of the movement, led by W. R. Roberts and R. S. Sweeney, saw a short cut in annexing Canada and using it as a base against England. In Chicago in 1863 a Fenian convention wrote the constitution of a Canadian republic and appointed a cabinet to govern it. Meanwhile Fenian agents, as D'Arcy McGee, himself a former revolutionary, kept warning the Canadian Government, began to reach across the border. In Canada, to avoid difficulty, the Fenians put on the face of other organizations; and it was said that 80 of their 700 cells were Canadian. Already in the fall of 1865 Fenian activity had brought out nine companies of Canadian volunteers to patrol the frontier and had enrolled New Brunswickers in the Home Guard. Part of the change-over in the November 1865 New Brunswick by-election was the result of the Fenian threat.

In the winter of 1866 two Fenian conventions were held. The first, in January, upheld the revolt-in-Ireland plan. The second, in February, switched over to the Sweeney-Roberts idea of an invasion of Canada. Nor did the Fenians lack for funds. Sentimental appeals for "dear ould Ireland" brought in barrels of money, as if ripe apples were falling from shaken trees, or as if modern labor unions were contributing to gangster bosses. As with some labor organizations of today, there was never any auditing of accounts. Raffles were held for prizes which no one won. Collections were taken up and any Irish man or woman who failed to contribute was not Irish. Even those who dared not join because of the Catholic Church's ban on secret societies, inclusive of the Fenians, sent in money.

Meanwhile, and not without the collusion of U.S. officials, arms and supplies from the demobilizing Union Army had been bought and sent north to depots along the Canadian border. A Fenian militia was organized. Officers were appointed and there was an extraordinary number of "colonels" and "generals." The Fenian "Secretary of War," "General" Sweeney, drafted an invasion plan. By it, Lakes Huron, Erie, and Ontario were to be occupied by Fenian navies while Fenian armies secured Canada West within two weeks and then seized Montreal. In the meantime a fleet from San Francisco was to "carry Vancouver Island and the Fraser River Country." The whole scheme was to cost $15,000,000 and utilize 30,000 men. When Canada was captured it was to be recognized by the United States as "New Ireland."

It was Irish romanticism at its talkative best. Yet, in view of the tolerant attitude of the United States authorities, the Fenian threat was more than turgid talk. Reports of their plans and activities poured across into Canada. It is likely that the Confederationists made no attempt to minimize the situation. In 1866 on March 7, in anticipation of an attack on March 17, St. Patrick's Day, Macdonald called up 10,000 of the Canadian militia. No attack came. As the excitement began to die down, the Fenians gathered their forces near New Brunswick between Vermont and Canada East and on the Niagara River near Buffalo. In spite of alarms, no one seemed really convinced that they would attack.

It was scarcely dawn of Friday, the first of June 1866. In Fort Erie, the somnolent village opposite Buffalo at the southern tip of the Niagara Peninsula, men, women, and children were still asleep. Someone heard movement and voices outside. Then there was a knocking at the doors. The villagers, in clothes hastily flung on, tumbled out, rubbing their eyes and gawking. The street was full of armed men in nondescript uniforms. Over them waved the green flag of the Fenians with a harp and a crown in gold on it.

The Fenians had reached Fort Erie by crossing the Niagara River on two rented tugs and two canal boats to Lower Ferry, about a mile below the village, while the American authorities looked on with an indulgent eye. It rather seems, in fact, as if certain groups in the United States waited hopefully to see if the invasion went according to plan before taking any action to check this inroad from their soil into the country of a peaceful neighbor.

In any case, following the old 1812–14 invasion route, over a thousand of the Fenians had been landed. Among them were many veterans of the American Civil War. The leader of the high enterprise was "General" John O'Neill, a lean sandy-haired man of average height who had won promotion in the Civil War. He and his men believed that all they had to do was to cross into Canada and the people would rise against "British tyranny." With that purpose in mind they had brought with them a goodly stock of extra arms and ammunition.

Full of this optimistic belief, O'Neill ordered the reeve, Dr. Kempson, to round up the villagers. Meanwhile, the Fenians had cut the telegraph wires. Two villagers who, less dumfounded than their fellows, tried to escape in a rowboat were brought back by warning shots. O'Neill announced his mission of "liberation," promised safety, and passed around a grandiloquent proclamation from "General" Sweeney. It told the gawking Canadians that the Fenians' only quarrel was with the "oppressors of Ireland" and offered them the "olive branch of peace and the honest grasp of friendship."

It was a disappointment when the announcement brought no recruits. But an army, even a Fenian one, must eat, and the villagers could at least feed their "liberators." As the June sun began to peek through the elms, the housewives and the staff of the local hotels were hot and flushed over the wood-burning ranges, readying pots of coffee and tea and huge mounds of fried ham and bread to carry out to the invaders. And then, as a final comic-opera touch, the Fenians, weary from their night crossing of the Niagara River and full of Canadian coffee, ham, and bread, instead of moving rapidly and decisively to secure the Niagara Peninsula, stretched themselves out in yawning sleep under the shade of the trees in the fields and orchards. Nothing could have made clearer their belief that this invasion was not a war but a picnic in which, as in the best of all Irish worlds, the whole of Canada would join to cheer them on as patriots and saviors.

There was nothing, however, of comic opera in the flame of resentment all over Canada West when the incredible news spread. The country was not altogether unprepared. On the preceding day, May 31, Macdonald, acting on information from his McMicken organization, had called out 14,000 of the militia. On the morning of June 1, while O'Neill's men dozed in the pleasant sun under the trees, the Queen's Own Rifles of Toronto, in their hot winter uniforms of green, were entrained and sent to Port Colborne at the south end of the Welland Canal, some eighteen miles west of Fort Erie. At Hamilton the 13th Battalion, gay in scarlet, was called up, and a force of regulars was gathered at St. Catharines at the north end of the same canal.

These were the first moves of the Canadians. Meanwhile, O'Neill, about 11 A.M., got his men together after their nap. Leaving a small force at Fort Erie, the last point to be vacated by the Americans in the 1812–14 war, he marched up the river road. But, after about three miles, he stopped at Newbiggin Farm near Frenchman's Creek. It seems that, in spite of all the fire-eating speeches and grandiose plans. O'Neill and his men had little stomach for anything except to be welcomed as conquering liberators.

The Canadians had not flocked in to join them as they had been told they would. Puzzled by this extraordinary contradiction between the dream and the reality, and hearing that hostile Canadian forces were gathering, at midnight O'Neill withdrew his men.

Fortunately for him, the Canadian command had no plans either except to fumble for the enemy and engage. On the next morning, the morning of June 2, O'Neill again advanced, this time as far as the Ridge Road, which, from a point some six miles north of Fort Erie, runs southwest like the hypotenuse of a right-angled triangle from the Niagara River to Ridgeway, a village between Fort Erie and Port Colborne on the south shore of the Niagara Peninsula. Getting word that Canadian troops were detraining at

Ridgeway Station, O'Neill moved southwest down the Ridge Road and occupied a strong position, not far from Ridgeway, known as Limestone Ridge.

The Canadian troops were some 400 volunteer militia of the Queen's Own, the 13th Battalion, and the Caledonian and York Rifle Companies. Most of them were youngsters with little training and no experience of war. Each man had thirty-five rounds of ammunition but, as ex-Sergeant Somerville of the British Army noted later, no greatcoats, knapsacks, mess tins, or water bottles. What was worse, they were led by a commander, Lieutenant Colonel Booker, who was equally inexperienced and, apparently, very nervous.

It was a clear June day. At about 7:30 A.M. the Canadians moved off, without breakfast, from Ridgeway Station up the Ridge Road. The plan, apparently, was for them to tramp up the road to engage O'Neill while another force, of 1700 men, chiefly regulars, under Colonel Peacocke, came in from the north upon the Fenians' rear and flank. To their left, as the volunteers advanced, was the gardenlike Niagara Peninsula country. There were fields of springing wheat and rye, crisscrossed by weather-beaten snake-rail fences. In the pastures, backed by woods, cows cropped the lush grass. There were oxeye daisies and yellow buttercups and among the fields sat the solid red-brick farmhouses. But on their right front, across a narrow ribbon of field and crowned with deep bush, the Limestone Ridge frowned at them.

It was too beautiful a morning for battle and death to seem real. But shots ahead told of the Fenians. The volunteers sifted out into the fields on both sides of the road and went forward, firing. "The line was well formed," O'Neill said later, "and the advance was brave."

Neither side suffered much damage. After a quarter of an hour, since the ammunition of the Canadian front line was running out, it was replaced by fresh volunteers. The Fenian main force was driven back on its reserve. O'Neill, afraid of the Peacocke troops to the north, decided to retreat to Fort Erie.

At this point, to the amazement of both sides, the bugles of the volunteers sounded the retreat. The Canadians fell back. Then, the bugles sounded the order to form squares to receive a cavalry attack. The Fenians now pressed on to fire at the massed volunteers. The result, with no one knowing why or what was happening, was that the volunteers broke. The Fenians chased them down the Ridge Road. On the other side of Ridgeway Station a train picked them up and took them back to Port Colborne.

It was only a confused skirmish. Nine Canadians were killed and thirty-seven wounded. The Canadian defeat cannot be placed on the shoulders of the militia. Though they were green troops, they were winning the fight when the amazing signal for retreat was sounded. Lieutenant Colonel Booker denied giving the alarm about cavalry. One explanation advanced is that some Fenian stragglers rode out of the bush on stolen horses. Ex-Sergeant Somerville came up with the suggestion that Colonel Booker had gone by parade-square drill—sound the advance, sound the retreat, form squares to receive cavalry, retire at the double.

In any case, on the Canadian side everything was utter mismanagement and confusion. On this same June 2, Colonel Peacocke's force of 1700 had been pushing on south from St. Catharines to secure the bridges at Chippawa over the Welland River and, presumably, to synchronize his attack with the advance from Ridgeway.

If so, he was too late. Finding the bridges already secured by volunteer militia, Peacocke marched on to New Germany, about eight miles south of Chippawa. At this point, Major Denison joined him with cavalry, the governor general's body guard.

No one, apparently, had thought of cavalry on May 31. Major Denison's orders to move, according to his own account, came only on the evening of Friday, June 1. By 8 A.M. of the next day he had his force under way by steamer from Toronto to Port Dalhousie at the north mouth of the Welland Canal. From Port Dalhousie a train took men and horses to Port Robinson on the Welland River. Thence, Denison pushed on via Chippawa and the Sodom Road to New Germany.

Meanwhile, O'Neill, after his victory of Ridgeway, still acting the completely puzzled man, decided, on hearing of Peacocke's advance, to dump the uniforms and rifles he had brought for Canadian recruits into the creeks along the way and to retreat again to Fort Erie. His hope was for reinforcements from Buffalo. When his men tramped once more into the village it was to find seventy-six bewildered Canadian soldiers there. This little group was the private adventure of Lieutenant Colonel J. Stoughton Dennis, the man whose surveying in Red River was, later, to set off the *métis* revolt.

By arrangement with Colonel Booker, while the Canadian

volunteers were marching to the Ridgeway skirmish, Dennis had gone up to Dunnville—near the mouth of the Grand River, again on the south shore of the Niagara Peninsula—taken the tug *Robb,* put on board the Dunnville Naval Company and the Welland Canal Field Battery, armed with rifles, and gone to Fort Erie.

The Fenians charged the Canadians, drove them behind a pile of cordwood, and captured most of them in full view of hundreds of cheering Americans on the opposite bank of the river. Their commander, Colonel Dennis, fled, apparently, at the first appearance of the Fenians.

In the meantime, Colonel Peacocke's force, with Denison's cavalry as the advance guard, had moved nine miles south from New Germany toward Fort Erie. As dusk fell, at a point where dark trees closed in the road on both sides, a Fenian picket was sighted. So the whole Canadian force was withdrawn a few hundred yards, skirmishers were posted, and infantry and cavalry slept in their ranks in the high green crops. No one had blankets or greatcoats. There were no rations and, for that matter, no water bottles, cooking utensils, knives, forks, or tents. The cavalry, Denison points out, had helped themselves to hardtack on the boat in the morning. That was all they had; and their only firearms were revolvers, with four to five ten-year-old paper cartridges for each man. John A. Macdonald, as Minister of Militia, plumed himself on his McMicken counterespionage organization. He had done nothing to put efficiency into the staff and organization of the Canadian militia.

While the troops slept the last act of the tragicomedy was being played. At Fort Erie, O'Neill and his Fenians realized at last that, far from having a triumphal picnic, they might actually get killed when morning came. The reinforcements they stretched out hands for did not come. This was chiefly because most of the ten thousand Fenians gathered at Buffalo had stomachs for only oratory and whisky. In addition, the American authorities had, belatedly, sent an armed revenue cutter, the *Michigan,* to patrol the river. As night dropped its curtain the Fenians in Fort Erie began to slip back across the river, some in boats and some paddling planks and some swimming. A few were drowned. Panic is infectious. "General" O'Neill shaved off his whiskers as a disguise and fled with the rest. The two hired tugs and two canal boats were sent across from Buffalo to remove the rest of the army. Now that the invasion had patently failed, the *Michigan* took these in tow. By morning only a few Fenian stragglers were left on the Canadian side.

Peacocke's troops did not know this. They had heard of the Ridgeway skirmish and there were wild rumors of thousands of Fenian reinforcements. Major Denison relates that when he was returning from an inspection of the sentries early on the next morning—it was Sunday, June 3—a voice called out:

"Is that you, George?"

The man who accosted him, disguised as a laborer with "a close fitting old cap pulled down over his head, a red woollen scarf around his neck . . . and a wild hunted look in his eyes," was Lieutenant Colonel Dennis, the man who had left his small force at Fort Erie to their fate. He was later court-martialed and acquitted, but with a certain dubiety.

When, finally, that morning the Canadians advanced on Fort Erie, it was to find the Fenians flown. The U.S. began to patrol its border. On the Canadian side there were charges and recriminations and a hot flush of shame that for two days a Fenian force had wandered at will through part of the Niagara Peninsula, stealing chickens and frightening farm wives, while the blundering Canadian command had let them escape, practically scot free.

There were no more raids over the Niagara frontier. But on June 4 some 1800 Fenians from St. Albans, the site of the 1864 Confederate incursion from Canada, crossed into the Eastern Townships of Canada East. They looted and swaggered. This time the American authorities seized the Fenian depots in Vermont and closed the border. The Fenians went back across the boundary except for a group who were captured, of whom a few were shot.

The grandiose Fenian invasion had turned out a colossal farce. But it stirred a hot anti-Americanism in Canada, a flame that was all the fiercer because of the bungling on the Canadian side. Over 20,000 volunteers turned out to guard the frontier. Nor did it calm the Canadian temperament that the Fenians, unabashed, continued their fantastic schemes and their grandiloquent threats. Those threats and another actual invasion with the same "General" John O'Neill involved, this time into Red River in 1871, hardened that resentment and suspicion of the United States which helped to make British North America into a nation.

Meanwhile, the Fenian threat had a potent effect on the election in New Brunswick which was to make or break Confederation. All during this spring of 1866, while the election was in the offing, the Fenians were drilling across the border within sight of the towns of St. Stephen and St. Andrews. No invasion came. But the constant menace was an argument for Confederation. The news of the June 1–3 invasion of the Niagara Peninsula, just as New Brunswickers were going to the polls, proved the clincher to campaign funds from Canada, and to the loss of Reciprocity and to the movement of volunteer regiments to points where they could best influence the vote. When the returns were all in on June 12, only two of the anti-Confederationists had been returned and Tilley had a smashing majority. In Nova Scotia, Tupper, as has been noted, had on April 17 managed to put through a resolution authorizing his government to continue to negotiate for federal union.

Confederation had been resurrected from the grave in which its opponents, only a year and a half before, had been prepared to lay it. The Fenians had blown the final trumpet to revive it from its deathlike coma. All that was needed was to push it through the Imperial Government.

3

The Westminster Palace Hotel, at the junction of Victoria and Tothill streets in the heart of London, looked out sedately over Westminster Abbey and caught a glimpse of the Houses of Parliament. Here on Tuesday morning, the fourth of December, beyond the reception desk, in a long room decorated in ornate Corinthian style, sixteen men (six Canadians, five New Brunswickers, and five Nova Scotians) sat down around a long table. It was a raw day outside and the room was chill. The English, then as now, were Spartan-like in winter heating.

This meeting was the final issue of the exuberant Charlottetown and Quebec conferences of 1864. Prince Edward Island and Newfoundland were missing, the former because it had refused Confederation, while the latter was still debating the question. George Brown, back in his Anglo-Canadian pasture, was missing, too. D'Arcy McGee had not been selected. But Galt was there, even though he had resigned from the coalition Cabinet the previous summer over the old sore of Separate Schools. He, Cartier, Tupper, Tilley, and, above all, Macdonald were the quintet who controlled the meeting. At the first session, on the motion of Tupper and Tilley, Macdonald was appointed chairman.

It was, undoubtedly, a moment of high drama. Yet there was a sort of weariness in the slumped shoulders of the men around the conference table. Confederation was a bride whose progress to the altar had been too long delayed. There was little left of the high enthusiasm of the Charlottetown betrothal, only a sense of dreary urgency. As the delegates sat here, they knew that Howe and Annand were also in London, pulling every possible string to defeat the marriage. Howe had even clipped and sent to Lord Carnarvon, the new Colonial Secretary, the self-righteous editorials of the previous August, in George Brown's *Globe*, about "Drunkenness in High Places," accusing John A. of being full-seas over at the time of the Fenian raid and so intoxicated during the last days of the Ottawa summer session that he had had to hold on to his desk to keep from falling.

It was a singularly sanctimonious action on the part of the cheerfully bibulous Tribune. Yet Howe's influence with certain political figures in Britain, such as John Bright of Birmingham, was not to be waved off. It had been fear of him which had made Tilley and Tupper so annoyed at Macdonald's delay in coming to London. The Maritimers themselves had sailed on July 19. John A. had dillied and dallied until November 14.

John A., as usual, had had a superb sense of timing. For during the summer, Russell's Whig government had been replaced by Derby's Tory administration, and Cardwell at the Colonial Office by Lord Carnarvon, later to be governor general of the Dominion. Carnarvon needed time to get the feel of his new office. Fortunately, he was as eager as Cardwell for Confederation. The chief reason for delay in Macdonald's mind was the necessity of getting Confederation through the British Commons and House of Lords in one concentrated campaign before delays could kill it. For this purpose John A. was undoubtedly pleased that all Britain was in such turmoil over electoral-reform proposals that the members of both houses had neither time nor thought for British North America. It might be insulting and ironical that the formation of a huge self-governing Dominion should be brushed off as of no account. But it would help to put Confederation through when, as it were, no one was looking. Now, on December 4, Macdonald was ready to act; and so were the others.

In this spirit the Conference set to work. No important changes were necessary in the 1864 Quebec Resolutions, except that provision was inserted for Prince Edward Island to enter, if that province changed its mind. By December 19, the task was pretty well finished with only one touch of excitement. On the night of December 12, John A. fell asleep in bed while reading and woke to find the bed, bedclothes, and curtains ablaze. He, Cartier, and Galt between them put out the fire. On Christmas Day the London resolutions went over to the Foreign Office. After the New Year a few changes in consultation with Lord Carnarvon were made. One was that the total of seventy-two senators could be increased by the Queen by the appointment of an additional three or six, divided equally among the three sections of the Maritimers, Quebec, and Ontario. And there was the choice of a name. John A. wanted "Kingdom of Canada." The Prime Minister and Foreign Secretary, the Earl of Derby, later characterized by Disraeli, his House of Commons leader, as dwelling "in a region of perpetual funk," feared the effect of "Kingdom" on the United States. As a compromise, the "Dominion of Canada" was selected.

The British North America Act to bring in Confederation was at last ready for the *imprimatur* of the British Government. On February 12 it was read in the House of Lords. By a happy coincidence, John A. Macdonald was himself entering on a new union. He had been a widower for nine years. In the early days of the London Conference, quite by accident, apparently, he met on Bond Street the sister, Susan Agnes Bernard, of his own secretary and long-time friend, Lieutenant Colonel Hewitt Bernard. A rapid courtship followed. On February 16 the two were married in St. George's Church, Hanover Square, by the Bishop of Montreal.

". . . All went off most aggreeably," Galt wrote to his wife, "the day was beautiful, and all were as happy as possible. . . . We afterwards lunched at our hotel. . . . There were rather a large party, four bridesmaids—Misses Macdougall, McGee, Tupper and Archibald [Galt was attempting a joke]—and about seventy guests."

The wedding was a pleasant augury though the bride and groom had only a two or three days' honeymoon at Oxford before John A. had to return to keep watch over the Confederation bill. On March 8 the British North America Act passed its final reading in a bored British House of Commons. Two and a half months later a royal proclamation announced that Confederation would come into effect on July 1, 1867. The long haul was over. A bloodless revolution had been effected. Even more important, the first step to a British Commonwealth of Nations had been taken.

There were still battles to come. In 1867 Confederation reached only as far as Lake Superior. The future of the Northwest and the Pacific West was still uncertain.

CHAPTER XIV

1867–73

Birthday of Confederation–The Dominion in 1867–Howe's Campaign for Repeal in Nova Scotia–Prince Edward Island Reconsiders

1

ON July 1, 1867, the weather god beamed. All across the new Dominion the sun shone in a sky of cloudless blue, though there was a breeze to temper the heat. In Ottawa, the capital, shortly after the midnight of June 30, the pealing of church bells and the dull thudding of a 101-gun salute banished sleep. When the sun rose, from Halifax to Sarnia, royal salutes of 21 guns began. All across the federation, too, the church bells rang and there were parades and the formal reading of the Queen's proclamation; though in Halifax and St. John the shops were hung with crepe.

Meanwhile, in the Parliament Buildings at Ottawa the first government of the Dominion was sworn in by Lord Monck. John A. appropriately, was the first Prime Minister. George Brown sat apart in Toronto, a dour dominie. But John A.'s Cabinet contained two Clear Grits, William McDougall and E. P. Howland, though Brown had had both of them read out of his party. Tilley was a cabinet member. Both Tupper and McGee had had to be excluded so as to solve John A.'s problem about a minister who would represent both Nova Scotia and the Irish Catholics. From Quebec, Cartier was the giant while Galt was Minister of Finance.

To signalize the event, Governor General Monck announced Macdonald as Knight Commander of the Bath with the inferior distinction of Companion of the Bath for Cartier, Galt, Tupper, McDougall, and Howland. Cartier and Galt were both so incensed by what they took to be a slight that they refused the decorations. Both had to be consoled, like babies, with better gauds. They were finally made baronets.

The official part of the ceremonies was completed by midday. Then, across the Dominion, but more particularly in what had been the province of Canada, the people went on holiday. In Canada East, renamed Quebec, it was flags and bunting and family parties, and a cricket game at Three Rivers. Canada West, which now had become Ontario, favored brass bands, regattas, races, and the like. In the more remote centers the farmers gathered in the local fairgrounds or picnic places for a program of sports and a country supper of salads, cold meats, pies, and cakes, at tables set up on trestles under the trees. As the soft July night floated down, the villages, towns, and cities were bright with Chinese lanterns on the porches and with fireworks and illuminations. The people, the inchoate mass without an articulate voice, sensed that something of significance had occurred.

2

What was it like, this infant empire of Macdonald's? In 1867, of its approximately 3,300,000 people almost half lived in Ontario, and if Quebec were added nearly 80 per cent were accounted for. By 1871, French-speaking Canadians were 31 per cent of the population; those of British origin, with the Irish predominating, 60½ per cent; and those of other national origins, only some 8½ per cent. The multiple mosaic of modern Canada had not as yet developed. But the ancient and modern tension between French Roman Catholic (about 42 per cent of the new Dominion's inhabitants were Catholics) and English Protestant remained a feature of Macdonald's new empire.

Statistics never convey the flavor of a vanished way of life. The whole of the Dominion was overwhelmingly rural, with 81 per cent of the population living outside the cities and towns. From the Maritimes, the wooden ships still whitened the harbors of the world. In Quebec and Ontario, the heart land of the new country, the frontier was still on the doorstep. Outside of the Eastern Townships, Quebec was pretty well limited to the habitant farms along the valley of the St. Lawrence. Except for the timber trade out of Quebec City, and except for the banks, colleges, merchants, shipping, and railways of Montreal, the life of French

Canada was still, as in the days of New France, the life of the parish and the farm. In Ontario, the only completely settled area was along the "Front" of Lake Ontario from Kingston to Toronto, with a depth northward of from twenty to, at the very most, a hundred miles, and in the southwestern peninsula to Sarnia and Windsor. Even in the settled areas there were swamps, frogs, mosquitoes, and flashing fireflies, and snake-rail, stump, and stone fences crawling over hill and dale. Frame and brick and stone houses betrayed prosperous farms. But along the back concessions and in the newly settled areas, it was still the log house and the log barn.

There was no flood of tourists. There were no paved roads. Along the Front and in the southwestern peninsula there were turnpikes and graveled roads, but in the back country the dirt trail and the corduroy road still led through the thick woods and the swamps, where the trees met above the ruts. Railroads, some of them already abandoned, crisscrossed the province. But, outside of the old-fashioned locomotives and the old-fashioned kerosene-lighted, plush-seated coaches they dragged, there were few machines. Here and there mowers and reapers were appearing, but in the back counties the scythe and cradle still cut the crops and oxen worked among the stumps. Wood was the universal fuel. The lamps were coal-oil lamps, though cast-iron stoves were ousting the picturesque fireplaces and the andirons and spits and kettles on the hobs. The women milked by hand. Hand-turned churns made butter. The spinning wheel whirred. Barn-raisings, cornhuskings, quilting bees, and threshings were community occasions, and so were the sugaring-off parties in the late March woods with the last snow still deep, though dirty, in the bush. In winter the bells of horse-drawn sleighs and cutters tinkled on the trails or, if the snow was deep, detoured through the fields. Snowshoe, skating, and tobogganing parties were the vogue. Farmers had to break open their own roads in winter and keep them in repair in summer. Life was still "self-help"—and government had not as yet emasculated independence with a beneficent paternalism.

Village and town life knew more of the amenities. In the village there was the kerosene-lighted general store with its kegs, barrels, bolts of cloth, and its conglomerate of odors—coal oil, the leather of harness, cheese, butter, eggs, spices, hard candies, "store-bought" cookies, stalks and strips of licorice—and usually a wicket for the mail. Rival centers were the blacksmith shop with the pungency of the burned hoofs of horses and the hissing of the red-hot horseshoe dipped in water, and the tavern with its sawdust and its smell of beer and whisky.

If there was a river with a dam and waterfall there would soon be a town with a sawmill and a gristmill and a drugstore, a doctor's and a dentist's offices, two or three rival stores, a local newspaper, a bank, three to four churches, and three to four taverns. In Ontario there was always an Anglican church and, quite often, a Roman Catholic place of worship and a struggle for the rest of the population between Presbyterian, Methodist, and Baptist, while minor sects scurried anxiously about the outskirts. The taverns, by a logical division, were one Grit, one Conservative, and one for neutrals. Often, too, in those departed days there was a cricket club.

Taverns were as frequent as today's gasoline stations. They were planted in every village and on every crossroad and they dotted the roads leading into the market towns. In the cities they stood as social centers on every other street corner. Yet it was also the age of unquestioning faith. Reprobates knew they were sinners and no two ways about it. So did the "backsliders." In Ontario the trinity of dissenter sins were drinking, dancing, and card playing—with smoking as a possible fourth. The camp meeting with its shacks and picnic grounds to accommodate hundreds of people and lasting for weeks—Dunkards or Bible Christians or Methodists or Baptists—were emotional orgies, precursors of those of the Billy Sundays and Grahams of more modern days.

The farm, the forest, and the fisheries ruled. In Ontario there were eight or nine cities, most of them overgrown towns of from 12,000 to 25,000 people, which had profited from the new factories sprouted by the Cayley-Galt tariff of 1858–59, factories which were turning out plows, implements, boots, shoes, cloth, cottons, and furniture. Quebec and Toronto both boasted about 60,000 people, Montreal some 100,000. Even in these, for that time huge centers, there were no buildings over three or four stories. There was a lack of paved streets and parks. There were a number of pretentious brick and stone mansions with huge elm- and maple-embowered grounds, but many of the homes were frame with frame verandas jutting out over wooden sidewalks. Milk and bread services and garbage collections were rudimentary. In the early sixties horse-drawn streetcars had appeared in Toronto and

Montreal, but the wealthy kept their own horses, carriages, and coachmen. Homes were gaslighted. In the better ones running water and the tin bathtub cleansed the body, but most people still got their water from a well in the back yard and their baths on Saturday nights in the family washtub.

Similarly, medical services tended to be elementary, and epidemics, such as smallpox and scarlet fever, were common. In Ontario, though not in Quebec, even the country districts had a school for at least part of the year. Books were few and school buildings and equipment not elaborate. The main furnishing was the hickory stick. In the Maritimes as well as in Ontario, there was a keen desire for education. Secondary schools, however, reached only a small percentage—but those who were taught, were taught well, chiefly in the classical languages and in mathematics. Somehow, that type of education produced leaders such as John A. Macdonald, Tupper, Tilley, Cartier, men who seemed to be better "adjusted" to life than the products of today's elaborately equipped omnibus schools with their neurotic emphasis on "personality development." In 1865 Ontario municipalities were forced to support high schools by taxes and girls were reluctantly permitted to attend. Colleges and universities had been established in all the four provinces long before Confederation. But it was not yet the theory that everyone ought to be gifted at birth with a B.A.

There was little that can be called Canadian literature or painting or music. The theaters did show plays from New York or London. These were for the cities. Average individuals, in default of TV, movies, professional sport, and motorcars, either made their own amusements or found sociability in the church or the tavern or both, and excitement in political meetings and revivals. There were plenty of newspapers, usually either in a double sheet, or four pages, which carried local happenings and, after the first transatlantic cable was established in 1866, columns of British, European, and American news. In Ontario everyone was a Grit or a Tory. In Quebec the picture was more complicated, with shades of political colors from *Rouge* to *Bleu.* In all the four provinces elections usually meant whisky, bludgeons, and fists, especially since there were no votes for women. Elections were the more exciting since, at the time, they were spaced over about a fortnight, so that there was opportunity for tensions to explode into riotous brawling.

In both Ontario and Quebec the life of the forest was still close to that of the farm. The white pine had not yet been stripped from the fringes of the settled areas. From December to April the timber cutting in the forests of the Ottawa, the St. Maurice, and the other rivers leading into the St. Lawrence held sway. A great many sawmills cut planks for the American market. But the timber trade from Quebec to Britain and Europe was still flourishing and the great rafts still floated down the St. Lawrence. In addition, Quebec shipyards were active. In 1863, for instance, they turned out 37 ships, 24 barks, 1 brig, and 3 brigantines.

The palm in shipbuilding, as usual, went to Nova Scotia and New Brunswick. These two Maritime Provinces were a fairly compact block of settlement, except that the interior of New Brunswick was, in 1867, largely forest country. Halifax, with 29,000 people and a long tradition, and St. John remained the two principal ports. As in the fifties, however, shipbuilding went on wherever there was a cove or a creek. In 1864, to give an example, New Brunswick turned out 163 vessels aggregating 92,605 tons; while at Yarmouth in Nova Scotia, from 1860 to 1869, 34 full-rigged ships, 104 barks, and a flock of brigs, brigantines, and schooners—the whole totaling 105,000 tons—were added to the Yarmouth fleet. Confederation might be a glum-faced subject in 1867 to Maritimers, but the high adventure of the "wooden ships and iron men" kept on, overshadowing the farms and even the fisheries.

3

Such was the color of the vanished way of life of the infant Dominion in the four provinces stretching in a narrow band from Halifax to Lake Huron. Far to the west was the province of British Columbia. Closer in distance was Red River Settlement. Before the Dominion could reach out its newborn hand to either, it faced the problem of a recalcitrant Nova Scotia. When the provincial elections were held on September 18, 1867, only two Confederationists were elected out of thirty-eight members. In the Dominion elections, completed on the same day, out of eighteen seats only one single solitary Confederationist, Dr. Tupper himself, survived the debacle. Howe, who was himself elected to the federal house, had won. Nova Scotia had turned thumbs down on Confederation.

In the rest of the new Dominion, however, John A.'s coalition government had carried the day. As a bonus, the redoubtable George Brown had been defeated in South Ontario. He never tried again for a seat in the House. When Parliament met in Ottawa on November 7, 1867, the titular leader of the Liberal opposition was, for a brief spell, John Sandfield Macdonald, the Glengarry Catholic, who was by this time the Premier of the new province of Ontario, since as yet there was no law against a man occupying a seat in both the federal house and a provincial one. Flanking him were Dorion the *Rouge* leader, Holton, the Montreal promoter, Alexander Mackenzie, the rock-ribbed Canadian Scot, and Edward Blake, a stocky young man with a plump face, a good mind, and a manner as exciting as a quadratic equation. Meanwhile, George Brown sat in the office of his Toronto *Globe* and woe betide the Ontario Liberal who strayed from the faith.

None of the titular leaders was of a caliber to trouble Sir John. What worried him was the dour phalanx from Nova Scotia, led by Howe. The fact that in the first session of the Dominion Parliament the bill to build the long-deferred Intercolonial Railway was passed made no impression on Howe and his cohorts. On February 14, 1868, with the first session still in progress, Howe sailed for England. On his heels followed Annand, the Premier of Nova Scotia, along with J. C. Troop and H. W. Smith, the aim of all four to persuade the Imperial Parliament to repeal the enforced incorporation of Nova Scotia into the Dominion. Tupper was hurriedly sent after them.

It was while Tupper and Howe were battling in England that the Dominion lost the first of its founder-fathers. On April 6, D'Arcy McGee, the poetic young Irelander turned patriotic Canadian and violent anti-Fenianist, about whom Josephine Phelan has written so eloquently in her *The Ardent Exile*, had been defending the absent Tupper in the House. Shortly after 1 A.M. Parliament adjourned for the Easter recess. It was a sharp, frosty night. A bright full moon hung cold in a luminous sky. Ice had formed on the ponds and on the Rideau Canal. McGee had left the House with Robert McFarlane. They parted at the corner of Sparks and Metcalfe streets. McGee, who was to celebrate his forty-third birthday on Easter Monday, walked with his quick nervous step along Sparks Street to his lodgings at Mrs. Trotter's boardinghouse. As he stooped to insert his key a shot rang out, fired at such close range that the powder singed his hair.

Had the assassin been lurking in a doorway near? Or had he followed McGee? McGee would scarcely have noticed. For who would have expected murder in the quiet town of Ottawa?

Will Trotter, the thirteen-year-old son of McGee's landlady, who was a page at the House, was also coming home. He heard the shot but did not see who had fired it. In fact, he scarcely realized that it was a shot. When he came opposite his home, on the other side of the street he saw a dark shadow by the door and thought it was a dog. His mother, who had opened the door in expectation of her son when she heard McGee approaching, had seen the revolver flash and the fall of McGee. But she was in a state of shock. Will Trotter crossed the road. Staring up at him was the face of D'Arcy McGee. Trotter turned and ran up to the Ottawa *Times* office.

"Mr. McGee has been shot," he cried.

The printer and deskman rushed down the street. A small crowd had already gathered. Dr. Robitaille, who also lived at Mrs. Trotter's, declared D'Arcy McGee dead. Shortly afterward, John A. Macdonald hurried up. The Prime Minister knelt by the body a moment. Then he helped carry it into the house.

McGee was a martyr to his Canadianism. The Fenians boasted of having "executed" him, and it was a Fenian, James Patrick Whelan, who on February 11, 1869, was hanged for it. All that Canada could do for the eloquent Irishman who had served her so well was to give him an imposing interment on his birthday, Easter Monday, April 13, and to proclaim a day of mourning.

The Confederation for which McGee had lived and, ultimately, died was not yet secure. In England, Howe used every trick in his not inconsiderable repertoire to get Nova Scotia out of it. By June his hopes were shattered. The Colonial Office rejected the request for the repeal of the Union Act and, in the same month, John Bright's motion for a Royal Commission of Inquiry into the Nova Scotian situation, a motion inspired by Howe, was decisively defeated in both the House of Commons and the House of Lords.

The stubborn Tribune realized that the game was up. Yet, with the whole of Nova Scotia believing in his ability to work magic, it was difficult to recant. He had an interview with Tupper in London. On the way back, not without design on Tupper's part, the two enemies traveled by the same boat. As Howe's fellow delegates watched suspiciously the old Tribune and the lion who had succeeded him played at shuffleboard together, with Howe staring out every now and then at the tossing gray wastes of the North Atlantic.

He still held out until, on August 1, 1868, John A. Macdonald himself came to Halifax accompanied by Tupper, Cartier, and John Sandfield Macdonald, who happened to be both a Liberal and an old friend of Howe. A friendly chat with Howe was managed on the next day, Sunday, August 2. There were few men, outside of George Brown and Oliver Mowat, whom John A. could fail to charm. Howe was no exception. It took until January 30, 1869, to complete the bargain. On that day Howe was sworn in as a cabinet member. The one new feature from all the furor was that Nova Scotia received the same increase in federal subsidies which had already been granted to New Brunswick.

To his anti-Confederationist followers, Howe was a leader who sold out repeal for a cabinet post. It is generally adjudged today that in his heart of hearts he had come to realize that his opposition had arisen from personal and unworthy motives. To recant openly was beyond him. He salved his pride by pointing to the better terms his capitulation had secured for Nova Scotia.

Nova Scotia had been captured. Newfoundland still hesitated, though as late as May 24, 1869, its delegates came to Ottawa and early in June of that year it was announced that satisfactory terms had been arranged. At the end, Newfoundland decided to stay out, a decision it was not to change until 1949.

Newfoundland was too distant from Canada's economic orbit to matter. Prince Edward Island, though, was a gap that was felt. Events favored the Dominion. The island got into financial difficulties in building its own railroad. On July 1, 1873, at the price of the Dominion's assuming the burden of the railroad, guaranteeing good ferry connections with the Intercolonial, and buying out the claims of the absentee landlords, P.E.I. joined the union. When, that same July, the governor general visited the new province, he passed under an arch of welcome at Charlottetown which read:

"Long Courted: Won at Last."

It might be added that in 1876, at long last, the Intercolonial, which Howe's dream in 1851 had almost secured, was completed. Now, a quarter of a century later, it was rapidly to become a white elephant, wallowing in government expenditures.

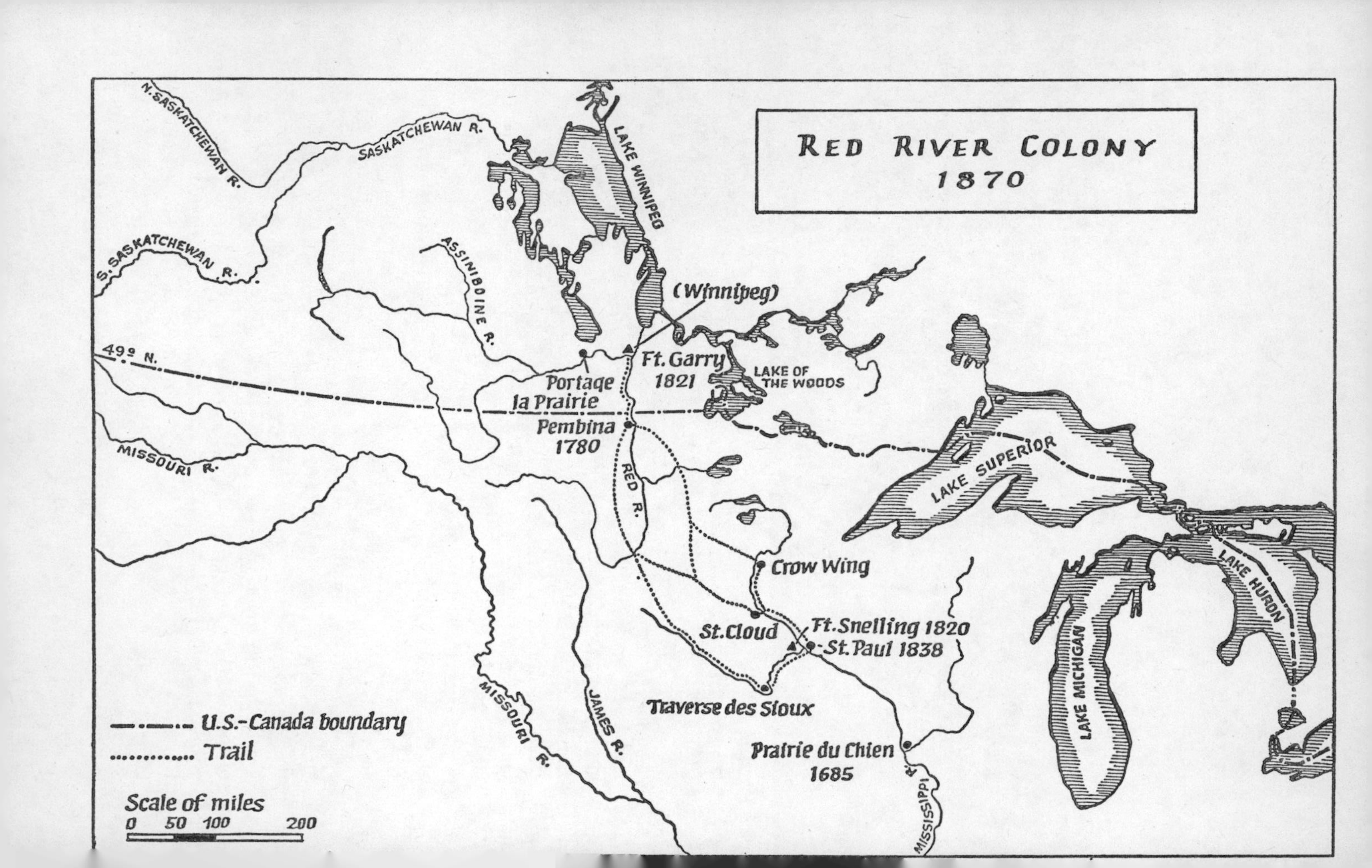
RED RIVER COLONY
1870
N. SASKATCHEWAN R.
SASKATCHEWAN R.
S. SASKATCHEWAN R.
ASSINIBOINE R.
LAKE WINNIPEG
(Winnipeg)
49° N.
Ft. Garry
1821
Portage
la Prairie
Pembina
1780
LAKE OF
THE WOODS
MISSOURI R.
RED R.
LAKE SUPERIOR
LAKE HURON
LAKE MICHIGAN
Crow Wing
St. Cloud
Ft. Snelling 1820
St. Paul 1838
Traverse des Sioux
Prairie du Chien
1685
MISSOURI R.
JAMES R.
MISSISSIPPI R.
U.S.-Canada boundary
Trail
Scale of miles
0 50 100 200

CHAPTER XV

1867–69

Canada Takes Over the Northwest—Manifest Destiny Tries to Block Her—Unrest in Red River and Louis Riel—McDougall Stopped at the Border

1

THE Dominion had been rounded out in the East. Long before Prince Edward Island was gained and while the dispute with Nova Scotia was still hissing angrily, Canada had reached out an ignorant and arrogant hand to garner the Northwest. Provision had been made in the Quebec Resolutions for its acquisition, though as late as March 27, 1865, John A. Macdonald, in a letter to Edward Watkin, president of the Grand Trunk, while agreeing that the route to the Pacific must be preserved from the Americans, thought that from every other point of view "the country is of no present value to Canada."

The remark is typical of the stupidity which gave birth to the Red River rebellion. But, if John A. had little enthusiasm for the Northwest, Galt, William McDougall, and the Grand Trunk were eager to secure it. On December 4 of 1867, at the first session of the new Parliament, McDougall, who with George Brown had been among the first exponents of Canadian expansion westward, introduced resolutions which led to an address to the Queen to turn over Rupert's Land to the Dominion. In October of the next year he and Cartier were sent to London to negotiate with the new H.B.C. of the Grand Trunk-inspired International Finance Company and the Imperial Government. Since the Canadians brought with them the old Clear Grit conviction that the Company had no rights whatever to Rupert's Land, while the H.B.C. relied on its 1670 charter, the Imperial Government had to cut both parties down to size. By March of the following year the terms were arranged. The fourteen items in the H.B.C.'s Deed of Surrender, which was to be dated November 1, 1869, included a cash payment of £300,000, retention of lands, totaling 450,000 acres, around its 120 posts, further land grants which ultimately amounted to 7,000,000 acres, and permission to carry on its trade without the imposition of any exceptional taxes.

The H.B.C. had at last surrendered Rupert's Land. On June 16, John A., realizing, apparently, at last what had been accomplished, wrote triumphantly to a friend:

"We have quietly, and almost without observation, annexed all the country between here and the Rocky Mountains."

2

John A. crowed too soon. Canada had taken over the Northwest as if it were a huge and vacant farm. The 11,500 inhabitants around Fort Garry were of no mind, as they conceived of it, to be bought and sold as if they were a herd of cows. And they had an alternative. The steamboats on the Red connected them with St. Paul, not with Canada; and St. Paul and the United States were holding out welcoming hands.

For, in the United States, Manifest Destiny, driven into the wings by the guns of the Civil War, was once more on stage. Even before that fratricidal conflict was over, the New York *Sun* had orated:

"From the Polar Sea to the Isthmus of Darien there will be in time but one Government. Canada, Rupert's Land, British Columbia, Mexico, all will have but one flag and eventually Cuba and her sister islands will join us."

It was rodomontade but the sort of rodomontade many Americans of the day liked to believe. To such an attitude the 1864–67 move to union had been a slap in the face. The interference of eastern American capitalists in the New Brunswick elections had been an attempt to throw a monkey wrench into the plans for Confederation. The March 1866 cancellation of Reciprocity had been another, since it was hoped in some quarters that the cancellation would force the eastern colonies to sue the States for annexation. In July of the same year, only a month after the Fenian raids, General N. P. Banks, head of the Foreign Relations Committee, urged on by Senator Ramsey, erstwhile governor of Minnesota, and by James Wickes Taylor, the long-term annexationist of St. Paul, had even introduced to Congress a bill to provide for "the admission to the Union of the States of Nova Scotia, New Brunswick, Canada East and Canada West, and for the organization of the Territories of Selkirk, Saskatchewan and Columbia."

Canadian protests led to the impudent bill being dropped. But the mouth of the American leviathan was gaping wide and hopefully. The Confederation of eastern British North America removed one of the plump chickens in prospect. There was still the Northwest and British Columbia. When, early in 1867, Seward, the U. S. Secretary of State, bought Alaska from the Russians for $7,200,000, the New York *Tribune* boasted on April 1 that "it [the purchase of Alaska] was, in short, a flank movement." "In the North-West," the article went on to state, there would be "a hostile cockney with a watchful Yankee on each side of him," so that the British would be glad to sell out to the States. It is significant of American thinking that Article XI of the Banks bill, already referred to, had provided for a payment of $10,000,000 to the Hudson's Bay Company "in full discharge of all claims to territory or jurisdiction in North America."

The jaws that slavered most were those of a Minnesota group, who, however, had support from Washington. Their leader was the James Wickes Taylor who in 1859, as an agent of the U. S. Treasury, had been commissioned to report on the route from Pembina to the British Columbia gold fields. From that time forward he had kept maneuvering for the annexation of the Northwest. The Sioux War had almost given an opportunity.

That war had been initiated by a long string of broken American promises. The final insult had come when in mid-August of 1862 an Indian agent told a chief, Little Crow, of the reservation Sioux: "If your people are hungry, let them eat grass."

On Monday, August 18, that agent lay dead in front of his store, his mouth stuffed full of grass. Before the next forty-eight hours were past, some 2000 white settlers were dead and more than 300 women and children were captives.

By mid-September the U. S. Army had broken the Sioux. Some fled into Dakota (organized into a territory on March 2, 1861); others slipped across the 49th parallel. The St. Paul newspapers wrote of Red River settlers "laughing at the impotent indignation of the Americans and boasting that the murderers were now under the protection of the British flag." Had not the United States been busy with the Civil War, her troops might easily have taken over Red River Settlement.

The Americans had failed to seize opportunity by the scalp lock. But with Confederation a fact Taylor redoubled his efforts to grab the Northwest before Canada did. In March of 1868 he persuaded the Minnesota legislature to protest against the transfer of the H.B.C. territories to Canada without a vote of its inhabitants. It also passed a resolution to the effect that the cession of the Northwest by Britain would satisfy the claims of the Republic against her. Long before this, in 1861, at the time of the *Trent* Affair, Taylor had told Washington that Minnesota alone was able to "hold, occupy and possess the Valley of the Red River to Lake Winnipeg." Then, in June of 1869, while John A. was pluming himself on his new empire, Taylor asked for and later received from Hamilton Fish, Secretary of the U. S. State Department, a commission as a "special agent" to work for the annexation of Red River. Even Jay Cooke's projected Northern Pacific Railway from Lake Superior to Puget Sound was brought into the argument. Of it, the U. S. Senate Committee on Foreign Relations said in 1868 that "it would seal the destiny of the British Possessions west of longitude 90 [running through the western tip of Lake Superior]. . . . They will be in effect severed from the new Dominion and the question of their annexation will be but a matter of time."

Taylor himself was determined that Canada was to end at Lake Superior. He had official backing in Washington. He also had a group of aides. Among these were "General" Oscar Malmros, the U.S. consul at Winnipeg, and the crippled "Colonel" Enos Stutsman.

Stutsman was a character fit for fiction. Born without legs in Indiana in 1826, by the time he was seventeen he was supporting himself as a teacher. After studying law and politics he moved to the frontier town of Sioux City and set up a real estate business. In 1866, at the age of forty, he was at Pembina as the U.S. customs agent. There the legless Stutsman also practiced law, built a hotel, became a friend of the *métis,* and mixed enthusiastically in Taylor's plans. Either in a buggy or in a specially made saddle, he traveled over the Red River trails, fishing in the troubled waters.

Through him and his other aides, Taylor, the St. Paul personification of Manifest Destiny, knew far more about the feelings of the Red River settlers than John A. and all his Cabinet. For by the summer of 1869 Red River was in a state of turmoil. Taylor and Stutsman licked their lips. Canadian stupidities seemed likely to throw the Northwest into the lap of the United States.

3

The man who spoke with passion and eloquence to a group of *métis* in a house at St. Norbert was stocky with a striking head covered with thick black hair. Under a wide brow his eyes were dark, intelligent, and almost hypnotic in intensity. All that marred the face was a nervous and twisting mouth.

The words that poured forth from the mouth held his audience entranced. In 1869 Louis Riel was only twenty-five years of age and he was only one-eighth Indian. He was of no particular use in the buffalo hunt. He could neither shoot well nor ride, like a true *métis*, as if horse and man were one. But he knew how to express to his fellow *métis* all their inarticulate fears, resentments, and ambitions. They were his, too.

Louis Riel's father was that "Miller of the Seine" who, in 1849, had helped force free trade on a reluctant H.B.C. His mother was a daughter of the first white child born in Red River Settlement. Louis Riel's own birthplace was St. Boniface, across the river from Fort Garry. As he grew up, Bishop Taché, impressed by the lad's intellectual precocity and religious ardor, found a patron for him in Mme. Joseph Masson of Terrebonne in Canada East. In 1858, at fourteen, young Riel began to study for the priesthood in the Sulpician College at Montreal.

There was no doubt of the boy's brilliance. It was marred by a strong ego and a moody irritability. He wrote turgid poetry. He resented discipline. Any opposition to his opinions brought a blast of rage. In the meantime his father had died. On an appeal from his widowed mother, without completing his religious training, Riel set out for Red River. En route he worked for some time as a salesclerk in a general store in St. Paul. In view of the number of *métis* in that cart-brigade center, and Taylor's interest in them, it is quite possible that he met that apostle of annexation. Quite certainly, later on, he was on close terms with Taylor's aide, Enos Stutsman. When, in mid-December of 1868, he reached his mother's cottage at St. Vital, it was to find that the only post for the brilliant Louis Riel was a job as a carter.

In his ten-year absence the winds of change had blown. There were steamboats on the Red River now. The Canadian Rifles had come and gone. Winnipeg had risen west of Upper Fort Garry as a collection of some twenty-five log shacks, which included two hotels, a saloon, and a butcher shop. The Canadian and American parties had come into being. They had done little more by their pulling and tugging than make the *métis*, and the English breeds, too, fearful about the titles to their farms. Then, in 1863, had come the sale of the H.B.C. to the Watkin-inspired International Finance Company.

That sale, without any consultation of the wishes of the *métis* had insulted them deeply. Were not they, the *Bois-Brulés,* the "New Nation," the true owners of the soil, having received it, by natural inheritance from their Indian forebears? As early as mid-March of 1860, when the *Nor'Wester* had published a statement by the old Indian chief Peguis that he had never sold the land of Red River either to Lord Selkirk or to the Company, the half-breeds had held an excited meeting in McKenney's log "Royal Hotel." The outcome was a statement that the half-breeds ". . . are natives; they are the present occupants; and they are the representatives of the first owners of the soil, with whom no satisfactory arrangement has ever been made."

"First owners of the soil"—there was the *métis* battle cry. Meantime, the H.B.C. wintering partners had not been considered either. Some of the chief factors and chief traders resigned. The rest grew slack in their control. Why freeze in winter and work night and day in summer for a soul-less Finance Company? When Governor Dallas, James Douglas' son-in-law, left Red River in May of 1864, William Mactavish, ill with tuberculosis but still governor of Assiniboia, the official name for Red River Settlement, loosened his fingers.

It was the moment for a strong hand and not the trembling fingers of a kindly but sick man. Violence bestrode the settlement and none personified it better than the titan John Christian Schultz, leader of the Canadian party. He and his half brother, Henry McKenney, had parted company when, after the failure of the Royal Hotel, a trading venture, McKenney and Company, had also come to grief. So in 1865 Schultz, among other enterprises, had taken over the *Nor'Wester* for a season. His half brother, however, got a judgment against him for his share of the debts of McKenney and Company. Schultz, declaring in the *Nor'Wester* that his half brother had "bullied and brow beaten" the court, refused to pay and was lodged in jail. His wife, a true titaness, got together fifteen of the Canadian party, overpowered the constable on duty, and freed her husband. He stayed free.

This was not the first time that the law of Governor Mactavish had been flouted. In 1863, when an opponent of the Company, the Reverend G. D. Corbett of the parish of Headingly, was found guilty on a charge of attempting an illegal operation on a maid-servant and sentenced to six months' imprisonment, the Canadian party, led by James Stewart, a schoolmaster, knocked down the jailer, broke open the padlock with a crowbar, and released him. When Stewart was imprisoned he, in turn, was freed.

Law and order was breaking down. Meantime, Schultz and his party agitated, now that Confederation was under way, for annexation to Canada. In the fall of 1866 the violent Schultz was joined by a new immigrant, Thomas Spence, an acquaintance of the enthusiastic D'Arcy McGee. Spence's lifework, as he conceived of it, was to lead Red River into the coming Dominion. On December 8, at ten-thirty of a frosty winter morning, in the court house beside Fort Garry, a meeting of five men, chaired by Spence, passed a resolution that the settlement was in favor of being received into Confederation, gave three cheers for the Queen, and dispersed. Meantime the American party had been forgathering in Emmerling's Bar. They rushed to the courthouse to pass a resolution for annexation to the United States. Their leader, Emmerling, however, had drunk too many toasts to his own hospitality. The meeting dissolved into uproar. But Spence's resolution, signed, curiously enough, by some two hundred people, was sent on to the Queen. Later, in January of 1868, Spence, having moved to Portage la Prairie, where he had opened a store, organized the "Republic of Manitoba" to hold the country for Canada and raised taxes to build a "Government House and Jail." But a cobbler accused the "President" and his "Council" of drinking up the taxes at the local tavern, the H.B.C. refused to pay the levy, and in answer to Spence's "Address to the Queen" came a letter to tell him the "Republic" had no force in law.

All this conniving and talking had upset the *métis* still further. The Canadian party kept them informed, exultantly, about the negotiations for the transfer of Rupert's Land to the Dominion.

Yet nobody consulted the people most concerned, the settlers. So, what was going to happen to their farms? And if an inrush of immigrants from Ontario, as was prophesied, followed on the acquisiton of Rupert's Land by Canada, would the newcomers seize the land?

These questions troubled all the settlers, and the *métis* in particular. The conviction that the Canadians were coming "*pour piller notre pays*" grew. Their priests were in sympathy with their flock. To a hierarchy which had built a French-speaking Catholic community on the banks of the Red River, an inflooding of immigrants from either the States or Ontario would destroy their work; and they knew better than their charges that in any meeting with civilization the *métis* frontier way of life would disappear. In 1867, after a visit to Canada, Bishop Taché himself had written to Cartier:

"*J'ai toujours redouté l'entrée du Nord-Ouest dans la Confédération parce que j'ai toujours cru que l'élément français Catholique seraient sacrifié. . . .*"

Into this muddied turmoil Fate flung, in the spring of 1868, battalions of locusts, which stripped Red River Valley of every touch of green. To add catastrophe to disaster, the spring buffalo hunt was an inexplicable but complete failure. The Council of Assiniboia voted £1600 for relief. The Company raised £500. Thanks to appeals in the *Nor'Wester*, £3600 came from the Dominion and £900 from the United States.

The Canadian relief scheme took the form of building the western end of the projected Dawson Route from Fort Garry to the Lake of the Woods. William McDougall, as Minister of Public Works, acted as if the settlement were already Canada's. He sent in a party under a surveyor, John A. Snow. Along with him came the young Charles Mair, who had already won himself a reputation as a poet in his native Ontario.

The whole party behaved as if Assiniboia were already an adjunct of Ontario. Snow and Mair lodged with Schultz, leader of the Canadian party. They found a job for the Confederation enthusiast Thomas Spence. The relief part of the scheme was to hire the half-breeds at £3 a month ($15), in provisions, for clearing bush from the right of way. The provisions orders were given on a store which Schultz had opened at Oak Point. Furthermore, some of the Canadians bought lands from the Indians near the *métis* settlement at the same Oak Point, and half-breeds who had squatted on some of the territory were, apparently, ejected. The *métis* were having their fears confirmed. The Canadians were coming "*pour piller notre pays.*" As a foretaste of the Riel Rebellion, the *métis* forced the Canadians to evacuate the land they had bought.

Two incidents, however, relieved the threat of tragedy. In one of them the road-building crew, when they had a dispute with Snow about wages, manhandled him and threatened to drown him. A ringleader was a violent young Ontario Orangeman, Thomas Scott, of whom more was to be heard later. Meantime, young Mair, the poet, had been writing graphic letters home. In one of them he poked fun at the women of the Red River.

"Many wealthy men," he satirized, "are married to half-breed women who, having no coat of arms but a 'totem' to look back to, make up for the deficiency by biting at the backs of their 'white sisters.' The white sisters fall back on their whiteness; while the husbands meet each other with desperate courtesies and hospitalities with a view to filthy lucre in the background."

To Mair's shocked surprise, the letters got themselves published in the Toronto *Globe*, and the *Globe* came out to Red River. When Mair appeared in Bannatyne's post office in Winnipeg, one woman pulled his nose, another his ears, and Mrs. Bannatyne lashed him out with a horsewhip.

Behind the comedy were the elements of disaster. When the news reached the *métis* that the H.B.C. had, in March of 1869, actually transferred Rupert's Land—and them—to the Dominion without consultation and without any assurance that the titles to their land would be respected, Red River seethed with dark resentment.

It was Louis Riel's moment. Young, ambitious, nursing both an inferiority complex and a deep resentment at a world which offered his brilliance only a carter's job, and, above all, at one with his own people in language, religion, and sentiments, he was able to express those feelings in passion-filled words. And the *métis* listened. More, they begged for him. It gave the sallow-skinned, hypnotic-eyed Riel a delicious sense of a power which, he could feel, was being exercised with the blessings of his church. For Abbé Ritchot, curé of St. Norbert, was his confidant and adviser, while at his side stood the lean, erect, thin-faced W. B. O'Donoghue, mathematics teacher at St. Boniface College.

O'Donoghue, who was to become for a while Riel's second self, was an Irishman a year older than Riel. Emigrating to New York, he had joined the Fenian movement. The failure of the raids into Canada had sent him traveling. At Port Huron, Michigan, he had met Bishop Grandin. Through the bishop had come the post at St. Boniface. There O'Donoghue had decided to train for the priesthood. He abandoned that decision in order to join Riel's crusade. The organization of the buffalo hunt and the cart train lay ready to their hands. By September 11, of 1869, Malmros, the U.S. consul at Winnipeg, was able to write gleefully to the U. S. State Department that "the mass of the settlers are strongly inclined to get up a riot to expel the new governor on his arrival about October 15th," and added that "if the settlers should raise from among themselves a small regularly armed force of, say, 1000 troops, it would form a nucleus around which volunteers from the North-Western States might collect."

4

Manifest Destiny was on the prowl. Meanwhile, McDougall, stuffed full of ignorance, was setting out from Ottawa to take over the new territory for the Dominion. Both he and John A. had been warned of the dark currents swirling in Red River. In 1868, the Anglican bishop of Rupert's Land, the Reverend Machray, had personally told John A. of the difficulties. In the next summer 1869, William Mactavish, while returning from England, had stopped over in Ottawa to suggest that care be taken. In the middle of July of the same year, Bishop Taché, on his way to an ecumenical conference in Rome, tried to make Cartier aware of the dangers, but, according to the Bishop, Cartier's impatient reply was that "he knew it all a great deal better than I did, and did not want any information."

Cartier, McDougall, and John A.—they all regarded the Red River settlers as "savages," and who bothered to consider the feelings of savages? The Dominion had already passed an "Act for the Temporary Government of Rupert's Land." By this act the country was to be governed by a lieutenant governor and a council of from seven to fifteen. It also provided that no changes in customary usages were to be made. No one, however, bothered to inform either the *métis* or the H.B.C. of the details of the transfer. Meanwhile, William McDougall had been chosen as governor of the Northwest, partly because of his long advocacy of its annexation but also because John A. found him a difficult colleague.

In any case, McDougall, at this time a heavy-set, heavy-jawed, somewhat pompous man, had no doubt that he would be received with the deference due him. The Northwest would not be officially part of Canada until December 1, the date set for its official transfer to the Dominion, yet in July, McDougall had sent out his old friend, that Colonel Stoughton Dennis who had made a fiasco of his 1866 encounter with the Fenians, to carry out a survey of the new territory.

To arrogance was added ignorance. The Red River farms, like those of Quebec, ran back in long narrow strips from the river with a hay "privilege" of two further miles into the prairie. Dennis, however, was ordered to use the American system, but, to quote William McDougall, "to make the individual sections 800 acres instead of 640" so as to suit "emigrants from Canada." When the *métis* saw the surveying crews busy laying out new sections which would cut right across their ribbonlike farms, to which most of them had only squatter's titles, they became certain their land was going to be taken from them. The whole country was in an uproar. Dennis wrote to McDougall about the difficulty. McDougall ordered him to go ahead. Dennis did his best to avoid a conflict. But on October 11 one of his crews, under Mr. Webb, ignorant of the "hay privilege," trespassed on the pasture land of André Nault, who was a cousin of Louis Riel, near St. Vital. André Nault came rushing out, waving his hands. He spoke only French. The survey party gestured him away. He went for help. Sixteen *métis* appeared. Their leader, a stocky, curly-haired young man, put a moccasined foot on the surveyor's chain.

"You go no further," he said.

Louis Riel had stepped from the shadows into the limelight. Five days later, on October 16, a meeting was held at St. Norbert at the home of Abbé Ritchot. On the twentieth, at a second meeting, at the home of John Bruce, the *Comité National des Métis* was formed with Bruce as the figurehead president and Riel as secretary. The organization of the buffalo hunt was now called into action. On the next day, forty *métis* horsemen gathered at St. Norbert and put up a barrier across the road from the frontier at the Rivière Sale. What the *métis* wanted, according to J. Y. Bown, an M.P. whose brother was by this time editor of the *Nor'Wester* (Schultz gave up his ownership in 1868), was payment to the Indians for their title to the land, recognition of their own claims and rights with 300 acres additional for each of their children, exemption from taxation for themselves and their descendants, lands set aside for the support of the Roman Catholic Church, an elective council, and the expulsion of Dr. Schultz and his aides.

In these terms one can see the hands of Louis Riel, Abbé Ritchot, and possibly Enos Stutsman. For these rights, as they felt them to be, the *métis* were prepared to defy the Dominion. James Wickes Taylor hoped they would.

It is ironical and yet symptomatic of Canadian ignorance that on the eighteenth of October, three days before the barrier at the Rivière Sale was set up, the old Tribune of Nova Scotia, Joseph Howe, now close to his sixty-fifth birthday, left Red River. Since he was to be appointed Secretary of State, with the new territory as part of his domain, he had taken a quick jaunt to Winnipeg. He had been wise enough to avoid Dr. Schultz. Since he had no official status as yet, he refused to speak at any public gatherings but, according to the diarist Alexander Begg, "many of the principal settlers visited the Hon. gentleman."

Howe was well known for his previous opposition to Confederation. Later, William McDougall accused him of being "the chief abettor if not the chief instigator" of the Red River troubles. The Toronto *Globe* was to declare that Howe had urged the settlers to follow the example of Nova Scotia and fight for "better terms."

That he was the "instigator" of the *métis* opposition is undoubtedly false. That he talked too much without any real understanding of what was going on is almost certainly true. The Tribune was always a man who tended to gallop off exuberantly in several directions. It is quite in character for him to have exhorted the principal men at Red River to fight for better terms as he had convinced himself he had done in Nova Scotia. The whole tenor of the evidence suggests that he was culpable of both ignorance and unthinking verbosity. But when he left Red River without reaching any understanding of the situation the last chance to avoid the consequences of Canada's stupidities was gone.

5

On October 11, the decisive day when Riel stopped the survey party, William McDougall was at St. Cloud in Minnesota, waiting for his baggage to catch up with him. For McDougall was traveling as a king to a new kingdom. He had left Ottawa on September 28. Included in his entourage were Captain D. R. Cameron and his bride, who was a daughter of Dr. Tupper, the Confederation leader; A. N. Richards, who had been Solicitor General of Canada West in 1864; G. A. N. Provencher, recently editor of *La Minerve*, the Montreal Conservative journal, and also nephew of Bishop Taché; and Alexander Begg, who is not to be confused with the Winnipeg diarist of the same name.

Of these men, Begg was to be Treasurer and Collector of Customs in the new kingdom, Provencher, the Secretary of the Council, and Richards, the Attorney General. As for Cameron, John A. had written in a letter to Cameron's father-in-law, Tupper: "I suggested to Howe that Cameron should be made one of the Council and . . . that his military experience would be of great value on the question of a military police." In a second letter, about salaries, he assured Tupper: "I shall . . . take care that Captain Cameron shall receive as much as anyone else except the Governor."

The posts in the new territory-to-be were being blithely parceled out. McDougall also brought his children with him. There were mountains of baggage in no less than sixty wagons, a group of servants, and three hundred rifles in cases, a fact which, when reported, did nothing to calm the tension among the *métis*. For, though McDougall did not know it, from St. Paul onward every step of his journey was being reported by *métis* riders. Cheerful in ignorance, McDougall set out from St. Cloud for Pembina. The trail was dry, the sky bright, and flocks of ducks, geese, and swans feathered the lakes. But weather can change rapidly in the West. When, north of Fort Abercrombie, Joseph Howe met McDougall it was snowing and the northeast wind blew chill.

Howe could at least have told McDougall that toasts to his arrival were not being drunk. Later, he claimed it was the weather which prevented him from doing more than suggest to McDougall that he had better go cautiously. But his failure to warn McDougall of the serious situation before him would seem to show either that Howe did not have any comprehension of the feeling in Red River Settlement or else that he felt guilty when he remembered incautious words of his own back in Winnipeg.

Possibly both motives influenced him. At any rate, after a brief exchange of greetings, Howe moved on toward St. Paul and an undistinguished career in Ottawa. His term on the stage was almost over. On May 10 of 1873 he was sworn as lieutenant governor of Nova Scotia. On June 1 of the same year he died. Few men have blazed more brilliantly and erratically than the "Great Tribune." But after his unsuccessful defiance of Confederation, the rest of his life was anticlimax.

Meantime, in October of 1869, McDougall, unwarned by Howe, pushed on into the snow. On October 30 he reached Pembina. At the American customhouse a *métis* sidled over to him with a note. When the portly McDougall unfolded it, his heavy jowls slackened, then clamped tight in rage. The note read:

A Monsieur McDougall.

Monsieur—Le Comité National des Métis de la Rivière Rouge intime à Monsieur McDougall l'ordre de ne pas entrer sur le Territoire du Nord-Ouest sans une permission spéciale de ce Comité.

Par ordre du président.
JOHN BRUCE,
LOUIS RIEL, *Secrétaire.*

Daté à St. Norbert, Rivière Rouge.
ce 21e jour d'octobre, 1869.

Ordered not to enter his kingdom: called "Monsieur"! What was this *Comité National des Métis?* Who was this John Bruce and this Louis Riel? How could such a thing have come to pass!

CHAPTER XVI

1869

McDougall Meets More Than His Match in Louis Riel

1

THE wheel of events had been set in motion. It was to spin further than anyone dreamed. McDougall called the note handed to him "rebellion," forgetting that, until the formal transfer of the Northwest to Canada on December 1, he was merely a private citizen. Brushing the *métis* warning aside, he and his party drove on that same evening to the H.B.C. post two miles north of the frontier. A letter there from Colonel Dennis told him of the barrier at the Rivière Sale. This gave McDougall pause. Next morning, a Sunday, he sent Provencher, the French Canadian and the nephew of Bishop Taché, to the barrier to discover what the situation was. The idea of discussions with ignorant half-breeds was disgusting to the belligerent Captain Cameron. Over McDougall's protests he loaded his bride, Tupper's daughter, and two servants into a surrey and also took off for the barrier. The baggage followed in another vehicle. At the barrier, Cameron found Provencher and a group of armed *métis*. Cameron, a fine figure of a man, stood up in the surrey, slapped his monocle to his eye, and roared:

"Remove that blasted fence!"

He may have impressed his bride. A group of the *métis* lounged forward. They took the horses by their bridles and abruptly turned them around. Cameron was jolted to his seat. Mounting their horses and motioning to Provencher, the *métis* escorted both Mars and Mercury back to the frontier. The baggage was allowed to go through to Winnipeg.

Meantime, at the H.B.C. post Colonel Dennis had arrived with a letter from Governor Mactavish advising McDougall to stay where he was. Then, on the afternoon of Tuesday, November 2, fourteen armed *métis* rode up, led by the six-foot-three Ambroise Lépine, "Adjutant General" of Riel's National Committee. They gave McDougall until 9 A.M. of the next day to get back across the border. At 6 A.M. that day, November 3, Provencher and Cameron arrived with their escort. McDougall was taken past the post marking the boundary and told:

"You must not return beyond this line."

It was highhanded but not "rebellion." In the St. Paul *Press* a dispatch from "Spectator"—who was almost certainly Enos Stutsman—reported that:

"A King without a Kingdom is said to be poorer than a peasant. And I can assure you that a live Governor with a full complement of officials and menials from Attorney-General down to cooks and scullions without one poor foot of territory is a spectacle sufficiently sad to move the hardest heart."

McDougall was like a bull with his horns caught in a wire fence. Seventy miles north was the mansion, "Silver Heights," which he had rented. At Pembina, with the prairie winter on the way, he moved into a 20-by-25-foot log cabin, owned by a half-breed, LaRose. There was only the one room. McDougall had it partitioned off for his children. Provencher took lodgings with Jo Rolette, the American fur trader, who was also one of Taylor's aides. Dr. Tupper's daughter found herself in a cabin six feet high.

McDougall gloomed and grumbled and through Colonel Dennis began to intrigue with the Canadian party to overmaster the *métis*. In the settlement all was confusion and conflicting rumors. The Canadian party tried to organize a posse to bring in McDougall. There were others who felt that the *métis* had gone too far. Governor Mactavish seems not to have cared. His authority was only temporary in any case—though it was the only legal authority in Red River. Besides, he was by now a dying man. Meanwhile, Riel rode the current of events, at first tentatively and then, when his canoe carried him, more confidently. On November 1 he had held a review of his forces. The muster roll was answered by 402 men, all bearing arms. Later another 100 horsemen came in. McDougall was sent back to Pembina, scouts were posted along the trail leading to the frontier, and all incomers and mail were examined at the barrier at the Rivière Sale.

All the while, Riel's eyes had been on Upper Fort Garry. Its stone walls enclosed Mactavish's residence, storehouses, men's quarters, workshops, a sales shop, and 390 rifles, while thirteen six-pounder cannon peered from its battlements. In olden days it had been garrisoned. Now only a night watchman kept guard.

Whoever held the fort held the settlement. On November 2, the day before McDougall was pushed across the frontier, Riel and 120 men walked in. When Chief Factor Dr. Cowan protested he was told that the *métis* had come to "protect it." Later the H.B.C. officials were accused of connivance with Riel. One can say that they made no real attempt to prevent the seizure of the fort and were rather glad than otherwise that Canada and McDougall were caught in a jam.

In seizing the fort, Riel had moved to open revolt against the one legal authority in the settlement. Yet the Council of Assiniboia was allowed to meet without interference and Riel kept his men under strict discipline with an oath not to touch liquor. Meantime, from the second to the seventh of November, McDougall wrote three frantic letters to Mactavish, demanding that he re-establish the peace and announce publicly the impending transfer of the government to Canada and himself. The advice of the Council and of Mactavish was for McDougall to return to Canada.

To McDougall, to slink back to Canada was impossible. He stayed on at Pembina, hoping to organize a counterforce among the groups hostile to, or suspicious of, Riel.

Riel let him fume. Up to this time his power had depended on the *métis*. Either on his own initiative, or, possibly, after consultation with Abbé Ritchot, O'Donoghue, and, quite probably, the legless Enos Stutsman, he decided that the "English" must be brought in. On November 6, by a notice printed in the *Nor'Wester* (after locking the editor, Dr. Bown, in a room in the plant) he invited the English parishes to elect twelve men to meet with his own council of twelve. His professed objective at this time was to compel the Dominion to negotiate with the whole body of settlers the terms of their entry into Confederation—a not unreasonable goal in view of Canadian bungling.

The combined meeting was held in the courthouse on November 16. The "English" were hailed by the *métis* with a *feu de joie* from an honor guard of 150 men, and a salute of twenty-five guns to signalize the importance of their coming. But gales of dissension blew. The English objected in particular to the stoppage of the mails and the seizure of the fort, while an official message from Mactavish deplored the violence which had been used and exhorted dispersal.

This document from the legal governor had a certain effect on the English. In spite of ominous bursts of temper from Riel, they wanted to allow McDougall to enter and then to present him with a list of grievances. To Riel, this was to turn over the keys before the settlers had achieved what they ought to have and, besides, it would mean the end of his own prominence. He refused. On the seventeenth, the conference was adjourned to November 22.

Meanwhile, the figure of Enos Stutsman was flitting in and out of the picture, so much so that his chief in St. Paul, Taylor, was able to write on November 16 to the U. S. Secretary of State that there would be armed resistance to Confederation, adding that he estimated that the "French Element" could put "1000 men into the field." Furthermore, two days later, Stutsman sent a dispatch to the St. Paul *Press* which said:

"Nothing short of a very liberal government, independence or annexation to the United States will satisfy the people."

How much influence the legless Stutsman exerted in these exciting days is difficult to determine. At any rate, when, on November 22, the conference resumed, he was again at Fort Garry.

Riel still refused to let McDougall enter the country. The *métis* leader was now obsessed with the notion of a "Provisional Government," with himself, naturally, at the helm. On November 23, the day after Stutsman's return, he seized the public accounts, took over some of the provisions and cash in the fort, stopped free ingress and egress from and into it, and put Mactavish under arrest.

From revolt, Riel was proceeding rapidly to a dictatorship. On the next day, when the English refused his idea of a provisional government, on the ground that they must first consult their constituents, the meetings were again adjourned, this time to December 1. But Riel promptly seized the customs.

By this time a consignment of pork, recently arrived at Schultz's house for Snow's road builders, had thrust itself into prominence, since whichever party held it could feed their followers. Riel put a small guard around the house.

There was also a group of "moderates," led by Alexander Begg, the diarist, and Bannatyne, the postmaster. This faction held hopeful public meetings on November 26 and 27. Their attempt was to persuade Riel to abandon his notion of a provisional government and to operate legally through Governor Mactavish, the Council of Assiniboia, and another council to be elected for the specific purpose of taking up terms of Confederation with Canada.

On the evening of the twenty-seventh Riel agreed to this proposal. There might have been peace except for the pork, the Canadian party, and William McDougall. For when Alexander Begg arrived at the downstream parishes on November 30 to announce to them the compromise which had been reached, he found, according to his account, some 250 Scottish and English half-breeds arming and drilling. Their ostensible purpose was to protect the pork from Riel. But the Canadian party was definitely implicated and it seems likely that this whole movement was directed from Pembina, with a view to overthrowing Riel by a *coup de main.*

On that same November 30, when he heard of the arming and drilling, Riel, quite naturally, retracted his promise. The moderates still hoped to repersuade him in time for the conference on the next day, December 1. But, again on that decisive date, November 30, McDougall was preparing an amazing move.

2

It was twenty below zero that evening. A wind, howling down from the Arctic, drove powdery snow in fierce gusts against the little cavalcade moving north from Pembina. There were seven of them in all in the sleighs, wrapped and bundled against the cold —William McDougall, Richards, Provencher, the Begg who was supposed to become Attorney General, and three others. The frost nipped at their toes and fingers. It flirted with their noses and cheeks. In the blizzard one couldn't see beyond the horses' heads.

It was the evening of December 1: If all had gone according to schedule, the Northwest would on this date be legally transferred to Canada and William McDougall would be no longer a private citizen but its legitimate governor. The party reached the frontier. In a storm such as this there was no one to stop it. It moved on to the H.B.C. post two miles north. The horses were tied with halters to hitching posts. The party gathered in a ring around McDougall. He pulled a flag from his pocket and gave it to an aide to hold. Another aide held a lantern. The wind howled. McDougall drew out a sheet of parchment, unfolded it with numb and fumbling fingers, and read aloud a proclamation from the Queen transferring the Northwest to Canada and appointing him, William McDougall, lieutenant governor. The ceremony over, the party untied the horses, tumbled into the sleighs, and drove back to Pembina to thaw themselves out.

The dice had been rolled across the board. As McDougall drove back to Pembina, Colonel Dennis was traveling north to Winnipeg. With him he carried copies of the Queen's proclamation which McDougall had read and a commission from that same McDougall as "Lieutenant and Conservator of the Peace," giving him power to raise a military force. Early in the morning of December 1, Dennis conferred with a number of people, among them Major Boulton, who belonged to his survey party, and the violent Dr. Schultz. Then, evading the *métis* guards, he hurried some twenty miles downstream to Lower Fort Garry, known as the "Stone Fort."

There were already, as has been mentioned, English and Scottish half-breeds arming in the downstream parishes. The Winnipeg Canadians, too, had been ordered to report to the Stone Fort. By the evening of December 1 there were some seventy men drilling at it, with Dennis passing out still more copies of the proclamation. Next day the Indian chief Henry Prince, who had been a delegate to Riel's conference and had objected to the carrying of arms at it, joined Dennis with nearly a hundred men in full war paint. Dennis kept fifty of these to guard the Stone Fort, rallied the survey parties to his banner, sent Webb (the man whose survey Riel had stopped on October 11) to Portage la Prairie to raise four companies of fifty men each, and divided the settlement into districts for drill and recruiting with Major Boulton in charge. Meanwhile those of the Canadian party who had come to the Stone Fort were sent back to Winnipeg with orders to remain quiet until the proper moment. The counterforce to Riel was being prepared.

McDougall, in fact, was gambling everything on the effect of his Queen's proclamation. If authentic, it automatically made Riel and his supporters rebels if they resisted his authority further. Both Snow and Mair of the road-building party had written urging him to issue it, and, Mair had added, "it will be responded to by five hundred men."

Incredibly, the proclamation and McDougall's commission had

been forged by himself. If the transfer to the Dominion had gone through as planned and as McDougall, lacking information, had believed, the forgery might not have been too serious. Ottawa, however, had let him down. John A. is said to have laughed when he heard of McDougall's being pushed back across the frontier. Gradually, however, as reports of Riel's doings came in, "Old Tomorrow" stopped laughing. On the twenty-fifth of November, the Colonial Secretary cabled from London a statement from Queen Victoria of her surprise that "certain misguided persons have banded together to oppose by force the entry of the future Lieutenant-Governor into Her Majesty's settlement on the Red River." The statement also ordered all complaints to be addressed to the governor general of Canada. On the twenty-seventh the governor general of Canada, Sir John Young, however, cabled London that the Dominion would not accept the transfer of the Northwest until the Imperial Government could turn it over in a peaceable state.

So, on December 1, McDougall was not, as he had believed, lieutenant governor. John A. had left him far out on a wintry limb. Meantime, "Old Tomorrow," now when it was too late, commissioned Lieutenant Colonel De Salaberry and the aged and beloved missionary to the Northwest, Father Thibault, to proceed to Red River to explain to the settlers that their lands and customs were safe. To his friend, Rose, he wrote that "we must construct a golden bridge [John A. was thinking of bribing the *métis* leaders] over which McDougall can pass into the country." To McDougall he sent instructions not to move until he received official word of the transfer and to keep Riel on as an officer in the police.

None of this reached McDougall until December 6. He realized then that he was on thin ice. But Riel, too, had no legal justification for his arbitrary actions. McDougall sat at Pembina and hoped.

By December 6, however, the dice were about to turn up snake eyes. On the first, in spite of the uncertainty caused by McDougall's "Queen's proclamation," Riel's conference, with at least six English delegates attending, had agreed to a List of Rights, believed by some to have been penned by Enos Stutsman. This list, published on the fifth, included demands for an elected legislature, a railroad within five years, the use of English and French as official languages, proper representation in the Dominion House, and as an American feature, the election of all sheriffs, magistrates, and the like.

Before its publication, apparently on the second of December, there was a proposal, once again, to send delegates to get McDougall's assent to this List of Rights and then to bring him in. But the news of the arming at the Stone Fort had coalesced the *métis* around Riel. He could afford to dismiss both the proposal and the English with contempt. The conference was, in fact, dissolved somewhat hurriedly. For by this time the pork in Schultz's house was becoming kegs of dynamite.

This was because the Canadians who had gone down to the Stone Fort had returned to Winnipeg in a state of ebullience. They had been told by Dennis to "wait for the moment." To wait was, for Dr. Schultz, impossible. Collecting, according to a letter from Boulton to Dennis on December 4, "70 men and 65 good arms," Schultz made his house, which was on the outskirts of the Winnipeg of that day, into a fortress. The proclaimed purpose was to protect the pork. It is more probable that the move was part of the over-all plan to effect a *coup de main* and seize Fort Garry and Riel. At any rate, on December 1, Captain Cameron had written John A. that "Mr. McDougall is sanguine that by tomorrow, Louis Riel, the rebel Secretary, will be a prisoner in the hands of loyal men. . . ."

To the *métis*, the Canadians at Schultz's house were pistols pointed at them. They poured into Fort Garry until, as Bishop Machray wrote Dennis on December 6, Riel had "over six hundred men . . . in arms." That day Riel posted guards around Schultz's house. The next day with three hundred men he moved out from the fort to the attack. Schultz tried to insist on terms. Riel gave the Canadians fifteen minutes to surrender and set up two cannon in the snow, pointing at the front door. The Canadians gave in. The forty-five who were still in the house were taken to Fort Garry and jailed. Three wives went along, among them the indomitable Mrs. Schultz, though she was so ill her giant husband had to pull her on a sled.

It was a strange cortege, that procession to the fort, with the *métis*, triumphant, riding herd, and Louis Riel almost beside himself with exultation. The women later took the freedom which had been offered them. It should be noted that among the prisoners was the violent Thomas Scott, the man who had threatened to dump Snow, the surveyor, into the water.

With this one event McDougall's plans were punctured and Riel sat tall in the saddle. On the next day, December 8, he announced a provisional government. On the ninth, Colonel Dennis issued a hand sheet ordering the "loyal party" to cease action. He himself, disguised as a squaw, fled south to Pembina. On the tenth, Riel, to the thudding of guns, raised a white flag emblazoned with a golden fleur-de-lis and a green shamrock (O'Donoghue's influence) over Fort Garry. All that the fumbling efforts of McDougall and of the Canadian party had achieved was to put Riel in complete control of the settlement.

Up to this point there can be little but admiration for Riel. Canada's mismanagement had left the *métis* uncertain as to what would happen to their farms and their way of life. Riel had set out to assure them of both. He had taken a quite reasonable stand that Red River would not agree to the transfer of authority to the Dominion or admit McDougall, even though he had been nominated as the governor-to-be, until direct negotiations with Canada got the *métis* what they wanted. Pursuing on the whole a careful and undeviating course and solidly backed by the *métis*, he had seized Upper Fort Garry, overridden attempts to raise a counterforce against him, established an illegal provisional government, and made himself dictator—and all this at the age of twenty-five.

It is clear that his actions were a revolt against the only legally constituted authority in the settlement, the governor and the Council of Assiniboia. But that authority had been undermined by the news of the impending transfer of government to the Dominion, and, in any case, the majority of the settlers agreed with Riel. The will of the people is often a partial justification, at least, for illegality. What was disturbing for the future of the movement which Riel had initiated were his fits of temper, the highhandedness of his acts, and his evident love of power, along with his touchy pride and the influence exerted on him by O'Donoghue, the Fenian, Stutsman, the annexationist, and Abbé Ritchot, the ardent ultramontanist.

Though it was a rebellion, it was as yet a bloodless revolt. The unanswered questions in December 1869 were Riel's final intentions and in what home Red River would, at the last, nestle. In St. Paul the hounds of annexation burst into full cry. The press reminded its readers of the bloodless conquest of Oregon by a few thousand settlers, whereas there were now 400,000 people in Minnesota. The freebooters along the American border—buffalo hunters, smugglers, wolfers, whisky runners, rustlers—began to drift along the wintry trails toward Pembina. Bishop Taché was to state later that Minnesota had pledged *"des sommes à un montant de plus de quatre millions de dollars"* for the annexation of Rupert's Land, and to Rupert's Land, Red River Settlement was the key and the door. In Washington the annexationist bloc, led by Senators Ramsey and Zachariah Chandler and Congressman Banks, had a resolution passed by Congress requesting full information from the State Department on McDougall's attempt to take over Red River "against the will of its inhabitants." The same bloc began to plan land grants to speed up a railroad from St. Paul to Pembina. James Wickes Taylor on December 30 received his commission as a special agent to report to the State Department on the situation at Fort Garry.

The threat of a railroad brought the Grand Trunk, which from the first had coveted the Northwest for its own expansion, into action. Its general manager, Brydges, wrote to John A. "Old Tomorrow," now thoroughly awake, wrote back that the United States would do anything "short of war" to acquire the Northwest. At Pembina the unlucky McDougall made one last attempt. He brought himself to write to Riel for an interview. There was no reply. On December 18, accompanied by Colonel Dennis and with his sixty loads of gear lumbering behind him, he set out for St. Paul, defeated and discredited. Inept, stupid, decisive at the wrong moment, only part of the fault was his. John A. must bear the major part of the blame. En route, on December 21, at 2 P.M., McDougall met Riel's matching antagonist, Donald Smith.

CHAPTER XVII

1870

Donald Smith Arrives as Commissioner from Canada—He Undermines Riel

FEW men have inspired more adulation or awakened more enmities than Donald Smith, later to be Lord Strathcona. He was a Scot. An occasional Irishman, such as D'Arcy McGee, may have flashed across the Canadian scene. Now and then an Edward Watkin may have surveyed it with an imperial eye. By and large, the history of English-speaking British North America in these years was the story of the Scots who dominated its economics and its politics—men such as George Brown, John A. Macdonald, George Simpson, James Douglas, and then Donald Smith and his cousin George Stephen. Part of the gray light which still broods over the Dominion of the North emanated from the rock-ribbed Scots who molded her—with John A. Macdonald as the one contrasting flame of Celtic fire.

As a sandy-haired lad of eighteen, Donald Smith had reached Montreal in 1838 with a letter from his uncle John Stuart, who had been an H.B.C. chief factor. George Simpson found a place for him sorting furs. From the first, however, the "Little Emperor" seems to have felt antipathy toward the new apprentice. Possibly, it was an instinctive feeling that here was his successor. Beckles Willson, in his biography of Lord Strathcona (an adulatory one, but Preston's picture gives a contrary note), suggests a more personal reason. Simpson's wife and cousin was twenty-six years his junior.

"When Mr. Smith came . . . in 1838," a fellow apprentice wrote, "Mrs. Simpson, who always took a friendly interest in the 'indentured young gentlemen,' . . . invited him to tea; she occasionally commanded his escort on boating excursions. Once, after the governor had returned after an absence at Red River, we heard that there had been a scene . . . one gentleman averring that he had heard the governor, in a highly pitched treble, declare that he was not going to endure any 'upstart, quill-driving apprentices dangling about a parlour reserved to the nobility and gentry.'"

Whatever the cause, Donald Smith spent seven years at Tadoussac, a king's post of the Company at the mouth of the Saguenay River, where furs were few and promotion slow, and then twenty years in a still more remote establishment at North West River on the Labrador coast. There he took to wife the daughter of Chief Trader Hardisty, a girl who had previously been married to a fur trader named Grant, in "Company fashion," that is, without benefit of clergy. That marriage was annulled in 1853. In the same year Smith took his father-in-law's place as chief trader and, despite the obstacles, made the territory turn over a profit. Ten years later, in 1863 (Simpson had been dead for three years), on furlough in London he made a favorable impression on the new owners of the H.B.C., the International Finance Company.

This was the beginning of a change in luck. On the way back to Labrador, via Montreal, he met his cousin and fellow Scot George Stephen, who was able to introduce him to acquaintances in shipping circles and in the Bank of Montreal. Smith had savings. He invested them in mortgages and industrial stocks and later became financial agent for a group of fellow officers. When in June of 1869, at the age of forty-nine, Smith came out of the Labrador wilderness to take over the H.B.C. Montreal District, he controlled enough capital to be a valued customer of the Bank of Montreal. In it, George Stephen was by this time an important figure.

It was a long apprenticeship for a man who was to die a multimillionaire. But it explains why Smith, though he believed in his "second sight," nevertheless always kept a careful eye peeled for whatever was of advantage to Donald Smith.

He had left his Labrador exile just in time for the Red River rebellion. Since the H.B.C. was involved, Smith watched events with disquiet, especially when rumors circulated that Mactavish, who was a personal friend, had connived at Riel's seizure of Fort Garry. There was a further reason. By this time, Smith was close to achieving financial control of the H.B.C. and he was anxious to protect his interests. On November 24 he offered John A. Company co-operation. On December 10, at John A.'s request (John A. thought, probably, that Smith held Simpson's old position, though Smith was actually only in charge of the Montreal District), he was appointed "Special Commissioner" to Red River. His instructions were to report on the situation, to do his best to pacify the country, and to act according to his best judgment.

The two other commissioners, Father Thibault and Colonel De Salaberry, had already left. The tall and taciturn Donald Smith, a man with a jutting nose, bushy eyebrows, and a huge thrust of a beard, set out from Ottawa on December 13 on a bitterly cold morning. With him he carried his credentials, a copy of the Queen's November 25 proclamation, a copy of a proclamation based on it from the governor general, Sir John Young, promising an amnesty, and a further letter from Young, in which it was stated: "The people may rely on it that respect and protection will be extended to the different religious persuasions, that titles to every description of property will be perfectly guarded and that all the franchises which have existed, or which the people may prove themselves qualified to exercise, shall be duly continued or liberally conferred."

Had these assurances been given to the Red River settlers as late as the previous summer, there would have been no rebellion.

Along with Smith went his brother-in-law, Richard Hardisty, who had Indian blood in his arteries, and Dr. Tupper, the Nova Scotian Father of Confederation. Tupper's mission was to bring back his daughter, the bride of Captain Cameron, from Pembina. The travelers went by way of St. Paul. There Norman Kittson met them—a momentous meeting for Smith and Kittson, though neither of them realized it. St. Paul swarmed with Fenians and with *métis* spies—a fact brought home to Smith when a note was thrust into his hand on December 17 as he was leaving his hotel. The note, signed "Phoenix," read:

> Beware how you indulge the vain hope that you will succeed where the Orangeman, McDougall, failed. The destiny of Red River is in its own hands, and is not to be tampered with by outsiders. An honest, true-hearted patriot [Riel] will soon be at the head of affairs. . . . Let not ambition or mistaken zeal place you in such a position that your lives may be forfeit! Pause now before it is too late! Your blood be upon your own

head. Remember this warning—the moment you attempt to cross the present American boundary line you will be in serious jeopardy.

It was made clear that Riel would know of Smith's coming. From St. Paul, Smith, Tupper, and Hardisty traveled to Breckenridge on a railroad called the St. Paul and Pacific, a fact Smith filed away to be fished out a few years later. A stagecoach carried them in two days to Fort Abercrombie. At their last dinner before the fort they ate broiled elk, the landlord of the inn taking them to an outhouse in which, Dr. Tupper relates, "six fine elk were standing like horses in a stall, all frozen stiff. . . ."

They still had two hundred miles to cover in a canvas-covered sleigh, drawn by two horses, while camping for the nights in the forest belt along the Red River and making a fire from the fallen timber. "There was about a foot of snow on the ground," Tupper recalls in his description of the trip, "which we cleared away with a shovel, put an india rubber cloth on the ground, our mattresses over that, and then our blankets and buffalo skin over all."

To Smith, it was like Labrador. They met and conferred briefly with the defeated McDougall, learning that Provencher was still at Pembina. On the twenty-fourth, "after a cold night and bad dreams" in the open, they covered the remaining miles to Pembina by 11 P.M. In eleven days they had managed the whole distance from Ottawa, in spite of stagecoach, cold, and horse-drawn sleighs. By their speed they had overtaken Thibault and De Salaberry.

It was Christmas Eve. Tupper found his daughter in bed. She sat up and said:

"What did you come for?"

Smith pushed on that same night to the H.B.C. post north of the border where, on December 1, McDougall had read his ill-fated proclamation. While he secluded himself there and De Salaberry stayed on at Pembina, Father Thibault went on to Fort Garry. Riel promptly put the priest under house arrest. Meanwhile the sturdy Tupper borrowed a dog cariole from the H.B.C. post and also traveled to the fort. He was after his daughter's baggage, which had been sent on to Winnipeg on the day her husband had been stopped at the barrier at the Rivière Sale. It was a typical Winnipeg winter day when Tupper reached the place—thirty below zero. He saw Riel and his priestly adviser, Abbé Ritchot. Anyone from the East was, to Riel, automatically under suspicion as a subverter and spy. Tupper was told to leave at once. However, he stayed for two days and got back his daughter's half ton of baggage, which, incidentally, was untouched and in good order. It is interesting to record that he met Riel's sister, a nun at St. Norbert, and found her so charming and dedicated to her church that he corresponded with her until her death many years later.

Tupper himself was excess baggage at the moment. The key man was Smith. After waiting two days and after taking the precaution of leaving his credentials and documents with Provencher at Pembina, Smith reached Fort Garry on the evening of the twenty-seventh. This, by chance, was the very day when, John Bruce having resigned, Riel had become "President" of his "provisional government." Riel, Smith tells us, promptly appeared. The two men faced each other, the young, eloquent, and somewhat unstable *métis* leader, and the cool Scot, almost twice his age, who never spoke once without having thought at least twice.

We are fortunate in having Smith's detailed account of his stay in Red River. According to him, he was introduced to "ten or a dozen" of Riel's council, then asked why he had come. Smith explained his Company position but also informed Riel that he held a commission from Canada to the people of Red River with credentials which he would produce at the proper time. Some authorities, however, believe that at first he concealed this latter fact. He was ordered to take an oath not to attempt to upset the government as "legally established." Smith refused but promised "to take no immediate steps to forcibly upset the so-called Provisional Government, legal or illegal as it might be," without first announcing his attention. The next day, in a letter to John A., Smith warned him that the drift was toward annexation to the United States.

The decision whether the Northwest was to remain British or become part of the United States now rested, in fact, in the ambition-heated hands of Louis Riel. The affair of the pork had crushed the Canadian party, except for a nucleus of resistance under Major Boulton of Dennis' survey party at Portage la Prairie. The flag of Riel's "provisional government" floated over Fort Garry. Riel himself was now "President." On December 10 the *Nor'Wester* and the *Red River Pioneer* had been suppressed, while on December 22 Riel had seized the funds of the H.B.C. As has been noted, when Father Thibault had reached Winnipeg, shortly before Smith's arrival, Riel had felt strong enough to put the revered cleric under house arrest for fear that he might influence the *métis* to favor Canada. Yet Riel and his advisers knew that in the spring a force from Canada could crush their resistance. He must therefore either manage terms with Canada, or agree to annexation to the States, or, as a third choice, set up an independent state and appeal for American backing.

In the New Year the current was still toward annexation. On January 7 Major Robinson, an American, was appointed as editor of the *New Nation*, a replacement for the suppressed *Nor'Wester*. Robinson editorialized vigorously for independence and ultimate annexation to the States. Taylor, as a U.S. secret agent to bring about this happy solution, was now in Winnipeg and so was O'Donoghue, the Fenian. Meantime, the St. Paul *Press* announced jubilantly that England would seize the opportunity of settling the American claims against her for the losses caused by the British-built Confederate raider, the *Alabama*, by "the cession of a country whose destinies God has indissolubly wedded to ours by geographical affinities which no human power can sunder, as He has divorced it from Canada by physical barriers which no human power can overcome." Washington did not speak so loudly. Still, it was clear that all the United States needed to walk in was an invitation from Riel.

What prevented Riel from giving the invitation? Some of his apologists have argued that he was threatening Canada with the States to get better terms for his *métis*. Others point out that the Roman Catholic hierarchy was just as opposed to an influx of Americans as to immigration from Protestant Ontario, since either would swamp their new Quebec. Possibly the best explanation is that Riel was a thoroughly confused, egotistic, and unstable, though brilliant, young man with the desire but, as was shortly to be proved, not the capacity for dictatorship. He was pulled toward annexation to the States by the Fenian O'Donoghue. The notion of an independent state for the "New Nation" of which he could be the head must have been compellingly attractive. Yet, like a sawdust rather than a real Caesar, he was childishly obsessed with the notion that the legality of his provisional government must be conceded, as if a dictator ever worried too much about legality. As its "President," he strutted about in a boiled shirt, a frock coat, black trousers, and beaded moccasins. He held on to the prisoners he had captured, chiefly, it would seem, because the possession of them heightened his feeling of power.

Instead of a consistent policy his course was fitted rapidly to what circumstances suggested, his main objective being, apparently, to hang on to his dictatorship, even at the cost of prolonging the troubles. He seems at times, in fact, to have had almost an undergraduate's excited view of how to conduct an insurrection.

In one determination, however, he was consistent—not to allow the commissioners from Canada an opportunity to effect any quick or peaceable solution of the revolt. Shortly after Smith's arrival Colonel De Salaberry had come in from Pembina with the credentials from Canada for Father Thibault and himself along with copies of the Queen's and the governor general's proclamations. Riel got hold of these papers. A glance at them told him that, if published, they would weaken his hold on Red River. So the two commissioners were brought before Riel's council, listened to, and dismissed. But their papers and credentials were not returned to them. Meanwhile, Smith was kept in confinement in Dr. Cowan's home inside Fort Garry, with permission to go outside the walls to exercise, accompanied by two guards, a privilege of which he did not avail himself.

The dictator was not quite astute enough for a man as skilled in deviousness as Smith. Smith was allowed to have visitors. Through these he spread the news of Canada's "liberal intentions" among the English settlers. He had also an emissary in his brother-in-law, Richard Hardisty, who was part Indian, spoke Cree, French, and English, and had many friends among the *métis*. Through him donations of money greased the way to a split among Riel's closest followers. Four years later, in 1874, Smith told the secretary of a select committee of the Dominion House that he had spent £500 among the French *métis* "whose assistance had been absolutely necessary in my position as Canadian Commissioner in 1869 and 1870."

Among the *métis*, in any case, the unaccustomed discipline began to pall. The jailers got drunk and the prisoners, whose possession as a proof of power was valued so highly by Riel, began to escape. There was an important jailbreak for instance, on the night of January 9, when twelve slipped outside the fort. Some were recaptured. Among those who got away to Portage la Prairie was the Ontarian and Orangeman the violent Thomas Scott. Early in January, too, Riel released several prisoners, on condition that they either left for Canada or took an oath of allegiance to the provisional government. Meanwhile, the English half-breeds began to grumble because all the prisoners were not released and the French *métis* to complain of Riel's dictatorial pose. On the fifth of January, Begg's diary records that "the Americans are rapidly losing ground if they ever had any"; on the fourteenth, that "it is said that there is a split among Riel's councillors on account of his overbearing attitude with them."

The wintry air hummed with intrigue, most of it Smith-inspired. Riel's reaction was an attempt on January 14 to get hold of Smith's credentials and papers. This may have been because, at last, Smith had revealed his commissionership. When he learned that Smith had left them at Pembina with Provencher, Riel asked for a written order for their delivery into the hands of a messenger from himself. Smith refused but agreed to send his brother-in-law, Hardisty, for them. "Immediately," Smith tells us, "I was placed under strict arrest, a captain's guard being assigned me, whose instructions were not to lose sight of me, day or night, and prevent me from communicating either verbally or in writing with any individual."

Riel's actions show clearly that it was his intention to clip Smith's wings by getting hold of his papers, too, and keeping them. Between two and three of the morning of the fifteenth, after Hardisty had left for Pembina, accompanied by a guard, Riel burst in on Smith. Standing over him, as he lay in bed, the *métis* leader again demanded a written order for the surrender of those papers to himself. The imperturbable Scot again refused. Then, forming a party of *métis*, Riel dashed off to intercept the papers.

Within his own party he was no longer trusted. At St. Norbert, he met Hardisty, who was being escorted by twelve sleigh loads of Riel's own followers as a guard; but these were followers who now trusted Smith rather than Riel. As the bewildered Hardisty looked on, a fierce quarrel flared, the half-breeds on each side shouting and shoving and pushing. During the melee Pierre Léveillé, one of Riel's own original supporters, took his "President" by the throat and put a pistol to his head. Riel, in turn, pulled out a pistol, crying out that he would not be taken alive in his own country. Abbé Ritchot, who was one of Riel's party, tried to intervene. He was pushed aside and told "not to interfere any further with matters unconnected with his spiritual duties."

It was all very French and very exciting. The quarrel over, the two opposing parties—both composed of Riel's followers—sped on to Fort Garry. When Riel opened the gate, Léveillé drove his sleigh through with Hardisty in it. Smith got his papers and demanded a chance to speak to the people of Red River. Riel and O'Donoghue protested. Léveillé's faction accused them of trying to force annexation to the United States. Riel's stammered reply was that this would happen only if the people wished it, but the statement does seem to show what had been in his mind. At last it was agreed that the meeting Smith wanted should be held on the nineteenth. Meantime, Riel's supporters guarded the fort and Léveillé's party guarded Donald Smith and the papers.

Why was Riel so anxious to seize Smith's papers and to prevent the Red River settlers from any official knowledge of Canada's offers? Was it because he intended to ask the United States to annex Red River? Or did he have an independent state in mind? Or was it merely the attempt of a petty despot to perpetuate his delicious feeling of power? In any case, it is clear that at this moment the last thing Riel desired was a quick and peaceable solution of the troubles.

CHAPTER XVIII

1870

The Meeting of January 19—Escape of John Christian Schultz from Prison—The Canadian Party Moves to Overthrow Riel and Fails—The Shooting of Thomas Scott

1

IT was twenty below zero that January 19. There was a wind to freeze the marrow. Yet by midmorning the rectangle of open ground inside the grim stone walls of Fort Garry was packed with more than a thousand buffalo-coated or capote-clad men and scores of women, come in from Red River Settlement on horseback, in sleighs, on foot. Their breath rose in frosty vapor. They stamped their moccasined feet and flailed themselves with their arms to keep warm. Icicles formed on the men's mustaches and beards. Here and there groups crowded around bonfires. Above them on the tall flagstaff floated the flag of the "New Nation." Before them was a small platform flanked by two Red River carts.

Finally a ragged salute was fired. The packed throng craned their necks. Out came Louis Riel, stocky and sallow, his mouth twitching nervously. With him was the tall, long-nosed Donald Smith. O'Donoghue, De Salaberry, and Father Thibault joined them on the platform. On the motion of Riel, Thomas Bunn, a highly respected English half-breed, was chosen chairman. It had been arranged that De Salaberry was to be interpreter for Smith. Instead, De Salaberry nominated Riel.

It was a remarkable meeting. For five hours, in spite of constant interruptions, Smith read his documents, and Riel interpreted. For five hours, in the open, in twenty-below-zero cold, the crowd listened. When the governor general's significant words promising protection to religion and to titles to property were read, there was a burst of cheering. There was "much protest on the part of Riel and his friends." But Smith got his message across. An altercation about the documents of Father Thibault and De Salaberry revealed that O'Donoghue had them in his possession. Toward the close of the meeting a Mr. Burke shouted up to Riel: "Release the prisoners," and the cry was taken up. Riel glared down at the crowd.

"Not just yet," he answered, and armed *métis* guards moved in to break up the demonstration.

Next day the crowd was even larger. Smith finished his reading of the documents, though at one time, as he told Sir John in his report, "armed men appeared on the ground and threats were freely used to me . . . with a view to preventing the information coming to the public."

Smith's own concluding speech was effective. Those two meetings, as far as the mass of the settlers was concerned, determined that Britain and not the United States was to have the Northwest.

Riel, whatever his previous, or future, intentions, was quick to go along with the tide. He moved, seconded by Bannatyne, the election of twenty delegates from each of the English and French sections to consider Smith's commission, the date to be the twenty-fifth of January. The meeting was then concluded by speeches from Abbé Ritchot, Bishop Machray, and Louis Riel, all breathing sweetness and light and harmony. On the twenty-second a penitent Riel, meeting with seceders from his followers, shed tears and convinced them all that he had no intention of annexing Red River to the States and that his only desire was a satisfactory arrangement with Canada. So all but ten of the group friendly to Smith left the fort.

The tears of the man who had tried to prevent Canada's offers from being made known to the settlers were really tears of frustration. As soon as he had the armed superiority again, Riel seized the remaining supplies of the H.B.C. He also hung on to the prisoners. On the next night, however, the night of Sunday, January 23, the indomitable Dr. John Christian Schultz screwed a gimlet, smuggled along with a pocketknife to him by his wife in a pudding, into the window casing of his cell. To it he tied a rope made by slicing the buffalo robe on his bed into strips. Then he squeezed his six-foot-four body through the window. Part way down, the gimlet pulled out. Schultz fell heavily into the snow, one leg twisted under him. He waited a moment, anxiously. The night was cold and Riel's guards were slack. Dragging himself to the wall, by boxes piled up, Schultz got over. Somehow, in spite of his injury, he staggered four miles through the snow and cold to Kildonan. There, Robert MacBeth, the father of the author R. G. MacBeth, though he was not even a particular friend of Schultz, hid him for four days while the red-blanketed horses of the *métis* streamed by with orders to shoot the escaped prisoner on sight. Then Schultz again began to organize resistance, in concert with Thomas Scott and Charles Mair at Portage la Prairie. The next act of the drama was in preparation.

2

Riel had lost the first round to Donald Smith. When the forty delegates met in convention on the twenty-fifth, the little Napoleon maneuvered to re-establish his position. There was no more talk of annexation to the States. Nor could anyone now be more loyal to the British connection than Riel. He concentrated on a new List of Rights for Red River, based on the December 1, 1869, List of Rights; and this time the hand of Abbé Ritchot can be seen guiding the pen.

But Riel was still Riel, a man who went into a temper when he was opposed. On February 4 he added a demand that Red River be admitted to Canada as a province. The delegates voted this down. When a second motion, that the transfer of Rupert's Land by the H.B.C. to Canada be considered "null and void" and that the transfer should be negotiated only with the people of Red River, was lost, Riel raged up and down the room in which the convention was meeting.

"The devil take it," he shouted. "We must win: the vote may go as it likes; but the measure which has now been defeated must be carried."

That night, still in Hitler-like rage, he burst into the room of the fatally ill Governor Mactavish, placed a guard over him, and threatened to have him shot if the ten Léveillé half-breeds, friendly to Smith, were not sent away from the fort at once. Then he stamped over to the house of the chief factor, Dr. Cowan, and ordered him to swear allegiance to the provisional government on pain of being shot within the hour. When Cowan refused he was dumped into prison and Smith was once more put under strict guard. If the H.B.C. officers had been apathetic in allowing Riel to seize control, they now realized they had let loose a mad jinni. Riel by this time was not a selfless patriot carrying through a coolly calculated policy. He was a juvenile delinquent with a gang behind him.

By the seventh of February, however, the List of Rights was ready. It was discussed with Smith, who managed, as he reported, to prune away some of the more objectionable features. The convention then voted to accept the invitation extended from Canada by Smith to send delegates to Ottawa. Father Ritchot, Judge Black, and Alfred H. Scott, a man close to the American party, were chosen.

At this point, Riel abruptly asked for recognition of his provisional government. The English delegates still objected. A party of four went to see Governor Mactavish. The fatally ill man answered: "Form a government, for God's sake, and restore peace and order in the settlement." The English withdrew their opposition. A provisional government—but this time one with the face of legality—was set up on February 10, with Riel as President.

It is a measure of the man's character that Riel went into a fit of delirious joy. Governor Mactavish and Chief Factor Cowan were freed. The guns of the fort banged out a salute. The skyrockets brought in by Schultz to celebrate the transfer to Canada traced blazing arcs in the sky to greet Riel as President. Winnipeg went on a "regular drunk."

In spite of the concession to Riel's vanity, Smith could feel that his job was accomplished. The imbroglio brought on by John A.'s inexcusable ignorance and slackness and McDougall's stupidities and arrogance was in a fair way to being calmed. True, Riel still retained some of the prisoners, who fed his sense of power. But on February 10 he had promised to release them. Two days later he did let sixteen go, after they had signed a pledge not to take up arms against the provisional government. He released the rest on February 15. A little patience, and a peaceable transfer to Canada would be assured.

3

Patience was a virtue foreign to Charles Mair, the poet, and Thomas Scott at Portage la Prairie and to John Christian Schultz at Kildonan. None of them can be blamed overmuch. They had seen a rebel seize power. They had been arrested by the *métis*, whom they despised. They had been held prisoners in a cold and uncomfortable jail and had escaped by their own efforts. What were insulted patriots to do, especially when their compatriots were still in prison? Sit down and let the rebel flap his wings and crow like a rooster? Larger issues? What did they matter beside honor and justice? Liberate the prisoners, that was the cry.

Major Boulton tried to hold back the Portage la Prairie hotheads, not because he was in disagreement but because common sense told him his forces were ill equipped to face Riel's buffalo-hunter marksmen. When they insisted on acting, he went along. On February 9 or 10, apparently (accounts of the date differ), a poorly armed group of some sixty men set out over the snow-covered trail from Portage la Prairie to Winnipeg. At the parish of Headingly, close to Winnipeg, a number of settlers joined them for a surprise attack on Fort Garry. But the Headingly delegate to the convention told them that the prisoners were about to be released. This created a certain amount of uncertainty, and so did a blizzard. Nevertheless, at 10 P.M. of February 14, a frosty moon shining down on the gleaming snow, the party set out. When they reached Winnipeg, realizing, apparently, that to attack Fort Garry's stone walls was suicidal, they surrounded the home of Henri Coutu on the rumor that Riel was there. A search drew nothing. The crusaders then marched north to Kildonan, where Schultz joined them with more than two hundred men and one small cannon, dragged from the Stone Fort. The party camped in the church.

Their chance of success was already gone. The threat from the Canadians brought the *métis* riding into Fort Garry. Soon Riel had at least six hundred riflemen around him. Donald Smith was furious. The moderates among the English were appalled. The patriotism of Schultz, Mair, and Scott might be laudable. But it endangered the peaceable settlement which had been effected, and it had again solidified the *métis* behind Riel. Meantime, the first blood of this curiously bloodless insurrection had been spilled.

It is all of a piece with the insanity of the whole affair that it was shed by a half-wit.

Parisien was a feeble-minded *métis* youth who had been splitting firewood at Fort Garry. He decided to visit his mother at Kildonan. As he came wandering in he was arrested by the Canadians as a spy. Parisien had no idea of what a spy was. On the morning of the sixteenth, seizing a moment when the guard over him was relaxed, he grabbed a rifle from a sled and ran off, a group of men after him. Parisien made for the thickets along the river. At that unfortunate moment young John Hugh Sutherland came riding along the ice, sent by his father to announce to the Canadian party the release of the rest of the prisoners the day before and to persuade them to disperse. Parisien thought he was being intercepted. His rifle flashed. Sutherland fell from his horse, mortally wounded. Parisien's pursuers came up and pounced on the *métis*. Sutherland, as he lay dying on the ice, pleaded for Parisien.

"The poor simple fellow," he is reported to have said, "was too frightened to know what he was doing."

But Parisien was felled with an ax blow and then dragged headfirst through the snow until Major Boulton, coming up, forced his followers to stop and got medical aid. The aid was too late. Parisien died.

It was an unfortunate incident. Meanwhile, Boulton's party on this same day, the sixteenth, sent in a demand for the release of the prisoners and an amnesty for all, inclusive of Dr. Schultz. We have Riel's reply:

Gentlemen,

The prisoners are out, they have sworn to keep the peace. We have taken the responsibility for our past acts. Mr. William Mactavish has asked you, for the sake of God, to form and complete the Provisional Government. Your representatives have joined us on that ground. Who will now come and destroy Red River Settlement?

I am,
Your humble, poor, fair and confident
public servant,
Louis Riel.

Along with this letter came a verbal assurance from Riel that, if the Canadians disbanded, they would be allowed to return home quietly. They were faced with superior forces. The prisoners had been released, although it is likely that the threat from the Canadians had speeded their freedom. There was pressure on Boulton's party from Bishop Machray and other clergymen not to disturb the peace. In confusion and with a let-down feeling the expedition broke up. Boulton, very carelessly in view of what he should have known about Riel, led the Portage la Prairie group past Fort Garry on their way home. As they struggled on foot through the piled-up snowdrifts O'Donoghue and Lépine rushed out on them with a force of horsemen, followed by half a hundred men on foot. Major Boulton and forty-seven others, among them Thomas Scott, were brought back to the fort and thrust into prison.

Here was Riel's opportunity to prove himself a statesman. Instead, the man who, when he thought himself in danger, had signed the plea to the Boulton party as "Your humble, poor, fair and confident public servant" proved himself a bullying megalomaniac. Boulton was immediately tried by an excited court-martial and condemned to be shot at noon of the eighteenth. The shocked intervention of the clergy postponed the execution until midnight of Saturday, the nineteenth. When Smith at 8 P.M. of that day saw Riel, the *métis* leader, beside himself with excitement and the sense of power, told him that "the English settlers and Canadians . . . had laughed at and despised the French half-breeds. . . . An example must therefore be made. . . ."

It took the Scot two hours to change the half-frenzied Riel's mind. His terms were that Smith persuade *les Anglais* to elect representatives to the provisional government. Another version, however, is given by R. G. MacBeth in his *The Making of the Canadian West.* According to him, the parents of that young John Hugh Sutherland who had been shot by the half-wit Parisien came to plead for Boulton's life.

"It is enough," Riel said, placing his hand on the mother's shoulder as she knelt before him. "He ought to die, but I will give you his life for the life of the son you have lost through these troubles."

The stagy acting suits the man who, as "President," paraded in frock coat and moccasins and had fitted his "government house" in Fort Garry with furnishings commandeered from Schultz's home. Nor is there anything in Riel's character to prevent him from having spared Boulton's life in two separate interviews. Then, in a rapid change that again reminds one of Hilter, he invited

Boulton to join his provisional government as the representative of the Canadian party.

Even before his court-martial of Boulton, Riel had condemned Gaddy, a half-breed who had rallied to Boulton's cause, to be shot. According to Gaddy, three times in the depth of night he was roused in his cell by armed men who pointed their rifles at him but, because they knew him, could not bring themselves to shoot. Danger livened Gaddy's wits. Working himself through a porthole of the bastion in which he was locked, he escaped. Meantime, Riel had horsemen scouring the snow-swept countryside for the man he hated, John Christian Schultz. The indomitable doctor, partly crippled though he was, by dog sled and on foot covered by way of Duluth the hundreds of miles between Red River and Ontario. Years later he was to be knighted and to become a lieutenant governor of the new province of Manitoba. Unfortunately, his escape only hardened Riel's determination that blood must be spilled to make Canada respect him.

4

Shortly after 1 P.M. of March 4, young Thomas Scott stood in prayer with Reverend Young, the Methodist minister, by the stone wall of Fort Garry. After a few moments the minister left him. Scott knelt in the snow. To one side was his coffin with a drape of white cotton over it. In front of him was a firing squad of six *métis*, all partially drunk. Behind them was a group of spectators. A command was spoken by André Nault, Riel's cousin. The rifles were raised and aimed. Three of them—no one knew which—were loaded with ball, the other three with blank charges. The command to fire was given. A ragged volley rang out. Scott fell to the snow, pierced by three balls. He was still alive. François Guilmette ran up and put a revolver bullet into his head.

What the spectators had watched was a sacrifice to the megalomania of a sawdust dictator. Scott had been a violent young man. He had been a ringleader of the attack on Snow, the surveyor. It was said that, months before McDougall's arrival, for some unexplained reason, he had attacked Riel with his fists in Winnipeg. Throughout the disturbances he had supported the Canadian party. He had escaped from his first imprisonment on January 9. When imprisoned the second time, he had been put in irons, for, according to Alexander Begg, the diarist, "having been indiscreet in the use of his tongue while in prison." Later, Bishop Taché, in trying to defend Riel, said that, when Coutu's house was surrounded by the Portage la Prairie party, Scott had entered it "with the intention of killing him [Riel] or, according to others, of seizing him as a hostage."

The good bishop's defense was very weak. Riel himself, according to Smith, told him that Scott had been "rough and abusive to the guards and insulting to him, Mr. Riel." There was Scott's real crime. He had been indiscreet enough not to treat Riel as if he were God Almighty and his *métis,* archangels. So Riel haled him before a "Council of War," presided over by Ambroise Lépine, under the charge of having taken up arms against the provisional government (as scores of others had done) and of having struck *"l'un des capitaines des gardes."* Riel acted as one of the three witnesses against Scott and as prosecutor as well. The accused man was not permitted to call witnesses. He was condemned to death in a burlesque of a trial. The French clergy did little, if anything, to save him. Smith's first hint of the affair was at 10 A.M. on the day of the execution, when Père Lestanc called on him, told of the imminent arrival of Bishop Taché (on the plea of the Canadian Government, which had sneered at his warning, the Bishop had cut short his visit to Rome), and then mentioned that the "conduct of the prisoners was very unsatisfactory" and that he was afraid "the guards might be forced to retaliate in self-defense."

What that meant, Smith did not discover until at 11 A.M. the Reverend Mr. Young, after a brief conversation with Père Lestanc in the hall, came and told Smith that "it was intended to shoot Thomas Scott." This time Smith's appeals failed.

As if conscious of his guilt, Riel refused Scott's body for burial both to the Reverend Young and to the Anglican bishop of Rupert's Land. No one knew where the young man was interred. The probable explanation seems to be that his coffin was sunk secretly and at night through the ice into the Red River.

The ghost of that murder, years later, was to lead Riel to the scaffold at a place which, in 1870, was called "Pile of Bones." What Donald Smith thought of it is seen in his statement: "After that date I held no communication whatsoever with Riel, except with reference to getting away from the country, which I was not allowed to leave without a pass."

Smith got his pass a fortnight later. On his way back to St. Paul he met J. J. Hill. Out of this meeting was to come, ultimately, the Canadian Pacific Railway.

Meantime, Riel was still riding high. When his former patron, Bishop Taché, returned, he was held for two or three days under house arrest in his palace. But the Bishop had brought with him the promise of an amnesty, though it should be noted that this had been issued before the murder of Scott. The Bishop completed the work Smith had done. It was decided to release the prisoners and send off the delegates to Ottawa.

Once they left on March 23 and 24, any notion of annexation to the States was, as Begg noted, "knocked on the head." The *New Nation* passed from the editorship of the American Robinson to that of Thomas Spence, the man who had once proclaimed the "Republic of Manitoba." On April 20, Riel, now a most loyal subject of the Queen, ordered that the Union Jack should replace the flag of the "New Nation" over Fort Garry. O'Donoghue, the Fenian, pulled down the Union Jack. Riel reversed the process. At last the Union Jack stayed, but O'Donoghue was permitted to take the flagstaff from Dr. Schultz's home—which was taller—plant it in the fort in front of Dr. Cowan's home, and fly the flag of the "New Nation" on it. As the two played their juvenile game the settlement began to return to normal. By the twenty-eighth of April the H.B.C. was open for business. Soon the steamer from Georgetown, the *International*, was tied up at the dock once more. Except for the provisional government and a small body of armed guards around Riel, the winter's nightmare was over.

There was one last flutter of life from the annexationists. In April the U.S. consul at Winnipeg, Malmros, wrote Washington to ask if he could "recognize" the provisional government, while James Wickes Taylor, the secret agent who had followed the Red River delegates to Ottawa, urged the same course. In the U. S. Senate, Zachariah Chandler demanded that Rupert's Land be recognized as an independent state and then annexed.

Wiser heads knew that the moment had gone by. In spite of bungling, Canada had won the Northwest. Both she and Red River, however, were to pay for their separate stupidities.

CHAPTER XIX

1870–75

Manitoba Becomes a Province—The Wolseley Expedition to Red River—A Fenian Raid—The Question of an Amnesty for Riel

1

RIEL, apparently, dismissed Scott's murder airily. Ontario felt otherwise. With Schultz, Mair, and others of those whom Riel had jailed fanning the fire, the flames of indignation leaped high. Punishment of the rebels was demanded. Inevitably, Quebec reacted in favor of their compatriots. The foundations were laid for a religious and racial dispute far beyond Riel's personal importance. Meantime, when Father Ritchot and Alfred H. Scott reached Ottawa they were arrested for complicity in Thomas Scott's murder and lodged in jail.

John A. got them out. When he and Cartier came to deal with the delegates, however, they discovered that demands for provincial status and denominational schools to be supported by public funds pro rata to the number of adherents (which meant, in effect, separate schools for Roman Catholics) had been added to the List of Rights as passed by the convention in Red River. John A. found himself squeezed between Cartier's Quebec supporters and the mounting demand for vengeance from Ontario. On April 29, when Sir Stafford Northcote, governor of the H.B.C., who was in Ottawa, came down for breakfast he was greeted by the words: "Bad news, Sir John A. has broken out again."

On Monday, May 2, however, John A. was in his place to put through the Manitoba Act. Then an attack of gallstones felled him. Cartier had to complete the job. Whatever criticisms may be directed at Riel as a dictator not big enough for the shoes he attempted to put on, his insurrection at least got Red River all that was demanded. It was made a postage-stamp province, only some 11,000 square miles in all. It should be recorded, perhaps, that, by extensions of its boundaries in 1881 and again in 1912, Manitoba was increased to its present area of 246,512 square miles. In 1870, however, though less than a twentieth of what it was to become, it received a lieutenant governor (who was also to govern the rest of the Northwest), a nominated upper house of seven, and an elected provincial assembly of twenty-four members. Two Dominion senators and four federal members were assigned to it with a provision for an increase as population rose. One new item was that its natural resources were to belong to the Dominion and not to the province. Yet, 1,400,000 acres of land were reserved for the half-breeds and their children, while all existing titles and occupancies were to be respected. Furthermore, denominational schools and the official equality of the French and English languages were granted, a feature which, years later, was to lead to the defeat of a Conservative government. The act received royal assent on the twelfth of May 1870. On the fifteenth of July of the same year the Northwest became part of Canada.

Riel had won. But with his other hand, to meet the protest in Ontario, John A. bestowed a military expedition.

2

Church bells were ringing on the banks of the Red River between Lake Winnipeg and Lower Fort Garry, twenty miles north of Winnipeg. There were cheers from the shore. Indians fired salutes. It was August 23, 1870, and the boats carrying the 1200 soldiers of Colonel Garnet Wolseley were moving upstream to the Stone Fort.

Wolseley, a slight, quick man with alert blue eyes, was an Imperial officer who was to go on to fame. Along with him was Captain Redvers Buller, later to be an unsuccessful general in the Boer War. The troops were a mixed force of Imperials and Canadian militia, the latter almost entirely English-speaking because French Canadians, except for a total of seventy-seven, had refused to enlist in the battalion which was drawn from Quebec. With the route through the United States blocked, it had taken Wolseley ninety-six days, or over three months, to bring his forces from Ontario to Red River. At Sault Ste. Marie the Americans had refused to allow a ship loaded with supplies through their canal, the only practicable one, so that the supplies had had to be portaged to Lake Superior and the men marched across. When the expedition reached Prince Arthur's Landing near Fort William, it was to find that only thirty miles of the Dawson canoe-and-portage route was ready. Wolseley bought and built huge boats. Then, cutting roads and portaging the boats wherever necessary on wooden rollers while carting along rifles, ammunition, food supplies, and even cannon and cannon balls, his troops began a fantastic trek through the wilderness. At Fort Frances an Indian chief, Crooked Neck, had to be bought off by presents of flour and salt pork. By the time the expedition reached Lake of the Woods the soldiers were a tough, work-hardened lot. Thence, Wolseley voyaged them down the difficult Winnipeg River to Lake Winnipeg. It all proved that, somehow, Canada must establish a better line of communication through her own territory to the Northwest.

When his troops reached Lower Fort Garry, Wolseley sent squads of his Imperials on foot along either bank while the rest stayed in the boats. There were rumors that Riel would resist. That night Wolseley camped six miles north of Winnipeg. That same night a terrific storm of wind and rain hit his camp, overturning tents and metamorphosing the countryside into a sticky mass of Manitoba "gumbo."

As Wolseley was advancing and then encamping, Riel, at Fort Garry, was pondering what to do. When the news came that Manitoba had been made a province and that until the new lieutenant governor arrived (he was to be not William McDougall but the Honorable A. G. Archibald of Nova Scotia) Riel and his provisional government were to rule, there had been ringing of bells and *feux de joie*. Riel began to work at a speech to deliver when the lieutenant governor appeared.

But the amnesty which Riel believed to have been promised seemed to be unaccountably delayed. Rumors of a cry in Ontario for punishment for Scott's murder began to filter in. It seemed suspicious, too, that, late in July, an emissary from Wolseley, Lieutenant William Butler, on arriving on the steamboat *International*, had jumped ashore before the boat docked and gone into hiding. Though Riel sent out to arrest him, the guards were not able to locate him. It was encouraging that when Butler finally came in to see him he brought a pacific message from Wolseley to be circulated in Red River. Riel would not have been flattered, however, by the description Butler, an Englishman, wrote of him:

"A short, stout man with a large head," Butler put down, "a sallow, puffy face, a sharp, restless, intelligent eye, a square-cut, massive forehead overhung by a mass of long and thickly-clustering hair, and marked with well-cut eyebrows. . . ."

If Wolseley was convinced that his mission was peaceful, the Canadian volunteers were of a contrary opinion. Reports came in to Riel that around their campfires they knew that their job was to avenge Scott and punish the rebel, Riel. O'Donoghue tried to persuade his leader to ambush the soldiers in the wilderness. Riel, who had by this time convinced himself that all his actions were justifiable, now stood out for peaceable union with Canada. His followers, uncertain of what would happen when the troops arrived, began to melt away.

So Riel waited at Fort Garry. On the twenty-third he and O'Donoghue led out two scouting parties to see if they could get information about the temper of the troops. They heard nothing to reassure them. When, at 1 A.M. of the twenty-fourth, in the midst of the wild gale, they returned to the fort, the members of the council began to disappear one by one until only Riel and O'Donoghue were left.

On that same morning at 6 A.M., Wolseley got his troops moving and landed at Point Douglas. Rumors were still flying. It was said that Riel had issued ammunition to his men.

Wolseley sent his Imperials plodding toward the fort. The sky was leaden. Mist shrouded the prairie. Each step was like drawing a boot from a quagmire. Stops had to be made to clean the gumbo from the clogged wheels of the carts and of the two brass cannon. The line of skirmishers glimpsed the stone walls of the fort through the mist. The north gate was closed. The cannon stared at them. At any moment they expected those cannon to belch flame. They did not know that Riel and O'Donoghue had been watching them approach. As the skirmishers reached the walls the two men hurried out the gate at the back, got together a temporary raft, and fled across the river. Scarcely had they left when two horsemen from Wolseley's force, moving around to the south gate, found it open. They dashed in and pulled up their steeds. The fort stood empty. Across the river, Ambroise Lépine with them, Riel and O'Donoghue were galloping toward the border and Pembina. The erstwhile dictator's first appearance on Canada's stage was over.

Wolseley had brought only his Imperials with him on the twenty-fourth of August. On the twenty-seventh the Canadians came in. Donald Smith, who had hurried up to Fort Alexander on Lake Winnipeg to meet the Wolseley expedition, was, as representative of the H.B.C., the temporary governor until Archibald arrived via the United States on the second of September. Lieutenant Butler gives a good description of the celebration.

"The miserable looking village [Winnipeg]," he wrote, "produced as if by magic more saloons than any of twice its size in the States could boast. The vilest compounds of intoxicating liquors were sold and for a time it seemed as if the place had become a very pandemonium."

On August 29 and September 3 the British regulars left for the East and, ultimately, England. Lieutenant Governor Archibald tried to establish order. But the vengeful Schultz was back in Red River and the Ontario soldiers knew why they had come.

The first victim of reprisal was Elzéar Goulet, who had voted on the "court-martial" to condemn Scott. He was imprudent enough to appear in Winnipeg on September 13. Two soldiers and a civilian chased him to the river. He tried to swim across but was stoned until he sank. François Guilmette, who had administered the *coup de grâce* to Scott, was killed near Pembina. André Nault, at whose farm, less than a year before, the survey had been stopped, was bayoneted and left for dead. He had given the signal to Scott's firing squad. Two or three others were also killed.

The real authors of the crime, Riel and O'Donoghue, escaped. They even returned to Red River. On September 17 they had a meeting with the *métis* leaders at the Rivière Sale, where the famous barricade had been. A petition to President Grant of the United States was drafted. Riel refused to sign it.

This split the friendship between the two men. O'Donoghue sent the petition to President Grant and then followed it to Washington. The freebooting senator from Minnesota, Ramsey, got him an interview with the President. When Grant gave no encouragement, O'Donoghue turned to the Fenians. "General" O'Neill of Niagara Peninsula fame came back with him to the borders of Manitoba. Their plan was to enlist the cutthroats and outlaws on the fringe of U.S. territory along with the thousands of unemployed railroad workers who were strung that winter of 1871 across the northern states. The belief was that a mere crossing of the border would cause a *métis* uprising.

Lieutenant Governor Archibald had, however, done a good job of pacification. On December 30 of 1870 the first provincial elections were held. Dr. Schultz, incidentally, was defeated by Donald Smith, who became M.P.P. for Winnipeg. When, on October 5, 1871, O'Donoghue—now, by the grace of the Fenians, "General" O'Donoghue—and "General" O'Neill crossed the border with thirty men, who, according to J. J. Hill, were "20 of the hardest looking roughs and ten Pembina loafers," they captured the H.B.C. post easily. They plundered it and loaded a wagon with provisions. But suddenly they saw Colonel Wheaton and twenty-three of his soldiers coming up.

"As soon as the Fenian leaders saw U.S. troops coming over the Canadian boundary," Hill recounts, "they at once dropped everything and fled. And such a flight! Some on foot and some on Indian ponies, with the wagon-load of provisions scattering to the woody banks of the Red River."

The crossing of the border by U.S. troops had been arranged between Washington and Governor Archibald by James Wickes Taylor, the erstwhile spy, who was now U.S. consul at Winnipeg and, in a change of heart, a supporter of the authority he had tried to prevent. The American troops captured ten of the Fenians, inclusive of O'Neill. That same afternoon O'Donoghue was picked up by *métis* and turned over to Colonel Wheaton. The prisoners were taken to Pembina, tried by an American court, and released.

This was the farcical ending of the Fenian raids. O'Donoghue, discredited, wandered south, got a job as a country schoolteacher in Minnesota, fell in love with an Irish girl, and on March 26, 1878, died of tuberculosis. The former treasurer of Riel's provisional government is buried three miles from Rosemount in Minnesota. O'Neill was to turn up once again following his *idée fixe,* this time, in 1872, planning an invasion of British Columbia.

3

But what of Riel? He had been in and out of Manitoba a dozen times before O'Donoghue's comic-opera invasion. Just before the arrival of the Fenians, Governor Archibald had issued a general mobilization order. The fear, of course, was of a *métis* uprising. (In the whole province there was only a garrison of eighty men at Fort Garry.) That the *métis* did not rise was due to Riel and to the Roman Catholic clergy, to whom, indeed, the Irish Fenian movement was anathema. Riel and Lépine, therefore, although at the time warrants for their arrest were out in Winnipeg, organized several companies of *métis* to defend the province. Because of the action of the U.S. troops these men were not needed. But, in gratitude, Archibald crossed the river to St. Boniface, reviewed the *métis* troop, and shook hands with Riel and Lépine, while pretending not to know who they were. The Toronto *Globe* accused him of shaking hands with murderers.

Riel, undoubtedly, hoped that this would help bring him an amnesty. Amnesty had become such a hot potato that even Sir John A. did not dare to handle it.

Before the murder of Scott an amnesty had been certain. Bishop Taché, indeed, continued to declare that the amnesty had been promised him, to cover all acts, including the killing of Scott. Father Ritchot also asserted that when in Ottawa as a delegate, after Scott's murder, he had received the verbal assurance of an amnesty from both the governor general and Cartier.

Whether such an amnesty had been promised verbally or not, Scott's death was soon blown up into such a flaming issue that John A. could only hem and haw. A "Canada First" movement in Ontario took up the Scott case as its banner. The *Globe* raised the shout of loyalty. The Orange Order, of which Scott had been a member, was in full cry. The Scott case was one of the causes which in Ontario on December 15, 1871, put the provincial Conservatives out of office, and the Liberals, under Edward Blake, into power.

The emotion in Ontario fired a counterreaction in Quebec. Soon the Quebec press was accusing the *Globe* and the *Telegraph* of striving for the "extermination of the French *métis* of Red River." Riel, "a man frank, just and noble, whom it is desired to crucify," became a hero, and Scott, "an ignoble victim who was about to plunge the steel during the night into the heart of his sovereign."

This sort of absurd emotionalizing and the equal hysteria in Ontario forced John A. to throw the red-hot iron of amnesty for Riel to the British Government. The British Government promptly tossed it back. John A. did nothing until the news of Governor Archibald shaking Riel's hand caused Edward Blake, the new

Premier of Ontario, to offer a reward of $5000 for the capture of Riel. Sir John was forced to move. Publicly, he said:

"Where is Riel? God knows. I wish I could lay my hands on him."

Privately, he sent $1000 to Bishop Taché to persuade Riel and Lépine to stay outside of Canada. A thousand was scarcely enough. The Governor and Taché on February 6, 1872, got Donald Smith to put up six hundred pounds to be repaid by the Dominion government. With this additional amount, Lépine and Riel were induced to leave Manitoba for a year.

Riel failed to keep the undertaking. When in August of 1872 the Dominion elections came on, he was nominated for the Manitoba seat of Provencher.

Elections in Manitoba in those days were as riotous as they are now, at times, in the province of Quebec. Donald Smith, M.P.P. for Winnipeg, was running in the federal seat of Selkirk, which included Winnipeg. A Mr. Wilson opposed him. Election day was a continuous series of fights. Two attempts were made to seize the pollbooks. At St. Boniface, Smith's supporters were attacked with pistols and ax handles. Before the day was over the militia had to be called out in Winnipeg. Even so, the chief of police was seriously wounded and the printing offices of both the *Manitoban* and *Le Métis* were destroyed.

Virtue seems to have gone out of Anglo-Saxons since those ebullient years. Elections, it will be remembered, were also dragged out for a fortnight. So it came to pass that Sir George Cartier was defeated in Montreal, and Sir John A. wired Governor Archibald:

"Get Sir George elected in your province."

Archibald and Taché went to Riel, got him and his opponent to withdraw, and Cartier went in. Naturally, Riel felt that Sir John A. was now under an obligation to him. No amnesty came. Then, in May of 1873, the great French Canadian, Cartier, died. His death removed from Canada one of its two principal Fathers of Confederation, a man who, most of all French-Canadian statesmen, perhaps, exemplified the strengths and failings of his compatriots. It cost Sir John A. his right hand. It likewise brought on a by-election in Provencher. Riel was elected by acclamation. When shortly thereafter, in 1874, another Dominion election followed the "Pacific Scandal," Riel was again returned.

Though he was at the time a fugitive from justice (the Grand

Jury of Manitoba had returned a true bill against him as one of the murderers of Thomas Scott), in an episode reminiscent of Gilbert and Sullivan, except for the underlying note of tragedy, he reached Ottawa in the spring of 1874, where the Liberal government of Alexander Mackenzie was now in power. With the help of a Quebec colleague, he actually signed the register of members.

After four days he left Ottawa and went into hiding in Montreal. Then Dr. Schultz, his old antagonist, by this time M.P. for Lisgar, got a motion passed expelling Riel from the House. At about the same time, Riel's adjutant general, Lépine, was at last caught, tried for the murder of Scott, and convicted.

This unloosed the flood. From all parts of the Dominion no less than 252 petitions for clemency bearing 58,568 names poured in. The final result was that on June 15, 1875, the new governor general of Canada, Lord Dufferin, on his own responsibility but doubtless with a huge sigh of relief from the then Prime Minister, Mackenzie, commuted Lépine's death sentence to two years' imprisonment and forfeiture of political rights. Shortly thereafter a bill was passed giving full amnesty to everyone concerned in the Riel Rebellion except Riel, Lépine, and O'Donoghue. O'Donoghue was left in the outer darkness. For Riel and Lépine the sentence was amnesty after five years' banishment from "Her Majesty's Dominions." Two years later O'Donoghue, just before his death, was granted forgiveness.

The amnesty had been too long deferred for Riel to regard it as mercy. It was his fixed conviction that he was a martyr.

CHAPTER XX

1864–71

British Columbia and Vancouver Island Separate and Again Unite—The Continuing Search for Gold—The Annexationist Party in British Columbia—The Pacific Coast Joins the Dominion

1

BY 1870 Canada reached as far as the Rockies. Beyond those shining ramparts the future of British Columbia was still uncertain. In 1864, when the era of James Douglas ended, the two colonies of Vancouver Island and British Columbia had, somewhat huffily, gone their separate ways.

Scarcely had the ship bearing Douglas away reached London when tragedy struck. Alfred Waddington of Victoria had taken up a charter to build a road from Bute Inlet, some two hundred miles north of New Westminster, to the Cariboo gold fields. On the night of April 30 the road workers were asleep in their tents. From the deep bush shadowy figures seeped out to surround the tents. At a signal knives and axes sliced through the guy ropes. The canvas collapsed. As the whites inside, startled and only half awake, began to shout and struggle, a blast of rifle fire blazed. Knives, stabbing through the canvas, finished the work. Of seventeen men, fourteen had been killed outright and two badly wounded. The canvas was pulled aside. The killers mutilated the corpses. Twenty-one Chilcotin Indian braves under Chief Klatsassin had avenged the rape of their women by the whites and their own treatment when they had been forced to feed on bacon rinds, bones, and tea leaves flung out from the work camps.

Later, the same band shot a ferryman and a lone settler and attacked a pack train. Here, of seven men, three were killed and three others wounded.

To New Westminster it was an Indian uprising. In high excitement punitive expeditions, at the cost of $80,000, were sent into the rugged and virtually unexplored Chilcotin country. It was some time before the authorities realized that only a small group of Indians was involved. Finally, eight braves surrendered. Two turned queen's evidence. Five were hanged. The far-flung Indian war turned out to be a damp squib.

This was only one of the troubles which plagued the new regime of Governor Seymour. Gold had founded British Columbia and had opened up the interior. By 1864, even though the Cariboo Road was operating, the first wild flush of excitement in that area was over. Deep diggings had replaced the surface mining and deep diggings meant investment of capital. The casual miners drifted to Wild Horse Creek in the Kootenay country, where nugget gold had been found. To give British Columbia merchants a chance at the profits, Douglas' Dewdney Trail was pushed at great expense into the Kootenay area. Before it could be finished, the miners had flocked north to the Big Bend of the Columbia River. Another trail in search of a market was built from Cache Creek on the Cariboo Road to Savona Ferry at the west end of Kamloops Lake. Thence a steamer ran to Seymour, the new gold camp which had sprung up over night.

The finds were disappointing. The miners drifted back to Idaho and Montana. The supplies freighted in by British Columbia merchants at a high cost, and bought and sold on credit, were a loss. By 1866 bankruptcy faced merchants and dealers and the gold roads seemed a loss, too. Depression ruled.

On Vancouver Island the same pall of gloom rested. Amor de Cosmos, the gadfly who had tormented Douglas, did a *volte-face.* He now shouted for union with the mainland. The Imperial Government obliged by the Act of Union of August 1866 with an expanded legislative council of twenty-three instead of fifteen and Governor Seymour to rule. On June 24, 1867, one week before ringing bells and slamming guns celebrated the first Dominion Day in the East, the first session of the Council of the United Colonies was held in the main barracks of the Royal Engineers at New Westminster. Victoria was chosen as capital. The British

Columbia of today, a huge, rugged, and scenic kingdom of 366,255 square miles, had finally been established. What its future was to be was still to be determined.

2

Both Canada and the United States were hot after the province which gold had made famous. The search for the yellow lure continued. The old creeks were revisited. Then, like hungry and industrious ants, the miners fanned out to the streams of the Far North. In 1869, gold was found on the creeks flowing into the Omineca River. Four years later a prospector, Thibert, discovered a new Eldorado in the almost inaccessible Cassiar country in the northeast tip of the colony. By the next year some 1600 men were mining on Dease and Thibert creeks. The returns were close to $1,000,000. In 1875 some 1300 claims in the same country produced $800,000. Two years later the biggest nugget ever found in British Columbia, a $1300 hunk of gold, was turned up on McDame Creek. Meantime the deep diggings of the Cariboo were still putting money into British Columbian pockets. In 1875, thirteen claims on Lightning Creek produced, officially, nearly $1,480,000.

For twenty years the search for gold was the principal mainstay of British Columbia. In the same period, although almost unnoticed, farming and dairying had been developing, especially on Vancouver Island and in the Fraser River delta. Coal mining continued, the salmon invited fisheries and the huge trees lumbering. North of New Westminster on the shores of the magnificent natural harbor of Burrard Inlet, tiny settlements were being made. In 1863, T. W. Graham had set up a sawmill which two years later was to become Moody's Mill, a nucleus for the settlement of Moodyville. Further up the inlet a seam of coal had been found at the inner neck of what is now Stanley Park and the place was called Coal Harbor. Soon Hastings Mill was established to the southeast of Coal Harbor. The camp that grew up around it was named Granville. Vancouver had been born.

The logical market for the slowly developing products of the colony was along the southern Pacific coast to the south. With the Hudson's Bay Company gone down the drain, there were no longer any real links of trade or transportation with Canada, while the mountains stood as a permanent geographical barrier. What ties of sentiment and memory existed were with Britain, and these were but feeble deterrents to the pull of the American Pacific coast. By 1867, too, British Columbia was squeezed between the States and the Seward-purchased Alaska. An annexationist party was formed in Victoria, with Dr. J. S. Helmcken, the man who had been surgeon at the fort there in 1849, as one of its principal leaders. To him and his followers, British Columbia was the natural passageway between Alaska and the American Pacific states, and there were visions of Victoria as the principal port north of San Francisco.

The United States was more than willing. In April of 1867 the press of New York spread the rumor that British Columbia would be ceded to satisfy the *Alabama* claims. Meanwhile the venerable London *Times* editorialized pontifically that if the inhabitants of British Columbia found it "more convenient to slip into the United States than into the Dominion . . . we all know that we should not attempt to withstand them."

Cheered by this support, in 1867 the annexationists presented a petition for union with the States, first to the Colonial office in London and then directly to President Johnson of the United States. The future of Red River and of the Northwest was, at that moment, also in the balance scales. The United States encouraged unofficial infiltration but was unwilling to risk an overt move.

Meanwhile annexationism had given birth to a counterreaction. The ebullient leader was the handsome, long-bearded Amor de Cosmos. On March 19, 1867, he got the Legislative Council to pass a resolution for British Columbia to enter Confederation. London replied that any action would have to wait until the future of Rupert's Land was determined. To Amor de Cosmos, opposition was a spur to action. By May of 1868 he had formed a Confederation League in Victoria with branches in New Westminster, Hope, Yale, Lytton, and Cariboo.

It was still a battle where all economic logic was on the side of the annexationists. Governor Seymour was apathetic. To add weight to Helmcken's party, on May 10, 1869, far to the south, Leland Stanford drove the last spike, one of gold, into the track of the Union Pacific, the first North American transcontinental. Its western terminus was San Francisco, and from San Francisco steamers ran north to Victoria. Two years before this, Jay Cooke had begun to build the Northern Pacific toward Puget Sound.

Who now could doubt where the interests of British Columbia ought to lie?

By this time the mercurial Amor de Cosmos had found an ally in John A. Macdonald. With the bargain for the Northwest completed, he wrote to the Colonial Office that now was the time to put "the screws on Vancouver Island, and the first thing to do is to recall Governor Seymour. . . . We shall then have to fight only the Yankee adventurers and the annexation party proper. . . ."

Fortune removed Seymour through a fatal illness on June 10, 1869, while on an expedition against the Haida Indians. Anthony Musgrave, who as governor of Newfoundland had striven to bring that colony into Confederation, took his place. There was a violent debate in the "goose pens," also called "bird cages," which Douglas had built in Victoria. Helmcken argued that British Columbia's interests must come first and that "ultimately not only this colony, but the whole Dominion of Canada may well be absorbed by the United States." Amor de Cosmos called for Confederation. "We are here laying," he said, "the cornerstone of a great nation on the Pacific coast."

In British North America in the nineteenth century the pull of British sentiment always overcame the logic of geopolitics. The vote was for Confederation. On May 10 of 1870 three delegates left Victoria to negotiate with Ottawa. Dr. R. W. W. Carroll and Mr. Joseph Trutch, who had made a fortune from the tolls over his suspension bridge on the Cariboo Trail, were two. The third, apparently on the same principle whereby the Athenians sent Nicias as one of the commanders of the Syracusan expedition which he had opposed, was Dr. J. S. Helmcken.

By the time the British Columbians reached Ottawa on June 10, the Manitoba Act had been passed and John A. was convalescing from his illness. Cartier handled the negotiations. Agreement was soon reached. The outstanding provisions were that Canada was to assume British Columbia's debt and pay her interest at 5 per cent on the difference between her debt and an estimated debt of $27.77 per head for a 60,000 population (the white population was about 10,000), that the new province was to be represented in the Dominion government by three senators and six M.P.s and that the Dominion should commence a transcontinental railway within two years and complete it within ten.

On July 20, 1871, British Columbia became, formally, part of Canada. What in 1850 had seemed a mere exercise in imagination had become reality. There was a Dominion stretching from sea unto sea.

That Dominion was not yet a true unity. In the East the Maritimes were still split off by geography and temperament from the St. Lawrence Valley. Nor was Confederation a strong enough magic to erase the deep-seated hatreds between Quebec Catholic and Ontario Protestant or to bridge the thousand miles of rock and trees between Ontario and the Northwest or to people the empty prairies and the rugged mountains. By 1871, the *disjecta membra* of British North America, except for Prince Edward Island and Newfoundland, had had the cloak of a single name tossed loosely over them. But Canada was as yet the name of a nation which was not a nation. The infant had still to grow from infancy to adolescence and thence to maturity.

CHAPTER XXI

1871–73

Fish and Politics in Washington—The Pacific Scandal Defeats the Macdonald Government and Delays the Transcontinental

1

IN 1867 John A. Macdonald had stood on a pinnacle of achievement. From such a peak all paths lead in only one direction. The first savage blow was the Red River insurrection. A second shock, though not as severe a one, was the defeat of the pro-Confederation forces in Newfoundland in December of 1869. Then came the discovery that the daughter born of his second marriage was not, and would never be, a normal child. On top of this, in the winter of 1870, to meet his debts, he had to mortgage all his assets to the Merchants' Bank of Canada. Finally, on May 6 of the same year, came the attack of gallstones which almost cost him his life. An ancient Greek would have said that Nemesis pursued him.

Meanwhile, in spite of the settlement of the Red River problem and success with British Columbia and the recovery of his health, another storm was brewing. This one blew in from the fishing grounds. The American cancellation of Reciprocity in March 1866 had nullified the privilege of New England fishermen to cast their nets and hooks wherever they pleased in Canadian and Newfoundland waters. In the seasons of 1866 and 1867 only a small fee was charged them. In the next two years the licenses were high and were evaded. In 1870, therefore, the Dominion decided to issue no licenses but to invoke the 1818 convention by which American fishermen could not take fish within the three-mile limit off the coasts of Canada. Fitting out six marine cruisers, the Canadians seized over 400 American fishing vessels which had broken the law.

The United States snarled like a dog driven away from its legitimate bone. In his annual message to Congress, President Grant referred scornfully to "the Colonial authority known as the Dominion of Canada," which as a "semi-independent but irresponsible agent has exercised its delegated power in an unfriendly way."

Until 1870 Great Britain had not paid too much attention to American protests about the fisheries or to their claims for compensation for the damage done by the *Alabama* during the Civil War. The Americans, however, though they seemed to regard the Fenian raids into Canada as a sportive exercise, had, quite rightly, taken strong exception to the *Alabama*'s activities. Senator Sumner had even calculated that the *Alabama* had prolonged the Civil War for many months and that, therefore, Britain should pay all the costs of the war for those months or else cede the whole of Canada in settlement.

It was the fantastic nature of the claims which had made Britain shrug them off. But in 1870 the empire of Napoleon III fell before Bismarck and Von Moltke like the proverbial house of cards. The balance of Europe was upset. Russia immediately denounced the clauses of the 1856 Treaty of Paris which had forbidden her to establish bases on the Black Sea. In consequence, Britain became abruptly anxious to secure her American flank. Before Canada could shake a puzzled head, Sir John found himself in Washington in the winter of 1871 as one of a joint British-Canadian commission to confer on the fisheries, the *Alabama* demands, the Canadian claims for damages done by the Fenians, and the long-deferred ownership of San Juan Island, south of Victoria.

For once John A. found himself cast as Little Red Ridinghood among the wolves; and the wolves were after the fisheries Red Ridinghood carried in her basket. By smirking coincidence the American representatives were headed by Hamilton Fish, the solemn-faced, big-jowled man who had done his best to swallow Red River Settlement. The five British commissioners were led by the Earl de Grey and Ripon, a handsome man with a scorn for colonials and a beard that would have graced any bull bison.

John A.'s hope was to trade the Canadian fisheries for a wide reciprocity agreement. The purpose of the Britishers was to sacrifice them for a general settlement of all the American-British difficulties. When they discovered that Macdonald was not ready to say "yes, sir," they regarded him with the amazement of gods who have been challenged by a mortal, and a barbarian at that. There followed a pretty little intrigue, not of the Britishers against the Americans, but of the Britishers against Macdonald. When the Britishers communicated with London behind Macdonald's back, it was right and proper. When John A. did the same, it was to Earl de Grey "treachery" and "slippery moral behaviour." To add to John A.'s indignation, the British Foreign Office had forgotten to put Canada's claims for damages from the Fenian raids on the agenda. The Americans, therefore, refused to discuss them.

The winter ran out as John A. squirmed and wriggled. Then the weeks dragged by in ideal spring weather, with entertainment and parties in between the meetings. Some wag quipped that the British high commissioners were a "High Commission on Joints." The Britishers then called themselves "High Joints" and their secretaries and aides "Cutlets." But to them Macdonald was a spoiled ham.

Finally, out of patience with a colonial who refused to hand over the fisheries he owned, the Gladstone government, which was in power in Britain, devised a masterpiece of chicanery. Earl de Grey was authorized to negotiate the sale of the fisheries over Macdonald's head but the articles affecting Canada were to take effect only when ratified by the Dominion Parliament. Macdonald knew that faced with a *fait accompli* there would be little that the Dominion could do. Red Ridinghood was caught. As a small concession, there was a "hint" that Britain might herself recompense Canada for her Fenian claims.

To appease the Americans, then, the fisheries were turned over to them for twelve years for a cash payment to be settled by arbitration (Canada, later, got $5,500,000 for them). Free navigation of the St. Lawrence *in perpetuity* was also given to the United States in return for similar Canadian rights on Lake Michigan and on three remote streams in Alaska. In return, the *Alabama* claims were submitted to an arbitration, which finally awarded the Americans $15,500,000, and the ownership of San Juan Island was referred to the decision of the Kaiser, who turned it over to the States.

It was another in the long series of negotiations in which British emissaries sacrificed Canadian interests on the altar of American appeasement. The Dominion was so indignant that the Washington Treaty was to lead ultimately to a demand that Canada handle her own foreign affairs. Meanwhile, all that John A. was able to salvage was a guarantee of a loan from Britain of £2,500,000 for railways and canals by way of compensation for the Fenian claims Britain had forgotten to press at Washington.

The loan was timely. For Canada now had to turn to the transcontinental promised to British Columbia. Already in 1871 Sandford Fleming, as engineer in chief with eight hundred men in twenty-one sections under him, had begun a costly and plodding survey of the route. Canada's Parliament had soon decided also to turn over the financing and construction to private enterprise with government cash grants and lavish gifts of Dominion lands to stir capitalists to action.

2

A transcontinental! Pickings! The hungry wolves began to slaver. In the United States, the fantastic Jay Cooke, who had emerged from the Civil War as America's principal financier, pricked up his ears. In 1867, attracted by prodigal governmental land grants, which were bigger than the combined area of six New England states, Cooke had added to his enterprises the Northern Pacific, scheduled to run from Duluth to Puget Sound.

What Cooke feared was a transcontinental competitor just north of the frontier. He began a campaign in newspapers such as the Montreal *Herald* against the Canadian project. Other promoters, however, began to gather around the loaded table. There was the Grand Trunk, which, ever since Edward Watkin, had dreamed of a transcontinental. There was Alfred Waddington, the British Columbian whose workmen had been slaughtered in 1864 by the Chilcotin Indians. From Chicago came a Prince Edward Island expatriate, George McMullen, a newspaperman and promoter. In Toronto that David L. Macpherson who, along with Gzowski, Holton, and Galt, had made a fortune from building the Grand Trunk west to Sarnia, was alerted; and Macpherson was a long-term friend of John A. He had, recently, indeed, raised a $67,000 "testimonial fund" to extricate Macdonald from his financial troubles.

Most potent of the gathering wolves was Canada's foremost businessman, the newly knighted Sir Hugh Allan of Montreal. He was, of course, a Scot. In 1853 he had built the first ship of what was to become the Allan Line. By this time, at sixty-one, in the fashion of present-day tycoons, he was president of the Merchants' Bank and president or vice-president of no fewer than twenty corporations. It is interesting to note that Donald Smith was also mixed up in a number of these concerns. In the immediate background but willing to take whatever bits fortune might toss their way were Cartier, solicitor for the Grand Trunk, and Sir Francis Hincks of the "ten-thousand-pound job" of 1854, now returned from his governorships to become Canada's Minister of Finance. Sir John did not know it, but he was to be cast in the role of Little Red Ridinghood once more.

The first offer to build, made by Waddington in July 1871, did not have enough substance. But along with Waddington came George McMullen, and McMullen, who had Chicago associates, soon managed to interest Jay Cooke and the other capitalists behind the Northern Pacific. In a misguided moment Hincks suggested to Allan that he contact McMullen. Soon Allan was leagued with McMullen's Chicago group and with a New York cabal. In the background was Jay Cooke. Out of the alliance came Allan's Canadian Pacific Railway Company, which offered to build the road. Macpherson, with Toronto and Grand Trunk backing, formed the Interoceanic Railway Company to bid for the job.

John A. was in the middle. Allan was powerful. But his American associates were suspect. It was believed that Jay Cooke's only interest in the contract was to use possession of it to delay the construction of the Canadian road so as to eliminate the competition to his Northern Pacific. Moreover, Macpherson was John A.'s personal friend, and Cartier, as solicitor for the Grand Trunk, protested strongly against any "*sacrée compagnie américaine.*"

To Sir John, an amalgamation of the two concerns, with the Americans ditched, was the answer. A charter for each of the two syndicates was passed. A third act was put through to empower the administration to confer land grants and cash subsidies on whichever company it selected. This was to be the club to force amalgamation.

Outwardly, Allan conformed. He pretended to drop his American associates. He offered to amalgamate with Macpherson if he were made president and assured of a controlling interest in the stock. Macpherson refused.

In reality, Allan was determined to seize the whole pie. Circumstances were favorable. There was an election coming up in August of 1872 and the Conservatives were on the hot seat because of the resentment over the loss of the fisheries and of the rabid dispute between Ontario and Quebec over amnesty versus trial for murder for Louis Riel.

In this situation Allan selected Cartier as the point of attack. The weapon was ready to his hand. Allan was president of the Northern Colonization Railway from Ottawa to Montreal and controlled the projected North Shore Railway from Montreal to Quebec. Both lines were designed to compete with the Grand Trunk, particularly since the Grand Trunk was purposing a transatlantic fleet to fight the Allan Line. Cartier, as a Grand Trunk man, had to oppose Allan's two railroads, but both were popular in Cartier's constituency, Montreal East. So Allan poured in money to defeat Cartier and wrote complacently to his American colleagues, who were putting up part of the funds, explaining how he had subsidized the newspapers, employed agents, and held meetings "until the strong French influence I succeeded in obtaining has proved sufficient to control the elections."

Cartier, who was suffering from Bright's disease, cracked under the strain. He endorsed Allan's demand for the presidency and the controlling interest in the stock. John A. was willing to concede the presidency. Meanwhile, Cartier in desperation had made further promises and had taken campaign funds up to $80,000 from Allan. Before long Allan had contributed a total of $162,500 to Cartier, Langevin, and Macdonald. Cartier got over half of this, but John A. himself received $45,000. On August 26, in the heat of the battle, John A. was imprudent enough to wire Abbott, Allan's solicitor:

"I must have another ten thousand. Will be the last time of calling. Do not fail me. Answer today."

It is scarcely surprising that at one point Allan wrote his American friends that:

"Yesterday we entered into an agreement by which the government bound itself to form a Company of Canadians, only according to my wishes. . . . Americans are to be carefully excluded . . . but I fancy we can get over that some way or another. . . ."

The Conservatives won the election but Cartier was beaten in Montreal East—and hence John A.'s appeal to Archibald to get him elected in Manitoba. Shortly afterward the French-Canadian leader left for London for medical treatment. Meanwhile, John A.

discovered that Allan had not, as he had promised, broken with his American associates. When he finally took the plunge it was not a plunge but a hesitant dipping of his toes in the water. But John A. was committed to Allan. When Macpherson still refused to amalgamate, a new Canadian Pacific Railway Company was formed with thirteen directors from all the provinces. These directors, properly guided, elected Allan president. John A., undoubtedly, heaved a sigh of relief in the hope that all the devious signs of political corruption were thrust under the rug. To that company on February 5, 1873, was given a charter, a subsidy of $30,000,000 in cash, and 50,000,000 acres of land. Before that date the election chickens had reappeared as threatening vultures.

3

It was on the night of December 31, 1872, that into John A.'s office in the East Block in Ottawa, walked George McMullen, the Prince Edward Island expatriate. Sitting down, he began to read to the Prime Minister the original contracts between Allan and the Americans, and, still worse, the letters from Allan to them, which incriminated Cartier and the government.

Sir John listened. He was too skilled and too poised to give away the consternation the letters caused him; even though they listed the amount of money Allan had disbursed and asked McMullen for a repayment of $343,000 spent during the election campaign. When McMullen had finished, John A. asked him what he had in mind.

The black-browed McMullen knew. Either let the government accede to the original bargain with the Americans or remove Allan from the new company. Otherwise, he stated, the Canadian public would be put in possession of the facts which proved a corrupt bargain between Allan and the Conservatives.

For once Old Tomorrow was high up a tree. To accede to either of the demands was to commit political suicide. Consequently, he strove to promote a private deal between McMullen and Allan. After two months of desperate anxiety, at a dinner in honor of Allan just before the magnate left for England to try to raise funds for building the railroad, it was whispered to Sir Francis Hincks that an arrangement had been made.

For once John A. had misjudged his man. McMullen wanted revenge as well as money. He had taken the first installment of

$25,000 of blackmail money from Allan and had turned over the correspondence to him. A few weeks later he sold copies of the same correspondence to the Liberals. Suddenly, on April 2, 1873, when Parliament opened, the Liberal member from Shefford in Quebec, Huntington, asserted that Allan's C.P.R. was really financed by American capital and that Allan had advanced large amounts of money—inclusive of American money (the damning adjective)—to cabinet members in return for the promise of the charter.

Huntington's motion for a committee of inquiry was defeated. Next day, with the solemn mien of injured innocence, John A. gave notice that he would move for such a committee. It was set up on April 8 and an Oaths Act to permit it to take evidence on oath was passed. This committee was adjourned to July 2 to await the return of Allan, Abbott, and Cartier from England. On May 7 its teeth were drawn when the Colonial Office ruled that the Oaths Act was *ultra vires*. When the committee did meet on July 2 and 3, it again adjourned until August 13 for the reassembling of Parliament.

Meantime, on May 20 came a cable to announce Cartier's death. On June 13 the burial of the great French Canadian took place in Montreal. The loss of his closest colleague was too much for Sir John. He took refuge in a drinking bout.

The "Pacific Scandal" was now poised over the Prime Minister's head. Allan had returned, unsuccessful, from London. On July 4 the waiting Liberals pounced. The Allan-McMullen correspondence with its damning proof of government corruption was printed simultaneously in the Montreal *Herald* and the Toronto *Globe*. John A. fought back. On the next day there was published a sworn statement by Sir Hugh Allan that, in effect, his letters were lies.

It had been a bitter pill for the magnate. He had gulped it down. John A. saw the chance to ride out the storm. Then, on July 18, the lightning struck. In the Toronto *Globe*, the Montreal *Herald*, and the Quebec *L'Evénement* appeared a statement from McMullen; a letter from Senator Foster supporting him; and the telegrams which Cartier and Macdonald had sent Abbott, Allan's solicitor, asking for money.

"I must have another ten thousand. Will be last time of calling. Do not fail me. Answer today."

John A. stared at those words of his. All Canada stared at them.

John A., like Francis Hincks, had committed the final sin. He had been found out. But how, John A. asked himself, could the Liberals have got hold of these telegrams? They were something McMullen had not had.

The answer was simple enough. While Abbott and Allan had been in England, Abbott's confidential clerk, George Norris, helped by another clerk from the office of J. A. Perkins, had burglarized Abbott's files; and Abbott had kept the telegrams to put pressure on John A., if necessary. Then, Norris had sold the telegrams to the gleeful Montreal Liberals.

It was not the first, nor was it to be the last, of scandals of this sort in Canadian politics. John A. had no illusions about the fate that awaited the man who had been found out. To make it worse, there was a new governor general. John A. went on a prolonged drunk.

4

It was Tuesday, November 4, 1873. Outside, it was a clear autumn night. Inside the Parliament Buildings in Ottawa, the Chamber was hushed. It had been jammed ever since Parliament met on October 23. It had been predicted that the government would resign. John A. had decided to fight. He had admitted to the committee of inquiry that he had received electioneering funds from Allan but had argued, quite reasonably, that all political parties accepted campaign contributions from interested businessmen. He had asserted that, whatever Cartier might have said, he himself had only promised Allan the presidency and had, further, compelled him to break with his American associates. And ought one, he urged, to pay attention to information bought from blackmailers and thieves?

In the House these arguments had a certain effect. It was also agreed that none of the money had gone into John A.'s own pocket. On the other side was the fact that, no matter how one sliced it, he had taken money from the applicant for a railway charter while the charter was still under advisement. Allan had, in effect, bribed Cartier, Langevin, and Macdonald and they had taken the bribe.

The fight swung back and forth. John A., however, failed to hurl himself into the struggle. He held back, sunk in liquor and a bitter consciousness of his own mistake. His majority dropped from a possible eighteen to a possible two. At last, when it was almost too late, on Monday, November 3, he spoke for five hours. When he sat down, after a brilliant exposition of what he had done for Canada, it seemed that he would win. But on this Tuesday evening, Donald Smith was to speak.

Smith had been John A.'s personal envoy to the Red River rebellion. He was a Conservative member. He was associated with Allan in a number of enterprises. It was known, too, that when the crisis over the Pacific Scandal came he had, while at Fort Carlton on the Saskatchewan River, received an appeal from John A. that: "Upon you and the influence you can bring to bear may depend the fate of this administration." In reply, Smith had made a record trip East.

So, as the big-nosed, bushy-browed Scot rose in his place, John A. and his Conservatives waited with confidence. There was an amendment to an amendment before the House. The first, an amendment to the Speech from the Throne, was one of censure of the government; the second, the one under debate, expressed confidence in the government. This second one was the one which must be passed if the government was to survive.

Donald Smith began with compliments for John A. The Conservatives relaxed. When the long-bearded H.B.C. man went on to say that he felt that the Prime Minister "was incapable of taking money from Sir Hugh Allan for corrupt purposes," the Conservatives cheered and thumped their desks. The crisis seemed over.

"But," Smith went on, and at the fatal word both Liberals and Conservatives jerked erect. To the stunned ears of the one party and the sudden jubilation of the other, he was saying that he would be most willing to vote confidence in the government, could he do so "conscientiously."

On that word "conscientiously" the Conservative government had foundered. John A. knew it. He leaped to his feet. As the Canadian Hansard records it, he shouted out that he "could lick that man, Smith, quicker than hell could frizzle a feather." If, as John A. claimed later, Smith had promised in a private conversation to support him, we can understand the Celtic rage. Smith denied the promise, insinuating that John A. had been too far gone in liquor to be compos mentis.

The government resigned. Alexander Mackenzie, the uncompromising incorruptible, became Liberal Prime Minister. In the ensuing election the Conservatives were reduced to seventy seats. In four years John A. had fallen from his pinnacle of power into the slough of defeat. The transcontinental had been defeated, too. Canada would have to wait for her ribbon of steel.

As an interesting footnote to the Liberal triumph, it might be recorded that in December 1873 John A.'s old antagonist, the rock-ribbed George Brown, was appointed to the Canadian Senate.

CHAPTER XXII

1873–78

Depression in the East–The Indian Treaties–The First Winnipeg Boom and the Migration of The Métis*–Days of the Stern-Wheelers on the Red River–Donald Smith and His Cousin Become Multimillionaires–John A.'s Return to Power–The Death of George Brown*

1

THE Liberals had won a Pyrrhic victory. For, in Europe, in the spring of 1872, the "Prussian boom," the one inspired by the defeat of Napoleon III in 1870, had collapsed. Depression reached its chilling fingers westward across the Atlantic. On September 30 of that year, in New York, Jay Cooke and Company closed its doors. Among the enterprises left bankrupt was the Northern Pacific, though it had already thrust 600 miles of rails westward like a blind worm seeking for a goal. It was ironical that, a year before the Canadian transcontinental was finally brought down, its success or failure no longer mattered to one of its chief opponents. By another of the seemingly blind fumblings of Fate, another abandoned Cooke railway, the St. Paul and Pacific, was later to prove the springboard to the C.P.R.

From the United States the depression leaped like a grasshopper into Canada. Prices of farm products shrank as if air had been let out of a blown-up pig's bladder. Mortgages fell on Ontario farms like autumn leaves. Though shipping held up in the Maritimes, the Dominion's revenues dropped. By 1873, when the Macdonald government went out of office, the public debt, inclusive of the provincial debts assumed at Confederation, totaled $100,000,000.

In the days before the welfare state and the big income tax, when each person was left to provide for his own old age or else trudge to the poorhouse, this figure seemed astronomical. So did a deficit of over a million a year when the total annual expenditure of the Dominion was around fifteen million, the budget today of a single moderate-sized Canadian city.

In 1873, to the stone-faced, pay-as-you-go Alexander Mackenzie, Canada's new Prime Minister, fifteen million dollars was not something to be handed over to some promoter or contractor in between drinks. British Columbia was howling for its promised transcontinental. But the Allan Company had been blasted out of its charter by the Pacific Scandal. In view of the depression, no other group of capitalists would touch the enterprise. So British Columbia, in spite of frustrated yelps, threatening secession, would have to wait. What Mackenzie decided upon was a bits-and-pieces method, using waterways wherever possible. By 1878 his government had spent $37,000,000. In return, it had over three million dollars' worth of surveys—not too valuable (Sandford Fleming, like a true engineer, was perfectly happy to go surveying till doomsday) a worthless Rainy River canal, and 710 miles of road in various sections, built or building. To get to Winnipeg from Fort William by the "Dawson Road" took seventeen changes from steamboats to wagons to open rowboats to steam tugs to stagecoach.

British Columbia, it seemed, would whistle in vain for its transcontinental, and the Northwest would remain permanently divided from the East. But, while the lugubrious Mackenzie was pinching pennies in Ottawa, the face of Manitoba and the Northwest was changing.

2

In 1870, Winnipeg, apart from the troops come to stamp out the embers of the Red River revolt, had boasted two hundred and twoscore inhabitants. Though Manitoba was now a postage-stamp province, Winnipeg had no parliament buildings. Its first Provincial Assembly met in March 1871 in the house of A. G. B. Bannatyne, the former postmaster, which had been rented for the occasion. It was a two-story frame building, standing at that time where the Banque Canadienne Nationale today looks down benignly on traffic-crowded Main Street. When, in 1873, the Bannatyne house burned down, the legislature removed to the newly built courthouse. There it stayed until 1884, when the old Parliament Buildings, on Kennedy and Broadway, now torn down, were ready. In 1871 the members themselves, except for a few such as Donald Smith, were frontiersmen, in rough suits, bright shirts, gay sashes, and moccasins. One of them, summoned to order for being drunk, called out:

"You may think me a fool, Mr. Speaker, but I am not such a fool as the people who sent me here."

Yet this legislature, rough and ready as it was, its mace fashioned from the hub of a Red River cart and the staff of the flagstaff of Colonel Wolseley's expeditionary force, was a triumph for Lieutenant Governor Archibald's moderate party over Dr. Schultz's vindictive "Loyalist" group. In the same year O'Donoghue's Fenian raid was squelched and the governor concluded the first Indian Treaty.

The Canadian Government had inherited from the British the voluntary purchase of the Indian territories and the settling of the red men on reserves. For this first treaty in the Northwest, to buy the land between "Thunder Bay and the Stone Fort" (Lower Fort Garry), whatever pomp was possible was trotted out. A thousand Swampy Crees and Chippewas gathered in tents around the Stone Fort. The lieutenant governor was in formal dress. Presents were exchanged with the chiefs. The guns thudded salutes.

In return for the surrender of their hunting grounds, the Indians received inalienable reservations on the basis of 160 acres for a family of five, a school in each reserve, an initial payment of $3 a head, and an annuity at the same rate payable in "blankets, clothing prints, twine or traps . . . or . . . in cash." The sale of intoxicating liquor to them was forbidden.

This treaty set the pattern for Treaties 2 to 7, which followed, except that in Treaty 3, in 1873, the grant of land was increased to 640 acres per family, the initial payment to $12 a head, and the annual payments to $5 per person, while chiefs and headmen got $25 and $15, respectively, each year along with suitable clothing triennially and medals and flags at the signing of the treaty. It was also provided that any bands requesting them were to be given hoes, spades, scythes, axes, saws, files, plows, harrows, and so on, a box of carpenter's tools, a yoke of oxen, a bull, and five cows. These terms, in turn, were applied to the following treaties. When Treaty 7 was negotiated in 1877, the Indian title was extinguished from the head of Lake Superior to the Rockies and from the 49th parallel northward roughly to the Nelson River, the height of land, and Lesser Slave Lake.

The Indians took a pittance for the vast territories they surrendered. Yet it can be said that, since the process was inevitable, the procedure was kinder and sounder than the wars and massacres south of the border.

The *métis* did not fare so well. The Manitoba Act had reserved 1,400,000 acres for the half-breeds and original white settlers. Governmental red tape, that curse of any civil service, almost strangled the arrangements for assigning the acreage. In many cases scrip for it was issued and the *métis* often sold that scrip for a few drinks.

Meantime, in 1872, a joint commission of the Dominion and the United States started an accurate delineation of the 49th parallel as far as the Rockies. In the same year the Dominion survey of the Northwest began from the 49th parallel northward. It was the square survey with the township as the unit. The township consisted of 36 sections of one square mile each with a road allowance of a chain in width. Each section had 640 acres in it. The meridians of longitude were numbered from east to west and the townships from south to north. By June 1873, 29,952 quarter sections, or 4,792,292 acres, had been laid out. Mackenzie's accession to power brought a halt until 1878, when the survey was resumed.

The *métis* saw the whole country being parceled into neat squares, like a huge checkerboard, most unlike their own ribbon homesteads. Besides, Manitoba was beginning to fill up. Some of Wolseley's Canadian volunteers were caught by the magic of the West. Other Ontarians, especially after the mortgages fell on their eastern farms, made the long trek to free land. Later, Scots came and a few Americans spilled across the border.

It was only a trickle compared with the tide of settlers pouring into Minnesota and into the Dakota Territory. Yet it was enough to make Winnipeg for a short space into a boom town. By 1873 it was tossing up hotels, stores, and houses overnight. Professor J. M. Grant, in Winnipeg as an aide to the surveyor Sandford Fleming, wrote back home:

"Nothing shows more conclusively the wonderful progress of Manitoba . . . than the fact that the Hudson's Bay Company sold at auction the other day in building lots, thirteen acres of the five hundred of their reserve around Fort Garry, at the rate of $7000 an acre."

The *métis* saw the waves of change beginning to roll in, the crest of each new one reaching a little further. Even before this, the mere approach of Wolseley's expedition had set some of them migrating. Now others began to move. Some drifted across the line to join their brothers in the States. There were, for instance, substantial *métis* settlements in what is today the state of Montana. There, later, Louis Riel joined them.

Others, however, made their way north and west to the *métis* hunting communities near Duck Lake and Fort Carlton in the strip of land between the about-to-merge North and South Saskatchewan rivers. Here as early as October 8, 1871, the mission of St. Laurent, near Fort Carlton, was established. As more and more *métis* fled from the advance of civilization, on December 10, 1873, a great assembly of all the *métis* in the Saskatchewan Valley was called together at St. Laurent by Father André, a name which, later, was to be associated with that of Louis Riel. At that meeting a provisional government, an ominous portent for the future, was formed. As its "President" for a year was elected a man of destiny, Gabriel Dumont.

Blunt and bluff, and a renowned buffalo hunter, Dumont was to prove himself, when his moment came, a tactician second to none. At the moment, he had eight "councillors" to assist him and a code of "*Lois et Regulations*" by which to rule. There were also, in accordance with the buffalo-hunting way of life, to which these *métis* had reverted, "captains" and "soldiers" on whom Dumont could call. As the Roman Catholic hierarchy had feared, the opening up of Manitoba to settlement was overwhelming the dream of some of them of a second Quebec along the Red River. By 1873 another *métis* community, strong in the faith, was being established along the Saskatchewan River. This community paid lip service to Canada. It claimed itself ready to dissolve its provisional government once Canada sent in magistrates and a force sufficient to keep the peace. When that moment did come, another Riel Rebellion flared.

In the early seventies, however, the migration of the irreconcilables among the *métis* rid Manitoba of a troublesome element. Meantime the new province's face was still turned toward St. Paul. Back and forth over the prairies the cart trains still crawled.

On the Red River the *International*, operated almost exclusively for the H.B.C., still threshed the muddy waters with its cumbersome stern paddle wheel.

It was soon to have a rival. When, in the early spring of 1870, Donald Smith traveled south from Fort Garry, as has been mentioned, he had met, driving a dog team north, that energetic Canadian, J. J. Hill, who in 1856, at eighteen, had arrived in St. Paul from Rockwood, near Guelph, Ontario. In the intervening years, Hill had poked his finger into a number of pies. In each case he had come out with a plum. By 1870 he was the leading freighter and forwarding agent in St. Paul. That year he was on his way to Fort Garry to see what opportunities might wait there for his Red River Transportation Company.

On such a man the H.B.C. monopoly of the steamboat traffic sat not as a silken veil but as an intolerable weight. Hill brought in Alexander Gregg, a famous Mississippi captain, to build a boat. In mid-April of 1871, Hill's *Selkirk* huffed and puffed into the dock at Fort Garry. Lining its rails were 115 passengers; in its hold were 150 tons of freight; and on Captain Gregg's lips was Hill's announcement of defiance to the H.B.C. and to Donald Smith, now the chief commissioner of its fur trade in Canada. Henceforth, Winnipeggers were told, all goods passing to Canadian ports through American territory must travel by a bonded carrier owned by an American. Hill was a naturalized American. The *Selkirk* was bonded. The *International* was not.

Smith, M.P. and M.P.P., a shrewd manipulator who had taken advantage of the drop in H.B.C. shares at the time of the sale of Rupert's Land to Canada and had become one of the principal shareholders in the Company, picked up the challenge. He transferred the *International* to Norman Kittson, who was also a naturalized American and was the H.B.C.'s forwarding agent in St. Paul. There was a short and vicious duel between the two boats. Then Smith took a second look. The result was an amalgamation of Smith, Kittson, and Hill. Kittson was put in charge of the river traffic. Soon he had a fleet of five steamers and twenty barges swimming back and forth along the Red River.

The three men whose operations were finally to form the launching base for the C.P.R. were now allied. In Winnipeg the news brought no joy to the merchants of the burgeoning boom. The Smith-Kittson-Hill combine meant high freight rates from St. Paul. The merchants in their turn, leaguing themselves with their

St. Paul brethren so as to get bonding privileges, in 1875 put two stern-wheelers, the *Manitoba* and the *Minnesota,* on the Red River. The Smith-Kittson-Hill trio promptly reduced their rates below actual costs. When this failed to shatter the merchants, Kittson, through his influence with the U. S. Customs, got the *Manitoba* detained at Pembina. It was released just in time to be "accidentally" rammed and sunk with its cargo by Kittson's *International.* The steamer was refloated at heavy cost. When it reached Winnipeg the sheriff was waiting to seize it for a small debt owed by the merchants. South of the border the same fate captured the *Minnesota.* The Winnipeg merchants tossed in the towel. They sold both boats to the Smith-Kittson-Hill combine. Rates at once returned to dizzy heights.

Such were the men who were, ultimately, to provide the core for the C.P.R., rugged individualists and no nonsense about fair play to competitors. It is interesting to note that Smith, now a millionaire, maintained one home, "The Cottage," in Ottawa. But he ruled the fur empire which Simpson had once governed from that "Silver Heights" mansion at Winnipeg which the unfortunate William McDougall had rented for the governorship he was never able to enjoy.

The seventies were the apogee of the paddle-wheelers on the Red River, even though their season was only five months in each year. While in the East the locomotives puffed along the iron tracks, in Manitoba the stern-wheelers, like huge shoe boxes with a threshing mill wheel propelling them, splashed their way through the turgid waters. Their boilers often broke down. Time after time they stuck their noses into mudbanks or into a point of the river. Sometimes they caught on fire. They stopped for stacks of wood piled on the bank, or to let their passengers stream off for a hunt. They carried freight and *métis* and rough-garbed settlers. They also bore gold-braided officers and frock-coated, wide-hatted Beau Brummells and ladies in the latest bustles. "Steamboat round the bend" brought the settlements along the Red out to cheer. At times schools were dismissed to let the children stare at the splashing leviathans. At Winnipeg there were special police to control the wild rush to claim shoes, oysters, church organs, printing presses, French wines, needles, and the hundred and one necessities or luxuries the boats carried.

This was not all their charm. In between the regular trips, on full-moon nights, flags flying, decks dressed with poplar branches, and fire buckets blooming with wild prairie roses, the steamers went out from Fort Garry dock to glide along the Red River. The fiddlers lilted and crooned. The dancing feet tripped the decks. The moon shone down. In the darkened corners lovers kissed. On such nights the problems of the present and the future seemed far away.

But on October 9, 1877, on a barge in front of her, the sternwheeler *Selkirk* pushed up to Winnipeg her own destruction, the wood-burning "Countess of Dufferin," the first locomotive to reach the Canadian Northwest.

3

The "Countess of Dufferin," long outmoded, stands today at the entrance to the C.P.R. station at Winnipeg. Behind her arrival on that October day of 1877 lay the casual toss of a coin. Behind the flick of the coin lurked, in turn, the demand of Winnipeg for a railway to St. Paul, a bankrupt railroad (the St. Paul and Pacific), and the shrewdness of J. J. Hill, Norman Kittson, and the canny Donald Smith.

Back in the fifties, like Canada, Minnesota had had its own frenzied railroad boom. The American Congress and the Minnesota legislature had vied with each other in giving away huge grants of public land to promoters who "all had their plates ready, should it rain porridge." Lines begun casually anywhere ended just as casually in virgin timber or on the empty prairie. Then came Jay Cooke and his vision of roads to tap the Red River Valley as well as of a Northern Pacific to run to Puget Sound. The collapse of his firm in the fall of 1872 had left his nascent railway empire a thing of bits and pieces.

The St. Paul and Pacific was one of the bits of debris. It had been chartered originally in 1857 as the Minnesota and Pacific but had been bankrupted through fraudulent construction contracts and then reorganized. By the end of 1870 it had been completed from St. Paul as far as Breckenridge, a total of 217 miles, and in that year Donald Smith had traveled over it on his memorable journey to the Riel Rebellion. Since its first reorganization it had been mortgaged, had had that mortgage foreclosed, and had been mortgaged again.

At this stage a syndicate of Dutch bondholders had been induced to buy some $20,000,000 worth of its useless bonds. When interest payments stopped in 1872, the Dutch bondholders, through their New York agent, Kennedy, applied for a receiver in bankruptcy. Jesse P. Farley of Dubuque, Iowa, was appointed.

Throughout its checkered history, the road had retained its valuable land grants and its charter to build a railway from Breckenridge to Pembina on the Manitoba border. Here was where that shrewd millionaire, Donald Smith, along with his cronies of the Red River Transportation Company, Hill and Kittson, scented opportunity. "When the St. Paul and Pacific Railway became bankrupt," writes Van Horne, who was to drive Canada's transcontinental across the prairies and the Rockies, "it occurred to Messrs. Smith and Hill that they might help the transportation difficulty and do something for themselves . . . by getting control somehow of the broken-down property."

Donald Smith was a man who looked far ahead. If the St. Paul and Pacific should finally be garnered in and built northward to the boundary, a Canadian line from Winnipeg to meet it would be necessary. As it happened, the Mackenzie government, which Smith's speech of November 4, 1873, had helped put into the saddle, decided to run the east-west line of its "bits and pieces" transcontinental not through Winnipeg but through Selkirk, further north. Smith protested on behalf of Winnipeg. To placate both him and Winnipeg, the Mackenzie government, on August 31, 1874, let a contract for a branch line to run south from Selkirk through Winnipeg to the international boundary, eighty-three miles away.

Thus, Smith had the prospect of his Canadian line, when and if he should need it. The first spike in that line, however, was not driven until three years later. For first there had to be the toss of the coin.

That spin of the coin came about because Smith had been importuning his cousin, George Stephen, to take an interest in the bankrupt St. Paul and Pacific. But by 1876 the Northern Pacific, back on its feet under new management and anxious to pick up the empire it had lost, was threatening legal action against the St. Paul and Pacific. Stephen, a tall gentlemanly man, somewhat lean and with stooped shoulders to suggest that he took his financial burdens seriously, pooh-poohed any thought of investment in such a road. Like a true Scot, however, he had prospered over the years. In that same 1876, as the president of the Bank of

Montreal, along with its general manager, R. B. Angus (another Scot, naturally), Stephen was in Chicago.

What had brought the two Canadians to the metropolis of the Middle West was the failure of a steel company in which the Bank of Montreal had invested. During the legal proceedings there was a week of inaction. The first impulse of the two was to visit St. Louis. Then Stephen remembered Smith and his St. Paul and Pacific. A dime was flipped between St. Paul and St. Louis. The northern saint won.

By this fragile bit of chance the two men were brought to St. Paul. Hill seized the opportunity. As the local agent for the receiver, Farley, he arranged for a special train to Breckenridge and back. The St. Paul and Pacific was in poor shape. The rails were of rusted iron, not steel, and the last stretch of them was simply laid down loosely on the level prairie. Again the unpredictable stepped in. Stephen, an Easterner, fell in love with the endless stretches of the fertile plains. There had been a plague of Rocky Mountain locusts for two years, so that not a smidgin of crop was to be seen. Hill pointed out that the locusts would not stay forever. Suddenly Stephen decided to make the plunge, especially since he could make use of the funds of the Bank of Montreal. He, Smith, Hill, Kittson, and Angus proceeded to show Americans how to make a killing.

The details of the story are too long and too complicated to be given *in extenso*. In brief, Farley, the official receiver in bankruptcy, and Kennedy, the New York agent of the Dutch bondholders, were taken into the picture. Farley, in fact, later brought suit against Smith and his associates for a share of the loot, which he claimed had been promised him for his help in persuading the Dutch to sell out; but the suit was thrown out of court because of Farley's fiduciary position. Meanwhile, Stephen made a trip to Holland to meet the Dutch bondholders. The final result was that the Dutch sold out an equity of some $28,000,000 in principal and interest for $6,000,000, while agreeing to wait for their money until the tangle was resolved.

The partners (Stephen, Smith, Kittson, Angus, and Kennedy) signed a joint note for the amount to the Canadian Bank, of which Smith and Stephen were directors, and included an extra $780,000 for contingencies. Money still had to be found to build enough road to secure the valuable land grants. The four Canadians put up $300,000, Hill and Kittson flinging into the pot everything they owned, even the deeds for their homes; while Stephen advanced a little under $700,000 from the Bank of Montreal.

Speed was of the essence, because an act of Congress had made it mandatory to complete the St. Paul and Pacific as far as the Canadian boundary well before the end of 1878, if the land grants were not to be forfeited. With Stephen supplying the credit and Hill driving the construction gangs, the railway was brought to Pembina with twenty-four hours to spare. Meanwhile, as has been noted, in 1877 the first spike in the Canadian line from Selkirk through Winnipeg to the frontier had been driven; and in October of that same year, steam up and whistle piping, the "Countess of Dufferin" chugged ashore at Point Douglas, just north of Winnipeg.

The next necessary move was to get control of the Canadian road. Donald Smith was the man for the job. In 1874 a bill had been passed prohibiting dual membership in the Dominion House and any provincial legislature. In consequence, Smith had resigned his seat in the Manitoba legislature. But he was still the Dominion member for Selkirk. So, in the spring of 1878, in the federal Parliament, he supported a bill to give an unspecified American railway company running rights over the Canadian line from the boundary into Winnipeg.

Everyone knew that this railway was Stephen's St. Paul and Pacific, and it was generally suspected that Smith had a financial interest in it. To John A. Macdonald, that last fact was all he needed to know. In his view, Smith had betrayed him during the crisis of the Pacific Scandal and John A. was not a man to forget such an injury. He attacked Smith, whose "conscience" had made him desert the Conservatives over their dealings with Sir Hugh Allan, for now supporting a measure in which he had a financial interest. He sneered that the bill was the way the Liberals were rewarding Smith "for his servile support."

Smith, now a man of fifty-eight, thought it over. On the last day of the session, May 10, he rose to repudiate John A.'s assertions. There followed a near riot in the House, with charges from Tupper that in 1870, when he and Smith were on their way to Red River, Smith had asked to be made a Canadian Privy Councillor and that at the time of the Pacific Scandal, Smith had telegraphed that he would support John A.; while Smith denied both charges and accused John A. of not being capable, during a personal interview with him, "of knowing what he was saying."

The House was soon in complete turmoil.

"Coward! Coward! Sit down," Tupper shouted at Smith.

Smith started again to explain why he had not supported John A. in the 1873 vote.

"That fellow Smith," stated John A., "is the biggest liar I ever met."

In spite of the furor, Smith got his way. On August 3, 1878, the St. Paul and Pacific was given the running rights for ten years over the line from the frontier into Winnipeg. On December 2 of the same year, amid fanfare and shouts, the rails from Winnipeg were joined to the steel ribbons running up from St. Paul.

Winnipeg at last had her route to St. Paul; while Smith, Hill, Kittson, Angus, and Kennedy held the keys to a treasure house. Now that the land grants belonging to the St. Paul and Pacific had been secured, Hill, who had influence in St. Paul, got through the Minnesota legislature a charter for a new company, the St. Paul, Minneapolis and Manitoba Railway Company.

This was in 1879. The partners were at last free to move in for the kill. New bonds of the new company were sold to the public, the Dutch bondholders were paid off, and the mortgage on the St. Paul and Pacific was foreclosed. The new company then bought all the assets of the St. Paul and Pacific at a bargain price. Of this new company, Stephen was president, Angus vice-president, and Hill general manager. By 1879, then, the new Midases, by means of their St. Paul, Minneapolis and Manitoba Railroad, were in undisputed possession of 667 miles of track, of which 565 were completed, and of a gargantuan grant of 2,500,000 acres of public lands.

Meanwhile, Fortune smiled its widest smiles. In 1877 the locusts had disappeared. The settlers flooded back. Land seekers jammed the platforms of the new company, and the group had the land to sell. They also had the rails over which to ship the No. 1 hard wheat which the land grew. The huge bonanza farms started. The profits came flooding in—and Stephen and Smith and their associates, while paying for the road with bonds sold to the public, had kept the stock for themselves.

The whole maneuver is a classic example of how the modern financial barons make the feudal lords seem like cave-dwelling amateurs. In 1879 the partners divided among themselves $15,000,000 of free stock in the St. Paul, Minneapolis and Manitoba, while selling the public $16,000,000 in bonds to pay for the road. For three years the group put their profits into expansion. In 1882 they issued to themselves another $2,000,000 of stock for nothing. A year later they paid to themselves $10,000,000 worth of bonds at ten cents on the dollar, a profit of $9,000,000. Apart from interest on these bonds and apart from dividends, the five stockholders of the Great Northern (as the railroad was renamed in 1882) cut up among themselves a Brobdingnagian melon of over $300,000,000—on an initial investment of $300,000. Seldom have modern promoters, while letting the public pay for the cost, been able to do better.

Such was the tale of the toss of a coin. Manitoba, as a result, was linked with Canada by rail, but via the States. The railroad across the Dominion still waited. And who would have thought, on that May 10 of 1878, when Donald Smith and John A. Macdonald barked at each other across the floor of the Dominion House, that within two years these bitter foes would be allied in building the Canadian Pacific Railway? But first John A. had to get back into power.

4

The Pacific Scandal of 1873 would have written finis to the political career of anyone but Sir John A. Macdonald. Yet, less than three years later, in that same 1876 when the flip of a coin had brought Stephen and Hill to St. Paul and the beginning of a fortune as big as a billionaire's dream, at eight-thirty of the morning of July 1, Dominion Day, a special train, jammed with between three to four hundred Conservatives, pulled out from the old Berkeley Street Station in Toronto. At eleven it reached the rustic and peaceful town of Uxbridge, north of Toronto. A huge crowd jammed its ordinarily quiet streets. John A. stepped from the train. A cheer split the air. Two brass bands (one had come from nearby Markham, the other was Uxbridge's own creation) blared a salute. An address of welcome was read to John A. The lanky, corncob-nosed ex-Prime Minister replied. A procession formed up. The brass bands thumped in front. The dignitaries followed in carriages. Behind came the mass of men, women, and children, the dogs barking excitedly on the edges. The procession moved under triumphal arches to the town's picnic ground, Elgin Park. There, under the tall elms, were long tables set up on trestles.

Anyone who is old enough to have seen an Ontario picnic in

the horse-and-buggy days prior to the First World War can visualize the scene. On those tables were plates of cold chicken, sliced tongue, hams, mounded heaps of glistening red strawberries, elaborately frosted cakes and equally elaborate pies—each housewife striving to outdo her neighbor—and huge jugs of iced lemonade and raspberry cordial. Around those tables, tucking in food that had a tang which the hygienic mass products of today's supermarkets fail to equal, were the people from miles around. There were the bank clerks, the "sports" of that day, in blazers and boaters. There were the town dignitaries in frock coats and bowlers, their wives in the conscious pomp of corsets, bustles, and flowered milliners' creations, each of these last an imitation of a section, at least, of the Garden of Eden. There were blacksmiths and farmers in their awkward Sunday best and their wives in the brown taffeta gowns and big hats of the period. There were the youngsters, the boys in unaccustomed boots and stockings and the girls self-conscious in dresses decked with buttons, bows, and fringes. Add the dogs, sneaking in for scraps, and the stamping and snorting and the jingling of harness from the horses and buggies and democrats ranged along the hitching posts, and it all totaled up to an audience made to order for John A.

The occasion for the meeting was the by-elections in the constituencies of North and South Ontario. During the meal, the Pacific Scandal a forgotten contretemps, the ex-Prime Minister toured the tables, greeting, with his politician's memory, the right man with the right word. Then, at 1:30 P.M., he mounted the freshly built wooden platform. Before him was an audience of several thousand in holiday mood, good-humored from food. They shouted to the tall elm tops as he took swinging cracks at the Mackenzie government's inability to halt the depression. He propounded the Conservative cure. The Conservatives won both by-elections.

John A. was on his way back. Just as in 1860 he had invented the public banquet, now he had pulled out of his sack of devices the political picnic. The 1876 climax came at Belleville, where 15,000 listened to him. Next year, in Dominion Square, Montreal, almost 50,000 hung on his words. It was clear that the tide had turned against the Liberals.

Depressions have overturned more governments than all the shoutings of ideals; and the Liberal Prime Minister was as unimaginative as his own rock-ribbed incorruptibility and bleak Scottish face. The one attempt to cure falling prices and the mortgages on Ontario farms had been George Brown's mission to Washington to negotiate another Elgin-Marcy Reciprocity Treaty. He seemed to have succeeded. But early in 1875 the treaty was repudiated by the American Senate.

Canada had to live with the depression but could not learn to like it. Meanwhile, Mackenzie failed to keep control within the ranks of his own party. His able, though humorless right-hand man from Ontario, Edward Blake, resigned from the Cabinet. In October of 1874, at Aurora, north of Toronto, he alienated the Orange Order by a speech in which, along with other vague generalities, he criticized the Imperial connection—always a dangerous thing to do in Ontario.

Blake was reflecting the views of Goldwin Smith, an ex-history professor from Oxford who, after a term of lecturing in the States, had settled in Toronto with the intention of becoming the "patron" of Canadian culture. Earnest young Canadians gathered around him. The ex-Oxonian stuffed their undergraduate heads with the usual assortment of high-minded but impractical notions. Among them was the pronunciamento that Canada's only salvation was to break with Great Britain. What Blake, strong in theory but weak in practicality, failed to remember when he spoke at Aurora was that there were in Ontario 2000 Orange lodges with, roughly, 100,000 members and 100,000 votes. His speech swung these votes back to their old allegiance, the Conservative party.

As if the depression and the loss of Orange support were not sufficient evils, in Quebec the Roman Catholic hierarchy chose these years for an all-out assault on "that insidious plague, Catholic liberalism." The hierarchy had always tended to resent the Quebec *Rouges*, from which Quebec Liberals were descended. The nudge toward an aggressive intolerance came from the triumph of ultramontanism "beyond the mountains (to Rome)" in Europe.

Ultramontanism was an attempt to revive the medieval authority of the Roman Catholic Church. In its official presentation in the 1864 Syllabus and Encyclical of Pius IX (the Pope who had been frightened by the 1848 year of revolution into reaction) many axioms of democracy were explicitly stigmatized as heresies. It was stated, for instance, that the Roman Catholic Church had the right to avail herself of force, that there should be no separation of Church and State, and that the Roman Catholic religion should be held "as the only religion in the State, to the exclusion of all other modes of worship." The Encyclical further condemned those who pressed for liberty of speech, conscience, worship, and of the press. Protestantism was declared not to be a religion. A true Catholic, it was said, could not abandon intolerance. Futhermore, since it was claimed that the laws of the Roman Catholic Church were binding even on heretics, it was held that no one, whether Catholic, Protestant, or unbeliever, had the right to read a book proscribed by the Roman Catholic Church. No marriages, naturally, except those solemnized by the Roman Catholic Church could be valid and no civil judge could annul a Roman Catholic marriage.

Such was the temper of the 1864 Syllabus and Encyclical, an attitude which still survives in Spain, Italy, some Latin-American countries, and, to a certain degree, in some circles in Quebec. To put the seal on ultramontanism, at the Vatican Council of 1870, in spite of the opposition of bishops from France, Germany, and Austria, on the eighteenth of July the doctrine of papal infallibility was promulgated.

Ultramontanism was followed by the collapse of papal temporal power in Italy and by struggles with the State in France, Germany, and Austria. In Quebec it was seized on with avidity by the medieval Bishop Bourget of Montreal. He had already banned the *Institut Canadien*, a *Rouge* literary society (to which the young Wilfrid Laurier belonged), for having forbidden books in its possession. In 1868 a member, L. A. Dessaules, gave an address before the Institut, urging tolerance and the union of men of all creeds in intellectual tasks. Though this suggestion does not seem radical today, the Bishop procured from Rome an edict depriving all Catholic sacraments from anyone who continued to read the report of Dessaules' address or who remained a member of the Institut. When in the next year a member of the Institut, Joseph Guibord, died, he was refused last rites and burial in consecrated ground. In 1875 a decision of the British Privy Council admitted Guibord's remains to the Catholic cemetery. The Bishop promptly declared his grave interdicted and separated from the holy ground. In the next year a servile Quebec legislature legalized his pronouncement.

To back up the Bishop, in 1871 a group of Quebec journalists and lawyers drew up a *Programme Catholique*. Its objective was to compel all Catholic electors to vote only for those candidates who pledged full adherence to Catholic doctrines in religion, politics, and social matters and who would agree to work for any change demanded by the bishops in the laws of either province or Dominion. To these ultramontanists, the state was to be completely subordinated to the Roman Catholic Church and was, in fact, to exist only to carry out its will.

The moderate wing of the Quebec Roman Catholic Church, led by Archbishop Taschereau, reacted against the ultramontanists. Yet even the Archbishop and his supporters joined in a pastoral letter in September 1875, signed by all the bishops, denouncing Catholic liberalism.

Ultramontanism exacerbated the split over the Riel amnesty question between French-Canadian Quebec and Orange Ontario. Then, in 1877, an Orangeman, Hackett, was beaten to death in Montreal during a Twelfth-of-July parade. The murderers were never caught. Mackenzie and the Liberals were blamed by the Orange Order for the failure.

It seemed, in fact, that whatever Mackenzie did was wrong. He backed the Scott Act, a temperance measure, and offended the powerful liquor interests. His advocacy of Reciprocity had alienated Canadian manufacturers. Then, when the 1878 elections rolled along, the best he could offer a country that was snarling over the depression was a "no change" policy.

John A. pounced. Later, his Ontario lieutenant, D'Alton McCarthy, was to admit that if the Liberals had gone in for a high tariff the Conservatives would have plumped for free trade as the depression's panacea. With "no change" as the Liberal banner, John A. trotted out "National Policy," which, by "a judicious readjustment of the tariff," was to "benefit and foster the agricultural, the mining, the manufacturing and other interests of the Dominion."

Like all good political promises, it seemed to offer jam for everybody's bun. Above all, those words "readjustment of the tariff" were visions of profit to Canada's industrialists. When the votes were counted on September 17, 1878, by an almost exact reversal of the 1873 verdict, the Conservatives had 137 seats to 69 for the Liberals. John A. sat again on the throne from which the Pacific Scandal had thrust him.

It was time. British Columbia was on the point of seceding from the Dominion, and in the Northwest events had almost cost Canada the prairies. It was still, however, to be two years before the transcontinental rolled forward.

5

Before that transcontinental drove forward, too, fate had removed a man who, in season and out, had urged the acquisition of the Northwest. The years had mellowed George Brown. They had not dulled his convictions. Though he never sat as an elected member of the Dominion House, his influence on Ontarian Liberals was a brooding potency. He was still the Presbyterian anti-Papist. At the same time, his vision of a powerful Canada never faltered.

For such a giant, it was anticlimax when, on the evening of March 25, 1880, he was shot in his office, not by any personal or political enemy but, almost accidentally, by a half-drunk, discharged employee. Brown overpowered his assailant. The wound was not believed to be serious. But complications set in. Early on May 10, the great nonconformist died. Some two months later, his attacker, George Bennett, was hanged.

In a way, in spite of the power he had continued to wield, Brown's life, too, had been anticlimactic since those high moments of June 1864 when, rising above factional politics, his greatness had set Canada on the straight road to Confederation. From that move, politically, not he but John A. had benefited.

There is no evidence that Brown ever regretted his generosity. John A. built Canada from coast to coast. But it was George Brown's towering directness and uncompromising vision of Canada's needs which gave John A. his opportunity. That vision, even after his death, must have approved of the transcontinental, even if Brown's principles would have disapproved of John A.'s methods.

CHAPTER XXIII

1874–75

British Columbia Threatens Secession–American Free Traders–The Whoop-up Country and the Cypress Hills Massacre–The Mounties March West–"Maintiens le Droit"

1

BY 1878 the sands of patience had run out in British Columbia. It had been promised a transcontinental to be begun at both ends of the Dominion within two years and to be completed within ten. What it had received had been a farcical turning of the sod on July 19, 1873, at Esquimalt (at that time the chosen western terminus), a plethora of Sandford Fleming's surveys, and bits and pieces of railroads in the East, none further west than Winnipeg.

Nor had its indignant yelps brought results. The "Rebellion" of 1874, when 800 Victoria citizens had stormed into the "bird cages" demanding the railway, had made Mackenzie send out James D. Edgar to try to placate the province. The parley ended in an uproar. Then, the Premier, G. A. Walkem, appealed to the Queen. This led to the "Carnarvon terms," suggesting that the Dominion build a railway from Esquimalt to Nanaimo at once, push on its cross-Canada surveys, construct immediately a wagon and telegraph line across the West, spend $2,000,000 a year at least, and complete the transcontinental by December 31, 1890.

The bill to build the Esquimalt–Nanaimo road was killed in the Canadian Senate by a majority of two–and it happened that two senators had recently been appointed by Mackenzie. British Columbia yelped again; and with the decline of the gold trade, it, too, was staring into the lackluster eyes of depression. In January

1876 the Walkem government was defeated for borrowing money from a Dominion which had defaulted on its obligations. That same summer the governor general, the Earl of Dufferin was sent out to see what an appeal to the British connection could do. He found arches set up with slogans, among which were "Carnarvon Terms or Separation." In June of 1878 Walkem came back into power on a policy of "Fight Ottawa." In August he introduced to the legislature a resolution for secession if the Dominion did not start the transcontinental by May 1879.

That resolution carried by a vote of 14 to 9. It was sent to Ottawa, and to London. Time, it appeared, had run out. But then John A. won the Dominion September election. Since he had lost his own seat in Kingston, he stood for Victoria and was elected. British Columbia decided to sit back and wait for what the old master would pull out of his magician's hat.

2

In the seventies British Columbia's temper had been getting shorter and shorter. In Manitoba there had been the migration of the *métis* to the valley of the Saskatchewan River, the Winnipeg boom (from 241 people to 8000 within a decade), the sternwheelers on the Red River, and in 1878 the junction of the rails at Emerson to link Winnipeg with St. Paul.

In those same seventies the face of the Northwest was changed almost beyond recognition. It was as if its destiny, having nodded sleepily for centuries, had suddenly awakened to furious energy. When her molding fingers paused, neither Indian nor buffalo roamed the prairies.

The first of the decisive days was July 8, 1874. On that date, with Mackenzie in power at Ottawa, from Fort Dufferin in Manitoba, just across the border from Pembina, the Mounties marched out, their faces turned toward the setting sun and the Whoop-up country.

The Americans had been the final creators of the newly organized and as yet untried "Force." Canada's stupidity and carelessness had also had a share in its genesis.

By the Manitoba Act the Northwest Territories were to be ruled by Lieutenant Governor Archibald of Manitoba with an emergency council of three. In 1872, his successor, Alexander Morris, was given a council of not more than fifteen and not less than seven, all appointees of the governor general.

To govern all the vast Northwest by such a method was to expect an infant to run a turbulent thousand-acre ranch. There were no armed forces. The few communities of whites and *métis* hugged the H.B.C. posts or the missions like frightened children. In all, there were only seven embryonic mission colonies in what is now Saskatchewan and Alberta. Except for buffalo-hunting camps, the rest of the settlements clung close to the H.B.C. forts. The missions and posts reached out from Manitoba westward as far as Fort Qu'Appelle and then swung up through the Touchwood Hills to the park-land country from Fort Carlton northeastward to Prince Albert and Fort à la Corne and westward to Fort Edmonton and Rocky Mountain House.

Inevitably the H.B.C. still traded for furs and applied what law and order there was. Equally inevitably, it was still an Indian land. The buffalo still roamed the prairies and the foothills. The Indians still fought their tribal wars. On December 22, 1873, Chief Factor Henry Hardisty wrote from Fort Edmonton:

"By the hunters who arrived today, I hear that the Crees have had a good whipping from the Blackfeet lately. It appears that a large party of Crees went . . . to steal horses and, seeing at a distance a few lodges, concluded to make a descent upon them but . . . it was a very large camp of the Blackfeet. The Blackfeet rushed out and chased the Crees into the South Branch of the Saskatchewan . . . and killed fifty-three of them."

The Blackfeet! These were the fierce Riders of the Plains among whom no fur company or missionary had been able to establish a permanent post. Their Confederacy tied together the Piegans, Sarcees, Bloods, and Blackfeet into a league which held sway from Fort Qu'Appelle to the Rockies and from the 49th parallel to the fur-bearing park-land and forest country to the north. They had never heard of the Manitoba Act and would have laughed if they had heard. Theirs was the buffalo. And theirs were the treeless plains and the foothills. They had the white man's horses and the white man's knives and guns. Except for rum and whisky, the buffalo supplied all their other needs—their meat, their tents, their clothing, and even, from buffalo chips, their fuel.

The white man made them another present, the smallpox. It was the great epidemics of 1837–38 and 1869–70 which broke the power of the Blackfeet, not the whites. The smallpox struck again in 1873. In the letter from Henry Hardisty already quoted, he mentions:

"I should think that between enemies and small-pox the different tribes of Indians who infest the plains must be gradually getting less. There is one tribe of Indians . . . called the Circees [Sarcees] . . . who are only left with one tent. . . . The tribe was supposed to have numbered sixty lodges last spring."

Even so, the writ of neither Canada nor the H.B.C. ran among the Blackfoot Confederacy. But by the early seventies, up from Fort Benton in Montana, the free traders had begun to push into the land which Canada had failed so far to make her own.

The Americans had a more restless foot and far less sense of responsibility than the Scots of the H.B.C. Their first entry into Montana had been in the Lewis and Clark 1804–6 expedition. The killing of two Piegans in a brawl on the Marias River etched a sharp hostility between the Americans and the Blackfoot Confederacy. For decades American traders attempting to cross the boundary were attacked and turned back. Meantime, in the forties the American Fur Company, moving up the Missouri, the river of which Senator Ingalls said that it was "a little too thick for a beverage and a little too thin for cultivation," had placed Fort Benton on its upper reaches. The Blackfoot country became a no man's land between the American traders and the H.B.C.

In 1864, however, the American Fur Company sold out to the Northwest Fur Company. The new company slackened the reins. First gold seekers and then free traders, whose only respect was for a quick profit, rushed in. The Blackfeet had been traveling north each year to trade at Fort Edmonton. Since 1860 the H.B.C., however, had pretty well abandoned the use of liquor in trade. The Americans offered rapid-fire rifles—and whisky. In 1869 two of them netted $50,000 among the Blackfeet, and the Helena *Daily Herald* commented: "Not very bad for a six months' cruise among the Lo family across the border." By 1870 the Blackfeet were carrying new repeating rifles, and in the next year they did not appear at the H.B.C. posts but traded with the Americans.

Thus, whisky and rifles had changed the whole current of trade in the Blackfoot country. Fort Benton, at the head of navigation, by this time had become the "Chicago of the North." Up to its docks splashed the stern-wheelers with goods for the Indian trade and for the gold fields to the west and southwest. Downstream went the pelts and the buffalo robes, over 100,000 in a season. At

Fort Benton there was a mile-long levee and a main street which was an almost continuous line of false-fronted saloons and hotels. Out from it surged the free traders, the wolfers, and the fly-by-night whisky runners. Back they came to drink up their profits in its saloons.

Two Fort Benton merchants financed the enterprises—Isaac G. Baker, a man with a clean-shaven upper lip, a Puritan's steel-trap mouth, and a beard and an acquisitive nose, and the alert-faced, mustachioed Thomas C. Power. They skimmed the rich cream of the trade among the Blackfeet. The wolfers and the free traders took the risks.

The wolfers were hated by Indian and free traders alike. In their search for pelts they spread strychnine bait indiscriminately, which the Indians' dogs swallowed as avidly as the wolves, so that the Indians often turned against all whites. Meanwhile, the wolfers fulminated against the traders for selling the Blackfeet rifles. At one time they organized a rough group of cavalry to try to drive the traders out.

The free traders, however, many of them ex-soldiers from the Civil War, were the true bane of the Blackfoot country. They were after buffalo hides, since eastern industry had discovered that, in addition to the market for buffalo robes, the hides could be cut into excellent belts for power machinery.

The annual buffalo hunts for pemmican and buffalo robes and coats had already made huge inroads upon the seemingly endless herds, both north and south of the border. Now, in the rush for the hides alone, while the meat was left stinking on the plains, in a few years the shaggy carpet of moving beasts was to be practically exterminated.

That fact was of no concern to the American traders, infected as they were with the white man's incurable and diseased hunger for quick and huge profits. They offered the Blackfeet rifles, axes, hatchets, blankets, calico, colored prints and cheap trinkets, beads, leather belts, and brass wire along with tobacco, tea, sugar, salt, and flour.

Their main staple was whisky. For the "whoop-up bug-juice" the Blackfeet would trade robes, pelts, weapons, horses, and squaws until they had nothing left.

The "bug-juice" was not even good whisky. One recipe from those days was to mix together a quart of whisky, a pound of chewing tobacco, a handful of red pepper, a bottle of Jamaica ginger, and a quart of molasses, dilute the whole with water, heat it to make it true firewater, and sell it by the mugful. Other traders mixed wine with water and dumped in tea leaves and tobacco. Another formula combined "Perry's Famous Painkiller" with Hostetter's Bitters, tobacco, and molasses and added a dash of red ink for color. Against this sort of offering the H.B.C. posts could not compete. The concoctions also crazed the Indians into wild orgies and killings. In 1872 Colonel Robertson Ross reported to Ottawa:

"The demoralization of the Indians and injury to the country from this illicit traffic is very great. It is stated on good authority that last year eighty-eight of the Blackfeet Indians were murdered in drunken brawls among themselves. . . . At Fort Edmonton during the present summer whisky was openly sold to the Blackfeet and other Indians trading at the post by some smugglers from the United States (these men had driven their wagons all the way from Fort Benton) . . . and on these traders being remonstrated with . . . they coolly replied that they knew very well that what they were doing was contrary to the law of both countries, but as there was no force to prevent them, they would do just as they pleased."

The main trail for this illegal traffic led north from Fort Benton to Fort Whoop-up, a post sited at the junction of the St. Mary and Oldman rivers, about eleven miles south of the present-day city of Lethbridge in southern Alberta. For the Americans were now taking over the land which Canada had left vacant. Standoff, near the merging of the Waterton and Belly rivers, is said to have got its name from Joseph Kipp and his traders "standing off" U. S. Marshall Charles D. Hard at that point. Slideout took its title from a report that a band of Blood Indians were on the warpath.

"We . . . had a few drinks of bug-juice," W. S. Gladstone, the ex-H.B.C. carpenter who had written about the digging up of the body of Chief Factor Rowand at Fort Edmonton, relates, "and got talking about what we would do. . . . A Dutchman in the gang said we had better slide out, so it has been called Slideout ever since."

There were other picturesque names for the American posts, such as Robber's Roost and Whisky Gap. The most imposing center, however, was Fort Whoop-up. It is said to have got its striking sobriquet from a Pennsylvania Dutchman who, when asked in Fort Benton how things were going, replied: "Oh, we're just whoopen-on-em-up."

Wherever its name came from, it was a permanent post, built of heavy squared timber in a rectangle with earth-covered roofs to prevent its being set on fire. It had two bastions, each mounting an antiquated brass cannon. There were loopholes in the walls; since, when the Indians came to after their drunken orgies to find themselves stripped of all their possessions, they sometimes attacked. Inside the walls were warehouses, cookrooms, living quarters, and a blacksmith's shop. Soon the whole area was called the Whoop-up country. It was from Fort Whoop-up that an oft-quoted but probably apocryphal letter was said to have been written to Fort Benton in the fall of 1873:

> Dear friend:
>
> My partner Will Geary got to putting on airs and I shot him and he is dead—the potatoes are looking well—
>
> Yours truly,
> Snookum Jim.

That letter sums up the spirit of Whoop-up.

At Fort Whoop-up itself the trader Johnny Healy had put down stubborn roots. It became evident that, if Canada failed to move, the Americans would take over the Blackfoot country by default. Meantime, even worse than the more or less established free traders were the small operators who would drive across the line with a wagonload of whisky, set up a one-night stand in a coulee, and decamp in the morning before their victims had recovered from their drunk. The Indians had been badly shattered by the great smallpox epidemics. Now, under the curse of the whisky trade, their demoralization was complete. In 1874 Father Scollen wrote:

"It was painful to me to see the state of poverty to which they had been reduced. Formerly they had been the most opulent Indians in the country; now they were clothed in rags and without guns." (For "Whoop-up bug-juice" the Indians would even trade back the rifles their buffalo hides had bought.)

It might be noted as a proof of the disintegration of the fierce Blackfeet that in 1873 Father Scollen had been able to found the first permanent Catholic mission among them, twenty-one miles southwest of where Calgary now stands. In the same year the two McDougalls, George and his son John, had established a

Methodist mission at Morley in the foothills country west of Calgary and halfway to Banff. Its log church still stands. It was near here that the Reverend George McDougall froze to death in a blizzard in the winter of 1876.

The two missions, however, could do little except protest against the cynical lawlessness of the Americans. Meantime, the reports of their infiltration into Canadian territory had led Sir John A. Macdonald to consider the formation of the Mounties. The final flick came from the May 1873 Cypress Hills massacre.

The Cypress Hills in southwestern Saskatchewan are a vestigial remnant of preglacial days. Here plants and insects which should be fossils survive. And here, another prehistoric survival, a group of American wolfers, found themselves early in May of 1873 in pursuit of horses which had been stolen from them when encamped in American territory five miles from Fort Benton.

The trail of the horse stealers had led to the Cypress Hills. There it was lost. T. C. Power of Fort Benton had a post at Battle Creek under a certain Abel Farwell. The wolfers, who were commanded by a man named John Evans, went to Farwell's post to anesthetize their disappointment with whisky. Two hundred feet away and across a creek was another post, under Moses Solomon. Near by was the camp of Little Soldier's North Assiniboins.

Both traders were hated by the Indians. To exacerbate the situation, on that pleasant Sunday of early May, with the spring birds caroling and the trees in a mist of green, both Indians and whites were drinking themselves thoroughly drunk. Shortly after midday, one of the wolfers, George Hammond, bawled out that a horse of his, which had been stolen and returned, had been stolen again. The Benton party rushed to the Indian camp. After an excited and drunken parley (the supposedly stolen horse was grazing on a hill near by) the whites, who, in fear of the Indians, had retired to a coulee three to eight feet deep which ran to within fifty yards of the Indian camp, fired a volley. The braves charged the coulee three times but were driven back. However, one of the wolfers was killed. The rest retreated to the trading post.

Their fire, however, prevented the braves from returning to their lodges. By nightfall the Indians were scattered. Then the Fort Benton men raged into the Indian camp. They found Little Soldier in hiding, killed him, cut off his head, and set it up on a pole. They raped whatever squaws they found and slew children along with adults. About thirty Indians in all—men, women, and children—were massacred. To make the butchery still more of a drunken outrage, Little Soldier's band had had nothing to do with the original stealing of horses.

It seems incredible that when these desperadoes returned to Fort Benton they were hailed as heroes who had taught Canadian Indians a needed lesson. The Cypress Hills massacre, however, did harden the resolution to send out a force to police the Northwest before the chaos became so complete that the Americans could march in. The Northwest Mounted Police (the name was not changed to the Royal Canadian Mounted Police until 1920) was set up by a bill brought in by John A. Macdonald. That bill was passed on May 20, 1873. The organization of the force took over a year. By that time Alexander Mackenzie had replaced John A. as Prime Minister. Meantime, however, Lieutenant Colonel French, an Imperial officer, was in charge as commissioner. Six divisions of fifty men had been authorized, each with a superintendent, an inspector, and a subinspector. Ordinary constables got a dollar a day, subconstables seventy-five cents. Superintendents were paid from $1000 to $1400 a year, and even the commissioner was set down to receive not more than $2600 annually and not less than $1000.

In spite of wages at which today's ditchdigger would scarcely trouble to sneer, by October of 1873 three troops had been recruited. This first contingent was sent by the vile Dawson Route to Fort Garry. The first regimental sergeant major, and also the first man to enlist, was A. H. Griesbach, who had served in the 15th Hussars and the Cape Mounted Rifles. It might be noted that his son, of Edmonton, became the Major General Griesbach of Boer War and First World War fame. Other men who were to win renown in the West were in this contingent—S. B. Steele, later to be a major general and knighted; Robert Belcher, after whom, as Lieutenant Colonel Belcher, the Belcher Hospital in modern Calgary is named; and Cecil Denny, later Sir Cecil Denny, whose reminiscences in *The Law Marches West* bring back the color of the early days of the N.W.M.P.

The first contingent drilled all winter. By April of 1874 most of the remaining men had been got together at the New Fort, Toronto, while horses for the whole force had been bought at an average of $150 per head. Men and horses left Toronto in June 1874 along with nine carloads of wagon and agricultural implements. Their route, however, was via St. Paul, to Fort Dufferin, near the present-day Emerson, Manitoba.

Here, the N.W.M.P. were assembled. Hence, on July 8, they set out. There were, according to the "Marching-out State" of that day, 275 red-coated cavalry in six troops. The troopers wore pill-box forage caps, with helmets tucked away for parade occasions. Below the scarlet tunics were black breeches with two white stripes (later changed to red and then to yellow, as at present) and high black-leather boots. Heavy dark-blue overcoats were in their packs. Their belts carried revolvers and cartridge pouches. Snider carbines were thrust into the boots of their saddles. Their mounts were carefully chosen to make an impression—A Troop rode dark bays, B dark browns, C bright chestnuts, D grays, E blacks, and F light bays.

3

Such was the force which had been organized to bring order to the Cypress Hills and the Whoop-up country and to enforce the law over a quarter of a continent, less than 300 men with the buffalo head as their insignia and "*Maintiens le Droit*" as their motto. It was too large a body to be completely ignored. It was far too small to be an army. Any concerted Indian attack could wipe out the whole of it. Behind it, as it moved out over the prairie, its destination Fort Whoop-up, followed 114 squealing Red River carts with their *métis* drivers, 73 wagons, 2 nine-pounder guns, 2 mortars, and a mélange of work oxen (142), bawling cows, steers, and calves, for meat and for breeding, 93 plows, harrows, and mowing machines.

The whole cavalcade stretched like a crawling, bright-headed snake for a distance of four to five miles. Most of the "Force" were Easterners, men green to the Northwest. Their line of march was, at first, strewn with broken carts and abandoned animals. When, on the twenty-ninth of July, the cavalcade paused at Roche Percée, some 270 miles out of Fort Dufferin, it took a whole day for the stragglers to come in.

Small as the "Force" was, it was now divided. From Roche Percée, part of Troop A was sent off under Inspector Jarvis north-westward to Fort Edmonton, which it reached on October 27. The rest set their faces toward the setting sun. It was still a tenderfoot march. Denny himself, for instance, while hunting antelope, rode his horse into a patch of alkali. His horse sank until only its head and neck showed and it took hours to extricate it. At last, on the twenty-fifth of August, the scarlet-tunicked riders sighted the Cypress Hills. They had already seen their first buffalo on the eighth of that month and, nine days later, had met the Red River hunters, their carts heavy with buffalo meat. Along with these was Père Lestanc, the priest who had tried to moderate Louis Riel. Now the buffalo increased. "There were places," Denny writes, "where as far as the eye could reach untold thousands were in sight, the country black with them." At last, on September 9, the N.W.M.P. came to the junction of the Bow and Belly (now Oldman) rivers, where Fort Whoop-up, according to their information, was supposed to be. No fort stared at them.

The Force was lost. Snow fell. There was ice on the water. Commissioner French's comment was bitter. "Here," he reported, "we were supposed to find luxuriant pasturage, a perfect garden of Eden, climate milder than Toronto, etc. As far as our experience goes, that vicinity for sixty or seventy miles in every direction is little better than a desert."

In the back of the commissioner's mind was the knowledge that on the twentieth of September in the previous year, this whole area had been covered by a foot of snow. Here he was with some 250 men lost in the middle of nowhere. Winnipeg was 800 miles to the east, Fort Edmonton over 300 miles to the north. With not even a railroad, much less an automobile or an airplane, to help him, these were formidable distances. Some sixteen miles up the Belly River a ford was found. Two scouting parties were sent out. The one with which Denny rode traveled up the Bow River. It saw thousands of snorting buffaloes swimming the river. It met a war party of fifty Assiniboins. Though the Mounties did not know it, that party had just attacked a group of white traders, had killed one of them, and had burned their wagons but had itself lost all its horses to a Blackfoot foray.

Such was life in 1874 just below present-day Calgary, A snowstorm hit the Mounties on September 15. Colonel French moved them through it to Milk River near the boundary line. Fort Whoop-up was still elusive. The nearest place for help was Fort Benton, a hundred miles away. On the twenty-second Colonels French and Macleod set out for it, after starting Troops D and E back East for their winter quarters at Fort Pelly on the Swan River in Manitoba. As the remaining Mounties waited, an enterprising Benton trader drove up with a wagon filled with canned goods, sirup, sugar, and the like. He charged $3 a gallon for the sirup and $20 for a sack of flour. The Mounties were again in touch with civilization.

Meantime, at Fort Benton contracts were made with the J. G. Baker Company to supply the Mounties. Until the railroad came, in fact, the forces in the Whoop-up country had to bring in their supplies by boat along the Missouri from Bismarck to Fort Benton and thence overland by the bull teams—twelve to fourteen oxen tugging forward three canvas-covered wagons to the pistol cracks of the bull whips. Those wives of the police who came West traveled the same route.

From the "Chicago of the North," Commissioner French set out to overtake Troops D and E in order to lead them to Fort Pelly and ultimately back to Fort Dufferin, a total round trip of 2000 miles. Colonel Macleod returned to his remaining 150 men. He brought with him the shrewd and colorful half-breed guide Jerry Potts. At last, on October 9, the N.W.M.P. came in sight of the long-sought Fort Whoop-up. A homemade flag flew above it. The Mounties wheeled their cannon into position. They moved in ready for a fight. All they found was one old man and three or four squaws. After this, Colonel Macleod established his first permanent camp, on an island in the Oldman River about a mile downstream from the center of the present-day townsite of Fort Macleod, amid a heavy growth of woods. Here the Mounties flung up a hasty Fort Macleod. The next spring, after being flooded out, they shifted it to the bank of the river about a thousand yards west of today's town. In the distance the Rockies gleamed in the sun. To the north and west were the heavily forested Porcupine Hills and to the south and east the buffalo-dotted prairies. Then the police turned to the job of enforcing the law.

Such was the famous trek of the Northwest Mounted Police, an achievement in itself, but one magnified beyond proportion by legend. In actuality, the plains had been crossed many times before this by missionaries, by the buffalo-hunting *métis*, by surveying parties, by travelers such as Milton and Cheadle and the wide-ranging Butler. The Reverend John McDougall in his *On Western Trails* recalls that once, when Inspector Jarvis was drawing the long bow, he pointed out to him the case of a French half-breed near Edmonton who in spring loaded his cart and, with his wife and children and his catch of furs and pemmican, made the round trip to Fort Garry; then, back at Edmonton, put up hay, fixed his winter quarters, and, again with his family, moved out two to three hundred miles into the plains to run buffalo, and yet took the whole thing as an ordinary spring, summer, and autumn's work.

The true achievement of the Mounties was not in their long march but in the law and order some 300 men enforced over the major part of what is now the provinces of Alberta and Saskatchewan. In the fall of 1874 there were only Colonel Macleod's 150 police to keep peace in the Whoop-up country. Their first capture, made by Inspector Crozier, set the pattern. He came upon Henry Taylor and Bond, the latter a Spanish Negro, some miles up the river, trying to escape south with several hundred robes and a quantity of whisky. The liquor was poured out. The robes, wagons, and teams were confiscated. The men, shepherded into Fort Macleod, were each given the choice of a $25 fine or six months' imprisonment.

The Americans howled injustice. Taylor finally paid his fine. Bond had no money. Unfortunately for himself, he escaped from the fort. In the spring his body was discovered by the Indians some thirty miles south. It was a strange fate, indeed, which brought him so far north to freeze to death in the trackless, snowbound prairie.

By ceaseless patrols such as these the Force killed off, or at least put a severe check on, the whisky runners. What was more important, these 150 men during that first winter won the confidence of the Blackfeet and their allied tribes. The Indians came to believe that the Mounties meted out equal justice to white and red men. The Blackfoot chiefs themselves understood the benefits of the suppression of the American free traders. On the occasion of Treaty 7 in 1877 the famous Chief Crowfoot said:

"If the Police hadn't come to the country, where would we all be now? Bad men and whisky were killing us so fast that very few, indeed, of us would have been left today. The Police have protected us as the feathers of the bird protect it from the frosts of winter."

By a combination of firmness and fair dealing the handful of Mounties kept better order in the vast Northwest than thousands of troops south of the border could enforce. A pathetic question posed to the Canadian Minister of the Interior a few years later while he was in Washington gives away the secret.

"How," the minister was asked, "do you keep your whites in order?"

While Canada delayed her transcontinental, the Mounties saved the West for her.

4

It is, perhaps, worth while to see through the eyes of the Mounties the Blackfeet in their last few years of untrammeled freedom. Decimated by the smallpox, their braves numbered about eight thousand. In summer they lived on the plains. They wintered in the wooded river bottoms. Their tents were floored with buffalo robes. They ate chiefly buffalo meat but had acquired a fondness for tea. Their tobacco was mixed with the dried inner bark of the red willow. Polygamy was the practice. Some chiefs had as many as twenty to thirty women, yet, unlike the Crees, the Blackfeet were jealous of their wives. Their tribal dances to the sun and to the buffalo were spectacular. Their over-all worship was that of the Great Spirit as manifested in the forces of nature and in animals. War with the Crees to the north and the Montana tribes to the south, often initiated by the sport of horse stealing, was one of their pastimes. Their dead were left in the forks of trees or in the lodges along the river bottoms with their possessions beside them and horses killed to accompany them to the Happy Hunting Grounds.

It was their misfortune, one which they shared with all the Indians of both the Americas, to meet with the white man's civilization before they themselves had left the Stone Age. Once again, as in all history, those who were less developed in the techniques of killing were brushed out of the way of "civilization."

It was among the Blackfeet and against the whisky runners that the N.W.M.P. were tempered into "The Force." At their first Christmas in Fort Macleod the Easterners learned to eat buffalo hump instead of roast beef and to dance with the half-breed belles. They also learned to put a stop to drunken Indian orgies and to hunt whisky runners in below-zero weather.

One of Denny's patrols in that winter of 1875 illustrates their work. Four Mounties in bitter weather traveled three days through deep snow to a creek at the foot of the mountains in pursuit of a trader who had been reported selling liquor to the Indians. On the last evening, while camping with a band of

Piegans, they found, confiscated, and spilled a five-gallon can of alcohol. When on the next day they reached the trader's camp, he had fled. The Mounties poured ten gallons of alcohol into the snow and seized 200 robes and a horse. Then they followed the trail of the trader. Though it was well below zero, they had to camp out that night without tent or covering but did manage a fire. Snow fell toward morning. The next night the patrol rode down into a heavy patch of wood on the river bottom. There, well concealed, was a log house with several sleighs about and a band of hobbled horses scraping away the snow to reach the grass beneath.

There was smoke from the stovepipe thrust out from the isolated cabin, miles away from anywhere. Denny and a sergeant pushed in. Three men looked up in consternation from their cards and liquor, while a couple of squaws stared at the police from the corner of the single room. The patrol arrested the men, dumped large stocks of liquor, and seized hundreds of robes along with packs of other pelts. They then shepherded the whole outfit over the weary miles through the cold and the snow back to the fort. Colonel Macleod fined each of the men $250 and, as usual, confiscated all their belongings. The squaws returned to the Piegan camp.

Episode after episode of this sort built the tradition that the Mounties always "got their man." In that same winter Colonel Macleod moved to bring to justice the authors of the Cypress Hills massacre. Accompanied by Captain Denny, Sergeant Cochrane, Subconstable Ryan, and the guide Jerry Potts, he set out for Fort Benton. It was March, but March in the Northwest can turn on the traveler like a wounded grizzly. During the second day, in twenty-below-zero weather, a blinding blizzard swooped down. On Potts' advice the party dug a deep hole in the north bank of the Milk River and crowded into it, with their unsaddled horses close by. Buffaloes, too, packed themselves under the lee of the bank for shelter. The men had no fire and it was deep below zero. At the end of thirty-six hours, rather than freeze where they crouched, they set out into the blizzard, riding and walking by turns. At one point Subconstable Ryan could not mount his horse because his buffalo-skin breeches were frozen stiff. Fortunately, by the next day the blizzard had howled itself out.

The attempt to bring the authors of the Cypress Hills massacre to justice became an international incident. By May 7, 1875, Colonels Macleod and Irvine were so successful in collecting evidence that the British minister at Washington asked for fourteen warrants for the Evans party. The U. S. Government ordered the Montana authorities to co-operate. On June 21, seven of the wanted men were picked up at Fort Benton. The extradition proceedings were held in Helena.

Local feeling, led by a group of Irish Fenians in Fort Benton, was all in favor of the accused, while the Montana newspapers defended the massacre as the sort of thing necessary to keep Indians in order. The men were discharged. Helena held a torchlight procession in their honor. Colonel Macleod was picked up by the local police on a charge of making a false arrest. He was, of course, freed, but when the leaders of the Cypress Hills butchery returned to Fort Benton, there was a public holiday "with flags flying, bands playing, and horses prancing." That evening at a mass meeting, the Fenian "Colonel" Donnelly, who had been involved in the invasion from Vermont in 1866 and the raid from Pembina in 1871, denounced Canada and its government. John Evans, the leader of the Cypress Hills party, promptly opened the Extradition Saloon. It was satisfactorily patronized.

The Mounties were not, as yet, checkmated. Three of the Cypress Hills gang (James Hughes, George Bell, and Philander Vogle) made the mistake of returning to the scene of their crime. The police nabbed them. They were taken to Winnipeg to be put on trial for the "wanton and atrocious slaughter of peaceable and inoffensive people." The accused turned to the U.S. consul, who was still none other than James Wickes Taylor, the special agent of the U.S. during the Red River rebellion. In Montana, James Evans collected $400 for them. The U. S. State Department took a hand. For one reason and another the trial was postponed for a year. In June of 1876 the prisoners were acquitted.

Their arrest and trial, however—and the legend that they had received stiff sentences—was the touch to convince the Indians that in Canada there was justice for the red man as well as for the white.

CHAPTER XXIV

1875–76

Beginnings of Settlement in the Blackfoot Country—Fort Calgary—Stern-Wheelers on the North Saskatchewan.

AN unforeseen corollary to the westward march of the law was the beginning of settlement in the Blackfoot country. By the end of the first winter, 1874–75, both the T. C. Power and I. G. Baker companies of Fort Benton had opened stores near Fort Macleod. An ex-whisky trader, Tony Chappelle, sold tobacco and candy and had two billiard tables. Soon there were other stores. Gladstone, the ex-H.B.C. carpenter, opened a carpenter's shop. A blacksmith set up for trade. So did a shoemaker. A couple of gambling dens for faro and poker, run by "Poker" Brown and "Ace" Sampler, who could take out the ace of a card at twenty-five yards with his pistol, completed the nucleus of a frontier town—and all within a few months.

These men came up the Whoop-up Trail from Fort Benton since, after all, the Mounties had to spend their dollar a day somewhere. Both Father Scollen and the Reverend George McDougall visited the post. McDougall's sons, John and David, had in 1873 brought some fifty head of cattle and horses to the mission post at Morley. (David was the trader son, while John was the preacher who trod in his father's footsteps.) Next year, while the Mounties were marching West, they had driven up a hundred head of steers and breeding stock over the long, wild trail from Fort Benton. What Methodist missionaries could do, others could imitate. During the fine summer of 1875, according to Captain Denny, a few cows were brought in from Fort Benton to an embryonic ranch on the Oldman River, three miles from Fort Macleod, by Joe McFarland and Henry Olson. Another ex-whisky trader, "Dutch" Fred Watcher, grew vegetables for the police on the Belly River. Near the fort itself, a subconstable, whose wife, along with Mrs. Macleod and two other wives, had made the long journey from the East via Fort Benton, resigned from the police and started to farm. The N.W.M.P. themselves opened a ranch-farm at Pincher Creek in the midst of the foothills, planting grain and setting up a depot of mares and stallions. Other settlers began to drift in.

The shape of things to come was slowly coalescing. That same summer of 1875 the police escorted the Imperial officer in charge of the Canadian militia on a tour from Winnipeg to Fort Edmonton and south from there to the boundary. Meantime, the N.W.M.P. had established Fort Saskatchewan, twenty miles northeast of Edmonton, and Fort Walsh in the Cypress Hills. In both cases small villages mushroomed around the posts. In September of the same bustling year Troop F from Fort Macleod chose the site of modern Calgary for a post. Captain Denny is almost lyrical about the view from the hill on the north side of the Bow, as it was then:

"Below us," he writes, "lay a lovely valley, flanked on the south by rolling hills. Thick woods bordered the banks of both streams; to the west towered mountains with their snowy peaks; beyond the Elbow stretched another wide valley, and heavy timber further west along the Bow. Buffalo in large bands grazed in the valley. . . . Our first sight of this enchanting spot was one never to be forgotten, one to which only a poet could do justice."

Today, less than a century later, those valleys house a great city, the city of the stampede and also the city of the offices which manage Canada's biggest oil fields. That city has crawled up over the hills on all sides and the buffalo are gone.

The building of the post here—first called Fort Brisbois and then by Colonel Macleod, Calgary, from an old castle on the Isle of Mull (the name in Gaelic is said to mean "clear running water") —took until Christmas. It was put up on the plateau of high ground at the forks of the Bow and Elbow. Half-breeds with Red River carts rolled down from Edmonton to build cabins on both sides of the Elbow. I. G. Baker's men from Benton threw up a general store with several log houses for dwellings. The ex-whisky trader Taylor, the man arrested by Inspector Crozier, brought in a billiard table from Macleod and tossed together a hall to house it, along with dances and the sale of homemade beer and candies. The Reverend George McDougall trekked in from Morley to erect a small church a little to the west of the fort for services on alternate Sundays. A small Hudson's Bay store, flung up in 1874 on the Ghost River to the west, was dragged in to be set up on the east side of the Elbow. It stocked flintlock muskets, H.B.C. capotes, pigtail tobacco sold by the fathom, carrot tobacco in three-pound rolls, and the H.B.C. heavy knife.

Calgary had been begun. For a touch of the old life, Denny records that in winter of 1876, while he was on a visit to Edmonton, the dogs were yelping for their frozen whitefish inside the stockade and bateaux were being built at the river's edge, while the warehouses were stocked to the roof with pemmican and the logs of the stockade were pitted with freshly made bullet gouges from the guns of drunken Indians.

Mounties, missionaries, and H.B.C. traders, these three forged the beginnings of settlement in a Northwest that was awaiting the transcontinental. But, except for the posts of the N.W.M.P. and the two missions of Father Scollen and the McDougalls, those settlements, avoiding the Blackfoot country, scattered themselves in the park land along the valley of the North Saskatchewan. The Catholics had missions for the *métis* at St. Laurent, near Fort Carlton, and at St. Albert, Lac la Biche, and Lac Ste. Anne—these three within reaching distance of Fort Edmonton. In the Fort Edmonton country, too, were the Methodist posts at Pakan (Victoria) and White Fish Lake (Pigeon Lake). At Prince Albert, northeast of Fort Carlton, in 1866 the Presbyterian Reverend James Nisbet had set up a mission for the English and Scots half-breeds. By December 16, 1878, Patrick Gammie Laurie, editor, owner, manager, and printer of the first newspaper in the Northwest, the *Saskatchewan Herald*, wrote that "within the last five years . . . Prince Albert . . . has been making great strides. . . . The buffalo-hunter is rapidly giving way to the farmer and the Indian trader to the merchant."

Meanwhile, in 1874 the surveyors of the projected telegraph line to the coast made their headquarters 160 miles upstream from Prince Albert, near the junction of the Battle River with the North Saskatchewan. From this came the community of Battleford. In 1875 the Northwest was given its own lieutenant governor to add to its own separate council, though the Dominion still kept control of the N.W.M.P., Indian affairs, and natural resources. Two years later Battleford became the capital.

It was the growth of the Saskatchewan Valley communities which in 1874 led the H.B.C. to put the *Northcote,* built to "swim in a heavy dew," on the North Saskatchewan. Soon five paddle steamers were churning the waters of that swift-flowing stream as far as Edmonton.

On a bright October day in 1876, a tall, gangling young man stood on the south bank of the North Saskatchewan and took his first look at Edmonton. Behind him on the level plateau, where the buildings of the University of Alberta now cast their shadows, was the bull team which he had helped prod across the prairie and through the park land all the weary miles from Winnipeg. Before the six-foot Frank Oliver lay the mile-wide curving valley of the river. Below him was the fast-flowing, mighty Saskatchewan, bordered by poplars and balm of Gilead in their dress of autumn gold, which were set off by dark clumps of fir and pine. Here and there were patches of cultivation in the flats along the river. On the opposite bank, flooded with sunlight, Fort Edmonton stood out, with shacks scattered above and below it.

"I was so impressed," Oliver was to write later, after he became a cabinet minister in Ottawa, "that at that moment Edmonton became home for me."

The young ox pusher was the genuine stuff from which pioneers are made. In 1873 he had moved from Peel County, Ontario, to Winnipeg. There he set type for the *Free Press.* Once arrived in Edmonton, he bought for twenty-five dollars the first lot ever sold there and threw up a log hut. He tried his luck as a trader. But printer's ink itched in his arteries. He had a small hand press sent out from Philadelphia by train and oxcart. His first masthead was carved from dry birch bark. On December 8, 1880, the first issue of the Edmonton *Bulletin* appeared. It contained advertisements for such items as grain shovels, gold pans, and a "yoke of young, well-broken oxen," a warning of a possible Indian uprising, and a flaming editorial against the alleged defrauding of a band of Stoneys of their treaty money. By this time Edmonton was a community of over a thousand people.

By 1880, too, ranching had made a beginning around Fort Macleod and High River south of Calgary. In that year the communities of the Northwest stretched in a great inverted and flattened *U* from Fort Qu'Appelle up to the valley of the Saskatchewan, along it to Edmonton, and then south to Fort Macleod. Within the circuit of that flattened *U*, except for Fort Walsh and Pile of Bones (where Regina now stands), was a huge vacuum (much of the southern areas of present-day Alberta and Saskatchewan) in which the Mounties were the only semblance of law and order. In 1876, their first commissioner, Colonel French, had resigned. He was replaced by Colonel Macleod. In that same year the control of the N.W.M.P. was transferred from the Department of Justice to the Secretary of State.

The Mounties had already proved themselves. They were soon to face a sterner test. For on June 25, 1876, far to the south of the border, at the Little Bighorn River, a ring of blue-coated cavalrymen broke at last before the charge of Sitting Bull's Sioux. The yellow-haired General Custer and 264 men of his Seventh Cavalry had been annihilated.

CHAPTER XXV

1876–83

The Mounties Face Sitting Bull—General Terry of the U. S. Army at Fort Walsh—Treaty 7 with the Blackfeet—The Massacre of the Buffalo and Starvation on the Plains—The End of Sitting Bull —Canadian Indians Herded into Reservations

1

THE Sioux outbreak had been sparked by American violation of an 1868 treaty. At the Little Bighorn, however, Sitting Bull (his real name was Sitting Buffalo) had won a battle and lost his war. The U. S. Army flung itself relentlessly after the victors. Many of the Sioux fled for sanctuary to their reservations. Many fought on. In December of 1876 the U. S. Army broke the Sioux in three major battles and eight skirmishes. During that same month about 500 braves with 1000 women, 3500 horses, and 30 U. S. Army mules crossed into Canada to camp at Wood Mountain, southeast of the Cypress Hills. On May 7 of the next year, Sitting Bull himself, with 135 lodges, joined the refugees. A few days later Major Walsh of the N.W.M.P. bearded him in his tent. The two men faced each other, on the one side the decisive and fearless Mountie, on the other the short, stocky Sitting Bull, with a powerful head and an expressionless face, pitted with smallpox scars.

It was a moment pregnant with danger. Around Sitting Bull were some 4000 war-hardened Sioux, the braves armed either with Springfields or with newer rifles, equipped with telescopic sights, captured from Custer's soldiers. Behind Major Walsh were, at most, 150 scarlet-coated Mounties. Across the line stood the U. S. Army, itching for an excuse to pour across the border. On the Canadian side of the frontier were the half-tamed Blackfeet and the Crees, a double-pronged threat. They might, in anger at the invasion of their hunting grounds, decide to attack the Sioux. Or they might cast their ballot to join with them in an all-out Indian war to exterminate the whites.

Both threats were real. On the eighth of July 1876, Denny, now a subinspector, had met the Blackfoot chiefs in council. They had told him that the Sioux, after their victory at the Little Bighorn, had sent them tobacco and the promise of horses, mules, and captive white women if they would join them in wiping out first the American whites and then their Canadian cousins. The Blackfeet had refused. Then, Sitting Bull had sent another message that, once the Americans were finished, the Sioux would attack both the Canadian whites and the Blackfeet. Denny had assured the Blackfeet of police protection, and Crowfoot had then told him he would raise 2000 warriors against the Sioux.

But who could tell what the Indian reaction would finally be? Moreover, fighting of any kind would give the U. S. Army their excuse to cross the line. A more immediate peril was the fact that if the Sioux decided to attack the Mounties, 150 men would be only a mouthful for 4000 braves.

All these thoughts were in Major Walsh's mind as he faced Sitting Bull. He gave no sign of trepidation. First he tried to persuade the chief to recross the boundary to the reservation the Americans claimed they were willing to offer him and his Sioux. Sitting Bull, quite understandably, refused. His argument was that long ago the Sioux had been British subjects, an argument advanced in Red River by the refugees from the 1862 Sioux War, and that they had been told that they could find peace in the "Great Mother's land." Walsh knew that he did not have the forces to drive the Sioux back across the line as the Americans were demanding, even if he had been willing to violate their right to sanctuary. He did not, either, have the troops or the food supplies to intern them. So he told Sitting Bull that he must keep the peace and not use Canadian territory as a base for raids into the United States. The Sioux accepted the ukase, just as if Walsh had 1500 instead of 150 men behind him. In Sitting Bull's mind, undoubtedly, was the knowledge that his refuge from the Americans would be safe only if he agreed to Walsh's terms.

The Sioux stayed, "Old Men of the Sea" around Canada's neck. At government level the Americans held that either Canada should drive the Sioux back into the rifle fire of the U. S. Army or else the Sioux were the Dominion's complete responsibility. Canada wanted to be rid of them but would not agree to U.S. forces following them into Canada. Finally, Ottawa persuaded the U. S. Government to send General Terry as the head of a commission to negotiate with Sitting Bull.

2

On October 17, 1877, the big hall of Fort Walsh in the Cypress Hills was as impressive as the Mounties could make it. There was a table on one side for the American correspondents, who had come all the way from Washington and New York to this outpost in the Canadian wilds. There was another table for the American commissioners, headed by General Terry, a courteous, quiet-mannered man, six feet six inches tall. Colonel Macleod, the N.W.M.P. commissioner, sat in state in full uniform with his aides. On the floor were buffalo robes for the Sioux.

Neither Terry nor the correspondents felt too secure. The Mounties had escorted them from the border to Fort Walsh. When they reached the post the Americans were amazed to discover only sixty police there, while near by were the lodges of thousands of Sioux, in a high state of excitement. That excitement had been raised to fever pitch by the arrival, just before the conference, of fugitives from Chief Joseph's band of Nez Percé Indians. The war with the Nez Percés had begun on June 13 of this same year at Slate Creek in Idaho. Somehow Chief Joseph, with only 350 fighting men, though encumbered by women and children and attacked by forces totaling 2000 soldiers, had managed to fight his way to the Bear Paw Mountains, only a day's journey from the Canadian border.

At that point, however, he was engaged by fresh troops and compelled to surrender. The arrival of the few Nez Percés who had escaped, showing their wounds, had roused the war party among the Sioux to a frenzy. The night before the date for the conference they had put on a war dance outside the walls of Fort Walsh, at which Chief Rain in the Face had shrieked to them to rush the fort and kill all the whites, and particularly the hated Americans. Terry and his fellow commissioners could not understand the calmness of Colonel Macleod and his sixty police.

Finally, all was ready. Colonel Macleod nodded to the Mountie at the door. Led by Major Walsh, Sitting Bull and his councilors stalked in. As the correspondents watched, and, later, reported to their papers, Sitting Bull, ignoring the Americans, strode across the room to shake hands with Colonel Macleod and his officers. Not until Macleod urged the Indian to give General Terry a fair hearing did Sitting Bull turn to face the American. Terry presented the American offer. If the Sioux would return they would have to surrender their arms and horses and go on a reservation. But they would not be harmed.

The Dominion's hope was that the Sioux would accept these reasonable terms. Sitting Bull, who by this time had come to enjoy the uses of publicity, refused them with scorn.

"You come here to tell us lies," he said in part, "but we don't want to hear them. . . . Go back where you came from. This country is mine and I intend to stay here."

The attempt had failed. Sitting Bull and his Sioux were to perch on the Mounties' doorstep like sticks of dynamite for four more years, until 1881. In those four years a single false step by the Mounties would either have precipitated a massacre of the police by the Sioux or have brought the U. S. Army across the frontier like hungry wolves. Fortunately for the Northwest, however, a month before the conference at Fort Walsh, Treaty 7 had been negotiated with the Blackfoot Confederacy.

3

That September of 1877 was the last pathetic gathering of the free tribes of the plains. From all over the country the Indians streamed in to Blackfoot Crossing, southeast of Fort Calgary and ninety miles from Fort Macleod. Their white lodges, some thousands of them, glimmered in the valley on the south side of the Bow River. Huge bands of horses and ponies, approximately 15,000 in all, grazed alongside the river or on the nearby hills. Dogs barked and fought. Children played around the lodges. The squaws, impassive, drew their water from the river and tended their cooking fires or watched the feathered braves galloping their horses at full speed either in furious races or simply firing rifles in the air. From a cautious distance a number of Crees and half-breeds stared at a show, which was not a commercial rodeo but a natural expression of the Blackfoot way of life. White traders, scenting profit, had trekked in. The unbiquitous Fort

Benton merchants, Power and Baker, had flung up temporary stores with log walls and canvas roofs. Chief Factor Hardisty of the H.B.C. had ridden down from Fort Edmonton. His brother-in-law, the Reverend John McDougall, along with his brother, David, the trader, had come in from Morley. An intelligent man such as the great Indian chief Crowfoot may have sensed the future. Few, if any, of his tribesmen realized that within a decade those proud Blackfoot warriors, galloping exuberantly along the valley, would be unwanted derelicts in the land they, at the moment, owned.

Into this milieu rode Governor Laird, the big florid man with the bull-like voice who, in 1865, had helped defeat Confederation in Prince Edward Island but who, later, had repented and was now the lieutenant governor of the Northwest.

He moved in amid pomp and circumstance, escorted by 108 police, 119 horses, and two nine-pounder guns. Even so, it took several days to make the treaty because of bad blood between the Blackfeet and the Sarcees. The terms were those of Treaty 6, which, covering the North Saskatchewan area, had been signed the year before with the Plains and Woods Crees, thanks largely to the peacemaking of the Reverend George McDougall. In addition to the terms of Treaty 3, which have already been noted, there was the presentation of a horse, harness, and wagon to each chief, a medicine chest for each band, and a grant of $1000 for three years for provisions for those Indians who engaged in agriculture. A further and, as it turned out, important clause in both Treaties 6 and 7 was one which assured aid and rations in case of "any pestilence" or "general famine."

On these terms, on September 22, 1877, the Blackfoot Confederacy signed away their title to the plains and the foothills. The Canadian commissioners were Governor Laird and Colonel Macleod. Among the Indian signers were Chiefs Crowfoot, Old Sun, Red Crow, Bear's Paw, and Morning Plume. There were floods of oratory. There were salutes. There was a sham battle, which came close to becoming a real one when five to six hundred braves, stripped to feathers and war paint and a blanket around their loins, circled the N.W.M.P. camp at a gallop, yelling and firing their Winchesters. Other treaties—8 to 11—were negotiated at later dates to extinguish the Indian title over the whole of the vast land northwest of Lake Superior. Treaties 6 and 7 were the essential ones. By them the plains and the valley of the Saskatchewan were flung open to settlement. Soon the Indians were being herded like cattle onto reservations. Their sun was setting behind the Rockies.

4

By an almost terrifying coincidence Treaties 6 and 7 were followed almost immediately by the all but complete disappearance of the buffalo. Centuries of Indian life had not depleted the herds. Even the annual hunts for pemmican had not seemed to make any particular inroad. But from 1850 onward the tempo of destruction quickened. The market for buffalo robes and salted tongues was established. The American traders gave the Indians repeating rifles and encouraged them to kill for the hides alone. Sportsmen began to travel to the plains of the American West to shoot buffalo for fun. A gargantuan slaughter crackled all the way from Arkansas to the Canadian park land.

The Indians were the first to note the diminishing herds. In 1859 the Stoneys told Dr. Hector of the Palliser expedition that "the buffalo could not be depended on as before." Three years later Milton and Cheadle, on their journey through the Canadian West, set down that the buffalo were often "far distant on the plain." Then, in 1869, the shining rails of the first U.S. transcontinental split the herd in two, while the spate of railroads reaching west of Chicago brought in a flood of surveyors, hunters, ranchers, and farmers.

They all shot down the buffalo. Even in Canada the increase in settlement, small though it was, meant more slaughter, for by 1878 there were more than a dozen homesteads on the Oldman and Belly rivers, near Fort Macleod, and at Pincher Creek and at High River, south of Fort Calgary.

The signs of the coming destruction were plain. The North American way of life, however, has always been characterized by a stupid and unthinking wastage of its natural resources. The huge massacre went on. In 1877 the Council of the Northwest Territories did forbid the killing by means of pounds, where the buffalo were driven, en masse, into a trap or over a cliff, and also slaughtering for sport or for the sole purpose of getting tongues, choice cuts, and robes.

Even these regulations were repealed in the following year.

Then, in that year, and in 1879, when the herd in its annual migration crossed the line to the south, the U. S. Army prevented it from returning north. Thus, in 1879, Dewdney, the Indian Commissioner, reported that a series of prairie fires "was started at different points almost simultaneously, as if by some preconstructed arrangement, and the country north of the boundary line was burnt from Wood Mountain on the east to the Rocky Mountains. . . ." The buffalo, of course, found no fodder in this burned-over stretch and stayed south; and it is generally believed that the Americans set these fires for this purpose. Meanwhile, General Miles deployed his troops between the boundary and the buffalo. In this way the herd was penned for the final kill into the region of the Missouri and the Judith Basin. In 1883, 150,000 robes were sold in St. Louis as the last kick of the thundering herd. Next year the supply did not exceed 300 and by 1888 the U. S. Game Report stated that only six buffalo were known to be in existence. Since that time conservation measures have kept alive a few of the humped cattle as vestigial remnants of the millions which once made the prairies tremble under their hoofs.

5

To the Indians of the Canadian plains and park land, the sudden and complete disappearance of the buffalo in 1878 was an inexplicable disaster. Their food supply had vanished overnight. The year 1878 and the next two years were the worst in the history of the plains. The proud Blackfeet were reduced to killing their horses and feeding on gophers and mice. At Blackfoot Crossing old people and children starved to death. Inspector Denny reports that he saw Indians eating grass and tearing a steer to pieces to eat it raw. At Fort Macleod 7000 were fed every other day from what the police could pass out. Up at St. Albert, Father Leduc came on a case of cannibalism. Starving and puzzled, the Plains Crees, Assiniboins, and Blackfeet joined the Sioux in hunting in the Cypress Hills and in raiding across the line in pursuit of the herd held there by the Americans. The U. S. Army soon blocked them. Others butchered the cattle of the ranchers around Calgary and Fort Macleod. In 1879, for instance, E. H. and George Maunsell drove in 103 head. Within a month the starving Indians butchered 44—and who can blame them?

Upon the shoulders of the Mounties fell the impossible task of keeping Sitting Bull and his Sioux pacified, of preventing the Crees and Blackfeet from flying at Sioux throats, of satisfying the American troops, of appeasing outraged ranchers, and of feeding the starving Indians and herding them onto reservations. For the Dominion, compelled thereto by the clause in Treaties 6 and 7 assuring the Indians of rations in the case of any "general famine," had taken a certain amount of action in the crisis.

Food was rushed to Forts Walsh and Macleod. Besides the supplies provided for in the treaty, 500 head of beef cattle were shipped out along with 91,000 pounds of bacon, 100,000 of beef, 20,000 of pemmican, and 806 sacks of flour. Further supplies followed in 1879, and in the year ending in June 1880 the total spent on these emergency rations was $157,572.22.

This amount, comparatively, was only a wagonload for a multitude. Hunger still gnawed at the Northwest like a throbbing canker. In June of 1879 Indians broke into the government store at Fort Qu'Appelle to seize flour and provisions. In the same year Sitting Bull, backed by a large following of chiefs and warriors, braced Major Walsh for supplies and provisions; this because Walsh had forbidden the Sioux to cross the border to steal horses and hunt buffalo, and the Sioux were starving. Walsh, losing his patience, denounced the chief and threatened him with imprisonment. Sitting Bull warned him that no man could talk that way to him. Walsh, his temper worn thin, cursed him. Sitting Bull reached for the knife at his belt. Seizing him, Walsh frog-marched him to the entrance of his lodge, flung him outside, and, in the presence of the Sioux's astounded followers, as Sitting Bull started to get to his feet, planted a hearty kick on his backside.

It was touch and go for a moment. When Sitting Bull let the moment pass, his spell over his followers was dissipated.

Hunger broke the Sioux. The policy of starving them out of Canada was initiated by John A. Macdonald when, in 1878, he came back into power. By July of 1880 Sitting Bull's men began to slip back across the line into the reservations the U.S. was holding for them. At last, at Fort Buford on July 19, 1881, the medicine man surrendered to the American authorities. In December of 1890 he was shot while resisting arrest for his "ghost dance" movement.

Canada could be proud of the way her slim force of Mounties had handled the Sioux when they first flooded across the line. The systematic starvation of them from 1878 to 1881 sheds no luster on her escutcheon. A brave and free people had been forced into surrender, not by battle or by persuasion but by the shabbiest of all tricks, denial of food for men, women, and children.

To get the Canadian Indians to go on their reservations was almost as difficult as to compel the Sioux into capitulation. The Blackfeet, under Crowfoot's persuasion, did accede. Even so, it was difficult to explain to the proud braves to whom the wide plains had been theirs, in freedom, that they must stay on the reservation and not interfere with the rancher's cattle or the farmer's crops.

The other tribes proved more difficult. In 1881 the Mounties were increased to a force of 500 in thirteen posts. At the same time they were instructed to get the Indians into reservations north of the now projected transcontinental line. The tribesmen moved to the reservations, found them not to their liking, and left. By October of that year 290 starving lodges were pitched around Fort Walsh. Among their leaders were Piapot, who was later to obstruct the transcontinental, and Big Bear and Little Pine, who were to become leaders in the 1885 rebellion. By January of the next year Dewdney reported that in the present provinces of Alberta and Saskatchewan there was 11,577 Indians on the plains, while some 5000 were near Fort Walsh and another 4000 were in the United States. When in the following spring these last, weak and starving, struggled back across the boundary, the situation was potentially explosive.

There had already been ominous flashes of trouble. In 1879 the first Mountie to be lost through Indian action, Constable Grayburn, was shot near Fort Walsh by an Assiniboin, Star Child. Star Child escaped across the border. Arrested in 1881, when he returned, he was given a fair trail and acquitted since the murder could not be proved. The police kept an eye on him. Shortly thereafter he was seized for horse stealing and condemned to five years in prison, where he died.

Yet the magic of the Mounties' name still worked. In 1881 Sub-inspector Denny with six police prevented a battle between some 1000 Blackfoot braves and an equal number of Crees at Blackfoot Crossing. The *casus belli* was the killing of a Cree by one of the Blackfeet. Denny persuaded the Blackfeet to surrender the killer and the Crees to accept the murderer and a payment of horses as full compensation. He reports that an American officer who had accompanied him stated that on his side of the line it would have taken a regiment of cavalry and a war to achieve the same result.

But in 1882 the Blackfeet for the first time resisted arrest. The victim was the third son of the famous novelist Charles Dickens. The son, Francis, was a slight, sandy-haired, quiet man with a deafness in one ear. He was sent to Blackfoot Crossing to arrest Bull Elk, who was accused of having fired a bullet past the ear of an agency butcher at Fort Macleod. Dickens made the arrest. Then he was knocked down and Bull Elk was freed.

Major Crozier promptly rode into the Indian camp with twenty police. Bull Elk was seized. All over the plains, however, there was unrest. For the Dominion had now decided to starve the Indians, too, into going to their reservations. The N.W.M.P. inspector at Fort Walsh, for instance, reported that the Indians there were "receiving two days' food to last them for seven days." There was nothing the inspector could do. The directive of the Deputy Minister of the Interior, Vankoughnet (an old friend of John A. Macdonald), was that "Indians at Walsh are to be kept on starvation allowance."

The policy worked. In 1883, except for a few irreconcilable bands, the Indians settled on their reservations. In the treatment of them some of the dragon's teeth which sprouted into the Northwest Rebellion had been sown. But, meantime, at last, the tracks of the transcontinental were being laid across the prairie.

CHAPTER XXVI

1878–84

Tariffs to Give Away—George Stephen and the Third Canadian Pacific Railway Company—Van Horne and the Gallop across the Prairies—Onkerdonk Blasts a Road through the Canyons of the Fraser—Financial Breakers and the $22,500,000 Story

1

IN September of 1878 the strong current of National Policy had carried John A. back into power. At sixty-three, the old master looked out at the political world with a somewhat weary yet amiable cynicism. Greed, prejudice, loyalty—these and other human motivations were to him the keys of a piano which he could now handle with a virtuoso's touch.

His own cheerful lack of hypocrisy remained. In November of that same year it was his duty to welcome at Halifax a new governor general, the Marquis of Lorne, whose wife, Princess Louise, was the handsomest of Queen Victoria's daughters. The governor general's boat was delayed by storms. So John A. locked himself with a few bottles of brandy in a room of his host's mansion (his host was that Honorable A. G. Archibald who had been the first governor of Manitoba and was now lieutenant governor of Nova Scotia), and no one could dig him out. It is said that when Archibald's secretary was sent in to tell him that the Marquis of Lorne's boat was entering harbor, John A., lying in bed, "pale and frowzled," raised himself on one elbow, pointed toward the door, and thundered:

"Vamoose from this ranch."

Yet he was on hand to take part in the interminable receptions for Lorne.

With the same disarming directness Sir John rewarded Canadian industrialists for helping him back into the Prime Minister's chair. His method was simple. Anyone who asked for an increase in tariff got it. New levies imposed a 10 per cent duty on partly manufactured goods and an average of 30 per cent on finished articles. Canadian manufacturers of textiles and of iron and steel products benefited. Imported blankets, for instance, were taxed at a rate of 41.4 per cent. Nova Scotia coal was protected by a tariff of fifty cents a ton. A small petroleum industry in western Ontario received a protective duty of over 30 per cent. For the profit making of a single firm turning out cheap clocks, a tariff of 35 per cent was imposed on all imported clocks. Tilley, who brought in this 1879 budget, could say with truth and smug satisfaction that it "would give ample protection to all who are seeking it. . . ."

By its tariff fence, to some apologists, Canada declared its intention of developing its own industries. To John A., the increases were, more probably, the golden shackles whereby he bound Canadian industrialists to himself and the Conservative party. In any case, that same fence has, ever since, penned in Canadian consumers, like patient sheep, for big business to clip; even though in these days the capital of those Americans whose products National Policy was supposed to exclude has leaped blithely over the barrier to share in the protection bonanza.

National Policy began the transformation of Canadian society into a plutocracy. It initiated a sort of socialism, of which the benefits are limited to the industrialists, though of late years the powerful labor unions have also declared themselves in on the cut, while by price fixing and monopolistic control the wastage of profits in a true "free enterprise" system is avoided. Tariffs, as one historian has remarked, are "easy on and hard off." The "infant" industries of John A.'s day are now bloated giants. The consumer still carries the high prices imposed by high tariffs.

In John A.'s day, however, fortune favored the new government. The sun began to blink through the clouds of depression. Prices began to rise. The 1879 harvest was lush.

The Conservatives, naturally, put the sunlight down to their National Policy.

"A citizen of Toronto," John A. is said to have observed unctuously, "assured me that his Conservative cow gave three quarts of milk more a day after the election than before. . . ."

He still had to walk a tightrope. Apart from support from manufacturers, and whisky distillers, and from the hopes of the outlying provinces, his power depended on the improbable union of Ontario Orangemen with Quebec zealots. In his Cabinet the Grand Master of the Orange Order, Mackenzie Bowell, rubbed knees with ultramontane Hector Langevin. Yet, in spite of the necessary political acrobatics, John A. never abandoned his dream of a Canada bound together, in defiance of economic geography, by a ribbon of steel. For a year and a half he continued Mackenzie's bits-and-pieces method. Then, at last, he was ready to move.

2

"Catch them," advised John A.'s old intimate, J. H. Pope of the Eastern Townships of Quebec, "before they invest their profits."

He was referring to the enormous fortunes George Stephen, Donald Smith, and their associates had garnered from their St. Paul and Pacific Railway venture. John A. listened. It had finally been decided, after many disputes and shifts, that the western terminus of the transcontinental should be not Esquimalt or Bute Inlet but Port Moody on Burrard Inlet, with the Fraser Valley as the last stage of the run. So, in the spring of 1880, a contract had been given to Andrew Onkerdonk, a young and brilliant engineer from San Francisco, to build the difficult 128 miles from Emory's Bar near Yale through the canyons of the Fraser up to Savona Ferry at the western end of Lake Kamloops. On May 14 of that year Onkerdonk began to force his way upstream with the old Cariboo Trail riding herd beside him. A ceremony was made for the first blast.

"After some congratulatory remarks for the Conservative Government and the Pacific Province by persons present," a report in the Montreal *Gazette* stated, "Mr. Onkerdonk, at the request of the Hon. J. W. Trutch, ordered the foreman to light the fuse—a grand success; the loud noise resounded in the Fraser Valley some distance, besides causing a heavy downpour of rain."

That blast served notice to British Columbia that it no longer needed to secede. The problem of who would build across northern Ontario and across the prairies and through the Rockies still remained. Various capitalists had approached John A., but they lacked backing. He himself had got in contact with the Grand Trunk. The Grand Trunk had answered that their board of directors would not be interested unless the line went through the United States as far as Winnipeg.

To Sir John, such a proviso was the ruin of his dream of an all-Canadian route. But now the Stephen syndicate, which had been joined by Duncan McIntyre, who controlled the Canada Central, a line projected from Ottawa to Nipissing, had made an offer to construct the transcontinental.

It was a strong combination. Apart from the private fortunes of the group, Stephen, it must be remembered, could also fling the Bank of Montreal behind the project. Yet one bone was sticking in John A.'s throat. Donald Smith was one of the syndicate; and Donald Smith had struck down John A. in the 1873 Pacific Scandal debate. Furthermore, in 1878 he had been elected, through calling himself a "Conservative," as a supporter of the Mackenzie Liberals.

That election was to be voided late in 1880 by the Supreme Court of Canada on charges of corrupt electioneering practices by Smith's agents. At the moment, however, to enter into any deal which included Donald Smith would be to wave a red flag in front of every Conservative bull. So it was decided to omit him.

With this condition established, a preliminary agreement for building the transcontinental was made in London with Stephen's group. On October 21, 1880, at Ottawa a formal contract was signed. The president of this third Canadian Pacific Railway Company was George Stephen, the vice-president Duncan McIntyre, the general manager Richard Angus. The names of Hill, Kittson, and Kennedy of the St. Paul and Pacific enterprise were also on the contract. Donald Smith's signature was conspicuously absent. According to Stephen, this omission made Smith behave "like a baby." Yet though he sulked in the wings, in one of the curious patterns of destiny, on that October 21 the defunct St. Paul and Pacific became the father of the C.P.R. Furthermore, when the list of the original stockholders was published, Donald Smith's name was down for 5000 shares. The other members of the syndicate were the London and New York firms of Morton, Rose and Co. and Morton, Bloss and Co. and the European firm of Kohn, Reinach and Co. of Frankfurt (which included the French Société Générale). The London and New York firms were in the picture because John Rose was a long-time friend of John A.'s. At one time, indeed, in early days, the two had put on shows in the United States with young Rose masquerading as a dancing bear and the young John A. solemnly squeaking out the accompaniment for the performance.

It was a different sort of music that John A. now offered. In return for building the transcontinental (it was to be completed by May 1, 1891) the Canadian Pacific Railway Company was, in brief, to receive $25,000,000 in cash, payable as construction proceeded, and 25,000,000 acres of land to be selected from the "Fertile Belt," that is, roughly, from the valley of the North Saskatchewan. In minor concessions the company was exempted from most forms of taxation, could import its materials duty-free (the high tariff fence was for the ordinary Canadian consumer, not for millionaires), and had permission to build whatever branches it wished. As a rider, there was a monopoly clause which forbade for twenty years the building of any competing line in the West between the transcontinental and the U.S. boundary. To prevent American control of the transcontinental there was a clause that the president and the majority of the directors were to be British subjects. For a bonus the Dominion tossed in the 710 miles of railroad already built or building and the cost of the surveys.

The total amount of money spent on the bits-and-pieces method had been $37,785,320, of which construction had swallowed some $28,000,000. Much of the construction, however, had been incompletely and extravagantly done, while a great deal of Sandford Fleming's elaborate and expensive surveys was of value only to mountain goats.

Even so, in these days before inflation made millions the equivalent of tens of thousands, the terms seemed princely. Edward Blake, who, on the retirement of Mackenzie, had become the Liberal leader, attacked them violently in the federal House. With support from the Grand Trunk, Blake and Richard Cartwright (Minister of Finance in the Mackenzie government) argued for the route through American territory as far as Winnipeg. Finally, in the middle of January 1881, the Liberals produced an offer from a group of Toronto capitalists to build an all-Canadian road for $3,000,000 and 3,000,000 acres less, while paying duty on all supplies and abandoning the exemptions from taxation and the monopoly clause. John A. had the votes. On February 1, 1881, the bill approving the contract with the C.P.R. passed by 128 to 49.

3

When, in 1869, the United States drove its first transcontinental to San Francisco it had a population of forty million of which three quarters of a million were on the Pacific coast and six million in the states between the Mississippi and the mountains. Nor was there any physical barrier between the East and the Rockies.

In 1881, Canada, in comparison, had a total population of some four million, a mere tenth of what the U.S. had had in 1869. In Manitoba there were by the 1881 census 65,954 people, while in British Columbia there were some 24,000 whites. To make the seeming folly of a transcontinental more patent, between the East and Manitoba were the thousand miles of uninhabited and apparently unproductive rock and muskeg of what is today northern Ontario and eastern Manitoba, while from Manitoba to the Rockies crouched only a few forlorn settlements. To compound the difficulties, the C.P.R. faced in the Rockies and the Selkirks a terrain considerably more rugged than anything across the line; and through these mountains no practicable route had as yet been found. Nor was there the modern equipment—giant bulldozers, fleets of trucks, giant cats, and the like—which makes the construction of a road such as the Alaska Highway comparatively easy. In 1881 engineers had to make do with manpower and giant powder. Not only was the C.P.R. a railroad in search of a population which did not exist; it also seemed to many a venture into the impossible by visionary ignoramuses.

In George Stephen the C.P.R., and Canada, had a visionary determined to make the dream come true. There was also the dynamic Hill, the St. Paul Canadian expatriate. The obvious place to make quick progress was over the prairies. So an office was opened in Winnipeg and Hill put two Americans in charge, A. B. Stickney as general superintendent and General Rosser as chief engineer. The Mackenzie government had, as noted, picked Selkirk north of Winnipeg as the crossing point of the Red River. But Manitobans wanted Winnipeg and the Winnipeggers themselves found the money for the Princess Louise bridge. On July 20, 1881, the first C.P.R. train steamed across it into Winnipeg.

Yet in 1881 only 161 miles of track were laid. In consequence, on December 31 "Hire 'em and Fire 'em" Hill replaced Stickney with William Cornelius Van Horne.

Van Horne, scion of an old Knickerbocker family, was a fortunate accident for Canada. Under forty, broad-beamed and a valiant trencherman, he had already made a formidable reputation as a railway man with the Chicago, Milwaukee and St. Paul road. To his friends, it seemed foolish to abandon an assured career for a visionary enterprise. After a trip to Winnipeg and a drive out over the prairies, Van Horne decided to accept the challenge; and his demands on those who worked for him were as vast as the meals he ate.

"If you want anything done," he once said, "name the day when it must be finished." To one of Sandford Fleming's protégés, J. H. E. Secretan, he gave the order to construct 500 miles of track in 1882, telling him, as Secretan relates it, that "nothing was impossible and if I could show him the road, it was all he wanted, and if I *couldn't,* he would have my scalp."

In actual fact, some 480 miles of track were put down that summer at the average, and in those days unprecedented, rate of over two and a half miles per day—and those rails stretched toward Calgary and the Kicking Horse Pass, not toward Edmonton and the Yellowhead Pass, as the original plan had been. The new route was over easier terrain and was a hundred miles shorter. The real reason for the change was fear of the Northern Pacific, south of the border. To leave too much of a gap between Canada's transcontinental and the frontier would be to invite the American road to throw spur lines into the untouched territory.

Yet when Van Horne started hurling his rails toward the Rockies, a feasible southern pass through the Selkirks, the rugged range which backstopped the Rockies, had not as yet been discovered. Another American, also hired by Hill, Major Rogers, was still in search of it.

Rogers, "a short snappy little chap with long Dundreary whiskers," was nicknamed "the Bishop" for his colorful profanity and was such an artist in expectoration that he was popularly believed to sleep with a chaw of tobacco between his jaws. He worked himself and his men to greyhound leanness that spring and summer. Following a hint from Moberly, the old H.B.C. man, he discovered, up the south fork of the Illecillewaet River, the western approaches to the pass later named after him. But he had not yet determined whether it was practicable from the east.

Meantime, in an act of faith, Van Horne drove surveyors, graders, bridgebuilders, and tracklayers with the tireless energy of a demon lashing forward sinners in hell. The whole contract as far as Calgary had been given to Langdon, Sheppard and Co. of St. Paul. The work was sublet to outfits averaging about a hundred men and forty teams each. Ahead went the surveyors. Behind came the graders, the bridgebuilders, and the tracklayers. Behind them, in turn, the construction trains steamed to railhead, each with a mile of track. Every stick of timber, every railroad spike, every pound of food, had to be brought to the end of steel.

Yet the pace was maintained and bettered. In 1883, for weeks in succession, the average rate was over three and a half miles every twenty-four hours, and on one red-letter day twenty miles were put down.

In those three years, from 1881 to 1883, the Canadian West boiled with action. To the rear of the construction camps Winnipeg was a blustering, booming city. As early as 1881, when the Marquis of Lorne visited it, it was possible to buy land for $6000 on Monday, sell for $7000 on Tuesday, and see the lot sold on Wednesday for $9000; and lots were staked out for miles beyond the city's outskirts. Wages were high. So were building costs. Hackney coaches charged a dollar a mile. Sealskin coats, diamond pins, and the popping of champagne corks signalized success. Even the unemployed were always drunk, because anyone and everyone would hand out a dollar to anyone. Meanwhile settlers were pouring in. In 1882 John A.'s only son, Hugh, moved with his wife and family to Winnipeg, and the Marquis of Lorne wrote complacently to the Colonial Secretary in London that "the number of people going to the West from Ontario alone will probably be twenty thousand this year."

While Winnipeggers rode the boom and drank champagne, out on the prairies villages sprang up alongside the rails like stinkweed. Regina, Moose Jaw, Swift Current, Maple Creek, and Medicine Hat shouldered onto the map. The construction camps swarmed with brawling "bohunks" as well as with gamblers, thieves, and bootleggers. The Indian braves hung around to steal horses while their squaws found the gangs profitable.

There were some Indians who feared, justifiably, that over those steel tracks would ride a horde of settlers. In 1883 under Chiefs Piapot and Long Man a large Cree band set their tents down on the construction line. The Mounties were summoned. There were only three of them, a sergeant and two constables. Yet these three gave the Indians half an hour to move with as much seeming confidence as if they were three hundred. The Indians sat where they were. At the end of the half hour, the three Mounties, with the Indians crowding around them and firing their rifles into the air, phlegmatically proceeded to flatten the tents. The Indians moved.

In the United States the Union Pacific had been built by an army fighting its way West through attacking Indians. In Canada, Van Horne found that all he needed to keep the peace were the Mounties, Father Lacombe, and the Reverend John McDougall—but to the Mounties must go the major part of the credit.

In this atmosphere of driving, swearing, sweating activity, Calgary, at that time a frontier post of some dozen log houses, was reached on August 10, 1883. By the end of the year the rails were at what is now Lake Louise Station and was then temporarily called "Holt City," after the chief engineer of this section, Herbert S. Holt, who was later to become the richest and most powerful of Canada's multimillionaires.

This point is at the summit of the Kicking Horse Pass. Fortunately, by luck and hard work in August of this same year Major Rogers had found his pass through the Selkirks. The C.P.R. could still drive westward. Meanwhile, work was also pounding forward east of Port Arthur and westward from the junction at Callander, Ontario, with Duncan McIntyre's Canada Central.

And, meantime, in the British Columbia sector of the route, Andrew Onkerdonk had also been forging ahead. For almost sixty miles from Yale to Lytton he blasted and bored his way. When white labor failed he imported Chinese coolies over the protests of British Columbians. When it proved difficult to supply the road and the men, he had the steamer *Skuzzy* built and with incredible difficulty had it taken upstream through the boiling waters of the Grand Canyon of the Fraser. At one point it took 150 Chinese, supplemented by the engines, hauling on a line, a steam winch pulling on a hawser, and 15 men on a capstan and a third hawser to drag the boat up against the rapids to the quieter waters above them. Similarly, to speed the work, dynamite was manufactured on the spot.

In this way the sixty miles of tunnels—fifteen in all—rock work, and bridges were completed. In 1882 the Canadian government added to Onkerdonk's contract the distance westward from Emory's Bar to Port Moody. Throughout that year and the next, the brilliant engineer drove forward with a total of some 6500 Chinese and 2500 whites blasting and constructing. By the end of 1883 the directors of the C.P.R. began to envisage the finishing of the road well before the due date of May 1, 1891.

4

In construction the tide of fortune was running full and strong. In finance and politics, rapids and treacherous canyons and ugly attempts to dam the flow threatened completion. In Great Britain, as early as 1881, there were violent onslaughts against what the magazine *Truth* called "The Canadian Dominion Bubble." To the south of the frontier, in the same year, the Northern Pacific strove to harass the C.P.R.'s plans by taking over Quebec's North Shore Railway between Quebec City and Montreal; while in Manitoba, it was behind the granting of a charter by the Manitoba legislature, in defiance of the C.P.R.'s monopoly, to the Manitoba and South Eastern Railway, intended to be a branch line of the American road.

The North Shore Railway threat was met by the C.P.R.'s buying the western section from Ottawa to Montreal. As for the Manitoba and the South Eastern, the Dominion government simply disallowed its charter. But, meantime, the C.P.R. had aroused the hostility of the Grand Trunk, both by grabbing the transcontinental and by invasion of the G.T.R. territory. The C.P.R. had, naturally, bought out McIntyre's Canada Central from Ottawa to Callander on Lake Nipissing (this road was finished in 1883). It also took over the Ottawa and Brockville. The North Shore Railway gave it entry into Montreal. Then, in 1883, it acquired lines running from Ottawa to Toronto and from Toronto to Georgian Bay and to St. Thomas, from which a road was later built to Windsor. Another to Sault Ste. Marie to link with the Soo lines was added.

This was carrying the war into G.T.R. preserves with a broadax. The G.T.R. countered by acquiring Sir Allan MacNab's old line, the Great Western, with its Michigan extensions, and the Midland Railway and its subsidiaries to the north and east, by building a tunnel at Port Huron under the St. Clair River (completed in 1890), by closing the London money market to its rival, and by fighting it on the New York Stock Exchange.

The C.P.R. financial road was as beset by difficulties as its route north of Lake Superior. To heighten its embarrassment, on May 3, 1883, J. J. Hill resigned from the directorate and sold his stock.

The bluff Hill had never been sold on the route north of Lake Superior; the more especially since a road via the States as far as Winnipeg could utilize his own St. Paul, Minneapolis and Manitoba Railway. When, toward the end of 1882, both Stephen and John A. insisted on an all-Canadian C.P.R., Hill, in a fit of pique, decided to pull out. With him went Kennedy, the former New York representative of the unlucky Dutch bondholders of the St. Paul and Pacific. Hill then turned his driving energy to a transcontinental of his own, the Great Northern. The C.P.R. had now two competing roads south of the 49th parallel. It had to keep thrusting spurs toward the line. Suddenly the C.P.R. was close to bankruptcy.

5

To detail the intricacies of C.P.R. financing would be to write a textbook in arithmetic. It had started life with a government grant of $25,000,000 payable as construction advanced, completed road and surveys valued roughly at $35,000,000, and a kingly land grant of 25,000,000 acres of the best lands in the Canadian Northwest.

Yet the land could have little value until the C.P.R. was finished and settlers poured in; while the cost of the main line alone was $50,000,000. In the meantime $100,000,000 had been authorized as capital stock. In 1881 the members of Stephen's syndicate bought $5,000,000 of this at par ($100 a share); and in May of 1882 they allocated to themselves $10,000,000 worth of it at $25 a share, that is, for $2,500,000, at a neat profit to themselves.

Meanwhile bonds on the security of the land grants were issued up to $25,000,000, of which, in 1881, $10,000,000 worth was sold on the London market at a rate of $92 a bond. Then in December of 1882, in the mysterious ways of high finance, $30,000,000 of the stock was turned over to a New York firm at $52½ a share. All together, the issuing of $55,000,000 worth of stock had brought some $23,000,000 into the treasury, to which should be added the close to $10,000,000 acquired from the sale of bonds or of lands.

This $33,000,000 drained away from the treasury as if someone had knocked a gaping hole in its bottom. There were the purchases of roads. There was the building of branch lines. Above all, there was the gaping maw of construction costs. As another flick of Fate's finger, from the beginning the C.P.R. had decided to pay a 5 per cent dividend on all the stock issued.

All this, with $45,000,000 of stock still to be issued, might not have been immediately serious, if the wolf of depression had not sneaked out of its cave. There was no spectacular onset. Instead, that summer of 1883, a slow but consistent drop in prices set in. The New York stock market began to act like a nervous spinster. In Winnipeg the hectic land boom collapsed like a tent when the center pole is cut. To pile disaster on insult, the wheat crop of the Northwest was destroyed by frost. Down in New York there was a sharp drop in the stock of the Northern Pacific. Suddenly, even as Van Horne drove his rails on toward the Rockies, the Stephen group found itself out of funds and in debt. They went to the government for help.

The first plan, to which John A. agreed, was for the government to guarantee for ten years a 3 per cent dividend on the $100,000,000 capital stock of the C.P.R. For this, Stephen offered to pay $15,000,000 at once, another $5,000,000 on February 1, 1884, and to make up the balance by securities and other assets.

Armed with this guarantee, on October 29, 1883, Stephen set out gaily for New York to sell the balance of the C.P.R. stock. He did not even get to first base. Returning to Ottawa, he proposed a government guarantee of a 3 per cent dividend for $65,000,000 of the capital stock, giving himself only $10,000,000 worth to sell. The Cabinet again agreed. Stephen paid over $8,710,240 of the new purchase price for the guarantee and set out for New York again. Once more he could not sell a share. For the Northern Pacific had by now been smashed into bankruptcy. All railroad stocks tobogganed. The best Stephen could do was to pledge the $10,000,000 for a $5,000,000 loan. With $16,000,000 either paid over to the government or pledged to it, the C.P.R. was worse off than before. Meantime, the monster of cost still gaped and there was a huge floating debt in New York. The Grand Trunk, which had barred off the London money market and had joined in beating down the price of C.P.R. stock, grinned in glee. The C.P.R. was, it seemed, within days of bankruptcy.

Ordinary mortals would have quit. Stephen, flanked by Donald Smith and Duncan McIntyre, refused to throw in the towel. To raise loans in New York and Montreal, all three pledged their securities, inclusive of their St. Paul, Minneapolis and Manitoba stock. At one time, their own collateral exhausted, McIntyre went around and begged securities from his friends. Even so, and even though Stephen was its president, on December 28 the Bank of Montreal, which was already heavily committed to the C.P.R., refused a further advance until Sir Charles Tupper, Minister of Railways and Canals, gave the bank a letter supporting Stephen's request.

In this sort of situation a crash seemed inevitable. In the middle of January 1884, Stephen approached John A. formally for a loan of $22,500,000; this to be secured by a mortgage on the main line of the C.P.R. In return he offered to complete the road by May of 1886 instead of 1891.

Sir John was in a quandary. The general election had been held in 1882. Thanks to the then continuing prosperity and by "hiving the Grits"—that is, by rearranging the boundaries of constituencies so that the Liberals were plethoric in numbers in those they were likely to win but scantily represented in formerly doubtful areas—he had won a comfortable majority.

But by now depression sat sullenly on Canada and would not stir its rump. The federal government, too, was worried in those naive days about a drop in revenues and a consequent deficit. John A.'s first reaction was to tell Stephen he might as well ask for the planet Jupiter as for a loan.

It is said that J. H. Pope, the man who had advised Sir John to catch the Stephen group before it spent its profits, woke the Prime Minister in the middle of the night to warn him that "the day the C.P.R. busts, the Conservative party busts the day after." At any rate, the proposal for a loan to the C.P.R. was bulled through the Cabinet and the caucus. On February 1, Tupper introduced the measure in the House. There was a bitter debate. The Grand Trunk lobbied against the bill. Ontario and Quebec Conservative members blackmailed the government for increased subsidies for their provinces as the price of their support. The C.P.R. bestowed plentiful largesse hither and yonder. Later, according to Preston, Donald Smith (now reconciled with Sir John) was to remark quietly: "They were a hungry lot in Ottawa then."

The debate went on and on. The C.P.R. directorate balanced on the razoredge of uncertainty. The creditors in New York pressed for payment and the payroll had to be met, but the Bank of Montreal refused to lend another copper. McIntyre was sent to New York to try to get $300,000. The C.P.R., which today can borrow ten to a hundred million by lifting a telephone receiver from its cradle, was a few days from bankruptcy.

On Thursday, February 28, the bill at last passed the House. Less than a week later, on March 5, Royal Assent was given. The floating debts in Montreal and New York were paid off. The sheriff was turned from the C.P.R. door. Van Horne could drive his crews forward. But Duncan McIntyre, convinced that the C.P.R. would collapse sooner or later, resigned his vice-presidency and was replaced by the bluff, square-faced Van Horne. Donald Smith, who had become a director in 1882, was taken onto the executive committee.

CHAPTER XXVII

1884–85

The C.P.R. Drives past Lake Superior and through the Mountains–Indians, Métis, *and Louis Riel–Battle at Duck Lake Saves the C.P.R.*

1

TO lay the tracks across the prairies had been a holiday in a peaceful glade compared to what now faced Van Horne. The original route north of Lake Superior, as surveyed by Sandford Fleming's crews, had cut far inland, but Van Horne had insisted that the line should cling close to the lake shore so that supplies could be brought by water. For this reason, late in 1882, Henry Beatty—father of the late Sir Edward Beatty, who became a dynamic president of the C.P.R.—was sent to Scotland, his job to order three steamers built in such a way that they could be sliced in half and brought through the canals to Lake Superior.

Today, along the northern rim of the lake the diesels lead the curling coils of the coaches carefully across wooded hills and valleys and over stream and muskeg and around the indented shores of bays and inlets as far as Port Arthur. The traveler who from the scenic domes looks out at vista after vista of beauty may forget the toil of the building unless he has a discerning eye. For this stretch of country is part of the prehistoric Laurentian Shield. The toughest of rock had to be blasted to find a route at water's edge. In one muskeg, seven tiers of rails, one after another, and three locomotives were sucked down by the seemingly bottomless muskeg. Again and again timber trestles had to carry the roadway high until the rock fill was tumbled down by train haul. At Jackfish Bay, two points a half mile distant from each other as a bullet flies are linked by the weaving in and out of three miles of track.

It was what Van Horne called "two hundred miles of engineering impossibilities." Ten thousand men ate hugely and worked as hugely. Beatty's three Clyde-built steamers were on the lake. So were nine others. A dynamite factory was built on the north shore and two million dollars' worth of it was used at the 1884 value of the dollar. One particularly obstinate mile swallowed $700,000 of C.P.R. funds.

In the West the maw of costs gaped just as wide. Here James Ross, a Scot from Cromarty, was in charge for the C.P.R. as far as Eagle Pass, while from that same pass to Savona Ferry the contract had been let to Andrew Onkerdonk, the energetic engineer who had built for the government from Savona Ferry to Port Moody on Burrard Inlet. According to his chief timekeeper, Dr. George W. Campbell, Onkerdonk used "any kind of a human being who could handle a pick and shovel. . . ." More and more of them were Chinese. At Yale everything ran wide open with gamblers and dance-hall girls to fleece the laborers.

In the eastern mountains, however, the N.W.M.P. under Superintendent Sam Steele were called in to keep order in the construction camps. Liquor was outlawed within twenty miles on each side of the railway line. From Calgary, Pat Burns, the cattle king, poured in beef to the camps.

It was a tough and violent life. In the Kicking Horse and Rogers passes gradients of 116 feet to the mile had to be made. Then there were the mountain avalanches to be overcome. To divert them, timber structures had to be flung up near the summits of the peaks and mile after mile of snowsheds, through some of which today's traveler still passes, reared to protect the tracks. There were mountain bridges to be painstakingly built. There were abysses to creep along. The tourists of the modern generation stare up wonderingly at castellated snow-covered peaks, with streams falling down their flanks like Tennyson's "slow-dropping veils of thinnest lawn," or down at wooded valleys dizzyingly far beneath, or marvel at rivers turbulent in mountain canyons or at the peaceful calm at sunset of mountain tarns. The road over which they travel was built with sweat and blood and also with a faith and an agony which was epic.

Epic, too, were the costs. By the fall of 1884 the $22,500,000 loan had disappeared as if into one of the muskegs north of Lake

Superior, or as if swept away by a tumbling avalanche from above Rogers Pass. Abruptly, the C.P.R. was again teetering on the edge of bankruptcy. In November, Stephen, Donald Smith, and Angus, by pledging Toronto, Grey and Bruce bonds to the amount of £77,000, raised a loan in Edinburgh of £50,000 to meet immediate emergencies.

This was only a temporary respite. Funds had to be found somewhere for the interest and dividends as well as for the balance of the construction. Stephen, who was in London, had a conference with John A. Macdonald, who while on a visit to England had, on November 25, received the Grand Cross of the Bath from Queen Victoria. Sir John promised government help, or Stephen thought he had. From London, Stephen sent his famous cable to his cousin, Donald Smith, in Montreal:

"Stand fast, Craigellachie."

Craigellachie was the great rock in the valley of the Spey River which had been in olden times the rallying point and the battle cry of the Clan Grant, to which both Stephen and Smith were bound by blood ties. They needed that battle cry in the bleak weeks that followed. In December the construction gangs at Port Arthur went on strike because the pay car had failed to roll up. In New York, C.P.R. stock dropped to 47½. To deepen the pit of depression, when in January John A. returned from London, it was to discover that his Cabinet, his party, and the whole of eastern Canada were inflexibly opposed to any further government "handouts" to the C.P.R. At the eleventh hour Stephen and Smith, by pledging more of their own funds, managed to put their hands on the $650,000 necessary to pay the January dividend of the C.P.R. stock, since otherwise that stock would have collapsed. On February 9, 1885, Stephen wrote to John A. that "we [Smith and I] have had to endorse a five months' note for one million dollars to provide the Company with current funds to keep it going for the next few weeks. . . . It is most important that no time be lost in arriving at a decision as to the rearrangement scheme, the three months' notes given a month ago to satisfy clamorous creditors will soon become due. . . ."

The "rearrangement scheme" was a proposal that $30,000,000 of 4 per cent bonds be issued in place of the $35,000,000 of unissued stock. John A. was forced to inform Stephen by telegraph that there was "little chance" of any help during 1885. To pile Pelion upon Ossa, news came that construction might be delayed in British Columbia by an anti-Chinese immigration bill. By March it seemed clear that the C.P.R., though almost completed, was going under. On March 26 Stephen, after a conversation with John A., wrote:

"The result of our conversation this morning has satisfied me that the government will not be able to see its way to extend to the C.P.R. Company the aid it requires. . . . I need not repeat how sorry I am that this should be the result of all our efforts to give Canada a railway to the Pacific Ocean. But I am supported by the conviction that I have done all that could be done to obtain it."

Stephen, sensitive and touchy—and who wouldn't have been? —was prepared to give up. But on that same March 26, at faraway Duck Lake in the then District of Saskatchewan, a force of N.W.M.P. and volunteers was being defeated by Louis Riel's *métis* and their Indian allies. George Stephen did not as yet know it, but Louis Riel had stepped in to save the C.P.R.

2

The Northwest Rebellion is a monument to the stupidities of government. In 1881, when the rails of the C.P.R. began to gouge their way westward from Winnipeg, Sitting Bull surrendered to the Americans. By that same year the buffalo were gone and the Dominion had begun to herd the Indians of the plains and the park lands into reservations, a task that was not fully completed even in 1883. For there were Indian bands who refused the reservations and remained a potential menace to settlement.

Meantime, the coming of the railroad was changing the face of the Northwest. As we have seen, there was a Winnipeg and Manitoba boom until the depression frost of 1883 killed it, while further west villages and towns were sprouting alongside the iron tracks. In 1875, along with its own separate government and council of five, it had been provided for the Northwest that when any district of 1000 square miles held a white population of 1000 a parliamentary representative went to this council. In 1882 the Northwest Territories were divided into four districts—Alberta and Athabasca for modern Alberta; Assiniboia and Saskatchewan for what was to become Saskatchewan. At first the capital was North Battleford. In 1883 it was shifted to Pile of Bones, incorporated the following year as the new and thriving railroad town of Regina with a population of some 500. When, in the same year of 1883, the Honorable Edgar Dewdney, the former Indian Commissioner, succeeded the Honorable David Laird as lieutenant governor, there were already six elected representatives on the council from the electoral districts of Edmonton, Lorne, Broadview, Qu'Appelle, Regina, and Moose Jaw; this last town having a riotous, floating railroad population of two to three thousand. In the next year sixty justices of the peace were appointed and there were seventeen Protestant and eleven Roman Catholic schools in operation.

The railroad was bringing in settlers. In 1884 Calgary, which the rails had reached the year before, was incorporated as a thriving, bustling frontier town. There was a rough and ready liquor trade for the construction gangs. The community had also become the hub of a surging ranching industry. Under the management of an old Imperial officer, General Strange, soon to figure in the Northwest Rebellion, a large ranch near the Blackfoot reservation on Bow River was stocked with horses. At the beginning of the killing, snow-deep winter of 1882–83, in anticipation of the construction gangs, some 12,000 cattle were driven to the Cochrane Ranch, about twenty miles from Calgary on the road to Banff. By spring scarcely 4000 were alive. Meantime, the Bar-U hustled in 3000 head of cattle all the way from Lost River in Idaho. By 1884, forty-one companies and individuals held ranching leases from a generous Dominion government from the 49th parallel up to Calgary, a total of 1,782,690 acres on which cowboys could sing "Home, Home on the Range" to the bawling cows and bellowing steers.

The great days of the open range had begun. The North-West Cattle Association was formed at Macleod. Among those who joined were six leaseholders who each held cattle baronages of 100,000 acres or more; and there were at least 40,000 head of cattle feeding off the prairie grass. The C.P.R. either bought the beef or carried it to market. Timber wolves were killed off by offering bounties of five to ten dollars a scalp. Wide-hatted, high-booted, spurred cowboys minced along the dusty or muddy or snow-drifted streets of Calgary, now become "cow town," and thronged its wide-open saloons. The Calgary *Herald* (begun in 1883) was added to the Edmonton *Bulletin,* the *Saskatchewan Herald,* the Prince Albert *Times* and *Saskatchewan Review,* the Moose Jaw *News,* the Regina *Leader,* and the Macleod *Gazette.*

Meanwhile, as it drove westward, the C.P.R. flung off tentacles toward the border, to hold its territory against the Northern Pacific and, later, the Great Northern. In Manitoba one line ran south along the west side of the Red River to meet with a branch of the St. Paul, Minneapolis and Manitoba at Gretna and then to swing westward a little north of the 49th parallel. Another poured southwestward from Brandon to within twenty-four miles of the frontier. Then it, too, veered to the west.

These branches opened up good farm land, besides serving notice that this was C.P.R. domain. In the south of present-day Alberta a coal seam was discovered at Coal Banks near old Fort Whoop-up. The coal was worked by the North-West Coal and Navigation Company, a venture headed by A. T. Galt, the onetime *Rouge* and Father of Confederation, who was Canada's first high commissioner in London, until he was replaced by Sir Charles Tupper. Coal for the nascent C.P.R. was shipped down the South Saskatchewan to Medicine Hat. In 1885 a branch from Dunmore on the main line to Coal Banks, now renamed Lethbridge, was finished. By 1886 Lethbridge boasted a thousand people.

A strong wind of change was blowing across the prairie and park land. Settlement to the north of the C.P.R. began to fill in. In 1880 there had only been five white families at Edmonton. The rest of the population were half-breeds. Newcomers began to squat along the banks east and west of the H.B.C. fort. A "Vigilance Committee" to which the sturdy quondam ox pusher turned publisher, Frank Oliver, belonged dumped shacks which were said to encroach on early settlers' claims over the bank into what was called the "Vigilantes' Depositories." By 1883, when the C.P.R. reached Calgary, there were 35 to 40 houses along Edmonton's straggling main street. Freight began to be teamed up the 200 miles from Calgary. A weekly stagecoach brought mail and passengers. An "express" journey between the two settlements cost $100, or fifty cents a mile.

From Calgary to Edmonton the only nucleus of whites was at the Red Deer River Crossing, about halfway between the two. Further east, apart from the older settlements along the North Saskatchewan at Battleford, Prince Albert, and St. Laurent and apart from the villages and towns budding along the C.P.R. rails, other pockets of settlement were being formed. Into the Yorkton area were brought Ontario farmers by the York Farmers' Colonization Company. The Temperance Colonization Company settled a group of Toronto Methodists in Saskatoon on the South Saskatchewan River. In 1883–84 Lady Cathcart sponsored a colony of Scottish crofters south of Wapella. Baroness Burdett-Coutts (the woman who had sent the first bride ship to Victoria) and Lord De Winton planted a Cockney accent in the midst of the prairies south of present-day Moosomin. Forty miles southwest of the same place was established Cannington Manor to train wealthy young Englishmen for farming in the West—a project which soon fell afoul of their liking for cricket, hunting, tennis, and horse racing.

Villages, towns, newspapers, ranching, and farmers—these were the first raindrops to herald to the Indians and *métis* the storm of change which was on the horizon. The buffalo had been swept from the Canadian West as if by a giant broom. The Indians, cooped up in reservations, saw the farmer and the rancher beginning to occupy the lands which had once been theirs. The average Indian did not understand, either, that by the treaties his title had been sold forever. On August 24, 1885, an Indian said in a council:

"The Indian . . . understood not the treaty. . . . He was then rich. . . . The Governor Morris comes and tells the Indian we . . . come here to borrow the country. . . ."

To heighten this sense of injustice, the Indians were expected to stay on the reservations unless they were given permits to leave. Nor were the first model farms and mission schools among them successful. Next, the Department of Indian Affairs, run by Vankoughnet, John A.'s old friend, decided to cancel all permits for Indians to leave their reservations. The final folly was the reduction of staff and rations; and this on the basis of a hurried trip to the West by Vankoughnet in the summer of 1883. Cecil Denny, by this time Indian agent for Treaty 7, narrates how he was ordered to dismiss his clerk and storekeeper and to do their jobs himself. He resigned. With a certain bitter satisfaction, he notes that his territory then had to be divided into three agencies with an agent for each. Each of these three agents received the same salary Denny had drawn and was "aided by a clerk, farm instructor, assistant and other subordinates."

Denny's case was only one instance of civil service bungling. The discretionary powers of the agents and farm instructors, who knew local conditions, and even of the Indian Commissioner, were reduced. Red tape strangled action. At Fort Pitt, for example, a government storehouse went two months without a padlock while the subagent wrote to the agent, who, in turn, had to refer the purchase to Regina for approval. Vankoughnet had, apparently, wandered off with Alice into Wonderland.

More serious than the red tape was Vankoughnet's decree that rations were to be issued to the Indians only in return for work and that these rations should be cut. The students at the Indian Industrial School at Battleford were reduced from a pound and a half of beef per day per pupil to a quarter of a pound. On the reservations the policy was to feed the Indians one day and to starve them the next. At Crooked Lakes, for instance, though 567 of 920 Indians had been receiving rations, the farm instructor was ordered to feed only the aged and infirm. The winter was a severe one. On February 18, 1884, Yellow Calf, followed by twenty-five armed tribesmen, rushed the warehouse. They knocked down, kicked, and stabbed the unfortunate instructor, and helped themselves. When forty police arrived they were stood off by the Indians. Vankoughnet's comment was that the previous instructor had evidently been "too lavish" with his supplies. He failed to see that his penny pinching was, ultimately, to stir an Indian war and cost the Dominion $5,000,000.

Vankoughnet was unimpressed by the Crooked Lakes incident. But the news that the Mounties had been blocked sped from camp to camp. Two Indian chiefs, in particular, hearkened to the story; Big Bear, leader of a band of recalcitrant Crees who had refused to sign Treaty 6, and the dignified Poundmaker, the tall, good-looking and intelligent man who was the most influential chief in the North Saskatchewan District. His reserve was on the Battle River. There, in June of 1884, rose the tepees of nearly two thousand discontented Indians under Big Bear and Poundmaker. Their pretext was a "Thirst Dance." In reality they were considering what to do.

Meantime, they demanded rations from Farm Instructor Craig. Under orders from Ottawa, he refused. An Indian followed him into the storehouse. He pushed the Indian out. The Indian seized an ax handle and struck him. Eighty-six police under that Superintendent Crozier who had starved out Sitting Bull's Sioux arrived. When, during a parley, he suddenly seized the wanted man, the Indians charged the Mounties, jostling the men and stabbing at the horses. One of the police was cut off, thrown down, and stripped of his arms. Crozier managed to get the arrested man inside the agency headquarters, which had been converted into a fort. He then had to toss out beef and flour to quiet the Indians.

The magic of the Mounties was wearing threadbare. The Indians collected again near Fort Carlton. The agent there had to issue rations and agree to an Indian council at which they could formulate their demands. Ottawa incompetence had made the Indians into flammable tinder. All that was needed was the spark to fire that tinder. That spark came. It was Louis Riel, a ghost, to change the metaphor, returned from the past to plague a John A. Macdonald who had learned but little from the 1869–70 Red River revolt.

3

It was cool but bright on that early morning of June 4, 1884, at the tiny settlement of St. Peter's Mission in the Sun River country of Montana below Fort Benton. With Louis Riel in one end of the cabin which he shared with another family was his wife, the shy, daintily shaped *métisse* he had married formally in April of 1882, and their two children, a boy of two and an infant daughter. Outside the sun was lighting up the peaks and crevices of Bird Tail Mountain. Along the stream near by, the willows burgeoned with sap. Over the prairie the tiny flowers were dots of color.

The fourteen years since 1870 had put weight on Louis Riel. A panoply of whiskers, beard, and mustache concealed the mouth. The real changes in the man were more deeply hidden; and the wife who watched him could not even guess at them. The Riel of twenty-five had been a brilliant if erratic young man whom the wine of power had led into deadly errors of judgment. The man of forty who sat there brooding had gone through the fire of tribulation and the slough of despond. When the Wolseley expedition had arrived at Fort Garry, he had learned all too sharply the loneliness of a deposed leader and the folly of trusting in politicians' promises. He, who had come to believe that all his actions were justified and were motivated only by affection for his *métis*, had found, as he had convinced himself, only injustice. When he had appeared in Ottawa as a member of Parliament in the spring of 1874, he had been swiftly forced into hiding and finally into exile.

A man who was much better balanced, mentally, than Riel might have succumbed to the strain. Riel, never too stable, had

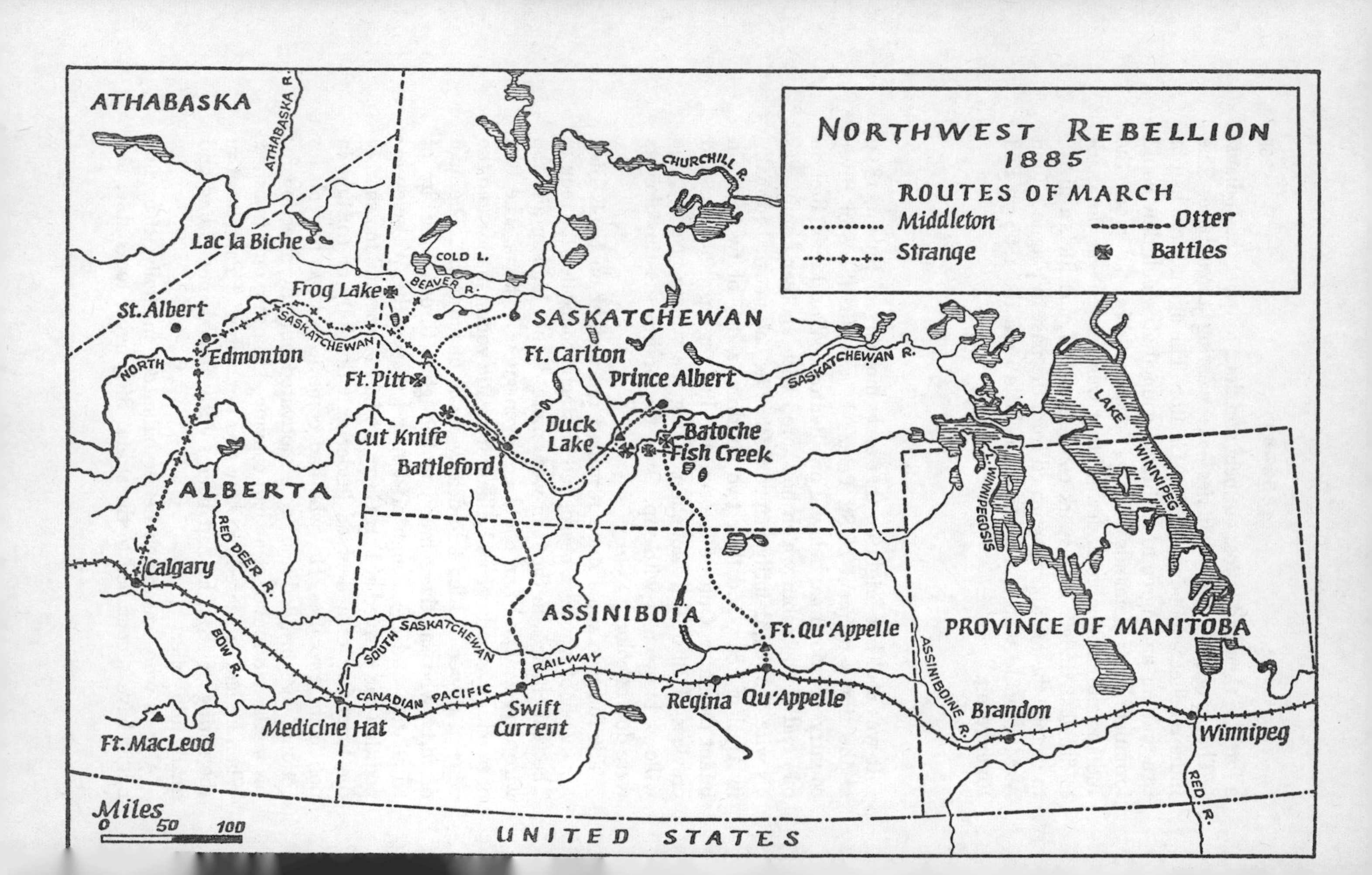
NORTHWEST REBELLION
1885
ROUTES OF MARCH
Middleton
Strange
Otter
Battles
ATHABASKA
ATHABASKA R.
CHURCHILL R.
Lac la Biche
COLD L.
BEAVER R.
Frog Lake
St. Albert
SASKATCHEWAN
Edmonton
NORTH
SASKATCHEWAN
Ft. Pitt
Ft. Carlton
Prince Albert
SASKATCHEWAN R.
LAKE
WINNIPEG
Cut Knife
Duck
Lake
Batoche
Fish Creek
Battleford
L. WINNIPEGOSIS
ALBERTA
RED DEER R.
Calgary
ASSINIBOIA
PROVINCE OF MANITOBA
Ft. Qu'Appelle
BOW R.
SOUTH SASKATCHEWAN
RAILWAY
ASSINIBOINE R.
CANADIAN PACIFIC
Swift
Current
Regina
Qu'Appelle
Brandon
Winnipeg
Ft. MacLeod
Medicine Hat
RED R.
Miles
0
50
100
UNITED STATES

cracked under it. On December 18 of 1874 he had seen his first vision, in which, he believed, a spirit appeared to him and, calling him "Louis *David* Riel," had told him he had a mission to fulfill.

From that moment forward Louis Riel signed himself Louis "David" Riel. Unwittingly, Bishop Bourget, the Montreal ultramontanist, whom Riel admired inordinately, fed the obsession. In letters which Riel henceforward treasured, Bishop Bourget, too, referred to a "mission." "God . . . will not abandon you . . . ," he wrote in one letter, "for He has given you a mission which you will have to accomplish in all points."

Wandering in exile, working as a day laborer in New York State, brooding over the injustice of his lot, seeing further visions, searching for the "mission," which at one point he conceived to be the setting up of a *métis* and Indian nation, Riel's mind, apparently, gave way. For some twenty months, under the name of Louis David, he was kept in asylums in Quebec at Longue Pointe and Beauport. In January 1878 he was released as cured. Shortly thereafter he fell in love, seemingly for the first time, with the blond and pretty sister of his friend Father Barnabé.

Yet there seemed to be no place or future in the East for Louis Riel. By November of 1878 he was again at Pembina. His five years of exile had two more years to run. While he had been in the East, in Manitoba those years had overwhelmed his people, the *métis*. They had fled from civilization, seeking refuge on the North Saskatchewan or in their camps in Montana.

So Riel followed them to Montana. He found his brethren still living their nomadic life. He joined with them as trader and hunter and organizer. Soon, as in Red River, he was their leader, protesting to Washington against what he took to be the denial of their rights. His letters to his eastern fiancée ceased. At some time in 1881 he took to wife the shapely *métisse* Marie Bellehumeur, a marriage solemnized formally, as has been noted, in April 1882.

When the first child came, Riel's wife, shy and adoring though she might be, asked for more security than the nomad way of life. Riel became a teacher at the tiny mission school of St. Peter's.

Yet he kept in touch with the dark currents swirling among the *métis* both in Montana and in the settlements along the North Saskatchewan. Nor had his "visions" ceased. Somewhere, someplace, he was sure, his "mission" waited. Marie did not know, really, the man beside whom she sat.

And later, on that June 4, 1884, the "mission" rode into St. Peter's. Four men, their leader the tough, bluff buffalo hunter Gabriel Dumont, who had been the "president" of the provisional government founded at St. Laurent in 1873 by Father André, had guided their horses over the long 700 miles from St. Laurent to St. Peter's Mission. Their purpose was to lead Louis Riel back onto the stage of history.

Behind that ride lay another story of governmental bungling. Father André's provisional government had been, perforce, dissolved when the Mounties brought law and order to the Northwest. But, meantime, from Manitoba more and more *métis* had migrated to the Saskatchewan settlements. True, by the 1870 Manitoba Act the Dominion had reserved 1,400,000 acres in that province for the *métis*.

This grant had been almost nullified by Ottawa's incompetence. Allotment of it did not begin until 1873. After that date there were constant changes in rules for eligibility and the size of allotments. The whole mess was not finally straightened out until 1886. Meantime, land scrip had been issued. Shrewd whites bought this up from the *métis* for from $40 to $60 for 240 acres and laid the foundation for fortunes for themselves.

This, and dislike of a settled life, had led to the emigration to the Saskatchewan Valley. The tale of governmental red tape and confusion traveled with them. As in Red River, the *métis* became anxious for the titles to their farms. Nor had they forgotten the claim that they were at least half owners of the soil by "natural right" along with the Indians. In 1878 from all *métis* settlements in the Northwest requests went to Ottawa for "a like amount of scrip and like land grants as in Manitoba."

John A. and his Cabinet were too exercised about "National Policy" and the like to worry about the half-breeds. Then, as in Red River, the square survey began to creep northward. Once again, the *métis* farms were in narrow strips with a river frontage on the Saskatchewan of from ten to twenty chains. The government had learned a little from the Red River imbroglio. In 1877 the holding of river lots was granted, and in that year and the next special surveys were made. But more *métis* moved in. With cheerful disregard of the square survey and of the sections reserved for schools and the H.B.C., they staked out new ribbonlike farms. At St. Albert, near Edmonton, these new farms were conceded. At St. Laurent and Prince Albert, recognition of them was refused.

To worry the *métis* further, they were told that, by the homestead regulations, they must register the farms which they had worked for a generation and then wait three years for their titles. The *métis* became pricklier and pricklier. In the early months of 1884 the Inspector of Dominion Lands, W. Pearce, did grant the white and half-breed titles at Prince Albert. But Pearce spoke no French. He turned the job of investigating the claims at St. Laurent and St. Antoine de Padoue (better known as Batoche) over to the Dominion land agent at Prince Albert. That agent did not report to Ottawa until October; and then his report was lost in the files until, on news of trouble in the Northwest, it was, in February of 1885, hurriedly exhumed and passed.

Even October of 1884 was too late. By the spring of that year the *métis* were as touchy as bears just come out from hibernating. They had seen the buffalo disappear. They had watched what had happened to the Indians, their cousins. The iron rails had gouged the prairies. Settlers were coming in; and they had no confidence in Ottawa. They wanted security. They wanted more. For they had thoroughly exaggerated ideas of what was due them—and these ideas included autonomy.

So they looked about for leaders. There was Charles Nolin, Riel's cousin. But Nolin had been suspect during the 1869–70 revolt and since then he had been a Minister of the Crown in Manitoba and so was not to be fully trusted. There was Gabriel Dumont. Dumont, though courageous and capable, was illiterate and no orator. Inevitably thoughts turned to Louis Riel. On May 6 a meeting in the Lindsay School House, south of Prince Albert, of whites, English half-breeds, and French *métis* decided to send for him.

This spin of the wheel of events was no surprise to Riel. Ever since reaching Montana he had kept in touch with the *métis* along the Saskatchewan. So a few days before the delegation arrived he received word that it was coming. The letter went on to say, significantly:

"Do not imagine that you will begin the work when you get here; I tell you it is all done, the thing is decided; it is your presence that is needed. . . . The whole race is calling for you."

On that June 4, when Dumont and his three companions (Moïse Ouellette, Michel Dumas, and James Isbister, an English half-breed from Prince Albert) found him, Riel was not unprepared. He led the four men to his tiny cabin. He listened, face impassive, as they extended their invitation. But to a man of forty, locked in a backwater, brooding on the past and on his "mission," it must have been as if he had been stumbling interminably through a dreary swamp and, suddenly, the swamp had disappeared and before him stretched a fair and smiling land, all his.

His decision was inevitable. Yet a strain of mysticism made him decide that, since on the fourth of June four men had come in search of a fifth, his own answer must wait until the fifth. On that morning he handed the delegation a written acceptance. In it was included the statement that the Canadian Government owed him 240 acres of land by the Manitoba Act as well as "five valuable lots on account of hay, timber and river frontage" and "if they only pay attention a minute they will easily find they owe me something else."

The "something else" came from Riel's conviction that the Dominion owed him compensation for his sufferings while in exile and also for the administration he had maintained in Manitoba until Wolseley's expedition arrived. Through this claim, as through a window, we can look at the feeling, not without reason, that injustice had been done him which was festering in Riel's soul.

The acceptance, further, referred to the numerical strength of the *métis* in Montana and his own influence with them. This may have been a hint at the possibility of a concerted *métis* movement. In any case, Riel wrote down that he would have to return in September to his Montana *métis*.

It is quite likely that this statement was put in so as to leave himself an avenue of retreat. But for the Riel who on June 10, his wife and two children and his few belongings in a Red River cart, rode north with Gabriel Dumont and his comrades, there was to be no return.

What sort of leader was he at that moment? He had several faces. There was the practical man who could organize and be so sweetly reasonable and yet, withal, breathe forth such a sense of power that he could charm the gophers out of their holes. There was the orator with the deeply resonant voice who could rouse others and himself to frenzy. There was the self-willed egotist who could brook no opposition. There was the cynic who later could offer his convictions for sale. Above all, coiled deep within him, was the obsession of himself as a chosen instrument of God to fulfill a mission.

The roots of that obsession were planted firmly in the religious mysticism which had always been deeply woven into Louis "David" Riel's being. By this time, however, he had become an unbalanced visionary, who was to believe himself inspired by God and to promulgate a heretical Roman Catholicism with Bishop Bourget as the Riel-selected Pope.

At first, however, Riel was all hypnotizing reasonableness. As on July 1, 1884, Dominion Day, he approached the broad valley of the South Saskatchewan at Batoche, by this time the main settlement of the *métis*, seventy of his compatriots streamed out to meet him on horseback, cheering and firing salutes. In the village itself hundreds more awaited him, among them old acquaintances, such as Louis Schmidt, who had been the secretary of Riel's Red River provisional government, and Charles Nolin, his cousin, with whom Riel was to lodge for three months. As he heard the shouts of joy and saw the arms raised to greet him on that bright July day, the heart of the returning exile must have swelled with joy and pride. The Riel of 1870 would have burst into surging words. The Riel of 1884 embraced Schmidt and Nolin, returned the greetings of those pressing in upon him, and proceeded up the trail toward the church, calm, smiling, affable. All the while, we may assume, his eyes were assessing the settlement which was to become the capital of his kingdom.

Batoche, originally, as already mentioned, had been founded as St. Antoine de Padoue, by Père Vegreville in 1881. It was about two hundred miles north of Regina and some forty miles southwest of the English half-breeds at Prince Albert. *Métis* cabins straggled for a mile or two along the rounded riverbanks on either side of the broad-flowing river. At almost the central point of the settlement there was a ferry, known as Batoche's Crossing. Here a few stores of log and frame hugged the riverbank. From the ferry a path, well-nigh a mile long, led up to the crest of the river valley. That crest was crowned by the church, with the parish house across from it. Six miles upstream at Gabriel's Crossing was another ferry, owned and operated by Gabriel Dumont.

It was a tiny place. Yet it was to blazon itself on the pages of Canada's history. Riel's arena was to be the whole of the Northwest and of the old province of the two Canadas. Here, at Batoche, was the center of that arena.

At first, though, Riel moved on quiet moccasins. The *métis* at Batoche and nearby St. Laurent were his. About ten miles due west, tucked between the South and North Saskatchewan rivers, was Duck Lake, where *métis* and Indians lived, and some ten miles west of it were the police at Fort Carlton on the North Saskatchewan. Prince Albert, to the north, was occupied by the English half-breeds, whom he must win over.

This was his immediate, if circumscribed, circle of action. Ultimately, however, that action must, in Riel's view, take in the Indians near Battleford, some two hundred miles upstream by the circuitous river route but almost directly west of Batoche. Above it again was Fort Pitt and beyond it an Indian reservation near Frog Lake, while some fifty miles to the northeast was Fort à la Corne.

All these places were merely names to those comparatively few Canadians who had heard of them. Soon Riel was to make them household words. At the moment, to his delight, he found that the English half-breeds and even some of the whites were behind him. A white settler, W. H. Jackson, the secretary of the Settlers' Union and a University of Toronto graduate, became Riel's shadow. Later, at Riel's request he was converted to Roman Catholicism. In one of Riel's first speeches, before a large audience at Red Deer Hill near Prince Albert, there was even a Thomas Scott among his hearers. This Thomas Scott was a Riel supporter.

To cap the triumph of his return, Riel was invited to speak at Prince Albert itself. He was fearful of possible hatreds among the "English" because of the killing of the other Thomas Scott. Father André, the beloved adviser of the *métis*, who was Oblate Superior at Prince Albert (the Oblates, it must be remembered, were ultramontanists, and the notion of a French Roman Catholic enclave along the Saskatchewan was attractive to them), urged him in a letter to "come" and "come quickly," telling him that he was "the most popular man in the country." (Opinions differ as to whether this letter from Father André was written about the meeting at Prince Albert or sent to Riel at St. Peter's Mission in Montana with Dumont, but, as Stanley points out in his *The Birth of Western Canada*, the reference in it to the "great disappointment to the people of Prince Albert" if Riel did not come seems to favor the former view.)

Riel went. The meeting, held on July 19, was *un succès fou*. The audience, we are told, was "struck with the quiet and gentle way he spoke to them." His major pleas were for free title to the lands the settlers had occupied, for representation in the Dominion Parliament, and for changes in the land laws. The means he advocated were constitutional.

The egotist and the visionary in Riel were still dormant or, at least, concealed. Jackson, the secretary of the Settlers' Union, issued a manifesto demanding provincial legislatures for the territories, a point Riel had also made. "There is no danger of Indian trouble," Jackson added, "as long as we can keep Riel in the country." Father André reported to Governor Dewdney that Riel had "acted and spoken in a sensible way." Big Bear and others of the Indian chiefs had an interview with him at Duck Lake. On September 24, with the approval of Bishop Grandin, who was in charge of all the Roman Catholic missions along the Saskatchewan, Riel inaugurated at Batoche *"L'Union Métisse de Saint Josèphe."* With whites, half-breeds, Indians, and clergy all behind him, Riel was on the crest of the wave.

Nor was his movement ill timed. As the depression grew gloomier and the C.P.R. struggled through the Rockies, agitation for Northwest rights mounted everywhere—for example, in places as far apart as Wolseley and Edmonton. In Manitoba, with disallowance after disallowance of railway charters and a harvest failure, there were threats of secession and even of rebellion. Riel so far was constitutional in his actions. On December 16, through Jackson, a petition was sent to the Honorable J. A. Chapleau, the Secretary of State, asking for more liberal treatment of the Indians, scrip and land patents for the half-breeds, representation in the Dominion Parliament and Cabinet, provincial control of natural resources, vote by ballot, modification of the homestead laws, a railway to Hudson Bay, and a reduction in the tariff. Into this omnibus petition—something for everybody—was thrust, by Riel himself, a complaint about the treatment of the 1870 Red River delegates to Ottawa and the nonpromulgation of the amnesty.

The petition must have been received. Sir John A. claimed in Parliament in March 1885 that it had never been transmitted to the government. Yet, somehow it did reach the Colonial Office in London. The truth might seem to be that Old Tomorrow, occupied by the crisis in C.P.R. finances, brushed aside both the petition and the ominously recurrent reports of trouble yeasting in the Northwest.

Among the prophets of disaster was that Charles Mair, the poet, who had been horsewhipped from Bannatyne's post office in Winnipeg by indignant ladies in 1869. For some years he had been living in Prince Albert with his wife and family. On several occasions in 1883 and 1884 he came to Ottawa to warn the government of an explosion to come. No one listened. When Riel arrived at Batoche, Charles Mair closed out his business and brought his family to Windsor in Ontario. There, until the rebellion flamed, he worked at his epic, *Tecumseh.* Then he joined Colonel Denison's cavalry as quartermaster.

Mair and all the other Jeremiahs, who included Superintendent Crozier of the N.W.M.P., might as well have spared their predictions of doom. Meantime, snags were thrusting up in the smooth flow of Riel's good fortune. Since many of his supporters were Liberals, the pro-government press in the West began to strike at him. In addition, the case of the murdered Thomas Scott was revived and anti-Riel passions began to flare. As the unkindest blow of all, the Roman Catholic clergy turned their faces from him. Father André, at first, appears to have approved of Riel. The higher hierarchy, remembering the issue of the Red River revolt, was suspicious, and all the more so because Riel's heterodoxy had begun to shine through the veneer; while the clergy on the spot became fearful of his influence over their flock. In December, Father Vital Fourmand at Batoche observed with a certain irritation that the *métis* regarded Riel as *"un Josué, un prophète, et même un saint."* Father André wrote to Governor Dewdney that Riel ought to be got out of the country. Dewdney himself, anticipating trouble, strengthened the Mounties at Prince Albert and placed a detachment at Fort Carlton. The governor, though a somewhat dilatory man, could appreciate that behind *métis* discontent, thanks to Ottawa, lay the specter of an Indian uprising.

4

The December wind swept the swirling snow over the valley at Batoche and along the ice on the river. It whistled down the chimney of Riel's cabin. The *métis* leader flung another log on the fire. Then he turned to stare again at Father André and D. H. MacDowall, Northwest Council member for the electoral district of Lorne. They had come to persuade him to return to Montana.

Riel had made that suggestion to his *métis* in the previous fall. The *métis* had begged him to stay. He had agreed. Now both his church and the government, even if unofficially, were asking that he leave. Riel paced up and down. Did he have a premonition of what was to come? Or was his offer only half in earnest? In either case, when he stopped, it was the cynical face of Riel which he presented. He told the two men, as MacDowall later wrote to Dewdney, "that if the government would consider his personal claims against them [and we must remember that reference to these in his letter of acceptance to Gabriel Dumont] and pay him a certain amount . . . he would arrange to make his illiterate and unreasoning followers well satisfied with almost any settlement of their claims for land grants . . . and also that he would leave the North-West, never to return."

He was asked how much he wanted. Riel listened to the wind a moment. His claim was, he said, for $100,000 but he would accept $35,000. "I believe myself," wrote MacDowall, "three thousand to five thousand would cart the whole Riel family across the border."

"'My name is Riel and I want material,'" Riel added, according to MacDowall, "which, I suppose," MacDowall went on, "was a pun."

Father André confirmed MacDowall's understanding of the interview. "Obtain for him four or five thousand dollars," the priest reported to Dewdney, "and I am bold in saying Mr. MacDowall and I will make him agree to any conditions."

Some apologists think that Riel was playing a game with Father André and MacDowall. It seems more likely that Riel, who had taken money to absent himself from Manitoba in 1871 and who was firmly convinced that what he was asking for was owed to him, meant what he said. Actually it was Canada's last chance to avoid the Northwest Rebellion—and Riel's last chance, too.

But the Furies were in full cry. No money was made available; and opposition had stirred the dormant madness in Riel. The whites were dropping away from him. The Catholic clergy, in his view of them, were proving traitors to his "mission" and to "True Religion." Nor had Ottawa deigned to answer the December petition. On February 4, 1885, the new Minister of the Interior, David Macpherson (another old friend of John A.'s), did wire Dewdney that the government had at last decided to investigate the half-breed claims for titles and land grants.

Promises from Ottawa were as old as last year's chestnuts. On February 24 Riel told a clamorous meeting of *métis* that he wanted to return to Montana. Opinions differ whether this was a sincere desire or the device of offering to resign in order to be begged to stay. Quite possibly it was Riel's final attempt to turn aside from the "mission" he believed God had imposed upon him.

The *métis* pleaded with him to remain. So, on March 2, did the English half-breeds. Riel agreed.

Thus was the die cast. From that instant Riel never looked back. On that same March 2 he demanded of Father André that he approve of the formation of a provisional government. When the priest refused, Riel denounced him to the *métis* as a police spy.

That which had been coiled within him had now taken control. From this point forward the signs of Riel's dementia are clear. What Riel had decided upon was to repeat the tactics of 1869–70, to form a provisional government, take over the country, capture hostages, and force the Dominion to treat with him. He forgot that the Saskatchewan was not Red River and that 1885 was not 1869–70. Delusions of grandeur and of God's certain help boiled through his mind—and the *métis*, even to the tough, realistic Dumont, were his to mold as he would.

His cousin, Charles Nolin, however, persuaded Riel to agree to a novena in the chapel at Batoche from March 10 to 19 to ascertain God's will. On Sunday, March 15, when Riel attended for the first time, Father Fourmand spoke against revolt, pronouncing that all who took up arms against constituted authority would be deprived of the sacraments.

At this opposition Riel boiled over. After the service he denounced the priest. The Spirit of God, he told the armed *métis*, as they milled outside the chapel, had left the Church of Rome and the Pope. The new Pope was Bishop Bourget.

At this pronouncement the *métis*, devoted to their church, hung fire. Riel drove forward. On March 18, aided by Dumont, he arrested a number of hostages. On the next day, which was the last day of the novena and also the Feast of St. Joseph, he shouted to the *métis* that a force of police was coming to attack them. This rumor is said to have had its origin with Lawrence Clark of the H.B.C. He, however, denied the charge.

Whatever the source of the report, it was to drive the *métis* where Riel wanted them to go. A provisional government was excitedly formed with Pierre Parenteau as president and Gabriel Dumont adjutant general. There was a council, too, called the *Exovidate* (to select one of several spellings from Riel's "Latin" for "the group from out of the flock"). That night Charles Nolin was arrested for treason (he had sided with the clerics) and sentenced to be shot. To save his life, he pretended to see the errors of his course and joined Riel. On the same day, in spite of the protests of Father Moulin, Riel seized Batoche church as his headquarters. The priests had already declared Riel *non compos mentis* and, therefore, incapable of receiving the sacraments. On Wednesday, March 25, Riel countered by renouncing the Roman Catholic faith and announcing a new religion. He ordered first Father Moulin and then Father Vegreville to become "chaplain" for the *métis* and the new religion. Both refused.

"Well, then," he told the *métis*, "I will be your priest."

The *métis* wavered. Such was the hypnotizing influence of Riel and the letters from Bishop Bourget which he showed to their illiterate eyes that they followed. Riel had defeated the Roman Catholic clergy.

But the English half-breeds of Prince Albert defected. Riel tried to win them back. On March 21 he wrote to them as "Dear Brothers in Jesus Christ" to tell them that "justice commands us to take up arms." On March 23 he begged them in a second letter for "the love of God" to help "save the Saskatchewan."

Rebellion had now flamed. The *métis* cut the telegraph wires. Trials were held and more hostages seized. Goods and ammunition were commandeered. When Superintendent Crozier, who was at Fort Carlton, twenty miles from Batoche, sent Thomas McKay, a half-breed from Prince Albert, and Hillyard Mitchell, the trader at Duck Lake, to negotiate with Riel, the new "David" replied with a letter demanding that the police at both Fort Carlton and Battleford surrender, warning Crozier that ". . . in case of non-acceptance we intend to attack you . . . ; and to commence without delay a war of extermination upon all those who have shown themselves hostile to our rights. . . ."

It may have been a bluff. The other *métis* leaders later said that their only intention was, by revolt, to compel the Dominion to pay attention to their claims; and it does seem that, at first, Riel strove to avoid bloodshed. Yet, with a man as obsessed as Riel had now become, it is difficult to tell exactly what was in his mind.

And blood was soon to redden the snow.

5

Nothing is drearier than a small settlement in Canada's wilderness when winter is still king. On March 26 the cold at Duck Lake was not too severe and a recent thaw had left the snow crusted. But the sky was cold and gray and as the day dragged by snow began to fall. The lake, about halfway between Fort Carlton and Batoche, that is, about ten miles from each, seemed a lost, bleak platter fringed by bare snow-vague willows and poplars. But there was excitement visible on its shore in the small clump of log cabins that clustered around Hillyard Mitchell's trading establishment and the church. Men were shouting and milling around. Some, mounting horses and led by Gabriel Dumont, were already riding toward the hill to the west. The rest, *métis* and Indians from the Cree reservation near by, partly on horseback and partly on foot, were getting organized. Among them Riel was rushing about, unarmed but carrying a large cross wrenched from the Duck Lake church. For news had just come that Superintendent Crozier's police and Prince Albert volunteers were on their way to Duck Lake.

On the other side of that hill the police and volunteers were moving stolidly forward through the falling snow. On the thirteenth of March, Crozier had wired Dewdney that a half-breed rebellion was likely "to break out at any moment." As a result, Commissioner Irvine at Regina had been ordered to move north to Fort Carlton with a hundred police as reinforcements. Meanwhile, Crozier had organized a body of volunteers at Battleford and had taken to Fort Carlton fifty Mounties and one seven-pounder gun. After Riel made his arrests and formed his government, eighty Prince Albert volunteers joined him; while others formed a home guard to protect Prince Albert itself.

As his attempts to negotiate with Riel prove, Crozier had no intention of hurrying into conflict, even after Riel's preposterous letter to him. But there were large government stores, including rifles and ammunition, at Duck Lake. Early on the morning of the twenty-sixth he sent Thomas McKay with a police escort thither to bring back the stores. Neither he nor Mitchell knew that, the night before, Dumont had led a force of *métis* to Duck Lake or that Riel had joined him. Three miles from the post McKay and the police were suddenly surrounded by Dumont and a band of mounted *métis,* accompanied by a few Indians. They demanded surrender. McKay refused. Since Riel had laid down a pronunciamento that the *métis* were not to fire unless fired upon, Dumont's men tried to provoke the police into shooting. But they retired to Fort Carlton.

By this time the reinforcements under Commissioner Irvine were only a few hours away. Crozier should have waited for them. But his "Irish" was up and his men were eager. With 4 officers, 53 police, 41 volunteers, and his seven-pounder, and taking sleighs along to bring back the supplies, he set out to teach the *métis* a sharp lesson. Dumont and his party, in fact, had scarcely got back to Duck Lake when a scout came riding in to tell them that the police were on the way. Dumont galloped off with 25 horsemen to intercept them. The rest, getting ready hurriedly, followed.

About a mile and a half from Duck Lake, the bluff buffalo hunter found the position he wanted. It was a low hill intersecting the road with ravines running forward on either side toward the police, while clumps of bush and willows provided natural cover. Here Dumont placed his men, hidden among the brush, and, in addition, occupied a log house to the right of Crozier's line of advance.

It was an excellent site for an ambush, and more and more *métis* accompanied by Riel were streaming forward from Duck Lake to join Dumont's advance guard. Meanwhile the Mounties and the volunteers were plodding on through the falling snow, which turned everything—road, ravines, hills—into an enveloping grayness. They mounted the first ridge which crossed the road and came down into the valley. They were within 150 yards of the next hill when suddenly Crozier's scouts came galloping back, pursued by mounted *métis*. Crozier halted his force. The *métis* halted, too. Crozier had the horses unhitched from the sleighs and taken to the rear. The sleighs themselves were drawn up across the road as a barricade. The police and volunteers, dismounting and also sending back their horses, took cover behind the sleighs.

While these operations were being carried out—and Crozier does not seem to have noticed the log cabin to the right of his line, concealed as it was by trees and snowbanks—Isidore Dumont, a brother to Gabriel, rode forward waving a white blanket. There was an Indian with him. Crozier and his interpreter, McKay, went forward to meet the two, intending to parley. As the parley began, the Indian snatched at McKay's rifle. A hand-to-hand struggle followed.

As to what happened then, accounts differ. The police account states that the *métis* fired first. Dumont, later, claimed that the police touched off the first shot.

That dispute does not matter too much. But as Crozier glanced around he perceived suddenly that a line of *métis* was in motion, coiling around his left flank. He realized that he had fallen into a skillful trap. Later, Dumont was to explain that the parley was intended to continue until the police were surrounded and could be forced to surrender. What Riel wanted was hostages as in Red River so as to compel the Dominion government to negotiate.

If that was his plan the Indian had spoiled it. Crozier spurred back to the barricade.

"Fire away, boys," he shouted.

The police poured forth a volley. Either in that volley or by the first shots, Isadore Dumont and the Indian were killed. Louis Riel, carrying the cross as his only weapon, cried to the *métis:*

"In the name of God the Father who created us, reply to that."

The battle was on. Crozier, a blunt, rather bullheaded man with little tactical sense, soon found that he had been outmaneuvered. His men were in the open. The *métis* and their Indian allies were under cover. Taking advantage of the ground, they were outflanking his left, while on the right the Prince Albert volunteers, when they tried to extend their line, came under fire from the log cabin. Crozier had his seven-pounder. It failed to be of much use. According to the police account, Crozier had it directed on the log cabin but found that the volunteers were in the line of fire. It was then turned on those *métis* who were encircling the left flank. After two or three shots a rattled gunner rammed in a shell before the powder and the gun was out of action.

It was only a tiny skirmish. It began to look like a massacre. Fortunately for Crozier's force, Dumont, spurring to within less than a hundred yards of the troops in his excitement, fell from a bullet gashing his scalp in true Hollywood fashion. A second of his brothers, Edouard, took command. The volunteers, stung by the sniping from the cabin, tried a charge against it. The charge failed.

After a half hour's fighting, Crozier, on a much smaller scale, was almost in Braddock's plight. His men, exposed in the open to fire from behind brush and willows, were almost surrounded. The falling snow cut down visibility. Shouts and fresh bursts of shooting showed that more and more *métis* and Indians were pouring onto the battlefield. Crozier gave the order to retreat. Somehow, though five of the transport horses had been killed, the rest, in the face of the *métis* fire, were brought up and hitched to the sleighs. With them and the seven-pounder, the police, leaving their dead where they lay, withdrew in what was almost a rout. If Dumont had had his way they would have been attacked and exterminated on their way back to Fort Carlton. But Riel, to his credit, intervened.

"For the love of God, no more killing." he cried. "There has been too much blood shed already."

As it was, Crozier had lost twelve dead and eleven wounded out of his small force of less than a hundred. The *métis* claimed that fourteen of the Mounties and volunteers were killed and wounded; while they reported a loss to themselves of only five killed, one of them an Indian, and three wounded. To complete Crozier's mortification, shortly after his return to Fort Carlton, Commissioner Irvine came in with 108 more Mounties.

And what of the *métis*? They swarmed back into Duck Lake with their booty, shouting and shooting in the air. Dumont had won the victory. To Riel went the credit. They hailed him as a prophet, a veritable David slaying the Canadian Goliath. They agreed with him that hell did not last forever. They agreed to whatever he said. Duck Lake had put Louis Riel on the pinnacle where he had longed to be. East and west and north and south the news of Duck Lake spread. To the north the recalcitrant Big Bear and Poundmaker stirred. Near Calgary the powerful Blackfeet were restless. The Indians around Edmonton began to look to their war paint. So did the tribesmen in the Qu'Appelle Valley. Was Riel truly a miracle worker? Had the time come to slaughter the whites and drive them out? At Fort Carlton, Commissioner Irvine prepared to abandon the post. At Prince Albert and Battleford and even in Calgary and Edmonton the whites, terrified, began to look to their defenses. Was an Indian war upon them?

The Northwest was in turmoil. In the East, on March 27 the news of Duck Lake blanched the face of Sir John. Tomorrow, for once, had been too late. But disaster could still be staved off.

For in March 1885 Canada had a transcontinental railway, except for a few gaps here and there. John A. had already, on the night of March 23, in view of the ominous rumblings in the Northwest, sent Major General Frederick Middleton, the Imperial officer who was in command of Canada's militia, to Winnipeg. As early as March 25 the Winnipeg militia, with John A.'s son, Hugh, among them, had started to move west. Now, Van Horne, who by chance was in Ottawa, promised to carry troops over the C.P.R., gaps and all, to Fort Qu'Appelle in eleven days on two days' notice, if he were given full charge of the operation.

A wire was sent to Father Lacombe at Calgary. Soon the revered "Black-Robe Voyageur" was speeding out on a locomotive to Blackfoot Crossing to use his influence with Crowfoot to keep the Blackfeet quiet. Father Lacombe succeeded. He wired John A. that the Blackfeet would remain loyal.

These were the first attempts to localize the prairie fire Riel had set blazing. Then, on Monday, March 30, in Hamilton and Toronto and Kingston and Montreal and Ottawa, the militia marched to the waiting trains. The skies were overcast. The rain fell. The bands played "Auld Lang Syne" and "The Girl I Left Behind Me," and the crowds cheered and the troops piled into the coaches. The machine to crush the prophet was being set in motion. Before it could operate, the wires brought news of fresh disasters.

CHAPTER XXVIII

1885

Abandonment of Fort Carlton—Poundmaker's Crees Besiege Battleford—Indians Massacre Whites at Frog Lake—Indians Occupy Fort Pitt—Troops Gather in the West and the C.P.R. Proves Its Worth—The Transcontinental Again in Difficulties

1

IT was a cold and hurried job, that night of March 27–28, preparing to leave Fort Carlton. Commissioner Irvine knew that the evacuation would put an exclamation mark after the victory won by the *métis* at Duck Lake. He felt he had no choice. This old fur traders' post had not been built for defense. It was on the river's edge and the three-hundred-foot bank behind it commanded the fort square from two sides. In addition, the Prince Albert volunteers were alarmed about their own homes and families.

All that night the men scurried to and fro. Every available sleigh was loaded with supplies. The rest of the stores were sunk through holes cut in the ice into the river. (The H.B.C.'s claims for losses here totaled $52,540.78.) Then, suddenly, flames flared up into the March night. In the N.C.O.s' quarters, hay used in making mattresses for the wounded men had been left too close to a hot stove.

The almost panic-stricken police and volunteers let the fort burn. From the surrounding darkness the *métis* scouts saw the red beard of the flames toss upward. As the last sleigh left at 4 A.M., they galloped in to check the fire. Then they streamed back to tell Dumont and Riel that the enemy were retreating. Dumont wanted to lead the *métis* to wipe out the police and the volunteers.

It was a counsel of sound military sense. Irvine's force was struggling in a long line, hampered with sleighs, along a tree-shrouded trail. They were so fearful of an assault that they did not stop even to water their horses until they were halfway to Prince Albert.

Riel once again refused bloodshed, almost as if his first experience with battle had sickened him. Irvine's men reached Prince Albert about 8 P.M. There, all was fear and near panic. The outlying settlers had flocked in. A stockade had been flung up around the Presbyterian church and the adjacent buildings. The men were armed and on guard.

The arrival of Irvine's force brought reassurance. Meantime the news of the defeat of the police flashed as if by signal fires across the snow-covered prairies. It sped north to the two thousand Crees and Stoneys on the reservations near Battleford. Riel's runners had already been there with tobacco, inciting to an Indian war. Those runners had told Red Pheasant, chief of one of the bands, that Riel was a god and in touch with heaven, that the Americans were coming to help him, and that they had better join the new prophet voluntarily instead of waiting until they were compelled to do so. Near Battleford, too, were the bands of Poundmaker and Little Pine. The runners had been to them as well.

Riel himself had also written the *métis* near Fort Battleford and Fort Pitt, asking them to "rouse up the Indians. Do what you can to put the Police of Fort Pitt and Fort Battle in an impossible situation." "David" might be averse to bloodshed under his eyes. He had no compunctions about unleashing an Indian war.

All the Indians near Battleford were already, thanks to governmental action, disturbed and dissatisfied and watching Riel to see what he would achieve. On March 28 they heard of the Duck Lake victory. It was the detonator to explode the dynamite. By the next day the Indians were in camp seven miles from the town. That night the settlers around took refuge in the fort. That same night the Indians raided the abandoned farms. From the fort's stockade the settlers watched the flames from their homes shooting up into the night. In the morning Poundmaker's and Little Pine's Crees, hideous in war paint, poured into the town itself.

The fort was on a hilltop some distance from the town. The Indians rode up to parley. They promised to return to their reserves if given clothing, sugar, tobacco, powder, and shot. Rae, the Indian agent, felt that he had to telegraph Dewdney for the proper authorization. By the time permission came the Crees had plundered the H.B.C. stores and the buildings of the town. Then the Stoneys, and a band of Assiniboins who had murdered their farm instructor and a bachelor farmer, poured in. From the stockade the settlers, 512 of them, of whom some 300 were women and children, watched the yelling warriors bedecking themselves with silk gowns and party bonnets, pounding silver to bits, ripping bedding to shreds, hacking pianos to pieces, reveling in an orgy of looting and destruction. Then they sat down around the fort and waited for it to surrender. Fortunately there was a three months' supply of food. It is again interesting to observe that, after Duck Lake, Riel wrote Poundmaker and his allies, saying in part:

"Praise God with us for the success He has granted us. Arise. Face the enemy. If you can take Fort Battle, destroy it. Save all the merchandise and provisions and come and join us. . . . Whatever you do, do for the love of God. Under the protection of Jesus Christ, the Blessed Virgin, St. Joseph and St. John the Baptist, and be certain that faith works wonders.

"Louis 'David' Riel, Exovede."

It would seem that by this time Riel's demented mind was reaching beyond the alleged purpose of forcing the Dominion to treat with him, to the fantasy of an independent Indian and *métis* nation. Certainly he had no hesitation in inciting the Indians to kill and plunder.

The settlers in Fort Battleford were luckier than they realized. Upstream from Battleford was Fort Pitt. About thirty miles northwest of it and some two hundred miles northwest of Duck Lake was the hamlet of Frog Lake. Here there was an H.B.C. trading post—being managed at the moment by W. B. Cameron—a subagency of the Department of Indian Affairs, with T. T. Quinn, of mixed Sioux and French-Irish blood, as the man in charge, six Mounties, and a Roman Catholic mission. Near by was the Plains Cree band of that Big Bear who had refused to go on a reservation and whose warriors had opposed the arrest of one of their braves by Crozier.

These Indians, starving and destitute, had spent the winter near the Woods Cree reserve. Finally they had yielded to Ottawa's decree of "no work, no food," and Big Bear had promised Quinn to go on a reservation in the spring. On March 18 the site for this had been picked at Dog Rump Creek.

Riel's runners had been to Frog Lake, too. Big Bear was shrewd enough to try to stick to peaceful measures. The war chief, Wandering Spirit; Imasees, Big Bear's eldest son; and a visiting Indian, Little Poplar, who was a born agitator, were all for violence. To them, on the same day, March 28, as the news reached Poundmaker and Little Pine, there came by some "moccasin telegraph" the story of the defeat of the police at Duck Lake, though the whites did not hear of it until two days later. As fate would have it, Big Bear was out hunting. Wandering Spirit, a violent, almost maniacal man, along with Imasees and Little Poplar, promptly held a council with the Woods Crees.

Big Bear returned on April 1. By that time his control of his warriors had been shattered. Meanwhile, on the thirtieth, the news of Duck Lake reached Fort Pitt. Here nagging chance had put the novelist's son, the precise Inspector Francis Dickens, in charge. On the next day he sent to advise the whites to leave Frog Lake but offered to come with his twenty-odd police to the post if this was desired. It was Quinn who, thinking he could control the Indians (his wife was a Cree), made the decision to stay. But it was agreed that the six Mounties should leave so as not to irritate the Indians. They went back to Fort Pitt.

Quinn was overconfident. On the evening of April 1, a mild, moist night, the whites heard the boom-boom of a drum from the Plains Cree camp and wondered what it portended. Early the next morning the braves in full war paint poured into the hamlet. They seized the rifles and the horses. Then, after looting a store and threatening the whites, they herded them, both Catholics and Protestants, to the Maundy Thursday Mass. Two priests, Father Fafard of Frog Lake and Father Marchand, who had come in a day before from Onion Lake, were conducting it. The warriors were moving restlessly in and out of the door at the back of the church. Suddenly Wandering Spirit, pantherlike in his lithe body and fierce features, war bonnet crowning his painted face and Winchester in hand, strode in. He moved almost to the altar and knelt there, Winchester butt on the floor, glaring up at the white-robed priests. He waited until the Mass was finished. Then, turning, he commanded the worshipers to leave. The whites were again herded together to the Indian agency building while the

Crees sacked the N.W.M.P. barracks. Wandering Spirit ordered Quinn, who was in the street, to go to the Cree camp. Quinn refused. Wandering Spirit raised his Winchester and shot him. Big Bear, who had been in the kitchen of the H.B.C. store, burst out of it, calling "*Tesqua! Tesqua!* [Stop! Stop!]"

It was too late. Maniacal bursts of firing cut down the whites. Besides Quinn, the two priests and six others, including the farm instructor and a *métis,* perished in those two or three savage minutes. Cameron, the H.B.C. man, through help from Indians for whom he had done favors, was saved. So were two white women, the newly made widows of Farm Instructor Delaney and J. C. Gowanlock.

These three were taken to the Indian camp. The two women were now by Indian custom the "wives" of the braves who had captured them. Two half-breeds, John A. Pritchard and Adolphus Nolin, by buying them, saved them from this fate. But they and Cameron remained prisoners of the Crees, not knowing when, at any moment, some chance mood of their captors might mean their death. One other white, Henry Quinn, the nephew of T. T. Quinn, warned by a friendly Indian, escaped to carry the news of the massacre to Fort Pitt. He merely confirmed news already brought to Inspector Dickens by the farm instructor at Onion Lake, George Mann, who had hastened into the fort with his family.

The tigers had tasted blood. Two other whites were added to the prisoners held by Big Bear's Crees. At Fort Pitt, Inspector Dickens was in a nervous position. The nearby settlers had come in. His fort, sited on the north bank of the Saskatchewan on the same side as Frog Lake, held about seventy people, of whom twenty-four were police. He set everyone to work. There was no stockade. But the windows and doors were barricaded with sacks of flour. Outlying structures were torn down to take away cover from the expected enemy. Carts and piles of cordwood were utilized to fill the gaps between the buildings around the central square. Even women, and among them the teen-age daughters of W. J. McLean, the H.B.C. trader, took post as sentries.

They all knew that the situation was desperate. The post was too isolated to expect help from anywhere. Like Fort Carlton, it was overlooked by a hill behind it. Still worse, its water supply, the river, was four hundred yards away; and there was not a single well. As the final flick toward panic, there were only forty rounds of ammunition for each Mountie and eighteen for each civilian. Each day the defenders scanned the level fields and the hill behind them, fearfully. Each night they huddled together, the eyes of the sentries straining out into the darkness, waiting tensely for the warwhoop to shrill.

On the seventh of April, Little Poplar, who had been to Battleford to scout the success of Poundmaker's Crees, arrived on the opposite bank of the river (which had now broken up from its winter ice) with nine tepees. He was forbidden to cross, though he seemed friendly. On the eleventh, in anticipation of retreat, the meticulous, red-bearded Dickens set his men to building a large scow. Two days later he sent out scouts toward Frog Lake.

Dickens was one of those men whose footsteps bad luck dogs. Scarcely were the scouts out of sight when Big Bear and 250 armed warriors appeared on the hill behind the fort. The Indians demanded surrender. Dickens refused, but acceded to their request to send out tea, tobacco, clothing, kettles, and a blanket for Big Bear, who had complained that he was "very cold." McLean then went out to parley with the Crees.

Next day the parley was resumed. McLean was decoyed into the Indian camp on the top of the hill. At this unfortunate moment the three scouts, still ignorant of the Indians' whereabouts, came past the Indian camp. Henry Quinn, who was one of them, had, indeed, warned the other two that the Indians might be between them and the fort, but Corporal Cowan refused to listen. The Crees burst out in pursuit. Cowan was killed. Constable Loasby was wounded but got to the fort. Quinn escaped but was chased away from the fort and captured the following day.

During this melee McLean had been made prisoner. At the order of the Indians he wrote to his wife telling her that the Crees demanded that all the civilians come into the Indian camp or else they would attack and burn the fort that same night. McLean's own advice to his wife was that she and the other civilians should surrender.

This may seem a strange suggestion. But McLean realized how feeble Fort Pitt's defenses were, and he knew that if it were taken by assault massacre would follow. Besides, he was an H.B.C. man who was intimately acquainted with many of the Crees, and in his favor were the centuries of fair dealing between the Company and the Indians. In fact, during the whole rebellion no H.B.C. personnel were killed by the Indians, though Cameron came close to it. It was the "government men"—the farm instructors and Indian agents—who paid with their lives for Vankoughnet's pinchpenny policies.

The civilians took McLean's advice. Hints in his letter, however, had made it clear to Dickens that he must now evacuate the fort. While the civilians, in accordance with another McLean hint, delayed their surrender to give the Mounties times to get away, Dickens had his men destroy whatever arms they could not take and pack food, ammunition, and weapons in the leaky scow at the river's edge four hundred yards away, the scow their own inexperienced hands had built.

Then, as the column of men and women, twenty-eight in all, straggled slowly and miserably up to Big Bear's camp, not knowing what the future held, the police, carrying the wounded Loasby with them, marched to the landing. When the scow was launched, water poured in through every seam. However, it carried them out of reach of the Indians to the other bank of the river. There the Mounties camped for the night. Next morning they were up at four-thirty. Snow was piling down and a hard, cold wind was blowing. The diary of Corporal Sleigh, the man who had been in charge at Frog Lake, relates that several men had been frostbitten during the night and that the clothing of all of them was frozen on their backs. It took seven days of fear-filled flight to get down to Fort Battleford in safety. They reached it at 9 A.M. of April 22.

Behind them, the Crees had swarmed into Fort Pitt. They stripped the stores. Much of the loot was comparatively useless—kegs of nails, woolen shawls, bolts of calico, and the like. There was even, as one curious item, Charles Dickens' gold watch which he had given to his son. When recovered later, it still had in it the miniature of Charles Dickens' wife and a lock of her hair. There was also much of more value to the warriors than Dickens' watch. It was the supplies plundered at Forts Carlton and Pitt which enabled the *métis* and Indians to keep on with their war.

What was more chilling was that Duck Lake, Fort Carlton, and Fort Pitt had blown away the legend of the Mounties' invincibility as if it were a puff of smoke. Warriors flocked in to join Big Bear. Panic gripped the whites as everywhere the Indians stirred restlessly. At Battle River Crossing, between Edmonton and Calgary, on April 8 the Indian agent abandoned the reserve. On the next day, every white except the Roman Catholic priest left. Two days later, Ringing Cloud's Crees pillaged the store and the houses. Similarly, on April 26, at Lac la Biche, northwest of Edmonton, the H.B.C. fort and the store were gutted; this after the arrival of runners from Big Bear. The *métis* there, though they refused to join the Indians, fled to the woods. In the same burst of fear, at Green Lake, northwest of Prince Albert, the inhabitants hurried a hundred miles downstream to Ile à la Crosse. Meanwhile, at Edmonton and Calgary there was rumor tramping on the heels of rumor. There was drilling of home guards. At Edmonton, Superintendent A. H. Griesbach was in charge. In Calgary the retired General Strange headed a home guard and a troop of volunteer cavalry. Similar units sprang up elsewhere.

The key to the south was the Blackfoot Confederacy. The evidence is that Riel's emissaries had been among them as early as the late fall of 1884. This fact makes it clear that, from the beginning of his movement, Riel had planned an Indian war. It also adds weight to the possibility that from the first he had hoped to form a *métis* and Indian state with Bourget as its Pope and himself as its divinely inspired leader.

The Blackfeet were restless. But, as has been noted, Father Lacombe had persuaded Crowfoot not to rise. Even when the news of the *métis* and Indian successes at Duck Lake, Fort Carlton, Frog Lake, and Fort Pitt flashed over the prairies, Crowfoot was able to keep his braves in check. For Ottawa, so lethargic and purse-tight in the previous years, had moved to localize Riel's insurrection with the celerity of a businessman scared about profits. Denny was asked to take charge of Treaty 7—and his influence among the Blackfeet was potent. Meanwhile, extra supplies of food were hurried to the dangerous bands in the Qu'Appelle Valley and to the Blackfoot Confederacy. Two carloads of flour and 15,000 pounds of bacon were, for instance, sent to Indian Head. Tea, tobacco, oxen, cattle, and extra rations, so lately locked jealously in the cupboard, were now scattered across the southern prairies with a suddenly lavish hand. In the same desperate haste, on March 30 commissioners were ordered to report on the *métis* claims, and on April 6 there was authorization to issue money scrip to them. What years of petitioning had failed to effect, Riel's rising brought to action in a couple of weeks.

What the Blackfeet noted most of all was the speed with which, by April 2, the C.P.R. had deposited the Winnipeg militia at Qu'Appelle. They and all the Indians in the south realized what

Riel had never understood—that in 1885 Canada had a transcontinental. That fact alone localized the insurrection. The successes of Riel and of the Indians were, in their moment of triumph, their knell of doom.

2

To crush the rebellion, 2011 combat militia, exclusive of the N.W.M.P. and the home guards, were put under arms in the West. In the East, 3324 were called out. The total official mobilization, inclusive of staff, transport, medical, and other corps, was 7982.

Since Riel never had more than 500 *métis* in his forces (Dumont in his story of the campaign sets the number he led at 350, of whom 200 were armed, but he probably minimized his count) and since not more than a thousand Indians ever went on the warpath, this mobilization might seem to be almost like swinging a sledge hammer to crush a mosquito. But at the time there were other bands of *métis* throughout the Northwest who might rise and all together some 20,000 Indian warriors. If the rebellion had spread, the 8000 men would not have been too much. As it was, it took all their effort to crush the comparatively few and ill-armed *métis* and Indians.

The eastern troops still had to be brought West. Van Horne had promised to deliver them to Fort Qu'Appelle within eleven days, in spite of 105 miles of gaps in the railroad north of Lake Superior.

He was as good as his word. Two batteries from Ottawa were the first to leave. Van Horne put down rails on the ice and snow wherever he could. For the rest, the men either rode in sleighs or walked across the trackless gaps, four in all, between Dog Lake—about midway between the present-day stations of Chapleau and White River, renowned as one of the coldest winter spots in inhabited Canada—and Nipigon. There were also more than a hundred miles which were still construction tracks, carrying only work engines and flatcars. Van Horne had four-foot walls nailed to these cars. But the artillery had to be continually unloading and loading guns. According to Lieutenant Colonel Montizambert, who was in command, there were sixteen of these operations; and one day the men rode "on flat cars eighty miles, with thermometer at 50 degrees below zero." Yet it took only four days to get those first two batteries—who were Canada's only regular troops—as far as Winnipeg. The rest of the forces which had got on board in the East on March 30 had still to come.

It was a late spring that year north of Lake Superior. When the first contingent of militia disembarked at Dog Lake, it was still twenty-five degrees below zero. There were not enough sleighs and most of the infantry had to walk. The situation was the same at the other three gaps in the line. The men ate hardtack and drank tea in the snow or, when the weather changed, in freezing rain. They slept in tents or under the sky. Some caught pneumonia. Others fell victims to snow blindness or rheumatism or pleurisy.

It was just as difficult for Colonel Denison's cavalry corps, the same corps which he had led into the Niagara Peninsula during the Fenian raid. This corps left Toronto on April 7 at 1:30 A.M. By April 9, at noon, they were at the end of the track. The infantry with them went on board sleighs. The cavalry had to unload, feed, water, and saddle their horses. They rode them from Dog Lake to Magpie River. Next day they were up at 6 A.M. to go on a further fifteen miles. Then the horses were led up gangways of railroad ties to the waiting flatcars.

That night was bitter weather, with six to eight inches of snow falling on the men and horses. At 4 A.M., once more the cavalry was at the end of track. In the cold predawn light the snow had to be brushed off and the horses unloaded and saddled up. After breakfast at a construction camp a mile away, there was a thirty-five-mile march on the ice across Lake Superior to Jackfish Bay. There was a savage north wind. With glare ice alternating with crust ice (a layer of ice through which the horses' hoofs broke to the firm ice beneath) and a lunch of cold corned beef and a hunk of bread, Colonel Denison's men scarcely appreciated the scenic beauty around them.

But they got through. By April 10 most of the eastern troops were in Winnipeg and some had already reached Qu'Appelle and Calgary. By April 15 Denison's cavalry, too, were on "mud flats" in Winnipeg amid falling snow. Riel's nemesis was gathering like a sullen thundercloud to the south of him. This thundercloud, except for its commander, General Middleton, was, unlike Wolseley's Red River expedition, entirely Canadian.

It was one of Canada's first expressions of a truly national will, unconnected with Britain and unaided by Britain. There were flaws in equipment. The first detachments entraining in the East were told to bring their own lunches, as if this were a picnic expedition. Many of the troops had to furnish their own boots, socks, shirts, and underwear. Saddles, harness, and blankets were of poor quality. There were even three types of rifles—Snider, Winchester, and Martin-Henry—so that three differing types of ammunition had to be stocked and issued. The medical service was almost completely inadequate. As in all Canada's wars, the Militia Department was caught unprepared; and contractors made fortunes out of the confusion. As another customary touch, hay at Qu'Appelle cost the Army twenty dollars a ton and freighters received ten dollars per diem while Canada's soldiers made do on fifty cents a day.

Yet, thanks to the C.P.R., the troops were on the spot—and within some twelve to twenty days of the outbreak of the insurrection. The tragedy of a general Indian uprising had, by this speed, been averted. The C.P.R. was no longer a dirty word.

3

It has been said that the C.P.R. ought to have put up a monument to Louis Riel. The effect on its fortunes was not immediately apparent. Though the opposition in the Cabinet to a C.P.R. loan now began to waver like a reed in the wind of a changing public opinion, John A. still dillied and dallied. Stephen had spent most of his time since December in Ottawa, lobbying and arguing and hoping. By this time he was almost at the end of his resources, spiritually as well as financially, and the C.P.R. was living from hand to mouth. At Beavermouth in the Rockies there was a strike because of nonpayment of wages, and three hundred men threatened to overrun the camp. Eight Mounties held them off. But trainloads of tracklayers were sent back and then work was halted until, on April 7, the pay car came through. During this same period, when it seemed as if the creditors would take over the almost completed C.P.R., Stephen in the C.P.R. board room in Montreal made what Van Horne later described as the finest speech he ever heard.

"Donald," he said to his cousin, "when they [the creditors] come, they must not find us with a dollar."

By this time the railroad, in putting troops into the West, had proved its worth. John A. still temporized, because some of his Cabinet were strongly opposed to aid for the C.P.R. On April 11,

Stephen, who was again in Ottawa, wrote to the Prime Minister that, if something were not done that day, it would be impossible for him "to carry on this struggle for life." Finally, humiliated and worn out, Stephen decided to give up the fight. As John Murray Gibbon relates it in his *Steel of Empire,* he checked out of Ottawa's Russell House. In the lobby he was stopped by the Honorable Frank Smith, minister without portfolio, who was the most prominent Irish Catholic in John A.'s following. Smith asked where he was going.

"No more Ottawa for me," Stephen answered. "We are going to assign tomorrow."

Smith argued with him until Stephen missed his train. Then Smith went to John A. and threatened to resign unless the remedial measures for the C.P.R. were put through.

The Irish-Catholic vote made Frank Smith a man of weight. Stephen stayed on, still hoping. By April 15 he was again in despair. He went back to Montreal. The next morning he received a wire from Van Horne:

"Have no means paying wages, pay car can't be sent out, and unless we get immediate relief we must stop. . . . Do not be surprised, or blame me, if an immediate and most serious catastrophe happens."

The C.P.R. was at last ready to topple into the abyss of bankruptcy. Stephen sent the information in cipher to J. H. Pope, Acting Minister of Railways and John A.'s political adviser. Pope passed it on to Macdonald. Old Tomorrow took a look. The railroad had put the troops out West. Public opinion was blowing more strongly in its favor. Above all, the road was still needed to carry supplies. He called a caucus of his party. His Minister of Finance resigned. John A. promptly put his own resignation on the table, to take effect if a loan to the C.P.R. were not approved.

This last move carried the day. On April 30 notice was given of resolutions to effect the loan for the C.P.R.

The final form of the proposals was that the $35,000,000 of unissued stock which could not be sold was to be canceled. In its place the same amount of 4 per cent 50-year first-mortgage bonds was to be authorized. To make the bonds salable, the government mortgage on the C.P.R. main line for $22,500,000 effected by the February 1884 deal was to be wiped out. In its stead the Dominion would take $15,000,000 of the new first-mortgage bonds as part settlement of the 1884 debt and advance a loan of

$5,000,000 at 4 per cent for 18 months on the security of the postal subsidy to the C.P.R. plus a further deposit of another $5,000,000 of the bonds. This would give the C.P.R. $5,000,000 in cash and also $15,000,000 of first-mortgage bonds to sell. On the strength of these proposals, a loan of $1,000,000 was advanced by the Bank of Montreal. The C.P.R. could still go ahead.

It was not yet out of the morass; even though it was making possible the crushing of the Riel rebellion. Politics is a slow horse, and John A., as a sign, possibly, of the toll taken by his seventy years, was almost stupidly obsessed by his Dominion franchise bill.

This bill was to substitute a uniform franchise law across the Dominion in place of the provincial franchise regulations which had, so far, determined the qualifications for the right to vote in federal elections. To John A., this bill took precedence over C.P.R. necessities. When the C.P.R. proposals were at last introduced on June 16, they met, as was to be expected, violent opposition from the Liberals, led by the serious-minded, cherubic-faced Edward Blake. As June and July dragged by, once again the C.P.R. was within three hours of bankruptcy for a few hundred thousand dollars. And this time, promises so often repeated would no longer assuage the creditors. At the twenty-third hour and fifty-ninth minute the proposals passed Parliament.

This was on the twentieth of July. Stephen went to England in fear and trembling to sell the $15,000,000 worth of bonds. This time Fortune decided to smile as if afraid to discourage her suitor too completely. Lord Revelstoke, the new head of Baring Brothers (which, through Grand Trunk influence, had previously refused to support the C.P.R.), took the whole issue at 91 cents on the dollar, payable within one month. A mountain, Mount Revelstoke, and a town of the same name enshrines his help.

The transcontinental was at last assured. Meantime, the Riel rebellion had been snuffed out.

CHAPTER XXIX

1885

The Campaign against Riel and the Indians—Relief of Battleford—Check at Fish Creek—Otter and Poundmaker at Cut Knife Hill—Dumont and Middleton at Batoche and the Capture of Riel—Frenchman's Butte and Big Bear's Escape and Surrender

1

IF, in April 1885, an observer in the not as yet invented airplane had swung over the western prairies, he would have seen the line of the railroad cutting a shining furrow across plain and coulee and from it at three separate points long columns of men plodding, like marching ants, northward. The general plan of campaign was sound. From Calgary on April 20 General Strange with 600 men moved north toward Edmonton. His objective was to overawe the Indians in between and to swing a left hook along on the North Saskatchewan at Big Bear's Indians. To the east a week earlier, on the thirteenth, Lieutenant Colonel Otter with three cannon, a Gatling gun, and a mixed force of 543 N.W.M.P. and militia had struck north from Swift Current for beleaguered Battleford. Still further east and again a week earlier, Major General Middleton had moved out from Qu'Appelle with the first units of his force to drive toward the heart of Riel's rebellion, Batoche.

Except for General Middleton and some of his staff, the troops were Canadian. The general was a veteran of the New Zealand Maori wars and of the Indian Mutiny. There was no doubt of his personal courage. That is almost all that can be said for his fitness to command Canadians. The old war horse had been put out to grass in Canada in a post supposed to be a sinecure. By this time he was paunchy, stodgy, self-opinionated, and openly contemptuous of the fighting abilities of the Canadian militia. He brushed off offers of help from the Mounties, although an instant's intelligent reflection would have told him that these men knew the country and the *métis* method of fighting. He was equally scornful of advice or help from any Westerner. Convinced that footsloggers win a war by plodding straight ahead in the good old British way, he put his cavalry in the rear to guard his communications. When he did employ mounted men he used corps of local scouts, such as two mounted units organized at Qu'Appelle, French's Scouts and Boulton's Scouts. (Boulton was the man who, back in 1870, had led the ill-fated Portage la Prairie expedition to Fort Garry and Kildonan against Riel.) The only men to whom General Middleton would give ear were the Imperials or former Imperials on his staff.

His closed mind almost nullified his superiority in numbers and in matériel. To do him justice, the transport system was faulty, his men were an unknown quantity (Middleton stayed four days at Qu'Appelle because many of the men in his 90th Battalion had "never pulled a trigger"), and the weather was against him. For, as he marched north, an icy Arctic blast swooped down to greet him. On the night of April 7, his men went to rest in tents. On the morning of April 8, it was twenty-three degrees below zero and the tent pegs had to be chopped out of the frozen ground with axes. Middleton must have felt that morning: "Why fight for such a country? Why not leave it to the Indians–and Riel?" In his mind, too, was the necessity of keeping casualties low for fear of public reaction against heavy losses.

Weighed down with these cares, he moved forward like a snail. It took him until the seventeenth of April–eleven days–to cover the 180 miles from Qu'Appelle to Clark Crossing on the South Saskatchewan, where he was overtaken by the Royal Grenadiers, bringing his strength up to 800.

At this point Middleton was about forty miles from Batoche. But he had no desire for speed. He waited several days for the H.B.C. steamer *Northcote* to come down from Saskatchewan Landing, near Swift Current, with supplies and two Gatling machine guns. With these latter was their demonstrator, Lieutenant Arthur L. Howard of the U. S. Army, from New Haven, Connecticut.

The Gatling machine gun had been invented in 1862 by the

man after whom it was named, Dr. R. J. Gatling. It was a multi-barreled weapon, somewhat like a giant and multiplied six-shooter, and had to be turned by a handle to bring each barrel in succession into play. Theoretically, it could fire up to 1200 bullets a minute. It had been used in the final years of the American Civil War and in the 1870 Franco-Prussian War. Howard had had five years of Indian fighting. At the moment, however, he was on leave from the machine-gun platoon of the 2nd Regiment, Connecticut National Guard, as a crusader for the gun. It mattered not to Howard against whom he fired the Gatling—and when he heard Canada intended to try it he offered his services. Later he was to be killed in the Boer War.

Neither the *Northcote* nor the Gatlings arrived. The steamer had, in fact, been held up on snags and sand bars in the shallow-flowing South Saskatchewan.

While Middleton waited, the well-trained Winnipeg and Quebec cavalry along with Denison's Ontario corps reached Qu'Appelle. Instead of sending them out to scout or to attack Riel's *métis* horsemen, the British general set them to guarding his supply depots—and that is where they stayed. Meanwhile, for some reason, known only to himself, he divided his 800 men into two columns to march toward Batoche on opposite banks of the unfordable river. In effect, he had reduced his effective striking force by half. Finally, with a weary sigh of reluctance, he set out again on his leisurely advance toward Batoche.

And, meantime, General Strange was on his way to Edmonton. Father Lacombe and the Reverend John McDougall traveled ahead of the column to reassure the Indians while Steele's cavalry scouts protected the convoy. It took ten days to reach Edmonton, with garrisons being peeled off en route at Red Deer and at Government Ford, near Edmonton. The chief difficulty was with General Strange's single cannon at Red Deer Crossing. The river was in flood and a raft had to be built to freight it over.

While General Middleton had been delaying at Clark Crossing, Colonel Otter's column had been advancing at full speed. Otter had added a wagon train of some 200 teamsters to his 543 men. He left Swift Current on April 18. Five days later, on the twenty-third, with Middleton still bogged down, Otter was within three miles of Battleford. The Indians melted away at his arrival. The next day, the day when Middleton finally decided to move,

Otter's troops marched into a Battleford that went wild with joy. For a month some 500 people, in fear of Indian massacre, had been cooped up in a fort of which the central square was 200 yards square. Now liberation had come.

2

And what of Riel and his *métis* during the weeks that the troops had been assembling and marching? His *métis* had the mobility which Middleton's tactics lacked. Dumont, the born general, had organized a detachment to raid down to the railroad and destroy the bridges. Riel put the finger of negation on the plan. Then, when Middleton began to march, Dumont planned a series of night attacks and ambushes. Riel stigmatized this as "*trop sauvage*" and besides, as in the case of the railway plan, he did not want to fire on "*nos amis Canadiens,*" that is, the French-Canadian troops from Quebec. Did Riel hope to win these men over?

No hope of design was too extravagant for the man Riel had now become. During these weeks of crisis, when he should have been considering either spreading the war vigorously and attacking or else preparing for defense, the *métis* leader had been lost in his dream of a theocratic state. Each day his *Exovidate* met at Batoche. Each morning it recited a prayer composed by Riel, whom it had formally voted to be a prophet. Certain practical matters were handled. The chief duty of the *Exovidate* was to confirm the prophecies of the new "David" and to announce them to the public. There was to be a new church, "the Living Catholic Apostolic and Vital Church of the New World," of which, naturally, Riel's admiration, Archbishop Bourget of Montreal, was "Pope." Hell was declared not to be eternal. It was decreed that the body and blood of Christ were only symbolically and not substantially present in the Host. The days of the week were renumbered; and the Sabbath was announced as the seventh day of the week.

The demented mystic in Riel was in control. He was certain that the Spirit of God spoke through him. Father Vegreville and three other priests were locked up in the parish house at Batoche for refusing the sacraments to *métis* in arms. When it came to defense, Riel evidently expected a miracle, though he would take no steps to make that miracle possible. God, he seems to have believed, would at the proper moment bring victory. Meanwhile, his whole policy was to wait until attacked and then to let the miracle happen. So, in a letter from the secretary of the *Exovidate* to an outlying commander, we read these words:

"The *Ex Ovidate* are of the opinion that Middleton and his troops ought not to be treated as extraordinary. It would be better to watch well their moves, to let them come when they please . . . and when they are near enough to strike, and then to work until, with God's and Christ's help, we have conquered them. A complete success over Middleton, we have to ask from Our Lady, the Blessed Virgin Mary, and let us aim at such decisive success."

The extraordinary thing is that the *métis,* and even the realist Dumont, remained under Riel's spell. One wonders what Riel's wife—or the wives of the *métis*—thought of it all. Few spectacles in Canadian history are more pathetic than that of the brave but deluded *métis* waiting like hypnotized rabbits as Middleton rolled along toward them ponderously like a half-asleep and grumpy bear. Had the *métis* been allowed their heads, as was to be shown, they could have shattered the pompous conceit of even a Middleton. But they crouched at Riel's feet; that is, until Middleton reached Clark Crossing.

Every step of Middleton's advance had been watched by *métis* scouts. There was even a *métis* spy, Jerome Henry, as a freighter in Middleton's wagon train. Finally, when the news came that Middleton had started forward from Clark Crossing, Dumont could no longer be restrained. Riel, who had an abnormal fear of Dumont's being injured ever since his adjutant general's wound at Duck Lake and who was also frightened of the embattled Mounties at Prince Albert to the north, gave in. On the night of April 23, Riel and Dumont led 200 *métis* and Indians south to intercept the Canadians, with Riel conducting religious services at the first stop. Here, however, a rider reached them with a report that police scouts had been seen near Batoche. Riel, with 50 men, went back. Dumont led 150 men, some of them armed only with shotguns, against the comparatively well-equipped Canadians, who had, too, three cannon.

Middleton knew nothing of their approach. His right column of 440 men was in camp some twenty-two miles south of Batoche. His left, of 373 soldiers, was across the river. Early that morning of the twenty-fourth, under a gray sky, Dumont with 20 men rode to within half a mile of the enemy camp. Then he prepared his "buffalo pound" for Middleton.

Seventeen miles south of Batoche, on the east side of the South Saskatchewan, Fish Creek, as it empties into the broad river, cuts a forty-foot-deep ravine across the prairie. Here, part way down the slope nearest the Canadian advance, Dumont posted 130 of his men, dismounted and concealed under brush in rifle pits so that they could fire up at an enemy silhouetted against the sky. His own 20 *métis*, he led on horseback further south to hide them in a coulee so that they could swoop on the Canadians' rear and herd them into the "pound."

It was the sort of tactics which, though Dumont did not know it, Hannibal had used some twenty-one hundred years before at the battle of the Trebia in northern Italy. Early on the twenty-fourth Middleton broke camp and moved forward. Boulton's Scouts were out in front. According to one account, they discovered horse tracks in the road left there by careless *métis*, and Dumont's 20 men ran into enemy fire. According to another, the scouts found traces of campfires, while at the same time some of Dumont's party fired on them. In either case, Dumont's score of men returned hastily to the coulee and thence, finally, got to the ravine. The attempt to surprise the Canadians had failed.

The fight was on. Middleton had no better plan than to bypass the coulee and to order his troops forward in solid line against the ravine of Fish Creek. Many of the *métis* had fled in panic. Dumont in his account claimed that he began the battle, if the tiny engagment can be dignified by that name, with 62 *métis* and Indians. Middleton thought he faced 280 men. The Canadians reached the lip of the ravine. The fire from the rifle pits drove them back. Middleton pushed two cannon forward. The guns could not reach the concealed *métis*. He sent a message to his column on the other side of the river to cross. They could find only one leaky scow; and it started to rain, a cold April rain.

Around noon the Canadians failed in a second attack. The battle settled down to a fire fight, except for occasional charges by the Canadians. The concealed *métis* suffered little; but the slugs from their shotguns tore gaping wounds in the bellies and heads of those Canadians they hit. One detachment, after a fruitless charge, was pinned down for three hours in six inches of water in a near slough. Some of the *métis* stragglers returned.

In midafternoon, when the sun appeared briefly, Dumont tried a daring maneuver. Firing the brush and grass at a point where the smoke would drive toward the Canadians, the *métis*, under cover of it, charged up to the militia to drop to the ground a few paces away and fire. Dumont said afterward that he hoped the raw militia would break. But they stood firm.

The *métis* withdrew to the ravine. The rain started again and an early darkness was settling. Some of Middleton's left column was by now across the river. The Canadian officers urged the British general to order an attack. Middleton, thinking of casualties, refused. Shortly thereafter 80 reinforcements from Batoche arrived. (Dumont had sent a man galloping for them when the firing began.) An hour later the Canadians began to withdraw. Ten of them had been killed and forty wounded. The *métis* claimed that they lost only four dead and two wounded. But fifty of their horses had been killed and they retreated swiftly to Batoche.

That was Fish Creek—a stalemate but, in reality, a victory for the *métis*. The engagement did not change Middleton's tactics. Instead, it confirmed him in his poor opinion of Canadian volunteers. For close to two weeks (from the night of April 24 to May 7) he holed up at Fish Creek, grumbling.

There was some reason for it. The medical service had proved to be practically nonexistent. Likewise he had to bring his left column back from across the river and to wait for two companies of the Midland Battalion and the Surveyor's Intelligence Corps, converted to cavalry. There was also the *Northcote*, and Middleton had a surprising plan for it.

On the other side, Riel had been stung to action by Fish Creek. It was as if he were waking from the dream. He went about aiding Dumont in preparing the defenses at Batoche. He wrote again to both Poundmaker and Big Bear. His plea was for Big Bear to join Poundmaker in an assault on Battleford, and he offered 100 wagons and horses to help him move more rapidly. After the capture of Battleford, both forces were to join the *métis* at Batoche.

Big Bear was in two minds about the proposal—or, rather, his band was split into two factions. From Fort Pitt the Crees had moved back to Frog Lake. As food began to fail, the Plains Crees wanted to kill off the miserable whites. The Woods Crees opposed. At last, about May 1, Big Bear's forces began to move slowly and falteringly toward Fort Pitt and Battleford.

After the relief of Battleford, Poundmaker had retired to his reservation. Riel's first messengers in March had spoken of American help and assured him that the prophet would, like a prairie blizzard, sweep everything before him. Now help was asked for. The intelligent, handsome Poundmaker replied briefly that he would send to Big Bear and wait for him a while before joining Riel. Then, on April 29, he sent a long letter to the *métis* leader asking about the "progress of God's work" and when the Americans would reach the Canadian Pacific Railway. In the same letter he requested ammunition and help to take Fort Battleford.

In reply, Riel told of the "victory" at Fish Creek and asked for "between two to two hundred and fifty men and even three hundred." His purpose, he told Poundmaker, was to finish with Middleton and so force Ottawa to treat with him. "Courage," he wrote. *"Venez-vous en tous."*

It was a despairing cry. Before it reached Poundmaker, that chief had troubles of his own.

3

Colonel Otter's smile was smug. While Middleton had got his nose well bloodied at Fish Creek, he himself had relieved beleaguered Battleford without firing a shot.

The success made Otter anxious for more glory. Bypassing his O.C., Middleton, on April 26 he wired the lieutenant governor for permission to attack Poundmaker. The objective was sound. Poundmaker was still in arms, and it was good policy to prevent a junction between him and Big Bear, with the possibility of both forces moving to Batoche to join Riel. Dewdney gave permission. So, on the afternoon of May 1 and through the night of May 1 and 2, Otter pushed 325 men (inclusive of 75 N.W.M.P.), 48 wagons, 2 seven-pounder guns, and his Gatling west from Battleford toward Cut Knife Hill.

Cut Knife Hill was where, years before this, Poundmaker and his Crees had defeated the Sarcee chief Cut Knife; and on the western slope of it Poundmaker had now pitched his camp. Otter's plan was to leap upon the Indians before they knew he had come.

It was only a partial surprise. Otter's column had marched until 7 P.M., had rested for four hours, and had then resumed the march under a spring moon that silvered the bluffs and sloughs and prairie to an almost otherworldly beauty. Finally, as dawn flushed the sky, his men were moving down the slope toward the creek that girdled Cut Knife Hill to the east. An Indian scout gave the alarm. At once, the troops, from the east, and the warriors, from the west, raced for the crest of Cut Knife Hill. The Mounties and the guns got there first.

At this moment the dice were loaded in Otter's favor. The Indians were disorganized, and had he flung the mounted police down upon the Indian camp, he might have won in a gallop. Caution held his hand. The seven-pounders and the Gatling did cut loose to do a certain amount of damage in the emptying tepees below them. But Otter decided to assemble his infantry, too, on the hill before attacking.

That was his error. The women and children in the camp had got to safety. The warriors, recovering from their initial shock, swarmed into the coulees fissuring the hill's slopes and, concealed by the trees and shrubs, worked around the Canadians. Within half an hour of the first shots, Otter's soldiers, exposed on the top of the hill, were under fire from three sides.

From this moment, although the Indians were outnumbered three to two, the final result was inevitable. The Gatling rattled out thousands of rounds at nondiscernible targets. The Indians used the old trick of raising war bonnets or rags on sticks to draw Canadian fire and then picked off the soldiers as they exposed themselves. One of those whom a bullet found was Corporal Sleigh, who had escaped both Frog Lake and Fort Pitt. A group of Crees even rushed the Gatling but were beaten back.

The seven-pounders saved the troops from being overrun. But they were ancient stock and no one in the Militia Department had checked their fitness. After about a hundred rounds from each the rotting gun carriages collapsed. The Indians by this time had worked around to the fourth side. The Canadians had marched all night. They had had no food. After seven hours of fighting, Otter abandoned his dream. One of the cannon was made usable by lashing it to a wagon tongue with ropes. By means of it and the Gatling a way for the retreat was cleared. The troops made it back to Battleford by ten o'clock on the night of May 2. But Jefferson and Father Cochin, two of the prisoners in Poundmaker's camp, felt certain that if Poundmaker had not restrained his braves from pursuit, the Canadians would have been decimated. The Cree chieftain undoubtedly realized by this time that, in spite of victories, there could only be one end to the war.

It seems almost a ridiculous anticlimax to record that after seven hours of fighting and the firing of thousands of rounds, only eight of Otter's force had been killed and fifteen wounded; while the Indians lost six dead and an undetermined number of wounded. The fighting in the Northwest Rebellion was mostly sound and fury. It could be said, however, that again the raw militia had fought bravely enough but had been badly led.

Otter nursed the wound to his vanity at Battleford. In Poundmaker's camp the war party was now in full cry. At last, like Big Bear, Poundmaker began to move toward Batoche, but slowly, like a man reluctant to go. On May 14 in the Eagle Hills below Battleford his Crees captured a supply train and took twenty-two prisoners. On the same day they beat back a party of scouts from Battleford, killing one man and wounding two others. These were Poundmaker's last successes.

4

In Batoche fear rode the wind. It showed in the faces of the women. It betrayed itself in the glances of the men up at the parish church. For the first time the *métis* began to wonder if Riel was the prophet and miracle worker they had believed him to be. And had it been unwise and sacrilegious not to listen to the priests? There had been three battles and three victories, that was true. But where were the bands of Poundmaker and Big Bear? The eyes of the *métis* went continually to the horizon, hoping. But no war bonnets gladdened their view.

There was one man whose courage did not falter—Gabriel Dumont. He might know in his heart that, once Middleton moved, the game would, in all likelihood, be up. He would not admit it. In these final days he, not Riel, was the actual leader. It was Dumont who had devised and built a skillful system of rifle pits and trenches. It was the bluff buffalo hunter who cheered the confidence of the *métis;* while Riel, according to his own diary, alternated from high confidence to despair, from plans for preparation to violent outbursts of temper, attributing, for instance, the loss of the fifty horses at Fish Creek to the *métis* fondness for horse racing. There is also a significant prayer for a treaty with the Dominion, good for the *métis* and Indians but also one in which Canada would pay him an indemnity, "not a little indemnity but one just and equitable before time and before me."

Such a man was clearly out of touch with reality. Yet on May 6, in a burst of clarity, he seems to have seen the truth, while putting the blame on the disobedience of the *métis*. "It [Batoche]," he wrote, "is going to fall into the hands of the conqueror for having first abandoned God. God also abandons it. It is all over with it."

Yet he still sent messengers to Poundmaker and Big Bear urging them to hurry. But time, even with a Middleton commanding, was running out. On May 27, at last, the British general came out of his shell.

Middleton had been waiting for the *Northcote,* with which he was to make his one imaginative gesture. It reached him on May 5. Middleton's plan was to convert this shoe box propelled by a paddle wheel into a gunboat and to attack Batoche by river and by land.

The *Northcote,* it will be recalled, had been built back in 1874 to "swim on dew." It had two decks with an exposed engine and boiler on the lower one and a cabin and pilothouse above, and its top speed, with the river as full of snags and sand bars as it was, reached about five miles an hour. On it Middleton placed 35 soldiers (among them John A.'s son, Hugh, who was ill with erysipelas), one cannon, and one of the two Gatling guns the *Northcote* had brought. Later heavy timbers were brought from Dumont's stables at Gabriel's Crossing, and the lower deck was fortified with a double wall of two-inch planks. Sacks of oats and the like formed the defenses on the upper deck and the pilothouse.

The gunboat was ready. All this had been reported by the *métis* scouts. Middleton's plan lacked the element of surprise.

On the early morning of May 7, then, Middleton moved from Fish Creek toward Batoche. His 850 troops were accompanied by teamsters and the like, raising his force to a column of over a thousand. There were 600 horses, 2 cannon, and a Gatling. It was a glorious day, bright and warm. The first spring crocuses were out, purple and yellow on the park land. At Gabriel's Crossing, six miles from Batoche, the troops halted and the steamer tied up to complete its fortifications.

Up to this point Middleton had been following the trail along the right, or eastern, bank of the South Saskatchewan. From Gabriel's Crossing onward, however, that trail ran through thick brush and willows and poplars. As it neared Batoche, where the river flows almost due north, the bold bank is flattened out to rise again beyond the village. Dumont, with a master's hand, had defended the southern approach to Batoche with a line of rifle pits along the edge of the bank. These reached southward for almost a mile. Behind them was the main position, along the range of hills parallel to the valley. Since the slopes of these hills were wooded and cut by coulees running toward the river, there was admirable concealment; and the pits themselves were three to four feet deep, with breastworks of earth and logs. In them Dumont had from 200 to 250 *métis,* among whom were a few Indians. His plan again was to shoot up at men silhouetted against the sky.

Such was the situation when at 5:30 A.M. of May 9 Middleton led out his force for the attack. Distrusting, with good reason, the river trail, he took his men in a wide circuit out into the prairie so as to come in against Batoche not from the south but from the east. At 7 A.M. the *Northcote* took off.

It was again an ideal spring day with the birds singing and the grass green and the willows and poplars budding into foliage. The rendezvous for the combined water and land attack had, according to the best evidence, been set at eight o'clock, though Middleton later claimed it was to have been at 9 A.M. In either case, somebody blundered; and the *métis* knew of the *Northcote*. Suddenly, as it reached the southern limit of Batoche, from both banks of the river rifle and shotgun fire opened.

The men on board were protected by the thick planks. Now was the moment for the land force to attack. It was still an hour away, following Middleton across the prairie. All the steamer could do was to run the gantlet, depending upon its Gatling to keep the *métis* back. As it reached the center of the settlement the captain, to his startled horror, saw the *métis* lowering the steel cables of the ferry fore and aft of the boat. In a moment he would be trapped. He ordered full speed ahead. The *Northcote* got through, literally denuded. The cable in front, crashing down, ripped off both its stacks, its mast, its two tall spars, and its whistle. The *Northcote* was a skinned rabbit. Fortunately, only three men on board were wounded.

The gunboat's brief career was over. As if in irony, precisely at nine o'clock, exactly an hour late, the advance guard of Middleton's force appeared over the prairie from the east. What his men saw was not the village, which was hidden in the valley, but the church, parish hall, cemetery, and two or three cabins, all on the crest of the hill above the valley. The advance guard occupied these. The troops followed. The guns and the Gatling were brought up. There was a brief parley with the priests and nuns who had been shut up in the parish hall. From them, apparently, the Canadians learned something of the resources and dispositions of the *métis*. Then the cannon began shelling the village at the river's edge. In front of the Canadians the hill sloped downward steeply to the valley. So far not a shot of defense had been fired. The Canadians moved forward to the rim of the dip. Abruptly, it erupted in bullets and shot full in their faces. The troops pulled back, taking the guns with them. Howard and the Gatling were the salvation of the withdrawal. But the *métis*, moving up by trenches to pits in the cemetery, attacked the left flank. The rest of the day went by in futile skirmishing.

That was the first day of the battle of Batoche. That evening Middleton withdrew his men to a zareba of wagons a few hundred yards east of the church. With a curious disregard for terrain, it was set in the middle of a plowed field.

The honors of the first day had gone to Dumont and his *métis;* and the next two days were, in general, a repetition of the first. Middleton, it must be recalled, had no confidence in his troops; and it was even rumored that he had sent off his aide, Lord Melgund (later to return to Canada as the Earl of Minto and its governor general), to ask for British regulars from Halifax. However, it must also be remembered that Middleton felt that he must keep casualties low. Moreover, the skirmishing tactics—advance each day and retire each night to the dust and dirt of the zareba—did use up what ammunition the *métis* had. By the third day many of them were reduced to putting nails, slugs, duckshot, and, according to Bishop Grandin, stones in their shotguns; while there were all too few cartridges left for their rifles.

It was Dumont's show. The women and children huddled in caves, dug into the riverbanks. Riel held services each morning, wrote prophecies, and devised new prayers, though he did go from pit to pit encouraging the defenders. On the third day, too, new messengers were sent to Poundmaker to beg him to hurry. And the *métis* still held out. There is something in their heroic stand with rifles and shotguns against four times their number and against cannon and a Gatling gun that catches at the heart. They were largely illiterate. They had listened too credulously to

Riel. In this, the sunset of their resistance, they were men fit to stand beside the bravest.

On the other side, the Canadians were chafing at the bit which Middleton had thrust into their collective mouth. The officers protested. On the fourth day, Tuesday, the twelfth, the British general decided to try a more elaborate maneuver. With 150 men, the Gatling, and one cannon he embarked on a wide sweep around the northeast flank of the *métis* position. At the sound of his cannon, Lieutenant Colonel Van Straubenzie, a former Imperial officer, was to attack straight ahead.

Middleton's cannon was heard only two or three times. Van Straubenzie concluded that something had gone wrong and did nothing. At noon—it was a bright day with not a cloud in the blue sky—Middleton marched back "in a towering rage." Ordering the Canadians to move out to skirmish again, he retired sulkily to the stockade to eat lunch.

The Canadian officers were now ready to take the bit between their teeth and run for it. They formed into skirmishing line—at the left the Midland Battalion of Port Hope, Ontario, under Lieutenant Colonel Williams, supported by Colonel French's Scouts; next to them the Royal Grenadiers from Toronto—some 260 men in all. The main force of the Canadians was in the zareba.

Williams, an M.P., had decided to end the affair. The word was passed along to the Grenadiers. The troops advanced as far as the church. Suddenly Williams led the Midlanders in a charge over the crest of the dip. The Grenadiers followed. Williams' men carried the pits on the left and the other battalion cleared the pits in front of them. The *métis* retired to the village on the water's edge. Williams himself led the charge to take it.

Later both Middleton and Van Straubenzie claimed credit for the order to charge. The evidence is against their claims. Lieutenant Colonel Houghton, deputy Adjutant General, points out that he was at lunch with Middleton when firing and cheering was heard. The general, he states, rushed out, saw that his troops were out of hand, and ordered up his other forces. (The cavalry and artillery were, for that matter, unharnessed and unsaddled.) These reinforcements took part in the final rush to the village and in the pursuit. It seems clear that the Canadians ended the battle by disobeying orders.

Once again casualties in this strange war were ridiculously light as compared to the thunder of the firing. In the whole four days eight Canadians were killed and forty-six wounded—a fact which rather destroys the legend that Dumont and his *métis* were veritable Robin Hoods in marksmanship. The *métis* losses were never accurately estimated. Dumont admitted that twelve of his men were killed but said that only three were wounded. It is thought that his losses were considerably higher. In the whole campaign about 70 of the troops were killed and some 130 wounded. It was a series of skirmishes rather than of battles.

Batoche ended the insurrection. On May 15 Riel surrendered. Dumont, the sturdy buffalo hunter, slipped through the net with ease to Montana. Twelve years later he was to die peacefully in bed at his farmhouse on the South Saskatchewan. Whatever may be said of Riel, Dumont's record remains unsmudged. Bluff, honest, and direct, he fought for a cause in which he believed with a skill and courage which puts the victor to shame.

5

After Batoche there were still the tag ends to clear. At Battleford, on May 26, Middleton, pompous and paunchy on a campstool, received the surrender of a dignified Poundmaker, who, on the whole, had fought the war like a gentleman. Big Bear was a more elusive animal. His march toward Battleford had been slow, partly because of dissensions between the Woods and Plains Crees. On May 26 the band was at Frenchman's Butte, a high conical hill only twelve miles east of Fort Pitt, holding a thirst dance, to restore harmony and to make new warriors, when scouts brought in the news that soldiers were at Fort Pitt.

This was General Strange's column, which, after reaching Edmonton on May 1, had swung down the North Saskatchewan. The white prisoners in Big Bear's camp hoped fiercely for liberation. But the Indians, hastily deserting the thirst dance, chose an excellent position on the crest above the forks of the Red Deer and Little Red creeks and dug rifle pits and trenches. On May 28 Strange attacked. He made no headway and he was determined not to "commit a Custer." Just as his cannon had found the range of the Indian trenches and the warriors were beginning to run, Strange ordered retirement. His losses were three men wounded. The Indians, too, retreated hurriedly. A few of the prisoners, including Cameron, escaped. The rest were dragged along with the band.

From this time forward it was a game of cops and robbers with the Indians outwitting the troops and their commanders. Major Steele's scouts did overtake the band at Loon Lake. The warriors fought a rear-guard action and got away. Then both Middleton and Strange chased the fugitives. Again Big Bear's band escaped by crossing a morass which Middleton's transport could not negotiate. The pursuit was abandoned. What saved the prisoners, who were by this time half starved and completely exhausted, especially the women and children, was that the Woods Crees, taking the prisoners with them, split off from the Plains Crees. The former made a deal with the H.B.C. trader McLean to arrange terms for them and released the twenty-seven prisoners. After sixty-two days of captivity, the whites set out for Fort Pitt, by this time 140 miles away, but overtook the troops at Loon Lake. On June 24 they reached Fort Pitt.

The prisoners were safe. Big Bear, his band dispersed, made his way through all the searchers back to Fort Carlton. There he surrendered on July 2 to Sergeant Smart of the N.W.M.P.

The rebellion was over. Punishment was not too severe. Of the Indians, eleven were condemned to be hanged. Of these, three were reprieved, but Wandering Spirit, courageous to the last, was one of the eight who went to the gallows. Poundmaker and Big Bear both got prison sentences, but in 1886 and 1887, respectively, were released. Prison, however, had taken its toll. Both died shortly after their release. Big Bear's son, Imasees, Little Poplar, and another murderer, Lucky Man, escaped, like Dumont, to Montana. In 1896 they were allowed to return to their reservations.

Of the *métis,* eighteen were imprisoned for terms of from one to seven years. Two whites, W. H. Jackson, the former secretary of the Settlers' Union, and Thomas Scott, the namesake of the Red River Scott, were tried but discharged.

The victor, General Middleton, was presented with a K.C.M.G., a grant of $20,000, and, later, a certain number of knowing smiles when he was accused of having collected too many furs as "mementos" of his campaign. The hero of the charge at Batoche, Lieutenant Colonel Williams, died by Fate's irony of fever at Battleford; though a statue in Port Hope, Ontario, commemorates his courage.

After the troops had left, there was still Louis Riel. What was to be done with him? Ontario shrieked that he was a traitor; Quebec cried to the skies that he was a hero and a patriot. In prison, as in the rebellion, he was a fiery sword to divide the Dominion.

CHAPTER XXX

1885–87

The Trial and Execution of Louis Riel—The Last Spike of the Transcontinental—Founding of Vancouver—The C.P.R. Girdles the World

1

THE Northwest Rebellion was the last defiant gasp of the old wide-ranging freedom of the prairies and the park land. It put a period to the hunter and the fur trader and the Indian. They were still to exist on the fringes, but the future belonged to the rancher and the plowman.

Yet the insurrection did bring to the Indian and the *métis* what they had demanded. There were better schools and better treatment for the red man. The bands which had remained loyal were rewarded with cattle, sheep, blankets, tea, tobacco, and money. The rebels were deprived of their arms, horses, and annual payments until the losses caused by their depredations were made good. Then they, too, benefited from the new deal.

The *métis* got their land titles and their scrip. Not that the latter did them too much good. As in Manitoba, they often sold their scrip for the price of a few drinks. Soon they, too, were to be scattered in small communities on the outskirts of the new West. Yet, as usual, the screeching wheel had got the grease which sweet reason would scarcely have squeezed out of Ottawa officialdom in a score of years.

The rebellion had shown great weaknesses in the Dominion's Militia Department's transport, hospital, and supply services; while Canada's contractors had made the usual fortunes out of camp equipment, clothing, saddles, and the like, of which much was of poor quality. Those profiteers who howled the loudest about their patriotism were too often the same men who raked in the taxpayers' dollars with the smuggest of smiles. The whole cost of the rebellion, as has been mentioned, was well over $5,000,000.

Yet for the first time, except for General Middleton, Canada had conducted a war, even if it was a punitive expedition rather than a war, completely on its own. Its own railroad had taken out the troops. Its poorly trained militia had fought bravely, in spite of fumbling leadership. Throughout Anglo-Canada there was a surge of pride and a consciousness of nationhood; and not only had French-Canadian troops shown themselves as good soldiers as Anglo-Canadians but it had been a French Canadian, the Honorable J. P. R. A. Caron, Minister of Militia, who had managed the whole operation. It was the Dominion's recurrent tragedy, however, that the aftermath of the rebellion was to stir in French Canada a hostility to which Anglo-Canada was all too swift to respond. Riel, defeated, was more potent than he had been as a prophet.

The tiny courtroom in Regina, fifty by twenty feet, was packed on that hot July 28 of 1885. A special table had been set up for a dozen newspapermen. There was a section reserved for the ladies. It, too, was jammed, all the women in their Sunday best, as if at the opera, and among them was the wife of General Middleton. At one side, imprisoned in their box, were the six men of the jury, all, as it was noted resentfully in French Canada, Anglo-Saxon and all Protestant. In the presiding seat sat Hugh Richardson, Stipendiary Magistrate of the Northwest Territories. In their appropriate places were the bewigged, begowned counsel for the prosecution and the defense.

All these were supernumeraries. The true center of the drama was the stocky, sallow-faced, bearded man of forty in the prisoner's dock. There was a scarlet-coated Mountie on either side. They were mere stage effects. Louis Riel, as always, dominated.

The trial had opened, technically, on July 20. Riel's counsel, four in all, had been sent him from a Quebec which was already passionate in his defense. After two days of argument and Riel's plea of "not guilty" to a charge of high treason, there had been adjournment to bring the doctors from the East who had treated Riel in the two asylums during his mental illness.

If Riel had lived today, there is but little doubt that he would never have been put on trial. Any alienist, in considering the strangeness of his delusions, would have ruled him *non compos mentis.*

But this was 1885, when violent insanity or obvious idiocy were the only evidences of mental aberrations which were understood, and when medical men themselves were none too clear about mental illnesses. Among Protestants, a man could rant and rave and, as long as his lucubrations were hallowed by the dragging in of God or the Bible, no one thought of questioning his mental balance; while if a man had "sold his soul to the devil" he was still accountable for his actions.

To add to the confusion, Riel, unfortunately for himself, had become an even more fanatic symbol than before of the deep rift between the English- and French-speaking Canadas. From the very first, the Quebec press had found excuses for the *métis* revolt. If this justification had been based on Ottawa's stupidly ignorant treatment of *métis* complaints, it would have been reasonable. But the newspapers turned it to a religio-racial cry. "They are hated," *L'Etendard* of Montreal proclaimed on April 1, shortly after Duck Lake, "for their French origins and Catholic faith. . . ." The French-Canadian militia were told that they were being sent against their brothers; while *La Vérité* exclaimed that the rebellion arose from "Orange fanaticism which would like the extermination of the French *métis* in the North-West. . . ."

At these attacks Ontario growled in fury. "If," said the Toronto *Evening News,* "she [Quebec] is to be a traitor in our midst, a thief in our treasury, a conspirator in our Canadian household, she had better go out."

In spite of the loyalty of the French-Canadian militia, in Quebec and Ontario every step in Middleton's campaign had heightened the flame of fanaticism dividing French Catholics and English Protestants. Riel's trial served to focus all this strife on him. In such a temperature justice finds it difficult going. If Riel was sane, he was guilty. There was no doubt that in the 1885 rebellion he had raised and led an armed revolt.

About this fact his counsel had no illusions. They based their defense on the allegation that the Regina court had no proper jurisdiction and that Riel was insane.

To Riel's particular delusion, the defense of insanity was to cut away his very *raison d'être.* If his "mission" were but a figment of a diseased imagination, where was he? From the very first he objected to the plea.

Yet there seems little doubt that he had a reasonably fair trial for the period in which he lived. To a jury and spectators and a world at large which had little understanding of mental imbalance, Riel seemed calm and collected. And, as usual, the medical authorities differed. Dr. François Roy testified that Riel was a victim of "megalomania." Dr. Daniel Clark, a Toronto alienist, stated that in his three examinations of him Riel had exhibited symptoms of insanity but admitted that he might have been putting on an act. Two other medical men believed him sane.

The jurors listened uneasily. They heard of the shrewdness with which Riel had bargained with Father André. They considered the premeditation in his incitement of a *métis* and Indian revolt. His "new religion" did not mean too much to their Protestant minds, to which Roman Catholic sacraments were all of a piece and "popery" at that. They leaned forward as Riel himself vigorously repudiated in what seemed an eminently sane manner any imputation of insanity and insisted that he had had a "mission" to remove the injustices under which his *métis* suffered. With relief they turned to the factual. Had or had not Riel stirred up and led armed rebellion? He had—so their duty was clear. On August 1, 1885, the jurors filed in. Their verdict was "guilty"; yet Riel had impressed them sufficiently so that they added a recommendation for mercy. Riel was sentenced to hang on September 18.

He was not to be hanged on September 18. An appeal by Riel's counsel to the Queen's Bench of Manitoba led to a confirmation of the verdict. Then there was a petition to the Judicial Committee of the Imperial Privy Council for leave to appeal to that Privy Council. Riel was reprieved to October 16, and then to November 12. Meanwhile the conflict over Riel's sentence reached hysterical heights. In Ontario the mere suggestion that Riel, the murderer of Thomas Scott and the leader of two rebellions, might escape his fate stirred the Orange lodges to frenzy. To Quebec, Riel was to be a martyr to Orangeism—and this in spite of his heresies. Petitions for clemency poured into Ottawa, not only from the French-speaking parishes of Quebec, Ontario, Manitoba, and the Northwest but from places such as New York, Chicago, and St. Louis. There were similar pleas from the Roman Catholics of England and France. The International Arbitration and Peace Association of London joined in the cry. Riel himself, as an American citizen, sent a petition to President Cleveland of the United States.

It is probable that all these cries for mercy hardened John A.'s heart. He knew he held a glowing political coal in his hands. If he pardoned Riel, he lost Anglo-Canada. If he let the sentence be carried out, French Canada would howl at his heels. In this dilemma it is likely that his personal dislike of Riel did something to tip the scales against the self-styled prophet. Twice Riel had upset the West. Twice he had, in effect, challenged John A. It was time for this thorn in his flesh to be pulled out, unless the appeal to the Privy Council saved him.

And then the Judicial Committee of the Privy Council refused Riel permission to appeal. The glowing coal burst into flame. Under pressure from his French-Canadian colleagues in the Cabinet, John A. again reprieved Riel to November 16 so that a commission of three might inquire into his sanity. Psychiatry was not yet a recognized branch of medicine. The commission was instructed to inquire "not as to whether Riel is subject to illusions or delusions but whether he is so bereft of reason as not to know right from wrong and as to be an accountable being"—and this *not* at the time of the rebellion but at the time they saw him.

To the medical, legal, and emotional world of 1885, John A.'s instructions seem to have appeared just and reasonable; John A.'s legal point being that the jury had found Riel sane and accountable for his acts during the rebellion. To the modern reader, instructions which ruled out investigation of Riel's mental state during the rebellion weighted the dice against him.

Two of the medical men found Riel "accountable." The other decided that he was not "accountable" in political and religious matters but able to distinguish "right from wrong" on "other points." For John A. this report closed the book. On Wednesday, November 11, the Cabinet concurred, though Chapleau of Quebec thought of resigning.

And now in French Canada the vials of wrath were upended and poured out. Before the cabinet decision was known, but was guessed at, Langevin, John A.'s party leader in French Canada since Cartier's death, was met at Montreal by five mutinous French-Canadian Conservative M.P.s. Next day a group of nineteen Quebec Conservative members telegraphed the Prime Minister that they would not accept responsibility for Riel's execution. The press on both sides spouted flames. Petitions for clemency again poured in. A spate of anonymous letters threatened John A. with death if Riel should hang. The Prime Minister reared back. "He shall hang," he cried, "though every dog in Quebec bark in his favor."

2

At Regina on the morning of November 16 there was a late autumn sky of brilliant blue, and on the flat prairie around the three-year-old town the hoarfrost sparkled in the sun. Inside the courtyard of the jail, on the top of a tall structure, Father MacWilliam and Riel, who had abjured his apostasy, were repeating the Lord's Prayer. The trap was sprung. Riel dropped to death but not to oblivion. Like Thomas Scott, he was to become a martyr. To the observer of today, though the circumstances around the execution of the two men were vastly dissimilar, both were put to death unjustly. Thomas Scott had been a victim of Riel's megalomania. At that time Riel, though unstable, could have been held responsible for his actions. By 1885, as the evidence of his delusions seems to show clearly, he was not accountable. By that time his execution was a judicial murder even though it was more legal than that of Scott. In a way, at Regina, the wheel of events came full circle.

In death, Riel was even more of a fiery sword to sever the two Canadas. In Ontario, where it had been written that "Ontario is not going much longer to be sat upon by those Frenchmen and the priesthood," there were grunts of satisfaction and parades and the burning of the "traitor" in effigy. In Quebec, frenzy rose to riotousness. At Montreal on November 22, six days after the execution, there was a huge meeting in the Champs de Mars.

Thousands crowded the square. There were three platforms decked with the Tricolor and the Union Jack. No less than thirty-seven speakers shouted themselves hoarse, denouncing the execution and even comparing Riel with Joan of Arc, who had been burned "by the ancestors of the men who hanged Riel." Among the speakers was Wilfrid Laurier, by this time the most important of the younger Liberals of Quebec. He asserted that "if he had lived on the shores of the Saskatchewan, he would have taken up a rifle to defend his property."

The most effective of the orators was Honoré Mercier, a rising young *Rouge* politician. Handsome, energetic, and somewhat unscrupulous, he claimed that Riel, a victim of the Orange Order, had died a hero, "who like Christ forgave his enemies." On the scaffold of Riel he erected his *Parti National,* one which amalgamated Liberals and Conservatives into a nationalistic French-Canadian party. It had three pillars—"our language, our religion, our race." From Mercier to Bourassa to Duplessis and his *L'Union Nationale* of today, that divisive cry has never left Canadian politics.

If, in Quebec, Riel's execution was a draught of poison to the Conservative party, in Ontario it was honey in the horn. When a motion deploring the carrying out of the death sentence came up in the Dominion House in March of the next year, seventeen French M.P.s bolted the Conservative party, but twenty-three Liberals supported John A.

In the Quebec provincial elections the Conservatives were not so fortunate. In the autumn of 1886 Honoré Mercier's *Parti National* won, though Mercier did not attain the premiership until January of the next year. Then, in the February 1887 federal elections, the Conservatives held only twenty-nine of Quebec's sixty-five seats. Twenty-six went to Laurier Liberals and ten to Nationalists and Independents. These last two categories were gradually absorbed into the two major parties. The final issue was that John A. had to settle for thirty-three seats from Quebec instead of his customary forty-five to fifty. Gains in Ontario and the Maritimes offset the losses. But in Quebec, Riel's execution had set the stage for the resurgence of a federal Liberal party. It is ironical that in the same month that the trap was sprung at Regina to array French Canada against Anglo-Canada, that gigantic effort to national unity, the C.P.R., was completed.

3

It was a raw misty day in the Eagle Pass, near the Columbia River in the midst of the peaks of the Gold Range, some 350 miles from Vancouver. A train had come to a stop, its engine panting in deep, muffled throbs. In front of it a group of men had gathered. At the side of one of the shining, unused rails, resting on a tie, was an iron plate with a hole in it.

Most of that group were roughly garbed workingmen. In the inner circle were a half dozen overcoated, top- or bowler-hatted executives. There was the nervous, energetic Major Rogers, whose discovery of this pass had made this route possible. There was Sandford Fleming, who had supervised so many surveys for the transcontinental, pontifical with his square white beard. There was the chunky Van Horne, whose dynamic energy had driven the C.P.R. across muskeg and barren rock and wide prairie and through the mountains to meet this day, the seventh of November 1885. His eyes, the eyes of all of them, were on that hole in the iron plate.

It was none of these three who stepped forward to grasp the waiting sledge hammer. Roadmaster Brothers put an iron spike in the hole. It was Donald Smith, white-bearded under his top hat, who lifted the hammer. His first blow glanced off the spike and twisted it over. Roadmaster Brothers yanked it out and put down another. This time Donald Smith, the Scottish lad who had once counted muskrat skins in a Montreal warehouse and now was a multimillionaire and one of the most potent, if not the most potent, man behind the scenes in the Dominion, tapped it home. After all the effort and the agonizing, Canada's first transcontinental at last linked East and West.

After the last spike was driven in, the group stood around. There was a feeling that this was a momentous moment and that something should be done to mark it. Van Horne was asked to make a speech. He cleared his throat.

"All I can say," he stated flatly, "is that the work has been well done in every way."

There was a short, embarrassed silence. From behind them the conductor called, half seriously, half as an attempt to give lightness to the embarrassment:

"All aboard for the Pacific."

The top- and bowler-hatted group turned and walked to the waiting train. The engine belched out puff after puff of black smoke in a series of strangled snorts. The wheels gripped the rails. They passed over the junction just made. The coaches dwindled down the tracks toward Port Moody. The spot they left was to be called, appropriately, Craigellachie, in remembrance of Stephen's wire in the black days to Donald Smith: "Stand fast, Craigellachie."

That was all. Not quite all. As the train diminished, a workman seized the sledge hammer.

"Now for the real last spike," he cried. Another followed him.

The outburst lasted until the tie was so studded with "last spikes" that no more could be driven.

There was another corollary to that last spike. Piers, Van Horne's secretary, had picked up the twisted spike, the one Donald Smith had marred. Donald Smith took it from him and had it split into thin strips. These he mounted with diamonds and presented to ladies related to the men responsible for the C.P.R. When other ladies clamored for a similar souvenir, Smith got another spike and had it divided into strips, which were similarly decorated with diamonds. But the second lot of strips were larger so that the original recipients could still strut condescendingly. Meanwhile, the spike Donald Smith had driven home was pulled by Roadmaster Brothers, for fear of souvenir hunters, and given finally to Sir Edward Beatty.

The story of the spikes contains another incident. The governor general, Lord Lansdowne, who was in the West in October expecting to be present at the ceremony, had prepared a silver spike. But Van Horne was none too co-operative and, besides, the furor raised by the question of Riel's execution took Lord Lansdowne back to Ottawa. This spike was presented by him to Van Horne.

With the driving in of the last spike the "North-West Passage by Land" for which Milton and Cheadle had argued, over twenty years before, had become a reality. On June 28, 1886, at 8 A.M, the first through train left Montreal to steam the 2905 miles (the C.P.R. was, at that time, the longest railroad in the world) to Port Moody. Cheering thousands watched the transcontinental—a conglomerate of colonist and first-class coaches—pull out from the station. A battery thudded out a fifteen-gun salute. To add to the sense of achievement, in spite of gloomy predictions, in March of this same year the Minister of Finance in John A.'s government had been able to announce the imminent repayment of the government loan to the C.P.R.—this by converting the $20,000,000 first-mortgage bonds held by the Dominion into cash (thanks to Baring Brothers) and by accepting $9,000,000 worth of C.P.R. lands (given to the company by the original subsidy) at a valuation of $1.50 an acre.

The impossible had been achieved. Even Great Britain woke up to realize the value of a quick route to the Orient. Both Smith and Stephen were honored with knighthoods. Van Horne, as an American, at first refused. In 1894 he, too, accepted a K.C.M.G.

from Queen Victoria. Later both Smith and Stephen were raised to the peerage, the one as Lord Strathcona and the other as Lord Mount Stephen. Even more enduring memorials are the two mountain peaks which carry the names of Donald and Stephen. The great venture of the transcontinental paid off in money and prestige to the men who had had the endurance and vision to outface the seemingly impossible.

The running time of the C.P.R.'s first through train was 137 hours as compared with the roughly 71 hours of the *Super-Continental* of today. In the same year, 1886, on July 11, its political architect, John A., along with his wife, stepped on board at Ottawa. He was seventy-one, yet he had never been west of Ontario. For the first time he was to experience the full extent of his empire.

Today, if one can strip away in imagination the enormous changes since 1886, one can visualize in part at least that upon which his eyes gazed. In northern Ontario he looked out at the league on league of willow and poplar and of fir and spruce and pine, and of winding streams and jeweled lakes. He gazed at the majestic reaches of Lake Superior. At Winnipeg he smelled the air like wine and breathed in the vitality of a city barely fledged but instinct with the growth to come. Here his son lived; and here he spent three days—receptions and a huge public meeting at the Roller Rink, where he announced the possibility of a steamer service to the Orient. He watched the almost empty prairie sweep by, mile after mile, under the huge inverted platter of its sky. At Regina, once Pile of Bones but now a raw and bustling town, he stopped for a weekend with Governor Dewdney. At that moment he must have remembered Riel. Then at Gleichen he paused for a meeting with Crowfoot, the proud old chief of the once-proud Blackfeet. Crowfoot was in his oldest clothes as a tribute to the recent death of his nephew, Poundmaker; and even as he faced Sir John the thought of the dead Cree chief must have lain between the two as an almost physical thing.

And then came the majesty of the mountains; through much of which, better to appreciate sights such as the Kicking Horse Pass, John A. and his wife rode the cowcatcher of the engine. Here, if anywhere the magnitude of the task undertaken when the contract for the C.P.R. was signed almost six years before must surely have overwhelmed them. Early on Saturday morning, July 24, the train brought them into Port Moody.

The empire had not as yet been completely traversed. A steamer, the *Princess Louise,* took them out of Burrard Inlet and over a sea darkening with night to Victoria. John A. had seen the Atlantic. At last his eyes, though wearied with age, could gaze out over the Pacific.

It is a journey which every Canadian should take at least once. Had John A. been able to make it earlier, there might, perhaps, have been no Northwest Rebellion. As it was, it drove home to him, as no other experience could have done, the vast emptiness of this part of the new Dominion which he, more than any other single man, had created. Yet Stephen, Donald Smith, Van Horne, and he had laid down the rails which, with good fortune aiding, could fill the empty land and make it truly Canadian.

To relate the whole story of the C.P.R. expansion is far beyond the space of this volume. In the East it reached, finally, to St. John and thence, by steamer and by rail through the apple blossoms of Annapolis Valley, to Halifax. The drive of its founders led, ultimately, to the Empresses furrowing the Atlantic from Montreal and Quebec to Liverpool and from Vancouver to the Orient. In Ontario its searching fingers stretched out to Windsor and Chicago and also, via Sault Ste. Marie, to Duluth and St. Paul and Minneapolis. From the Twin Cities in 1902, the C.P.R. ran through the northwestern United States over the Soo Line to Estevan and Moose Jaw. In western Canada, though in 1888 John A. bought back the C.P.R. monopoly, it crisscrossed the prairies with a network of tracks. In the mountains its branch lines hunted out the valleys and the lakes and connections south of the 49th parallel. But none of its farseeing moves were more important to Canada than its creation of Vancouver.

To the modern observer, it seems impossible that the surveyors for Canada's transcontinental should have preferred Port Moody, at the head of Burrard Inlet, to the village, small and rough though it was, which had grown up around Hastings Mill near Coal Harbor at the eastern neck of Stanley Park. Here, within the First Narrows, was a commodious and almost landlocked harbor. To the north, the mountains gazed down in splendor. On the southern shore on the whale-backed almost-island between the inlet and the Fraser, there was room and to spare for wharves and yards as well as huge trees for building. The whole of the British Columbia coast marries mountain to sea in beauty. The village which was once called Gas Town—from that *rara avis,* a garrulous Yorkshireman nicknamed "Gassy Jack," who had put up a hotel, the Deighton House, near the sawmill and the shacks—and was now Granville, added to that marriage fertility of soil as well as space and the majestic firs and cedars.

Yet it seems to have been pretty well disregarded until that tough old realist and romanticist Van Horne took a look at it. Port Moody uttered cries of anguish. Its citizens brought suits in court to prevent the change of terminus. But Van Horne had made up his mind, though one of his stipulations was that Granville be renamed Vancouver.

The mere hint of the C.P.R.'s arrival brought a rush of settlers and a land boom as fantastic as that in Victoria when the 1858 flood of gold seekers poured in on her. On April 6 of 1886, the city of Vancouver was incorporated. By June of that year it was a bustling eager little city with a dozen hotels, half a score of real estate offices, several restaurants and grocery shops—in all, about seventy places of business. And then on Sunday, June 13, disaster leaped.

It was a typical Vancouver day that morning of June 13—warm but with a fresh breeze from the west. Over to that west the C.P.R. crews were clearing land. The smoke from the fires drifted over the frame homes and the frame business street. In those days most Vancouverites went to church. After services there were sailboats on Burrard Inlet and picnics on the North Shore under the mighty trees. Then, suddenly, at 2 P.M. the wind rose to a gale. Before church bells could more than peal out an alarm, fire from the west had pounced on the wooden buildings of Vancouver. Before an hour was over, all that was left, except for the Hastings Mill and a few small buildings, were smoking heaps of ashes.

An unknown number died in the inferno. The survivors, who had saved only what they could snatch, stood and stared at what had been their homes and places of business. Yet on June 29 the Vancouver *Advertiser* was able to report:

"At 2:30 P.M. on Sunday, the 13th of June, the city was completely destroyed by fire; at 3 o'clock on Monday morning teams were delivering lumber upon the site. . . ."

In this spirit Vancouver rose from its embers. On May 23 of 1887, the year of Queen Victoria's Golden Jubilee, the first C.P.R. train steamed into it, though to this day Port Moody remains, technically, the official terminus.

C.P.R. ambitions reached out beyond Vancouver. While John

A. was at Victoria on his western trip, the *W. B. Flint* brought into Fort Moody a cargo from Yokohama of 17,400 half chests of tea. On July 30, 1886, the first tea train left for Montreal. The route to Cathay had been opened and the C.P.R. wanted its share. A mail contract to the Orient, involving a total subsidy of $60,000, was granted. The C.P.R. at first chartered vessels for its trade. Then three Empresses were built. The first of these, the *Empress of India*, reached Vancouver in 1891. Meantime, the C.P.R. had begun hotels at Vancouver and Banff as well as the Château Frontenac in Quebec City. Steamships, hotels, the sale of lands, railroad extensions—from a transcontinental the C.P.R. swiftly stretched out its arms to girdle the world. But it had been conceived and built, in essence, by three Canadian Scots and by an American Knickerbocker turned Canadian. From this time forward, in finance and politics, it and the Bank of Montreal became dominant features in Canada's history. Through these two, by the close of the nineteenth century Montreal had reaffirmed its victory over Toronto as the transportation, trade, and finance center of the Dominion—and that politician who expected to survive found he needed to reckon with both.

CHAPTER XXXI

1887–91

Expansion—British Columbia and the Kootenay Boom—The Battle For Provincial Rights—The Fisheries Again—Imperial Federation and Commercial Union—John A.'s Last Election

1

IN the United States, transcontinentals were the natural expression of its westward march to a continental empire. In Canada, the C.P.R. was a thumbing of the nose at economic geography. By it, John A. and those who thought as he did served notice that the Dominion intended to become a nation in its own right. Its trade was to flow east and west, not north and south.

In modern days that dream of a separate nationhood has been increasingly vitiated by the importation of American capital, by the spilling across the frontier of American mores, and by the American need of Canada as her northern shield against Russia. In the closing years of the nineteenth century the dream was still possible. The C.P.R. tied together the *disjecta membra* of Canada. It also by its "all red" route contributed to British imperialism and did its share toward creating the notion of a British Commonwealth of Nations. At the same time its steel rails began to open up northern Ontario and to settle the Canadian West.

In northern Ontario nickel was found at Sudbury, and the rich mine of Silver Islet was discovered near Port Arthur. But the real "march of the metal men" was to wait for the next century. At the moment the chief interest was in lumbering.

Similarly, on the prairies, the big jump in settlement was to come later, though in 1891 the C.P.R. did run branch lines to Fort Macleod and to Edmonton, and in 1890 the Qu'Appelle, Long Lake and Saskatchewan Railway, which was taken over by the C.P.R., linked Regina with Saskatoon and Prince Albert. Inevitably, along these and other extensions settlers farmed and villages and towns planted hopeful feet.

It was in British Columbia, that home of gold rushes, however, that the first excitement flared. The coming of the transcontinental led to the spread of farming in the Fraser delta and, indeed, along its whole valley, as far as the railroad tapped suitable land. New towns put in their roots. Settlements were begun in the Okanagan fruit district and in the Thompson River country. In 1890 the C.P.R. flung out the Shuswap and Okanagan Railway, and in 1891 it tossed a line from Mission to Huntingdon on the U.S. boundary.

Meantime, on Vancouver Island, Victoria had achieved both its graving dock at Esquimalt (paid for by the Dominion in return for a block of 3,500,000 acres in the Peace River area) and its long-sought Esquimalt-Nanaimo Railway. To build this road the Dominion offered an area of 1,900,000 acres in the southeast part of the island, which had been turned over to it by the province, and a grant of $750,000 in cash.

The terms attracted a rugged individualist, Robert Dunsmuir. Dunsmuir, beginning with a wagon, a cart, and a coal seam which he mined himself, had built himself into a magnate. Now, in the offer of the money grant and of nearly two million acres of the finest of timberland together with its coal and all other mineral rights, the whole free from taxation, he had discovered his own Cathay. He built the road, and on August 13, 1886, while on his visit to Victoria, John A. himself tapped in the last spike.

British Columbia, along with its new port, Vancouver, was set for a rapid expansion in its mines (a year after the first train steamed into Port Moody the Nanaimo coal mines produced 413,360 tons), its fisheries, its lumbering, and its trade; and in 1890 the province itself rushed into an orgy of railroad building. But sober development was too dull for the "Kingdom of the Pacific." In 1887 on Toad Mountain, in the southeast corner of the province, the Hall brothers discovered the fabulous Silver King; and Nelson, on Kootenay Lake, was born.

In British Columbia, to find a mine was to shout "Food!" to starving men. Within a year prospectors swarmed like eager bloodhounds over the whole tumbled terrain of the Kootenays. Then Red Mountain, at today's Rossland, yielded gold in the Lily May mine. In 1890, on that same mountain, Le Roi, War Eagle, and Centre Star came into being.

These three mines, along with two others, were staked by Joe Bourgeois and Joe Moris. Back at Nelson the assay values were meager, and they also discovered they could hold only four claims. So they offered the fifth at the price of paying the recording fee of $2.50 for all five, a total of $12.50, to the deputy recorder, Eugene Sayre Topping. Topping, miner, sailor, and writer, took the chance; only he changed the name of his claim from Le Wise to Le Roi. That claim in eight years paid $725,000 in dividends. As the miners swarmed in, a young man, Ross Thompson, took over 160 acres near the mines and laid out a townsite. Thus, Rossland got its start.

The boom was on. In 1891 the silver-lead-zinc ledges of the Slocan country to the north came in. The Slocan Star paid out $300,000 in five years, while between 1897 and 1904 the Payne returned dividends of $1,438,000. The same ores were found in the East Kootenay. Along the boundary line copper-gold mines rewarded the prospectors, the most famous being the Granby, which in 1908 shipped out 23,505,009 pounds of copper. Near Fort Steele (founded in 1887 for a brief stay of N.W.M.P. under Major Steele) in 1892 huge deposits of lead-zinc made the North Star and Kimberley mines famous.

The whole southern part of British Columbia as far as Vancouver Island boiled with prospectors. On the coast the Britannia mine, north of Vancouver was discovered. Near the boundary and in the Kootenay area smelters bloomed at places such as Grand Forks, Nelson, Revelstoke, and Trail. In those boisterous days Rossland, which now drowses in respectability, was for fifteen years the center of a rough and tumultuous life. To it—to quote a contemporary record—"merchants, hotel-keepers, doctors, lawyers, gamblers, painted women, and all the rag-tag and bob-tail of civilization gravitated. . . . Boomers of every description were seen coming down the hills and up the valley. Tents mushroomed and the scent of whip-sawn tamarac and fir was everywhere."

Rossland and Nelson were only two of the brawling towns to prove that British Columbia could still house characters as colorful as those of the days of the Cariboo Road. Into the hurly-burly came a young American speculator, F. Augustus Heinze.

Heinze was of the stuff from which legends are made. He got contracts for ore from the Rossland mines, built a smelter at Trail where Trail Creek empties into the Columbia, and then put down a narrow-gauge railroad from Rossland to Trail. The equipment was brought from Utah, and the private coach of Brigham Young, the great Mormon leader, became a plush-lined passenger car on the new run.

The scent of profits brought other railroads searching, and notably J. J. Hill's Great Northern. The C.P.R. pushed in with a network of roads plus a fleet of river and lake steamers. Meantime, the coal fields of the nearby Crow's Nest Pass were found—the aggregate thickness of the seams running to 125 feet. The C.P.R. shoved in a line from Fort Macleod, which ultimately was continued to Vancouver; while in 1895 the smelter at Trail was secured under the charter of the Columbia and Western Railway.

The steamers are now gone from the lakes and rivers they used to furrow, and the railroads and towns have settled to a more decorous life. Yet the huge Consolidated Smelters at Trail occasionally think back to their origin, and in the whole Kootenay country there is still the memory of the days when at a dinner in the Allen Hotel at Rossland the napkins were hundred-dollar bills.

2

In 1887 five angry men met at Quebec. Four were Liberal premiers and one was Conservative. The fury of all five was directed at the Dominion government and, therefore, at John A. Macdonald. Their objective was so to strengthen provincial powers that each province would become, in effect, a separate state. It was beginning to seem, even at the moment when an ebullient and successful transcontinental was reaching out more and more cords of steel to tie Canada together, that the union of 1867 was to end in disunion.

The anger of John Norquay, Premier of Manitoba, was easy to understand. There was depression and high freight rates in his province. The high rates were blamed on the C.P.R. monopoly. Yet the Dominion kept disallowing every charter for a railway to break the constricting bond. Bluff half-breed Norquay, Conservative though he was, had no confidence in John A. If the Dominion would not yield to reason its power of disallowance must be dynamited.

The Premier of Nova Scotia, the tempestuous W. S. Fielding, was just as easy to comprehend. His province was the press-gang sailor on the Confederation ship. And what had Confederation fed to Nova Scotia? A duty of fifty cents per ton on coal (later increased to sixty cents). That was all. It had been blocked off from its natural market in the New England states. The Intercolonial had brought merely a few crusts of trade instead of the heaped-up platterfuls which had been promised. Manufacturing had become concentrated in central Canada. All Nova Scotia saw of the bonanza of industrialism were Ontario drummers robbing its poverty-stricken pockets with goods priced high under a sheltering tariff. Meantime, the dingy iron freighters were rapidly replacing the white sails of the trim full-rigged clippers. Nova Scotia's economics had sailed into the doldrums and stuck there. Her young men, with no place for them at home, were slipping across the line into the United States. In the year before this Fielding had won a sweeping victory in a provincial election, and his platform had been "Secession!"

His fellow Maritimer, the Premier of New Brunswick, a somewhat colorless man, had also tagged along. In A. G. Blair's province the stands of pine were at last depleted. For the same reasons as in Nova Scotia, the young people were draining away southward. Yet Norquay, Fielding, and Blair found Honoré Mercier of Quebec, the Premier who had called the conference together, somewhat puzzling. It was a little difficult to assess what he was really after. His *Parti National* had swum into power on the tide of protest flung upward in French Canada by Riel's execution. Whether or not it was realized fully that behind the *Parti National* lay Quebec's recurrent dream of a separate Roman Catholic, French-Canadian Laurentian state, it was difficult to understand Mercier hobnobbing with that Oliver Mowat whose Ontario had ravened for Riel's death.

Mowat had come to the conference with victories over John A. thrust into his pocket. Ontario was in his pocket, too. Since 1872 he had been its premier—and his reign was to last until 1896. In the old days, though he had once been John A.'s pupil, he had been a Clear Grit follower of George Brown. As such, he had been one of the founders of Confederation.

But, except for that unique genius, John A., once an Ontarian, always an Ontarian. Precise, efficient, capable, as full of conscious rectitude as Sir John was of political savoir-faire, Mowat was the walking embodiment of Ontario's smug feeling that in population, Anglo-Saxon stock, territory, wealth, and Puritan Protestant morals it was the head and body of the dog and the rest of the Dominion the unimportant tail. John A.'s theory of Canada demanded a strong and overriding central government with the provincial legislatures mere city councils. To Mowat, Ontario was an independent kingdom. As such, he felt, it possessed the right to manage all affairs within its own borders, while criticizing with a condescending superiority the conduct of other provinces not so blessed with character; while for the Dominion to disallow Ontario legislation was an insult not to be forgiven.

John A. and he had locked horns years before, on that memorable occasion in the legislature of the two Canadas when, jumping from his seat in white-faced Celtic rage, Macdonald had rushed over to the priggish Mowat, crying: "You damned pup, I'll slap your chops." Since 1878 they had met in duel after duel.

One of their battles, perhaps appropriately, had been whether the Dominion or the province should control the sale of liquor and all the patronage that went with it. In 1877 Mowat had passed a Liquor License Act giving Ontario jurisdiction. When John A. returned to power in 1878, he put through a Canada Temperance Act, by which the Dominion handled liquor licenses. A Fredericton bootlegger, Russell, contested this law on the ground that it conflicted with the provincial law.

John A. won this round. The Privy Council ruled his Canada Temperance Act *intra vires*. Flushed with success, and to clip further the wings of "Mr. Mowat, that little tyrant," the Prime Minister in 1883 shoved through the Intoxicating Liquors Act, which gave to Dominion commissioners the perquisite of regulating the sale of beer, wine, and spirits. But in that same year the Privy Council, with a fine impartiality, in the case of *Hodge v. The Queen* ruled Mowat's 1877 Liquor License Act also *intra vires*. Mowat, in his turn, promptly pushed through an Ontario bill imposing heavy penalties on any provincial tavern keeper who took out a Dominion license. John A. disallowed it. Then, a year later, the Privy Council ruled against the validity of Macdonald's 1883 Intoxicating Liquors Act. To Mowat went the final victory.

There was the same sort of quarrel over the Ontario 1881 Rivers and Streams Act. This was a somewhat comic bill put through a Liberal legislature to permit a Liberal lumberman to float logs downstream over improvements made in a waterway by his Conservative rival. John A. disallowed this bill three times. Mowat had it passed a fourth time. This time it stuck. For in 1884 the Privy Council declared Mowat's bill *intra vires.*

By decisions such as these the British Privy Council gnawed away at Macdonald's concept of a strong central government. Mowat's biggest victory was in thrusting Ontario's frontiers north and west. The territory which he claimed for his province was no mean one. It was 144,000 square miles of what had once been regarded as worthless rock and muskeg but was beginning to be vaguely realized as a storehouse of lumber and minerals. In the summer of 1878 the Mackenzie government, just before it went out of office, awarded the region which is now North Ontario to Ontario.

John A. canceled the award and referred the matter to the Privy Council. The Dominion was represented by Macdonald's Ontario wheel horse, D'Alton McCarthy, and a battery of lawyers. Mowat, himself a lawyer, appeared in person for Ontario. He won. In the summer of 1884 he returned to his province laden with the spoils of conquest. Ontario was to have her boundaries pushed north to James Bay and west to Lake of the Woods. At the Quebec Conference Mowat was the dominant man.

The immediate effects of the conference were not imposing. British Columbia and Prince Edward Island had failed to attend; and John A., though an invitation had been sent to the Dominion to be present, simply wrinkled the nostrils of his generous nose faintly, as if there were skunks hiding out in the cabbage patch. A number of resolutions were passed which, if carried into effect, would have meant that each province was to fly off into its own separate orbit. Then the angry men went home.

The waves they had stirred went on swelling. In 1888 the Prime Minister attempted to pacify Manitoba (the hapless Norquay had meantime been replaced by the Liberal Greenway) by buying out the C.P.R. monopoly, that is, that no lines should be constructed for twenty years between the C.P.R.'s main line and the 49th parallel. The price was a Dominion guarantee of the interest at 3½ per cent of a new $15,000,000 issue of C.P.R. bonds. Another long-term result of the conference came from its proposal that there be a readjustment of the subsidies to the provinces. This suggestion was seized on. Ever since that conference the provinces, and in particular Ontario, have looked upon the Dominion as a miserly multimillionaire who, having greedily seized the main sources of revenue, must be cajoled or forced to surrender to the provinces their dues; quite forgetting that the monies for such subsidies must come from the taxpayers' pockets.

To imagine, however, that after the conference Quebec and Ontario became cooing doves would be to underestimate both. In the February 1887 federal election, in spite of the Riel hysteria, the Roman Catholic hierarchy of Quebec had still come out for the Conservatives. To them, the Liberals were still tainted by the fatal *Rouge* vice of toleration. Mercier, a former *Rouge*, decided that his *Parti National* must be washed whiter than snow. To win over the hierarchy, in 1888 he put through the legislature his Jesuits Estates Bill.

In the days of New France the Jesuits had been granted large estates. In 1773, however, the order had been suppressed by a papal brief. Consequently, when in 1800 the last surviving Jesuit died, the estates were confiscated by the Crown. Thirty-three years later they were transferred as an endowment for education to the legislature of Lower Canada; and education in Lower Canada was pretty largely in the hands of the Roman Catholic Church, though Protestant education was managed by the Protestant clergy. In the sixties, however, the Jesuit Order, having been re-established, pressed for compensation for its confiscated property. The Roman Catholic bishops of Quebec put in counterclaims on the ground that the property in Quebec of an order suppressed by the Pope belonged to their hierarchy.

In the midst of this welter, Mercier's bill, as a compromise satisfactory to all, arranged for the province to provide $400,000 to extinguish all claims (the Protestants got $60,000), this money to be divided among the Jesuits, Laval University, and the Roman Catholic Ecclesiastical Corporations according as the Pope might decide.

"As the Pope might decide." The bill might have seemed to be none of Ontario's business. But not with those words in it! The Orange Order put on the garments of wrath. The Protestant press and clergy joined in denunciation of the Pope's authority being invoked to settle affairs in a Canadian province. By January of the next year petitions were pouring into Ottawa to disallow the Quebec bill. John A. refused. In March the "noble thirteen," led by D'Alton McCarthy, the Conservative wheel horse among the

Orange lodges of Ontario, tried to force disallowance in the House, but were defeated.

Defeat merely added fuel to the fire. An Equal Rights Association (for Protestants) was formed in Toronto by 800 delegates. D'Alton McCarthy himself went out West to speak on what to him was a simple question: Shall this country be English or French? From this tour in the fullness of time was to come the 1890 Manitoba repeal of denominational schools.

In Canada both French Catholics and English Protestants have toes with corns on them. Meanwhile Mowat, like an industrious beaver, continued to whittle away at the Dominion's powers. The villain of the piece was the Privy Council. At first it had upheld Sir John A.'s contention that by the British North America Act the provinces were restricted to local spheres of action, particularly since all "residuary powers" were reserved to the Dominion.

In a curious way, however, the defeated South took revenge on Canada for Canadian help to northern armies during the American Civil War. After that war the Attorney General of the Confederacy, Judah P. Benjamin, a strong proponent of States' rights, went to England. A man trained under him, Lord Watson, became a Privy Councilor. He was the man who in judgment after judgment gave the nod to provincial rights over Dominion rights. Thanks to the Privy Council's reversing its earlier attitude, Mowat achieved for Ontario and all the provinces the power to appoint Queen's Counsels, unlimited jurisdiction over penalties and punishments prescribed by the province, and the like. In 1896, in announcing Ontario's Local Option Act *intra vires*, Great Britain's Privy Council even declared that the general residuary powers reserved to the Dominion, in Section 91 of the British North America Act, "ought to be strictly confined to such matters as are unquestionably of Canadian interest and importance and ought not to trench upon provincial legislation with respect to any of the classes of subjects enumerated in Section 92."

In this way the Privy Council practically nullified the intent and purpose of those who framed Confederation. Instead of Dominion powers being paramount, provincial rights were exalted. The relationship between the Dominion and the provinces was made more similar to that between the U.S. federal government and the states of the Union. In the two world wars, Ottawa retrieved something of its dominant authority. In peacetime, however, the provinces tend to become feudal kingdoms.

In modern Canada provincial rights plus economic and religio-racial sectionalism are powerful centrifugal forces which act against national unity. The first of these disintegrating influences is owed to Mowat and the Privy Council.

3

The year of the Quebec Conference and of the entry of the first C.P.R. train into Vancouver and of the discovery of the rich mines on Toad Mountain was also the year when that perpetual nuisance, the fisheries question, once more came to a boil. In 1885 the United States, annoyed by the arbitration award of $5,500,000 to Canada for the rights she had surrendered by the Washington Treaty, announced the abrogation of the fisheries clause in that treaty.

Thus the 1818 Convention, excluding American fishermen from fishing within the three-mile limit or from bringing their vessels into Canadian ports for any purpose except for repairs, shelter, wood, or water, came back into force. The Dominion decided to seize those American vessels which broke the regulations. Immediately the Republic protested vociferously; though in 1886 it blandly treated the whole Bering Sea as a closed preserve for American fur-sealers and pounced on British Columbian vessels for "poaching."

So once again, in 1887–88, there was a Washington Conference with Tupper representing Canada. The Americans refused to discuss the Bering Sea question. Furthermore, when a fisheries treaty was reached the American Senate threw it out. Only Canada's forbearance in continuing a *modus vivendi* whereby American fishing vessels were admitted to her ports on a payment of a license fee kept the peace. The United States showed no similar forbearance about Canadian fur-sealers in the Bering Sea.

The Bering Sea imbroglio was centered around the fact that the rookery of the fur seals was the Pribilof Islands in that sea. These islands had been leased by the United States to the Alaska Commercial Company. In defense of that company's attempt to maintain a monopoly of the fur-sealing industry, from 1886 to 1893 American revenue cutters seized vessel after vessel of the British Columbian fur-sealing fleet, even though those vessels were in the open sea.

It was a strange action for a nation which, presumably, had

fought the War of 1812 to establish the "freedom of the seas." However, in 1892, the United States agreed to submit the question of pelagic fur-sealing to a tribunal of arbitration sitting in Paris. This tribunal ruled that the Americans could not treat the Bering Sea as their private preserve. But, to protect the fur-sealing industry, it did prohibit any sealing within a zone of sixty miles around the Pribilof Islands and any sealing at all in the months of May, June, and July north of 35 degrees latitude and west of 180 degrees longitude. Moreover, after long and tortuous proceedings British Columbians, in 1896, received compensation for their seized vessels.

To complete the story, in 1911 Canada, in return for refraining from pelagic fur-sealing, received 10 per cent of the Japanese profits from fur-sealing and 15 per cent of the take by each of the Russian and American fleets. The important feature, however, of the Washington Conference of 1887–88, was that Canada had dominated the joint British-Canadian delegation. For, since the days of 1871, when the Earl de Grey and Ripon had blithely tossed Canada's interests to the American wolves, a tremendous transformation had taken place in Britain's attitude toward Canada.

4

Eighteen eighty-seven was also the year of Queen Victoria's Golden Jubilee. In the celebration of that event all the ancient pageantry of the United Kingdom blazed forth to honor Victoria, Queen by the Grace of God, the Defender of the Faith, and the Empress of India. That ceremonial, in conscious pride, likewise celebrated the new British Empire, the one on which the sun never set. In the same year the first colonial conference was held. For the colonies were no longer "millstones," to recall Disraeli's petulant words, but jewels to hang around Britain's neck; and the author of this new imperialism was Benjamin Disraeli, Lord Beaconsfield, himself.

By 1887 Disraeli was six years dead. Through his romantic shrewdness, the Suez Canal shares had been bought for England, Egypt had become a British protectorate, Queen Victoria had been proclaimed Empress of India, and Lord Beaconsfield at the Congress of Berlin had forced Russia and Turkey to accede to Britain's arbitration.

The Empire and pride in its world-wide power had never stood higher. In 1886, in opening the Colonial and Indian Exhibition at South Kensington, the Queen, like a Hindu maharaja or a Pharaoh of ancient Egypt, sat on a throne of hammered gold.

Behind the pomp and pride lay a widespread extension of commercial and political power. Africa was being parceled out among the European powers with Britain putting her lion's paw on the choicest pieces of the meat. In January of 1885 she had suffered a check in the Sudan when Wolseley's expedition to save Chinese Gordon from the Mahdi had failed to reach Khartoum in time. But Egypt was being benevolently administered by Sir Evelyn Baring (Lord Cromer) of the Baring Brothers firm. In the ripeness of time Kitchener, at Omdurman in 1898, was to crush the Mahdi and his Kiplingesque Fuzzy-Wuzzies and to add to Cecil Rhodes' vision of an all-red Cape-to-Cairo route. With Africa and India to supply her with raw materials and markets, with Hong Kong as her door of entry to the Orient, with possession after possession girdling the globe and her trade pushing its way into South America, these years were the high point of Britain's political and commercial hegemony.

In such an atmosphere the self-governing Dominions became adjuncts to Britain's power and proofs of her wisdom; or, more picturesquely, by the side of the British lion were ranged the cubs, now almost full-grown. This was the thought behind the first Colonial Conference. Three years before this, too, the Imperial Federation League had been formed in London. It soon migrated to Canada. There it was welcomed warmly by the "loyalists." Its aims were, in general, reciprocal preferential tariffs between the Old Country and the self-governing colonies, their participation in the costs of Imperial defense, and a close-knit Imperial Council to tie the Empire together. This concept collided head on with "Commercial Union."

Commercial Union was a nostalgic glance backward to the 1854 Elgin-Marcy Reciprocity Treaty. From 1879 to 1883 John A.'s National Policy had basked briefly in the warmth of returning prosperity. Then the bleak winter of depression clamped down again. The building of the transcontinental had been a few sticks of wood on the fire. The metals boom in the Kootenays gave British Columbia something to which to stretch out its fingers. But from the Rockies to the Atlantic there was a chilling cold.

As always, Canadians looked longingly across the border. The United States, too, was suffering from depression, but, to Canadians, with the markets for their grain, lumber, fish, and other primary products restricted and with not enough jobs to go around, the economic climate there seemed warmer. The result was emigration across the line. In the East as in the West, in many a household there was a vacant chair "for the boy in the States." Even the French Canadians swarmed across the boundary into Maine and Vermont. In 1870 there were nearly half a million Canadians in the United States. By the end of the century that number had risen to about 1,200,000. Worse still, it was the young people who went. It was Sir Richard Cartwright who commented wryly that Confederation, which had begun "in Lamentations, seemed to be ending in Exodus." An inevitable consequence was that, in spite of immigration and births, increase in population went forward at a snail's pace. In 1871 (the Dominion census was taken in the first year of each decade) Canada had had 3,689,257 people. Twenty years later there were only 4,833,239 souls; though in the same period the States had advanced from 38,558,371 to 62,947,714.

Lack of increase in population, lack of jobs, poor prices for primary products, high prices behind Canada's tariff fence for manufactured goods—by 1887 many Canadians had had it. Even if it meant throwing themselves into the maw of the Republic they wanted "Commercial Union."

As it happened, the climate south of the border was for the instant favorable to the notion. The Democrat Grover Cleveland was President and his party favored tariff reduction. Butterworth of Ohio made himself the proponent of Commercial Union in Congress. Samuel Ritchie, an American businessman with Canadian interests, and Erastus Winman, New York financier and ex-Canadian, propagandized for it. In Canada the farmers, the fishermen, and the lumbering interests shouted for what was Reciprocity under another name. Both the Liberal *Globe* and the Conservative *Mail* got on the band wagon. Goldwin Smith, the pontifical patron of Canadian culture, the man who had been the mentor of the 1874 Canadian Firsters, became the prophet of the new movement. By this time he had convinced himself that instead of independence Canada's future was to be absorption by the Republic. The *Farmers' Weekly Sun* was established by him to enlighten the darkness of the back concessions. In the United States there was, at this time, an agrarian revolt against high tariffs, an uprising which found expression in the Grange Co-operative movement. There were no "Granges" in Canada. But the Farmers' Institutes of Ontario took the cue from their American brothers; while the left wing of the Liberal party came out whole hog for Commercial Union in a speech by Sir Richard Cartwright at Ingersoll on October 20, 1887. Depression makes any cure seem worth trying.

The counterreaction was inevitable. The Canadian Manufacturers' Association was stung to the marrow by the possibility that through Commercial Union their captive consumers might escape into fields where prices were lower. The powerful C.P.R. and Bank of Montreal saw the wreck of their all-Canadian transcontinental. For why should goods flow east and west through Canada if the tariff fences were obliterated? In behind these potent economic powers was flung the Imperial Federation League, now led by D'Alton McCarthy. Their opposition to any form of reciprocity was given an assist by a brief lifting of the depression in 1888. Canada was tugged two ways by the opposing forces which always pull at its people—the British connection and the economic advantages of union with the Republic.

In 1888, however, there was also a presidential election to the south of the border. Both candidates, Cleveland, the Democrat, and Harrison, the Republican, knew one sure way to get votes—twist the lion's tail.

This time the tail was Canada. Alarmed by the headway Harrison was making among the anti-British Irish, after the Republican Senate had rejected the fisheries bill, Cleveland even asked Congress for the power to proclaim complete noncommercial intercourse with Canada, as if it were Red China of today.

The Republican, Harrison, was elected. His Secretary of State, Blaine, was an anti-British jingoist. By the next year, while blandly stating that the United States had never asserted that the Bering Sea was a mare clausum, he was seizing British Columbian fur-sealers venturing into it, as if it were. Then, on October 6, 1890, the Republic put into force the McKinley tariff with import duties so high that many Canadians believed it to be an attempt to starve them into annexation by annihilating the market for their primary products. A month later, however, in the peculiar way in which the United States Constitution works, a Democratic low-tariff Congress was returned. So Blaine did an about-face. In December he informed Lord Pauncefote, the British ambassador, that he had a "strong desire to conclude a wide Reciprocity Treaty."

5

From his throne at Ottawa, the old master, John A., had been watching all these alarums and excursions with weary and disillusioned eyes. Despite Quebec's revolt he had won his election in 1887. Since then he had ignored the Quebec Conference, had bought back the C.P.R. monopoly in the West, and had refused to enter into the bitter dispute between Protestant and Catholic over the Jesuit Estates Bill. It must have seemed to him by this time that his Canadians were a singularly stupid people. At Confederation the country had perched on a pinnacle of hope. Yet, in spite of a union which had seemed to be the dawning of a new and sunlit day and in spite of a transcontinental which should have filled them with confident pride and a fresh sense of unity, what John A. beheld were the same bitter antagonisms of race and religion, the same sectionalism of Maritimer, French Canadian, Ontarian, and now of Westerner and British Columbian, each hugging himself to himself, the same uncertain wavering between Britain and the States, like that of a child wondering to which shopwindow to turn. And, meantime, the strong powers he had pre-empted for the Dominion government were being nibbled away, stick by stick.

There were consolations. Canada had its own high commissioner in London, and Britishers were more chary of signing away Canadian rights. It was pleasant, too, to be courted instead of scorned by England; while, at home, whether Canadians realized it or not, the expedition to quench the Riel-lit fire had shown an over-all Canadian national consciousness.

Yet all that he had achieved so far was, or so it must have seemed, the mere framework of a Canadian nation. Were Canadians now willing to abandon their painful step-by-step progress for the economic advantages of Commercial Union? And would, this time, Reciprocity mean absorption by the great Republic?

Many Conservatives, some Liberals, and all Imperialists believed firmly that it would. It seems doubtful that John A. Macdonald had any such conviction. There appears to be no doubt that since Confederation he, more than any single man, had seen the vision of a separate Canadian nation from sea to sea and, in spite of his bewildering shifts and turns, in spite of errors, in spite even of his amiable disregard for venality and his cynicism about human motivations, had clung firmly to that vision. When it came to any single issue, such as Commercial Union, it had been Sir John's experience that something would usually turn up, if one waited long enough. For Sir John was the most devious of opportunists. In the meantime, within a month or so there would be an election to win and the depression was settling down again.

So, on December 13, acting on the suggestion made to Lord Pauncefote by Blaine, John A. sent to London and Washington proposals for a discussion on reciprocity with the States. Even John A.'s long experience of American duplicity had scarcely prepared him for Blaine's next action. On January 16 of the next year the Conservative *Empire*, getting wind of what was in the air, reported that the United States had approached Canada about improvement in trade relationships. Twelve days later, not to Sir John or to Lord Pauncefote or to anyone in an official position, but to Edward Farrer, one of the editors of the Liberal *Globe*, Blaine repudiated all his suggestions to Pauncefote about a "wide Reciprocity Treaty." Further, in reply to a letter of the same date from a congressman, Blaine stated that "there are no negotiations whatever on foot for a reciprocity treaty with Canada. . . ."

It almost seemed as if Blaine were in a pact with the Liberals of Canada to defeat the Conservative government. On the very eve of a general election John A. and his Conservatives stood, apparently, convicted of having made tentative explorations toward that "Commercial Union" which the Liberals were boosting. Blaine's *volte-face* made it difficult to argue that those explorations had been in answer to an American invitation. The one saving fact was that the proposals had been merely exploratory.

That was the out John A. seized. He looked about him. Manitoba and the Maritimes were alienated, but Tupper might be able to hold the latter and the C.P.R. could bring pressure on the West. In Quebec, Honoré Mercier and his Cabinet had been dismissed for corruption.

John A. Macdonald was wise enough to know that this fact did not mean that Quebec would return en masse to the Conservative fold. The Anglo-Saxon voter may demand a veil of hypocrisy over benefits to an individual or his friends from possession of political power. The French Canadian, more realistic, has always believed that to the victors belong the spoils. Still, Mercier's fall did hold out hopes. It became evident to the master politician that if a more or less even break could be secured in Ontario, where the farmers were all out for the Liberals and Commercial Union, the Conservative ship might yet be saved. So Tupper was summoned from his high-commissionership in London to help carry the battle. On February 17 he and Sir John faced a huge meeting in the Academy of Music in Toronto.

That meeting looked up hopefully at the old man. The Liberals were already baying hot on the scent of victory. Could John A. at seventy-six, tired and not too well, pull one last spell from his magic bag to block them? They did not know that chance and that Edward Farrer, who had so gleefully reported in the *Globe* Blaine's repudiation of any offers to initiate trade discussions with the Conservative government, had already given John A. his magic words.

Farrer, though an editor, seems to have been a singularly simple Canadian in a den of American sharpers. At the request of an American friend he had set down in a pamphlet Canadian-American relationships as they should be viewed by an American. With an enthusiasm worthy of a professor expounding an academic thesis, he had analyzed how the United States could bring Canada to its suppliant knees by measures such as tonnage duties on Canadian vessels, suspension of bonding privileges, and the lopping off of the C.P.R. connections at Sault Ste. Marie. As a final act of political folly, he had had a few copies of the pamphlet printed. But there was in Toronto that outstanding Imperial Federationist and stout upholder of the British connection, Colonel Denison, the refreshingly direct man whom we have met as a cavalry leader during the Fenian raid and the Northwest Rebellion. By cloak-and-dagger methods some of the proof sheets of Farrer's fatal pamphlets had come into Denison's hands. Thence they went into John A.'s bag.

Before the great audience in Toronto he pulled them out. He read extracts. Here, he thundered, was the proof that there was "a deliberate conspiracy, by force, by fraud, or by both, to force Canada into the American union." And who were implicated in this conspiracy of disloyalty? The Liberals!

And what of himself? "A British subject I was born," John A. Macdonald trumpeted, drawing himself up to his lank, frail height, his mop of silver hair an aureole in the light, the nostrils of his massive nose quivering, "a British subject I will die."

The theme was set. In the Conservative campaign that disloyal thing, Commercial Union, was tossed into the cesspool and National Policy was nailed to the mast beside the Union Jack. "The old flag," the Conservative orators shouted, "the old man, the old policy."

The slogan worked. Though in Quebec the Conservatives had a majority of only five seats, the C.P.R. in the West and Tupper in the Maritimes, helped out by generous patronage, retained those sections of the country. Most important of all, the Liberals who had seemed likely to sweep Ontario were held to an even split. The over-all Conservative majority was thirty-one. John A. had done it again. But it was for the last time.

6

A hush seemed to lie over Canada. It was as if people waited with held, incredulous breaths. For a whisper had sped outward from Ottawa across the Dominion. "John A. is dying," that whisper had murmured.

It seemed impossible. Like Homer's Nestor, John A. had outlived two generations of articulate-speaking men and now ruled over the third. It mattered not whether the Canadian were Liberal or Conservative, French- or English-speaking, passionate devotee or bitter foe, in every man and woman there was the sense of a historic moment, the imminence of the end of an era.

John A. had been struck down by illness on February 24 in the midst of the election which his strategy won. His convalescence had been slow. As always, however, with that remarkable vitality of his, he had recovered enough to be present in his seat when Parliament opened on April 29.

But the frail body had been overtaxed. On May 12 the Prime Minister suffered a minor disability in speech and a slight twisting of one side of his face. His physician advised a complete rest. John A. refused to take it. There was a warning stroke on the morning of May 28. On the next day at four o'clock there was a second and a massive one. John A. was paralyzed.

And now Sir John lay dying. That was the hush which rested over Canada. Yet he held on to life. Canada began to stir. There was, even on June 4, a rustle of hope.

The hope was only a flicker. As sunset faded away on June 6 and darkness and sleep settled down over the Dominion, for John A., too, the last sleep came.

They gave the old warrior the honors due him. The body lay in state in Ottawa, first in his home at Earnscliffe, then in the Senate Chamber of the Parliament Buildings. On June 10, in long procession it was escorted between shops and houses draped in black and purple to St. Alban's Church and, after the service, to the waiting train—the locomotive, too, a C.P.R. locomotive, hung with purple and black, as was every locomotive and station along the transcontinental which he, Stephen, Smith, and Van Horne had built. The train of mourning carried him back to the gray limestone homes of Kingston.

The body lay in state again in the city in which John A. had grown up and practiced law, in the heart of that constituency which he had represented—except for the years from 1878 to 1887—since 1844, first in the legislature of the two Canadas and then in the Dominion House. Finally, on June 11, in bright sunlight, with thousands in the funeral cortege, it was laid in its last resting place, in Cataraqui Cemetery, near his mother and father and his first wife, Isabella, and their first child. John A. had passed from life but not from memory.

He had died, quite literally, in harness, and he had stamped his imprint on Canada and on North America. For a breath short of forty-seven years, politics had absorbed him almost completely. In his domestic life, tragedy had stalked him—the death of his first-born, the illness and death of his dearly beloved first wife, the sick disappointment in the failure of his daughter by his second wife to develop normally. Financially, he had been forced for many years to struggle with creditors. Others might be venal. John A. did not use politics to make money. Money to him was not that important. Rather, as with any man who sees into the meaning of the universe further than his nose, even if it be as generous a one as Sir John's, to consider the making of money as the main preoccupation of life and material possessions as the measure of success was to John A. Macdonald ignoble. It was to nullify the spark of the sublime in humanity, to reduce that element in him which seeks to reach to the stars to a greedy fumbling for the materialistic. John A. would have agreed with Tennyson that a man's reach should exceed his grasp, or what's a heaven for? But to reach and grasp for money and not for a vision was beneath him, even though he understood, condoned, and used for his own purposes that money-grabbing instinct which so often characterized the Canadian magnates of his day.

For, of necessity, Macdonald was a master politician. With a complete cynicism he manipulated lesser men according to the preoccupations which ruled them. To that Macdonald, any and every means to win elections and to keep the Conservatives in power could be, and were, used. He knew the stupidities, loyalties, and overpowering prejudices of the common man. Like every master politician, he cajoled, flattered, browbeat, and herded the mass, knowing that to win elections the appeal must be not to reason but to emotions. No Canadian, before or since, has been so capable of reconciling warring prejudices or of harmonizing incompatibilities.

Yet there was another Macdonald. That Macdonald had an over-all vision and dream of the Canadian future. It was this Macdonald who, in spite of errors implicit in his cynicism or in his belief that time would solve all problems, founded the Liberal-Conservative party and became the architect of Confederation and dreamed the transcontinental. Yet these contributions, which founded and shaped the Dominion, would not have been possible without Macdonald the master manipulator. One facet was necessary to the other.

And then, to Macdonald the domestic man and the politician and the statesman must be added the Macdonald who was the great nonconformist, the urbane cosmopolitan, the civilized non-hypocritical Canadian who regarded dogmas and doctrines as the caves in which his average compatriot took refuge from reality and his own inadequacies. This was the Macdonald who forced a stodgy and bourgeois Canada to accept his bottle and his earthy stories and to vote for him nonetheless.

But now he was dead. An epoch was ended. The throne was vacant. Who would fill it? Four baronets tried it—Sir John Abbott (the former solicitor of Sir Hugh Allan of Pacific Scandal fame), Sir John Thompson, a convert to Roman Catholicism who died in 1894 while in London, Sir Mackenzie Bowell, former Grand Master of the Orange Order, and, finally, in a last effort to maintain Conservative hegemony, the old lion, Sir Charles Tupper. In the wings waited the true successor, Wilfrid Laurier.

ERRATA

Page 414, line 35, for Tennyson, read, Browning.

CHAPTER XXXII

1891–1900

The Rise of Laurier—Separate Schools in Manitoba Dish the Conservatives—The "Ministry of All the Talents"—Queen Victoria's Diamond Jubilee—Canada and the Boer War

1

JOHN A. MACDONALD, the Scot Canadian, had erected the grand but unfinished design of a Dominion from the Atlantic to the Pacific. It was left to Wilfrid Laurier, the French Canadian, to complete the structure. Unlike John A., a migrant to Kingston at the age of five, the man who was to be the new master of Canada had his roots thrust deep into Canadian soil.

In that stout Carignan-Salières Regiment which had come to New France in 1665, there had been a François Cottineau, *dit* Champ-Lauriers, possibly because of an ancestral field of *lauriers* in his homeland. From him young Laurier was the sixth-generation descendant.

Before his time the Lauriers, a prolific family, had hewed out habitations for themselves along the mouth of the Ottawa River. But Laurier's own father, Carolus, had settled on a farm newly cut from the forest near the frontier village of St. Lin at the foot of the Laurentian Hills to the north of Montreal.

Here on November 21, 1841, the future Prime Minister was born, not in a log cabin but in a home close enough to it to conform to the Canadian variant of the Lincolnesque myth. His childhood was a quiet one, fishing for trout, hunting for partridges and rabbits, roaming the as yet uncorrupted countryside, getting his primary schooling in the parish school at St. Lin. Fortunately for the young Laurier, there was in his French-Canadian father a streak of nonconformism. When the boy was eleven he was sent for two years to live in a Scottish settlement at New Glasgow, about eight miles west of St. Lin. Here he went to a co-educational school under, finally, an able teacher, Sandy Maclean, a man said to be almost as eager for the music of poetry as for his glass of whisky. The playground and the school taught Wilfrid Laurier that use of the English language which was to help fit him for the prime-ministership of double-tongued Canada. From Sandy Maclean he acquired a taste for English letters and British institutions. From his contact with the Murrays, a devout Presbyterian family, and others like them, he achieved a religious tolerance unusual for a Catholic of his period.

Thereafter, for seven years his training was at the College of L'Assomption. His schooling was in that same classical curriculum which had prepared John A. for leadership. The emphasis was on Latin, Greek, and French, though there was a certain dosage of English, mathematics, scholastic philosophy, history, and geography. Fortunately for young Laurier, vocational and exploratory subjects, with a nibble at each, had not yet cluttered up the program. What was taught was taught thoroughly and there was no wastage of time on courses in guidance or in the development of personality.

At the age of twenty he moved on to Montreal to study law. His father had a bias toward liberalism. Young Laurier was, therefore, articled to a firm headed by a prominent *Rouge,* Rodolphe Laflamme. As a brilliant student at McGill he became the class valedictorian. There followed a short time in a law office. Then, because of his health (Laurier, like John A., would never have qualified for a rugby football hero), at the advice of Antoine Dorion, the then leader of the Quebec *Rouges,* in 1886, the year before Confederation, he moved to the new settlement of Arthabaskaville in the Eastern Townships to practice law and edit *Le Défricheur.*

Here came his first definite brush with the Roman Catholic hierarchy. At L'Assomption he had caused headshakings among the good fathers by taking the affirmative on a resolution that the French kings ought to have permitted Huguenots to settle in Canada. In Montreal he had become a member and a vice-president of Bishop Bourget's bête noire, *L'Institut Canadien.* At Arthabaskaville, *Le Défricheur* fell under the ban of the priests and had to be discontinued. Laurier's counterblow in 1871 was to become Liberal M.P.P. for Arthabaskaville (John A. had been twenty-nine when he first became member for Kingston). It is significant that in this period of his career, when the Protestant Salvation Army made its first appearance in Quebec, and its drum beating was interfered with, Laurier, though a Roman Catholic M.P.P., announced: "The Army must be allowed to march; if necessary I will march at the head of its procession."

In that attitude was prefigured the Laurier who, in broad tolerance and love of liberty, could rise above race and creed. And in politics he had found his true vocation. By 1874 he was a Dominion member in Alexander Mackenzie's Liberal government.

Laurier supported amnesty for Riel. What soon made him prominent in Quebec, however, was his unswerving opposition to Bishop Bourget's ultramontanism. It was in 1875 that the joint pastoral, already referred to, of all the Quebec Catholic bishops gave the Catholic clergy authority to declare that to vote for a Liberal was a sin. In a by-election at Chambly a priest went so far as to declare to his congregation that "as Catholics you cannot . . . vote for a Liberal, nor for a moderate Liberal, for moderate is only another term for sin."

For a devout Catholic, as Laurier was, to speak out against the bishops took courage. In June of 1877 in an address to *Le Club Canadien* at Quebec City, he stated flatly that the right of ecclesiastical interference in politics ceased when it encroached on the voter's independence. It was a fitting tribute to this stand that in this same year he became Minister of Inland Revenue in the Mackenzie Cabinet.

The 1878 elections made this post as brief-lived as John A.'s first cabinet position in the 1844 Draper-Viger administration. But from this time forward, Laurier was the Liberal banner bearer in Quebec.

Riel's execution put him on the spot. Though in the Champs de Mars meeting he had taken an extremist position, in the House he was more statesmanlike. In two powerful speeches he pronounced a scathing indictment of government stupidity in dealing with the Northwest. At the end of the second address even the government benches, like the ranks of Tuscany, could "scarce forbear to cheer." Edward Blake, leader of the Liberals, stated that "it was the finest parliamentary speech ever pronounced in Canada since Confederation." The Conservative Thomas White declared:

"I think it is a matter of common pride to us that any man in Canada can make, on the floor of Parliament, such a speech as we listened to last night." Laurier's father and whisky-loving Sandy Maclean had both builded well.

Those silver-tongued speeches made it inevitable that, when Blake resigned the Liberal leadership in 1887, Laurier at the age of forty-five should take his place. The second of the great statesmen who dominated Canada in the nineteenth century and the first decade of the twentieth had stepped fully on stage. Even old John A. gazed at the French Canadian with a wary respect which he had never accorded the unexciting Blake.

Such was the making of the man who waited as the four Conservative successors to John A. tried vainly to put on the old master's boots and to don his mantle. The continuing depression made their efforts as pitiable as those of choristers in a freezing rain. But the Conservative ship finally foundered on that perennial and dangerous rock in all Canadian politics, the religio-racial reef. The particular jagged point which pierced the vessel was the question of denominational schools in Manitoba.

2

Those provinces, such as Nova Scotia and, later, New Brunswick, in which all schools supported by public funds were nonsectarian were fortunate. In Manitoba denominational schools, though not demanded by the List of Rights drawn up by the February 1870 Riel convention, had been thrust into the negotiations at Ottawa by Father Ritchot. In consequence, in the Manitoba Act, not only had French been made an official language along with English but, though the province had been given control of its own educational policy, there had also been a proviso that no law should be passed to prejudice any right or privilege with respect to the denominational schools which any class of persons had by law or practice at the time of the union.

The proviso was, in actuality, to insure that Roman Catholic Separate Schools would be supported by public funds. A further safeguard was a right of appeal to the Dominion government against any provincial act or decision affecting the privileges of any religious minority, Catholic or Protestant.

Thus, in Manitoba, as in Quebec, a sectarian system of education was set up with Catholic and Protestant schools dividing the funds for education according to the number of pupils of each faith.

Protestant schools, because of the differing sects, almost always became public schools. But in Manitoba, as in Quebec, the Roman Catholic clergy from the first achieved a tight control of their schools as places to instill the Roman Catholic faith. Over the years, however, immigration made Manitoba predominantly English-speaking and Protestant.

Then came the Jesuit Estates Bill in Quebec and the Equal Rights Association in Ontario. In 1888 its leader, McCarthy, as has been recorded, carried his campaign against French-Catholic influence into Manitoba and the Northwest.

His speeches fanned a fire already smoldering. In the Northwest Territories, where the issue turned on the official use of the French language, the final compromise was that, apart from the courts and the territorial ordinances, where French was still to be used, the Northwest Assembly could decide the language of its own debates and records.

Manitoba had more power and could go further. In 1890, under Mr. Greenway's Liberal administration, by a provincial statute French was abolished as an official language and a single system of state-supported, nonsectarian schools as in Nova Scotia was instituted, though it was provided that nondenominational religious teaching could be given during school hours.

The Roman Catholic hierarchies of Manitoba and Quebec hit the ceiling and climbed all over it. They demanded that the Manitoba Schools Act be disallowed. John A., at this time still the helmsman, gained time, as usual, by suggesting that the act be tested in the courts.

When all the moves and countermoves had been ground through the slow-moving mills of legality, the final decision by the Privy Council was that, though the period for disallowance of the act was long past, the Dominion government could receive an appeal from the Roman Catholics of Manitoba and, if it wished, could pass "remedial legislation" to put Separate Schools back into the province. This was during the regime of Mackenzie Bowell. As a former Grand Master of the Orange Order, his strength rested on Protestant Ontario. Yet he was asked to coerce a Protestant Manitoba government in favor of a Roman Catholic minority of 20,000 in a population of 150,000. On March 21, 1895, he fell into the trap. He issued an order in council instructing

Manitoba to restore to its Roman Catholics their Separate Schools with the right to share proportionately in the public funds and to be exempted from taxation for any other schools. In June, Manitoba refused to obey.

The stiffest voice for disobedience was that of Manitoba's Attorney General, Clifford Sifton. Behind him lay a family history of Irish Protestantism and Brownite anti-popery. His father, an ardent follower of George Brown, after various business ventures had in 1881 settled down near Brandon as a farmer. Young Clifford, heir to a Protestantism as militant as Quebec and Manitoba Roman Catholicism, graduated from Victoria College in 1880 at the age of nineteen as gold-medalist in mathematics and class valedictorian. Two years later he began to practice law in Brandon. A tall, fair young man, intelligent and a convincing speaker, the early West was tailored for his talents. In July of 1888, at the age of twenty-seven, he was elected as a Liberal to a Manitoba legislature in which the Liberals held twenty-eight of thirty-eight seats and Thomas Greenway was Premier. By May of 1891 Sifton had shouldered Joseph Martin out of the attorney-generalship.

What with disputes over railways, the schools question, and a strong opposition led by an ex-Liberal, R. P. Roblin (grandfather of the present Premier of Manitoba), both Sifton and the Manitoba government sat on a hot seat. But Sifton was insistent that Manitoba had the right to determine its own educational policy, particularly since denominational schools had been foisted on the province by Father Ritchot's secret list of rights. Furthermore, the province argued, if Roman Catholics were to have the right to levy on the public funds for their denominational schools, then that right must be extended not only to Anglicans, Presbyterians, Methodists, and Baptists, but to Mennonites, Lutherans, and every other Christian sect.

So the fiat of the Dominion government to restore denominational schools was refused. Mackenzie Bowell then gave Manitoba until January of 1896 to reconsider its refusal under the threat of remedial legislation. In December of 1895 the Manitoba government appealed to its electorate on the question. The government got a thumping majority. Only five opposition members survived the debacle. Manitoba had declared for the second time (the first was in the 1892 provincial election) in the most definite of terms that nonsectarian public schools were what it wanted on its educational platter.

One might have thought that this election would have settled the question. By this time, however, the evil spirit of religio-racial strife had been conjured up. Apart from the extreme language used by the Catholics of Manitoba, the hierarchy in Quebec, always more Roman Catholic than the Pope, would not listen to anything but unreason. On the other side, Ontario Protestants, already unhappy over the encroachments of Separate Schools in their own province, rose up in wrath.

Mackenzie Bowell was, as John A. had so often been, in the middle. With Riel, John A. had grasped the Quebec nettle. Mackenzie Bowell, though Orangeman and Protestant, decided to close his hand tight around the Ontario-Manitoba thorn; even though his government, by the constitution, had to go to the country by April 25, 1896. One may well ask why. John A. would certainly have managed delay. Mackenzie Bowell, though a Protestant, appears to have been convinced that the Roman Catholic minority of Manitoba was in the right. In the early part of 1896 he tried to push through the Dominion House a remedial bill to re-establish, in effect, Roman Catholic Separate Schools in Manitoba.

Bowell found that he had bit off more than Conservative unity could chew. Seven members of his Cabinet revolted. Bowell tried to form a ministry without them. The seven rebels picketed possible candidates and even put surveillance on trains reaching Ottawa to make sure that no cabinet strikebreakers came rushing in. At last, Sir Charles Tupper was recalled from his high-commissionership in London to take charge. He tried to bull through the bill and ran into insurgent Conservatives and Laurier.

Laurier himself squirmed on a prickly seat. Fourteen Catholic Liberals from Quebec bolted his party over the remedial bill. There was also heavy pressure on him from the hierarchy. A letter from Father Lacombe, the famous western missionary, speaking for the Roman Catholic bishops, was sent to him and published throughout Canada. That letter warned Laurier that if the Conservatives were overthrown over the remedial bill, "the episcopacy, like one man, united to the clergy, will rise to support those who have fallen to defend us.'"

The threat was clear. The Laurier who had objected to ecclesiastical interference with a voter's independence refused to allow the hierarchy to dictate to him in things political. In Parliament, after referring to the threats he had received, he pointed out that, as leader of the Liberal party, he represented "not Roman Catholics alone but Protestants as well" and declared that his stand would be one which could appeal "to the consciences of all men." Then, instead of any equivocal amendment, he moved a six months' hoist of the remedial bill, a motion tantamount to a rejection of it. At that moment Laurier proved his greatness. In what affected Canada as a whole, he was a Canadian first and a Roman Catholic second.

His stand, combined with the revolt in his own ranks, forced Tupper into an election.

3

Seldom has there been as topsy-turvy a scene in Canada as the 1896 election. The Conservatives, whose stronghold was Protestant Ontario, were upholding the coercion of a Protestant Manitoba; Laurier, a French Canadian and a Catholic, was opposing that coercion, his argument being that a sunny smile could achieve more than a cold north wind. To make it still more an "Alice Through the Looking-Glass" sort of campaign, the Roman Catholic hierarchy was supporting the Orangeman, Bowell, and the Protestant, Tupper, and pouring out their wrath upon the Catholic French Canadian, Laurier. Bishop Laflèche, the ultramontanist of Three Rivers, declared that no Catholic could, without sin, vote for Laurier. Archbishop Langevin of Winnipeg called on every true son of the Catholic Church to stand by the Conservatives. A *mandement* was even read ordering the faithful to vote *Bleu.*

Would Quebec follow the hierarchy? That was the key question. When the votes were counted the French Canadian proved that race counted more than creed; and, possibly, some French Catholics were weary of the long attempt of their church to dictate their politics. From Quebec's 65 seats, 49 Liberals were returned; while in Ontario only 43 Conservatives were elected. Manitoba, ironically, went Conservative by 4 seats to 3. But the rest of the West turned to the Liberals, and the Maritimes broke even. There was a clear majority, 118 seats out of 213. Laurier, by courage, had led the Liberals out of the dark swamps of opposition into the cheerful seats of power.

What was he like—this new master magician? When, in August 1896, Parliament met, the curious saw a neat, clean-shaven man with silver hair fluffed back on either side of a bald domelike head. He was elegantly—in fact, almost fastidiously—dressed. His eyes were alert, his mouth sensitive and mobile. About him like a mantle was flung an aura of aloofness. There was in Laurier none of John A.'s "soft sawder" or jaunty earthiness. No one ever saw him as other than a courtly gentleman; and his private life was equally dignified and reserved. He was almost an adult Little Lord Fauntleroy; except that he radiated a special and enthralling charm.

Yet there was nothing Fauntleroyish about his management of either the Liberal party or the Dominion. As time went by, his colleagues were to discover that he was as stubborn and as calculating as Sir John. Like John A. and Pericles, he was more interested in the broad vision than in the details, in moderation and compromise than in the stand-or-fall convictions of men of lesser intelligence. There was also a touch of "Old Tomorrow" in his belief in the healing value of time and in his fondness for old faces and old loyalties. But he could be ruthless when he deemed it necessary, and anyone who challenged his control of his party met short shrift. What made him most similar to Macdonald was that Laurier, too, was a passionate nationalist.

The first task was to find a solution to the Manitoba school question. It was quickly achieved. The province itself amended its school legislation. The provisions were that:

(*a*) Religious teaching could be given in the last half hour of any school day by any religious denomination on days to be arranged, if this was authorized by the trustees or requested by the parents of a specified minimum of children—but children of other faiths than the one being taught were not required to stay.

(*b*) Wherever there were in rural school districts 25 Roman Catholic children and in urban schools 40, on petition a Catholic teacher was to be hired. The same rule applied to Protestants.

(*c*) If ten pupils spoke French or any other language than English as their native tongue, a bilingual teacher was to be hired.

To the Roman Catholic hierarchy, these concessions were dry crusts. Their onslaughts on Laurier grew more and more virulent. Finally, a number of Catholic Liberals appealed over the heads of the bishops to Rome. The Vatican, as a rule, knows when to compromise or retreat. A papal envoy, Monsignor Merry del Val, was sent over. Charming and of Spanish descent, this prelate soon told the bishops, gently but firmly, to pull in their horns. A papal pronunciamento forbidding further overt participation in Canadian politics was issued. The Roman Catholic civil war was ended.

Meanwhile, Laurier had assembled what was called the "Ministry of All the Talents," a ministry in which, by the way, besides the clean-shaven Laurier, there were three who wore only mustaches. For, after a century of concealment, men's faces were coming out of hiding.

In that Cabinet were three provincial premiers—John A.'s old opponent, Mowat of Ontario, Fielding, the Nova Scotian secessionist, and Blair, his coadjutor from New Brunswick. In this way the Liberals of those provinces were welded into the Laurier machine.

Notable among the other members were William Mulock, the dignified jurist from Ontario, and Clifford Sifton, Manitoba's strong man. A place was found for the venerable Sir Richard Cartwright. He expected the portfolio of Minister of Finance. That plum went to Fielding. For Cartwright back in 1891 had come out for Commercial Union and Laurier was shrewd enough to make peace with the Canadian Manufacturers' Association, the C.P.R., and the Bank of Montreal. The Liberals had, as late as 1893, pronounced against any kind of protection. They now settled for Galt's pious hypocrisy of 1859, "Tariff for Revenue." In the April 1897 budget, as a sop to the farmers, duties on binder twine, barbed wire, and Indian corn were abolished; tariffs on flour and sugar and some agricultural implements (but not on expensive mowers and binders) were reduced; and a provision was included to lower the protection on goods controlled by trusts and combines. What was even more pointed, the reference to a possible reciprocity with the United States, always a part of previous budgets, was omitted. The Free Trade Liberals, now that they were in power, had recognized the facts of life. They had been converted, overnight, to "National Policy."

Another straw to show the reconciliation of the Liberals with the C.P.R. and, for that matter, with Canada's bankers and industrialists, was their confirmation, in his seventy-sixth year, of Sir Donald Smith as Canada's new high commissioner in London. Meantime, in the same budget of 1897, the Liberals, the party which had been accused of desiring annexation to the States, made provision for a preferential tariff, a reduction finally of 25 per cent, for imports from Great Britain. That gesture coincided with Queen Victoria's Diamond Jubilee.

4

The Diamond Jubilee was the apotheosis of Queen Victoria. It was also the last great magnificence of the second British Empire. For almost the last time, everything was for the British best in a world dominated by the *Pax Britannica.* To London in those early summer days of 1897 came Hindu potentates, African princes, queens and kings from the Pacific islands, and the Prime Ministers of the self-governing colonies. Through its streets surged every color and nationality from Britain's far-flung possessions. There were dinners, receptions, addresses, and reviews of troops. Donald Smith was raised to the peerage as Lord Strathcona and Mount Royal, and Laurier became Sir Wilfrid Laurier. In the great Jubilee Procession a picked Canadian contingent of scarlet-coated Mounties, Denison's Governor General's Body Guard Cavalry, Canadian Grenadiers and Highlanders marched behind Sir Wilfrid though London's crowded and cheering throngs.

The Empire was at its blazoned peak. Behind the brilliance and the feasting the Colonial Secretary, Joseph Chamberlain, the arch-priest of the new imperialism, was conducting the third Colonial Conference. His objectives were clear. He was eager for a close-knit Empire, one tied together by a unified defense system, a customs union, and an Imperial Council; and the key to this golden dream was Canada's Prime Minister, Sir Wilfrid Laurier. In these days Canada was courted as never before. "With Canada's lead," pronounced the London *Daily Mail,* "we stand at the threshold of a new epoch in the history of the Empire."

It was a long shout and a holler from the days of the Little Englanders. The course of history might well have been greatly changed if Chamberlain had won. Though Laurier in public spoke expansively once or twice of an over-all Imperial Council, in the conference itself, when it came to putting on the shoe, he preferred, like John A., Canadian autonomy to centralization. What he and the other Prime Ministers were fumbling toward was a union, under the symbol of the Crown, of a commonwealth of free and self-governing nations. Chamberlain did not cease his attempts. Yet his failure to win his dream in the year of Queen Victoria's Diamond Jubilee was never to be retrieved; and it is possible that what finally determined Laurier's stand was the thought of French-Canadian votes.

What was achieved was agreement on a Pacific cable, penny postage throughout the Empire (though in Canada the penny has now become five cents), and an arrangement to restrict immigration from Asia. Yet the glittering pageant of the Empire on parade and the attention paid to him, a French Canadian, does seem to have confirmed Laurier's belief in British institutions. Two years later the Boer War was to test the ties the Diamond Jubilee had forged.

To Canada's oldest generation of today, the Boer War is yesterday's newspaper. They may not remember Majuba Hill in 1881, when the Boers won independence for the Transvaal and the Orange Free State, or the Cecil Rhodes-inspired Jameson Raid of 1895–96 or too much about the discovery of gold at Johannesburg or of the refusal of the franchise to the "Uitlanders" who paid the taxes. But from 1899 to 1902, Kruger, Cronje, "Slim" Joubert, Botha, and De Wet were household names. So were Buller, Baden-Powell, and Lord Roberts, as well as Kimberley, Ladysmith, and Mafeking and the battles at the Modder River, the Tugela, and Paardeberg. For this was the first Imperial war in which Canadians took part as a Dominion force.

The Boer War was the attempt of a patriarchal, Old Testament people to dam the tide of expanding British commercialism. At the time few in the Empire saw it as such. French Canada shrugged its shoulders and turned back to its farms and its church bells. To Anglo-Canada, it was a clarion call to patriotism. For, when war erupted on October 9, 1899, with an ultimatum to Britain from Paul Kruger, President of the Transvaal, British forces in Natal and Cape Colony were, as usual, inadequate. In no time at all, British territory was invaded, and Mafeking, Ladysmith, and Kimberley were under siege. Press and public, outside of Quebec, demanded that Canada send a contingent.

When in 1884 Britain had asked for a Canadian contingent in the expedition which was too late to save Chinese Gordon at Khartoum, all John A. would do was to permit the Mother Country to recruit in Canada at her own expense. The final upshot had been 400 voyageurs, chiefly French Canadians, to help transport Wolseley's expedition up the Nile.

But 1884 was not 1899. Laurier looked about him. In French Canada, at the first suggestion of a contingent, apathy turned to bitter opposition. The habitant in 1812 had proved that he would fight, and fight well, in defense of his own country. When it came to Britain's wars, there was no pull of blood to stir his pulse. As in World Wars I and II, so in 1899 French Canada could almost have doubled for Ireland's "Ourselves Alone."

But Anglo-Canada was aflame. Once again Laurier decided that the majority should rule. Within three days after the declaration of hostilities, a Canadian contingent was authorized. What John A., the Scot Canadian, had refused, Laurier, the French Canadian, gave. On October 30, only twenty-one days after Kruger's ultimatum, the Second Royal Regiment left Quebec on the Allan liner *Sardinian*. It was a sunlit day. On the docks a huge crowd was waving handkerchiefs and flags and singing "God Save the Queen." The troops waved back, filled with a sense of excitement and high adventure. Cape Diamond stood out bright and clear as the vessel pulled away. There were puffs of smoke and dull thuds as the guns of the citadel slammed a salute. The whistles and sirens of the river craft shrieked and hooted. Tugs and boats bedecked with flags escorted the *Sardinian* down the St. Lawrence; and its shores were daubed with the crimson and gold of autumn beech and maple. In that small contingent was the prelude to the Canadian soldiers of World Wars I and II.

It was the expression of a dawning nationhood. In French Canada, however, the sailing of the *Sardinian* revivified its own characteristic "nationalism." At Ottawa, Henri Bourassa, the ultramontane grandson of the fiery old rebel and anticlerical Papineau, resigned his federal seat in protest. In the ensuing by-election he was returned by acclamation. Soon he had resurrected Mercier's *Parti National*.

Laurier did not listen to the Bourassa threat. A week after the first contingent sailed a second was authorized. This time a regiment of Mounted Rifles and three batteries of artillery sailed off. For already it was clear that the war would be no picnic excursion. The Boers, tough mounted riflemen, knew the country and what they were fighting for. In the "black week" of December 1899, the armies attempting to relieve Ladysmith and Kimberley were defeated, as was the force defending Cape Colony. The most serious check was the Boer victory at the Tugela River over General Sir Redvers Buller, the same Buller who in 1870 had accompanied the Wolseley expedition to Red River. Boer marksmen, in a natural position of great strength, cut down the British troops moving, as in the American Revolutionary War, straight forward in frontal attack across the river and up the hills on the other side.

The Boer victories made Europe snicker. The German Kaiser sent congratulations to Kruger. The United States, which had just finished its Spanish-American War, owed Great Britain a debt of gratitude for its help against German interference and kept reasonably quiet. Throughout the Empire, however, a wave of unreasoning patriotism stirred. Lord Roberts, a quick, active man, who had made his name in the Afghanistan War of 1879–81, was appointed commander in chief, with the six-foot phlegmatic Lord Kitchener of Omdurman fame as his chief of staff. Troops, and among them Australians and New Zealanders, as well as Canadians, poured into South Africa. British generals learned new tactics the hard way. In Canada a battalion of infantry was raised to garrison Halifax and to release the Leinster regiment. Out of his immense wealth, Donald Smith, Lord Strathcona, contributed the funds to raise and send the Strathcona Horse, a force of picked men drawn chiefly from the West.

In all, Canada sent over some 7300 men, all volunteers. Sir Arthur Conan Doyle spoke of Smith-Dorrien's 19th Brigade, of which a Canadian regiment formed a part, as "probably the very finest brigade in the whole army." After the decisive engagement at Paardeberg, Lord Roberts reported that "a most dashing advance made by the Canadian Regiment and some engineers . . . apparently clinched matters."

The surrender of Cronje's army at Paardeberg on February 27, 1900, settled the war. The great emotional release came in June on "Mafeking Night," when the news of the relief of that beleaguered town lighted bonfires from Melbourne to London to Toronto and Vancouver.

With the relief of Mafeking the war of pitched battles was over. Brave Boer commandos, led by Botha, Smuts, De Wet, and De La Rey, kept the struggle going for another two years. At last, by the May 1902 Peace of Vereeniging, the Boers became British subjects. Seven years later the Union of South Africa was a self-governing Dominion, and a Boer, General Botha, was its Prime Minister.

It was on January 22, 1901, when the Boer War had degenerated into guerrilla raids, that Queen Victoria died. She had become as much of an institution in the Empire as John A. Macdonald, in a smaller sphere, had been in Canada. With her death, a world epoch ended. Before her accession in 1837, there had been a drift toward republicanism in Great Britain. At the end of her reign, the monarchy was once more firmly established.

It was a new type of monarchy. Although Queen Victoria had never hesitated to express definite opinions to her ministers on all public questions, she had abandoned the attempt of her predecessors to govern. Parliament now ruled, and the monarchy was on its way to becoming a beloved symbol of unity. In its withdrawal was its salvation.

But if the monarchy had retreated from the political sphere, Queen Victoria's impact on the mores of the age had been all the more notable. Gone were the open crudities and bawdiness of the Georges and the Williams. As the years went by, Victorian respectability clamped down more and more firmly. This did not mean that there was the less bawdiness. But it and its ribald companions were swept under the rug. In the Victorian era the outward appearance was what mattered. It was with almost a sigh of relief that England, when Edward the Seventh came to the throne, at first surreptitiously and then more openly, loosened the tight stays of its Victorian corsets.

In 1900, however, the Queen still lived, and in Anglo-Canada there was a thrill of vicarious pride at the achievements of her volunteer troops, fittingly blown up by a clamant press. With the long leagues of sea between, there was little realization of the sun-baked battlefields or of the angry whine of Boer bullets smacking into living flesh or of typhoid killing off the troops as if they were unconsidered amoebae. What Anglo-Canada saw was the proof that her sons were as good soldiers on an Imperial battleground as any in the Empire, including the British themselves. It is a curious commentary on humanity and human affairs that war, more than any other human event, appears to be the best fertilizer for a nascent nationhood. It was in the midst of this surging pride that Laurier's government went to the polls.

In Quebec the Bourassa extremists attacked Laurier viciously for participation in Britain's wars. In Ontario, the leader of the Conservatives, Sir Charles Tupper, still vigorous though he was in his eighties, assailed the French Canadian as anti-British, while in Quebec he declared that Laurier was "too English for me."

But the sun was shining brightly for Sir Wilfrid. For by 1898, abruptly, the long winter of depression, which had lifted briefly in 1889 to 1891 only to settle down still more frigidly, had been replaced by the surging warmth of prosperity; and that boom showed no signs of lessening. For the first time there were evidences of a real influx into the Canadian West; while the famous Yukon gold rush was by now in full spate. The Liberals lost fourteen seats in Ontario. They gained in the Maritimes, in the West, and even in Quebec. Laurier went back with an increased majority.

Their defeat made the Conservatives change horses. Tupper was replaced by another Nova Scotian, Robert Laird Borden, a direct, heavily mustached man, who was to prove a forceful antagonist. The age of Laurier, however, was firmly established. In his first term he had faced the Imperial Conference and the Boer War and had emerged from both with a strengthened Canadian nationalism. In his second lease of power, he had to grapple with the other menace to Canadian nationhood, the Republic to the south.

The problem was the long dispute about the Alaska boundary. What brought that dispute to the soreness of a boil was the gold rush to the Yukon.

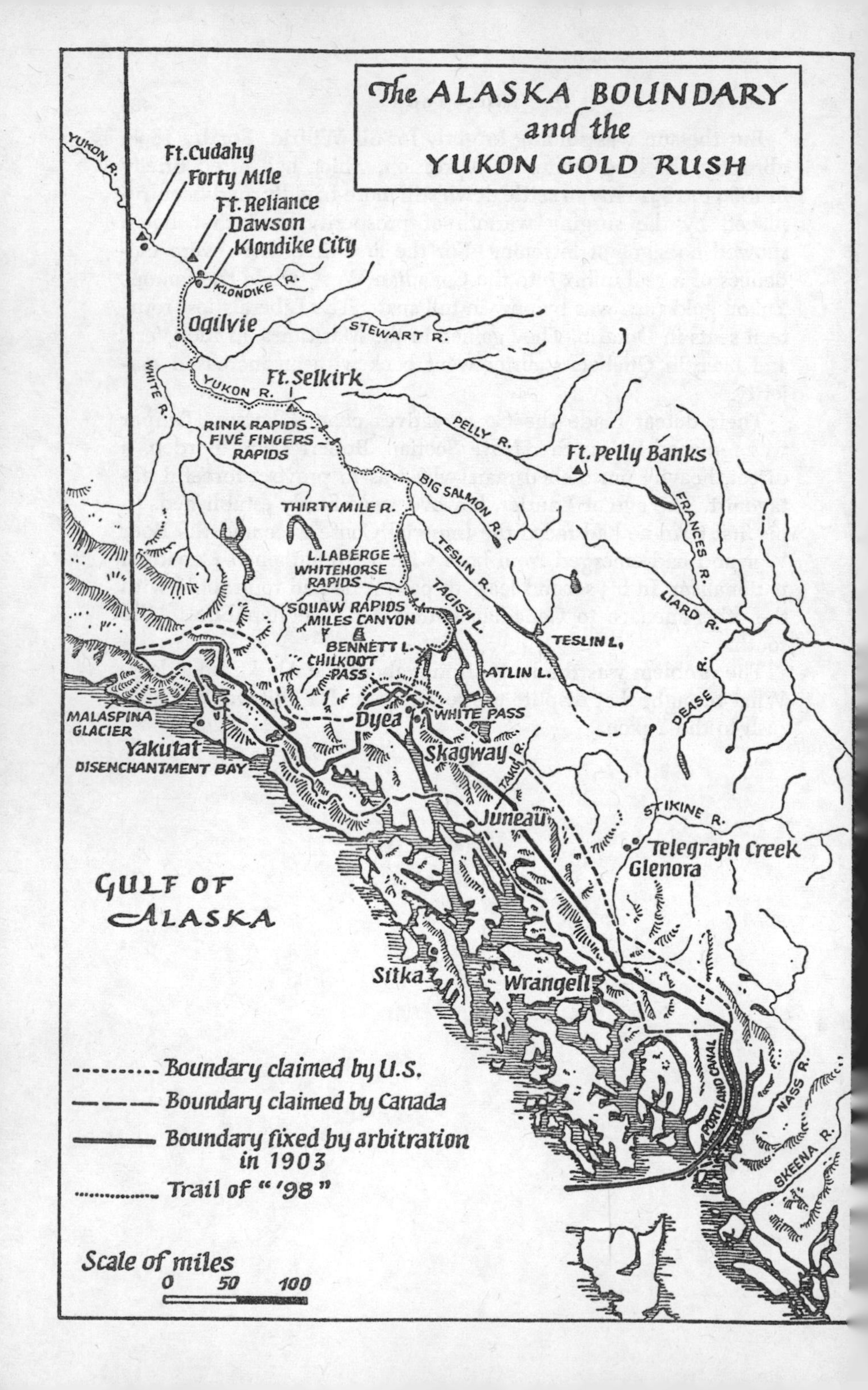
The ALASKA BOUNDARY and the YUKON GOLD RUSH
YUKON R.
Ft. Cudahy
Forty Mile
Ft. Reliance
Dawson
Klondike City
KLONDIKE R.
Ogilvie
STEWART R.
WHITE R.
Ft. Selkirk
YUKON R.
PELLY R.
RINK RAPIDS
FIVE FINGERS RAPIDS
Ft. Pelly Banks
BIG SALMON R.
THIRTY MILE R.
FRANCES R.
TESLIN R.
L. LABERGE
WHITEHORSE RAPIDS
TAGISH L.
LIARD R.
SQUAW RAPIDS
MILES CANYON
TESLIN L.
BENNETT L.
CHILKOOT PASS
ATLIN L.
MALASPINA GLACIER
Dyea
WHITE PASS
DEASE R.
Yakutat
DISENCHANTMENT BAY
Skagway
TAKU R.
Juneau
STIKINE R.
Telegraph Creek
Glenora
GULF OF ALASKA
Sitka
Wrangell
Boundary claimed by U.S.
Boundary claimed by Canada
Boundary fixed by arbitration in 1903
Trail of "'98"
PORTLAND CANAL
NASS R.
SKEENA R.
Scale of miles
0 50 100

CHAPTER XXXIII

1896–98

The Mounties Come to the Yukon–Klondike Gold–The Gold Rush of '97–Sifton and the Alaska Boundary–The Winter of 1897–98 at Dawson–"Soapy" Smith at Skagway

1

THE Yukon is a wedge-shaped segment of the frozen North. Its base rests on the 60th parallel and the rugged northern frontier of British Columbia. Its tip touches the Arctic Ocean. To the east are the Northwest Territories and the great Mackenzie River plunging toward Aklavik and Coronation Gulf. On its western flank American Alaska hems it in.

Here, for two months a brief, hot summer flares. There are another two to three months of spring and autumn. For the rest of the year, the desolate wastes and barren peaks and tree-snapping cold make it, veritably, the land "God gave to Cain." In early days the ubiquitous H.B.C. had planted a few posts in it. After Seward's 1867 purchase of Alaska, the Company and Canada, too, seemed content to leave the Yukon to the wolves, to the scattered bands of Eskimos and Indians, to the Alaska Commercial Company, and to the gaunt-eyed, hollow-cheeked prospectors who panned its creeks and rivers.

World War II drove the Alaska Highway northwestward from Edmonton to cut through British Columbia to Whitehorse and Fairbanks. In the eighties and nineties, however, the highway—and that only from the breakup of the ice in late May to the freeze-up in October—was the Yukon River.

That river's sources are but a mere fifteen miles from the splash of Pacific tidal waters on the beaches at Dyea and Skagway at the tip of the almost hundred-mile fiord of the Lynn Canal. Yet to find salt water it courses north and then westward through the Yukon and Alaska for some 2500 miles. At last, fed into a mighty stream by tributary after tributary, it pours into the ice-cold Bering Sea. Some seventy miles north of its mouth on an island is St. Michael, its port of entry.

In the days before the Alaska Highway, the river was the front door to the Alaska and the Yukon. There was also a backdoor approach over the passes from Dyea and Skagway to the upper reaches of the same stream.

Until August 1896 and George Carmack, however, the Yukon remained unwanted and more or less unknown. True, as early as 1887, the stalwart, incorruptible William Ogilvie, sent in by the Dominion to survey the boundary between Alaska and the Yukon, reported that there were some three hundred prospectors, chiefly Americans, just inside the Canadian frontier, either at Forty Mile Creek or further upstream. By 1893, too, the posts of two rival companies perched along the river. The old established one, the Alaska Commercial Company, with headquarters in San Francisco, was represented, more or less loosely, by Harper, Mayo, McQuesten, and a French Canadian from New York State, Joe Ladue. In charge of the other, the newly formed North American Trading Company, roosted that J. J. Healy who, years before, had, from Fort Benton, set up the Fort Whoop-up which had been the goal of the 1874 Mounties' westward trek.

The boats of these two companies were already churning up the Yukon for some 1500 miles to supply the mining camps. In 1894 a new gold strike at Birch Creek added to Forty Mile another center, 170 miles downstream from it, called Circle City.

It was a rough life and a lonely one at both Circle City and Forty Mile. There were saloons. There were dance halls. In the long winter, when the sun dipped down behind the horizon and stayed there, there were squaw dances and shootings and rough-and-tumble fights, and the only law was in the Miners' Meetings.

But in that same year of 1894 two Mounties, Captain Constantine, a thick-set "square-shooter," and Sergeant Brown, came to Forty Mile. Ogilvie's report to the Dominion, plus letters from Healy to Superintendent Sam Steele of the N.W.M.P. and from a Church of England bishop, William Bompas (a name which seems, somehow, suitable), to Ottawa, shared in bringing them in.

Their purpose was to assert Canadian authority to the disgruntled miners. What was still more galling, they collected customs dues on the traders' goods.

It was the first appearance of the law. The Mounties left and the miners sighed in relief. The next year, however, Captain Constantine found himself appointed Agent-General of the Yukon. Groaning, undoubtedly at malignant fate, with twenty officers and men, and Mrs. Constantine, he made the long journey by ocean steamer to the Yukon's mouth and thence by river boat up to Forty Mile. Logs cut sixty miles upstream were floated down to build a post close to the cluster of shanties and saloons. It was at that time the northernmost station in the British Empire. In the same year Ogilvie returned to his cold and prosaic job of surveying.

The Dominion government must have had a premonition. The story of Carmack's discovery of coarse free gold on Bonanza Creek on August 16 of 1896 has been told and retold. Carmack, whose first two names, George Washington, were, apparently, somewhat of a misnomer, was a sleepy-eyed, somewhat pudgy wanderer who had skipped ship at Dyea at the head of the Lynn Canal and had drifted into the Yukon. There he took to himself an Indian wife, a drooping Indian mustache, and the nickname of "Siwash George." Except for a gaunt, dour, mustached, unshaven Bluenose, he would probably have spent the rest of his life with his Indian friends, fishing for salmon, cutting saw logs, and packing loads over the Chilkoot Pass.

Henderson, the son of a lighthouse keeper on Big Island, off the north coast of Nova Scotia, was a dedicated prospector. For some twenty-three years he had lugged pick, shovel, and pan through New Zealand, Australia, Colorado, and Alaska before he drifted, in 1894, down the Pelly River into the Yukon. The yellow will-o'-the-wisp still evaded him. In the Yukon he was grubstaked by Joe Ladue, who was at this time, in loose association with Harper, running a trading post and saw mill at Ogilvie (named after the surveyor) near the point where Sixty Mile Creek joins the Yukon River.

For two years Henderson searched the creeks of the Indian River, one of the tributaries of the Yukon. To the north was a helmet-shaped hill called the Dome. The Creeks on its far side emptied into still another Yukon feeder, the Klondike, a name derived from the Indian name *Thron-diuck,* meaning "Hammer-water," called so because the Indians had hammered in stakes for nets across its mouth to catch the silver-scaled salmon that leaped in it. One day Henderson panned a creek on the other side of the Dome, found eight cents' worth of gold, called it Goldbottom in pathetic hope, and persuaded four other miners to join him.

By midsummer the five had $750 in gold. Henderson went to Ogilvie for supplies. On his return journey, because the Indian River was, at the moment, too shallow for his skin boat, he took the other route, via the Klondike.

By such accidents history is made. On the flats along the shore, busy at salmon fishing, were Carmack, his wife, and two Indian friends, Tagish (also called "No Good") Charlie and Skookum ("Strong") Jim. The second man deserved his nickname. Of him, Ogilvie, the Dominion surveyor, relates that he once packed 156 pounds in one load up the 35-degree slope of the Chilkoot Pass.

To Carmack, Henderson, after the custom of the country, gave an invitation to Goldbottom but added a dour remark about not wanting any Indians staking claims on it. He went on his way. About a score of days later, according to Ogilvie, who discussed the whole story with all four men, Carmack and his Indian friends set out for Goldbottom. By a second accident they traveled from the Klondike not by Goldbottom but by the nearer Rabbit Creek, two miles up from the mouth of the Klondike. Goldbottom, however, did not attract them, and Henderson refused tobacco to the Indians, though they offered to pay for it. Henderson also claimed later that he had advised Carmack to try Rabbit Creek for gold. In any case, on the way back, again more or less by chance, a half mile below the junction of Rabbit Creek with one which was soon to be called Eldorado, Carmack's party panned the gravel. In the bottom was four dollars' worth of gold. The three did a wild dance by the banks of the stream.

Then they staked claims. Skookum Jim stayed to guard them. Carmack and Tagish Charlie rushed to Forty Mile to Constantine's post to record them. En route he shouted his news to everyone he met. By the morning after his arrival Forty Mile was a deserted camp. Rabbit Creek was renamed Bonanza. No one thought to send word to the gaunt Henderson, working doggedly on Goldbottom Creek over the ridge.

It was to be a strike to out-Cariboo the Cariboo. From every nearby camp in the Yukon and Alaska the prospectors surged toward Bonanza. Within five days its narrow valley was a trampling mass of miners, staking claims or jumping them. The constables from Fort Cudahy near Forty Mile arrived early. Even Mountie discipline dissolved in the excitement of gold. Every redcoat staked (as they had a right to do) and most of them made fortunes. By the end of August practically the whole of Bonanza was claimed. A group of latecomers wandered up Bonanza's "pup." Each of the claims staked that day on that "pup," renamed Eldorado, was to produce more than a million dollars' worth of gold. Then, in September, Andrew Hunker found gold on Hunker's Creek, the other fork of Henderson's Goldbottom. As for Henderson, he only learned of the strikes when it was too late. He had missed fortune by a creek bed—and quite possibly because of his prejudice against Carmack's Indian friends.

It was, perhaps, symbolic that, though a Canadian and an American were co-discoverers of Klondike gold (Henderson later received a pension of $200 a month for his share in the find), it was the American who reaped and dissipated the fortune and the Canadian who was left out in the cold.

Ladue, the man who had grubstaked Henderson, was more fortunate. Hurriedly moving his goods and sawmill to the mouth of the Klondike, he and his partner, Harper, bought 178 acres of the mud flats on the north side of that river. In January 1897, Ogilvie laid out a townsite on those flats. It was titled Dawson, after the director of Canada's Geographical Survey.

From that townsite—with lots finally selling up to $12,000 apiece—his sawmill, and a saloon, Ladue reaped his share of the golden harvest, though, unfortunately, he was to die of tuberculosis in New York State in 1898. To make the irony more poignant, Ladue had returned to marry the sweetheart whose parents, years before, had refused his suit because of his poverty. The same plague had carried off his partner, Harper, in the previous year.

Meantime, in September of 1896, Carmack's "moose pasture" had not as yet been proved. The old-timers, the "sourdoughs," were skeptical. Only the top gravel at the edge of the creeks had been panned. To discover whether the claims had real value or not, shafts, as in the Cariboo, had to be sunk from fifteen to thirty feet to bedrock. In the Yukon, even in July and August, only about two feet of earth ever thaws. So the muck had to be shoveled away, and the ground heated by fires for digging, until the "pay dirt" was reached. A few pans would be washed. Most of the potential paydirt, however, had to be hauled up the shafts to wait in dumps until spring. Then, when the ice went out and the valleys became quagmires, it was time to put the dump through the rough wooden sluices to find out if one had hit fortune or not.

It was grueling work for an uncertain reward. Many of the sourdoughs hinted darkly at "skim" diggings—take off the top layer and then there would be nothing. This led to some strange quirks of chance. Half the fabulously rich claim "Thirty" on Eldorado, for instance, was sold for a sack of flour to "Big Alex" McDonald. From this and a hundred other ventures, he was to become for a space the "King of the Klondike," with $20,000,000 as his own, only to die, penniless, in a log cabin in the wilderness.

Similarly, "The Lucky Swede," Charlie Anderson, while on a drunk in Forty Mile, bought "Twenty-Nine" for $800. Next morning he tried to get his money back and failed. From that claim came over $100,000.

By a not so strange coincidence it was often the "cheechako," the tenderfoot, who made a fortune. There was, for instance, the handsome, wavy-haired Austrian, Stander, who discovered Eldorado, made his pile, and dissipated it on a dance-hall girl. His partner, Berry, died a millionaire.

Berry, a California fruit farmer, was, in 1896, making his second try at the Yukon. This time he had brought a bride with him to Forty Mile. Since his luck was out, he was working as a bartender when Carmack came in with news of his strike. Berry staked a claim on Bonanza. Later, he traded half of it for half of Stander's "Discovery" claim on Eldorado. That fall Berry reached bedrock. His first test pan gave him fifty-seven dollars. During that winter, as Berry's hired men dug out the prehistoric creek bottom which was Eldorado's wealth, Berry's bride, whenever she wanted money, simply washed a few pans from the dump and picked out the nuggets.

By the time November came the richness of the strike was proved. The miners from the nearby camps had already rushed in. In January, when the news reached downstream to Circle City in Alaska, it soon became Goldsmith's "Deserted Village," though of a far different vintage. In below-zero cold, its men and dogs strained over the four hundred desperate miles to Dawson. In the midst of that exodus was the dapper Tex Rickard, later to become synonymous with Madison Square Garden in New York. In that same month, too, at the miners' request Ogilvie made a survey of the claims on Bonanza and Eldorado.

That winter shacks and dump heaps multiplied along the snow-covered creeks like ugly excrescences and fire on fire sent up its smoky flames into the Arctic night as if this were another and a northern *Inferno*. Everywhere, men worked with tense excited faces, as if, in truth, each minute had sixty golden seconds. They lived on beans. They snatched fitful sleep in ice-cold cabins. In Dawson, close to 1500 men, isolated from the world as surely as if they rode an ice floe in the Arctic Ocean, crouched, eating their dogs and drinking whisky at fifty cents the glass. There was money. Berry's spring cleanup brought him $130,000. There was nothing to spend it on.

And then, on May 14, the ice went out. Two days later the first boats came in. For during the winter and spring the news of a strike in the Yukon had sifted along the river and over the passes. In a twinkling, Dawson City and "Lousetown" on the other bank of the Klondike became a forest of tents. The newcomers brought food. Bacon, worth in those primitive days eleven cents a pound, sold for seventy-five cents. Tea was priced at two dollars a pound, high even for today's inflation. When in June the first river boat steamed in bringing whisky and food, the whole raw town of some 2500 people went on a gigantic binge. Yet this rush was merely the prelude. For the great outside world did not, as yet, know of the Yukon.

2

"Gold! Gold! Gold! Gold!"

That was the headline splashed across the front page of the Seattle *Post-Intelligencer*. "Stacks of Yellow Metal!" was another. For reporters had gone out to meet the *Portland* off Cape Flattery, and on the *Portland* were sixty-eight miners from the Klondike with gold dust in their pokes. When the *Portland* docked on Saturday, July 17, 1897, it was greeted by a solid mass of humanity. Half in awe, half in envy, they watched as the gaunt, unshaven men came down the gangway, each toting, or having toted, his pile of gold. There was Ladue, the French Canadian. There was Berry, the erstwhile fruit farmer, with his $130,000. There was Mrs. Berry, who had brought out $10,000 in nuggets as souvenirs. All in all, close to two million dollars' worth of gold was aboard that ship.

Meanwhile, down at San Francisco, on July 14, another boat, the *Excelsior,* had already landed fifteen Klondikers. The crowd had followed them as they had shambled to Selby's Smelting Works on Montgomery Street. They laid half a million dollars' worth of dust and nuggets on the counter.

"The nuggets," the San Francisco *Call* related, "are reported as big as potatoes. A boy picked up one that weighed twenty-one pounds. It was worth $5,700."

Before such tales, even a Texan was seen to swallow twice and keep silent. "A Ton of Gold" was the headline that flashed across the United States and Canada and around the world. A rush to make even the Cariboo stampede seem a pallid Sunday-school excursion was in the making. For 1897 was the fourth year of the deepest slump the North American continent had so far seen. After a brief lift in 1890 and 1891, prices had plunged still lower. Gold was scarce, and it was in 1896 that Bryan had cried: "You shall not crucify mankind on a cross of gold."

Mankind was being crucified. There were millionaires and hobos. There were champagne baths for the gilded beauties of the nineties, but for "Coxey's army" of unemployed there was only a fruitless march on Washington. Both Canada and the United States seemed frozen, economically. Banks were failing, credit was nonexistent, and merchandise moldered on the shelves. The fog of depression, particularly in the western part of the continent, was thick and deep.

The news of the Klondike strike was like a yellow sun breaking through the fog. Klondike fever swept the continent as if carried on a roaring wind. It hit hardest in the United States, the traditional land for excesses. Livery-stable youngster, bank manager, milk-wagon driver, factory hand, businessman, mayor, college boy, teamster—butcher, baker, and candlestick maker—every mother's son and many a mother's daughter set their faces toward the Klondike. Those who could not go themselves strove to finance a partner. Those who prey on others—the con men, the dance-hall owners, the pimps, the gamblers, the thieves, the saloonkeepers—these, too, pulled up stakes with eyes set on a richer lode of profit. Among the first to move was the erstwhile crime king of Denver, the man who had won his sobriquet by selling soap bars which seemed to be wrapped in ten- or twenty-dollar bills to suckers for a dollar. There were others who stayed at home to form Klondike companies of all sorts and descriptions, such as the venture to travel to the Yukon by balloon.

Seattle and San Francisco were thronged. Goods moved. Prosperity returned in a blaze shed by Klondike gold. When the *Portland* sailed back for St. Michael, the port of entry for Alaska and the journey to the Yukon River, the passage rate had been upped from $200 to $1000. When the *Excelsior* pulled out from San Francisco, 10,000 people watched her steam through the Golden Gate.

Canada was not immune to the fever. From all over the East and West trainloads of gold seekers poured into Edmonton or Vancouver, or found their way by boat to Victoria. Stores as far east as Winnipeg were cleared of robes, picks, shovels, and the like. In the streets of Vancouver dog teams were trained for the frozen North, and robust men mingled with beardless youths and gold-crazed women. Some had tons of equipment; some had none. All along the Pacific coast of both the States and Canada every available horse or dog or mule or even elk and reindeer was bought for a pack animal. All along the coast, too, every ship that could swim was pushed into the water and loaded with gold seekers. Canada's new Minister of the Interior, Clifford Sifton, issued a warning that the Dominion would not be responsible for supplying the Yukon with food. The warning was as useless as a lone shout against a buffalo stampede.

The first mad rush, the rush of 1897, was on. Even in that year the frenzy reached out to Great Britain and Europe, to South America and the Orient. Before it died it was to bring men from almost every country and nation to the Klondike. And before it dissipated, too, the Klondike rush was to do its part in ushering the boom of the late nineties and early nineteen hundreds.

3

Meanwhile, all that summer of 1897, either by river steamer up the Yukon or by the route over the passes, gold seekers and dance-hall girls and eager searchers after profit came drifting into Dawson. The boats piled up three and four deep along the river front. Some three hundred rough shacks were flung together, but it was chiefly tents which spilled out over the flats. The Mounties, increased to 80, had put up a post. Later, a force of 150 Winnipeg constables was imported. There was a "Front Street" facing the Yukon, a street six inches deep in slime. Along it were hotels, stores, and a dozen saloons and gambling dens. Dance-hall girls, sharpers, adventurers, traders, bearded sourdoughs, and shaven cheechakos ebbed and flowed along it. Back of Front Street, in what came to be known as Paradise Alley, and over in Lousetown were the cribs of the prostitutes.

Behind all the feverish bustle in the land where the summer sun shone twenty hours in the day, and the mosquitoes and "no-see-ums" were a torment, was the yellow dust catching in the riffles of the sluices on Bonanza and Eldorado and the other creeks. The harpies, male and female, were eager for their share. Already in that summer the Northern Saloon—merely a plank floor with a tent covering—was taking in $3000 a day. "Why save?" the scornful Klondikers cried. "There's more where that came from."

Yet, though rough and tough, Dawson was never a wild West town with six-shooters blazing and desperadoes in control. For everywhere stalked the scarlet coats of the Mounties.

As in the British Columbia gold rush, it was a new experience for most of the incoming horde. The older prospectors, accustomed to United States regulations, with Miners' Meetings as the only justice, chafed and raged. By the summer of 1897, the Canadians had both a Gold Commissioner and a customs man at Dawson. The Americans protested the miners' licenses ($10 each) and the annual renewal fee (in 1897, $100, but later reduced to $15). They objected to the $15 recording fee. The royalty tax (10 per cent on the gross output of claims under $500 and 20 per cent if over that amount) left them almost speechless with fury, even when later the $500 limit for a 10 per cent tax was increased, first to $2500 and then, in March 1899, to $5000. Then there was the 100-foot frontage (later raised to 250 feet) of claims as compared with the American 500 feet, and the regulation that each man could stake only one claim in the whole Klondike area.

The Americans felt that they had moved from a man's world into a Sunday school. To turn the knife in their discontent, the Dominion also calmly collected from all incoming non-Canadians a 35 per cent import duty, on an average, on the goods they brought with them.

The Americans talked revolt. The Mounties went their way,

imperturbable. Clifford Sifton, the Minister of the Interior, was equally bland-faced. His attitude was that the Dominion was spending annually $396,000 on the Yukon, chiefly to maintain law and order, and deserved to have its expenditure recouped. The Americans might complain. But the Mounties, in one of their finest performances, kept the peace. All through the rush they let the dance halls and the gambling dens run wide open, except that on Sundays the gamblers were closed down. No man was allowed to carry a gun. Crimes were checked before they could blossom. Major offenders had to take the first boat out. Minor ones sweated on the woodpile. As in Victoria under Douglas, order was maintained.

By the summer of 1897, too, the Mounties had established customs posts on the Canadian side of the passes and at Lake Bennett where the trails from Dyea and Skagway converged. That summer nineteen boats were overset in the rough water below Lake Tagish and at least two hundred people were drowned.

On the orders of Canada's Minister of the Interior, the Mounties were that winter to move to the summits of the passes. For the Klondike gold strike had fanned the Alaskan Panhandle boundary dispute with the United States, which had been smoldering for some time, into a red-hot problem.

The line of that boundary depended upon the British-Russian treaty of 1825. That treaty, drafted in blithe ignorance of the terrain, presupposed a continuous range of mountains paralleling the coast along the Panhandle. Its decisive clause stated that if the summits of the mountains were more than ten marine leagues (about thirty-four and a half miles) from the shore, the boundary would follow the windings of the coast but "never exceed the distance of ten marine leagues therefrom."

There was no continuous range of peaks parallel to the coast; and that coast was deeply indented with fiords, some of which, as in the case of the Lynn Canal, reached as much as 100 miles inland. The United States controlled the coast. It demanded an unbroken strip of land following all the windings, a solution which would cut off Canada from the sea all along the Panhandle.

Canada might have agreed like the meek lamb the Republic expected her to be, had it not been for the Klondike. Now she wanted a port to give her a Pacific ingress to the Yukon. There was more than the gold involved. Victoria and Vancouver were battling against Seattle and San Francisco for trade to the new Eldorado. So Canada argued that there was a range of mountains which, though somewhat askew, was the one envisaged in the treaty. It also urged that "coast" meant the main Pacific coast and that, in consequence, the boundary ought to be a straight line, ten marine leagues from the Pacific Ocean itself but not from the indentations. Such a line would make the heads of the fiords Canadian and give her ports, and notably the ports of Dyea and Skagway.

The Americans in fact, however, if not in law, held these ports. Sifton assembled a group of officials for the Yukon—among them as commissioner that Major Walsh who had tamed Sitting Bull. Like a good general, however, he decided to see something of the problem for himself. In the last week of September 1897 the whole party set out from Ottawa for the long trek. On October 9 the government steamer *Quadra* disembarked them at Skagway.

The whole beach was already cluttered with the 1897 rush. Sifton looked up at the towering mountains. He decided to go in by the Chilkoot Pass. After moving past Lake Bennett as far as Lake Tagish, he left Major Walsh to set up posts and returned via the White Pass. Walsh himself, caught by the October freeze-up, was not to reach Dawson until June of the next year. Meantime, from Ottawa, in spite of the protests of Seattle and San Francisco, Sifton persuaded the American Government to allow customs subposts at Dyea and Skagway for the entrance of Canadian vessels, and for Canadian goods to be carried in bond to the Yukon border, though this second concession required a payment of $6 a day and expenses to an American escort. The Mounties, however, were permitted to pass freely back and forth over the passes. The boundary of the Yukon backdoor entrance was, however, still in dispute. The Americans claimed it was at Lake Bennett on the Yukon side of the passes. In the spring of 1898 they assembled a military force at Portland, intending to send it up to Skagway and over the passes to seize the territory in dispute. Sifton took a leaf from the American book. He dispatched secret orders to Superintendent Perry of the N.W.M.P. to hurry in Major Steele and forty men to plant outposts at the summits of the passes. This was done in February of 1898. "It would have taken twenty years of negotiating to get them [the Americans] out," he wrote on April 1 of that year to Commissioner Walsh. As it was, the American expedition never sailed.

4

And meantime, the rush of 1897 had hit the beaches at Skagway and Dyea like a tidal wave. Some of the passionate gold seekers, it is true, had taken the long way around by ocean steamer and river boat to the creeks of gold. The price of this journey was too high for most of the adventurers. They chose the "Poor Man's Route" for as low as $75 up the Pacific coast to the Lynn Canal. After its almost 100-mile well-nigh due-north plunge from the ocean, the Lynn Canal stretches out two searching fingers. The one to the left ends at Dyea at the outlet of the Dyea River; the other pauses at Skagway, which is set beside the mouth of the river of the same name. In front of both towers the mountain wall, notched by the two passes. The precipitous Chilkoot Pass faces Dyea. From Skagway the route is over the White Pass. The trails from both passes meet at Lake Lindeman. Thence most gold seekers went on to Lake Bennett, there to build boats for the 750-mile water road to Dawson.

Neither Dyea nor Skagway was equipped to handle the 1897 rush. At the former place, a mere Indian village, there was no wharf, and the goods—horses, sheep, dogs, goats, bales of hay, barrels of whisky, lumber, drums of kerosene, all the conglomeration which cupidity or inexperience had suggested to the adventurers—were tossed into the sea to swim, sink, or be carried in by the tide. On the narrow apron of the beach the gold seekers scrabbled for their gear.

Skagway, on the other arm, was, at first, the same story. But Skagway possessed a wider beach, and soon long fingers of wharves snaked out into the water. By the fall of 1897, however, both ports were a welter of tents, hotels, saloons, brothels, and gambling joints plunked down in the mud with dead horses underfoot and dogs everywhere—and there were no Mounties to keep the law.

From the feverish confusion on the beaches two long lines of men that autumn strove desperately to surmount the passes and reach Lake Bennett before the ice stopped the route to Dawson. Up the valley and through swamps and mudholes and canyons, a bobbing column of men and horses made for the trail that led around the precipitous flank of a hill, called Porcupine, to the summit of the White Pass. Each man had a ton of goods or more to freight—the year's supply of food, which the Mounties demanded; the saws, axes, and the like to build their boats; gold pans, shovels, picks, and quicksilver for the yellow fortune they expected to dig; furs, blankets, matches, and whatever fancy dictated. The horses were to pack this freight. They died in the mud-holes and bogs. They slipped from the narrow mountain trails. Soon the whole Skagway Trail was paved with the rotting carcasses of horses, some three thousand in all. Alongside that trail was scattered, like the debris of a routed army, pile after pile of the goods brought so many hundreds of miles and with such high hopes. Of five thousand men who tried the Skagway Trail that fall, barely a tenth reached Lake Bennett. Finally the trail was closed while men strove to slap a corduroy road into the mud and slime.

Hundreds of the defeated left for home. Other hundreds waited stubbornly until winter would make the trail passable again. Then, amid the falling snow, the black line of men and sleds began to plod forward again, like lemmings on their relentless march toward extinction. The supplies had to be moved forward in lots—usually for six miles at a stretch. This meant that for a ton of goods a man had to make about twenty trips for each six-mile stage. As the snow kept falling and was packed down on the trail, as anyone who has seen a road in winter in deep-snowed North Ontario will realize, the pathway rose, a hard and slippery ridge, above the deep drifts. A man could slide from it and stumble waist-deep in snow, losing his place in the solid, blank-eyed moving line and cursing his fate in helpless rage.

It was like the frenzy which, centuries before, had driven the hysteria-filled Children's Crusade to its fate, only this time the lure was the glitter of gold, not the splendor of the Cross. Over the precipitous Chilkoot Pass a still more frightening and frenzied traffic crowded. The Chilkoot was the shorter route. Up from the hand's breadth of beach at Dyea the trail led up the wooded river valley to the beginning of the mountain wall. From this point there was a frightening canyon and then a patch of woods. Thence the path zigzagged upward to the foot of the Chilkoot Pass.

That autumn and winter, ephemeral and roaring tent cities blossomed along the road to the hoped-for Eldorado—Canyon City, Pleasant Camp, and Sheep Camp, which was at the end of timber and at the base of the pass. When winter came, and snow and cold and blizzards with it, the traffic thickened. All along the roadway were hurrying men, each moving his ton of supplies antlike, inch by inch and foot by foot, until he got it from Dyea to the circular plateau on which Sheep Camp was planted. Among those men and in the three "cities" were professional packers, both Indian and white, cardsharpers and thieves, saloon and restaurant keepers, and the like. The would-be miners were, to them, a Promethean carcass which, picked bare, constantly renewed itself.

And then came the pass, rising up at a 35-degree slope. There was, finally, a cable-and-pulley arrangement to hoist goods to the summit. Few could afford this luxury. Most had to trudge up it, helped by 1500 steps cut in the ice and a rope. It took six hours, freighting from fifty to a hundred pounds on one's back, to make a single ascent. Then, piling the goods at the top, where a blizzard always seemed to blow, each man turned to slide, tobogganlike, to the bottom, prepared, like a second Sisyphus, to start the ascent again.

That line of bent figures, toiling upward against the white snow, became the trade-mark of the Trail of '98, the summation of what frenzied human endurance could achieve. There was a piano packed in bits and pieces over the Chilkoot Pass. Even more startling were the two steamboats and a sawmill freighted in sections over the trails. When Sophocles once wrote that there was nothing too difficult for men, he prefigured the Trail of '98. And along that trail that winter came another author, Jack London, with books in his kit instead of food and blankets. All in all, that fall and winter, some 22,000, almost all of them men, made the desperate journey up over the two passes.

5

Meanwhile the winter of 1897–98 had clamped down on Dawson City, isolating it once again from the outer world. The main tidal wave was still on the way. Yet enough of a trickle had reached the raw and brawling camp along the Yukon at the Klondike's mouth before the freeze-up so that some five thousand people in tents and cabins had to wait out the long darkness and the soul-shattering cold. The incredible richness of the creeks had been proved. The wealth of bench claims on ledges on the hillsides which concealed the bed of a prehistoric stream had been discovered by a cheechako. The pokes were full of gold dust. There was plenty of liquor. But food was in short supply. For the last boats up the Yukon had been stranded far down the river by dropping water and the ice.

The sturdy and single-minded Inspector Constantine issued a warning for those without supplies to leave. A number did go out on the last boats. Even as those boats left, the last of the advance guard of the stampeders from the passes were inching their way under a gray October sky amid cakes of floating ice to Dawson City. They found near starvation. As hunger mounted, the N.W.M.P. offered each man who would walk it back to Dyea or Skagway a three months' ration. Some nine hundred made the 750-mile journey through the freezing cold. One of them was sent on to Washington to tell of Dawson's plight.

Congress bubbled over with sympathy; $200,000 was appropriated for the relief of the starving miners at Dawson. In the somewhat fuzzy-minded way in which relief organizations sometimes operate, it was decided to bring reindeer from Norway and to walk them in to Dawson. In the end, 539 reindeer were actually bought (a bonanza to the grinning Norwegians, but why not let the crazy Americans spend their money?) and transferred by steamship and railroad to Haines Mission, near Dyea and Skagway, to start their trek to Dawson. There were Finns, Laplanders, and Norwegians to herd them over the trails. Most of the reindeer died; 114 of them, walking skeletons, straggled into Dawson a year later in January of 1899.

The Dawson of the 1897–98 winter had to make do with what it had. A fifty-pound barrel of flour soon went as high as $100 and a sack rose from $15 to $75. The lowly bean sold for $1.50 a pound.

If food was scarce, the Dawsonites, like the ancient Lydians told of by Herodotus, pieced out their hunger with fun and games. The saloons roared with business. Most popular of them all was the Monte Carlo, run by "Swiftwater" Bill Gates. In November 1896 he had walked down from "Thirteen," Eldorado, with 200 pounds of gold dust in his poke. During the autumn he had brought from Seattle a mahogany bar with all the trimmings and a covey of dance-hall girls. His bartender was Alexander Pantages, who, later, was to start a chain of vaudeville theaters across the United States and Canada. Swiftwater himself had already won renown as the man who, in the spring of 1897, had paid her weight in gold

(134 pounds) to a dance-hall girl, Gussie Lamore, for her promise to marry him.

Gussie, who was already married, evaded her promise skillfully. The disconsolate Swiftwater then married her sister, as the first of several matrimonial escapades. Part of the fascination of Dawson City for the modern age is that here was a life which actually lives up to the motion-picture extravaganza.

By the time the ice went out even the perfervid gaiety had worn thin. On June 8, 1898, at last, the first boat with supplies came in.

In the meantime some 10,000 adventurers had piled up during the winter at Lake Bennett, and more and more were struggling over the passes to join in the mob swarming in the sprawling tent city along the lake. As spring came it was like a scene in Technicolor. There was the smoke from thousands of campfires. There was the emerald of the lake, and along its shores a mass of feverish men whipsawing the trees into lumber while others hammered together their rude craft. And there were, too, in this strange city, restaurants, barbershops, hot baths, saloons and the offices of lawyers, doctors, dentists, and the like.

By May, for some twenty-six miles along the shores, the boats were packed four, five, and six deep. From the tops of a forest of hand-placed masts, weird flights of towels and bandanna handkerchiefs tossed in the wind. When on May 30 the ice broke, an armada of some eight hundred boats, chiefly homemade scows, set off on the 750-mile race for Dawson, and the dream of wealth. With more and more awkward boats plunging into the lake and with more and more newcomers surging over the passes and into the sprawling city of canvas, all the elements of disaster hovered.

In the Yukon, however, the Mounties were in control. They had relief stations on the American side of the passes. By February their customs posts crowned the summits. The redcoats moved calmly through the turbulence along Lake Bennett. At the exit from the long, narrow lakes at Tagish, there was a registration post. As the impatient gold seekers cursed and bellowed, the Mounties calmly saw to it that on each boat a number was painted and the name and address of each person in each craft entered in a registration book.

The delay dammed the tide. The boats stretched back for four miles. But by check posts every twenty-five miles the police kept track of possible upsets or loss of life. If a boat failed to stop when so ordered, a shot was fired across its bow. The Yukon was not to be the scene of the riotous disorder which ruled in Dyea and Skagway. In all, by the Mounties' count, 7080 boats passed Tagish Point during the summer of 1898 and the passenger total was close to 28,000.

The chief dangers to the boats were the five-mile run through the boiling waters of the red-walled Miles Canyon, with its whirlpool and a still narrower gorge beyond, followed by the Squaw Rapids, full of jutting rocks, and the Whitehorse Rapids. Here many lost their lives. When in June of 1898 Major Steele reached this stretch (the commissioner, Major Walsh, had gone on to Dawson) more than a hundred boats had already been smashed, ten persons had been drowned, and several hundred other boats were milling together.

With characteristic vigor Steele straightened out the jam. A Mountie, Corporal Dixon, was placed in charge. No woman or child was allowed to board the boats. They had to walk, but police escorted them. Furthermore, each boat, after inspection and approval by the corporal, had to carry a registered pilot.

The gold seekers cursed but obeyed. From that time forward not a life was lost. All summer long, from the beaches at Dyea and Skagway over the passes and down the lakes and rivers, the flood tumbled on to the Klondike.

6

Nothing shows more strikingly the contrast between Canadian and American frontier life in the closing years of the nineteenth century than the reign of the king of gangsters in Skagway. The king was Jefferson Randolph Smith, known as "Soapy," the erstwhile boss of crime in Denver. In the fall of 1897 he brought his bland and bearded face, five of his cronies, and his ingratiating talents to Skagway.

There was no doubt that Soapy had a way with him. The United States Government made his path even easier. At Dawson were the Mounties. In the whole of the chaos at Dyea and Skagway there were that fall no police and merely six marines; and these forlorn representatives of the law were empowered to act only in case of a riot.

Soapy looked about him. In Skagway there were already twenty-five saloons. (There were to be seventy by the next year.)

There were brothel keepers, thieves, con men, murderers, sharpers, all preying on the glassy-eyed gold seekers.

It was a chaos which called for a better arrangement. Soapy opened a saloon, named with stark simplicity "Jeff's Place," and rapidly brought order out of turmoil. In a remarkably brief time there were two or three hundred desperadoes behind him. All the vice and crime of both Dyea and Skagway was properly organized. There must have been a certain sense of humor in the man. To face a "Vigilance Committee" of 101, he set up his own "Law and Order Committee" of 303, or, as it is sometimes given, 317.

Under Soapy, gambling, selling liquor, and prostitution became virtues, and robbery, along with every kind of knavery to divorce men from their money, a business of respectability. No man with a poke of gold or a purse of money was safe. His sharpers met the boats, and they mingled with the toiling lines mounting the passes. His robbers thieved in the saloons and in the streets. If violence was needed, it was applied.

"Skagway," wrote Steele on his way through on February 14, 1898, to take command of the Mounties at the passes, "is the roughest place in the world. Gambling hells, dance-halls and variety theatres are in full swing. 'Soapy' Smith with his gang of one hundred and fifty ruffians runs the town and does as he pleases. . . . Robbery and murder occur daily. . . . Shots are exchanged on the street in broad daylight. At night the crash of bands and the shouts of 'Murder' mingle with the cracked voices of singers. . . . In the dance-halls the girl with the straw-colored hair trips the light fantastic at a dollar a set. In the White Pass . . . the shell game expert plies his trade while, frequently, some poor fellow is found lifeless on his rifled sled . . . powder marks on his back, and his pockets inside out."

Soapy, however, had his admirers. He dispensed violence with one hand and charity with another. There were hundreds of ownerless and starving dogs—this because to ignorant gold seekers had been sold every breed and type. Soapy began a "save a dog" movement and kept six himself; while he also contributed to churches, supported widows and orphans (some of them bereaved by his men), and sent out twenty-dollar bills as Christmas gifts. In May of 1898, when the news of the sinking of the *Maine* in Havana Harbor reached Skagway, he raised a company of infantry to avenge it and was miffed when the U. S. Government refused the contribution. The Fourth-of-July parade was led by "Grand Marshal" Soapy Smith on a pony with his guards following him—and Governor Brady of Alaska made the speech of the day. Four days later, because of revulsion set off by the robbery from a miner (who, by chance, was a Canadian) of a small poke of $2700, Soapy Smith was shot dead by a courageous vigilante, Frank Reid. It was tragic that Reid also died. But he had, at last, put an end to the king of gangsters.

It is significant that Soapy tried to send agents to Dawson with the intention of adding to his pickings. They were hustled out of the Yukon so fast that the only breath they used was in clambering back. The American way was in 1898 too lawless for Canadians.

CHAPTER XXXIV

1898–1903

Other Routes to the Klondike—Theodore Roosevelt's "Big Stick" and the Alaskan Boundary Dispute—Canadian Reaction

1

THE Trail of '98 over the Chilkoot Pass was the one which caught at men's imaginations. Apart from the ocean-and-river passage, and from several other routes north and south of the Chilkoot and White passes, there were perfervid attempts to drum up business for all-Canadian routes.

The first all-out drive was by Clifford Sifton himself. On the British Columbia–Yukon border was Lake Teslin; and from Lake Teslin there was a water passageway to Dawson. So in January 26, 1898, he signed a contract with Mackenzie and Mann (later to build a transcontinental) to thrust a railroad from Telegraph Creek, on the Stikine River—to which boats could run up through the Alaskan Panhandle—to Lake Teslin, a hundred and fifty miles away.

Telegraph Creek was at the end of a long, overgrown trail which in 1865 had been cut by Western Union through the wilderness from Ashcroft, near Kamloops.

Sifton failed to get his railway bill through the Canadian Senate. All through the spring and summer of 1898, however, gold seekers cut their way north to Telegraph Creek. Some of them even had tickets on the nonexistent railroad.

Others pushed up the Stikine River to the same point. There was a thousand miles before them all. Of seven thousand who tried this route to Dawson, less than half reached the Klondike.

Even so, they were luckier than the two thousand who tried the odyssey from Edmonton. This road to the Klondike had been publicized vigorously by the Edmonton Board of Trade and by Arthur Heming—whose paintings of the North are still well known—as the "old fur traders' route." It was 2500 weary miles at least from the then little settlement on the banks of the North Saskatchewan to Dawson, but Heming, the complete optimist, declared that all that was needed was "a good constitution, some experience in boating and camping and $150." Two months, it was said, would get you to the land of gold.

What Heming and the Edmonton Board of Trade failed to mention was that on their portage-and-water route the tough H.B.C. men and the Nor'westers had traveled in light canoes paddled by Indians and had either lived off the land or got supplies from the fur traders' posts along the way. To send greenhorns toting a ton of supplies to portage over the muskegs and rocks and to tempt the boiling rapids of the rivers in homemade boats was to condemn dozens to death.

Not that any warnings could have stopped the gold seekers. The C.P.R. dumped them in trainloads in Strathcona (now South Edmonton). They swarmed across to the north bank of the Saskatchewan. Their tents bloomed on the level stretches. The saloons were jammed and the merchants sold out their stocks. Then, in ignorance and enthusiasm, the eager horde started north. Some tried the trackless path via Whitecourt, Grande Prairie, and Fort St. John, where today the automobiles speed along the Alaska Highway. Thence they struggled over the weary leagues still waiting between them and Dawson.

The great majority plodded by differing trackways to Athabaska. There they built scows and sailed and portaged their way to Lesser Slave Lake. By the spring of 1898 there was a solid line of boats moving along the seventy-five miles of that lake.

From it some groups portaged across to the Peace River to battle up it as far as Fort St. John, whither the first route had led. They still had hundreds of miles to go. Most of the boatbuilders, however, tried Heming's route by the Slave River to Great Slave Lake and thence down the mighty Mackenzie River. Just above the Mackenzie delta is a feeder from the west, the Peel River. By this time the argonauts, if all the windings of the journey are reckoned, had traveled almost 2500 miles from Edmonton but still had to tug their boats hundreds of miles up the Peel and its tributaries, such as the Rat and the Wind, to cross the mountain divide between the Mackenzie and the Yukon. Many of these men spent two years on this route and had to winter in desolate camps. Many, inevitably, died. Many others turned back. Of the two thousand who started from Edmonton in their quest for the golden will-o'-the-wisp, only a corporal's guard from all the routes reached their goal before the 1898 freeze-up. In the spring of 1899 the miserable remnants of the Edmonton contingents staggered into Dawson, walking skeletons. All together only thirty of the whole two thousand reached the Klondike.

Edmonton prospered. So did the H.B.C. posts along the route. As a by-product, some of those who turned back began the settlement of the up to then unconsidered Peace River country.

That settlement and Edmonton's prosperity was fed by the bones of dead men whitening among the mountains or in the sloughs and muskegs.

2

By the summer of 1898 the population of Dawson City had ballooned, like a bloated spider fed to bursting, from five to thirty thousand. Under the midnight sun a restless, searching crowd moved ceaselessly up and down its dusty or muddy streets. There were two banks, the Bank of British North America and the Canadian Bank of Commerce. In the second of these a clerk, looking like any other clerk, was working. He was Robert Service. With eyes that took in all the amazing picture, he watched the dog and horse trains packing in the gold from the creeks, a sight so ordinary that by this time the Dawsonites never turned to look. He saw cucumbers selling at $5 apiece, radishes at $1 each, eggs at $36 a dozen, and apples matching radishes in price. In an age when $1 a day was big wages, laborers were making $15 a day; and carpenters got today's wages—up to $25 and $30 a day—but had to work for it.

The high wages were a salvation. For when the rush of '98 poured in, it was to find practically all the claims already staked. There were Scots. There were Australians. There were South Americans, Italians, Hindus, Chinese, and Egyptians to mingle with the Canadians and Americans. The tents and cabins covered the flats (some two hundred acres of them) and climbed up the slopes of the high hill to the east and north. On Front

Street, along the Yukon, all that summer there was a feverish building program. Through the eyes of a Londoner, Price, sent out by the *Illustrated London News,* we get a vivid sketch. "Try and picture for yourself," he wrote for his readers, "a wide flat stretch of marshy ground with a background of high hills, on the shore of a mighty river rushing by; and cover this shore with as many tents of all shapes and sizes as your imagination can picture. In the water along the beach . . . place hundreds of the roughest of wooden boats and see a big and motley crowd of men and women and children, in all sorts of conditions of garb . . . ; and above all a blazing sun and plenty of dust blown about by a persistent wind, . . . and you have Dawson, the golden city, as it appeared to me as I landed on the 14th of June, 1898."

It impressed Price, too, that "many very smartly dressed women were to be seen, looking strangely out of keeping, . . . for the men were absolutely the roughest, ruggedest and most unkempt lot I have ever seen . . . with their long boots, faded yellow flannel coats and slouch hats. . . ."

It was a city of incongruities, contrasts for which Robert Service was to have an observant eye. The Mounties ruled with a light hand. There were the Salvation Army lasses. There were itinerant musicians to make the perpetual day hideous. There were also the ladies of the evening in Paradise Alley and in Lousetown, now renamed Klondike City, each with her name over her crib. The saloons ran twenty-four hours a day. All the important ones had separate gambling rooms—faro, rouge et noir, roulette, poker, blackjack, dice. Five thousand dollars in a single poker pot was common. Fortunes were made and lost on the spin of a wheel or the flick-over, face up, of a card.

The very dust of Dawson seemed to be impregnated with the gold fever. In the more pretentious establishments, such as the Mascot or the Pavilion or Swiftwater Bill Gates' Monte Carlo, there were shows—and admission was a drink. There was vaudeville. There were variety songs, songs that, more than any other single thing, perhaps, make evident the gulf between now and then—"Put Your Arms around Me, Honey"; "Two Little Girls in Blue"; "After the Ball"; "Genevieve"; "There'll Be a Hot Time in the Old Town Tonight"; even "Only a Bird in a Gilded Cage."

The Gay Nineties had their epilogue in Dawson. After the shows came dancing; and the dance-hall girls made a drink obligatory at the end of each dance, and got a chip, worth twenty-five cents, for each drink they sold. Each dance, naturally, ended almost as it began.

There was nothing too good for Dawson. There were circus freaks in the plush saloons-*cum*-gambling-*cum*-attractions-*cum*-dancing, and specialty acts such as "Lady Godiva," "Little Egypt," and a man who was hanged twice a night. In the Opera House, boxers and wrestlers alternated with New York shows, notable among them *Camille* and *Uncle Tom's Cabin,* while champagne at $40 a quart was the only drink served. By a sensitive interpretation of the Dominion's Blue Laws, though saloons, bakeries, laundries, and the like were closed down on Sundays, theaters and places of entertainment of all kinds were left open and drinking in them was not a breach of the Lord's day observances.

Dawson City was as close as Canada ever came to the Barbary Coast; except that the Mounties prevented riots or any serious crime wave, even in the wild summer and winter of 1898. In Dawson stick-ups were rare and no one ever locked his cabin door. By the next year the place had become respectable with zinc bathtubs, pianos, billiard tables, and Brussels carpets in the hotels. The surest sign of the change was an unofficial Council of Ladies (wives who had moved in to tame a too masculine society), which presided over social activities and the virtues.

Their very presence announced that the peak of the boom was over. In 1899 gold was found at Nome in Alaska and eight thousand miners left Dawson in the first week of the rush.

Production with, as in the Cariboo, companies instead of individuals operating continued. In 1898 there was ten million dollars' worth of gold from the creeks. The next year the take rose to sixteen million, and in 1900, the peak year, to twenty-two and a quarter. By 1905 the output had dropped to $7,162,438.

Population went down even faster. By 1901 the whole of the Yukon had 27,000 people in it, of which Dawson housed less than 6000.

The Klondike fever had a more lasting effect than a first casual glance might indicate. The gold production and the trade involved in the stampede did its share toward stirring the boom days of the late nineties and the early years of the twentieth century. Over and beyond this, just as the Cariboo rush publicized and opened up British Columbia, so the Yukon and Alaska swam into the world's ken.

The gold rush also became one of the legends by which a pattern of nationhood is welded together. To the Americans, the

Trail of '98 became folk history because in the odyssey of individual after individual was shown the heroism and the endurance as well as the unreasoning folly and complete depravity of humanity. In that terrific experience a man was either shattered into the weakness he was or toughened to an evil which he had not realized was within himself, or to a fiber finer than his dream.

To Canadians, the Trail of '98 and the amazing characters brought to their full growth by the forcing house of Dawson were American rather than Canadian, except insofar as Robert Service's verse made them feel something of its romance. What the Klondike gave to Canada was a realization of unsuspected resources in her refrigerated northland and a pride in the achievement of her Mounties. The Klondike was a part of the picture which made Laurier exclaim prematurely: "The twentieth century is Canada's." It also led at last to a settlement of the Alaskan boundary dispute.

3

The first years of the twentieth century were the age of Teddy Roosevelt of the staring spectacles, the walrus mustache, the superabundant, extroverted energy, and the "Big Stick." Americans at their most imperialistic seldom realize their imperialism. But Roosevelt at an early age had come under the influence of two imperially minded fellow countrymen, Mahan and Josiah Strong.

Mahan, the author of the classic book on the influence of sea power, was more than a historian. His self-appointed task as a publicist and politician was, as Beard states in his *Basic History of the United States*, to convert the U.S.A. to world-power politics.

Equally ambitious for his country was the missionary Josiah Strong. It was his Kiplingesque belief, to quote Beard, that "the Anglo-Saxon race was chosen by God to civilize the world" and that the major part in this laudable crusade "belonged to the United States." Two of the chief converts to the theses of Mahan and Strong, as pointed out by Beard and also by Faulkner, in his *American Economic History*, were Henry Cabot Lodge, a senator since 1893 and the grandfather of the present American representative to the United Nations, and Theodore Roosevelt, the scion of an old Dutch family. With him and with Lodge it became a tenet that the U.S.A. should throw its weight around. In the depression year of 1895 Roosevelt, as quoted by Beard, wrote to Lodge that "the country needs a war."

The blowing up of the American battleship *Maine* in Havana Harbor early in 1898 was like a God-given answer to this prayer. Out of it was puffed up rapidly the Spanish-American War, ostensibly to liberate Cuba. Decadent Spain had no chance against the vigorous Republic. The Americans occupied Cuba and Puerto Rico, destroyed the Spanish fleet in Manila Harbor on May 1st—with Britain, figuratively, holding America's coat for her by warning off interference from a German squadron—and then seized the Philippines. In the same year on July 7, the United States annexed the Hawaiian Islands.

The eagle was screaming a new note, the note not of the old continental imperialism but of world imperialism. In the peace treaty with Spain, Puerto Rico, Guam, and the Philippine Islands became American territory. Cuba, theoretically independent, was virtually a U.S. protectorate. The Philippines rebelled, demanding independence. The United States, still not calling herself imperialistic, crushed the rebellion in a savage three-year war.

The success of the Spanish-American War put the Republican McKinley back as President for his second term. Roosevelt, the hero of the "Rough Riders" and of the charge at San Juan Hill, went in as his Vice-President. An assassin's bullet in September 1901 removed McKinley. Unexpectedly Roosevelt sat on the throne.

Under Roosevelt, world imperialism became formal American policy. There had been a commission on the Alaskan boundary dispute which had dissolved in 1899 without reaching a solution. Britain now suggested a tribunal with an outside arbitrator, the same sort of tribunal which President Cleveland had demanded from Great Britain in a dispute over the boundary between British Guiana and Venezuela. For, by an extension of the Monroe Doctrine, the United States was now asserting that Central America and South America were both under the cover of her umbrella.

Britain had given way over the boundary dispute. Furthermore, in the extraordinarily tender consideration of American feelings which characterized her even in her days as the dominant world power, she had conceded the Panama Canal. Here again American imperialism had been displayed. By the 1850 Clayton-Bulmer Treaty it had been agreed that Britain and the United States should join in building the canal. But in 1900 and 1901 the United States, feeling her oats, demanded that Britain withdraw; the only concession to her rights being that the canal should be open to the ships of all nations at the same rates. When the Americans turned to building it, Colombia, to which the canal area belonged, made difficulties. To Theodore Roosevelt, it was time for the Big Stick. In 1903 an American-inspired revolt wrenched the Republic of Panama away from Colombia. It was with this complaisant satellite that the United States made her canal treaty.

Britain may have expected that her concessions over both the British Guiana–Venezuela dispute and the Panama Canal would lead the United States to agree to a joint tribunal with an outside arbitrator to settle the Alaskan boundary dispute. But no! An outside arbitrator was fair and just when the interests of Britain and Venezuela were concerned. It was not to be endured when the United States herself was in the picture. The furthest Roosevelt would go was to agree early in 1903 to a mixed tribunal of "six impartial jurists of repute," three from each side, each of whom was to take an oath that he "will impartially consider the arguments and evidence presented to the tribunal and will decide thereupon according to his true judgments."

Canada, in view of her long and unhappy experience with British-American negotiations, regarded this proposal with a wary eye, like a fox walking around a trap in which he has lost a toe or two more than once. Britain, however, accepted and offered a commission of two Canadians and one Englishman. With some reluctance Laurier agreed. The Canadian nominees were Sir Louis Jetté, formerly a judge of Quebec's Superior Court, and Mr. Justice Armour of the Supreme Court of Canada. Mr. Armour's death, however, meant that he had to be replaced by Mr. A. B. Aylesworth, K.C. Britain appointed the Lord Chief Justice of England, Lord Alverstone.

These three could be regarded as "impartial jurists." But the U. S. Senate was on the point of refusing to sanction the tribunal unless it could be assured that Canada's claim would not have a chance. In a charmingly frank memoir, in fact, Henry Cabot Lodge wrote that the Senate "could not agree to having anybody on the Tribunal who would yield to the Canadian claim." So, in confidence, as Lodge tells us in the same memoir, the names of Roosevelt's three appointees were disclosed to it. They were Elihu Root,

Secretary of War, who had already pronounced against the Canadian claim, Senator Henry Cabot Lodge, who had publicly stated that the Canadian position was baseless and trumped up, and Senator George Turner of Washington State, in which lay Seattle, the rival of Vancouver and Victoria for the trade of the Yukon. Turner, too, had already committed himself against any concession to the Canadians.

These men were, undoubtedly, able, if predatory, negotiators. They were not "impartial jurists." The Senate was now quite willing to agree to the tribunal. As the American press stated gleefully, "the chances of convincing them [the three U.S. appointees] of the rightfulness of Canada's claim are about the same as the prospect of a thaw in Hades." Canada burst into a storm of protest. No one heeded.

Even so, when the tribunal met in London, it seemed at first that the discussions would end in an impasse, with three on either side of the fence. To Roosevelt, in all negotiations in which the U.S. was concerned, there had to be a 100 per cent victory for the Americans and a zero for the other party. He was as dogmatic as a fundamentalist. To him, America's case in Alaska was "ironclad"; while Canada had come "dangerously near blackmail." So he began to chafe at the delay. In March 1902, before the tribunal was even agreed to, he had already ordered his War Department to send troops to southern Alaska, as quietly as possible; and later, in a cheerful disregard of anybody's feelings, he announced that, if the decision had gone against the United States, he would have seized the territory under arbitration and held it by force.

A man who, as his daughter, Alice, said of him, had to be the "bridegroom at every wedding and the corpse at every funeral," Roosevelt was determined that the decision should go in favor of the United States; nor did he care how that decision was obtained. Since the tribunal was deadlocked, the obvious maneuver was to force Lord Alverstone to change sides. On July 16, Roosevelt wrote Lodge that a decision must be reached before Congress met in November, or else he would have to recommend action.

The Canadians still held out, though Sifton, Minister of the Interior, who was handling the Canadian case, had no illusions about the final issue. On August 30 Lodge reported that the Canadians were so stupid they would not yield gracefully and that "England is in such mortal terror of Canada that I feel more than doubtful in regard to it."

Roosevelt now decided to wave the big stick. He wrote to Justice Oliver Wendell Holmes, who was on holiday in Britain, to inform him that if agreement was not reached he would get Congress to give him authority "to run the line as we claim it" and to use troops for enforcement. Holmes was told he could tell Joseph Chamberlain, the Colonial Secretary, what Roosevelt had said, "though, of course, it must be privately and unofficial." He also wrote to Henry White, secretary to the U.S. embassy in London, to give the British Prime Minister, Lord Balfour, the same news.

Against this kind of diplomacy, the Dominion had no chance. The British Government, as Roosevelt put it complacently later, "tipped the wink" to Lord Alverstone. Changing his views overnight, he shifted to the American side. By the so-called compromise line, the United States received practically its full claim. Its strip was narrower in some places than the ten marine leagues it had claimed. But its major contention was accepted. In the Alaskan Panhandle from 54° 40′ to 60° Canada was blocked off from any port of entry to British Columbia or the Yukon. The Dominion was presented with two unimportant islands in the Portland Channel.

The two Canadian commissioners refused to sign the award. Across the Dominion there was a burst of rage. It was not directed against the Americans. The Americans, in the Canadian view, were greedy and grabbing. But that Britain should have once more given away what the Dominion had come to consider as Canadian territory, that was something not to be endured. A bitter gibe in the Toronto *News* illustrates the sense of betrayal.

"Lord Alverstone (to Canada): 'Is there anything more that I can do for you?'

"Canada: 'We would like to go on drawing breath.'

"Lord Alverstone (to Messrs. Root, Lodge and Turner): 'Any objection to our young friend continuing to use the atmosphere?'

"Messrs. Root, Lodge and Turner (cheerfully): 'Not at all, just now.'

"Lord Alverstone (with a judicial air): 'My decision is that you are entitled to the temporary use of all the air not required for United States' purposes.'"

There had been the same wave of indignation after the 1842 Webster-Ashburton Treaty and the 1871 Washington Treaty. This time the anger was deeper and more dangerous. Canadians had become convinced of their own importance and conscious of themselves as a people. In the fourth Colonial Conference of 1902, Laurier, as Prime Minister of the senior Dominion, had led the opposition to Chamberlain's second attempt to establish an Imperial Council with wide taxation and legislative powers (inclusive of taxation for a unified defense and legislation for free trade) over the whole empire. To be brushed aside now as of no account bit deep. Laurier himself told Parliament (italics mine):

"I have often regretted, Mr. Speaker, and never more on the present occasion, that we are living beside a great neighbor who I believe I can say . . . *are very grasping in their national actions,* and who are determined on every occasion to get the best in any agreement they make. I have often regretted also that while they are a great and powerful nation, we are only a small colony, a growing colony, but still a colony. I have often regretted also that we have not in our own hands *the treaty-making power which would enable us to dispose of our own affairs. . . .*"

To the United States, the victory over the Alaskan boundary was of no more importance than for a millionaire in a gold-plated Cadillac to have made a pedestrian jump back to the sidewalk. To Canada, it was another insult to store away in bitterness until sometime, somehow, a day of reprisal might come. If Americans today are surprised occasionally, when they think of Canada at all, to discover that the United States is sometimes regarded with a wary suspicion, they ought to review the case after case in which their statesmen have casually pushed the Dominion out of the way.

The resentment against Britain was that of an adolescent who has been betrayed by its own parent. The Alaskan boundary decision was a sting to sharpen Canada's feeling that she must handle her own foreign affairs. In 1880 John A. had set up a high-commissionership in London. In 1909 Laurier established a Canadian Department of External Affairs. By this move he served notice that Canada was now a nation in her own right.

Meantime, a tide of immigration was, at last, pouring into Canada's westland. For, finally, in the late nineties, after hope long deferred, circumstances and the man to make use of them had met at the decisive moment. The man was Clifford Sifton, the Minister of the Interior who had reacted so swiftly to the Klondike gold rush. The circumstances had had a long gestation in the womb of Destiny before a happy star brought them to birth.

CHAPTER XXXV

1896–1910

Its Destiny Overtakes the West—Sifton Hunts for Settlers—The Barr Colonists—The Dominion Catches a Prickly Porcupine in the Dukhobors—Two New Transcontinentals—Prosperity Built on Wheat—Alberta and Saskatchewan Are Born—The Development of the Prairie Westerner and the First March on Ottawa

1

IT may seem strange that the story of Canada's western boom of 1896–1914 should begin around 1842 with David Fife, a farmer near Peterborough, Ontario, examining a sample of wheat which had been sent him from Scotland by a friend. It was a hard wheat, with a glint of fire in its coloring. Thinking it fall wheat (wheat to be planted in the autumn and reaped the next summer), Fife seeded it in September of that same year. Only three plants came through the winter and, according to legend, a cow ate two of the three. Fife, realizing at last that the strange wheat was spring wheat, put the remaining few grains into the soil the next April and carefully preserved the increase for seed. One fact intrigued him. This wheat (he called it Red Fife) was not only harder than other spring wheats, it also ripened ten to twelve days faster.

In that fact, though Fife never knew it, was the future of the Canadian West. For in the West fall wheat was usually winter-killed and spring wheat always ran the risk of being nipped by an early September frost.

Accident had brought the wheat to Fife. (His friend had

picked it up casually and did not know its genesis, though it is believed to have been wheat from eastern Europe.) It took another accident to carry it to the Canadian West. In 1868 a plague of grasshoppers devoured everything green in Red River Settlement. Seed wheat had to be brought in from the American Middle West. Thither settlers from Ontario had carried David Fife's strain of wheat. So the seed that came up to Winnipeg was Red Fife, the wheat tailored to order for the short growing season of the Canadian prairies. It seems almost too pat that in 1876 the first export shipment of wheat ever to leave the Canadian West was 857¼ bushels of Red Fife, for seed, bound for Ontario on board the stern-wheeler *Minnesota.* It seems even more incredible that the first overseas shipment in 1884 was a thousand bushels of the same "No. 1 Hard" from Brandon in Manitoba to, of all places, Glasgow in Scotland. By such happy accidents the prosaic becomes surrounded by the aura of destiny.

From Manitoba the quick-maturing Red Fife spread over the Northwest. It pushed the country possible for wheat growing further north. More was to come. In the Saunders family the Dominion had discovered cerealists who were devoted scientists. For some sixteen years the father, William, and the son, Charles, collected early ripening spring wheats from all over the world and crossed the strains. In 1904, from all their researches, Charles Saunders selected a single head of wheat. That wheat was Marquis, which ripened eight days earlier than even Red Fife. Five years later Marquis was thrusting the wheat belt of western Canada still further northward. (Later discoveries provided even better strains.)

Red Fife made possible the thousands of acres of golden grain bowing before the winds across Canada's prairies and park land. Before the first shipment of it went overseas there was another flick of Destiny's finger. In 1878 the new roller-milling technique for making flour was discovered. Before this time the hardness of Red Fife had been a blemish. Now it became a virtue, especially for mixing with softer strains. From this time forward, under the Dominion system of grading wheat, which was accepted in Great Britain, western Canadian No. 1 Hard sat at the top of the heap.

The right strain of wheat and the invention of roller milling were only two of the developments which seemed to wait in the Book of Destiny for the right moment. By 1896 there was the Oliver chilled-steel plow for shearing the tough prairie sod, the McCormick and Massey-Harris binders for quick reaping of the boundless acres, and the grain elevators for storage. Even more important for the scanty rainfall of the Canadian West, to the south of the border the technique of dry farming with its use of the summer fallow had already been mastered; while the bonanza farms of Minnesota and the Dakotas had introduced a one-crop, mass-production method.

All this, and the railroad, too, was ready to hand before 1896. Yet Destiny still hesitated. In what is now southern Alberta the high-booted cowboys rode the open range or rubbed elbows at the 135-foot bar of Calgary's Alberta Hotel. By 1900, in fact, there were around 115,000 head of cattle roaming the short-grass country. Driblets of settlers came into Manitoba and the Northwest Territories from Ontario or from across the line. In 1887, for instance, forty Mormons led by Charles Ora Card made the long trek from Cache Valley in Utah to the country south of Lethbridge. Clusters of Europeans—German-speaking Mennonites from Russia, Icelanders, Scandinavians, Hungarians, Austrians, Germans, Rumanians, and so on—also formed pockets of homesteaders.

Yet, though Canada was offering 160 acres of free land to every immigrant, and though the C.P.R. land department and various land companies made effort after effort, settlement went at a turtle's pace. In the fifteen years from 1881 to 1896, in the whole of the vast immensity from Lake of the Woods to the Rockies only 56,520 homesteads were taken up, and of these, 16,326 were canceled. In 1896 itself, the year the Laurier government came to power, the total immigration into the Dominion was a beggarly 16,835 people. There was the attraction of the States. There was the long bleakness of Canada's depression. From 1882 to 1897 the wholesale-price index dropped from 112.1 to 75.6, and in 1893 wheat brought 64¼ cents a bushel, the lowest price since the fourteenth century. In spite of the epic of the transcontinental, it seemed as if Destiny had taken a slantwise look at the Canadian West and decided to pass it by.

Instead, after its long journey down into the pit of hard times, the world was already gathering strength for a swoop upward. Gold and optimism had both been in short supply. Now came the spectacular discoveries of the yellow metal in South Africa (1893–96) and the Klondike (1896–98). Confidence returned. Prices began to climb, and from 1897 to 1907 the wholesale-price index rose from 75.6 to 96.2. The Spanish-American War did its part in restoring prosperity. But, for Canada, the great and unrealized factor was the industrialization and urbanization of much of Europe and the United States. Factory workers need bread and cities are parasites on the bounty of the soil; while No. 1 Hard was just what the doctor ordered for mixing with the softer wheats of Europe and eastern North America.

So the clamor was for wheat and yet more wheat. At this moment, too, free land in the United States gave out like a cow which has been milked too long. The land-hungry emigrants from Europe had to turn their faces, at last, to the neglected Canadian prairie. Even in the middle western United States, with land selling at $50 to $75 an acre, many a farmer's son was ready to look across the border for a free homestead.

It all added up to Canada's opportunity. In Clifford Sifton the Dominion had a man to seize Opportunity by nape and rump and bundle her into the house.

He was a somewhat cold man, vindictive toward his enemies, ruthlessly efficient (the Sifton political machine in Manitoba rode over opposition roughshod), and almost scornful in his directness. His eyes looked out at the world with the uncompromising arrogance of one who knows his own ability and intelligence and does not trouble to conceal his contempt for lesser minds. To him, red tape and circumlocution were both anathema. Yet he was passionate in his convictions, a man who in 1905 resigned his cabinet post overnight when he thought Laurier had double-crossed him about Roman Catholic Separate Schools. Above all, he believed with all his being in the Canadian West; and he had the practicality and drive to make his dream come true.

2

Settle! That was Sifton's clarion cry. He stopped the policy of land grants for railroads. He compelled the railway companies, and particularly the C.P.R., to select at once the millions of acres which had already been allocated to them so that he himself would know what he could offer to newcomers. He straightened out the free-land regulations, one important change being that a young man could continue to live at home and still take out a homestead. He put a subagent into every developing district so as to cut red tape. He abolished the Dominion Land Board at Winnipeg and transferred its functions to an official at Ottawa so that it would be under his own thumb.

Nor did he wait, passive, for settlers to come. The C.P.R. and the land companies felt the strong wind that was Sifton blowing. With their co-operation the new Minister of the Interior sent lecturers to fall fairs in the middle western states to sound the trumpet for western Canada. A shower of pamphlets backed them up. In 1897 he opened nine state agencies south of the 49th parallel, increased by 1914 to twenty-one, with sheaves of western wheat on display. By 1902 he was advertising the Canadian West in some seven thousand American agricultural periodicals, with a total circulation of over seven million. Canada had long been losing her people to the Republic. Now immigration did an about-face. American editors were taken on joy rides through the Canadian West while the crops were at their best. Then in 1899, some six hundred members of the National Editorial Association were given a free jaunt. So were selected groups of land seekers.

The campaign brought the Americans (a goodly number of them returning Canadians) across the line in coveys. The same vigorous assault was made on Britain; though, instead of land seekers, selected British M.P.s were given free trips to the "Granary of the Empire." Among them was a bright young man from Wales, David Lloyd George—and no one could guess that he would be Britain's famous Prime Minister of World War I.

Settle! Sifton thrust searching fingers into Europe. Immigrants from Scandinavia were desirable but hard to get. A few Belgians responded to the carrot of free land and practically no Frenchmen. Germany, annoyed by Canadian efforts, protested officially against "the attempt to lure our fellow-countrymen to this desolate, sub-arctic region. . . ." But in the province of Galicia, in the pre-World War I Austro-Hungarian Empire, there were emigrants and to spare. The North Atlantic Trading Company, an organization of steamship and booking agents, was given a bonus of $5 for each head of a family and $2 for each individual brought to Canada. There was opposition. Sifton declared stubbornly that he thought "a peasant in a sheepskin coat" was "good quality."

It took a year or two to get results. In 1897 there were some 32,000 immigrants as compared with the 16,835 of the previous year. Once the tide began to roll, it soon increased to a torrent. During the fifteen years of the Laurier administration (1896–1911) over 2,000,000 newcomers found their way to a Canada which by the 1901 census had boasted only 5,371,315 souls and by 1911 was up to 7,206,643. Of this flood, in round figures, 38 per cent came from the British Isles, 34 per cent from the United States, and 26 per cent from Continental Europe. By 1914, when the First Great War dammed the tide, over three million immigrants had poured into the Dominion, although about half of these either leaked southward to the States or returned home.

Most of the newcomers sought the West. Along with them went a horde of eastern Canadians, chiefly from Ontario. Between 1901 and 1911 Manitoba increased from a population of 255,211 to 455,614, while what is now Alberta and Saskatchewan swelled from 164,281 to 867,095. The lure was free land. To quote Skelton in his *The Day of Sir Wilfrid Laurier:* "In 1908 a Wales was given away; in 1909 five Prince Edward Islands; while in 1910 and 1911 . . . a Belgium, a Holland, a Luxembourg and a Montenegro [Albania] passed from the state to the settler."

Statistics do no more than indicate the vastness of the incoming. They do not make vivid the unending stretches of the "Great Lone Land" or its bleak emptiness under the winter's snow or the feeling of insignificance many an immigrant felt when he found himself in the middle of nowhere with only a tent or a soddy to cover him. For the Americans, the migration was comparatively easy. They knew the wide skies over the prairies. Most of them were merely moving from old farms to new. Some were in hopes of making a killing in a few crops of wheat from the virgin soil. The majority came to stay.

Nor did they come in as paupers. In prairie schooners, their families and chattels with them, they poured into southern Saskatchewan. They rolled into the ranching country around Calgary and into the black-earth central Alberta. By 1916 in that province around 18 per cent of the people were of American provenance. With them they brought the technique of dry farming.

For those who moved in from Britain, the transition was more difficult, especially if, as in the case of the Barr Colonists, they came, not from Scotland's moorlands, but from England's cities.

3

It was April 10, 1903, when an old Boer War transport, *The Manitoba*, floundered up the Bay of Fundy, toward St. John, New Brunswick. On deck, still pale from a storm-tossed trip over the gray North Atlantic, was a hodgepodge of furriers, hatmakers, shopkeepers, lawyers, and the like, with a few farmers tossed in for seasoning. They and their families had left an England that was green with spring, hypnotized by the siren voice of an Anglican cleric, the Reverend I. M. Barr. On board the troopship most of them had had to sleep on bunks in the cargo hold. There was little or no privacy. The food had been execrable, the water not fit for drinking, and the toilet facilities deplorable. Now they looked out at bleak shores and the untidy houses of St. John.

A good many were already regretting their venture into the new land. When they came ashore it was to discover that their heavy baggage, sent on by freighter, had failed to arrive on that freighter. (The mystery of the missing baggage still remains a mystery.) Complaints against the Reverend Barr began to shrill to a crescendo. But the C.P.R. trains were waiting. The immigrants piled in. The coaches were "colonist" cars with wooden slats instead of cushioning for seats. Grumbling and ill at ease, the former city dwellers stared out at the seemingly endless leagues of trees and snow and rock in North Ontario. From Winnipeg onward they gazed out at a prairie that still waited for spring. So slow was the train that some of the colonists claimed afterward that one could shoot a rabbit through the window, jump off, pick it up, and climb on again a few coaches to the rear.

It was April 17 when the first three trainloads reached the then tiny town of Saskatoon, only to find that their remaining baggage had again failed to arrive. The rage against the silver-tongued Reverend boiled over. But another and more determined ecclesiastic, the Reverend G. E. Lloyd, had taken over.

"We have not come," he told his fellow countrymen, "all this way to quit."

So the hatmakers and the tradesmen and their families camped two weeks in tents by the C.P.R. tracks until their baggage caught up with them. Meanwhile they cleaned Saskatoon's stores, and the farmers round about, out of tea, jam, dried apples, bacon, bucksaws, ammunition, butter, horses, and oxen. Then they began the journey to the site arranged for them just over the boundary between Alberta and Saskatchewan.

It was a trek of greenhorns. Their wagons, loaded too high, overturned their baggage into the first slough or mudhole. Spilled coal oil spoiled food. Late spring blizzards and unseasonable below-zero weather hit them. When they did reach their homesteads among the scrub bush, they had to live in tents and soddies. Nor did they know how to farm. One story, probably apocryphal, tells of them planting potatoes by placing carefully two sods, tent-like, over each one.

It was a far cry from England's neat fields and trim lawns. Yet the Barr Colonists stuck. Today the Lloydminster they named after their leader is the center of a thriving countryside, rich with prosperous farms and dotted everywhere with bobbing rockers bringing crude oil to the surface. The faith Sifton had in western Canada was more strongly based than he knew.

It was the predominance of Ontarian, British, and American settlers which kept the West English-speaking. The immigration from Europe made it somewhat the proverbial melting pot. Europeans, naturally, tended to settle in blocks according to their national origin. Little Icelands, Germanys, Ukraines, Denmarks, Italys, Austrias, Belgiums, and Polands dotted the prairie and the park land.

Of all these newcomers, the greatest surge was that of the Ukrainians from Austria-Hungary's province of Galicia. Between 1897 and 1914 more than 200,000 of Sifton's sheepskins came to the Dominion. Most of them settled in the West. They filled out Manitoba. They poured into what was soon to be Alberta, around Fort Saskatchewan, Lamont, and Beaver Lake (now Star). They were sneered at for their illiteracy, their strange customs and costumes. But they knew how to farm and they were not afraid to work. The men made themselves stakes on the railway construction gangs or in the lumber camps or in the coal mines. The women joined in tearing a living from the soil. In their settlements in those days there was the sod house, the bake oven in the open, and women and children working in the fields.

It was said that they would never be assimilated. Today Canadians of Ukrainian ancestry are soldiers, lawyers, doctors, mayors, members of Parliament, and the like, as well as industrious farmers. Not all of Sifton's experiments, however, turned out so happily as his "sheepskins."

4

On May 21, 1903, near Yorkton in Saskatchewan, a farmer's wife looked out of her door and gasped. A group of men, stark naked in the sun, were strolling casually down the road toward the town.

About the same time a startled Mountie rushed hurriedly back to Yorkton. When the nude Adams (there were twenty-eight of them) were a mile away, about a hundred townsmen, led by the police, surrounded them. The paraders refused to dress. There was a ludicrous scene as the police, townsmen, and farmers tried to get clothes onto men who held their arms and legs stiff and twisted their bodies about. Finally, partly clothed, they were herded into Yorkton's Immigration Hall and later sent to Regina jail for three months for indecent exposure.

In the same month, two hundred and fifty miles northwest of Yorkton, English-speaking villagers and farmers bugged their eyes out at some thirty nudes, women as well as men this time, drifting by in broad daylight. The Mountie who was summoned hurriedly was of a realistic and, one may suspect, humorous turn of mind. According to J. F. C. Wright in his detailed study of the Dukhobors, *Slava Bohu*, he inveigled the naked men and women into a house that evening, nailed the door open, and hung a lantern in the doorway. It was a hot, damp night. The mosquitoes of the West, those which the Overlanders of '62 had described as being "as big as hummingbirds," rushed to the feast. Before morning the Eves and Adams had their clothes on.

The nude parades were the protest of the radical faction of the Dukhobors, the "Sons of Freedom," against all authority and, in fact, against anything connected with civilization. Canada was shocked to the depths of its nonsophisticated soul. The Dukhobor radicals were so pleased at the furor that thenceforward, at the slightest provocation, they flung off their clothes. One of their most spectacular exhibitions was in Fort William, which seventy-eight of them had reached in a "pilgrimage" from Saskatchewan on November 1, 1907. On New Year's Day 1908, in subzero temperature, as Fort William's citizens gaped, or snapped photographs, twelve men and women paraded, naked, down the snowy streets. This was a little too exuberant, even for the "Head of the Lakes." The nudes were herded into a poolroom, draped with blankets, and taken back in horse-drawn cabs to the deserted Anglican parsonage (it had later been a brothel) in which the "Sons of Freedom" were staying.

Long before this the Dominion had reluctantly realized that an experiment in practical philanthropy had turned slightly sour. The Dukhobors were a pacifist sect which had sprung up in Russia during the seventeenth century. They had survived persecution after persecution before, in the nineties, another attempt to make them conform brought them to the notice of the writer and somewhat fuzzy-minded theorist Count Leo Tolstoi. Tolstoi, like many crusaders, saw only what he wanted to see. To him, these ignorant peasants were living communally in a state of "early Christian anarchy," rejecting all authority but that of God, and doing right according to their own "reason and conscience." The pacifist Quakers were deeply impressed. So were many other "do-gooders." Pressure was put on the Czar's government. The Canadian Government and the C.P.R. were induced to co-operate. In 1899 some 7400 Dukhobors (the name means "Spirit Wrestlers") were brought to Canada, with the promise that they would not be called upon for military service. They were given homesteads in Saskatchewan near Yorkton and between Saskatoon and Prince Albert. Canada's Minister of the Interior, Clifford Sifton, even spent a few self-congratulatory days in their settlements.

The Dukhobors were hard workers. Most of them, like two other pacifist sects, the Mennonites and the Hutterites, believed in communal ownership. A good many of them, especially when they broke away from the strict tenets of their faith, ultimately became good citizens. Many of them, however, rejected all authority except that of their leader. For what no one had realized at first was that the basic belief of the Dukhobors was in a "God-Man," in whom the spirit of Christ took residence. At the time of their migration to Canada their current "God-Man" was in exile in Siberia. He was Peter Vasilivich Veregin, a handsome, bearded six-footer with a hypnotic voice and a compelling personality. In 1903 he was finally allowed to come to Canada.

To the Dukhobors, except for a few unregenerates, the voice of Peter Veregin was the voice of Christ. It did not matter that he himself lived luxuriously or that he surrounded himself with a covey of good-looking maids. What he preached, they did. To them, he forbade education, the registering of their homesteads, and the taking of the oath of allegiance. To the Canadian Government, he spoke with another tongue, promising co-operation.

Between the two tongues, the Dominion was completely baffled. Schoolhouses burned. Machinery was destroyed. There was nude parade after nude parade. Wright, in the book already referred to, tells of the embarrassment, on July 13, 1929, of a young volunteer fireman in Kamsack, Saskatchewan, who was helping to disperse a parade of Adam and Eve Dukhobors, when he came face to face with a young schoolteacher, whom he had escorted to dances and movies, standing naked and angry before him.

The "Sons of Freedom" were an annoyance to Peter Veregin, though they themselves were persuaded that his opposition to them meant only that their "Christ" was testing them. Another thorn in the leader's flesh was the "Independents," who tended toward individual ownership of their farms or, at least, of their stock and implements, and were ready to swear allegiance to the Dominion and the King.

Veregin kept the rest of his subjects illiterate and under his thumb. Thus in 1907, when, after seven years, the Dominion at last demanded that the Dukhobors fulfill the law and Veregin's followers refused, some 100,000 acres reverted to the Dominion, though a kindly government allowed each head of a family to retain fifteen acres for himself and fifteen acres for each member of his family.

Veregin had an answer to this move. He bought land with communal funds in British Columbia. In 1909 he began to transfer his devoted dupes to Brilliant, near Nelson, and to Grand Forks, fifty miles further west. It is instructive to record that by this time even the Quakers had become disillusioned with their pets.

In this way Canada's westernmost province was gifted with a problem which is as yet unsolved. Peter Veregin himself was blown to bits between Castlegar and Nelson in 1924 by an explosion, still inexplicable, in a railway coach. His son and successor, Peter Petrovich Veregin, was then brought over from Russia, He proved to be even more flagrant in his scorning of the taboos he imposed on his followers, such as the prohibition of tobacco and liquor, and in his collection of money from them. Under him more and more factions rent the Dukhobors. The present "Christ" of the cult, Stefan Sorokin, lives in luxury in Uruguay, South America, on lavish contributions sent him by his Canadian followers.

There is a general feeling that most orthodox Dukhobors may ultimately be more or less assimilated, though among the radicals, until recently, there was refusal to send children to school and there is still the nude parade at the dropping of a hat or of a pair of trousers. The burning of schoolhouses and the dynamiting of homes and railway tracks still enliven British Columbia—a practice generally blamed on the "Sons of Freedom," who center at Krestova.

5

The Dukhobors were one of the few sour apples Sifton imported. Meanwhile, in the decade and a half between 1899 and 1914 the tide of immigrants changed the face of the West. It was not only the homesteads curling up their thin smoke where formerly there had been only the gulls and hawks and songbirds or the prairie dog and rabbit. There were the hamlets which grew into villages and towns. There were the gaunt elevators pointing bleak fingers to the wide, flat sky. There were the frantic land booms and the towns burgeoning into cities. To take a few examples between 1901 and 1911, Winnipeg's population swelled from 42,340 to 136,023, Regina's from 2249 to 30,213, Edmonton's from 2626 to 24,900, Calgary's from 4392 to 43,704, and Saskatoon's from a mere 113 to 12,000. The population of the whole area now covered by the three prairie provinces increased from 419,492 to 1,322,709. In that golden decade the foundation for today's swift surge forward of the Canadian prairie West had been laid.

And there were the railroads. The C.P.R. thrust out branch lines. The Grand Trunk, under its energetic American manager, Charles M. Hays, began to cast longing glances westward at the opportunity it had, in 1880, scorned. Two native-born Ontarians, Mackenzie and Mann, began to dream of a second transcontinental.

Laurier was not averse. In the early years of the twentieth century, as in Drake's England or Periclean Athens, anything seemed possible. When the smoke of intrigue cleared, the Grand Trunk came out on top of the heap. As in the two previous railroad booms, the government was more than kind to the railway magnates. The final deal in 1903 was for a transcontinental 3550 miles long from Moncton, New Brunswick, to Prince Rupert well up on the coast of British Columbia. The eastern half—the more expensive—was (as in the case of the Trans-Canada Pipeline) to be built by the Dominion. Then, for no apparent good reason, it was to be leased to the Grand Trunk for seven years for nothing and after that for forty-three years for 3 per cent of the cost. The western half was to be constructed as the Grand Trunk Pacific with the government guaranteeing the principal and interest on the greater part of the bonds.

Laurier's Minister of Railways, A. G. Blair, who was closely linked to Mackenzie and Mann, resigned over the deal. It was also one of the main issues of the 1904 election. Laurier came through with a smashing victory, carrying 139 seats of a House of 214. The eastern half of the new transcontinental cost $160,000,000 instead of the estimated $60,000,000. The western section ran to $140,000,000. Yet it did bring results. The eastern division, running far north of all settlements, rediscovered the forgotten clay belt of northern Ontario, and farmers began to dribble in. A spur was also thrown to Fort William to give another shipping outlet for western wheat. Furthermore, by 1910 the main line had reached Edmonton and over 1200 miles of branch lines had been begun. When, finally, in 1914, the rails reached Prince Rupert, access was given to the halibut fisheries and to the mineral and timber resources of northern British Columbia. Meanwhile, in imitation of the C.P.R., the Grand Trunk had built hotels and elevators and had launched fleets of steamers on the Great Lakes. But in 1915 the Grand Trunk refused to accept its lease on the eastern half. The Dominion was forced to take it over as far as Winnipeg as a nationally owned railroad. Ultimately, thanks to greedy shareholders, the whole system went bankrupt and became Canada's property. Such was the final end of the road conceived first by Howe and Hincks in the fifties and grabbed off by Jackson *et al.* and the Galt quintet.

And what of Mackenzie and Mann? Canada did not need a third transcontinental any more than today's earth needs another satellite circling it. But Mackenzie and Mann, along with two fellow contractors, James Ross and that Herbert Holt who had built the Lake Louise section of the C.P.R. and was shortly to become Canada's dominant multimillionaire, had discovered how to make the Dominion, the provinces, and the public lay golden eggs for them to pick up.

To detail their amazing operations is beyond the space of this volume. Their basic device was to build their roads with subsidies enticed from governments, Dominion and provincial, and with money from bonds sold to the public and guaranteed by the Dominion or provincial parliaments. (For the road from Edmonton to Vancouver the Dominion gave cash subsidies totaling $21,000,000 and then another $45,000,000, while for their Canadian Northern transcontinental, the amazing total of the guaranteed bonds was $245,000,000.) Then Mackenzie and Mann and their small group of associates assigned the bulk of the stock in all their roads—and thus ownership of them—to themselves as a tribute to their own sagacity. In 1896 the Mackenzie-Mann group had possessed the charter for one railroad of about 130 miles from Gladstone in Manitoba to Lake Winnipegosis—a road that began practically nowhere and ended nowhere, and which, when completed, was run by thirteen men and a boy. By 1914 they were the proud possessors of almost 10,000 miles of track as well as of elevators, hotels, express and telegraph companies, iron mines near Lake Superior, coal mines in Alberta and in Vancouver Island, steamers between Montreal and Bristol, along with whaling interests, halibut fisheries in the Pacific, and sawmills on the British Columbia coast. To acquire this empire none of the group had risked or invested a nickel except in the original 130-mile road.

The Laurier administration is often held up as a proud contrast in purity to the corruption of John A.'s years of office. But seldom has any cabal received more gifts from government than the Mackenzie-Mann group. They were, literally, government-made millionaires. Nor were they to be the last of that favored group on whom the Dominion's administrations, federal and provincial, shower wealth at the expense of the taxpayers.

In the case of Mackenzie and Mann, the tight money of early 1914, following the Balkan wars, forced a slight disgorging. To get the final subsidy of $45,000,000 to complete their transcontinental to Vancouver, they had to turn over $40,000,000 of their $100,000,000 in capital stock to the Dominion and to allow Parliament to put one representative on their board of directors. Three transcontinentals had proved too much even for Canada's golden decade and a half. When the Canadian Northern, too, was declared bankrupt (though not Mackenzie, Mann, Ross, or Holt), the way was prepared for the merging of the Canadian Northern and the Grand Trunk into the present-day government-owned transcontinental.

Nor did the C.P.R. stand still. By 1914 it had under its control more than 18,000 miles of tracks. It employed directly 9000 men with a monthy payroll, at pre-World War I prices, of $5,000,000. It reached into the United States with over 5000 miles of roads. Besides its lake and Pacific-coast steamers, its red-and-white flag floated over liners in Liverpool and Trieste, in Hong Kong, Yokohama, and Sydney, Australia. It, too, had its elevators, its express and telegraph companies, and its sleeping cars and hotels.

In addition, it possessed its huge landholdings in the West, which it developed systematically and efficiently. In 1914 its assets were valued at over $800,000,000, a far shout indeed from the day it almost went bankrupt for the lack of $300,000.

War was soon to cast a cloud over the Dominion. But in the years from 1900 to 1910, in spite of the Triple Entente and the Triple Alliance and in spite of the Russo-Japanese War of 1904–5 and the Agadir incident, there did not seem to be even a shadow to mar the golden sunlight over Canada's westland. Everywhere the railway construction gangs were sweating as they pushed forward branch after branch until from the 49th parallel to Edmonton and Prince Albert a network of lines like a crazy spider's web gave a certain amount of depth to the prairie West. And everywhere, too, there were the golden fields, spread over generous-acred farms as far as eye could reach under the blue bowl of the sky, or the smoke from the engines of the far-ranging threshing crews, or the lines of wagons carrying wheat to the elevators, or the long trains crawling through the lonesome night to Fort William.

In these years the West was a one-crop country. Wheat was king. There was no huge carry-over as now, and fortune and a winter in California was always the promise of next year's crop. Meantime a grain-transportation system second to none had been devised. From the huge terminal elevators stretching out into the water at the head of the lakes like rows of tubular monsters in close embrace, lake freighters, "iron troughs with a lid on them," carried the fire-red wheat over the lakes and through the canals (deepened to fourteen feet; and there was by this time a Canadian as well as an American canal at Sault St. Marie) to other terminal elevators at Montreal. There the steel-hulled ocean freighters took over. It is a proof of the success of Sifton's policies that from 1900 to 1906 wheat production on the prairies rose from 18,129,182 bushels to 117,364,000. In 1915 even that huge amount almost trebled to 342,000,000 bushels.

6

Prosperity seemed as certain and as endless as it was to seem in the years preceding "Black Friday," October 29, 1929. At the halfway mark of the golden decade Canada took another great stride toward nationhood. Like Zeus begetting Athena, she created out of the Northwest Territories as far north as the 60th parallel the two new provinces of Alberta and Saskatchewan. Sir Wilfrid, accompanied by the governor general, Earl Grey, took his first trip West to inaugurate them.

At Edmonton, the capital of the new Alberta, the great day was September 1, 1905. A photograph of the occasion shows Sir Wilfrid in frock coat, his fluffy white hair an Einstein-like aureole to frame his head, on the speaker's stand. That stand, decked with red, white, and blue bunting and capped with the royal crown, stood in the flats along the North Saskatchewan. Behind was the wide river and the high and wooded southern banks of the great valley. In front rose the bastions on which the H.B.C. fort and the nascent city stood. Above was the noon sun in a sky of cloudless blue. Behind the speaker's stand were the scarlet-coated Mounties on their sleek horses and the Indians from the Hobbema reserve in full war regalia. In front and at the sides were crowded some 20,000 cityfolk and farmers. As Sir Wilfrid finished speaking, the cheering seemed to re-echo through the winding valley.

There was the same cheering and, *mutatis mutandis*, the same sort of ceremony two and three days later at Regina on September 3 and 4. Those three days put the seal on the development of the prairie West.

It had been a long road, indeed, since the 1670 charter of the "Adventurers of England." There had been the fur empire, the greatest the world has ever seen. There had been Lord Selkirk's 1818 Red River Settlement as the first organized attempt to transform the romance of the buffalo and the Indian and of the wide-ranging trappers and voyageurs into the duller life of the plowman and the grain grower.

That attempt had seemed to stagnate. But with Confederation and under the pressure of the forceful Americans to the south, the pace of change had quickened. Among those who listened to Sir Wilfrid were men who could remember when the Mounties first marched West, or when the shaggy mantle of the buffalo still drifted across the plains and the park land. To such men, the building of the C.P.R. and the Northwest Rebellion were yesterday's memories.

There were also many whose childhood recollections went back to Ontario or to Minnesota and the Dakotas or to Great Britain or to Europe. These were not as yet wedded to the West, or if they had spoken the marriage lines, that marriage was still uneasy.

To those from the middle western states, the scene was not too different from that which they had known. For the others, their hearts were divided between enthusiasm for the opportunities offered by this new, crude land and longings for the tall trees and the smaller, more manageable fields of their homeland or for the teeming cities which their youth had known. As one result of the great immigration, most Westerners had come from someplace else. That fact made for restlessness. When it was combined with the wide spaces and the pioneer life, it tended to develop a freer, more openhanded, and more open-spoken type of man. There was a certain flamboyancy in the air. A Frank Oliver, the former ox pusher (in 1905 he succeeded Sifton as Laurier's Minister of the Interior), could write: "While the Saskatchewan runs downhill, while coal will burn or timber grow, or the seed produce after its kind, they [the people of Edmonton] ask no favors of anyone, but with their own hands will build up in this country the best province of the Dominion of Canada," and not be accused of boasting. A Bob Edwards could take potshots, in his *Eye-Opener*, at all the sacred cows and, though the pious raised their eyebrows, his fellow citizens chuckled over statements such as "the Trinity of Canada is the C.P.R., Clifford Sifton and the Almighty." The law of libel, in fact, meant little to a man who in 1906 could comment about a show in Calgary that:

"Zinn's dancing girls . . . did big business. . . . Although the wages of Zinn is death, many of the girls of this company seem to be laying up treasure in their stockings where neither moths nor flies do corrupt."

Edwards had a special field in a "frontier city," where the cowboys still lingered and where many a remittance man still walked the streets. Sifton, quite wisely, refused to open up the ranching land to homesteaders; but, after his 1905 retirement, pressure forced the move. In Edwards, indeed, was the authentic spirit of the homesteading West, frank, direct, and openhanded to the point of extravagance. To the Easterner, the Westerner was a "blowhard," typified by an R. B. Bennett, who was sometimes called "the wind bag of the prairies." In his own opinion the Westerner "thought big"; though, by the constant and curious contradiction of frontier life, the West was also the home of a puritanism and religious fundamentalism more rabid than Ontario's smugness or Quebec's medievalism.

It was inevitable that in a wheat-growing country the Westerners should be radicals and free traders. The prairie farmer looked across the invisible 49th parallel. He saw his Dakota or Montana or Minnesota counterpart driving binders or seed drills or plows that cost tens of dollars less. Why, he began to ask, should the western farmer be a milch cow for the protection-bloated eastern Canadian manufacturer? He stared at the railroads and grumbled at high freight rates and high elevator dues.

And he did something about it. The freight and passenger rates were from 1903 forward controlled by the Board of Railway Commissioners (now renamed the Board of Transport Commissioners). To protect themselves against the grain dealers and the elevator companies, as early as 1901, on December 18, the Territorial Grain Growers' Association was formed. From this came the Grain Growers' Associations of Manitoba, Saskatchewan, and Alberta, and a seat on the Winnipeg Grain Exchange, and farmers' co-operative elevator companies.

When Sir Wilfrid visited the West again, in 1910, deputations of argumentative farmers turned what was to have been a triumphal progress into a debating tour. On December 16 a huge delegation, having descended upon Ottawa in the first of the "Farmers' Marches," demanded from Parliament an increase in the preference for British goods and reciprocity with the United States. The Liberals discovered an adder in their bosom.

So did the Canadian Manufacturers' Association (reorganized in 1900). It might have been thought that by this time Canadian industry was old enough and big enough to do without tariff protection. Canadian industrialists, however, had no intention of facing competition for the Canadian market. That, they still felt, ought to be their own high-fenced pleasance. Canadian finance and the transcontinentals agreed—and there was always the flag to wave.

CHAPTER XXXVI

1896–1910 (Cont'd)

The Industrial Revolution in Canada—The Maritimes and British Columbia—Sifton's Resignation over Separate Schools in Alberta and Saskatchewan—Canada and the United States Reach an Accord—Chinese, Japanese, and Hindus—British Columbia—Laurier's Concept of Canadian Independence—Canada in 1910—From Disunion to a Nation

1

IN the sixties the stand-bys of Canadian industry had been the flour mill, the sawmill, and the woolen mill. There had been a number of other nascent plants. The Massey Company had begun making farm implements around the middle of the nineteenth century, and there had been the manufacturing of harness, boots, clocks, buggies, wagons, and the like. In the field of processing farm products, cheese and butter factories had also begun to operate in the sixties. By the eighties these had spread all over Ontario and Quebec and into the Maritimes. There was even an amusing competition in making huge cheeses. The town of Perth, Ontario, finally carried off the prize with a giant cartwheel 28 feet in circumference, 6 feet high, and weighing 22,000 pounds.

It was in 1860, too, at Merritton, Ontario, that the looms of the first big cotton textile mill began to rattle. By 1881 there were nineteen mills bringing out $4,000,000 worth of cotton goods. In heavy industry, four years later the amalgamated Massey-Harris Company was shipping binders, mowers, and the like as far as

Germany and Asia Minor, while the Dominion was also producing its own locomotives and rails.

The same year 1881 saw five pulp mills in operation, while in the Maritimes, in the next year, the Nova Scotia Steel Company was producing Canada's first steel ingots. Two years later, 1883, during the building of the C.P.R., near Sudbury in Ontario a huge body of copper-nickel ore was discovered.

By the time 1900 rolled around, industry in central Canada was ready to seize upon the first decade of the new century for its own. By happy chance, just as Red Fife had made possible the farms of western Canada, so the discovery of hydroelectric power made feasible an "industrial revolution" in an Ontario and Quebec which had but little coal to turn the whirring dynamos which generate electricity.

It was in 1895 that the first hydroelectric power flowed out over the wires from Niagara Falls. Eleven years later the Hydro-Electric Power Commission was established. Quebec, too, had its plentitude of waterfalls. The pulp and paper industry burgeoned into stinking but active mills. So did other industries. Moreover—abruptly, as it seemed—the mineral treasures of the seemingly barren North Ontario burst on man's ken.

It was in 1903, when Ontario was driving the Timiskaming and Northern Ontario Railway up to the settlers in the great Clay Belt north of Lake Nipissing, that the rich silver deposits at Cobalt were found. In the next few years gold turned up at places such as Porcupine, Kirkland Lake, and Timmins—not free gold as in British Columbia or the Klondike, but gold which had to be hunted for deep in the bowels of the Pre-Cambrian Shield, that ancient formation of the oldest rocks in the world, by diamond drills and well-financed companies. Mowat, when he fought with John A. Macdonald for the possession of the rocks, trees, and lakes, had been prescient.

It all added up in these years to a surge of prosperity and to a growing concentration of Canada's industry and banking in the area from Three Rivers through Montreal and Toronto to Windsor; and Montreal was also the terminal point for the golden tide of Canada's western wheat. In banking, the Canadian trend was to a few monster houses, whose buildings, along with those of life insurance companies and the giant industrial corporations, were to become the real temples of the Dominion—though one should probably also include the railway stations of that era. Between

1886 and 1914 the Dominion's 41 banks had been reduced to 22, with some 3000 branches throughout Canada.

There was the same huddling together in industrial capitalism. Between 1909 and 1911, 196 firms were concentrated into 41 combinations, and the capital involved rose from $125,000,000 to $335,000,000; while interlocking directorates put tremendous economic power into the hands of a few favored individuals. Monopoly capitalism, as in Britain and in the States, had come into existence; and there was no Teddy Roosevelt in Canada to bluster about the iniquity of "trusts"; though in 1910 the Dominion did pass a Combines Investigation Act to look into complaints about monopolies and price fixing.

Of this industrial, financial, and railway empire, Montreal was king, though there was a subking in Toronto. The only cloud in the sky, until the revolt of the western wheat grower, was the appearance of the trade union. John A. Macdonald had been the first to give unions a legal status (in 1872); and in 1886 the Trades and Labor Congress of Canada was formed.

Yet it was, during this era, only a small cloud. By 1914, out of a Dominion labor force of about 850,000, some 166,000 were in unions; although as early as 1907 the Lemieux Act forbade strikes or lockouts until a mediation board had operated.

This sudden surge forward of industry in 1900–10 meant, naturally, urbanization in central Canada. In those years, over the whole Dominion, in spite of the expansion of farming in the West, rural population increased by less than 600,000 while urban went up by 1,260,000; and the percentage of city dwellers rose from 36 per cent to 45 per cent.

It is not strange, then, that by 1910 the farmers of the prairies felt they were simply milch cows for the industrialists of the East. Nor is it curious that, when they saw that a binder cost roughly a hundred dollars less across the invisible boundary line, they howled for the fence of protection to be torn down. The industrialists did nothing to still the shouts. It was their pleasant habit, then as now, to charge the Canadian consumer for goods manufactured in Canada very nearly the United States or British price for those goods plus the amount of the tariff. The extra profits went into their pockets. The quip that the Canadian tariff system is designed to feed fat a few prize hogs while the consumers, except in modern days for the labor unions, feed on the droppings, has enough truth in it to engender bitterness. As Stephen Leacock observed in his *Canada: The Foundations of Its Future,* "the huge infants" of Canadian industry "rolled off their mother's lap," but there was no drop in protection for them.

The Westerners, as it turned out, had no more chance of lowering the tariff fence which penned them in than a sheep has of jumping over a twelve-foot stone wall. Meanwhile central Canada in these years knew a golden age of which the traces have never left it. In Ontario, on the farms, wire fences and brick houses, except for the back concessions, tended to replace the snake rails and frame dwellings. (Wire fences were touted as preventing "drifting," that curse of winter roads in the "snow belt" north of Toronto.) The towns were elm- and maple-shaded hives of a quiet and solid prosperity. The most of Quebec, sunk in its French-Canadian dream of the past, changed but little. But Montreal and Toronto had become metropolitan centers with electric streetcars and electric lights and a wealth that was Victorian in its dignity and assurance. Their businessmen knew that, no matter what Ottawa might devise, the true heartbeat of Canada's economic life was strong and influential in their cities. With a confidence that was not misplaced, they continued to skim off the cream of the prosperity. In these years Canada moved rapidly toward a plutocracy.

The Maritimes did not share in the Laurier boom except insofar as when the larders of the rich are full to bursting, poor relations are sure to get a few leftovers. The days of the wooden ships were long past, and so was the carrying trade of the Bluenoses over the Seven Seas. Coal mining and the making of steel profited from the protection of the tariffs. Otherwise, the Industrial Revolution did little to compensate them for the loss of the natural market along the New England coast. Their farming remained stationary and their lumbering and fishing had to adjust to new techniques. The Maritimes, like the prairies, were critical of the wealth of central Canada.

On the other ocean, however, the almost separate kingdom of British Columbia was as lusty in its growth and prosperity as the prairies. Gold had brought its mainland to birth. Gold had been the dancing will-o'-the-wisp to lead the white man into its uttermost recesses. To change the metaphor, it had also been the province's lifeblood for a space. By the early years of the twentieth century, as we have seen, along with Kootenay gold, Kootenay copper, lead, and zinc had outstripped the almost forgotten Cariboo. British Columbia's agriculture could not compete with the prairies, and in the West the orchards of the Okanagan had not yet displaced the fruit from the Niagara Peninsula. There was still the halibut off the province's shores and the terrific rush of the salmon up its rivers. Between 1901 and 1914 the value of British Columbia's fisheries almost doubled.

And then there were her huge trees. The prairie West had at this time only one arrow in its quiver—wheat. British Columbia had half a dozen. The giant cedars and Douglas firs had made lumbering as natural as fishing for her inhabitants. The filling up of the prairies handed them a new market. The growth of the pulpwood industry gave them another. And the province had water power and to spare. It is significant that, though St. Catharines had the first electric street railway in Canada (1897), Vancouver was only three years behind with the second.

Coal, metals, huge trees, salmon and halibut, fruit, rich agricultural land, tumbling waterfalls—to these rich products the kingdom of the mountains and the sea added a scenery and a climate with which the newcomer fell in love. By 1891 the 10,000 whites of Confederation had swelled to some 98,173. In the next census (1901) that figure had almost doubled to 178,657. By 1911 it was up to 392,480, a far halloo indeed from the three bona fide settlers and the score or so of H.B.C. men who on March 11, 1850, had watched Richard Blanshard inaugurated as the first governor of Vancouver's Island. Victoria, by 1910, was already becoming a cup of English tea on a shaven lawn. Vancouver, however, was by this time a bustling, hustling port of over 100,000 people. It did not yet fully control its hinterland. But it was thrusting out grasping fingers; and meantime into its magnificent harbor steamed ships and freighters from San Francisco and Seattle, and liners from the Orient bringing silk and tea and the Chinese, Japanese, and Hindus against whom British Columbia raised up hands of protest.

Such a city cannot help but be cosmopolitan. Furthermore, in spite of the transcontinentals, without which British Columbia would have been lost to the Dominion, the province tended to look to the south and to the Orient, rather than to the prairies and to eastern Canada. The British Columbian is often more British than the Britisher. He is also, quite often, more western than the Westerner. An easy camaraderie, a touchy pride, a sense of separateness, these are mingled in him, and the last of the three proves that in this far western province the mountains and the pull of the sea have been almost too much for the ribbons of steel. Even today the British Columbian approaches the rest of Canada as if it were a foreign country, and a somewhat less blessed one. Sifton's peopling of the prairie West had spilled an excess into British Columbia. It did not cure the economic sectionalism which the geography of the Dominion imposes.

In these years, however, Canada began its true career as an exporting nation. In 1890 only four of its exports had topped $5,000,000. In 1911 there were fifteen over that amount. Primary products headed the list. Wheat (which had scarcely been a trickle in 1890) was in first place with $52,600,000 worth; lumber came second ($33,100,000); cheese, third ($21,600,000); fish, fourth ($15,200,000); silver, fifth ($15,000,000); then followed in order wheat flour ($14,900,000), cattle ($10,800,000), and meats ($8,000,000).

The Laurier regime, then, was the birth of modern Canada in economics as well as in the growth of a Canadian nationalism and independence. In the process, the silver-plumed orator shed two cabinet ministers. Blair, as has been seen, resigned over the transcontinental. Sifton, a much more serious loss, locked horns with his leader over that ancient source of strife, Roman Catholic Separate Schools. The occasion was the creation of Alberta and Saskatchewan, immediately after the November 1904 elections. The cause was a curious political slip by Sir Wilfrid, a man who was usually sensitive to the feelings of his Protestant compatriots.

2

The 1875 act had given the Northwest Territories sectarian schools, both Catholic and Protestant. By 1901, however, the territories themselves, cheered by the example of Manitoba, had installed a system whereby the first school in any school district had to be a public, nonsectarian school. Thereafter, if a minority wanted a sectarian school (which, almost always, meant a Roman Catholic Separate School) it could establish it and levy on its own religious adherents for its support.

But—and this was the "but" which infuriated the Roman Catholic hierarchy, which wanted all Catholic schools to be under the control of the priesthood—such schools had to use the same curriculum, the same inspectors, and, in general, the same textbooks as the public schools; and qualifications for teachers were the same. The only real concession to Roman Catholicism was that the last half hour of each day could be used for religious instruction; and here a conscience clause protected any pupil whose parents did not want him or her to stay for it.

Sifton, as an ardent Protestant, preferred to leave the soon-to-be provinces the power to put in whatever educational system they wished. But the Catholic members of the Cabinet put on the pressure to save, at least, what Catholicism had. When Sifton went off for a holiday in the southern United States, it was his understanding that the 1901 educational setup was to be included in the act to establish Alberta and Saskatchewan. As it happened, Fielding, another strong Protestant, left at the same time. As soon as the two were out of the road, Laurier, with the gleefulness of a youngster let out to play, put the 1875 school clause into the new act. This clause tied the two new provinces to sectarian schools, Protestant and Catholic, under ecclesiastical control, as in Quebec. The net result on the prairies would have been a rigid division of the school population into Catholics and Protestants, with, finally, two sectarian schools in each district, to say nothing, later, of Greek Catholic schools and the like. Religious strife would have been intensified.

Did Laurier regard himself as the indispensable man? Or was he, at sixty-three and a bit, atoning to his church for his attitude on the 1896 Manitoba Separate Schools question? At any rate, the act, with this clause in it, passed the first and second readings in the House, and Sir Wilfrid himself delivered a passionate eulogy on the superiority of sectarian schools over public schools.

And then Sifton rushed back from the States and the roof fell in. On the night of February 26, 1905, he saw Sir Wilfrid. Next day he resigned from the Cabinet. The Orange lodges and the Protestants fell in behind him. Fielding returned and threatened to resign. On the other side, the Catholic hierarchy and Henri Bourassa, that ardent Quebec nationalist who had campaigned against a Canadian contingent in South Africa, urged Sir Wilfrid to stand firm.

Laurier, like a youngster caught raiding the cooky jar, backed away from the religious strife he had evoked. He accepted an educational clause drafted by Sifton himself. The amendment put the 1901 system into effect.

The uproar, however, dragged a tail of consequences behind it.

On the one side, Bourassa and his narrow Quebec nationalism was strengthened. On the other, the breach with Sifton was never really healed; and, later, at a crucial moment he was to turn on Laurier and rend him. For Sifton never forgot a slap in the face.

3

In the second half of the first decade of the twentieth century, however, in spite of a faint odor of skulduggery left among Protestants by his attempt to foist sectarian schools on Alberta and Saskatchewan, the sun still blazed golden for Laurier. In the 1908 elections he carried 134 seats out of the 221 in the House. To the south the United States, with the last boundary dispute settled and the terrible Teddy away in Africa after lions and elephants, seemed to have decided to accept Canada as running her own show. "Manifest Destiny" was, at last, dead, and the Republic's venture into dollar diplomacy in Central and South America and into world-power politics and global imperialism was engrossing her. From this time forward the ignorance of her citizens about their neighbor to the north was to become as profound as that of most Britishers.

This lack of interest might be—and was—a source of irritation to Canadian self-consciousness. Too often her people behaved like a youngster jumping up and down because Big Brother pays no never mind. But it made for an amicable relationship which was underlined by the 1909 International Joint High Commission. Its six members, three each from Canada and the United States, were given complete authority over the use of all boundary waters, over other questions arising from the boundary, and over such other problems as the two countries might refer to them. The curious thing is that after all the indignant squalls from both sides during previous disputes, this commission has, without any fuss, been able to settle peacefully all the questions submitted to it.

In this new mood of co-operation the much gnawed bone of the North Atlantic fisheries was, in 1910, referred to the Hague Tribunal. Its decision in favor of Canada was received without a single scream from the American eagle. It was during Laurier's regime, in fact, that the fiction of the friendly frontier became a reality.

Even more important was the final achieving under Laurier of, in effect, the final steps in independence. Over the years since

Confederation, the governor general had, bit by bit, been demoted from a voice in Canadian politics (as in John A. Macdonald's days) to a symbol of the Throne. British troops had been withdrawn from the Dominion and so had the British commander of Canada's permanent force and militia. By 1905 the naval bases at Halifax and Esquimalt had been taken over.

In defense, Canada was now to drive her own horse and buggy. Similarly, in 1909, with the establishing of the Dominion's Department of External Affairs, Laurier served notice that from this time forward Canada expected to handle her own foreign affairs. Never again, as in the Washington Conference of 1871 or in the Alaskan boundary dispute, was the Dominion to be "let down" by the tendency of British negotiators to sacrifice Dominion interests to Anglo-American amity.

Laurier soon discovered that independence in this sphere could be a blade which might cut the hand that wielded it. One of the toughest questions his government had to handle was the immigration of Chinese, Japanese, and Hindus into British Columbia.

Canadians, in spite of their boasts, are no more tolerant, when the baby is on their own doorstep, of the colored races than their neighbors to the south. It was the American engineer, Andrew Onkerdonk, who had brought some 6500 Chinese coolies into British Columbia to work on the western section of the C.P.R. From the first, the whites objected. The Chinese were industrious. The complaint against them was their low standard of living, which meant that they would work for wages at which a Canadian would sneer. Moreover, they opened restaurants and other businesses as family enterprises and bankrupted their white competitors. And their customs and costumes were different. Foreigners, the British Columbians howled, were doing Canadians out of a living.

It was the same cry which on the prairies was raised against the "bohunks" on the construction gangs of the railways; and which is still on occasion shouted today against immigrants from almost anywhere. Even in loyal Ontario in the eighties, there were signs "No Englishmen need apply." To this economic pinch was added that unreasoning prejudice which is based on a difference in color. On March 13 of 1885 the British Columbia government refused to allow Chinese to land.

The John A. Macdonald government had to act. What it did was to impose on Chinese immigrants a head tax of $50 per person, except for officials, merchants, or students. The Chinese kept coming. In 1901 the Laurier government raised the tax to $100 and in 1904 to $500.

This solved the Chinese problem to a certain extent (though in 1910 some 1600 Chinese came in) and left no aftertaste, since no one anywhere cared too much whether Chinese were excluded or not. The Japanese were a yellow problem of a somewhat different hue. When the United States, back in 1854, forced Japanese ports open to American trade, in the curious deviousness of Fate, she thereby gave birth to a phenomenon which was to become a business and ultimately a military and naval rival. At first there was admiration for Japanese cleverness. When in 1904–5 Japan, a yellow David downing a lumbering white Goliath, won the Russo-Japanese War, Anglo-Saxons burst into a storm of applause.

In 1906, however, some 3000 of them emigrated to British Columbia. The next year there were 7600 of the cheerful victors over Russia. Vancouver's admiration swung rapidly to race hatred. In September of that year the city exploded into riots. The looting whites swept through the Chinese quarter. Then shouting Japanese routed them.

What was the Dominion to do? Laurier and his Cabinet knew that the comparative emptiness of Canada was like a huge juicy roast to the overcrowded, poverty-stricken, land-hungry countries of the Orient. Apart from the prejudices of the British Columbians, if the Dominion was to be kept white and predominantly Anglo-Saxon (and in the world as it has so far developed, Canadians had the right, if only of possession, to make that demand), Japanese immigration had to be checked. Japan, however, in addition to having a touchy pride, was an ally of Great Britain—and Canada, though virtually independent, was part of the Britain-led Commonwealth of Nations.

The solution here was a "gentleman's agreement," limiting immigration, which was negotiated with Japan. Even so, the failure to exclude the Japanese completely cost the Laurier government in the 1908 elections every federal seat in British Columbia except one.

The Hindus were an even more difficult set of fish to fry. For they, too, were citizens of the Empire, and in 1907 more than 2000 of them entered the far western province. It was William Lyon Mackenzie King, on stage as Laurier's Minister of Labor, who found a characteristically Machiavellian solution. There was no direct line of steamships from India to Canada. So in 1908 a clause was put into the Immigration Act barring immigrants who did not come in a direct journey from their homeland to the Dominion. When, however, in 1914, 376 Hindus challenged this ruling by chartering a ship direct to Vancouver, they were not permitted to land. Canada was to remain white, no matter what.

On the whole, the Laurier government did reasonably well in these essays in international diplomacy; and Britain did not interfere. For, by this time, Chamberlain's notion of a close-knit Empire was as dead as the proverbial dodo. Out of the ashes, however, like a phoenix, had at last arisen the fully developed idea of a union of self-governing nations under the British flag. There was Australia, where in 1900 the separate colonies had been united into one Commonwealth. There was New Zealand; and self-government had also been granted to the Transvaal, where in 1910 the Union of South Africa became another great Dominion. And there was Canada. A Laurier who, like John A. Macdonald, had sheered away from the Chamberlain dream of an Imperial Council and the rest of it, was thoroughly willing to join in a British Commonwealth of Nations.

It was an idea which pleased all but the extremists of Imperial Federation on the one side and the Bourassa nationalists on the other. There was still one flaw in the concept of it. As the world wagged then, and as it wags now, independent nations had to be prepared to look after their own defense. Canada had taken over control of her land forces. But, though part of an Empire whose power depended on control of the seas, like a bride who still looks to mother, she expected Britain's fleet to be her shield, just as in modern days she huddles under the protection of Uncle Sam's air umbrella and hopes it is leakproof.

The British Admiralty had, for years, attempted to persuade the Dominions to make contributions to Britain's fleet. In 1909, under the threat of German naval construction, the Admiralty changed its tune. It pleaded for separate naval units from the Dominions. Laurier once more proved himself a Canadian and not a narrow Quebec isolationist. In January of 1910 he introduced a bill for a Canadian navy of six cruisers and five destroyers, a navy which, as he pointed out, could act independently or be used, if Parliament so decided, to assist Britain. The Imperial Federationists, who wanted a direct contribution to Britain's fleet, opposed. So did Bourassa's Quebec following. In 1910 Quebec still perched where it had sat in 1850. "Ourselves alone" was still its battle cry. But the bill passed.

It was in support of this bill that Laurier expressed the new independence of Canada, which he himself, more than any other single man, had brought about.

"I do not pretend to be an Imperialist," he stated, "neither do I pretend to be an anti-Imperialist. I am a Canadian, first, last and all the time. I am a British subject by birth, by tradition, by conviction—by the conviction that under British institutions my native land has found a measure of security and freedom which it could not have found under any other regime."

To him, as he declared it in another part of his speech, the true conception of the British Empire was "the conception of new, growing, strong and wealthy nations, each one developing itself on the line of its own needs and conditions, but all joining in the case of a common danger, and from all points of the earth rushing upon a common enemy."

In that statement was the explanation of the British Commonwealth of Nations as Laurier conceived of it. Yet he made it clear that Canada, in his opinion, though "at war and liable to attack" if England were at war, need not necessarily take part in all of England's wars. "That," he asserted, "is a matter which must be determined by circumstances, upon which the Canadian Parliament will have to pronounce and will have to decide in its own best judgment."

It was in accord with this pronouncement of Laurier's that, in the Second World War, Canada was not officially at war until, on September 10 of 1939, its own Parliament had so declared. In Laurier's words was a typical Anglo-Saxon illogicality which, so far, like so many illogicalities, has worked in practice—independent nations who yet, in spite of independence, band together in war. Those words, however, meant that Laurier had achieved complete Dominion autonomy, that in foreign as well as in domestic affairs he had preserved for Canada independence of choice—to be, in a paraphrase of Kipling's words, "daughter in her mother's house, but mistress in her own," even to handling her own foreign affairs and to deciding whether or not to declare war.

And so the cycling decades had come round to 1910. It is a good year in which to take our last view of Laurier. In 1910 he still sat firmly on the throne; and the silver-plumed knight had become as much of a symbol of Canada to his generation as John A. had been to his.

It was a different sort of a symbol; and one in keeping with the new seriousness and dignity of the Dominion. John A.'s earthiness, slapdash humor, political connivings, and bouts with the bottle had suited the era he had dominated, an age of raw effort and wide expansion, when even the Maritimes and the central provinces were still but a step from the backwoods. Laurier, however, in his touch of reserve and his Old World courtliness, typified the senior Dominion of the Commonwealth in its youthful manhood, when it was still not quite sure what fork to use at table. Laurier was what it wanted to be, not what it was. He knew what fork to use; and his aureole of white hair had become the banner of a new Liberalism which was not too different in its nationalism and in its tariffs from John A.'s Liberal-Conservatism. That Liberalism gave more of an ear to the rights of the provinces. It had its radical, free-trade wing. But in 1910 it was still on good terms with manufacturers, bankers, and railway promoters, and, like John A., Laurier depended on a union of French-speaking Catholics and English-speaking Protestants for his majority.

John A. had awakened either hatred or love. The great French Canadian inspired respect and even reverence—and this from English as well as French. The basic secret of both was the same. Each rose above race and creed to put Canada first. John A. had been the architect of Confederation and of a Dominion from sea to sea. Laurier, through Sifton and Frank Oliver, peopled the empty stretches of that Dominion. That was a secondary achievement. His true place in history is as the author of Canadian independence. For he was the statesman who cut an immature "Johnny Canuck" loose from Britain's apron strings and set him gently but firmly to walk along a path he had to blaze for himself.

4

And what of the Canada over which he ruled? The Western world was still in the horse-and-buggy days, and in the bicycle-and-railway era, even though the automobile had appeared and the first, almost antediluvian, airplanes had lifted themselves falteringly into the air. (The first airplane flight in the British Empire was made at Baddeck, Nova Scotia, on February 23, 1909, by a Canadian, J. A. McCurdy, who, fifty years later, attended a re-enactment of his flight.)

On the west coast there might be hurry and bustle as the huge trees crashed and the saws whined or as the fishermen swarmed after the leaping salmon. Over the prairies there might be binders, staggered one behind the other, cutting the yellow fields, each of them as big as an Ontario farm. In Ontario, however, still the heart land of the Dominion, life had not changed too much in essentials since the days of Confederation. On the farms, seed drills, mowers, binders, and steam-engine-pulled threshing machines had replaced the sowing by hand and the scythe and the flail or the horsepower thresher.

But the farmer still worked from sunup to sundown, and the social activities of the rural community still centered around the church. The tavern, however, had fallen into disrepute, and "local option" had sobered the countryside. The villages still featured the general store and the church and the blacksmith shop, with the drugstore as a new attraction. Roads had improved. They were graveled and kept up by "road work" put in by the farmers themselves. True, the "party" telephone had made its appearance (Graham Bell, a Canadian, invented the telephone at Brantford in 1876), and most farmers took a weekly newspaper and, occasionally, even a daily. One had to go to the back concessions, too, to see the log house and the log barn, though these and the snake-rail and pine-root fences still persisted not too far from Toronto.

It was in the towns that one realized more fully the gradual changes since Confederation. They were solidly built and prosperous with one or two basic industries on which their wealth rested. But their tempo was sleepy as compared with today's hectic rush. There might be bicycles everywhere, since from the turn of the century the bicycle became one of the favored methods of transportation. Slow-moving horse-drawn vehicles were still the rule; nor had Ontarians as yet forgotten how to walk. The residences of the well to do were roomy brick and stone houses set in spacious grounds, and modern plumbing was not, in those days, for everyone. Lake excursions were a habit, and the summer cottage and the regattas had made their appearance. For the most part, however, people still had to provide for their own amusements. And they were also expected to work. A modern man would, probably, discover his own vacuity if he were thrust back into 1910.

The cities, such as Toronto or Montreal, moved at a faster speed. They had electric street cars and electric street lighting, and three- and four-story business blocks, paved streets, and sidewalks, and, for that day, large populations (the 1911 census gave Montreal proper 470,480 people and Toronto 376,538). Horse-drawn traffic and bicycles traversed those sidewalks, and there seemed, somehow, to be more time.

In sports, track and field was still pre-eminent and the Indian runner, Longboat, gave a fillip to it. Rowing was one of Canada's prides. Cricket, however, was losing out to the new game, baseball, and tennis, a "lady's game" at that time, was coming to popularity. The first decade of the twentieth century also saw the heyday of the Dominion's "national game," lacrosse, until excessive roughness killed it off. A new and typically Canadian game, however, ice hockey, was ready to replace it in popular favor.

There had been games of this "field hockey on ice" as far back at least as 1855. In 1885 the first league was organized at Kingston, and in 1890 the Ontario Hockey Association (still operating) was formed. Three years later the governor general, Lord Stanley, offered the Stanley Cup for amateur competition. By the first decade of the twentieth century every little town and village had its natural ice rink and every pond and river dam was crowded with youngsters with hockey sticks on skates. A new national game, fast and skillful, which was to become an article of export, had been born—though in these modern days, in its homeland, the roughness and overorganization thrust into the sport by professionalism seems to have ushered in a decline in its popularity at its "ice roots." In 1910 almost all sport was amateur; nor had the day of the spectator sportsman as yet arrived.

The popularity of sport was in itself a sign of increasing leisure and maturity. So was the spread of education. Quebec tended to remain backward. In Ontario, however, some 84 per cent of its ten- to fourteen-year-olds were attending school. Even in the new prairie provinces, with their heavy admixture of European immigrants, the percentages in Alberta and Saskatchewan were 66 and 65. For the whole of Canada, the average was almost 78 per cent. Furthermore, in both the public and high schools there was not, as yet, any trace of the American-invented "soft" curriculum of the present.

In higher education, to the long-established colleges and universities in the East were added the provincial and nonsectarian

Universities of Alberta and Saskatchewan, in 1908 and 1909, respectively. Manitoba had begun a provincial university in 1877, but its development waited until this same decade. Meanwhile, the geologist Dawson and the medical man Sir William Osler had won international reputations, and it was a Canadian engineer, Sir Sandford Fleming, who was responsible for the inauguration of Greenwich time in 1903. Years before this, in 1882, the Marquis of Lorne had encouraged Canadian scholarship by founding the Royal Society of Canada.

In 1910 higher education was still an eager goal for the brilliant and the hard-working; and it was quite usual for students, in deciding upon their lifework, to take into account what service they might render to humanity. The materialistic had not, as yet, overshadowed the idealistic. In consonance with this attitude, the churches maintained a powerful influence on the community. In the early twentieth century, in spite of Darwin and of the "Higher Criticism," it was pretty largely the age of an uncritical faith; though the idea that knowledge through education could cure the ills of humanity was gaining ground, an idea which, unfortunately, presupposed a high level of intelligence in the masses.

As has already been suggested, the eastern part of the Dominion, in particular, had become much more decorous over the years. There was the Lord's Day Act of 1906 to make Sunday in any Canadian city, except, perhaps, Montreal, an exercise in dreariness, especially for the stranger. Quebec fundamentalism and the Dissenter Protestant obsession with its quartet of sins (drinking, dancing, smoking, and cardplaying) put a gray tinge on mores even if the slums remained. It may seem incredible that a girl who wore bloomers while riding a bicycle was regarded as "fast," that bathing suits were tents, that men wore nightgowns, and that rouge was only for a woman of the streets. Such were the accidental stigmata of the period to make the modern wonder how many of his taboos, costumes, and customs will be rendered ridiculous by time. In 1910, however, the Dominion was still a custodian of Victorian prudery.

Of culture, in the definition which limits the word to the arts, there was comparatively little which was distinctively Canadian. The shadow of Britain hung over the land. Painting and sculpture were generally imitative; although Cornelius Krieghoff's studies of habitant life could be termed "Canadian," and one sculptor, Louis Philippe Hébert, born in the Lake Megantic district of Quebec in 1850, was in 1911 made a *Chevalier de la Légion d'Honneur* of France. His statues of Maisonneuve (Montreal) and Champlain (Quebec) are still ranked as excellent.

Literature, as is natural, made somewhat more progress. In this field, French Canada has often shown the way to the Dominion. So by 1865 the Crémazie Circle (begun about 1850) found its finest expression in the writings of Fréchette. His swelling periods appear to owe something to Victor Hugo. His inspiration, however, was his native Quebec.

In English-speaking Canada, the first truly Canadian poetry began in 1880 with the publication of *Orion and Other Poems* by Charles G. D. Roberts. New Brunswick gave Roberts and his cousin, Bliss Carman, to the Dominion. Archibald Lampman and Duncan Campbell Scott joined these two to form the Ottawa Valley group. All four were absorbed by the moods and colors of the Canadian landscape (still a safe subject for Canadian writers), and though their style tended to be imitative of Shelley, Keats, Swinburne, Tennyson, and Arnold, their pride was in Canada.

Mention should also be made of Pauline Johnson's touching lyric poetry. Service's *Songs of a Sourdough* and the like and Drummond's habitant verse belong in a different category.

Prose literature in any country is likely to be a later development than poetry. William Kirby in his *The Golden Dog* (1877) and Gilbert Parker in his *Seats of the Mighty* had turned to the Canadian scene. Similarly, Roberts went back to Acadia for his stories. He, also, along with Ernest Thompson Seton, made stories of animals popular. In the last years of the nineteenth century and the first decade of the twentieth, Ralph Connor (the Reverend Charles Gordon) set a vogue in his *Black Rock*, *The Man from Glengarry*, and *The Sky Pilot*. Her *Lords of the North* established Agnes Laut as a Canadian author. Names such as Marion Keith (*Duncan Polite*), Nellie McClung (*Sowing Seeds in Danny*), and L. M. Montgomery (*Anne of Green Gables*) show that the Canadian scene was beginning to stir a desire to express it.

It cannot be said, however, that there was any efflorescence of Canadian culture. The Athenian achievement in sculpture, architecture, literature, and, probably, in painting in the century after Marathon finds no parallel in the first forty-three years after Confederation. It has been argued that the Dominion was too preoccupied with its materialistic problems to have time for culture. It might be added that its admiration of all things British was a drawback, while in things cultural the sad fact is that the problems Canadian writers try to express have usually been anticipated a quarter of a century before them by American authors. In any case, though by 1910 Canadians had begun to achieve a definite sense of nationhood, the stirrings of that nationhood were only beginning to be expressed in the arts.

5

Even though the arts lagged, constantly turning their heads toward Britain and Europe to see if "teacher" approved, the Dominion which in 1867 had been an experiment was by 1910 a fact. There were weaknesses. The bitter antagonism of race and creed was still a running sore. A sullen Maritimes, a faraway British Columbia, and a prairie West cursing the industrial East were economic rifts which made all too evident the difficulty of defying economic geography.

Still, if one looked back to 1850, the achievement in the sixty-year period had been enormous. At the halfway mark of the nineteenth century the feeble and scattered colonies of British North America had seemed likely to be swallowed by the United States. Even at Confederation there had been only four provinces joined together, with their less than three and a half million people straggling in a thin band from Halifax to Lake Huron. Yet in the forty-three years since 1867 the thrust northwestward of Manifest Destiny had been repulsed and the Dominion had pushed first a ribbon of steel and then a narrow carpet of people across the continent to the Pacific. Thanks to what seemed a series of almost fortuitous occurrences, but thanks, also, to the vision and energy of a few men, it had achieved a Canada stretching from ocean to ocean.

In the same period its people had won through to a sense of nationhood. The Canadian in Quebec has always been a Canadian, even though he is primarily a French Canadian with the weaknesses a separate nationalism inside a nation always brings. The English-speaking Canadian, however, was still tugged by two pulls—his uneasy fascination for the United States and his admiration and love for the British tradition. There was in 1910, as was shortly to be proved, a third emotion in him, a latent anti-Americanism, which, in a way, was the strongest factor in making him Canadian. Yet he had become conscious that he was a Canadian and there was a growing pride in that fact.

Like every other nationalist in any other nation, he was inclined to stress his own virtues and minimize his own faults. He believed that he was steadier, more sensible, and more virtuous than the American and more capable and progressive than the Britisher. Above all, in this first decade of the twentieth century, he had an enormous pride and confidence in the future of his country. To him, by the accident of the American Revolution or the failure of Britain's negotiators, had been left all that seemed barren, cold, and uninhabitable in North America. Out of that heritage he had framed a nation—and at this moment, so he felt, the possibilities of that nation were unbounded. Faith in the future of the Dominion and pride in the stubborn task which had been stubbornly achieved made him a Canadian.

If, by 1910, Canada had become a nation, two men had been chiefly responsible. There had been other actors on the Canadian stage—George Brown, Joseph Howe, George Etienne Cartier, Donald Smith, Louis Riel, George Stephen, and the like—who had in one way or another contributed to Dominion from sea unto sea. The two towering giants from 1850 to 1910 were still John A. Macdonald and Wilfrid Laurier. Without the one, Canada might well have ended at Lake Superior. Without the other, the structure of nationhood would not have built so solidly. In no other period of Canada's story is it so clear that men who, like Winston Churchill, meet their moment of destiny make history.

SELECTED BIBLIOGRAPHY

Bibliographical Note. The writer of this history is fortunate enough to have traveled widely across Canada and to have seen a number of the sites described in the text. Microfilms of some of the newspapers of the period have been consulted, and a number of articles have been read. Of these latter, only two, which were of special help, have been listed. In general, the Bibliography is restricted to those works which seemed helpful; whereas books which were dipped into only for corroboration of this point or that have not been listed.

BALDWIN, L. D. *The Stream of American History.* New York: American Book Company, 1952.

BANCROFT, H. H. *The Works of Hubert Howe Bancroft* (Vol. XXXII: *History of British Columbia*). San Francisco: Bancroft, 1883–86.

BEARD, C. A., and MARY R. BEARD. *A Basic History of the United States.* Philadelphia: Blakiston, 1944.

BEGG, ALEXANDER. *History of British Columbia.* Toronto: William Briggs, 1894.

——. *Red River Journal and Other Papers Relating to the Red River Resistance of 1869–1870.* Edited and with introduction by W. L. Morton. Toronto: Champlain Society, 1956.

——. *Ten Years in Winnipeg: A Narration of the Principal Events from the Year A.D. 1870 to the Year A.D. 1879, incl. by Alexander Begg and Walter R. Nursey.* Winnipeg: Winnipeg Printing and Publishing House, 1879.

——. *The Creation of Manitoba, or A History of the Red River Troubles.* Toronto: Hovey, 1871.

BERTON, PIERRE. *The Golden Trail: The Story of the Klondike Rush.* Toronto: Macmillan, 1954.

——. *Klondike: The Life and Death of the Last Great Gold Rush.* Toronto: McClelland & Stewart, 1958.

BREBNER, J. B. "Joseph Howe and the Crimean War Enlistment Controversy between Great Britain and the United States," *Canadian Historical Review,* XI (Toronto: University of Toronto Press, December 1930) 300–27.

BROWN, GEORGE W. *Building the Canadian Nation.* Rev. ed.; Toronto: Dent, 1950.

BRYCE, G. *A Short History of the Canadian People*. Toronto: William Briggs, 1914.

BURT, A. L. *A Short History of Canada for Americans*. Minneapolis: University of Minnesota Press, 1942.

BUTLER, SIR WILLIAM FRANCIS. *The Great Lone Land: A Tale of Travel and Adventure in the North-West of America*. 17th ed.; Toronto: Macmillan, 1910.

CAMERON, W. B. *Blood Red the Sun*. Rev. ed.; Calgary: Kenway Publishing Company, 1950.

CARELESS, J. M. S. *Canada: A Story of Challenge*. Cambridge: Cambridge University Press, 1953.

CHAFE, J. W., and G. R. M. LOWER. *Canada: A Nation*. Toronto: Longmans, Green, 1948.

COATS, R. H., and R. E. GOSNELL. *Sir James Douglas* (Makers of Canada Series, Vol. XX). Toronto: Morang, 1909.

CREIGHTON, DONALD. *Dominion of the North*. Toronto: Macmillian, 1957.

——. *John A. Macdonald: The Young Politician*. Toronto: Macmillan, 1952.

——. *John A. Macdonald: The Old Chieftain*. Toronto: Macmillan, 1955.

——. *The Story of Canada*. Toronto: Macmillan, 1959.

DAFOE, JOHN W. *Clifford Sifton in Relation to His Times*. Toronto: Macmillan, 1931.

DAVIDSON, W. M. *Louis Riel: A Biography*. Calgary: The Albertan Publishing Company, 1955.

DENISON, LT. COL. GEORGE T. *Soldiering in Canada*. Toronto: Morang, 1901.

DENNY, SIR CECIL E. *The Law Marches West*. Toronto: Dent, 1939.

DOYLE, SIR ARTHUR CONAN. *The Great Boer War: A Two Years' Record, 1899–1901*. New edition; London: Smith, 1901.

FAULKNER, H. V. *American Economic History*. 7th ed.; New York: Harper, 1954.

GIBBON, JOHN MURRAY. *Steel of Empire*. Toronto: McClelland & Stewart, 1935.

HAMMOND, M. O. *Confederation and Its Leaders*. Toronto: McClelland, Goodchild & Stewart, 1917.

HATTON AND HARVEY. *Newfoundland*. Boston: Doyle and Whitney, 1883.

HAYDON, A. L. *The Riders of the Plains*. Toronto: Copp, Clark, 1926.

HEDGES, J. B. *Building the Canadian West: The Land and Colonization Policies of the Canadian Pacific Railway*. New York: Macmillan, 1939.

HINTON AND GODSELL. *The Yukon*. Toronto: Ryerson, 1954.

HOWARD, JOSEPH KINSEY. *Strange Empire*. New York: William Morrow, 1952.
HOWAY, F. W. *British Columbia: The Making of a Province*. Toronto: Ryerson, 1928.
HUGHES, KATHERINE. *Father Lacombe: The Black Robe Voyageur*. Toronto: William Briggs, 1911.
HUTCHINSON, BRUCE. *The Fraser*. Toronto: Clarke, Irwin, 1950.
——. *The Struggle for the Border*. Toronto: Longmans, Green, 1955.
KELSEY, VERA. *Red River Runs North*. New York: Harper, 1951.
KIRKLAND, E. C. *A History of American Economic Life*. 3d ed.; New York: Appleton-Century-Crofts, 1951.
LEACOCK, STEPHEN. *Canada: The Foundations of Its Future*. Montreal: Gazette Printing Company, 1941.
LE BOURDAIS, D. M. *Nation of the North: Canada Since Confederation*. Toronto: Methuen, 1953.
LEWIS, JOHN. *George Brown* (Makers of Canada Series, Vol. XIX). Toronto: Morang, 1909.
LOWER, A. R. M. *Colony to Nation: A History of Canada*. Toronto: Longmans, Green, 1946.
MACBETH, R. G. *Policing the Plains*. Toronto: Hodder and Stoughton, 1921.
——. *The Making of the Canadian West*, 2d ed.; Toronto: William Briggs, 1905.
MCDOUGALL, JOHN. *In the Days of the Red River Rebellion*. Toronto: William Briggs, 1911.
——. *Forest, Lake and Prairie*. 2d ed.; Toronto: Ryerson, 1910.
——. *Saddle, Sled and Snowshoe*. 3d ed.; Toronto: Ryerson, 1910.
MACEWAN, GRANT. *Eye Opener Bob*. Edmonton: Institute of Applied Art, 1957.
MCINNIS, EDGAR. *Canada: A Political and Social History*. Toronto: Rinehart, 1947.
MACKAY, DOUGLAS. *The Honourable Company*. Rev. ed.; Toronto: McClelland & Stewart, 1949.
MCKELVIE, B. A. *Pageant of British Columbia*. Toronto: Thomas Nelson & Sons, 1955.
MACNUTT, W. S. *Days of Lorne*. Fredericton: Brunswick Press, 1955.
MOBERLY, H. J. *When Fur Was King*. Toronto: Dent, 1929.
MOIR, GEORGE T. *Sinners and Saints*. Victoria: Wooding, 1947.
MORTON, A. S. *A History of the Canadian West to 1870–71*. Toronto: Thomas Nelson & Sons.
MORTON, W. L. *Manitoba: A History*. Toronto: University of Toronto Press, 1957.
——. *The West and Confederation* (Historical Booklet No. 9). Ottawa: Canadian Historical Association, 1958.

NEEDLER, G. H. *Louis Riel: The Rebellion of 1885*. Toronto: Burns & MacEachern, 1957.

OGILVIE, W. *Early Days on the Yukon*. Ottawa: Thorburn and Abbott, 1913.

ORMSBY, MARGARET A. *British Columbia: A History*. Toronto: Macmillan, 1958.

PHELAN, JOSEPHINE. *The Ardent Exile*. Toronto: Macmillan, 1951.

PRESTON, W. T. R. *The Life and Times of Lord Strathcona*. London: Eveleigh Nash, 1914.

ROY, J. A. *Joseph Howe: A Study in Achievement and Frustration*. Toronto: Macmillan, 1935.

SANDWELL, B. K. *The Canadian People*. London: Oxford University Press, 1941.

SHARP, PAUL F. *Whoop-up Country: The Canadian-American West, 1865–1885*. Minneapolis: University of Minnesota Press, 1955.

SKELTON, O. D. *The Day of Sir Wilfrid Laurier*. Toronto and Glasgow: Brook, 1916.

——. *The Life and Times of Sir Alexander Tilloch Galt*. Toronto: Oxford, 1920.

——. *The Railway Builders*. Toronto and Glasgow: Brook, 1916.

STANLEY, G. F. G. *The Birth of Western Canada: A History of the Riel Rebellion*. Toronto: Longmans, Green, 1936.

STRACHEY, LYTTON. *Queen Victoria*. New York: Harcourt, Brace, 1921.

TANSILL, C. C. *Canadian-American Relations, 1875–1911*. Toronto: Ryerson, 1943.

——. *The Canadian Reciprocity Treaty of 1854*. Baltimore: Johns Hopkins, 1922.

WADE, M. S. "The Overlanders of '62," *Archives of British Columbia*, Memoir No. IX (Victoria, 1931).

WALLACE, F. W. *Wooden Ships and Iron Men*. Toronto: Hodder and Stoughton, 1925.

WILLSON, BECKLES. *The Life of Lord Strathcona and Mount Royal*. London: Cassell, 1915.

WINSLOW, KATHRYN. *Big Pan-Out*. New York: Norton, 1951.

WRIGHT, J. F. C. *Prairie Progress*. Saskatoon: Modern Press, 1956.

——. *Saskatchewan, the History of a Province*. Toronto: McClelland & Stewart, 1955.

——. *Slava Bohu: The Story of the Dukhobors*. Toronto: Farrar & Rinehart, 1940.

INDEX

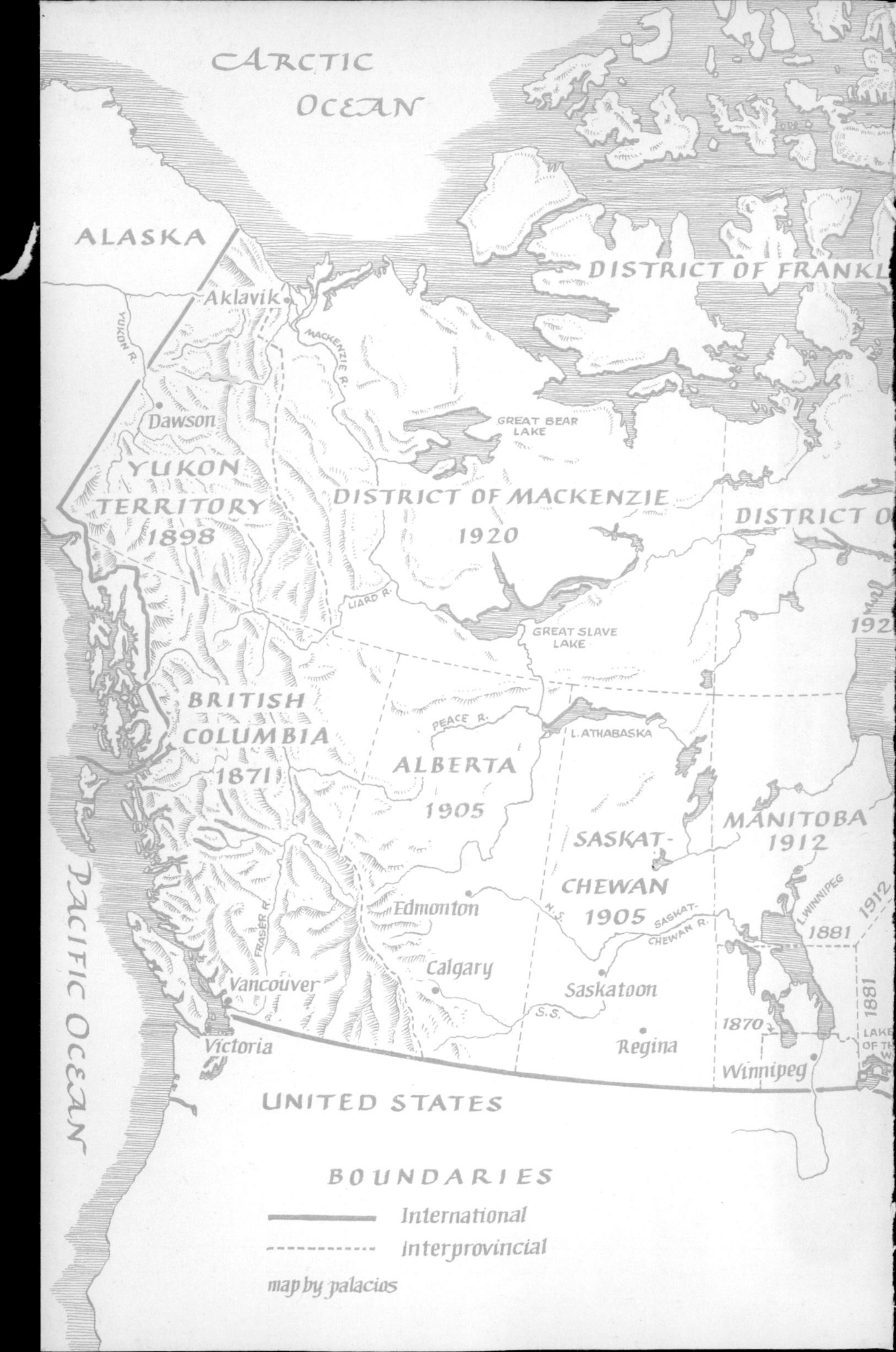

ARCTIC OCEAN
ALASKA
Aklavik
YUKON R.
MACKENZIE R.
Dawson
YUKON TERRITORY 1898
GREAT BEAR LAKE
DISTRICT OF FRANKL
DISTRICT OF MACKENZIE 1920
DISTRICT O
LIARD R.
GREAT SLAVE LAKE
BRITISH COLUMBIA 1871
PEACE R.
L. ATHABASKA
ALBERTA 1905
SASKAT-CHEWAN 1905
MANITOBA 1912
L. WINNIPEG
1912
1881
PACIFIC OCEAN
FRASER R.
Edmonton
N.S.
SASKAT-CHEWAN R.
Calgary
Saskatoon
Vancouver
S.S.
1870
Regina
Victoria
Winnipeg
UNITED STATES
BOUNDARIES
International
Interprovincial
map by palacios